Aging and Society
A Canadian Perspective

Sixth Edition

Mark Novak
San José State University

Lori Campbell
McMaster University

NELSON / EDUCATION

NELSON EDUCATION

Aging and Society: A Canadian Perspective, Sixth Edition

by Mark Novak and Lori Campbell

Vice-President and Editorial Director:
Evelyn Veitch

Editor-in-Chief, Higher Education:
Anne Williams

Executive Editor:
Laura Macleod

Executive Marketing Manager:
David Tonen

Developmental Editor:
Liisa Kelly

Photo Researcher:
Kristiina Paul

Permissions Coordinator:
Kristiina Paul

Senior Content Production Manager:
Anne Nellis

Production Service:
KnowledgeWorks Global Limited

Copy Editor:
Karen Rolfe

Proofreader:
Saravanakumar Dharman

Indexer:
Chris Dregnan

Production Coordinator:
Ferial Suleman

Design Director:
Ken Phipps

Managing Designer:
Franca Amore

Interior Design Modifications:
Peter Papayanakis

Cover Design:
Peter Papayanakis

Cover Image:
Tom Grill/Getty

Compositor:
KnowledgeWorks Global Limited

Library and Archives Canada Cataloguing in Publication

Novak, Mark W.
   Aging and society : a Canadian perspective / Mark Novak, Lori Campbell. —6th ed.

Second-4th eds. have title: Aging & society. Includes bibliographical references and index.

ISBN 978-0-17-650043-6

1. Aging—Canada—Textbooks. 2. Older people—Canada—Textbooks. 3. Older people—Canada—Social conditions—Textbooks. I. Campbell, Lori D. (Lori Debra), 1953– II. Novak, Mark W. Aging & society. III. Title.

HQ1064.C2N68 2009   305.260971   C2009-902387-3

ISBN-13: 978-0-17-650043-6
ISBN-10: 0-17-650043-X

Contents

Chapter 9   Finances and Economics   185

Chapter 10   Retirement and Work   210

Chapter 11   Housing and Transportation   231

Preface

Many changes have taken place in Canadian gerontology since the fifth edition of this text was published: new researchers have entered the field of aging; the government has released many reports that summarize studies of health, housing, and pension reform; and consortia of researchers and research centres have published the results of their studies. This body of knowledge will shape future social policy.

As the 21st century unfolds, the study of aging will increase in importance. Canada's population will have more older people than ever before, and they will make new demands on Canada's health care, retirement income, and housing resources. They will also bring new interests, new skills, and a new perspective on aging. People young and old will need to understand the realities of aging in this new age.

This text has an underlying theme: successful aging. The text presents a full picture of aging—problems and all—but it emphasizes the opportunities and advantages of later life. This theme makes more sense today than ever before. Longer life, and more years of activity and good health, have changed the landscape of old age. Late old age still brings physical decline but better health and nutrition at every stage of life, along with advances in medicine, extend the active years of middle age. The saying "60 is the new 40 and 70 the new 50" may have begun as clever remarks but they do describe the reality of aging today for more and more people. Few older people today (aged 65 and over) fit the stereotypical image of the poor and decrepit senior.

Researchers Turcotte and Schellenberg (2007, 8) say that as the Baby Boomers turn 65 "it is possible that a new definition of 'senior' will replace the current one. What it generally means to be a senior, for seniors themselves as well as for society in general, could go through an important redefinition." Better pension plans, better health, more opportunities for personal expression, and social engagement all have transformed later life. This text documents that transformation and the new landscape of aging today.

Some years ago French gerontologists used the term "the third age" to describe this new stage of life. This phrase defines a time of life between adulthood (the Second Age) and old age (the Fourth Age). It refers to the healthy active years around retirement before old age sets in. Moen and Spencer (2006, 128) define this as a time of transition, a "*midcourse* between the career- and family-building tasks associated with adulthood, but before any debilitating infirmities associated with old age" (emphasis in the original). This stage may begin in the 50s and go on to age 80 or more.

Two phenomenon led to the emergence of the Third Age today. First, demography: more people than ever before live in the Third Age. And as the Baby Boom generation ages, it will swell the older population. Baby Boomers will look and act more like people in middle-age than like the stereotypical older person. Second, longevity: people on average live longer today than ever before. And they will live these added years, sometimes called the "longevity bonus," in better health than past generations (Moen and Spencer 2006, 128). Add to this changes in technology that allow people to stay productive longer, opportunities to stay engaged through volunteer work, and the practice of life-long learning. All of these changes mean that Third Agers will remain active and engaged in second careers, leisure, and social service. They will redefine the concept of retirement and of later life.

Moen and Spencer (2006, 134) call the traditional view of old age "outdated," and "obsolete." The old model no longer fits the complexity of the Third Age. The rapid social change at the start of the 21st century—technological change, a globalized economy, unstable work careers, demographic change, convergence of male and female career opportunities—calls for new models to fit new patterns of social experience.

The existence of the Third Age as a large-scale phenomenon causes some rethinking of assumptions about aging. In the past, older people who took part in athletic events seemed like odd specimens. Today, large numbers of people in their 50s and older run marathons, take up surfing, and climb mountains (a 71-year-old Japanese man summited Mount Everest in the spring of 2007). Erdman Palmore (2005), a renowned gerontologist, tells us that on his birthday every year he bicycles the number of miles that equal his age (75 miles in 2005). These Third Agers shatter the stereotype of old age.

Social institutions such as business and industry will need to adapt to this new population of Third Agers. As Baby Boomers retire from the workplace they will leave behind a labour shortage. The smaller age groups behind them will provide fewer workers, changing the way that business and industry view retirement and the retiree. Some companies will rehire retirees, others will give people incentives to delay retirement.

On my campus an interim president came out of retirement for two years to manage the campus while we searched for a new leader. The campus then hired our administrative vice-president, who delayed retirement, to serve as our new president. He then brought back a retired senior administrator to serve as vice-president to manage a troublesome unit. These administrators all had many years of successful experience, quickly assumed their new roles, and brought the campus to new heights of stability and achievement. This pattern will occur more and more often in varied industries and institutions in the years ahead.

Third Agers will engage in activities that express their interests and passions. In some cases they will create institutions to meet these needs, as well as programs such as life-long learning institutes and new volunteer opportunities.

This edition of the text also links the generations through the life course perspective. The emergence of the Third Age demands this approach. It blurs the meaning of retirement and old age. It asks for a view of aging that looks at the whole of adult life—the discontinuities (e.g., retirement) and the continuities (e.g., life-long learning). A life course perspective shows where and how a person's life has continuity and how the generations depend on one another. Many Boomers will play the role of caregiver to their aging parents and to their children and grandchildren. At the same time they will deal with their own retirement and health issues. Older people will affect the younger generations through their use of services, their social contributions, and their ability to improve society as they age.

As Baby Boomers enter the Third Age they will put pressure on existing programs and services. The Canadian pension system, other pension programs, and health care systems will have to adapt to this large number of older people. In general, these systems and others may shift the cost of programs and services to the individual, marking a change from the way that programs and services developed during the 20th century. During the past century government and corporate programs increased benefits to older people; however, the 21st century will ask people to take more responsibility for their own pension planning and health care costs. This text reports on these changes in social policy and their impact on older people.

The sixth edition of this book has the same goals as the first five. First, we want a readable book—one that students can read without stumbling over social science jargon and dense academic prose. We have defined most technical terms within the text so that students will not have to flip to a glossary or interrupt their reading by looking at footnotes. We also present examples, charts, and graphs to illustrate difficult points. This edition includes key terms and study questions that students can use to review and test their knowledge. These study aids will free students to think about the ideas contained in the text. This edition includes suggested readings at the end of each chapter, as well as websites, so students can access additional information on topics of particular interest to them.

Second, we want a text that presents aging in the context of Canada's history and social life. In the past, gerontology instructors had to use U.S. texts in their aging courses, and each year they had to delete large sections of the text from the assigned readings. Canadian students don't need to know how many older people live in Arizona, the workings of the U.S. Social Security system, or the differences between aging black, white, and Hispanic Americans. These are interesting topics, but Canada has its own geographic regions, social policies, and mix of cultures and ethnic groups. Canadian students should first learn about aging in their own country.

Third, we want a text that describes Canada's social institutions—its health care, income, and housing systems—as well as its family and community life. Canadian students should know, for example, that their health care system provides free health care benefits to all older people and that the retirement income system provides a basic income to older Canadians. These systems create a social safety net for older people and provide the basis for a decent old age today.

Canadian students should also know that older adults face problems in their society. Many Canadians hold negative stereotypes about older people (look at the number of lotions designed to hide wrinkled skin); the fast pace of modern society often pushes older people to the sidelines (imagine trying to cross a six-lane street if you have arthritis in your legs); and some groups of older people (many of them very old women) still live in poverty. Canadian society needs improvement. Students need to know what parts of the social system work for older people and what parts work against them. *Aging and Society: A Canadian Perspective* gives students the facts about aging and helps them sort through and understand the issues surrounding aging today.

This new edition has a fourth goal: to improve on the fifth edition. Many instructors and students across the country have used the fifth edition. We too have used it in our classes with hundreds of students. Our students and our colleagues have commented on what they liked and did not like about the text. We have used their comments to improve the text and create this new edition.

As in earlier editions, this one refers to classic Canadian studies and the most up-to-date facts and figures on aging in Canada. Research findings and other information within each chapter are clearly referenced to make it easy for students to locate the original academic sources. The text also contains exhibits that present case studies of older people today and discuss current issues in the field. This edition also has some new sections that reflect new research in the field of aging. Where appropriate, the new edition makes reference to the impact of technology on seniors' lives. This includes the use of computers to maintain contact with family members and to join new communities.

Chapter 1 contains information on intergenerational equity and societal ageism. We have brought this material forward so that students can learn, early in their reading, about the sociopolitical context of aging. Chapter 2 includes information on current research activity in Canada and a section on information literacy—an emerging issue in our computer age. It also discusses the challenges researchers face when they collaborate with community partners. Chapter 3 contains up-to-date demographic facts and new material on aging around the world. It provides new information on aging in developing nations. Chapter 4 contains thoroughly updated information and statistics based on the latest Canadian data. Chapter 5 looks at how physical activity, health promotion, and self-care can improve health and well-being in later life. It contains expanded sections on nutrition and stress reduction. Chapter 6 contains more information on creativity and on healthy adaptations to change. Chapter 7 contains expanded discussions of ethnicity and aging with a focus on Aboriginal elders. Chapter 8 discusses health care reform. It documents the continuing increase in home care and the growing interest in long-term care. It also discusses the growing interest in health promotion programs and practices.

Chapter 9 contains the latest information on pensions in Canada. It shows that financial inequality continues to exist between single women (many of them widows) and men in later life. It also documents the shift in responsibility for pension savings from companies to individuals. Chapter 10 describes the ongoing redefinition of retirement. Many people move in and out of the work force after retirement from their mid-life career, blurring the lines between work and the traditional meaning of retirement as an end to work—and a growing percentage of seniors say they never plan to retire. Chapter 11 contains new information on homeless seniors, an expanded discussion of supportive and enriched housing, and more material on housing for rural seniors. The chapter also looks at issues related to gender and driving a car in later life. It discusses the challenges older people face when they must stop driving.

Chapter 12 updates information on how older people spend their time. It documents the many leisure activities that now occupy seniors' time, including the growth of interest in sports and fitness. Chapter 13 remains divided into two major parts. Part One (Family Life) contains new information on remarriage and challenges that older couples face in late-life marriage. Part Two (Social Support) contains more information on gender and caregiving by spouses and adult children. It also contains new material on the social support benefits of pets for older people living in the community and in long-term-care settings. The final chapter, Chapter 14, discusses the ongoing controversy around euthanasia and physician-assisted suicide. It also includes an expanded section on widowhood and its impact on the surviving spouse.

This edition, like those before it, documents the aging of Canadian society. It shows the issues that occupy our thinking and the ways that society and individuals have adapted to aging. The first edition, published nearly 25 years ago, laid down many of the issues discussed here. That edition looked to the future and saw a growing number of older people and recognized that Canada would have to reshape its policies and programs to meet their needs. Later editions tracked the changes that took place as Canadian society aged.

This edition continues that tradition. But the projected issues of the past exist as real challenges today. Canada has become an older society. Income inequality, early retirement, community-based health care, the importance of active living, and family caregiver burden all affect more people than ever before. We are now seeing the first of the Baby Boomers entering later life. As it ages, this generation will make new demands on society, requiring new responses. The sixth edition of *Aging and Society: A Canadian Perspective* points to some of the emerging issues in aging and to the challenges that lie ahead.

ORGANIZATION

This book begins by describing large-scale (macroscopic) changes in society. It then shows how these changes affect people and social institutions. It concludes by showing how individuals respond to these changes and how individuals' actions give new direction to society. The structure of the book reflects a dialectical model of social change.

Part 1, Gerontology Today (Chapters 1 and 2), introduces students to the field of aging. It shatters many of the myths people have about aging and shows the range of topics gerontologists study. It also describes the theories and methods gerontologists use when they study aging.

Part 2, Historical Change (Chapters 3 and 4), looks at the changes in Canada's history and demographic structure that led to population aging (the increased proportion of older people in the population). It also places aging in Canada in a world context.

Part 3, Maturational Change (Chapters 5, 6, and 7), looks at individual aging—the physical, psychological, and developmental changes that come with age.

Part 4, Institutional Change (Chapters 8 through 14), examines Canada's institutions—the health care, social security, and housing systems as well as the family, the community, and the institutions responsible for death and dying.

SPECIAL FEATURES

A number of features make this both a useful and an easy-to-use book.

First, the chapters are organized into topics that most instructors cover in their courses. Each chapter represents a unit of study and presents the facts and issues related to one topic (e.g., housing or health care). This division allows instructors to use this text in either a one- or a two-term course. Instructors of a two-term course are able to use the entire book, while those teaching one-term courses can assign specific chapters and know that a topic will be covered in depth. A one-term course, for example, might include those chapters that deal specifically with population aging and Canada's social institutions (i.e., Chapters 1, 3, 4, 8, 9, 10, and 11).

Second, each chapter starts with an outline of the chapter's contents and an introduction to its main themes.

Third, each chapter contains graphs, charts, and excerpts from other publications. Some of the exhibits present controversies in the literature; others contain case studies that show the human side of aging. Most graphs and charts have accompanying explanations that describe them and show their relation to the text.

Fourth, each chapter concludes with a series of main points that summarize the text, a list of study questions, and an annotated list of important sources students can consult for further reading. This edition also includes key websites that contain useful and dependable information.

Fifth, the book concludes with a reference list of all the sources referred to in the text, in alphabetical order by author surname. Many sources now refer to websites. Students can use these web addresses to gather more information on a topic.

GENERAL ACKNOWLEDGMENTS

Anne Williams, Editor-in-Chief of Higher Education at Nelson Education Ltd., and Laura Macleod, Executive Editor, guided us through the early stages of this project. Liisa Kelly, the Developmental Editor on this project, worked diligently to get this edition out on time. Like all good editors, Anne, Laura, and Liisa cleared away technical and editorial problems so that we could focus on the research and writing. Anne Nellis served as Senior Content Production Manager, and Kristiina Paul coordinated the book's text and photo permissions. Karen Rolfe and Saravanakumar Dharman capably handled copy-editing and proofreading, respectively. We thank them for their support.

The librarians at the Martin Luther King Memorial Library at San José State University helped with interlibrary requests and database searches. Dean Ruth Kifer supervises an exceptional staff who worked hard to get the resources needed to complete this text. We thank them all for their support.

Sharon Cancilla, Zeni Espinosa, and Nadia Elliott from my office helped me (Mark Novak) to find the time to work on the text. They cleared my calendar, rearranged meetings, and helped me to find days when I could finish the text as the deadline approached. I thank them for their patience and good cheer.

Dr. Steve Zlotolow, Associate Dean of International and Extended Studies at San José State, deserves special thanks. Steve works in the next office. We interact throughout the day. His frequent, "No problem. Everything's gonna be OK" helped me keep focused on this work. Steve often held the wheel of the ship on days when I had to give full attention to completing the text. He's a great colleague, friend, and fellow mountain climber. I appreciate his willingness to help me find time for this work.

Canadian colleagues in the field of gerontology contributed to the core knowledge assembled in this text. We cannot thank them all here, but we want to acknowledge that they helped make this a better text.

AUTHOR'S ACKNOWLEDGMENTS

Lori Campbell

I wish to thank Mark Novak for his incredible support, patience, and kindness on this project. I feel deeply privileged to have had the opportunity to again work with, and learn from, such a fine and inspiring person and academic. Mark demonstrated an unwavering commitment to the project, a genuine concern for the academic needs of students, and an amazing generosity and sharing in the collaborative process.

To my sisters, Jane Levy and Lynn Campbell, thank you for your wonderful support and friendship. To my "2Ps," Payton and Paris, who have grown into such enchanting young women—bright, funny, and most dear. Thank you for bringing such joy and delight into my life.

To my husband, Michael Carroll, thank you for your unconditional love, support, and encouragement in all I do—academically and in life. I feel truly fortunate to share my life—and our dogs Barkey and Bronney—with such a remarkable and loving person. My heart could have no warmer or happier haven than it has with you.

I dedicate this book in most loving memory of my parents, Leon and Dorothy Campbell, who demonstrated to me what it truly means to care about family and others, and how to live and age with strength, spirit, compassion, and humour. I owe them much more than I could ever express.

Mark Novak

My wife, Mona, helped me by reading the chapters and preparing the summary points, key terms, and study questions at the end of each chapter. She has made the book more useful to students. My son Daniel helped with the preparation of the references. I thank both of them for their time and their careful work.

It has been a pleasure working with Lori Campbell, my co-author, and sharing ideas with her as we went along. She has been a friendly critic, a careful scholar, and a hard worker. She has brought many new insights and resources to the text. Students will benefit from her knowledge and her sensitivity as a teacher.

I owe special thanks to my mentor and close friend, Hans Mohr. His intellectual integrity inspires all my work. I can never repay him, only thank him for his support and friendship.

I dedicate this book to my family—my wife, Mona, and my sons, Christopher, Jonathan, Sean, and Daniel; and Chris's wife Shona and Jon's wife Judy. I have some newer family members who deserve mention—my grandchildren, Tobin and Shea. I hope this book will guide them as they age and will help them give exceptional care to their aging parents and grandparents. All of them deserve credit for lightening my spirits with their good humour and love.

© Tim Bieber/Getty Images

Chapter

1

Aging Today

INTRODUCTION

Everyone needs to know about aging. First, all of us are getting older. While some of us are over 65 already, most adults not yet 65 will become part of the older population between now and the year 2040. We will want to make old age as good a time of life as it can be.

Second, when those of you who are younger students reach middle age, your parents, aunts, uncles, neighbours, and older friends will have grown old. You will want to know about aging so that you can help them live the best old age possible.

Third, more people work with the elderly than ever before, and more will find themselves working with the elderly in the future. In 2005, Canada had 4.2 million people aged 65 and over. Older Canadians make up more than 13.1 percent of the population today, and experts predict that this proportion will grow to 9.8 million people or 24.5 percent of the population by 2036 (Turcotte and Schellenberg 2007). Nurses, social workers, teachers, family counsellors, and even travel agents will have more and more older people as clients.

An older population will also put new demands on Canada's **social structures**. Sociologists define a social structure as a relatively stable pattern of social interactions. The family, the education system, and the health care system all fit this definition, and they will change in the following ways as Canadian society ages:

- More Canadians will live in three- and four-generation families. And many people will become grandparents while they are still active in their careers.
- Schools and universities will attract more older students than ever before. These students will want flexible schedules. They will also need different kinds of teaching methods and different courses.
- The health care system will also change. The current system favours the treatment of acute (short-term) illness, but older people tend to have chronic ailments such as arthritis, hearing problems, and diabetes. An aging society needs to prevent illness before it occurs.

Gerontology is the discipline that systematically studies aging. It looks at the subject from two points of view: how aging affects the individual and how an aging population will change society. This chapter describes (1) myths and realities of aging, (2) stereotyping and attitudes toward aging, and (3) ageism and social policy.

MYTHS AND REALITIES OF AGING

Jessie Taylor called for a cab and headed downtown for her last appointment of the day. She works for the provincial office on aging. She monitors nursing home standards and teaches staff ways to improve patient care. Jessie is 63 years old. She has a sturdy figure, a pixie grin, and a mop of gray hair. As she got out of the cab, the driver got out too. He grabbed her elbow, ushered her across the street, and deposited her on the sidewalk. "You can't be too careful crossing the street these days," he said, then smiled and waved goodbye. Jessie says that when she goes to her local supermarket, the checkout clerk often asks other customers to wait a moment while she checks Jessie's things through. Then one of the workers helps her to her car with her groceries.

All of this used to surprise Jessie. After all, she works at a job like everyone else, drives her own car when she travels out of town, and serves as a leader in her profession. Yet sometimes people treat her like a frail old woman. People see her kind face, gray hair, and wrinkles, and they want to help her. They imagine that she needs help doing simple things because of her age. I asked Jessie whether she ever told people that she didn't need their help. She said that sometimes she does, but she doesn't want to discourage these people from helping someone in the future who may need their help, so often she goes along and grins to herself.

Jessie knows about stereotyping and **prejudice** toward older people.[1] She knows about it firsthand, and she observes it every day in her work. She also knows that stereotypes can be useful. They help us get along in a complex world where we know only a fraction of the people we see and meet every day. But stereotypes can lead to problems.

Stereotypes can lead us to misjudge people, to treat them inappropriately, and, in the case of older people, to assume that they need help. Stereotyping can also lead to prejudice, a negative attitude toward a person, and to **discrimination**, unfair treatment based on prejudice rather than merit.

Gerontology has two goals. First, scholars and researchers work to produce accurate knowledge about aging. Second, professionals who work with older people apply this knowledge to create a better life for their clients. Academic gerontologists try to decrease prejudice and stereotyping by presenting the facts about aging.

---

1. The terms "old," "elderly," "aged," and "senior" in this text refer to people aged 65 and over unless another age is given.

Studies show that many people hold incorrect views of aging today. Researcher Erdman Palmore (1977) first devised a "Facts on Aging Quiz (FAQ)" to study knowledge about aging. By the late 1990s more than 150 studies reported the use of the original and later versions of the FAQ. Researchers and educators have used this quiz with people from a variety of backgrounds. Studies report that factual knowledge of aging improves with education (Palmore 2005). People with a high school education or less, for example, average 57 percent correct. Undergraduates do somewhat better, averaging 64 percent. Gerontology students and faculty on average score 83 percent (Palmore 1988). A study in Canada by Greenslade (cited in Palmore 1988) found that nurses with no gerontology training scored 61 percent correct, but a group with training in geriatrics scored 83 percent.

Matthews, Tindale, and Norris (1985) gave a modified version of Palmore's quiz to public health nurses and also to students and faculty at the University of Guelph (see Exhibit 1.1). They found that the people with the most knowledge about aging scored best on the quiz. Undergraduate students just completing a gerontology course scored highest. Students in an introductory human development course scored lowest. Their results suggest that when people learn about aging, their knowledge of old age improves.

A study at the University of Western Ontario medical school (Diachun et al. 2006) divided students into three groups—a group that learned about aging in the classroom, an experiential group that met older people, and a control group that had neither educational option. The study found that after one year, compared to the control group, both the classroom and the experiential group reported better attitudes toward older people.

Consider the following myths and the facts that gerontologists have found to replace them.

Myth: People feel lonely and lost in retirement. They often get sick and die shortly after they retire.

Reality: Few people face sickness or loneliness due to retirement. Genoe and Singleton (2006), for example, conducted in-depth interviews with a group of male retirees (age 72 to 86) in Eastern Canada. The men in the study said they found meaning in life through

---

● Exhibit 1.1

FACTS ON AGING QUIZ

Try the following quiz to see how much you know about aging in Canada. The quiz is based on Palmore's "Facts on Aging: A Short Quiz" (1977), but it incorporates suggestions made by Canadian researchers who have revised Palmore's work (Matthews, Tindale, and Norris 1985). The answers are on page 17. You will find the facts to support these answers throughout this book.

True or False?

1. At least 15 percent of the aged in Canada are living in long-stay institutions (e.g., nursing homes, mental hospitals, homes for the aged).

2. British Columbia has a higher proportion of older people in its population than any other province.

3. Older people today have less contact with their families than older people had in the past.

4. Older people stand a higher risk of criminal victimization than people in other age groups.

5. Memory declines with age.

6. A decline in sexual vigour in older men is usually due to hormone deficiencies.

7. Retirees more often feel depressed, bored, and ill than those who keep working.

8. Most older people in rural areas depend on public transportation to get around.

9. The body's systems go into a steady decline from age 40 on.

10. The majority of older people have incomes below the poverty level (as defined by the federal government).

Source: Reprinted with permission from the *Canadian Journal on Aging*.

volunteering. They also said that recreation activities like acting, dancing, and playing cards kept them in touch with their community. Some people retire because of poor health, and this may account for the myth that retirement causes poor health (Taylor & Doverspike, 2003). In most cases, retirement has little, if any, effect on health, social activity, life satisfaction, or happiness. And in some cases the health of workers improves when they retire. Many retirees now start new careers, take up volunteer work, or go back to school. Some even return to work.

Myth: People in older age groups face a higher risk of criminal victimization than people in younger age groups.

Reality: Older people face a lower risk of criminal victimization than any other age group. Ogrodnik (2007, 6) reports that "according to the 2004 General Social Survey (GSS), seniors were three times less likely than nonseniors to experience a victimization in the 12 months preceding the survey (10% versus 31%)."

Young people aged 15 to 24 experienced the highest rates of violent crime victimization for assault, sexual assault, and robbery. They had a rate of 226 per 1,000 persons in 2004. People aged 65 and over had a rate of only 12 incidents per 1,000 persons in that year (a rate almost 20 times lower than for the youngest age group). Victimization for violent crime decreased steadily with each older age group. The same trend applies to personal property theft (Turcotte and Schellenberg 2007). Ogrodnik (2007) reports that in violent crimes almost two-thirds of older victims knew their attacker. And most often a family member, friend, or acquaintance engaged in the criminal act. This can occur, for example, when a caregiver becomes frustrated and angry. Still, only a minority of victimized older people experienced an injury due to victimization.

The 2004 General Social Survey found that nearly all seniors (92 percent) reported feeling satisfied with their safety from crime (Ogrodnik 2007). This figure increased from 89 percent in the 1999 GSS. A small percentage of older people (17 percent) reported fear of crime during their time alone in the evenings, and 21 percent felt very or somewhat worried about walking alone in their neighbourhoods. Nathalie (2001; also Ogrodnik 2007) found that compared to younger people, older people tended to stay home because they feared crime.

Older people do face relatively high rates of certain kinds of crimes. For example, compared to younger people, they run a higher risk of being victims of fraud. Crime surveys in Canada report that people aged 65 and over make up over half the victims of fraud. People aged 60 and over make up three-quarters of the people

defrauded of more than $5,000. And a large majority of this group gets cheated more than once (National Advisory Council on Aging 2001a).

The National Advisory Council on Aging (NACA) reported a number of conditions that create a higher risk of fraud among older people. These included lack of information, social isolation, and lack of wariness in business relations. Donahue (2001, 36) reports that ethnic- minority seniors face further risk due to the language barrier, trust in Canadians, trust in their ethnic community, and fear of reprisal. One minority respondent in Donahue's study said, "Even if we know it is fraud, what can we do? We do not know the channels to fight. We do not know the language."

The Internet provides a new channel for crooks to cheat older people. A method called "phishing" targets people with computers. The thieves send an e-mail that appears to come from a bank or a major online business like Amazon. The e-mail asks the person to click on a link to verify the information about his or her account. The thieves' computer then redirects the person to a fake site that collects the login and password. This gives the thieves access to the person's online account. Computer fraud may increase against older people as computers becomes more a part of their daily lives. (RCMP 2007).

Some fraud-prevention programs have begun for older people. Project PhoneBusters, a national program in Canada, handles complaints of telemarketing fraud from people of all ages. The RCMP reports that people aged 60 and over made up 40 percent of telemarketing and lottery scam victims in 2006. The total loss to all victims came to over $1 million or $4,835.21 per person on average. A group called SeniorBusters works with Project PhoneBusters to advise and support senior victims of fraud.

Myth: Most old people live in institutions.

Reality: Only 7.4 percent of older people in 2001 lived in an institution—a nursing home, hospital, or other long-term care facility. Turcotte and Schellenberg (2007) report that, compared to men, women run a higher risk of institutionalization at every age in later life. And the likelihood of institutionalization increases with age. Only 2.1 percent of men and 2.3 percent of women aged 65 to 74 lived in an institution in 2001. However, more than one-third (35.4 percent) of women aged 85 and over, compared to only 22.6 percent of men in that age group, lived in an institution in 2001.

Institutionalization rates have slowed over the past several decades. In 1981, for example, 8.8 percent of older people lived in an institution. By 2001 that figure had dropped to 7.4 percent (Turcotte and Schellenberg 2007).

Today, most institutions house the very old, sick, and frail elderly people with few social supports, who cannot live on their own. Current moves in Canada toward increased community care may lead to less institutionalization in the future.

ATTITUDES TOWARD OLD AGE

People hold many **stereotypes** about old age. Sociologists define a stereotype as an exaggerated and often prejudiced view of a type of person or group of people. People who hold a stereotype do not check to see if it is true. If they meet someone who does not fit the stereotype, they think he or she is an exception. Stereotypes often have some basis in truth, but they exaggerate and distort the truth. Often they lead to discrimination.

When it comes to old age, we hold both positive and negative stereotypes: the wise old farmer and the kindly grandmother, the dirty old man and the sex-starved spinster. Grant and his colleagues (2001) asked 240 men and women aged 18 to 86 in Newfoundland about how they thought an older person would respond to a set of attitude questions. Younger people in the study thought that older people would give socially and politically conservative answers. People in the study thought that liberal views would decrease with age. The researchers conclude that both young and old people hold traditional age stereotypes (see Exhibit 1.2).

In another study, Ryan and her colleagues (1998) found that, compared to younger telephone users (mean age 22 years), older telephone users (mean age 73 years) reported fewer problems using the telephone. Still, younger people in this study believed that, compared to a 25-year-old, a 75-year-old would have more trouble using the telephone. A study of undergraduate students' attitudes toward eyewitness testimony also found ambivalence toward older people (Brimacombe et al. 1997). The study found that undergraduates rated older adults as honest, but as less credible witnesses than younger adults.

Many of our stereotypes consist of negative views of older people and old age. Sometimes the stereotype leads from prejudice (an attitude) to discrimination (an action taken against someone). Page (1997, 59) had an elderly woman call to rent an apartment. He then had a young woman and a young man each make a similar call. In a fourth case a young man called on behalf of an older woman. Page found that the elderly woman and the young man calling on behalf of an elderly woman got three to four times more negative responses than the two younger people. He concludes that "persons identified as elderly still face the prospect of rejection."

Hess (2006, 384) reviewed the psychological literature on aging stereotypes. He found that overall "the literature suggests an underlying negative component to most categories of older adults." Laboratory studies of attitudes about aging, for example, find a consistent bias

---

● Exhibit 1.2

A NEW MYTH ABOUT AGING

A student passed the following story along to us. She said she heard it from someone who heard it from a Nova Scotia fisherman. Maybe it will become a part of our Canadian mythology about aging.

The ferry between Cape Breton and St. John's was having a rough passage. The seas were so rough that the captain decided that it was too dangerous to take the boat right to the dock. Instead, he anchored in the harbour. He manoeuvred the boat so that passengers could get off, but he kept the boat far enough from the quay walls to keep the boat safe. The crew set up a makeshift gangway made of wood planks and a rope handrail on either side. The heaving of the boat and the springiness of the planks made the passengers reluctant to cross to the shore. The crew and shore personnel persuaded and encouraged the passengers to get them to cross. At last, a small, frail-looking old lady came from below. She hesitated to cross the gangway, but finally she worked up her courage and inched across. Many people watched her make her way and the people on shore almost carried her the last few feet. People began to cheer as she set herself on the shore. Then she turned to face the boat; she cupped her hands and called, "It's all right, Mother. You can come down now."

against older people (Hummert et al, 2002). Nosek and colleagues (2002) compared subjects' attitudes toward race, gender, and age. They found stronger negative associations with age than with race or gender.

Nosek and colleagues (2002) also found that older adults showed just as strong an age bias as did younger adults. A study by Bieman and Bouchard (1998) found a similar result. They studied peoples' assumptions about memory and aging. They found that younger people *and* older people in the study saw memory success as more typical of younger people. The subjects in the study saw memory failure as more typical of older people, and they linked this failure to lack of ability and worry.

Thornton and Light (2006, 276) describe a way of talking that they call "**elderspeak.**" Elderspeak refers to "a specialized speech register resembling baby talk in addressing older adults." This form of speech uses few clauses, shorter phrases, more filler phrases (e.g., "like," "you know"), words with fewer syllables, slower speech, and longer pauses. Elderspeak also includes the use of words like "dearie," "cutie," and "sweetie." Institutional workers may use words like these to address residents (Hess, 2006). Stereotyping drives elderspeak. The speaker assumes that the older person has low mental ability or some other impairment. Elderspeak has a negative effect on the older person; it creates low self-esteem, it reduces a person's ability to communicate effectively, it decreases the quality of interaction, and it reduces the older person's sense of control (Thornton and Light, 2006).

Levitt and Dubner (2005, 79) in their book *Freakonomics,* describe a TV show called *The Weakest Link.* On this show contestants vote to eliminate other players. In the early rounds weak players get eliminated because they lack the information needed to help the others succeed. In the later rounds players get eliminated if they know too much because they increase the competition. Levitt and Dubner found that: "Elderly players [on the show] … are victims of taste-based discrimination: in the early rounds *and* late rounds, they are eliminated far out of proportion to their skills. It seems as if the other contestants—this is a show on which the average age is thirty-four—simply don't want the older players around."

A study of older people treated in the hospital for congestive heart failure points to discrimination based on age. Cujec and colleagues (2004) found that, compared to younger patients, older patients with heart failure had higher rates of death. But, in spite of this higher risk of death, older patients less often were

admitted to special care units. They less often had a specialist or subspecialist review their case. And they less often received beta-blockers and other medications after discharge. The researchers leave open the question of whether more aggressive therapy would have reduced the older patients' mortality rate, though they say that beta-blockers and other related drugs would probably have benefited the older patients. This study points to age bias–related to treatment of older people. Other studies support this finding. Alder and colleagues (2002) found that, compared to older men, older women who had heart disease received less aggressive treatment.

Dr. Robert Butler, first Director of the National Institute on Aging, coined the term ageism (1969). **Ageism** refers to prejudice against older people. Butler says that ageism comes about because the young and the middle-aged feel distaste for aging. They see old age as a time of weakness, sickness, and dying. Ageism also comes about because people know little about old age, and because what they know is based on myth and fear. Palmore (1994) considers it one of the three great "isms" of our day (along with racism and sexism).

In Canadian society today, people learn to be prejudiced against the old. These negative views come from many sources (see Exhibit 1.3). Cruikshank (2003, 138) found negative attitudes toward older women in fairy tales and folklore. These tales often portray older women as witches. According to one folk saying, "if the devil can't come himself, he sends an old woman." Cruikshank discusses how, in *Gulliver's Travels*, Jonathan Swift created the Struldbruggs, a people who grow old but never die. Gulliver's interpreter calls them "peevish, covetous, morose, vain, talkative." He describes them as selfish and impotent, and Gulliver says they are "the most mortifying sight I ever beheld; and the women are more horrible than the men."

Berman and Sobkowska-Ashcroft (1986, 1987) reviewed the treatment of older people in great books from the Bible to those of the 20th century. They found that comedies almost always make fun of older people. Wortley (1998) found negative attitudes toward women in some ancient Greek poems. These poems especially criticized courtesans who relied on their beauty in their youth. Overall, in philosophy, literature, and the theatre, Berman and Sobkowska-Ashcroft found that "negative traits outnumber positive traits by about two to one" (1986, 141).

Jokes present a negative view of old age and older people as well. Palmore (1971) conducted a classic study

● Exhibit 1.3

WHAT IS IT LIKE TO BE OLD?

We cannot know the answer to this question until we reach old age ourselves. But Professor Paul Baker of the University of Victoria set out, at age 33, to learn about aging firsthand. In the story that follows he describes his experiment with old age.

"You're too young to be a gerontologist. How can somebody who's only 33 know what it's like to be 83?" This reaction from one of the few older students in my course on the sociology of aging bothered me. My first instinct was to haul out my academic/scientific defenses and claim that you don't have to be an X to study X's (be they old, female, black, or handicapped).

But I was left with the uncomfortable feeling that maybe she was right, maybe I was missing some of the more subjective and emotional aspects of aging by working only with "hard," "objective" data. Then I ran across John Griffin's classic book, *Black Like Me*, written in 1961. Griffin dyed his skin and passed as a black man in the southern United States for a month. His book showed how different the world was for a black man, and made a lot of white people realize what racism meant at the human level.

So, how could I become old? The answer was obvious: the same kind of makeup that turned Dustin Hoffman old in *Little Big Man* might work for me, and, with the help of a makeup artist in Vancouver, plus some old clothes, a cane, and a grey wig, I made the transformation. The makeup took several hours to apply, and hurt like hell going on and coming off, but it worked.

My main interest was in experiencing society's reactions to an old man. I walked around in Victoria and Vancouver about a dozen times, in different places, at night and during the day. And what I found was pretty much what I expected; a few people go out of their way to help the old, a few turn their backs, and most people simply ignore them.

One "young" woman (my own age) waited patiently for me as I struggled up the stairs at the Victoria Institute of Gerontology, held the door open, and said, "Have a nice day." I felt very uncomfortable: I was really a young, healthy male but was masquerading as a decrepit old man; I actually felt like I was a "burden" and almost told her I could open doors for myself, even if I was old.

On the other hand, I was shoved off the sidewalk in front of the Empress Hotel by a large, noisy bunch of tourists. It may have been accidental, but I felt angry and frustrated. On crowded streets I could no longer stride along and know that other people would move aside. I had to be on the defensive, anticipating others' moves. Crossing busy streets became a totally different experience. I hung back so that the crowds could bolt across as soon as the light changed, and then I shuffled along, keeping my eye on the cars, which seemed like racehorses just itching for the gates to open. The lights always started flashing "DON'T WALK" before I was across. What was I supposed to do, the bunny hop?

I experimented with getting in and out of cars and using buses. The basic lesson I learned was that the world gets bigger and faster for an old man, and I became acutely aware of this dramatic change because I was really young, and hadn't gradually accepted the inevitable changes of aging.

I discovered a sense of comradeship of the old, who had the time to sit and talk. I also found a subtle difference between old Victoria and big Vancouver: it seemed easier to be old here, partly because of the size and pace, but maybe also because in Victoria we have so many old people. I think we have learned to be a little more patient.

Would I do it again? Probably not . . . pretending to be old hurt my back, my legs, my feet. It was hard to explain to friends and neighbours what I was doing. I think I'll wait for old age to creep up on me slowly, and, in the meantime, I think I have gained a better understanding for my old friends.

Source: Paul Baker, 1983, *Old Before My Time* [videotape], distributed by the Centre on Aging, University of Victoria, Victoria, BC V8W 2Y2. Reprinted by permission of Paul Morgan Baker.

of attitudes to older people in humour. He looked at 264 jokes taken from 10 popular joke books. He found that one-quarter of the jokes took a positive view of aging and about one-fifth took a neutral view, but more than half of them showed a negative attitude to aging or the aged. Jokes relied on several stereotypes about older people—"loss of physical or mental abilities; loss of attractiveness; loss of sexual ability or interest; and age concealment" (Palmore 2005, 87). Palmore also found a double standard in jokes about age. Jokes about women, more often than those about men, portrayed older people negatively. A study by Bowd (2003) supports Palmore's work. Bowd chose more than 4,000 jokes from three published joke books. He found that 102 of these jokes presented a stereotype of the older person. The jokes included stereotypes of impotent men, unattractive women, and childishness in old age.

These jokes project our own fears about aging onto older people. But do these fears have a basis in fact? Studies generally find high life satisfaction among older people. The Canadian Community Health Survey sampled 25,000 community-dwelling Canadians aged 15 and over in 2002 (Statistics Canada 2003u). The older age group had the highest proportion of people who felt very satisfied with life. They also showed the lowest proportion of people who felt dissatisfied or very dissatisfied with life. George (2006) reviewed the literature on life satisfaction. She says that in both short-term and long-term studies, life satisfaction in old age remains high.

Married seniors, those in good health, those with more education and better income all report high life satisfaction (Clarke et al. 2000). Michalos and his colleagues (2001) compared the life satisfaction of the general population in British Columbia with the life satisfaction of older people (aged 55 to 97). They found that, compared to the general population, on almost all dimensions older people reported higher levels of life satisfaction. The older people in the study did not feel stereotyped and they said they felt that someone really cared about them. The study of aging shows that old age has its compensations. Older people in Canada have guaranteed incomes, subsidized housing, and free medical care. They also get reduced rates on buses, hotels, and car rentals. Other bonuses include tax breaks, free tuition at many universities, and financial support for recreation programs.

The research shows that Canadian society has an ambivalent view of aging: ageism exists alongside care and concern for older people. The study of aging shows that the attitudes of others cause some of the worst problems older people face. McMullin and Marshall (2001) studied garment workers in Montreal. The workers said

they felt that the owners' ageist attitudes and actions put pressure on them and in some cases forced them to retire. They felt that the owners and managers gave them less credit for their experience than they deserved, and that the owners focused on decreases in their speed and strength.

The owners and managers denied any ageist attitudes. They said they focused only on productivity and outcomes. But the researchers found that the owners gave the older workers the hardest jobs. They did not adapt the speed of the work to accommodate older workers who worked at slower speed than younger workers. The researchers say that the owners and managers used the decline in speed and precision of older workers as an excuse to force them out of work. A more flexible attitude and an appreciation of the older workers' contribution to the workplace would have allowed older workers to stay at work.

Other studies of attitudes toward older workers show that ageism in the workplace exists. Underhill, Marshall, and Deliencourt (1997; cited in Marshall 2001, 7) asked counsellors at Human Resources Centres of Canada about employers' attitudes toward older workers. Sixty-two percent of the counsellors agreed that "employers believe that older workers should step aside" and 50 percent agreed that "employers believe that older workers have low productivity"; 84 percent agreed that "employers discriminate against older workers in hiring practices." Marshall (2001, 7) concludes that ageist beliefs "are so widespread as to affect the working opportunities of middle-aged and older individuals."

A study by Palmore (2004) asked older people in the United States and Canada about their experiences of ageism. He found that, compared to the Americans, Canadians reported more experiences of ageism.

Kalish (1979) described a **new ageism**. This refers to the belief that older people need special treatment due to poor health, poverty, and lack of social support. Binstock (2005) calls this a **compassionate stereotype**. This stereotype attempts to create sympathy for older people. It led, in part, to the creation of many social policies that benefit older people today. But this view of aging doesn't give a true picture of later life. And it works against older people by reinforcing the negative stereotypes of old age. A Montreal woman, for example, said that "older people are infantilized," she said, "to the point where they are addressed by the informal 'you' (in French), called by their first names" (Richard et al. 2005, 27).

Older people today face many of the traditional stereotypes about old age. But, as the population has aged, a new form of prejudice has emerged. This type of ageism focuses on the cost of having an older population.

AGEISM AND SOCIAL POLICY

Stereotypes and ageism most often focus on the individual. They exaggerate the physical and mental changes that come with age. But ageism can also focus on population aging. This type of ageism reflects a fear of an aging society (Binstock 2005). Some commentators have begun to express this new form of ageism. They see the new generation of older people as a burden on Canadian society. They fear that an increased number and proportion of older people will lead to higher costs for pensions and health care. And they fear that this will lead to economic and social collapse.

Gee and Gutman (2000, 6) cite some examples of this attack on the older population at the beginning of their book *The Overselling of Population Aging: Apocalyptic Demography, Intergenerational Challenges, and Social Policy*.

- Barbara Beck, writing for *The Globe and Mail* on December 29, 1995, wrote, "the deal between the generations is under severe threat, as the costs of state pensions rise. Many countries are running out of people to pay those contributions. . . . But the argument between the generations is not just about pensions. Medical expenses, too, will burgeon as people get older."

- Shawn McCarthy and Rob Carrick, writing for *The Globe and Mail* on April 11, 1998, said, "faced with the daunting demographic challenges of an aging baby-boom . . . Canadians—younger ones in particular—are skeptical . . . the CPP [Canadian Pension Plan] will be around for their retirement. And they have every reason to worry."

- Edward Greenspon, writing for *The Globe and Mail* on October 3, 1996, wrote, "Canadians have rarely received so few benefits for their tax dollars, and the difficult times are just beginning. The consequences of this will be profound: tense interregional conflict, *clashes between young and old people*, and if things get really bad, class warfare [emphasis added by Gee and Gutman].

These writers play on the public fear of an aging society. They stereotype the older population as dependent, unproductive, and costly. And they speak in apocalyptic terms as if population aging will lead to the collapse of society as we know it. "In line with this ideology," Rozanova and colleagues (2006, 380; citing Gee and McDaniel 1993) say, "older adults are stereotyped as unproductive greedy geezers, are blamed for public debt loads, and are portrayed as a threat to the sustainability of public programs."

Discussions of aging within this worldview often come down to the issue of the fair distribution of resources to the older and younger generations. Rumblings in the Canadian press and in public debate suggest that Canadian society shows concern about generational equity. Connidis (2001, 253) points to calls for "deficit reduction, downsizing, and cost cutting in public and private spheres" as evidence that Canada, like the United States, sees older people as the source of increased costs.

A study of newspaper articles in *The Globe and Mail* by Rozanova and colleagues (2006, 381) found apocalyptic comments that echo these concerns. The researchers say that in their study, "older adults were portrayed as a burden on their families and on society. Seniors were described as unproductive, dependent, and in need of support and care … Seniors, even if healthy at the moment, were portrayed as a time bomb that would sooner or later damage society due to the rising costs of the health care system …" In one article, Bernard Lord (cited in Rozanova et al. 2006, 381), Premier of New Brunswick, echoed the apocalyptic theme, "… Canadians," he said, "are going to face some tough choices as they deal with the needs of an aging population …"

Townson (2006a, 214) says that "In the recent past, neo-liberal think-tanks and commentators in Canada did their best to whip up inter-generational conflict." This took place in the debate over pension reform. Supporters of privatization of pensions used fear of a large older population to argue for decreased government pensions. But Clark (1993) believes that Canada will avoid intergenerational conflict. Clark says that broad-based social programs in Canada create a sense of common interest. For example, Canada's national health care system serves people of all ages. For this reason, it tends to unify national concerns around good health regardless of age. Clark says that "what is interpreted in the U.S. as a crisis is simply seen in Canada as a challenge to good government" (498).

A study by Stone, Rosenthal, and Connidis (1998) shows that influential Canadian researchers take a broad view of **intergenerational equity**. They look beyond public exchanges of funds (such as Canada's Old Age Security program) to include parent–child exchanges of informal supports. They also look at the mutual exchanges (of money and services) between adult children and their aging parents. And they look at support levels and types of support given and received by many age groups. Some studies conclude that "*over the life course, private exchange of supports between parents and children is not balanced. It heavily favours the children*" (66; emphasis in original). Up to age 70, older people give more support to their children than they receive. And they continue to give to their children throughout their lives.

These findings question the U.S. model of inter-generational relations. In the U.S. view, each genera-tion looks at what it has put into the system and judges whether it will get back more or less than it put in. Stone and his colleagues support a long view of exchange. They propose that giving and receiving over the life course strengthens social bonds between the generations. They see children's dependence on parents over most of a life-time as a normal part of social and familial life. And they see giving to parents in later life as a way for the young to pay back their parents for this support. They propose that we view this as "a foundation of social cohesion." Childless older people can experience this same bond with nieces, nephews, and the children of friends.

Myles (2000) reports little influence of the intergen-erational equity controversy on Canadian policy or on public opinion. Northcott's research supports this view. He studied the attitudes of the public toward the idea of an aging crisis. He concluded that population aging would not necessarily lead to intergenerational conflict (Maurier and Northcott 2000).

A background paper written for the Canadian Federal, Provincial and Territorial Committee of Officials (Seniors) (Edwards and Mawani 2006) presents a bal-anced view of intergenerational relations in Canada. The report calls for "**a society for all ages**," a theme endorsed by the Federal, Provincial, and Territorial Ministers Responsible for Seniors.

> This intergenerational approach addresses the growing tendency to isolate different age groups, particularly at the beginning and later stages of life, and encourages intergenerational programs, practices and policies. These initiatives have become increasingly popular because the benefits to old and young participants are visible and immediate. All of the key informants who were interviewed in the preparation of this paper recommended increased support for intergenerational activities to enhance healthy aging (10).

This debate over the cost of an older population will continue. And the growing size of the older popula-tion will draw attention to the costs of public pensions, health care, and other services. Blaming older people for this shift in resource allocation will not lead to a better life for older or younger people. Longino (2005, 83) says that the challenge of an older population "can generate creative answers, many of which are unknowable ahead of time." Gerontologists can provide the public with good information about the costs and the benefits of social policies.

We all have parents and grandparents. We'll all be old someday. We want to live in a society that cares for people at every age.

A NEW VIEW OF OLD AGE

Stereotypes and ageism give a simplistic picture of individual and societal aging. Research shows that older people live rich and complex lives that contradict the stereotypes. For example, most people aged 50 to 70 have good incomes, little or no mortgage, and no children to support. They have money to spend, better educa-tion than past generations of older people, and active lifestyles. Recreation programs, education, and travel services appeal to this group. The corporate world has begun to see older age groups as a market for new goods and services.

Retail companies, insurance companies, and travel companies, for example, now market services and prod-ucts to the needs and desires of seniors. Foot and Stoffman (1998) report that Baby Boomers will pay for quality and service when they buy a product. Ikea, the furniture company, for example, now offers delivery and assembly services that benefit older customers.

Companies have developed drugs to improve male sexual potency, chemical treatments to hide wrinkles, and new hair colours to enhance older women's looks. Foot and Stoffman (1998) report that beer makers have created new premium brands for older consumers. A recent beer ad, for example, shows liquor store owners and bartenders refusing to serve 20-something cus-tomers. The ad ends by saying "Only people aged 30 and over can appreciate the taste of ..." Foot and Stoffman say that clothing makers have redefined the sizes of clothing in order to salve the egos of older customers. "Even men's waist sizes have been relaxed by some man-ufacturers who are putting 32-inch labels on pants that fit comfortably around spongy 34-inch waists" (132). All of these products support a new model of later life. They meet the needs of older people who see themselves as active, energetic, and engaged. This view of later life rejects the image of aging as decline.

Women make up a large segment of the mid- to later-life market. Milner (2006) says that 8 million Canadian women make up the 40-and-over age group. These women feel satisfied with life, self-confident, and empowered. Milner says that, to attract this wealthy market segment, companies should focus on the mature woman's desire to look and feel good. Companies like Gap that served the youth market have begun to discover the mature consumer. Gap created Forth & Towne, a new chain to serve the older woman. This move follows the lead of Chico's, a retail chain that successfully targets mature women.

One company, Unilever, the maker of Dove beauty products, has taken a bold step to attract older consumers. It created a new line of products called "Pro Age" that help people look good without denying their age. The advertising for the Dove products features full-figured women who are not professional models. Unilever takes a risk in promoting a product that helps people look their age (rather than deny it). After all, millions of Americans get Botox treatments each year, use anti-aging makeup, and buy toothpaste to whiten aging teeth. Nancy Etcoff, a psychologist at the Harvard Medical School consulted on the study that led to the new Dove products. She says, "We're seeing a real shift in how people are approaching beauty. Up to now, it's been about fighting aging with everything you have. Now you have a chance not to" (cited in Tsiantar, 2007, 1–2).

Rozanova and colleagues (2006, 379) found "successful aging" as a theme in their study of *The Globe and Mail*. They found that many articles described older people as "wealthy, active, healthy, youthful looking, pursuing stay-young activities." Television shows now sometimes feature single, independent, older women. The Rolling Stones, in their 60s, tour and produce albums. Jane Fonda in her 70s and Cher in her 60s promote fitness through aerobic exercise videos. One TV commercial has an elderly 90-pound saleswoman carry a 200-pound man out of a store to try her pizza because he "only goes out for pizza."

The May/June 2009 issue of *AARP The Magazine*, contained articles on the elder wisdom, personal finances, and health. You might expect to see these articles in a magazine for seniors. But it also contained articles on travel, gourmet food, divorce, and job loss. These articles reflect the interests and lifestyles of older people today.

Some critics believe that this new positive view of later life creates a new stereotype. Katz and Marshall (2003), for example, note that our consumer society pressures older people to use drugs and products to remain sexually and physically youthful. They say that this promotes an impossible ideal that ignores other ways to age. According to these researchers, many of the new images of aging marginalize the very old, older people with disabilities, and older people with a different view of aging.

Studies of the media support this concern. McHugh (2003) studied advertisements that promote retirement in Arizona. These ads portrayed older people as active, energetic, and upper middle class. But the ads excluded images of disabled or poor older people. These ads subtly distinguish two kinds of older people—haves and have-nots. Calasanti (2005,10; also Hurd 1999) says that "through activity one demonstrates productivity and hence social worth." A less active person—either due to personal preference or illness—gets rejected as old. Rozanova and colleagues (2006, 376) call this "intra-generational ageism." The ads distinguish between "us," the healthy active older person who will live the good life. And "them," the poor and disabled who live on the margins.

A number of authors say that claims of agelessness or youthfulness in spirit deny the uniqueness of later life. For instance, Gibson (2000) objects to this view of a youthful mind inside an aging body. She says that older people should feel proud of their experience, wisdom, and freedom from their youthful mistakes. Andrews (2000) also challenges the idea of a youthful self within an aging body. This mind–body split, she says, rejects the aging body. She says that older people and society should embrace aging in all its forms. Cruikshank (2003, 168) proposes "frankness about decline and loss of capacity." She argues against the "false cheerfulness" of the more upbeat view of aging.

AGING AS DISEASE—ANOTHER FORM OF AGEISM

As you can see, ageism takes many forms. It shows up in literature, advertising, jokes, and attitudes. Even the promotion of health and activity, or "successful aging" in later life can support ageism because it rejects people with chronic illness, disability, low income, or visual signs of physical decline (gray hair and wrinkles). This view of healthy aging links physical decline to disease—an abnormal state of aging. Calasanti (2005, 9) says that aging looks avoidable and like a personal failure from this point of view. "... to appear unhealthy," she says, "is to have failed and to deserve one's fate; one ought to have changed one's lifestyle or diet." Calasanti says that the older person who shows signs of aging (or even someone who chooses to live a contemplative lifestyle), from this point of view, deserves their fate and the poor treatment they receive. "Not to resist signs of physical decay," she says, "may be perceived as evidence of moral decline" (Calasanti 2005 citing Jones and Pugh, 2005, 254–55).

Rozanova and colleagues (2006) show that both ageism and the overpromotion of active aging lead to the same end. They both stereotype the older person and create a one-dimensional ideal of later life. Both views of aging exclude the many ways that people can and do grow old successfully. For example, some people will choose a less than active lifestyle; for example, people in nursing homes or those "who prefer contemplation or are simply sedentary." Poor people and minority group members may lack the resources to live a stereotyped "successful" old age (Minkler and Holstein 2005).

Bayer (2005, 14) says that "'positive aging' soon equates with anti-aging"—a denial of aging. A study by Hurd Clarke and colleagues (2007) shows that women feel ambivalent about the pressure to look eternally young. Men may also feel pressure to look younger and more virile. But they less frequently turn to cosmetic solutions.

The medical profession, along with questionable marketers, joins in the attack on the aging body. Bayer (2005) for example, refers to the "cosmeceutical" industry. Cosmeceuticals refers to the combination of cosmetics and pharmaceutical substances. Together these substances promise to fight the effects of aging on the skin and in the body. Botox and plastic surgery promise solutions to sagging skin and wrinkles.

Older people today can feel caught in a bind. Society expects people to act young as they age. But they might prefer to let the signs of aging show. Clarke (2002) looked at older women's views on beauty in later life. The women in this study felt the pressure toward thinness exerted by the modern fashion ideal, but they rejected the current ideal of extreme thinness. They preferred a more rounded body shape for themselves. These women also emphasized the importance of inner beauty. They found beauty in an individual's personality, relations to others, and inner happiness. Clarke concludes that social ideals shape an older woman's view of herself: "ageist norms … denigrate older women and older women's bodies" (440). But, she says, older women can and do challenge these norms. "Many of the women in my study," she points out, "provide an important example of how oppressive social values can be resisted and how individuals may … offer alternatives to ageist interpretations of later life" (440).

Hurd Clarke and colleagues (2007) found this same tension between societal expectations and personal beliefs. The researchers interviewed 44 women aged 50 to 70. They asked the women about their views on beauty in later life. These women viewed natural aging—without the use of hair dye and makeup—as a worthwhile goal. But most of the women engaged in what the researchers call "beauty work." They endorsed the use of cosmetics, anti-wrinkle creams, and even cosmetic surgery to produce a "natural" look as they aged. And most of these women used these methods to look young. The researchers conclude that ageism in Canadian society leads women to cover the signs of aging.

The debate about good aging shows a healthy interest in redefining old age. It captures the diversity of later life as older people and Canadian society work out new ways to live in the Third Age. Still, more change needs to take place in society and in our attitudes in order to have a more balanced view of later life. We need to allow for many ways to grow old. Some people want to engage in energetic activities that we associate with youth. Other older people define later life as a time to use their wisdom, share their memories, and offer community leadership. Some people will live vibrant healthy lives into late old age. Others will live with chronic illness. Some will seem youthful to us, others will look old. No single right way to grow old exists. And none of these ways should meet with social rejection.

Education as an Antidote to Ageism

Hess (2006) reviewed the research on attitudes toward older people. He found that people with more knowledge about aging had a more positive view of later life; they could see things from the perspective of the older person. Also, people who had personal contact with older adults tended to stereotype less. Negative stereotypes come into play most often when we know little about a person or group (Funderburk et al., 2006).

Hagestad and Uhlenberg (2005; Hendricks 2005) say that the separation of age groups in modern society perpetuates ageism. Typically young people and older people spend little time together and know little about one another. Studies show that more positive interaction between older and younger people decreases ageism. Knapp and Stubblefield (2000) assigned students in a psychology of aging course to work with older people in the community. Students also interacted with fellow classmates aged 55 and over. Students kept a journal and discussed their experiences in class. The researchers compared these students with a control group in a criminal justice course. The researchers conclude that interaction with older people in class and through service learning led to more realistic and positive views of older people.

Roth (2005) describes a volunteer program for university students. Students spent time interacting with residents of a nearby long-term care facility. The program asked students to learn about the residents' view of life. Students wrote weekly reports that reflected on their experience. The researchers conclude that the students developed a more positive view of frailty and later life. These programs show the value of interaction between the generations. Knowledge and satisfying contact with older people lead to a more positive view of aging (see Exhibit 1.4). The number of education programs for undergraduates and health care professionals has

● Exhibit 1.4

EVENTS TODAY'S CENTENARIANS HAVE WITNESSED IN THEIR LIFETIME

Year	Age in that year	Event
1914		World War I begins
1918		World War I ends
1918	10–20	Canadian women win right to vote
1927		Lindbergh makes first transatlantic flights
1929		Stock market collapses and Great Depression begins
1931	20–30	Penicillin discovered
1939	30–40	World War II begins
1945		World War II ends
1946		Baby Boom begins
1949		Newfoundland becomes a province
1952		CBC broadcasts first television show coast to coast
1972	60–70	State-funded universal medicare exists across Canada; all provinces comply with national standards
1980	70–80	Era of the personal computer begins
1990	80–90	Dot-com stock market bubble
2001	90–100	World Trade Center bombing and terrorism threat worldwide Broadband
2006	100+	Internet, the World Wide Web, and mobile communications create a global community; concern about global warming takes hold

This chart shows the tremendous amount of change that the oldest Canadians have witnessed in their lifetimes. Centenarians today played an active role in many of these events, including the Great Depression and World War II. These changes and many others have shaped and reshaped their world. World events have also shaped the older person's character and personality. This view of the past century challenges the belief that older people resist change and can't adapt to a changing world.

What changes have occurred in your parents' lifetimes? In your own? Create a chart that lists the changes you've witnessed in history, technology, and society. How have you responded to these changes? Can you guess what changes you will witness in the future?

Source: Adapted from Statistics Canada, 2002, "Time Line: The Events Today's Centenarians Have Witnessed in Their Lifetime," http://www12.statcan.ca/english/census01/Products/Analytic/companion/age/timelinet.cfm, accessed May 7, 2009. Reprinted with permission.

increased in the past few years. These programs will lead to better treatment of older people and a more balanced view of aging today.

A CANADIAN VISION OF AGING

Some changes in Canadian society suggest that ageism will lessen over time. First, Canada will have more older people in the future. Many of them will live in good health until late old age. They will serve as role models for younger people. They will demonstrate the many ways that people can age successfully in Canada today. Second, compared with earlier generations, people will enter old age with more education and technical knowledge. This will allow older people to remain a valuable part of their communities and of the workforce (if they choose). The generation gap in the past, in part, reflected an education gap between the generations. This will lessen in the future. Third, the small size of younger age groups may open opportunities for older people to work at later ages if they choose. This would provide some older people with better incomes in later life. And it would decrease the stereotype of the older person as dependent, obsolete, and irrelevant.

Finally, attitudes toward older people have improved in recent years. And Canadians hold a more realistic view of aging in the future. Palmore (2005, 90), who has studied ageism in society for more than 30 years, holds an optimistic view of the future. "Most trends in our society and culture will push us toward reductions in ageism … I believe that 'we shall overcome' ageism!"

Canada has taken steps to decrease and eliminate ageism. The federal government has created a National Framework on Aging (NFA) Vision Statement. Canada, it states, is "a society for all ages, promotes the well-being and contributions of older people in all aspects of life, recognizes their valuable contributions and reflects the goals of elimination of ageism in all sectors" (Health Canada 1998, 6). The NFA consulted with seniors across the country on the key principles that a society for all ages should embrace. The consultation groups came up with five core principles: *dignity, independence, participation, fairness,* and *security.* The Federal/Provincial/Territorial Ministers Responsible for Seniors approved these principles and saw them as key to the development of policies for seniors.

CONCLUSION

Canada's government and people have dedicated themselves to the elimination of ageism. However, this goal can't be achieved through a policy statement, the stroke of a pen, or a speech. Canadians need to understand that people of all ages make up the fabric of a good and just society. And a high quality of life at all ages benefits everyone. The more Canadians understand about aging, through research and public discussion, the more Canada can realize the vision of a society for all ages.

Gerontology can play an important role. It can help us understand the facts and the issues about aging. It can move discussion from fear, stereotype, prejudice, and discrimination to understanding. Gerontology shows that old age forms a normal part of the life cycle. Nearly all of us will enter old age some day. And we'll bring with us the attitudes and experiences of a lifetime. Gerontology can help overcome ageism by presenting a more balanced and accurate view of aging and older people. It can change people's attitudes toward aging and give them more knowledge about their families, their friends, and themselves.

Summary

1. The growth of the older population in Canada has made aging a major social issue—one that will affect all of us.

2. Gerontology has two goals: first, to increase our knowledge about old age and, second, to improve the quality of life in old age. In Canada today, these goals take the form of scholarly research and the practical application of research findings.

3. Canadians have both positive and negative images of aging and older people. Many of these stereotypes have little basis in fact. Negative attitudes can lead to prejudice and discrimination against older people.

4. Population aging has led to a new form of ageism. Some writers scapegoat the older population and blame older people for rising pension and health care costs. These writers predict economic collapse and intergenerational conflict. They propose a reduction in support for older people. Gerontologists refute these claims and present a more balanced view of Canadian society in the future.

5. New images of aging have begun to emerge. These include the image of the ever-youthful person; the active, engaged senior; and the older person who accepts aging and the physical changes it brings.

6. A growing population of healthy and active older people will lead Canadians to rethink their views of aging. Gerontology tries to replace stereotypes with facts, information, and a clearer understanding of later life.

7. The Canadian government supports "a society for all ages." This concept proposes an ideal society in which people of all ages can get the social support they need—and people can live full and happy lives at every age.

Study Questions

1. Why should students know about aging? How will an aging population affect social structures like education, health care, and the family?

2. What is ageism? Where do negative attitudes toward aging come from? How can people develop a more positive attitude toward aging?

3. Define the term "gerontology." What are the two main goals of this discipline?

4. State three common myths about aging. Explain why these myths are false.

5. Why do some writers predict intergenerational conflict? Do you think this will take place in Canada? Why or why not?

6. Explain why older consumers have become a force in the marketplace. What types of products do older consumers prefer? How has the image of the older consumer changed in the past few years?

7. What troubles some older people about the image of later life as an extension of youth? What response have some seniors made to the image of the older person as ever-youthful?

8. What do policy makers mean by "a society for all ages?"

Key Terms

ageism   prejudice against older people. (6)

compassionate stereotype   a stereotype that attempts to create sympathy for older people, but does not give a true picture of later life. (8)

discrimination   unfair treatment of a person or group based on prejudice. (2)

elderspeak   a simplified speech like baby talk that some people use when they speak to older people. It stems from stereotyping older people as slow-witted. (6)

gerontology   the discipline that studies aging systematically. (2)

intergenerational equity   the call for a smaller proportion of public support for older people; based on the belief that older people use a disproportionate share of public resources. (9)

new ageism   the belief that older people need special treatment due to poor health, poverty, and lack of social support. (8)

prejudice   being biased against someone or something; a negative judgment formed beforehand without knowledge of the facts. (2)

social structures   a relatively stable pattern of social interactions. (2)

society for all ages   "promotes the well-being and contributions of older people in all aspects of life, [it] recognizes their valuable contributions and reflects the goals of elimination of ageism in all sectors." A society for all ages has five core principles: dignity, independence, participation, fairness, and security. (10)

stereotypes   an exaggerated and often prejudiced view of a type of person or group of people. (5)

Selected Readings

Butler, R. N. *The Longevity Revolution: Benefits and Challenges of Living a Long Life*. New York: PublicAffairs, 2008.

> An informed and thoughtful look at the issues raised by individual and population aging today.
>
> The author updates many topics he has covered before—ageism, intergenerational conflict, and the aging of society. He also covers scientific facts on the aging body. This leads to a detailed discussion of the health care system and the challenges society faces in the years ahead. An excellent study by one of the leading gerontologists today.

Gee, E.M.T., and G. Gutman, eds. *The Overselling of Population Aging: Apocalyptic Demography, Intergenerational Challenges, and Social Policy*. Don Mills, ON: Oxford University Press, 2000.

> This book presents articles by Canadian gerontologists on pension reform, health care, caregiving, and family life. The articles challenge the myth that population aging will lead to social conflict and economic collapse. The writers show that through social planning Canadian society can respond to the challenges of population aging.

Grabinski, C.J. *101 Careers in Gerontology*. New York: Springer, 2007.

> This book describes career paths in gerontology for mid-career job-changers, postsecondary students, and even high school students. It outlines the schooling and credentials needed for various careers. It offers insight into job opportunities that gerontology students may overlook—clothing design, law, travel, etc. The book also presents interviews with people who work in these fields. This book provides a good way to stimulate your thinking about career opportunities in gerontology.

Maurier, W.L., and H.C. Northcott. *Aging in Ontario: Diversity in the New Millennium*. Calgary: Detselig Enterprises, 2000.

> A close look at aging in one Canadian province. The study focuses on the diversity of the older population and presents a factual analysis of aging today. It also shows how gerontologists look at aging and how their work can give a clear understanding of later life.

Websites to Consult

Canadian Seniors Partnership

http://www.seniors.gc.ca/content.jsp?lang=en&contentid=25

> In November 2001, a group of decision makers from the federal and provincial governments and the volunteer sector formed an association that is committed to bringing about a transformation in the way programs and Canadian seniors, their families, caregivers, and supporting service organizations access services. The Seniors Canada On-line website (http://www.seniors.gc.ca/h.4m.2@.jsp?lang=eng) is a visible result of what collaboration across governments can achieve.

Guide to Government of Canada Services for Seniors and Their Families

http://www.seniors.gc.ca/content.jsp?&font=0&contentid=100&lang=en

This guide provides information about Government of Canada services and programs for seniors and their families.

National Seniors Council (Canada)

http://www.seniorscouncil.gc.ca/en/home.shtml

The National Seniors Council has been established to advise Canada's government on all matters related to the health, well-being, and quality of life of seniors. The site contains reference to government speeches and to publications on aging.

Answers to Quiz in Exhibit 1.1

All 10 statements are false.

Chapter

2

Theories and Methods

© istockphoto.com/Robert Lerich

INTRODUCTION

Thirty years ago, the Gerontological Society of America (GSA) and the Association for Gerontology in Higher Education (AGHE) set out to define the discipline of gerontology (Foundations Project 1980). They asked 111 scholars, researchers, and professionals in the field to describe a basic education program in gerontology. These experts came from such different disciplines as biomedicine and economics, and their descriptions of the exact content and boundaries of gerontology varied. But they did agree that three broad areas of study should make up the core of a gerontology curriculum: biomedicine, psychosocial studies, and socioeconomic-environmental studies. Now, three decades later, these areas remain central to the study of aging. The first area, biomedicine, looks at the changes in physiology and health that come with age. This area includes studies of the biochemical causes of aging, studies of reaction time and stress, and studies of Alzheimer's disease and other types of dementia. Experts disagreed least about the curriculum content for this area; this may be due to the long tradition of biomedical research on aging.

The second area, psychosocial studies, examines the changes that take place within individuals and between individuals and groups. This includes studies of memory, learning, and personality, as well as research on family and friendship ties, and recreation and leisure activities of older adults.

The third area, socioeconomic-environmental studies, concentrates on the effects of aging on social structures such as health care and education. It also looks at the effects of social structures on the aging individual and includes the study of income policies, health care systems, and formal social supports.

Social gerontology includes psychosocial, socioeconomic-environmental, and practice-related research. It looks at aging from the points of view of both the individual and the social system. Social gerontologists often take an interest in physical and health care changes that come with age. But the focus of the social gerontologist differs from that of the physiologist or biochemist. When social gerontologists look at biological or physical change in old age, they ask how these changes affect the individual's social life or society as a whole. They want to know how diseases in old age affect hospital costs or how changes in lung capacity affect a person's ability to work.

They also want to know how a social norm such as retirement affects an older person's health, how changes in family life in Canada affect the psychological well-being of older adults, or what counselling methods work best with new retirees. Researchers use a variety of methods to examine these and other questions. And they have begun to give added attention to gerontological theory (Bengtson, Rice, and Johnson 1999; McMullin 2000; Powell 2006). This chapter will look at (1) the theories that gerontologists use to guide their research and to interpret their findings, (2) the methods researchers use to gather data, and (3) current and future developments in Canadian research on aging.

THEORY IN THE STUDY OF AGING

Social gerontologists use theory to guide research and to interpret the results of their studies. A good theory helps a researcher choose research methods, questions, and samples. Bengtson and his colleagues (1999, 5) see the primary value of theory as providing "a set of lenses through which we can view and make sense of what we observe in research." They identify four ways that theory is valuable to researchers. Theory

1. allows for the integration of new knowledge with information that is already known on the topic or issue;

2. provides a framework for the explanation of findings;

3. predicts outcomes in future research; and

4. provides practical information for the development of social programs and interventions.

Theories create a structure that explains why things happen the way they do. For instance, research shows that women get more of their retirement income from public pension sources than men. Why does this difference exist? And is this an important finding or a trivial fact? Theory offers a framework for explaining research findings and for building knowledge and understanding. Feminist theory, for example, would trace this difference to gender inequalities in the workplace. Women have less opportunity to pay into private pension plans during their middle years. This forces them to rely on public pension sources in old age, and it forces some women to live in poverty. A life course perspective would see the issue differently. It would focus on women's choices and the circumstances they face throughout life. Women, for example, take on caregiving tasks. And this affects their patterns of employment and their pensions.

Theory gives an interpretation to the facts. But no one theory in gerontology can explain all the facts about aging. And sometimes a researcher will use several theories to explain the results of a study. Authors often select theories to fit their sense of how the world works. If you know the assumptions that underlie a theory, you know the strengths and limitations of using that theory, and you know the biases that each theory brings to the explanation of results. The theory used will guide the collection of data as well as how that data is interpreted.

Social gerontologists have generally used sociological or social-psychological theories in their work. Sometimes they have adapted these theories to fit the study of aging. Theory helps to disentangle the effects of history, biology, and social life on the aging person.

Two Levels of Theory

Theories describe all sorts of human activity and relationships, from individual attitudes to societal structures. The following discussion categorizes theories by placing them into a framework (see Exhibit 2.1), and

also gives examples of how gerontologists apply these theories in their work.

Gerontologists often classify theories into two categories or levels of theory: (1) micro level and (2) macro level. But be aware that sometimes these levels overlap and some theories bridge both categories.

Micro-level theories focus on individuals and their interactions. They are used to explain phenomena such as the relationship between adult children and their parents, changes in memory with age, and the effect of negative attitudes on an older person's self-image. **Macro-level theories** "examine social structures or structural elements as they influence experiences and behaviors" (Bengtson, Burgess, and Parrott 1997, S76). Macro-level theories explain phenomena such as the effect of industrialization on older people's status, the history and impact of public pensions, and how gender and income affect older people's well-being. Critics of micro-level theories say they focus too much on people's actions and interactions. They ignore or take little account of economic conditions and social policies.

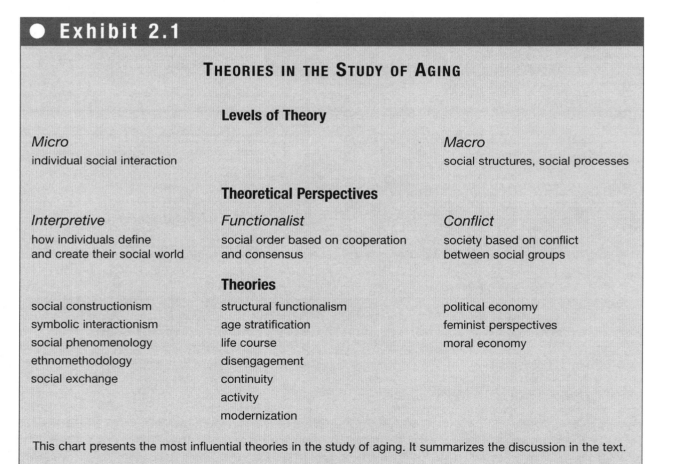

● Exhibit 2.1

THEORIES IN THE STUDY OF AGING

Levels of Theory

Micro
individual social interaction

Macro
social structures, social processes

Theoretical Perspectives

Interpretive
how individuals define
and create their social world

Functionalist
social order based on cooperation
and consensus

Conflict
society based on conflict
between social groups

Theories

social constructionism
symbolic interactionism
social phenomenology
ethnomethodology
social exchange

structural functionalism
age stratification
life course
disengagement
continuity
activity
modernization

political economy
feminist perspectives
moral economy

This chart presents the most influential theories in the study of aging. It summarizes the discussion in the text.

Critics of macro-level theories say that this approach tends to minimize people's ability to act and overcome the limits of social structures.

Three Theoretical Perspectives

Both micro- and macro-level theories can take one of three perspectives: (1) the interpretive perspective, (2) the functionalist perspective, or (3) the conflict perspective.

The Interpretive Perspective

The **interpretive perspective** focuses almost exclusively on the micro level of social life. It looks at how people define situations, how they create their social world, and how they relate to one another in daily life. Historically, social gerontologists have made the least use of this perspective, although interest in this approach has increased significantly in the last few decades. Theories within this perspective include social exchange theory (Homans 1961; Liang, Krause and Bennett 2001), the symbolic interactionist perspective (Mead 1934), social phenomenology (Berger and Luckmann 1966), and ethnomethodology (Garfinkel 1967). The term "social constructionism" has come to represent many of these interpretive approaches (Neugarten 1985; Bengtson, Burgess, and Parrott 1997; von Kondratowitz 2003). It has its foundations in the early work of Max Weber (1905/1955) and George Herbert Mead (1934).

Mead, for example, said that objects and events have no meaning in themselves. People give them meaning through everyday interaction. Grey hair can be a sign of wisdom in one society but a sign of decline in another. People give meanings to objects and then base their actions on these meanings. Some people will refuse to wear a hearing aid because to them it symbolizes decrepitude and weakness. The interpretive perspective views the individual as a creator of social order and organization. This perspective asks the question, "How is a recognizable, predictable social order created?" (Berger and Luckmann 1966; Garfinkel 1967; Schutz 1967). The interpretive perspective can give a good understanding of how people interpret their social world, how they interact with one another, and why they do what they do.

Canadian gerontologists have used this approach to study a range of issues including how caregivers for people with Alzheimer's disease maintain their identity in the face of caregiving stress (MacRae 2002); the self-identity of women with osteoporosis (Wilkins 2001); and the social construction of elder abuse and neglect (Harbison and Morrow 1998). These studies demonstrate some of the strengths of an interpretive perspective.

For example, MacRae (2002) used a symbolic interactionist framework to study caregivers of people with Alzheimer's disease (AD). She looked at how family members help a parent or spouse cope with the loss of self that the disease causes. MacRae found that family members employ a number of strategies to help their relative preserve some of his or her former identity. One strategy involves concealing the diagnosis from others to avoid the label of "dementia." A second strategy involves interpreting inappropriate behaviour as caused by the disease and not by the "real person." A third strategy involves assisting the relative with dressing and grooming so he or she will present an unchanged image of self to others. These strategies help family members preserve the identity of their relative. MacRae shows that this process takes place through daily interactions between the caregivers and the family member who receives care.

A symbolic interactionist perspective helps us recognize that objects and behaviours can have more than one meaning. MacRae's research, for example, shows that family members can help a loved one with dementia look normal when he or she enters the social world. Also, MacRae's work shows that members of the same family often have different interpretations of how much the person with AD has changed and how much of the person's former self remains. MacRae (2003, 414) concludes that "while selves are at risk because of the effects of AD, whether identity is lost or retained is very much dependent upon 'the eye of the beholder.'" MacRae's work demonstrates the value of using an interpretive perspective to study identity maintenance in the case of people with Alzheimer's disease.

The interpretive perspective has weaknesses as well as strengths. For example, it gives only the subjective or individual point of view on social life. It tends to ignore the connections that exist between micro-level social interactions and the larger social forces or structures in society, such as the health care system. This means that it cannot answer many of the "big picture" questions that gerontologists ask. The interpretive perspective, for example, cannot tell us how health care policies will have to change to serve an aging society. It also says little about power and conflict between social groups. For example, it cannot explain income inequality between men and women in old age or the effects of ethnicity on social status in later life. Fortunately, the functionalist and conflict perspectives allow gerontologists to examine these questions.

The Functionalist Perspective

The **functionalist perspective** fits within a **positivist worldview**. It holds that social order is based on consensus, cooperation, and shared norms and values.

Within this perspective, all parts of society serve a role or function to keep society in a state of balance or equilibrium. While the interpretive perspective asks "How do people create their social world through interaction with one another?," the functionalist perspective asks, "What is the structure of the society that people live in and how do the parts of this structure function?"

The structural functionalist theories that grew out of Emile Durkheim's work in 19th-century France best express the traditional functionalist perspective (Parsons 1937; 1951). Durkheim's studies, such as *The Division of Labor* and *Suicide,* serve as models for this approach. Structural functionalist theories treat society as a system that consists of social institutions such as the family, the military, and educational institutions. These systems keep society in a dynamic equilibrium. They adjust to one another as the system responds to internal and external pressures. For example, a structural functionalist would say that the increased number of women in the labour force has led to a decrease in the number of full-time family caregivers for frail older people. This, in turn, has led to more community care programs sponsored by government health services. The health care system has changed to meet new family demands, and this change serves the useful function of restoring society's balance.

Structural functionalism sometimes draws the analogy between society and a living organism, like the human body. Just as our bodies adjust to an increase in our blood sugar, so society adjusts to changes in its internal condition. An increase in the number of older people, for example, may lead society to increase funding to health promotion programs, or to invest more resources in long-term care homes. Structural functionalism predicts that when there is change, society will attempt to create an orderly transition to a new, stable state.

Structural functionalism also assumes that shared norms and values shape individual behaviour. People conform to these norms through social pressure, but also through their belief in society's underlying value system. The values expressed in the commandment "Honour thy father and mother" show up in everyday behaviour and in social policies. Failure to honour or respect a parent may lead to informal sanctions, such as criticism from a sibling or grandparent. Extreme neglect of a parent may lead to the charge of abuse and legal sanctions. Functionalism draws connections between large-scale (macro) social structures and individuals' social roles and actions.

Finally, structural functionalism assumes that society changes or evolves in a positive direction. It explains social problems as dysfunctions, and it proposes to correct these dysfunctions through the use of experts in planning and the helping professions. So, for example, society uses social workers, counsellors, and other experts at shelters and resource centres to deal with the problem of homelessness among older people.

Historically, gerontologists used the functionalist perspective more than any other perspective in their study of aging. Gerontology's most influential early theories—disengagement theory (Cumming and Henry 1961), activity theory (Neugarten, Havighurst, and Tobin 1968), continuity theory (all discussed in Chapter 7), and modernization theory (Cowgill and Holmes 1972, discussed in Chapter 3)—all rely on structural functionalist assumptions. Riley (1971, 1987; Riley, Foner, and Waring 1988; Riley, Johnson, and Foner 1972) also produced a dominant theory based on structural functionalist principles: age stratification theory.

Age stratification theory, also called the "aging and society paradigm" (Riley 1994; Riley, Foner, and Riley, Jr. 1999), "focuses on the role of social structures in the process of individual aging and the stratification by age in the society" (Bengtson, Burgess, and Parrott 1997, S81). Age stratification theory focuses on the movement of **age cohorts** over the life course. It identifies similarities and differences between and among different age cohorts. Gerontologists define an age cohort as a group of people born in the same period of time. All the people born between 1950 and 1955, for example, form an age cohort. According to age stratification theory, people in each cohort move or flow through society's predetermined **age grades** as they age. Childhood, adolescence, and young adulthood are all age grades in Canada. A new age grade, "the Third Age" has emerged recently in Canada. This occurs after retirement but before physical decline and dependence takes place in late old age.

People born in the same period experience the transitions from one stage to another at roughly the same time. They also experience the same historical events at the same time in their life course. People who are in their 60s today, for example, experienced the cultural changes of the 1960s in their late teens and early 20s. These people still have an interest in the music of that period, and "classic rock" radio programs cater to this large group. People in their 50s today lived through the 1960s as children. They may recall the events of that decade, but the cultural, social, and political turmoil of those years had less effect on them, and left less of an impression.

Age stratification theorists say that society also changes as people age, so the norms and roles learned by each new cohort change as society changes. The norms of adult behaviour that people learn in their childhood, for example, may no longer fit when these same people reach adulthood. Many older people today were taught in their childhood that sex outside marriage was immoral. Now, due to the death of a spouse or the influence of changing values and lifestyles of their children and grandchildren, many older people have changed their views on sex outside marriage. Similarly, many younger people will rethink their own values as they age and as society changes.

Age cohorts constantly move along as if on an escalator. As one group leaves an age grade, a new group takes its place. Each age grade (childhood, adolescence, young adulthood, and so on) places expectations on its members and offers people new roles. Also, each successive cohort brings new norms and values to its age grade.

This leads to a dialectic between individuals and societal structures. Changes in norms and values bring changes in social organizations. These changes, in turn, shape the process of aging. For example, new cohorts of older people, with interests in travel and lifelong learning, will affect the traditional programs offered in senior centres. Some senior centres will close because they don't meet the demands of these new older adults. Others will remain open by adapting their programs to meet the changing needs and interests of newer cohorts of older people. These changes in programs will also change the way younger and middle-aged people think about later life.

Age stratification theory relies on many of the assumptions of the structural functionalist approach to aging. First, it assumes that norms and values influence individual aging. Second, it describes the relationship between the individual and society as a feedback loop. Change begins with an individual cohort or with large-scale historical or social change. These changes then lead to change in other parts of the social system. Third, the theory tends to see society as a homogeneous set of structures and functions that all people experience in the same way.

Age stratification theory has a number of strengths. First, it has helped to separate age differences (between cohorts) from age changes over the life course (aging). Second, it highlights the impact of historical and social changes on individuals and cohorts (Bengtson, Burgess, and Parrott 1997). Third, it shows the relationship between aging and social structures. Bengtson and his colleagues (1997, S82) say that age stratification theory "provides new ways to explore differences related to time, period, and cohort."

This perspective also has its weaknesses. For example, people of the same age do not all experience the world in the same way. An elderly Chinese woman who has just arrived in Canada will see the world differently from an elderly French-Canadian man born in Montreal. The age stratification theory overlooks each person's interpretation of the world. It makes little reference to individual control or action. The theory also makes little reference to the tensions and conflicts between social groups in society or to issues of power.

There is also little focus in age stratification theory on how characteristics such as gender, social class, race, and ethnicity can create inequalities within age cohorts. For example, it says little about the differences between growing old as a poor black woman compared with growing old as an upper-middle-class white male. Such variations within cohorts may have a greater influence on people's lives and their experiences in aging than the norms and values related to their age grade. A person's race or gender will lead to different behaviours and to different experiences in and responses to socio-historical events. A person's race or gender will also shape the choices he or she has available. For example, a policy change such as a decrease in government pension payments will have different effects on poor older women and wealthy older men.

Although age stratification theory has its limits, it has made a major contribution to our understanding of aging. It orders many complex phenomena and helps us to see the relationship between the individual and society.

The **life course perspective**, a functionalist approach, bridges the micro- and macro-levels of analysis by incorporating social interaction and social structure within its framework (Bengtson, Burgess, and Parrott 1997). In this way, the life course perspective overcomes some of the limitations of age stratification theory. Researchers use this perspective to explain (1) the continuity and change in individuals' lives over time, (2) age-related and socially recognized life transitions, and (3) the interaction of social life, history, culture, and personal biography (Bengtson, Burgess, and Parrott 1997; Moen & Spencer 2006; Settersten 2006). At the micro or individual level, the life course approach looks at how events and conditions early in life can affect later life. At the macro or societal level, the life course approach shows how social change and historical events can create differences between cohorts (Elder 2000; Elder and Johnson 2003; Settersten 2003).

Researchers tend to agree that no unified, systematic approach to the life course exists. Rather, a life course perspective merges theoretical approaches from many disciplines, including sociology, anthropology, and psychology (Settersten 2006). The life course approach recognizes variety in life course patterns and differences between and among age cohorts. It also recognizes diversity within age cohorts due to differences in race, ethnicity, social class, and gender (Elder and Johnson 2003). This approach takes into account the diversity of roles and role changes across the life course. The life course approach recognizes aging as a lifelong, dynamic, interactive, and multidirectional process. For example, an older person may show some loss of memory over time, but may stay physically active, and may take up new activities in later life. Aging involves both continuity and change—decline in some areas of life, stability or improvement in others.

The life course approach looks at **transitions** and **trajectories**. Transitions refer to changes in social status or social roles (when those changes occur, how long they last, etc.). Transitions include marriage, divorce, remarriage, widowhood, and parenthood. Work-related transitions also occur; for example, getting a first job, changing careers, or retiring. Trajectories refer to long-term patterns of stability and change. They often include many transitions. One person's marital status trajectory may involve the transition to marriage, a subsequent divorce, then a remarriage, and finally a transition to widowhood. Another person's marital status trajectory may involve only one marriage for life. This latter trajectory involves only the transition to a first marriage and, for one of the couple, the transition to widowhood.

Many Canadian researchers use the life course approach (Stone and Harvey 2001; Wister 2005). Ploeg and her colleagues (2004), for example, explore intergenerational financial transfers from parents to their adult children and grandchildren. These researchers find that parents often provide financial help to their adult children. This often occurs when the children go through a life transition like marriage or the purchase of a home. McMullin (2005) studied paid and unpaid work in a three-generation family. She found strong links between the generations. In particular, the needs of children and older family members often shaped middle-aged women's work lives.

The life course approach has made a number of contributions to the study of aging. First, it bridges the macro and micro levels of analysis by recognizing the importance of social structures and historical context, as well as individual experiences and meanings. It helps us to understand the diversity within and between cohorts. Second, the approach brings together sociological, psychological, anthropological, and historical approaches to the study of aging. Third, the life course approach highlights the interdependence of people's lives over time. It also shows the complexity of individual life paths.

Finally, the life course approach understands aging as a dynamic process that takes place throughout life.

The life course perspective appreciates the link between earlier stages of adulthood and later life. Research on topics like diet, health and illness, family life, and work all show the impact of earlier life conditions on old age. For example, women more often than men show an interrupted work history. This leads to lower incomes for women in mid-life, but also poorer pensions and lower incomes in old age. Likewise, a divorce or the decision to stay single may lead to fewer family supports in later life. The decision to have children may mean more available informal support in old age. Poor nutrition in childhood can lead to poor health in old age.

The life course approach has some limitations. Its broad focus on society, culture, and the individual makes it hard to define as a single theory. Furthermore, as Bengtson and his colleagues (1997, S80) say, "it is very difficult to incorporate into a single analysis the many contextual variables … that this approach identifies." And, although this perspective bridges the micro and macro levels of analysis, life course research remains, predominantly, micro-oriented. Still, the life course approach encourages us to think about the many individual and social forces that affect aging.

The Conflict Perspective

The conflict perspective holds that society consists of conflicts between dominant and subordinate social groups. Historically, few gerontologists have used the **conflict perspective** in their work. But in recent decades an interest in this perspective has developed. For example, researchers understand that social and structural inequalities experienced earlier in life can lead to poverty and other disadvantages in later life. Also, studies show that women are more likely than men to earn less income, work part-time, or have disrupted work histories due to child care or care for other family members. Public and private pension programs tend to reward those with higher incomes and stable work histories. This means that many women will be financially disadvantaged in their later years. Researchers who use the conflict perspective study the causes of poverty in later life, women and gender discrimination, the multiple disadvantages facing older ethnic and Aboriginal people, the ideology of aging as a social problem, and pensions and policies.

The **political economy theory** that grew out of the work of Karl Marx exemplifies the conflict perspective. This theory focuses on conflict and change in social life. It traces this conflict to the struggle between social classes and to the resulting dominance of some groups in society and the subordination of others.

Marxist theory says that, for example, if managers view older workers as slower and weaker, they will also see these workers as less useful to industry as they age. Therefore, companies will tend to fire or retire older workers and replace them with younger workers who will work faster and for lower wages (McMullin and Marshall 2001). Today's information technology (IT) age links youthfulness with technical expertise. As IT workers age, they become marginalized from technical positions (Comeau and Kemp 2007). It is young workers (typically young males) who are most desirable in the IT industry. As Comeau and Kemp (2007, 229) suggest, "these links between youth and computing skills may be the rationale for recruiting young people for technical positions—they are also paid less and have worked more in an environment of competitive global capitalism."

Political economy researchers also study aging in the modern state. They examine the structural conditions in society that create inequality in old age. Gerontologists have looked at such diverse issues as powerlessness of older people (Kam 2003), globalization and aging (Fry 2005), and the structural situation of women and retirement (Zimmerman et al. 2000).

The political economy approach traces the origins of older people's problems to the political and economic structure of capitalist society. This perspective also looks at how social programs and policies for older people serve the interests of middle-aged, middle-class professionals. These programs and policies can reinforce class, gender, and racial inequalities in later life. Estes (2001) calls these **interlocking systems of oppression**. By this she means that none of these characteristics—gender, race, or social class—is experienced independent of the others. And, together, they structure opportunities that individuals are given or denied.

Early work by Myles (1984) used the political economy approach to study pensions in Canada and other liberal democracies. He traces the development of modern, state-run pension plans to the struggle between labour and the owners of industry and business—what Marx identified as "the means of production." Workers today expect pensions to form part of their wage package, but many employers want to pay as little for pension benefits as possible. For this reason, employers support government pension programs. This allows them to pay less into their workers' pension programs.

For this reason Canada's *Old Age Security Act* of 1951 gained the support of industrialists. More recently, labour unions have played an important role in deciding pension entitlements. In the 1980s, Myles (1984) found that increased labour union organization led to better public pensions, as did the increased political power of working-class parties and the right to strike. He also found that the electoral process itself led to better pensions. Political parties pay attention to have-not voters when an active electoral process exists. Today, more than 25 years later, these findings remain true.

Myles's (1984) early work remains important for understanding the historical roots of pensions in Canada. It also shows the strengths of the political economy approach in understanding aging. First, it places the study of aging in the context of large political, historical, economic, and social forces. Second, it views public pensions as the outcome of a struggle between competing groups. Third, it predicts that economic and political forces will shape future changes in public pensions.

The political economy approach looks beyond the individual to understand the forces that shape individual aging today. It broadens gerontologists' understanding of aging and offers another way to interpret the origins and effects of social policies. More recent work by Myles (2000), for example, examines the distribution of income among older Canadians. It looks at income in the context of recent improvements in Canada's public and private retirement income system. Myles finds that, since the early 1980s, the average income of older Canadians has increased significantly, particularly among lower-income seniors. And this has decreased income inequality among older Canadian.

The political economy approach emphasizes the impact of history, economics, and the political structure, on individuals. It shows how the state and social policies can increase or decrease social inequalities (Estes 2001; Quadagno and Reid 1999). It shows how race, ethnicity, social class, and gender can intensify inequality. Further, it looks at different dimensions of powerlessness—social, economic, and political. Walker (2005) and Phillipson (2003) anticipate a move to a more "international" political economy of aging to help us better understand the relationship between aging and the state in an era of increasing globalization.

Critics of the political economy approach say that it overemphasizes the poverty and problems older people face. It also tends to view the individual as the product of political and economic forces, and pays little attention to individuals' interpretations of social life. It says little about the ways that individuals shape their world through their interactions with others. As Bengtson and his colleagues (1997, S83) say, this perspective too often "paints a picture of all elders as powerless, forced to exist under oppressive structural arrangements with no control over their own lives."

Feminist approaches, within the conflict perspective, bridge the micro and macro levels of analysis. They recognize the importance of social interaction and social structure in the study of aging. A feminist framework holds that society is gendered by nature. Feminist social gerontologists believe that gender defines social interaction and life experiences, including the experience of aging. Furthermore, within a patriarchal system (such as North American society), gender-based inequalities are created and perpetuated. This results in social advantages for men (for instance, higher wages and better pensions) and disadvantages for women (higher rates of poverty in old age). A feminist approach recognizes gender as a social organizing principle, not just a category on a census form (Calasanti 2005).

Feminist theorists criticize other theories of aging and aging research for not focusing enough on gender relations or on women's experiences. They say that gerontologists need to explore women's experiences without constant reference to the experiences of men. In turn, mainstream feminist theory has been criticized for ignoring aging issues and the experiences of older women and older men (Calasanti 2004a). Hooyman and her colleagues (2002) state that researchers and practitioners need to find new approaches to address gender, race, and class inequalities that exist throughout the life course.

Feminist research in aging has focused on many unique issues: mother–daughter conflict (Ray 2003), "double-duty care" by female health professionals who care for older parents (Ward-Griffin et al. 2005), the health of older men (Calasanti 2004a), and identity and the aging body (Twigg 2004).

A feminist approach has made several contributions to the study of aging. First, the feminist approach recognizes the importance of social structure, social interaction, and individual characteristics (primarily gender, but also race, ethnicity, and social class) in shaping a person's experience of aging (Calasanti 2004b; Calasanti and Slevin 2001). Second, the feminist approach presents a more inclusive picture of aging and older adults by focusing on the majority of the older population—women—and on issues that are relevant to women's lives. Third, feminist theories of aging challenge the traditional focus on men in research and the ageist biases in "mainstream" feminist theories that ignore issues of age (Calasanti and Slevin 2001).

Nevertheless, feminist approaches have some limitations. They are too diffuse to form one unified "theory." Also, some gerontologists say that feminist theories remain biased or value laden. These authors see gender as too narrow a focus for the study of aging. (This view has begun to change as gerontologists realize the links between gender, race, ethnicity,

social class, and age (Calasanti 2004b)). Furthermore, feminist theories have been criticized for the so-called feminization of aging. Critics say that feminist theories deny the gendered nature of aging for men and overlook experiences important to older men (Calasanti 2004a). Feminist theories have also been criticized for their preoccupation with the problems and disadvantages older women face. They have overlooked the positive experiences of aging for many women and their contributions to society. Still, feminist approaches have made gender an explicit theme in the study of aging and later life.

Further Developments in Gerontological Theory

Theories try to make sense of the complex, multidimensional facts of aging. The theories discussed here show that no single explanation of aging can account for everything we know. But we must have theories in order to understand the mass of detailed information that researchers gather. A statement made by Bengtson and his colleagues (1997, S84) more than a decade ago remains true. They state that "theory is not a marginal, meaningless 'tacked-on' exercise to presenting results in an empirical paper. Rather, cumulative theory-building represents the core of the foundation of scientific inquiry and knowledge" (see also Biggs et al. 2003).

What theoretical ideas have emerged in social gerontology in recent years? What approaches will emerge or grow in the years ahead? Many researchers and theorists support the wider use of interpretive frameworks for studying aging. **Narrative gerontology** offers one new framework (Kenyon, Ruth, and Mader 1999; Randall and Kenyon 2004). This approach seeks to understand the "inside" of aging. It studies the stories that people tell in order to organize and make sense of their lives. These stories create meaning around their experience of aging (Randall and Kenyon 2004, 334). Becker (2001) used the narrative approach to study older people who live with chronic pain. Other writers have studied the life stories of people with dementia and terminal illness (Basting 2003; Kuhl and Westwood 2001). Narrative gerontology shows that people "compose" their lives through their life stories. These stories get retold, revisited, and reinterpreted, as people age.

Moral economy theory, a complement to political economy theory, grew out of the work of E.P. Thompson in England (Thompson 1971). Political economy theorists and researchers have begun to use this perspective to explore issues like retirement, long-term care (Minkler and Estes 1999), and community volunteerism (Narushima 2005). This approach to the study of aging looks at the shared moral assumptions held by members of a society. Studies that use this approach look at values such as justice and fairness in society and how they affect social policies. The moral economy theory is concerned with the social consensus that underlies issues such as justice between the generations, pension entitlements, and access to health care.

Critical gerontology emerged to address limitations in mainstream gerontological theory. Estes (2003; also Katz 2003), for example, criticizes mainstream theory for not "'looking within' to examine and question its under-lying and "taken-for-granted" assumptions about aging. It does not question "what is missing, ignored, or denied" (Ray 2003, 34) within aging theories and research. Ray (2003) makes the distinction between "theory" and "crit-ical theory." Theory helps to guide research and interpret research findings. Critical theory questions these find-ings, as well as the structure and method of inquiry. Ray (2008, 97) believes the role of critical gerontology is to "cast a critical eye on society and the field of gerontology itself." Critical theory is essential for the growth and development of gerontology. It reminds "us that all theo-ries are partial, that other meanings are always possible, that meaning-making itself is an exercise in power and authority, and that we promote some meanings at the expense of others" (Ray 2003, 34).

Researchers predict an increased focus on the polit-ical economy perspective, interpretive approaches such as phenomenology and social constructionism, critical and feminist approaches, and life course perspectives. Theory will remain central to studying aging. Bengtson and his colleagues (1999, 18) say that "theory is the compass with which to navigate through vast seas of data. It is the means by which data are transformed into meaningful explanations, or stories, about the processes and consequences of aging." Gerontological theories offer many explanations of aging. Their variety reflects the many dimensions of gerontological research. Each of these perspectives gives us a different insight into what it means to age.

RESEARCH ISSUES AND METHODS

Research Issues

Gerontologists also use a number of methods that help them study the process of aging. The proper use of these methods ensures that researchers come up with reliable and valid findings. Improper use can lead to faulty and confusing results. The following discussion will give a glimpse of the methodological issues that

gerontologists face in trying to study continuity and change in later life.

Gerontologists generally place changes in old age into one of three categories:

1. **age effects** due to physical decline. These changes appear with the passage of time. They include an increase in the body's fat-to-muscle ratio, a decline in lung elasticity, and decreases in bone density. They also include environmentally caused changes such as wrinkled skin and cataracts caused by the sun.

2. **cohort effects** related to the time of a person's birth. A cohort refers to a group of people born around the same time (usually within a five- or ten-year period). People born in a certain cohort often share a common background and experience of the world. People born just after World War II, for example, are in the cohort that was the first to be exposed to large doses of television. This new technology shaped their entertainment habits and lifestyles. In compar-ison, those born in the early 1990s spent their youth playing video games, text messaging, and listening to music on their iPods. This technology has shaped entertainment habits and lifestyles that differ from those of their parents' or grandparents' generation.

3. **period or environmental effects** due to the time of measurement. This category includes social or his-torical effects on measurement, such as an ongoing war, changes in health habits (for example, increased exercise), or changes in health care policies. These effects have different influences on different age cohorts.

Gerontologists try to disentangle these effects in order to understand the causes of aging. They use a number of research designs to look at these three effects in their attempts to understand change in later life.

Studies on aging done in the 1960s supported many of the negative stereotypes of aging. Much of the early research on aging used a **cross-sectional research design**. This type of method studies people from many age groups at one point in time. Studies done in psy-chology at that time, for example, found that older age groups, compared with younger age groups, scored lower on intelligence tests. This finding was seen as support for the view that people get "simple-minded" as they get older. But these early studies tended to confuse differ-ences *between age groups* (cohort effects) with *changes due to aging* (age effects). In the 1980s, research by Baltes and Schaie (1982) found that younger people had more education than older people. This, they said, accounted for some of the differences in younger and older people's test scores.

Most researchers who study aging today still use a cross-sectional design (Neuman and Robson 2009). This method allows researchers to gather data in a short time at a relatively low cost. It also allows policy makers to assess and meet the needs of different age groups fairly quickly. Researchers in a single study can ask a broad range of questions that give a detailed snapshot of many age groups at one point in time.

Still, this method causes problems. As the early intelligence studies show, cross-sectional studies can confound cohort effects (such as lower education levels in older cohorts) with age changes (such as changes in intelligence due to increasing age). The findings from cross-sectional studies cannot tell us whether aging (maturation) leads to changes in intelligence, health, or any other conditions or behaviours that change over time.

Longitudinal research designs attempt to overcome this problem. A longitudinal study looks at a single group of people at two or more points in time. For example, a longitudinal study of how aging affects intelligence might test the same group of people at 10-year intervals. These results give a truer picture of the effects of age on intelligence, because this kind of study avoids the problem of trying to compare different cohorts (e.g., people with different educational backgrounds due to the historical conditions in their childhood).

Gerontologists use longitudinal studies when they want to learn about age changes, but this method also creates problems. Environmental changes (period effects)—such as historical events, changes in the economy, or changes in political values—can confound changes due to aging. Longitudinal studies involving older people face special problems. These include loss of study participants due to death, illness, and moving; inability to respond due to chronic illness or cognitive decline; and a shift in the sex ratio in the study due to the deaths of more men than women in later life. These examples show the kinds of problems gerontologists can face when they search for the causes of change in later life.

A third method, **time-lag comparison design**, tries to overcome the problems raised by simple cross-sectional and simple longitudinal designs. Time-lag studies look at different groups of people of the same age at different points in time (e.g., 70-year-olds in 1989, 1999, and 2009). This type of study tries to measure differences between cohorts. Like cross-sectional and longitudinal methods, the time-lag method also presents problems. It confounds cohort effects with environmental ones. If a research study finds that 70-year-olds in 2009 visited doctors less often than 70-year-olds did in 1989,

this difference may be because of the better health of 70-year-olds in 2009 (a cohort effect) or it may be because of a change in the health care system, perhaps higher costs to users (an environmental effect).

Wister (2005) used a combination of research designs to study the health of Baby Boomers over time. He looked at major chronic illnesses, physician visits, and lifestyle behaviours within each cohort. The data, drawn from major Canadian health surveys over a 22-year period (1978/79 to 2000/01), allowed him to identify changes in health and lifestyle patterns over time for different age cohorts. This type of study also permitted a comparison of Baby Boomers' health today (e.g. people in their 60s) with 60-year-olds' health at earlier points in time (e.g. 10 years ago): a time-lag comparison.

Each type of study creates problems when it comes to interpreting results. In addition, longitudinal and time-lag studies pose practical problems. First, they often take many years to complete—years during which researchers must wait before they can show results to granting agencies or to the public. Second, they are expensive to maintain (Neuman and Robson 2009). The cost can force the researcher to apply for new grants for each wave of the research. The researcher must compete with all other applicants, but cannot tailor sample size or limit the research to fit new funding conditions. Third, subjects in longitudinal studies drop out (or die), biasing results in later rounds of the study (Alwin et al. 2006).

Longitudinal studies of disease face this problem (Vogler 2006). Those who die during a study leave a healthier, less diseased group behind. This group no longer represents the original sample's characteristics. This confounds the study results. Fourth, longitudinal studies require institutional support. The time needed to complete a longitudinal study can be so long that researchers themselves may die or move before the study ends. For this reason, some longitudinal studies take place through a research centre or university. The institution can see the study through and provide a home for the data.

Gerontologists have solved some of these problems by turning simple cross-sectional and simple longitudinal designs into **sequential designs**. Researchers create sequential designs by looking at a series of cross-sectional studies during a longer longitudinal study. The cross-sectional studies allow for quick data collection. The longitudinal study provides a check on cross-sectional findings. These two methods together also provide time-lag data on the sampled members of same-aged groups at different times.

The Aging in Manitoba Longitudinal Study (AMLS) offers this option to researchers. It provides comparable data on health and health care needs for a random sample of older people in Manitoba at different times (McKeen, Chipperfield, and Campbell 2004; Chipperfield, Havens, and Doig 1997). In this project, which began in 1971, three independent cross-sectional studies were conducted (in 1971, 1976, and 1983). The groups were then followed over time (1983, 1990, 1996, and 2001). This method produced both cross-sectional and longitudinal data (within a sequential design). With data now from more than 9,000 participants over 30 years, the Aging in Manitoba Longitudinal Study is the longest and most comprehensive continuous population-based study of aging in Canada (National Advisory Council on Aging 2006).

This type of study allows researchers to compare the needs of different age groups in a given year (e.g., 66- to 75-year-olds and 76- to 85-year-olds in 2001). It also allows researchers to study the changes in these groups' needs over time (e.g., whether the needs of the sample of 66- to 75-year-olds have changed between 1990 and 2001). The researchers can also see whether social changes have affected all age groups (e.g., whether all groups of older people used hospitals more in 1990 than in 2001). They can then separate period effects—effects due to social conditions at the times of measurement (e.g., new medical care policies)—from effects due to aging (such as the need for more medical care as a person ages).

The AMLS data has led to dozens of research studies. One study compared self-reports of functional ability with performance-based observations (Finlayson et al. 2003). Another study analyzed the relationship between negative emotions and health service use by older people (McKeen, Chipperfield, and Campbell 2004). Yet another study looked at the link between perceptions of control and health outcomes (Chipperfield et al. 2004).

Salthouse (2006) says that only longitudinal studies allow researchers to assess the long-term effects of interventions. For example, it may take years for an exercise program to affect health in later life. An immediate effect of the exercise program (e.g. an improved self-image) might lessen and disappear over time. Only by following participants over time can researchers assess lasting benefits of the program. Salthouse admits that long-term studies cost a lot and consume time and energy. But they provide the only accurate assessment of an intervention's lasting effect on the process of aging.

These complex designs still do not completely untangle time of measurement, age, and cohort effects, although they do give researchers more information about the group under study. Attempts to neutralize variables takes a great deal of time and effort. Without the effort, the researchers could make a fundamental error in understanding. But, even with it, the researcher still has to explain, for example, the specific historical events that led to changes in health care use or how these events translated themselves into different behaviours. Whatever method the researcher chooses, logical reasoning and judgment must be used to make sense of research findings.

Types of Research Methods

Gerontologists use not only psychological tests and surveys to study aging, but also other research methods such as interviews, participant observation, and content analysis. Researchers in each dimension of aging (biomedical, psychosocial, socioeconomic-environmental) have their preferred methods.

Pharmacologists, chemists, and neurophysiologists use laboratory techniques and controlled experiments to study aging; historians use libraries, archives, diaries, and even paintings; literary scholars use plays, novels, and poetry. Social gerontologists use surveys, personal interviews, focus groups, community-based action-research, and case studies. Some studies require more than one method—a questionnaire survey of a large population, for example, may include a psychological test, and an anthropological field study may include the study of a society's literature and history as well as a measurement of the people's physical condition. Research on health service use might involve a mailed survey to community-dwelling older adults as well as face-to-face interviews with a subgroup of that population.

Researchers have recently expanded their interest in certain research issues and methods. Most Statistics Canada publications, for example, routinely include separate information on age groups over 65 (e.g., groups aged 65 to 74, 75 to 84, and 85 and over). This approach recognizes that we need more information about the growing population of very old people. It also recognizes that age cohorts among the 65-and-over group often differ from one another. Smaller age groupings give more information about differences among older people. Researchers also focus more now on the differences between men and women as they age. Studies of health, retirement, widowhood, caregiving, and social life, among other topics, all show the importance of gender differences in later life. Gerontologists' interests continue to grow and expand. As this happens, researchers will develop and use the methods that best address their questions.

Quantitative and Qualitative Methods

Social gerontologists use both quantitative and qualitative methods in research on aging. **Quantitative methods** remain the dominant approach in much of the gerontological research. But the use of qualitative methods is growing as is the use of **mixed methods**. Mixed methods or **triangulation** refers to the use of two or more methodological approaches in a research study. For example, a study might use a survey questionnaire (quantitative method) as well as face-to-face interviews (qualitative method), or face-to-face interviews and focus groups (two qualitative methods).

Quantitative methods emphasize relationships between and among factors (variables) through numerical measurement (quantity, amount, frequency) (Del Balso and Lewis 2008; Neuman and Robson 2009). Quantitative studies often gather data through surveys or questionnaires. Researchers then summarize responses into numerical values for statistical analysis. Examples of Canadian studies that use quantitative methods include research on income inequality and life expectancy (Prus and Brown 2008), gender inequality in the wealth of older Canadians (Denton and Boos 2007), older adults' perceptions of health care and health care delivery (Shapiro, Tate, Wright, and Plohman 2000), and adult sons' level of involvement in care for parents (Campbell and Martin-Matthews 2003).

Researchers who use **qualitative methods** seek to understand the social experience of individuals from the subjects' own perspective. Qualitative research does not use statistical procedures or quantification of the data to report findings. Rather, "qualitative research is characterized by a verbal or literary presentation of data" (Del Baso and Lewis 2008, 40). Qualitative research uses many methods, including interviews, life histories, field observation, case studies, and content analysis. Qualitative research tends to use an interpretive theoretical approach to understand these data.

Neuman (2003, 146) says that "instead of trying to convert social life into variables or numbers, qualitative researchers borrow ideas from the people they study and place them within the context of a natural setting." Researchers try to understand the meanings people bring to social interactions. A key principle of qualitative research is to give voice to the study participants. Examples of Canadian qualitative studies include research on older women's perceptions of beauty interventions and "natural" aging (Hurd Clarke and Griffin 2007), the unwritten rules that guide inheritance decisions (Ploeg et. al. 2007), paid and unpaid work patterns in multi-generational families (McMullin 2005), and conceptualizations of gender and masculinity in men's care of older parents (Campbell and Carroll 2007; Carroll and Campbell 2008).

Quantitative and qualitative methods each have their strengths and limitations (see Exhibit 2.2). Quantitative methods, for example, allow researchers to gather a great deal of information on a wide range of issues. Moreover, researchers can analyze a sample and generalize results to a larger population. But quantitative researchers use very structured research questions that give respondents limited response choices. This kind of research offers little opportunity to capture the "rich description" of individuals' subjective experiences or perceptions of their social world (Lincoln and Guba 2000; Neuman and Robson 2009).

Qualitative methods allow researchers to capture the complexity of social interactions and behaviours. These methods study how individuals understand and give meaning to their lives (Del Balso and Lewis 2008; Neuman and Robson 2009). They allow for the words and subjective experiences of participants to be heard. Qualitative research also has its limits. Researchers often use small sample sizes, a practice that limits generalization to a larger population. Some researchers combine both quantitative and qualitative methods in one study (Neuman and Robson 2009).

Integrating Research and Practice

Gerontologists hope their research findings will improve the lives of those they study. For example, many studies report on the sources of health and well-being in later life. These studies can help people live longer and healthier lives. They also can help agencies and organizations that promote healthy aging and they can help health care professionals to better serve their clients. Researchers face the challenge of how to make their findings usable in the wider community.

Lewis and his colleagues (2005) promote the use of research data by staff who work with dementia patients. These researchers prepare manuals and present workshops on how to apply research evidence in practice. The workshops also identify barriers to adopting best practices. These include a shortage of staff or resources (structural factors), communication gaps (organizational factors), and a lack of knowledge or a resistance to "buy-in" by the staff (individual factors). The researchers call for more organizational support for educational workshops and standardized practice.

Information Literacy: The Challenge of the Internet

When it comes to food, you know the difference between a fast food burger and a meal made by a trained chef. You also know the difference between a quality running shoe and a flimsy copy. Sometimes we rely on a brand name to get the quality we expect. Sometimes past experience or education has taught us to tell the quality of one thing

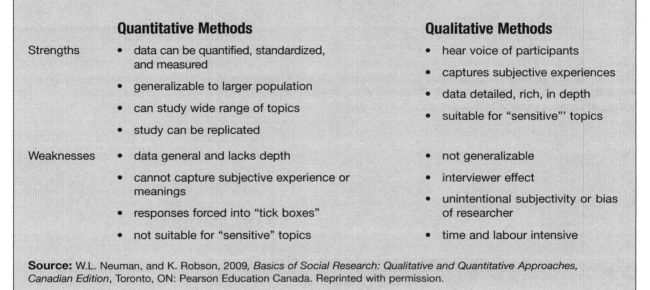

Exhibit 2.2

STRENGTHS AND WEAKNESSES OF QUALITATIVE AND QUANTITATIVE METHODS

The following table summarizes some general advantages and disadvantages of qualitative and quantitative methods, based on Neuman and Robson (2009).

	Quantitative Methods	**Qualitative Methods**
Strengths	• data can be quantified, standardized, and measured • generalizable to larger population • can study wide range of topics • study can be replicated	• hear voice of participants • captures subjective experiences • data detailed, rich, in depth • suitable for "sensitive"' topics
Weaknesses	• data general and lacks depth • cannot capture subjective experience or meanings • responses forced into "tick boxes" • not suitable for "sensitive" topics	• not generalizable • interviewer effect • unintentional subjectivity or bias of researcher • time and labour intensive

Source: W.L. Neuman, and K. Robson, 2009, *Basics of Social Research: Qualitative and Quantitative Approaches, Canadian Edition*, Toronto, ON: Pearson Education Canada. Reprinted with permission.

from another. But when it comes to information many people remain largely illiterate.

A widely accepted definition of information literacy (Campbell 2004, 2) is the one put forward in the 1989 Final Report of the American Library Association's (ALA) Presidential Committee on Information Literacy. It states that, "To be information literate, a person must be able to recognize when information is needed and have the ability to locate, evaluate, and use effectively the needed information." Information literacy is a vital skill for anyone who wants to understand aging today.

In 1994, the Canadian government created the Information Highway Advisory Council (IHAC). This group set out to address challenges of "**digital literacy**" in a growing digital information age (Whitehead and Quinlan 2002). A report from the IHAC three years later states that "computer and Internet literacy is a necessary precondition for success in the emerging knowledge society and economy (Industry Canada 1997, cited in Whitehead and Quinlan 2002, 2).

The World Wide Web serves as a storehouse of information on aging (Neuman and Robson 2009). At the touch of a button an older person, a student, or a scientist can call up masses of information. But the Web offers no guide to the quality of the information retrieved. For example, by typing the word "aging" into the Google search engine, the top ten websites retrieved include Wikipedia (the free encyclopedia), the National Institute on Aging, ScienceDaily: Healthy Aging News, Geriatrics and Aging, and the Canadian Centre for Activity and Aging. These sources each provide information on aging, on a variety of topics. But the quality of information on these sites varies.

The government source, the U.S. National Institute on Aging, for example, links to information about research grants, scientific findings on aging, and practical information on health. It also offers links to research reports and announcements of conferences. This site provides a high standard of information quality. The scientific reports have passed inspection by top scientists. The Canadian Centre for Activity and Aging is affiliated with a major Canadian university, hospital, and health research institute. This site provides academic and practical information that promotes active, healthy aging for older Canadians. It includes information on research projects and publications, physical activity programs and other community resources, as well as links to numerous active aging and health service sites.

But all information has a bias. The National Institute on Aging, an American government site, for example, takes Western scientific knowledge as a cornerstone of truth. Someone skeptical of the government's goals, someone skeptical of scientific methods and findings, or someone who wants a more personal view of aging will question the value of this site.

Wikipedia, an encyclopedia created by a community of users and changed constantly by those users, does not claim to offer true or valid knowledge. The managers of the Wikipedia site admit bias in the listings and explicitly warn readers. However, Wikipedia comes up as one of the "top ten" Internet sites retrieved on the topic of "aging." This means that many Internet users look for their "aging" information on this site.

Wikipedia shows sensitivity to the quality of the information it provides. This is good. But it leaves the reader to sort out the truth from the misinformation. For example, at the time of printing, a section on the cognitive effects of aging is only five sentences long. A link to cognitive impairment provides three sentences. This further links to three paragraphs on Alzheimer's disease. And this entry has many further links. These entries provide a mix of information—some useful and some of little use—to a student, a researcher, or a caregiver who needs more knowledge. This site leaves it to the reader to sort out the accurate from the inaccurate information.

Wikipedia shows the strengths and the weaknesses of Web-based information. It offers a lot of information, it allows a reader to surf from one topic to another according to his or her needs, and it offers information from a wide range of authors. But it offers no expert review or screening of the information. The Wikipedia community members can change any information they consider inaccurate. But Wikipedia leaves it to the reader to decide on the validity and reliability of the information. Wikipedia might serve as a starting point for research, but it can mislead a naïve reader with little experience in a field.

ScienceDaily provides a third example of information available on the web. It sits somewhere between the government sources and Wikipedia on the reliability scale. The site states that it selects news releases from: "leading universities and other research organizations around the world. Each news release is posted in its original form, with a link to the organization's home page ... In this way, ScienceDaily [delivers] science news in its original,

unedited format directly from the source (in this case, the news bureaus and public affairs offices of major universities and research institutions) (ScienceDaily 2009)." The reader can then go to the source of the news release for more detailed information.

A close look at the bottom of the ScienceDaily home page gives information about the editor. This information attempts to establish his credibility; it state that he worked as a science journalist, for leading universities, and for the National Institutes of Health. Still, the site accepts advertising, and this could bias the information presented. For example, the editor chooses which items to report. Does the editor subtly or overtly choose news items to attract or keep advertisers? Would the editor leave out an item that reflected badly on an advertiser? The reader needs to keep these questions in mind.

A researcher or student needs to use varied sources to get a more complete picture of scientific research on aging. Some useful academic information is not available on the Internet, or is available only through paid subscription. Also, unlike academic journals that sit on library shelves for years, Internet sites can vanish without a trace. And although the Internet provides quick and easy access to a wealth of useful information on aging, one must take a critical view of information provided on the Web.

Ethical Issues in Research

Research studies on human subjects face ethical challenges. And studies of certain frail or vulnerable groups pose unique problems. Researchers need to recognize the ethical implications of studying vulnerable older people, such as those living with Alzheimer's disease or another cognitive impairment (Karlawish 2004; Sevick et al. 2003).

Researchers need to consider at least three ethical issues: (1) the need for informed consent, (2) the need to guard subjects against harm or injury, and (3) the need to protect individuals' privacy (Neuman and Robson 2009).

Informed consent means that the researcher tells the subject the facts about the research and gets written permission from the subjects before they participate in a study. Individuals must freely give their consent without any coercion. They need to understand that they can decide not to answer any questions without explanation. And they need to know that they can withdraw from the study at any time.

Researchers must also guard against doing harm or injury to study participants. This includes physical harm and psychological harm. A person might feel embarrassed or upset at some questions they feel they have to answer. Research questions might force participants to recall events that are unpleasant or traumatic. Researchers need to minimize risk to participants throughout the research process (Neuman and Robson 2009).

Researchers also seek to protect participants from potential harm by protecting their identity. Researchers can do this by making sure that data analysis cannot reveal an individual's identity. The researcher should also promise to keep personal information confidential. This means securing information in a location that only he or she can access.

Older people with Alzheimer's disease or other types of dementia present special challenges in research. For example, they may not be able to give true voluntary informed consent (Bravo et al. 2005; Neuman and Robson 2009). If the mental competency of an individual is in question, the researchers must get written permission from someone who has the legal authority to make such decisions. A family member or staff member in a nursing home may have this authority. Permission from a substitute decision maker allows for research at all stages of the disease (Karlawish 2004). In most provinces in Canada, substitute decision makers can provide permission through court-ordered guardianship, power of attorney, and advance directives (Bravo et al. 2005).

Universities and other funding agencies have ethics review boards to evaluate potential risks that participants might face. The ethics review board must approve each study, weigh the potential risks and benefits, and then give permission for research to proceed. This process protects participants from potential harm and ensures that researchers act ethically and responsibly in their research.

THE FUTURE OF GERONTOLOGICAL THEORY AND METHODS

What theories and methods will gerontologists use in the future? First, gerontologists will create new and more sophisticated quantitative methods, including structural equation models, longitudinal factor analysis, and multivariate effects models. As computer power increases and as gerontologists apply methods used in other social sciences, gerontologists will be able to test new and more complex theories.

Hendricks (1997) proposes the use of theories from natural science—chaos theory and catastrophe theory—to explain aging. These theories and models question the assumptions of linear, probabilistic analyses that gerontologists use today. Hendricks challenges gerontology "to develop mind-sets and measures that address the possibility of non-linear processes" (205). This approach would include the study of unpredictable and dramatic changes in individuals' lives and in their families, work, and neighbourhoods. It would also include a study of how people modify their life course through their own interpretations of their lives.

Second, gerontologists will continue to link the micro and macro levels of theory. Age stratification theory, life course approaches, and feminist theories come closest to doing this now, although they have their limitations. They try to explain a great deal, but they remain broad or abstract. Researchers support the further development of political economy, life course approaches, feminist theories, and interpretive approaches, including phenomenology and social constructionism. These theories allow gerontologists to stand back and analyze social processes. These approaches reveal hidden sides of aging and explore ways to create a good old age.

Third, qualitative methods will continue to grow in importance in gerontological research. Qualitative methods can explore the experience of aging at a time when more and more people will want to know about that experience. Neuman and Robson (2009, 358) say that "qualitative approaches give a voice to research participants in a way that is not possible in quantitative studies." Qualitative research prizes the richness and diversity of everyday social life. This type of research takes us into the world of older people and their communities. It reveals their experiences of later life.

Fourth, technology will continue to expand research opportunities. Laptop computers allow researchers to enter interview data in the field. Wireless Internet connection gives researchers access to online information from countless locations. Video recording technology allows researchers to observe behaviour without a researcher present. This method allows researchers to gather data throughout the day, and a number of researchers can observe and analyze the same data. Researchers have used this technology to study wandering behaviour and the causes of falls in nursing homes.

Fifth, studies in the humanities will add new methods to gerontological research such as linguistic analysis, the study of paintings and photos, autobiographical analysis, and narrative gerontology. New topics of interest in the future will lead to new approaches to the study of aging. Researchers will develop new methods as they work to answer new questions about aging. They will choose the method that best suits their needs and allows them to answer their research questions.

Large-Scale Gerontology Research in Canada

Gerontology research in Canada has been undergoing some important shifts. For example, attempts have been made to bridge the gap between anglophone and francophone gerontologists in Canada (see Exhibit 2.3). Further, the past 20 years have seen an increase in national studies conducted by interdisciplinary teams. The federal government funded most of these studies and continues to be a major source of funding for research on aging.

An important source of government funding for health-related aging research is the Institute of Aging (IA), a pillar of the Canadian Institutions of Health Research (CIHR). The IA is a community of researchers from universities and hospitals across Canada. It also includes practitioners, volunteer health organizations, and older adults themselves. They share a common goal: to increase our knowledge about aging, promote healthy aging, and address the challenges of an aging population.

The IA studies a broad range of topics "from the causes, prevention, screening, diagnosis, treatment, and palliative care of aging-related diseases and conditions, to support systems, health services and health policy…" (CIHR Institute of Aging 2008). The IA has become a national leader in addressing the health needs of Canada's older population.

The Institute on Aging led the launch of The Canadian Longitudinal Study of Aging (CLSA), as part of the CIHR's Canadian Lifelong Health Initiative. This study will follow a random sample of 50,000 men and women from across Canada, aged 40 and older, over a 20-year period. The research team includes researchers from the social sciences, psychology, medical

---

● Exhibit 2.3

ANGLOPHONE AND QUEBEC GERONTOLOGY: TWO SOLITUDES?

Anglophone Canadians have often overlooked francophone research, as have other North American scholars. In part this is due to the fact that francophone researchers often publish their work only in French and publish in research reports rather than in refereed journals. For these reasons, their work has not reached the wider North American academic community. Lesemann (2001, 58) says that English-Canadian and Quebec gerontology exist as "two solitudes." He remarks on the "comparative lack of knowledge of one another that seems to exist … despite the efforts at collaboration that have been made over the years" (58). He traces this lack of knowledge to the impact of politics and culture on research and scholarship. McPherson (2001) says that language also forms a barrier to collaboration. Relatively few English-speaking scholars today can work in French and so they know little about Quebec gerontology.

A special supplement of the Canadian Journal on Aging (CJA) (2006), containing all of the official abstracts of the VIIIᵉ Congrès international francophone de gérontologie et gériatrie held in Quebec in October 2007, attempted to bridge the gap between anglophone and francophone gerontologists. The journal printed all of the abstracts in French. The CJA wanted to give the Anglophone academic community "an opportunity to see what our Francophone colleagues around the world are doing across the various topics that are of interest to gerontologists and geriatricians" (Rosenberg 2006, 2). Even anglophone gerontologists who could not read the abstracts in French could at least learn about the topics of interests to francophone colleagues.

As the abstracts in the CAG supplement show, francophone researchers have conducted numerous community studies that could interest a wider audience. They have also conducted social and social-psychological studies that speak to important issues like arthritis pain and functional limitations among older people (Bourgue et al. 2006), family caregivers' assessment of the quality of geriatric services (Roberge et al. 2002), and women's perceptions of physical activity and aging (Beausoleil and Martin 2002). Anglophone gerontologists could benefit from wider exposure to this research.

and clinical research, population health, and health services.

The study will collect medical, psychological, social, and economic data. Analysis will go on throughout the 20-year span of the study and the project will share findings with the public. The study will "examine health patterns and trends and … identify ways to reduce disability and suffering among aging Canadians" (Canadian Longitudinal Study of Aging 2008).

The Social and Economic Dimensions of an Aging Population (SEDAP) is a multi-disciplinary research program located at McMaster University. The first SEDAP program (SEDAP I) ran from 1999 to 2004. It involved 28 academics from four Canadian universities. The second phase of SEDAP (SEDAP II: Canada in the 21st Century: Moving Towards an Older Society), runs from 2005 to 2010. This project now involves 46 researchers from 14 Canadian universities, and three universities abroad. It also includes more than 50 graduate students and postdoctoral fellows (SEDAP Website 2008).

SEDAP I and II received funding from the Social Sciences and Humanities Research Council (SSHRC). These projects produced a wealth of academic research related to a wide range of social and economic issues. Researchers have studied ethnicity and health (Kobayashi, Prus, and Lin 2008), poverty among older Canadians (Milligan 2007), urban and rural differences in health service use by older Canadians (Conde and McDonald 2007), and the economic cost of retiring to provide family care (McDonald, Sussman, and Donahue 2007). The research produced by SEDAP researchers provides valuable information and insights about the challenges and rewards facing Canada as its population continues to age. It will also help shape policies and programs to improve the lives of older Canadians.

In 2003, another major interdisciplinary project entitled "Workforce Aging in the New Economy: A Comparative Study of Information Technology Employment" received funding from the Social Sciences and Humanities Research Council (SSHRC) in the amount of $2.9 million. This multidisciplinary, cross-national study examines the growth in information technology, employment, and workforce aging in Canada, the United States, the European Union, and Australia. A number of academic papers, book chapters, and reports have come out of this project. Study topics include employment incentives and disincentives for older workers in Canada (McMullin and Tomchick 2004), age and masculinity in the information technology industry (Comeau and Kemp 2007), and stereotyping older workers and retirement (Henkens 2003). This research, focusing on the workplace in the new economy, will help countries, including Canada, respond to an aging workforce and diversity in the workplace.

These research projects show a trend toward large-scale, interdisciplinary research among Canadian researchers. Collaborative studies save money by pooling researchers' skills and resources. They also create interdisciplinary teams that can carry out sophisticated analyses of large data sets. This research, and the many other studies conducted by researchers throughout Canada, expand our knowledge and understanding of aging. They also help governments, social service agencies, and professionals to plan better programs for older people.

CONCLUSION

Research in gerontology now goes on in many disciplines, including biology, economics, social work, political science, health sciences, psychology, and sociology. Researchers also have access to the latest gerontology research through the use of online databases. Still, more research on aging in Canada needs to be done. For instance, a review of the abstracts for the 2008 annual meeting of the Canadian Association on Gerontology (CAG) (2008) shows that researchers presented more papers on health-related issues than on any other subject. A review of the Ageline database in 2008 found a strong focus on income, caregiving, and health issues. Government funding for research on these policy-related issues, in part, explains the concentration on these topics. But we also need to know about healthy older people because most older people live healthy, active lives.

Social gerontologists now see the need to focus on the social conditions that lead to good aging. Lesemann (2001, 65) reports that, compared to the past, Canadian researchers now look at "the strengths and resources available to the older person … [in order to] make them more autonomous." He notes the improvement in older peoples' lives due to better social supports, better income, and greater understanding of later life. This will lead to more questions for researchers. For example, what do people of different ethnic backgrounds need as they age? Do the needs of people in rural areas differ from those of people in cities? Do older people have unique educational needs? How do they learn best? How will early retirees use their time? Researchers have begun to ask these and other questions about aging.

Summary

1. Three broad areas make up the field of gerontology: biomedicine, psychosocial studies, and socioeconomic-environmental studies. Social gerontology includes psychosocial and socioeconomic-environmental studies, as well as practice-related research.

2. Gerontologists use theory to guide their research and to interpret their results. Micro- and macro-level theories exist. They include interpretive, functionalist, and conflict theories. Each theoretical approach gives a different and valuable insight into aging.

3. Gerontologists have developed methods to distinguish age effects (changes due to age) from changes in groups due to differences in cohorts, historical events, and the effects of repeated testing.

4. Gerontologists also borrow methods from traditional disciplines such as biology, chemistry, history, philosophy, and anthropology. Researchers have begun to shift their interests as their knowledge grows. New statistical reports now present separate statistics for the oldest age groups. New critical methods of analysis have also emerged as gerontology has grown.

5. Gerontologists use both qualitative and quantitative methods for studying aging and older adults. They use methods that suit their research questions and their discipline. Methods include surveys, face-to-face interviews, focus groups, and case studies, among others.

6. The Internet offers quick and easy access to a wealth of information. But it provides no "quality control" on that information. Further, some useful academic information is not available online. Researchers, students, and the public need to assess the quality of information they retrieve from Internet sources.

7. Researchers who study older people often face unique ethical challenges. Those who study frail or cognitively impaired older adults must take special care. They must ensure the willing participation of people in their studies. All researchers must be aware of important ethical concerns: the need for informed consent, the need to guard their participants against harm or injury, and the need to protect participants' privacy.

8. Many Canadian gerontologists take part in large provincial and national studies. These studies, often funded by the government, provide opportunities for multi-disciplinary research. These studies take place over long periods of time and allow researchers to conduct individual, cohort, and time-lag analyses. These studies will provide information to guide practitioners and policy makers.

9. Gerontology today is one of the fastest-growing fields of study. It can make old age a better time of life by increasing knowledge about aging, as well as help modify and create social structures that meet the needs of older people.

Study Questions

1. List and describe the three main areas that make up the field of gerontology. What areas does social gerontology include? Compare the major focus of the social gerontologist with the focus of the medical gerontologist.

2. Explain the function of a sociological theory. Gerontologists classify theories into two categories. Define these two levels of theory and the three perspectives that these levels of theory can take. Critique each of these perspectives.

3. State the major characteristics of gerontological theories. What theoretical ideas may emerge in social gerontology in the future? Where will future theorists look for new theoretical insights?

4. What is the most significant problem with using a cross-sectional method to gather gerontological data? How can researchers overcome this problem?

5. What are the benefits of using a longitudinal research design? What are the weaknesses?

6. Discuss the strengths and limitations of qualitative and quantitative methods.

7. List at least six methods that gerontologists use to study aging.

8. Discuss the benefits and challenges of using the Internet to gather information on the aging process and older people.

9. What are some important ethical issues that researchers need to consider when conducting research with older people?

10. How does gerontological research benefit society?

Key Terms

age cohort a group of people born in the same period of time. For example, all the people born between 1950 and 1955 form an age cohort. (22)

age effects an effect on a person's life related to physical decline or change due to the aging process. (27)

age grade a concept used in age stratification theory to describe a period of life defined by society, such as childhood, adolescence, and young adulthood. (22)

age stratification theory a theory that focuses on the movement of age cohorts over the life course and on "the role of social structures in the process of individual aging and the stratification by age in the society" (Bengtson, Burgess, and Parrott 1997, S81). (22)

cohort effects an effect on a person's life related to the time of the person's birth. (27)

conflict perspective a perspective that holds that society consists of conflicts between dominant and subordinate social groups. (24)

critical gerontology theoretical approaches that look "within" theory and research to critically examine and question the underlying and "taken-for-granted" assumptions about aging. (27)

cross-sectional research design a research method that studies people from many age groups at one point in time. (27)

digital literacy refers to computer and Internet literacy in a growing digital information age. (31)

feminist approach an approach that views gender as a defining characteristic in social interaction and life experiences, as well as in the process and experience of aging; gender is seen as socially constructed, with men being more advantaged than women in society. (25)

functionalist perspective a perspective that holds that social order is based on consensus, cooperation, and shared norms and values, and that all parts of society serve a role or function to keep society in a state of balance or equilibrium. (21)

interlocking systems of oppression "macro level connections linking systems of oppression such as race, class, and gender" (Estes 2001, 13). (25)

interpretive perspective   a perspective that focuses almost exclusively on the micro level of social life. It looks at how people define situations, how they create social order, and how they relate to one another in daily life. (21)

life course perspective   a functionalist approach that bridges the micro- and macro-levels of analysis by incorporating social interaction and social structure within its framework. (23)

longitudinal research design   a research method that looks at a single group of people at two or more points in time. (28)

macro-level theories   theories that "examine social structures or structural elements as they influence experiences and behaviors" (Bengtson, Burgess, and Parrott 1997, S76). (20)

micro-level theories   theories that focus on individuals and their interactions, and that are used to explain phenomena such as the relationship between adult children and their parents, and the effect of negative attitudes on older people's self-esteem. (20)

mixed methods   also known as triangulation, refers to the use of more than one research method in a research study; for example, combining a quantitative survey with qualitative interviews, or two qualitative methods such as interviews and focus groups. (30)

moral economy theory   a theory that focuses on shared values and social norms that shape popular beliefs in the legitimacy of certain practices and policies; this theory complements political economy theory. (26)

narrative gerontology   an approach that seeks to understand the "inside" of aging by examining the narratives or life stories that people tell in order to organize and make sense of their lives, and their experiences of aging. (26)

period or environmental effects   an effect on a person's life due to the time of measurement. This would include historical, social, or environmental effects, such as an ongoing war, changes in health habits (e.g., increased exercise), or changes in health care policies that have different influences on different age cohorts. (27)

political economy theory   a theory that focuses on conflict and change in social life. It traces this conflict to the struggle between social classes and to the resulting dominance of some groups in society and the subordination of others. (24)

positivist worldview   theoretical perspective based on the belief that knowledge is built by studying observable facts and their relationship to one another. (21)

qualitative methods   research methods that include in-depth interviews, analysis of the content of documents or artifacts, and field observation. Researchers use these methods to understand individuals' social world and experience from the subjects' own perspective. (30)

quantitative methods   research methods that use statistical methods and mathematical models to analyze data that include census data, national social surveys, and epidemiological studies. (29)

sequential design   a research method that looks at a series of cross-sectional studies during a longitudinal study. (28)

time-lag comparison design   a research method that examines different groups of people of the same age at different points in time (e.g., 70-year-olds in 1989, 1999, and 2009). (28)

trajectories   long-term patterns of stability and change that often include many transitions. (24)

transitions   changes in social status or social roles such as marriage, parenthood, divorce, remarriage, and widowhood. (24)

triangulation   also known as mixed methods, refers to the use of two or more methodological approaches in a research study; for example, a quantitative method and a qualitative method, or two qualitative methods. (30)

Selected Readings

Biggs, S., A. Lowenstein, and J. Hendricks. eds. *The Need for Theory: Critical Approaches to Social Gerontology.* Amityville, NY: Baywood Publishing Co. 2003.

> This book brings together theorists who have advanced theory in social gerontology. The authors examine a range of substantive issues that shape the process and experience of aging. They use a variety of theoretical frameworks, including social constructionism, feminism, and political economy.

Denzin, N., and Y. Lincoln, eds. *The Sage Handbook of Qualitative Research,* 3rd edition. Thousand Oaks, CA: Sage Publications, 2005.

> An excellent and comprehensive resource on qualitative methods. Topics include ethics and politics in qualitative research, critical ethnography, and feminist qualitative research. A useful reference for a wide audience, including undergraduate students, graduate students, academic instructors, and researchers.

Neuman, W. L., and K. Robson. *Basics of Social Research: Qualitative and Quantitative Approaches, Canadian Edition.* Toronto: Pearson Education Canada, 2009.

> This text introduces students to the basics of social research, with a focus on qualitative and quantitative methods. It demonstrates the value of combining approaches. The authors include data and examples from Canadian research studies.

Websites to Consult

Canadian Association on Gerontology (CAG)

http://www.cagacg.ca/whoweare/200_e.php

> The CAG produces the *Canadian Journal on Aging* and organizes an annual meeting of predominantly Canadian researchers and practitioners. The website provides links to sites that report on international aging issues. The organization also announces meetings, conferences, and educational programs of interest to gerontologists. The site contains information for students as well.

SEDAP II: Canada in the 21st Century: Moving Towards an Older Society

http://socserv.mcmaster.ca/sedap

> This website provides online access to research papers that cover a wide range of social and economic issues facing Canada's aging population and older Canadians. SEDAP II (the Social and Economic Dimensions of an Aging Population) is the second phase of a 10-year, national, multidisciplinary, and multi-university program of research.

AgeLine Database

http://www.aarp.org/research/ageline/

This website allows you to search for articles, books, government reports, and other publications on topics related to aging. You can search by keyword, author, title, and more, as well as limit your search by year. The database contains thousands of sources along with abstracts of their contents. Some sources allow you to immediately download a full-text copy of the document. In other cases you can track down the source (e.g., a Statistics Canada document).

© Courtesy of Lori Campbell

Chapter

3

Aging Then and Now

INTRODUCTION

In Laurel Creek, West Virginia, old men retire to the porch. They watch the traffic go by, they talk to friends and neighbours, and they arrange for part-time work. Life on the porch in the early years of retirement allows a man to keep in contact with the community. When a man gets older and his health fails, life on the porch allows him to draw on his social credit. People stop to check on him, and they make trips to the store to get his groceries. If bad health keeps him indoors, his absence from the porch alerts people that he may need extra help. When a man nears death, he may come out to the porch to receive last visits from friends and neighbours. Life on the porch keeps a man part of the community until he dies (*Human Behavior Magazine* 1977).

Life on the porch matches an ideal we have of late old age. It reminds us of another time, a time when people grew up and died in the same town, when neighbours knew one another well, and when the young respected the old. Today, many people feel that old age has become devalued. We push old people aside in retirement, advertisers tell everyone to "think young," and even birthday cards make fun of aging. One card reads, "Roses are red, violets are blue, thank goodness I'm not older than you." It seems that in the past people enjoyed old age; not so now because older people get little respect or attention.

Has old age become worse over time? Did simpler societies offer a golden age to the old? Or do we just like to believe things were better in the past?

Social gerontologists try to answer these questions. They take two approaches: some gerontologists study past societies to see how they viewed and treated older people; others study modern societies to see how different social structures lead to different experiences of old age. This chapter will examine both points of view. It will look at (1) how aging differs in different types of societies, (2) how social structures affect aging, and (3) how aging today differs from aging in the past.

FOUR TYPES OF SOCIETIES

Sociologists Gerhard and Jean Lenski (1974) describe four stages of sociocultural evolution. These stages correspond to four types of societies: hunting and gathering, horticultural, agricultural (agrarian), and industrial. They also list specialized types of societies, including herding and fishing societies. Recently, sociologists have described a new sociocultural stage: the postindustrial society. This chapter will look at

four major societal types: (1) hunting and gathering, (2) agricultural, (3) industrial, and (4) postindustrial societies. Each type has a unique social organization and exists today. These types also represent a historical evolution from the simplest to the most complex forms of social life. A look at these societies will show the impact of social organization on the status and treatment of older people. This review will also illustrate how aging has changed over time.

Hunting and Gathering Societies

Humans lived in hunting and gathering bands for a million years or more and settled into agriculture between only 10,000 and 20,000 years ago. People in hunting and gathering societies survive by gathering wild plants and by stalking or trapping wild game. These groups (sometimes as few as 20 people) move constantly from place to place in search of food. They resemble an extended family. Their technology is simple, consisting mainly of bows, spears, and fire, and they have no permanent settlement.

Most simple societies underwent rapid change in the 20th century. Industry has destroyed many of their habitats, and some groups find themselves confined to reserves. Other groups have adapted to new technologies and new opportunities and now work for the large companies and government projects that use their land. These contacts have led to changes in traditional nomadic life. The discussion below refers to traditional hunting and gathering life as it existed in the past and where it exists in the present. Where possible, the discussion compares traditional life with life for these people today.

Archaeologists estimate that people in hunting and gathering societies had a short life expectancy by modern standards. For example, before the Europeans arrived, Aboriginal peoples in Canada may have had an average life expectancy of 30 or 40 years (Northcott and Wilson 2001). Cowgill and Holmes (1972) report that these societies defined a person as old by age 45 or 50; and Simmons (1960, 1970), in a study of 71 contemporary simple societies, says that people in these societies are considered old at 50 or 60 years of age. He estimates, on the basis of scarce data, that these societies rarely had more than 3 percent of their people over age 65. Therefore, when the terms "old" and "elderly" are used here in connection with simple societies, they refer to people 50 to 60 years old.

Early work by Cowgill (1972) and Press and McKool (1972) present four conditions that led to support for an older person in simple societies. First, the person needed an important role to play in social life; second, the older person must have lived near and fit into his or her extended family; third, he or she must have controlled some important material or informational resource; and fourth, the group must value collective rather than individual development (Sokolovsky 1990). Few simple societies fulfill all these conditions, so treatment of older people varies among them.

Researchers have found one condition more than the others leads to a good old age in primitive societies: The old have high status when their contribution to subsistence outweighs their cost to the group. Older people do well when they still have a valued role to play in the culture. Their ability to give to the group depends on two things. First, the culture must offer alternative roles for older people to play as they lose their strength, and, second, the older person must have good health.

Canada's Inuit serve as a good example of a present-day hunting and gathering society. They live in a climate that demands physical strength to survive, but they love and respect their elders and encourage their older members to take part in social life as long as they can. Men, for example, "retire" slowly from work. As a man loses his strength, younger male members of the community or household do more of the winter hunting. The older man may then take shorter hunting trips or teach the young how to hunt. Older Inuit women have an easier time moving into old age than do men (this is true of women in most nomadic societies). They pass the heavy work on to younger women and spend more time taking care of the children.

Collings (2000, 2001) found that a good attitude and the ability to manage decreased health defined successful aging among the Inuit. Successfully aging older men and women find their own ways to adapt to decreases in their strength. Older men will start to hunt early in the spring in order to stockpile food for the winter. They may also strike a bargain with young hunters; for example, the older man may fix the gear while the younger man hunts. Older women sometimes adopt children. The Inuit allow their elders to play new roles in society as their health and strength decline. They value their old as much for their knowledge and wisdom as for their work. A person gives something to the group when he or she recalls and passes on the knowledge of Inuit lore. This social role makes the old person useful to the group and improves his or her status and treatment in the community.

Not all groups make these accommodations for older members. The Chipewyan, for instance, who live in Canada's northern prairies, have no roles for older men to play. The Chipewyan do not place a high value on knowledge of tribal lore or craftwork. A man has status when he succeeds at hunting, but when he stops hunting, he loses respect and power in the group, and

people label him "elderly." Men will do anything to avoid this label. Some continue to hunt even when their health fails. Sharp (1981) reports the case of a man who had just recovered from a heart attack and had emphysema but still went into the bush alone. His wife worried that he would kill himself through overexertion, but he would rather risk his life than be called old. Most of these simple societies have changed in the recent past due to contacts with the modern world. Elders no longer rely on their contribution to group survival for their well-being. Today, they get government pensions. Pensions give elders new status and provide a source of income for their children. At the same time, the cash economy leads to less respect for older people. Modernization has decreased the role of elders as educators and caregivers to their grandchildren. In some cases, children (who learn English in school) cannot understand their grandparents' language.

Researchers report that hunting and gathering societies distinguish between two different stages of old age. In the first, a person retires from the heavy work of middle age, but he or she still has good health. In the second stage, the older person gets sick or becomes confused or frail. Simmons (1960) calls people in this second group the "overaged."

In traditional Inuit society, older people kept their status as long as they do some useful work for the group. Their status dropped if illness made them dependent. People made fun of the frail elderly, said nasty things to them, or ignored them. The overaged got the worst cuts of meat, had little money, and had to do without trade goods. A stranger might have taken in an Inuit who outlived his or her spouse, children, and close relatives, but this person would get little respect and would have to do the worst work.

The Inuit also abandoned their aged when they became liabilities to the group. They did this as a last resort and encouraged the older person to make the decision. But sometimes the group would withdraw its support rapidly, thus hastening death (Holmes and Holmes 1995).

Simple societies vary in how they treat the aged and treatment of the aged often depends on how much an older person contributes to or takes from the group.

Agricultural Societies

People in agricultural societies live on food produced from farming the land. These societies have more complex technologies than hunting and gathering societies. They also have more complex social structures, including social classes and bureaucracies.

Humans settled into villages and cities for the first time in the Middle East, China, and India about 10,000

● Exhibit 3.1

Do Nomadic People Abandon Their Elders?

In any nomadic society, if people live too long and become decrepit or demented, the group may abandon or kill them.

Jacob Bronowski (1976) shows this in his film series and book *The Ascent of Man.* In Iran, he follows a nomadic group called the Bakhtiari on their yearly journey to their summer pastures. The tribe climbs over six mountain ranges, through high passes and snow, until it reaches the Bazuft River.

Bronowski says the test for the group comes at the river. The Bazuft, a trickle in summer, swells each year with melting snow and spring rain. The group—men, women, and animals—must swim across. For the young, crossing the Bazuft stands as a test of adulthood. For them, life begins, but for the old, Bronowski says, life ends. The camera records in detail the struggle to cross the river. The current batters horses, donkeys, sheep, goats, and people. The young men swim for their lives and help the animals get across. But then the camera pulls back to focus on two figures among the rocks—a dog and an old man. The dog races back and forth looking from the man to the group below. The man sits silently with his back against the rocks watching the tribe cross the river. No emotion shows on his face. He no longer has the strength to cross the river, and the tribe will go on without him. "Only the dog is puzzled to see a man abandoned," Bronowski says. "The man accepts the nomad custom; he has come to the end of his journey" (1976, 64).

Life in many nomadic cultures demands this kind of choice. The tribe must move on to survive, and the old, who cannot keep up, get left behind. This man accepts his fate. He may have left his own parents to die in the same way. This dramatic case shows the dark side of life in primitive society. "In a vigorous community," Colin Turnbull (1961, 35–36) says, "where mobility is essential, cripples and infirm people can be a handicap and may even endanger the safety of the group."

A study by Maxwell and Silverman (1977, 37) found that 80 percent of the societies that did not value the elderly lived as nomads for at least part of the year. The harsher the environment, the greater the chance a group will kill or abandon its aged. Killing the aged shows up most often in societies that have irregular food supplies, move often, and live in severe climates (Simmons 1970, 240).

---

years ago at the end of the last Ice Age. For the first time in human history, societies gathered a surplus of food. In these societies, older people often owned property, and they used property rights to get support from the young.

As a general rule, in agricultural societies, those with land command the most respect, those without land the least. All over the world, property rights create a legal dependence of the young on the old. Old people among the Gwembe Tonga of Zambia get power by owning livestock and land (Colson and Scudder 1981). Older people among the Etal Islanders of Micronesia gain respect when they own property. The Etal look down on old people who hold on to all their land, but they think of a person as foolish if he or she gives it all away. The land serves as an inheritance bribe (Nason 1981).

Agricultural societies in the past sometimes expressed their dislike for the aged. Greek playwright Aristophanes mocked the old in his plays; Aristotle derided the way most people grew old (although he thought a philosopher could live a good life even in old age). Greek poems mock older people who want to hold on to youth (Wortley 1998). And in the Renaissance, Machiavelli portrayed the old man as a lecherous fool in his play *La Clizia*. These writings show a special dislike for older people who deny aging.

Tension between the generations sometimes surfaced in song. An Austrian folksong (Berkner 1972, cited in Fischer 1978, 69) says:

> Papa, when will you give me the farm?
> Papa, when will you give me the house?
> When will you finally move to your little room
> And tend your potato patch?

Studies of English Canadians in the late 19th century show the same tensions between the young and the old. Historical accounts indicate that parents gave a great deal of thought to how they would pass their land down to their children (Gagan 1983b; Mays 1983), and the children, who worked to improve the family farm, sometimes into their 30s, expected to get it as a reward for their work. In 1853, Susannah Moodie wrote that "death is looked upon by many Canadians more as a matter of … change of property into other hands, than as a real domestic calamity" (Moodie 1853, cited in Gagan 1983b, 185).

Ontario farmers kept intergenerational tension low by passing the land down before they died (a method still used today) (Keating 1996). Older people stayed on the land with the inheriting child and his family. Getting the land early in life must have reduced some tensions between the generations, but it created others. Selling the land to the young risked the older generation's old-age security. When they did sell the land to their children, parents often kept a few acres for themselves to maintain their independence in old age.

In Canada in the early 20th century, the family provided most of the support to older people. Snell (1996) says that older people with little income or poor health often went to live with a child or grandchild. Snell reports that in some cases children moved into their parents' house to care for them. In other cases, the older and younger generations moved to live near each other in order to ensure support for the elderly parents. Sometimes the elderly parent moved from one child's house to another's in order to spread the costs and benefits of parent care. Scattered historical reports show that older people who lived with their children often helped with gardening, household repairs, or child rearing. This exchange of support characterized family life in rural Canada.

Prentice and her colleagues (1996) report that, in New France in the eighteenth century, an older woman who gave up her farm to a younger family member often received a pension. For example, a woman who lived in the Richelieu valley in 1760 got a pension for "heat, light, clothing, and houseroom." She also got "16 minots (bushels) of flour, 1/4 minot of salt, and 120 pounds of salt pork." Another pension allowed a woman "two pairs of French shoes every year" (44). These pensions provided older women with some support.

In the 1850s in Canada women had few rights to ownership of the land. Widows did have a right of dower to one-third of her husband's land. But a husband's will could ignore this right, so land often passed down to a son when the woman's husband died (Benoit 2000). This left a widow with only a small pension. And this pension sometimes depended on her willingness to stay widowed. "Control 'from the grave' continued in many farming regions well into the 20th century" (Prentice et al. 1996, 124).

The content of farmers' wills in Ontario, like those in New France, suggests some worry about future security. Wills stated exactly what the inheriting son was to do for his parents. One will describes in detail the kind of food ("flour, pork and butter and milk, potatoes and other vegetables"), the kind of firewood ("plenty of good wood ready for use"), the transportation ("a horse and buggy"), and the cash ("$100 a year") that a son had to give his mother for the rest of her life (Gagan 1983b, 186). Snell (1996, 75, 101) says that parents used "maintenance agreements to gain support from children, based on the fear that such support would not otherwise be forthcoming."

Treatment of the aged in agricultural societies differed by social class. The elderly who owned land in these societies had power until they died. For this reason, older people who owned land commanded the greatest respect in societies from Canada to traditional China (Ikels 1981). (In rural areas today land still gives the older people influence over the young) (Kind et al., 2004). The poor and landless lived less well and got little respect. In rural areas today land still gives the older people influence over the young (Kind et al., 2004).

These reports about aging in agricultural society give the impression that many older people lived in poverty but this wasn't true in Canada. Canadian historians report that most older people "lived independently and were capable of maintaining themselves" (Montigny 1997, 52). Those who needed help got support from their families and neighbours. Indeed, "intense poverty in old age was still the exception" (Haber and Gratton 1994, cited in Myles 2002, 327). That meant that most people in poverty had no working adult children to help support them.

McDaniel and Lewis (1997 cited in McDaniel 2003) studied family life in pre-Confederation Newfoundland. Because of its isolation from mainstream Canadian society, pre-Confederation Newfoundland provides a good example of family life in a traditional society. McDaniel and Lewis found that few older people at that time lived in multi-generational extended families, most older people lived alone or with their spouse, and multi-generational households occurred when families faced poverty or when the older person provided the support. In the past, contrary to the stereotype, older people often provided support to the young.

McDaniel (2003) says that researchers need to do much more research on aging in simpler societies in the past. She says that "not nearly as much is known about intergenerational relations in families past or present as might be expected." Generalizations about societies in the past often miss the variety and dynamism of actual family. Some examples of daily life emerge from the historical record. They show that the direction of support in families can flow from young to old or old to young depending on the time and circumstances. McDaniel says that "people are products of their times and contribute, or not, to children, elders, and society only insofar as they are able, whatever culture or the time dictate" (McDaniel 2003, 44).

In Canada community support softened the effects of poverty or isolation in old age. Snell (1996) reports on many cases in the past in which neighbours and friends support an older person in need. They provide a room and food or at least try to get the older person formal help. But most families had little extra to give to older family members. So a poor older person in a household might push the limits of family and community support. For instance, a farmer in eastern Ontario took in a 73-year-old widower, and provided the man with room and board in return for some light chores. But, the farmer says, the man "cannot do much ... [and] we would like to be free of him" (Snell 1996, 62).

Prentice and her colleagues (Rubio and Waterson 1986, cited in Prentice et al. 1996, 124) report on another case in Ontario from the 1905 diary of Lucy Maud Montgomery. She writes:

> Uncle John and Prescott have been suing grandmother shamefully all summer. In short, they have been trying to turn her out ... Grandmother's absurd will put her completely in their power—the power of selfish, domineering men eaten up with greed. Grandmother told them she would *not* leave the home she had lived and worked for sixty years and since then Uncle John has never spoken to her or visited her.

In its treatment of older people, agricultural society, appears to be a mirror image of primitive society. In the simplest societies the old had no wealth, but they received respect as long as they gave to the group. The !Kung San roam the Kalahari desert throughout their lives and have little property. The young revere their elders as storytellers, spiritual leaders, and healers. In agricultural societies, the elderly got the most respect if they owned property and kept it from their children until late in life or until they died. In such a society, "a firm hold on the strings of a fat purse was one effective compensation for declining physical powers" (Simmons 1970, 46). The old may be respected in this kind of society, but they are not always loved.

The current picture of life in preindustrial society shows that most older people maintained a decent standard of living, although some people faced hard times in old age. The existence of poor older people and their marginal condition argue against the idea of a golden age in pre-industrial society.

Modern Industrial Society

The agricultural revolution created a new form of society. Agriculture produced a surplus of food and gave rise to the first cities. It created social classes and based status on ownership of property. This kind of society dominated until the middle of the 18th century, when three interrelated changes began to reshape social life: (1) industrialization, (2) urbanization, and (3) the demographic transition.

These changes took place over 200 years, and they affect society still today. They began at various times in different places, and sometimes one type of change—economic change, demographic change, or a change in values—had more influence on a society than another. Scholars still argue over which change came first in which society, but taken together these three changes revolutionized social life and led to a new age of older people.

Industrialization

By the 19th century, most of Europe had begun to industrialize. Industry began to use steam and water power to increase productivity, the factory system gathered workers and raw materials in cities, and transportation systems spread the production of factories to all classes and countries. Some countries industrialized before others, and some more quickly, but by 1850 industrialization had changed the shape of European society.

Industrialization both caused and resulted from the breakup of rural life. Cottage industries, where small groups of workers in villages produce mostly for local needs, failed as the factories produced more and cheaper goods. At the same time, parents could no longer keep their sons on the farm with the promise of future inheritance. As death rates declined, families had too many sons who wanted the land; the younger sons had to move to the city to find work, and the city welcomed them as a cheap source of labour. The new pace of work and life in the city freed young people from traditional ties and beliefs, and led to a decrease in the status of older people.

Industrialization decreased the status of older people in another way. Companies looked for ways to get the older, supposedly less effective, worker out of the workplace. Retirement rules, supported by both labour and management, forced older workers out of work. Management liked retirement because it allowed them to release workers who were costly because they had seniority. Unions supported retirement because in return they won seniority rights (rules about being first hired, last fired) from management.). In short, unions traded older workers' right to work for younger workers' job security. Retirement expressed in a formal rule the decline of the older person's status in industrial society.

Snell (1996) points out that these changes came about gradually in Canada. Workers with little in the way of savings continued to work. And those who worked had an income similar to the incomes of younger workers. Only in the 1930s and 1940s did modern patterns of retirement emerge in Canada. Still, over time, older workers found that work became harder to find. They often had to take work in low-paying and marginal jobs as janitors or household labourers. Some people complained about discrimination due to their age.

Urbanization

Canadian society changed from a rural to an urban one between 1851 and 1950. During the 19th century, both men and women migrated to the cities. Accounts of this time say little about the elderly.

Katz (1975) gives one of the few reports on what life was like for older people in a Canadian town. He studied Hamilton, Ontario, between 1851 and 1861. He found that men who owned land had the most security in old age, and men aged 60 and over were the largest group of landowners. Still, after age 60, Katz shows, a man's power began to decrease, and men over 60 had a greater chance of having less land from one year to the next than any other group. Men 60 and over were also the least likely to have a servant (a sign of wealth). After age 60, Katz says, even landowning men often "decline[d] into difficult circumstances" (63).

In small businesses and on farms older people could adjust their work to suit their health and strength, but in industrial cities older people had to meet the demands of the workplace or quit. No public pensions existed in the 19th century, and many older people in the cities had no private savings. In addition, they often had to take the lowest forms of work, move into public homes for the aged, or live in poverty, especially if they were without children.

In North America, urban life undermined traditional society in another way. The cities supported a market system in which individuals could accumulate wealth outside the family structure. Inequality in society began to grow as some individuals gathered wealth for themselves through trade. Those who were successful turned from public affairs to private concerns. This focus on the self broke some individuals' communal bonds, including those that linked the older to the younger generation.

Synge (1980), who studied working-class families in Ontario in the early 20th century, found that city life made old age an uncertain time. Young people earned their own wages and gave money to their parents while they lived at home. But when these children grew up and moved out, parents lost this income. Few social services existed for older people, and an unmarried daughter often looked after her parents as they aged. Families sometimes passed the job of care from one child to the next. Synge reports the case of one old woman who lived for periods of time with each of her children for her last 25 years.

Katz (1975) found that few older people in Hamilton lived with their married children, and the poorest households were least likely to house an older relative. Only 8 percent of households in 1851 and 10 percent in 1861 had adults of two or more generations. "Only when old age and loneliness were combined would a parent move in with her children" (254).

Katz also found that, from 1851 to 1861, 58.8 percent of women aged 60 to 69 were widowed, almost double the rate of men. Women of the poorest social class (Irish Catholic women) faced an eight-times greater chance of widowhood than women of the highest class (Canadian-born Protestant women). Poor widows had little or no savings and no pensions from their husbands. The poorest women, especially those without children, would finally be recipients of charity (a special charity, the Ladies' Benevolent Society, was created to help them) or live in a "house of refuge and industry."

Snell (1996) found that in the late 1800s Ontario built a network of poorhouses or houses of refuge that served poor older people. Similar houses existed in Nova Scotia, New Brunswick, and Newfoundland. These institutions began by serving all poor people—orphans, unwed mothers, and older people—but over time, more and more of these homes focused on care for older people. Poorhouses gradually became homes for the elderly and were an important public response to the needs of older people.

On the surface, the new freedom and equality in urban industrial Canada made all people more alike, but for the old they often meant a decrease in status. Yet, studies of the past show the complexity of urban life and of family relations at the time. Recent work in the United States, for example, shows that older people in cities sometimes continued to serve as a resource for their children (Haber, 2006). Older people in cities, for example, often provided living quarters in their own home for adult children and grandchildren. Older women in families sometimes provided a babysitting service so that their children could work. Multiple-generation households in cities in the 1860s in the United States. served the needs of young and old, and combined the assets of children and parents.

Some older widows moved to cities from the countryside to improve their economic status and quality of life. Haber (2006) says that these women, who depended on their adult children in a rural setting, could live on their own in the town or city. They could hire servants to care for themselves or take in boarders to help pay expenses. For these women and their families, urban life led to more freedom and opportunity. It freed people from the limits of life in the countryside and it created new relations between the generations. More research on Canadian life in the past will no doubt turn up new information about social relations between the old and the young.

The Demographic Transition

The demographic transition refers to the changes in population that led to a high proportion of older people among the developed nations (of Western Europe and North America). This transition, which took place in North America at the end of the 19th century along with industrialization and urbanization, was a three-stage process. The stages outline how European and North American societies shifted from a youthful to an older population structure.

Stage 1: 1300–1750 Before the 18th century, population had been relatively stable. High birth rates were balanced by high death rates. French studies of the 17th century estimate that there were about eight children to a normal marriage and that about 70 percent of the households had children. Children made up 45 percent of the French population at that time (compared with half that rate in industrial societies today).

Only a small number of people lived to old age in preindustrial society. Figures exist only for scattered populations before 1800, but they give some idea of the

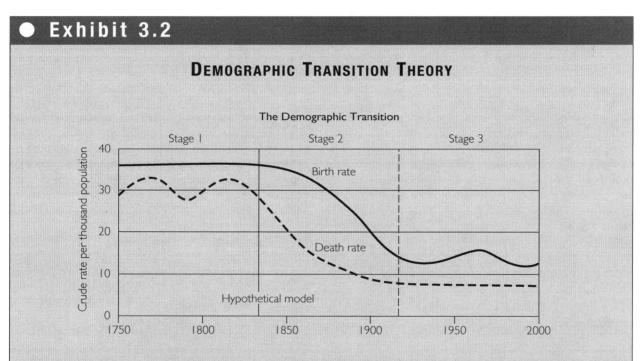

● Exhibit 3.2

DEMOGRAPHIC TRANSITION THEORY

The Demographic Transition

Stage 1: Demographic transition theory says that before industrialization, societies had high birth rates and high death rates. Population size stayed small because of the high (though variable) death rates. The proportion of old and young in society also stayed stable.

Stage 2: Industrialization led to a decrease in death rates. Birth rates stayed high, and the population grew in size. These societies had a growing proportion of young people.

Stage 3: Further into industrialization the birth rate dropped. Death rates remained low, and population size stayed stable. The birth rate sometimes fluctuated (as with the baby boom of 1944–1965). Society had a growing proportion of older people.

Source: Chart based on personal communication with W.W. McVey, 1987. Courtesy of Wayne McVey.

proportions of people 65 and over. A national census in Iceland in 1703 reported 4.6 percent of the population was 65 and over; Belgrade in 1733 reported 2.1 percent; and Nishinomiya, Japan, in 1713 reported 6.6 percent. A listing of counties in England from 1599 to 1796 showed people aged 65 or over made up between 1.4 percent and 6.4 percent of the population. Rarely did the 65-and-over population top 10 percent in any place in Europe.

Stage 2: 1750–1850 Three phenomena caused rapid population growth in Europe from 1750 on, and also changed the proportion of young and old people in society. First, the death rate decreased, because war fatalities decreased, the cycle of epidemics ended, improved hygiene in cities led to better health, border controls stopped the spread of disease, and food supplies increased due to better climate and more open land.

Second, the birth rate stayed high and in some cases increased. New lands opened in Canada and earlier marriages took place in the countryside. Young people in the cities, who did not have to wait for their parents' land, married young. Better nutrition and more opportunity led people to have more children.

Third, the number and proportion of young people in the population began to grow and the total population increased.

Stage 3: Early 20th Century to the Present Both the birth rate and death rate in Western Europe had declined by 1900, completing the transition to an aging population. The biggest change in death rates came from improvements in the general standard of living. Diet and hygiene in the cities improved. Clean underwear, soap, coal for heat, and glass in windows all helped people stay healthier. Improved housing and more efficient treatment of water and sewage decreased disease. As the standard of living rose, the virulence of disease, and therefore the death rate, declined.

These changes led all social classes to decrease the number of children per family. Middle-class families led the way. They had smaller families to ensure that their children would have the money needed to remain in the middle class. Rural families followed the trend later in order to ensure that each of their children would get a good portion of land.

From 1850 onward, the proportion of older people in developed nations grew.

Industrialization, urbanization, and the demographic transition put an end to almost all of the following conditions, each of which had supported the high status of older people:

1. ownership and control of property;

2. a monopoly on special knowledge;

3. ancestor worship and a high value placed on tradition (in which the old provide a link to the gods);

4. society organized around kinship and family;

5. small, stable communities;

6. high mutual dependence of group members;

7. small numbers of older people; and

8. special roles for the aged.

In the past two centuries, the economy, the structure of family life, and the relations of the old to the young changed. Old age became more common, but it also lost its privileged status (Fischer 1978).

Modernization Theory

Some researchers believe that a sharp break occurred in some societies as they moved from an agricultural to an industrial way of life, affecting affected all social institutions and social relations. **Modernization theory** holds that this shift to an urban life, with high technology and complex institutions, led to a decrease in the status of older people.

Some social scientists refer to the shift from agricultural to urban society as a process of modernization. Modernization is "the transformation of a total society from a relatively rural way of life based on animate power, limited technology, relatively undifferentiated institutions, parochial and traditional outlook and values, toward a predominantly urban way of life based on inanimate sources of power, highly developed scientific technology, highly differentiated institutions matched by segmented individual roles, and a cosmopolitan outlook which emphasized efficiency and progress" (Cowgill 1974, 127).

Cowgill and Holmes (1972) theorize that the status of older people decreases with increases in modernization. They reviewed studies of 14 contemporary societies from around the world. These ranged from a study of the Sidamo of southwestern Ethiopia, to two studies of Israeli society (one of a kibbutz), to a study of the aged in the U.S.S.R. Cowgill and Holmes found that small numbers of older people, ancestor worship, low social change, extended families, a value system that emphasized the importance of the group, stable residence, and low literacy (where the group values the old for their knowledge) all lead to high status in old age. In modern societies, where such conditions are reversed, older people have low status. The authors concluded that these trends support modernization theory.

Other writers, many of them historians, have criticized modernization theory. They say that the theory compares the present, with its problems, to an idealized past. He shows, to the contrary, that the treatment and status of the aged varied from time to time and from place to place before modernization (as it varies today among simpler societies). O'Rand (1990) says that modernization theory cannot account for the complexities of social change. It misses the differences within the older population based on age cohort differences, socioeconomic differences, and historical conditions. Within a single society, researchers often find ambivalent feelings toward the aged.

The latest research shows an even more complex picture of aging in the past. Haber (2006) says that aging differed by time and place in the past (and even today). She shows that an example exists to contradict almost any general statement about old age in the past. The experience of aging and of life in the family differed by time, place, gender, ethnicity, economic status, economy

of the region, family life-cycle stage, and many other variables. Historians continue to sort out the different experiences of older people. Their focus has moved from the study of broad societal differences to the experiences of older people under specific conditions. This work gives us more detailed knowledge of aging in the past.

"In the future, then," Haber (2006, p.73) says, "the work of historians has the promise to contribute to a meaningful and multifaceted understanding of what it was like for men and women in the past—of different classes, regions, ethnicities, and cultures—to experience the realities of growing old."

Postindustrial Society

Countries such as Canada have gone through the industrial revolution and have developed service-based **postindustrial societies**. Today, some people in these

---

● Exhibit 3.3

THE COAST SALISH PEOPLE: A CHALLENGE TO MODERNIZATION THEORY

Modernization theory describes a single path from premodern to modern society. It also describes a single outcome for older people: a drop in status. The Coast Salish people of the Pacific Coast of North America show an alternative to modernization theory. They show how people can respond to events and shape their future.

Miller (1999) researched the role of grandmothers in Coast Salish tribes in the 1980s and 1990s. He found that some grandmothers did lose status as they aged. Tribal custom speaks of respect for elders. But elders who did not control resources or who did not make a contribution to the group lost status.

But Miller also found that some grandmothers gained status with age. These women play an important role in tribal culture. Their status comes, in part, from recent changes in tribal life. And their status questions the universality of modernization theory.

Miller calls these women "political grandmothers." They hold office and play a role in the political life of the community. They also preserve traditional practices and the right to tribal membership. This gives them

control of fishing rights (the key to material well-being in the tribe). All of these roles give these grandmothers power and prestige in their community.

Also, young people show a new interest in Indian identity and tribal culture. This has led to higher status for certain elders. Miller says that grandmothers "who have ritual knowledge and control (i.e., knowledge of Indian names, shamanistic abilities, or influence over the process of initiation into dancing societies) are in demand and are valued in their communities" (1999, 106–7).

Political grandmothers who hold office link their political role to traditional roles held by women in Coast Salish society. They emphasize their work as teachers and mentors of children and grandchildren in the tribe. These grandmothers also speak out in public. They remind tribal members of their genealogy, traditional values, and cultural practices. These women remain active in public life until late old age. The tribe admires them for the care they gave their families, for providing income to the family, and for their knowledge of tribal customs (Miller, 1999).

Sources: Amoss, P. T. (1981). "Coast Salish elders." In P. T. Amoss and S. Harrell (Eds.), *Other ways of growing old: Anthropological perspectives* (pp. 227–247), Stanford, CA: Stanford University Press; and Miller, B. G. (1999). Discontinuities in the statuses of Puget Sound grandmothers. In M. M. Schweitzer (Ed.), *American Indian grandmothers: Traditions and Transitions* (pp. 103–124). Albuquerque: University of New Mexico Press.

societies still live badly in old age—they have poor housing, poor nutrition, bad health, and little money. Also, studies show that negative attitudes toward the aged still exist today.

Kastenbaum and Ross (1975, 5) say that people in Western societies feel ambivalent about aging. They call this an "approach-avoidance dilemma." They say that limited resources and the physical decline that come with old age make it unattractive in all societies. On the other hand, most people know and like older individuals, and at all times in history younger people have cared for and loved their aged relatives and friends.

In spite of some negative attitudes toward old age, older people as a group in North America live materially better lives than older people at any time in history. Major improvements have taken place in private and public pension programs. These include Canada's Old Age Security, the Canada Pension Plan, and free nationwide health care coverage for the elderly. These programs increase older people's independence and freedom.

AGING IN THE WORLD TODAY

The United Nations (UN) recognizes the demographic challenges faced by developed and developing nations. It declared 1999 the International Year of the Older Person (IYOP). Canada's motto for that year was "Canada, a society for all ages" (Canada Coordinating Committee 1999). The UN focused on four themes: raising awareness of aging, looking beyond 1999, reaching out to younger people, and networking between nations on policy and research. This last theme—networking between nations—will grow in importance as nations struggle with common issues. Countries can learn from one another, though the diversity of governments, cultures, and economic systems in the world will force nations to look for unique solutions. Chappell (1999a, 1) says that the IYOP reflected a new paradigm in the study of aging. "The new paradigm," she says, "promotes the life course perspective, age integration, and the inter-relatedness of aging and development." This perspective puts the life of the individual in the social, historical, and economic context of society. It looks at aging as the product of social as well as individual (biological and physiological) forces.

The U.S. Bureau of the Census calls the global increase in the number of older people "a social phenomenon without historical precedent" (American Association of Retired Persons [AARP] 1998, 7). In 2000, about 16 percent of the population of developed nations such as the United States, Australia, the United Kingdom, and Canada were over age 60 (United Nations 2002).

Australia, Western European countries, the Russian Federation, Japan, and Canada had 12 percent or more of their populations over age 65. Europe had a greater proportion of older people than any other continent. One projection estimates that the United Kingdom, for example, will have nearly one-third of its population (29.4 percent) aged 60 or over in the year 2025.

This increase in the older population will be caused mostly by a decrease in birth rates and, to a lesser extent, by increased longevity. Italy reports the lowest birth rates in human history. It now has more people over age 60 than under age 20 (United Nations 2002). The United Nations (2002) reports that by 2050 Italy may have as many people aged 60+ as people in the work force. Developed nations, which will see increases in health care and pension costs, have a number of options. For example, they can change pension policies and encourage people to work longer, raise taxes to cover increased costs, or increase the national debt (Anderson and Hussey 2000). Whatever approach they choose, developed nations will all have to provide more services to their aging populations.

Developing nations (such as the Latin American, Asian, African, and Middle Eastern countries) make up three-quarters of the world's population, and they too will see changes in their population structures. These countries have relatively young populations, with large numbers of children and proportionately few older people, some with as few as 3 percent of the population aged 65 and over (e.g., Bangladesh and Afghanistan) (United Nations 2002). But the death rates in these countries have begun to fall and many more people now live into old age.

The low proportion of people aged 65 and over in developing nations, compared with that in developed nations, tells only part of the story of aging in these countries.

First, the United Nations (2002) projects that between 2000 and 2025 the world population of older people (65 and over) will nearly double to more than 800 million people. About two-thirds of the world's older people will live in developing nations (AARP 1998). Today, "Hong Kong, Singapore and China are all witnessing the fastest population aging the world has ever seen" (Chi 2001, 119). In 2025, the UN predicts that about 86 percent of the older people in the developing world will live in Asia.

Second, the developing countries will show the greatest percentage increase of older people. The UN says that between 2000 and 2050, the 60-and-over population in developed countries will increase by 70 percent. But the 60-and-over population in developing countries will more than quadruple in this same time. Nearly 80 percent of the world's older population will live in the less-developed countries in 2050 (United Nations 2002). These nations will also see increases in their oldest old populations (people aged 80 and over).

Third, the developing countries have to spread their scarce resources among all age groups. This often means few public services to meet the needs of their aging populations.

China: A Case Study of Population Aging in a Developing Nation

China began its one-child-per-family policy in 1979. This policy aimed to decrease population growth. Although

---

● Exhibit 3.4

ELDER POPULATION INCREASES, AGED 65 AND OVER FROM WORLD AND MAJOR REGIONS, 2000–2050

	Increase (Year 2000 as [in millions])			Population (base = 100)	
	2000	*2025*	*2050*	*2025*	*2050*
World	421.0	838.7	1,492.1	199	354
More developed*	171.0	261.0	325.6	153	190
Less developed**	250.0	577.7	1,166.5	231	467
Africa	27.0	58.6	138.5	217	513
Latin America and Caribbean	30.0	71.0	142.5	237	475
South America	20.3	48.6	95.8	239	472
North America	38.9	71.1	95.6	183	246
Asia	214.6	483.3	922.7	225	430
Europe	107.4	148.3	183.2	138	171
Oceania	3.1	6.3	9.5	203	306

*More developed: Europe, Japan, North America, Australia, and New Zealand.
**Less developed: Africa, Asia (excluding Japan), Latin America/Caribbean, Melanesia, Micronesia, and Polynesia.

This table (1) shows the distribution of older people worldwide; (2) allows for a comparison of the size of older populations that each country and region will have to deal with; and (3) shows the growth rate of the older population in each region. This growth rate gives an idea of how much demographic change each society will undergo.

This table shows that, worldwide, the less-developed countries have a larger number of older people than the more developed countries (although they have smaller percentages of older people). It also shows that the older population will increase in the less developed countries at a faster rate than in the more developed countries.

In 2000, for example, Asia had five and a half times more older people than North America. This reflects the larger size of the total Asian population. Projections show that the Asian older population will increase at a faster rate than the North American older population. This reflects increased life expectancies in Asian countries. By the year 2050, compared to North America, Asia will have more than nine and a half times more older people.

Source: "Medium variant data. Population Division of the Department of Economic and Social Affairs of the United Nations Secretariat," *World Population Prospects: The 2006 Revision Population Database.* http://esa.un.org/unpp/index.asp?panel=2, accessed December 29, 2008. Reprinted with permission.

● **Exhibit 3.5**

REFLECTIONS ON AGING IN AFRICA

Novelist and travel writer Paul Theroux travelled by land from Cairo to Cape Town. He detailed his journey in his book *Dark Star Safari: Overland from Cairo to Cape Town*. During his travels he passed his 60th birthday. This caused him to examine the meaning of age and aging—for him and for the people he met. In the excerpt below Theroux reflects on what aging means in the African context.

"I decided to avoid any birthday celebration. I was so self-conscious of my age that I often asked Africans to guess how old I was, hoping—perhaps knowing in advance—they would give me a low figure. They always did. Few people see elderly in Africa. Forty was considered old, a man of fifty was at death's door, sixty year olds were just crocks or crones. Despite my years I was healthy, and being agile and resilient I found traveling in Africa a pleasure. I did not seem old here, did not feel it, did not look it to Africans, and so it was a great place to be, another African fantasy, an adventure in rejuvenation.

"You are forty-something," Kamal had guessed in Addis. The highest number I got was fifty-two. Little did they know how much they flattered my vanity. But no one was vain about longevity in Africa, because the notion of longevity hardly existed. No one lived long and so age didn't matter, and perhaps that accounted for the casual way Africans regarded time. In Africa no one's lifetime was long enough to accomplish anything substantial, or to see any task of value completed. Two generations in the West equaled three generations in African time, telescoped by early marriage, early childbearing, and early death.

"In southeastern Uganda I wrote in my diary: I do not want to be young again. I am happy being what I am. This contentment is very helpful on a trip as long and difficult as this."

Source: P. Theroux, *Dark Star Safari: Overland from Cairo to Cape Town.* Boston: Houghton Mifflin, 2003. 197–98.

the government has relaxed the policy somewhat in recent years, China will age sooner and more quickly than other developing nations.

China had a total population of 1.3 billion people in 2000. Demographers expect the population to grow to almost 1.5 billion people by 2050. Over these same 50 years the population aged 65 and older will grow from 88 million in 2000 to 341 million in 2050 (United Nations, 2002). Retirees at mid-century will make up about one-third of China's population, or 430 million people (*The New York Times*, 2007). Zhang (2001, p. 12) says that "China has a population that is aging … so fast that it has outpaced industrialization and modernization." Experts call this "one of the greatest demographic changes in history" (French, 2006).

At current rates of population change, China will get old before it gets rich. It will have to deal with the issues of a developing nation such as feeding its people, privatizing industry, and growing its economy. At the same time it will have to deal with issues of a developed society such as creating pension and health care systems to care for its older population.

China today has the largest population of older people in the world. It also has the largest share of the world's oldest old (aged 80+). These figures raise questions about China's ability to respond to its rapidly aging population. For example, the elderly support ratio (the number of people aged 65 and over per 100 people aged 20 to 64 years old) will double between 2000 and 2030 from 12 to 26. And its parent support ratio (the number of people aged 80 and over per 100 people aged 50 to 64) during those same years will more than quadruple from 3 to 14. For women this ratio will grow more than five times from 5 to 28. These crude figures suggest that Chinese society and its citizens will need to provide more support for its older population in the years ahead. Most of these older people (about 76 percent of all older Chinese) live in rural areas.

Rural older people depend almost entirely on family support. But illness and frailty can place a burden on family caregivers. This leads to stress and sometimes to family breakdown. Also, younger people often move away from their families. More older people than ever before live on their own, especially in cities. The Chinese Association of Senior Citizens reports that more than 25 percent of older people in China live alone or with only their spouse (Zhang, 2001). These people face poverty, and they may lack a family support network. Osnos (2007, 7A) interviewed Zhang Junrui, a 79-year-old who retired from a state-owned factory in Beijing. Zhang says that "for elderly people, the biggest issue is to avoid getting sick … Because savings might not be enough."

Chinese tradition puts the responsibility for care on the family. But in urban centres, this can also lead to burden and burnout. A study in Beijing found that 50 percent of families report financial, emotional, or other hardship in caring for their older relatives. This pressure will grow in the future as small young families care for four to eight older relatives. An increase in the very old population (80+) will put a further burden on the young. The very old population will increase almost six-fold from 16 million in 2006 to 94 million people in 2050 (Johnson, 2006). Li Bengong, the executive deputy director of the China National Committee on Aging says, "The situation is very serious … We have weak economic capability to cope with the aging of the population." (Johnson, 2006, 20A).

Like other developing nations, China will find it hard to meet the needs of its growing older population. The high cost of building and running long-term care institutions will limit their growth. Also, older people in China prefer to stay at home and receive support from their families. China has begun to develop home care options that fit its culture and meet the needs of its aging population.

The increased number and proportion of older people in China and their need for support will lead to social change. Kinsella and Velkoff (2001, p. 79) say that in the near future China "may anticipate a social and economic fabric radically different from that of today."

Further Issues Facing Developing Nations

Developing nations like China face other problems as well. When nations develop, the young often move to the cities (Oppong 2006). The young feel less tied to the land and feel less obliged to care for their elders. This leaves the aged in rural villages with little family or social support (Chi 2001; Gureje et al. 2006). Also, changing gender roles lead women to work outside the home, so older people are left without the family supports that former generations could rely on. Villages lack communications, transportation, supplies, and services that the elderly need. Modernization in India, for example, leaves elders without the support of tradition or the presence of modern social services (Bhat and Dhruvarajan 2001).

Older workers sometimes return to their home countries after years of working in another country. They have no work, no skills, and no pensions, and will grow old in poverty (DeLehr 1988). In rural settings, old people must work as long as they have the strength. In larger centres a growing number of older people survive by "scratching out a living from rubbish dumps or peddling goods on the streets" (DeLehr 1988, 7). She predicts things will get worse unless these countries develop basic services to help older people.

New problems have arisen that further place older people at risk. AIDS now plagues many developing countries. Canada's National Advisory Council on Aging (2002) reports that in Thailand two-thirds of the adults with HIV-related illnesses receive care at home from their 60- and 70-year-old parents. African elders face similar challenges. The AIDS pandemic in Africa has

This old Masai woman offers decorative beads and earrings for sale in a native Masai village in western Kenya. Developing nations will see a rapid increase in life expectancy and in the number of older people in their populations. Few people in these societies have pensions. Like this woman, they will have to work in old age to earn a living.

hit the working-age population, leading to the loss of middle-aged caregivers for African elders. Eke (2004) reports a collapse of the bonds between the generations. AIDS has left many older Africans as the sole caregiver for their orphaned grandchildren (Oppong 2006). "In some parts of Africa," the AARP says, "AIDS is actually called the 'grandmothers' disease'" (AARP 1998, 19).

Developing countries need more information about their older populations, and they need to plan for an aging society. Countries with social programs and pension plans in place will need to adapt these programs to serve more people (Chee 2000; Oh and Warnes 2001). Gerontologists need new theories of aging to explain the changes taking place in these countries (see Exhibit 3.6) and new plans for social change to fit the needs of an aging world.

Solutions that fit Western developed countries do not necessarily fit developing nations (Apt 2002). Katz says that even the Western view of aging does not fit many nations' needs. He says that the Western, problem-centred approach to aging makes traditional views of old age look "ineffectual and disorganized" (Katz 1996, 3). Western gerontology "is premised on moral and social

understandings of the individual vastly different from those of India [and other developing nations] and is designated for different political, economic, and cultural realities" (3). Western societies evolved away from family-centred supports for older people. Developed countries created pensions and other welfare programs for their older citizens. But this approach requires an economy and political system that supports these programs. In the developing nations of sub-Saharan Africa, for example, family support and family relations in many cases provide the only support for older people (Oppong 2006).

Developing countries have neither the social services nor the economic resources to help the elderly poor. Nor can these countries afford the housing, health, or welfare services for the old that Western countries have set up. This means that many older people in these countries will face economic and social hardship.

CONCLUSION

Did older people live better lives in the past than they do today? Can we learn something about aging from

---

● Exhibit 3.6

CONTROVERSY: MODERNIZATION VS. DEPENDENCY THEORY

Modernization theory views developed industrial societies as the model for developing countries. But developed countries' solutions often do not fit the needs of developing societies. Therefore, some theorists propose an alternative theory of aging—dependency theory.

Dependency theory uses a critical Marxist approach to the study of aging. It says that the social and economic structures in a society create the status of the old and that to understand the developing world gerontologists have to understand aging with regard to the economic relations between nations. Dependency theory looks at the societal and world-wide forces that decide the fate of older people.

Dependency theory begins with the fact that structured inequality exists between developed and developing societies. Developing, or peripheral countries, now depend on developed, or core, countries for their economic well-being. The peripheral countries of Latin America, Africa, and Asia produce raw materials, crops,

and manufactured goods for core countries. Core countries decide what peripheral countries should grow or make for the core country's markets. This keeps the peripheral country dependent and poor, and disrupts its economic, familial, and political life.

Younger people in core countries move off the land to work in the cities. Also, the gap between rich and poor people in these nations grows. Families grow less food for their own use, and begin to grow cash crops for export. This makes it harder for them to support large families that include older members. Older people also lose status in these societies because their knowledge does not serve the core nation's needs. "Old people do not simply become out of date, they are made obsolete. If one goal of gerontology is to upgrade the quality of life for older people in any given society, then it must first understand the structural imperatives that have shaped their control over potential resources" (Hendricks 1982). Dependency theory adds this understanding to the study of aging and society.

past societies? Will aging in the future differ from aging today?

The latest research shows that aging differed by time and place in the past (and even today). But one thing holds true, regardless of the historical period: all past societies had fewer older people than societies today. We cannot look to the past for ways to create a good old age today. The large number of older people in the world today is a new phenomenon. As Laslett (1976, 96) says, "It calls for invention rather than imitation."

In the future, as in the past, aging will differ between societies. Developed nations will have the best chance of creating a materially satisfying old age for their people. Developing countries will struggle under the burden of more people, old and young. Shrestra (2000) notes that, unfortunately, care for the old has a low priority among public policy concerns in many developing countries.

Aging populations will challenge all countries in the world. In 2002, the UN published its "International Plan of Action on Ageing." This strategy calls for improved attitudes toward older people, more effective policies, and more supportive communities. The UN looks to governments worldwide to achieve these goals. But the economy, political system, culture, level of development, and age structure of a society will all affect how governments respond to this challenge.

Like other countries, Canada cannot copy past societies in its treatment of older people, but it can learn something from the past and from simpler societies. Wherever older people have had valued roles to play in their societies, they have lived respected and purposeful lives. Canada can make this a goal of its policies.

Summary

1. Culture, custom, and the economic life of the group all influence how a society treats its older members. A study of four types of societies—hunting and gathering, agricultural, industrial, and postindustrial—shows that treatment of the aged differed in the past from time to time and from place to place. None of these societies created a golden age for older people.

2. Like most societies, past and present, modern Western societies show an ambivalence toward the aged. Negative stereotypes exist, and some discrimination against the aged takes place. Modern societies also offer older people independence, a high standard of living, and many opportunities for life satisfaction.

3. Developed nations have a high percentage of older people and will have to shift resources to serve the changing needs of their populations. Postindustrial societies show an ambivalence toward older people. They provide pensions and services but also show prejudice toward older people.

4. Modernization theory predicts a decline in the status and treatment of the aged in modern society compared with societies in the past. Some studies that compare developed and developing countries today support modernization theory, but critics of the theory argue that it oversimplifies life in the past, ignores differences in treatment of the elderly within societies, and undervalues the opportunities for a good old age today.

5. Developing countries have large numbers of older people, even though older people make up a relatively small percentage of their populations. This increase in the numbers of older people presents developing countries with problems of service delivery and health care support.

6. Population aging has become a worldwide challenge. The response a nation makes to the challenge will depend on its traditions, culture, level of development, and economic strength.

Study Questions

1. Identify and describe the four major types of societies. How are older people treated in each of these societies?

2. What are the four conditions that lead to support for an older person in simple societies? How do these conditions determine the way these societies treat older people? How has modernization affected the status of elders?

3. How did older people command status and respect in agricultural societies? What kind of tension did this create?

4. Define the process of modernization. What three changes created the modern industrial society? How did these three things influence the status and treatment of older people? Why do some researchers criticize modernization theory?

5. Explain why older people in developed countries live better materially now than at any time in the past.

6. What problems will the developing countries face as their older populations grow in size?

Key Terms

modernization theory   this theory holds that a shift to urban life, with high technology and complex institutions, leads to a decrease in the status of older people. (49)

postindustrial society   a society such as Canada's that has gone through the industrial revolution and become a service-based, complex society. (50)

Selected Readings

Bengtson, Vern L., and Ariela Lowenstein, eds. *Global Aging and Challenges to Families*. Hawthorne, NY: Aldine de Gruyter, 2003.

> This book contains writings from authors around the world. The chapters explore the relationships that exist between older people and their families. The articles collectively challenge the belief that older people use more resources than they contribute to their families or to society. The book shows that family structures have changed due to population aging, and families contain more living generations than ever before. The book documents the complex exchanges that now take place between the generations.

Hermalin, Albert I., ed. *The Well-Being of the Elderly in Asia: A Four-Country Comparative Study*. Ann Arbor: University of Michigan Press, 2003.

> This collection of articles looks at the demographic changes taking place in four Asian societies: Philippines, Singapore, Taiwan, and Thailand. It compares health care needs and services, the economic well-being of older people, work and intergenerational transfers, and housing among other topics. It provides good comparisons of countries at different stages of development.

Journal of Cross-Cultural Gerontology. Editor-in-Chief: Margaret A. Perkinson. Springer, Netherlands.

> This journal publishes articles on aging throughout the world. It includes three types of articles: (1) articles on history, anthropology, sociology, political science, health, biology, and other topics that describe aging in non-Western societies; (2) articles on Western societies that compare ethnic minority or subcultural groups (e.g., Vietnamese, Turkish, etc.); and (3) comparative studies of different types of societies (e.g., socialist vs. capitalist systems). This journal covers the most pressing issues related to aging around the world.

Websites to Consult

CanadaBenefits.gc.ca

http://www.canadabenefits.gc.ca/f.1.2cl.3st@.jsp?lang=eng&geo=99&catid=11

> This site provides links to information about benefits available to seniors in Canada (including the Canada Pension Plan and Old Age Security systems). It demonstrates that, in spite of some ageist tendencies, Canada provides a wide range of resources to support older people.

Seniors Canada

http://www.seniors.gc.ca/home.jsp?userLanguage=en&displayCat=ALL

This site serves as a portal for information about topics that range from computers and learning to end of life decision making. It also provides a connection to seniors' networks throughout the country.

National Advisory Council on Aging (NACA)

http://intraspec.ca/rc2006_e.pdf

This website contains information about the *Seniors in Canada: 2006 Report Card.* Each year the NACA gathers data on health, housing, income, and other topics related to seniors' quality of life. The NACA then rates progress on this topic by comparing the most recent data with the past year's findings. It provides a good readable overview of seniors' lives today.

AARP International

http://www.aarpinternational.org/

This site includes a topic called "Aging Everywhere." The site provides links to publications and data on aging throughout the world. It contains information in the form of interviews, news, and research reports. You can search a library of information by key word or world region. This site is rich with up-to-date information on aging in other parts of the world.

© Walter Hodges/CORBIS/MAGMA

Chapter

4

Aging in Canada

INTRODUCTION

When people think about aging, they think about their family members, their friends, or themselves getting older. But societies age too. From 1901 to 2001, Canada's population grew almost six-fold (Statistics Canada 2003o). During this same period, the older population grew by more than 13 times, more than twice the rate of the general population. The proportion of people aged 65 and over rose from 5 percent of the total population in 1901 to 13.7 percent of Canada's population in 2006 (Health Canada 2001a; Statistics Canada 2002b; Statistics Canada 2007d).[1]

This makes Canada's population one of the oldest in the world. And demographers expect Canadian society to age even more in the next 50 years.

This chapter will look at (1) why Canadian society has aged, (2) the population structure of Canada today, and (3) the impact of population aging on health care and pension programs.

CANADA COMES OF AGE

Canada is a relatively young nation compared to European countries. Until the late 1800s, less than 5 percent of our population was aged 65 and over (Norland 1976). The country then aged gradually through the first part of the 20th century. In 1951, Canada had 7.8 percent of its population over age 65 (Lindsay 1999). By 2000, Canada had 3.8 million people, or 13 percent of its population, aged 65 and over (Health Canada 2001a). By 2056, the portion of Canada's population aged 65 and over could be over 27 percent of the total population, more than five times the proportion of older people in 1901 (Turcotte and Schellenberg 2007).

What caused Canada to age in the 20th century? What will keep it aging in the years ahead? And what effect will population aging have on Canadian society? A look at Canada's population, past and present, will answer these questions.

Demographers study three conditions that affect a population's size and structure: immigration, death rates, and birth rates. Each of these demographic forces caused the Canadian population to age from the mid-1800s to the present.

---

1. Most studies use the population aged 65 and over to measure population aging. We will use this figure (unless otherwise noted) to allow for a comparison of different societies, past and present.

Immigration

Of the three demographic forces—immigration, birth rates, and death rates—immigration played the smallest part in the aging of Canada's population. It also affected different parts of Canada in different ways. Waves of immigration in the early 20th century brought new groups of young adults to Canada. Between 1901 and 1911, 1.5 million people arrived in Canada, as many as in the previous 40 years combined. Immigration in the first decade of the 20th century accounted for 44 percent of Canada's total population increase in those years (Statistics Canada 1981). Most of these immigrants came to Canada as children or young adults (20 to 34 years old). These young people (and the families they raised) helped keep Canada's population young at the start of this century (see Exhibit 4.1).

Immigration continued to add to Canada's population until the start of the Great Depression. Between 1901 and 1931, successive waves of immigration brought from 3.5 to 4.5 million people to Canada. These immigrants did more than simply increase the number of people in Canada; they also changed the face of Canadian society. Immigrants before 1900 came mostly from the British Isles, but Leacy (1983) reports that Canadians of "other European" origin rose from 37 percent of the European-born population in 1881 to 43 percent of the same population in 1911. Germans, Norwegians, Mennonites, Doukhobors, Chinese, and southern and eastern Europeans arrived in large numbers. Most of these immigrants were young males.

Many of the eastern Europeans, along with Icelanders and Mennonites, settled on the Prairies. Manitoba in the 1880s and Saskatchewan around 1911 had high birth rates due to the large number of young immigrants in their populations (Henripin 1972). This large wave of immigration partly explains the drop in the proportion of people over age 65 in Canada from 5 percent in 1901 to 4.7 percent in 1911 and 4.8 percent in 1921. This same group of immigrants increased Canada's older population as they aged. The Census of Canada (as cited in Turcotte and Schellenberg 2007) reports that in 2001 52 percent of all immigrants aged 65 and over had arrived in Canada before 1961. Many older immigrants came to Canada during World War II and the first years after the war.

Immigration accounts for about 6 percent of Canada's growth from 1946 to 1978. The proportion of foreign-born people in the older population reached a peak of 38.8 percent in 1961. The proportion of immigrants in the older population then dropped to 28.4 percent by 2001 (Norland 1994; Turcotte and Schellenberg 2007). In part, this reflects a counter-trend

● Exhibit 4.1

THE AGED POPULATION, CANADA, 1851–2041
(ABSOLUTE NUMBERS AND PERCENTAGES)

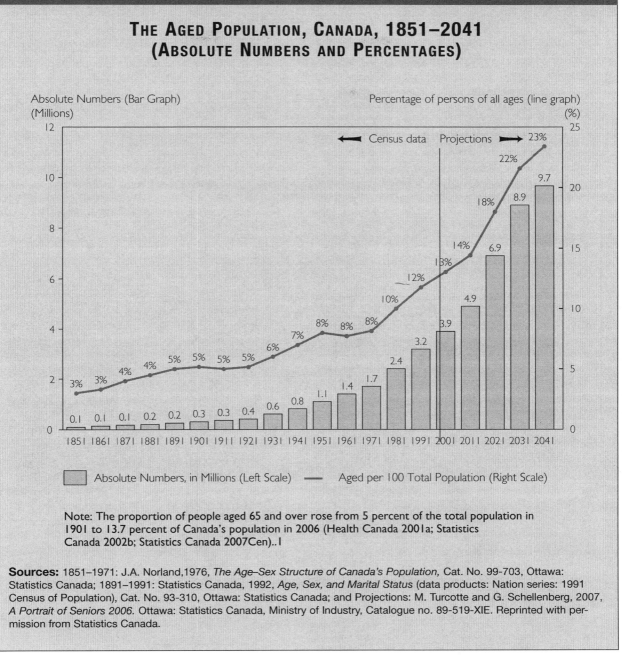

Absolute Numbers (Bar Graph)
(Millions)

Percentage of persons of all ages (line graph)
(%)

← Census data   Projections →

Absolute Numbers, in Millions (Left Scale) — Aged per 100 Total Population (Right Scale)

Note: The proportion of people aged 65 and over rose from 5 percent of the total population in
1901 to 13.7 percent of Canada's population in 2006 (Health Canada 2001a; Statistics
Canada 2002b; Statistics Canada 2007Cen)..1

Sources: 1851–1971: J.A. Norland,1976, *The Age–Sex Structure of Canada's Population,* Cat. No. 99-703, Ottawa:
Statistics Canada; 1891–1991: Statistics Canada, 1992, *Age, Sex, and Marital Status* (data products: Nation series: 1991
Census of Population), Cat. No. 93-310, Ottawa: Statistics Canada; and Projections: M. Turcotte and G. Schellenberg, 2007,
A Portrait of Seniors 2006. Ottawa: Statistics Canada, Ministry of Industry, Catalogue no. 89-519-XIE. Reprinted with per-
mission from Statistics Canada.

to the immigration of older people to Canada. By age
75, Denton and Kusch (2006, 14) say, "net migration is
actually negative." This means that more immigrants
in the oldest age groups leave Canada than arrive. We
know little about why people leave Canada in late old
age. They likely return to their home country, probably

to enjoy their traditional culture in their old age and to
die in their homeland. Denton and Kusch call for more
research on older immigrants.

Older people comprise only a small percentage of
the total immigrant population admitted to Canada; they
made up only between 2 and 4 percent of all immigrants

and refugees between 1995 and 2004. Nearly all (91 percent) immigrants aged 65 and over today came as family members of Canadian residents (Turcotte and Schellenberg 2007).

More recent immigration patterns will change the character of Canada's older population in the future. In the period before 1961, most of Canada's immigrants—almost 90 percent—came from the United Kingdom or Europe (Chard, Badets, and Leo 2000, cited in Lindsay 2000b). This pattern shifted dramatically between 1981 and 2001. The proportion of immigrants from Western and Northern Europe and the United States decreased by almost half (from 45.5 percent to 24.6 percent), while the proportion of immigrants from Asia rose more than two and a half times (from 13.9 percent to 36.5 percent) (Turcotte and Schellenberg 2007).

By the early 1990s, the largest portion of immigrants came from the developing countries of Asia, the Caribbean, South America, and Central America. During this period more than half of immigrants came from East and South Asian countries, including India and China, particularly Hong Kong (Statistics Canada 2001a). Immigrants from mainland China made up the largest number of immigrants in the 1990s (Chui et al. 2007).

Compared with other demographic forces, immigration has little effect on the aging of Canada's population. In 2006, for example, most immigrants were between the ages of 25 and 44. The median age of immigrants who arrived in that year was 29.8 years. This came to 9 years lower than the median age in Canada that year (38.8 years). But only 252,000 people immigrated to Canada in that year (a rate of 8 per thousand). Canada has maintained this low rate of immigration since 1990. If present immigration trends continue population aging will continue in spite of immigration (Chui et al 2007).

Fertility, not immigration, causes population aging or rejuvenation. But immigration does increase the diversity of Canadian society, and it creates new challenges for families, communities, and groups that serve older people (Gee, Kobayashi, and Prus 2004).

Death Rates

The **death rate** is the number of deaths per 1,000 people in a population. By the late 19th and early 20th centuries, death rates began to drop across the country. The most reliable figures for this period come from Quebec. Henripin and Peron (1972, cited in Beaujot and McQuillan 1982) say that the crude death rate (total number of deaths per year per 1,000 people in a given area) in Quebec dropped by half from 24 per 1,000 in 1871–75 to 12.9 by 1921–25. These figures probably overestimate the drop in death rates for

Canada as a whole because historians say that Canada's large cities still suffered from high death rates (Artibise 1977; Cross 1983); however, a steady, if not dramatic, decline did take place. Life expectancy at birth rose from 41.9 years for men and 44.2 years for women born in 1851 to 60.0 years for men and 62.1 years for women born in 1931. Life expectancy at age 65 had increased to 78 years for men and 78.7 years for women by 1931. This meant that more people lived longer and that more lived into late old age.

Life expectancy increased steadily for men and women of all ages between 1941 and 2001 (except most recently for women aged 85 and over) (see Exhibit 4.2). Infants during this time gained the most years in life expectancy. **Infant mortality rates** (the death rates of children less than one year old) decreased dramatically over the 20th century. By 2004, the infant mortality rate had fallen to about 0.5 percent of live births (compared to about 10 percent in 1921) (Parliament 1987; Statistics Canada 2007e).

Control of childhood disease, better prenatal care, and improved nutrition account for most of this change. Lavoie and Oderkirk (1993) say that in the mid-19th century epidemics of cholera (in 1832), typhus (in 1846–49), and smallpox (in 1885–86) led to high infant and child mortality. Nagnur and Nagrodski (1988, 26) report that "infectious and parasitic diseases, including tuberculosis, accounted for almost 15% of deaths in 1921; in 1986, however, only about half of one percent of all deaths were the result of these diseases." From 1931 to 2003 in Canada, life expectancy at birth increased from 60 years to 77.4 years for men and from 62.1 years to 82.3 years for women (Martel et al. 2006).

Since 1979, Canada has also seen a drop in the most common cause of death in adulthood—cardiovascular disease (which includes ischemic heart disease, strokes, arterial disease, hypertension, and rheumatic heart disease) (St-Arnaud et al. 2005). People in the oldest cohorts show some of the greatest improvements in life expectancy. Dumas (1990, 64), for example, says that "the most spectacular progress [in the extension of life expectancy has been] realized at very advanced ages." Between 1921 and 2001 men aged 85 and over showed a 37 percent increase in life expectancy and women showed a 63 percent increase in life expectancy.

As a result of this trend, between 1981 and 2005 the proportion of Canadians aged 75 to 84 in the population increased from 2.8 percent to 4.6 percent. This age group is expected to grow to 9.7 percent of the population by 2041. Between 1981 and 2005 the population aged 85 and over also increased. This age group nearly doubled its share of the population, growing from 0.8 percent of the population in 1981 to 1.5 percent of the

● Exhibit 4.2

EVOLUTION OF LIFE EXPECTANCY BY AGE AND SEX, CANADA, 1921–2001

| | At Birth | | At Age 65 | | At Age 85 | |
Year	Males	Females	Males	Females	Males	Females
1921*	58.8	60.6	13.0	13.6	4.1	4.3
1931*	60.0	62.1	13.0	13.7	4.1	4.4
1941*	63.0	66.3	12.8	14.1	4.1	4.4
1951	66.4	70.9	13.3	15.0	4.3	4.7
1961	68.4	74.3	13.6	16.1	4.6	5.0
1971	69.4	76.4	13.8	17.6	5.0	5.9
1981	71.9	79.1	14.6	18.9	5.2	6.6
1991	74.6	81.0	15.8	20.0	5.5	7.0
2001**	77.0	82.0	17.0	20.5	5.6	7.0

* The 1921 figures exclude Quebec, and the 1921–41 figures exclude Newfoundland.
** Based on three-year average from 1997 to 2001.

This table shows a steady increase in life expectancy at birth, at age 65, and at age 85 from 1941 to 2001 for both sexes, with one exception: life expectancy at age 85 for women levelled off for 2001. Note that women have a longer life expectancy than men at every age and in each time period. This may be due to differences in lifestyles, habits, or the environment (e.g., working conditions). Recent figures show a change in life expectancy between the sexes. Compared to women, between 1981 and 2001, men at birth and at age 65 gained more years in life expectancy. Changes in work patterns and lifestyles for men and women may account for this change. For example, women have entered the workforce in large numbers. This may add to the stresses they face and this may translate into smaller gains in life expectancy.

Source: Adapted from M. Turcotte and G. Schellenberg. 2007. *A Portrait of Seniors 2006. Ottawa: Statistics Canada, Ministry of Industry.* Catalogue no. 89-519-XIE, Tables 2.1.1 and 2.1.2. Based on Statistics Canada, Life Tables, Canada, Provinces and Territories, Catalogue no. 84-537-XPB; Canadian Vital Statistics, Birth and Death Databases; and Demography Division (population estimates) and Statistics Canada, Vital Statistics—Death Database; Estimates of Population by Age and Sex for Canada, the Provinces and the Territories.

population in 2005 (Turcotte and Schellenberg 2007). Statistics Canada projects that when the Baby Boom reaches later old age in 2056, the group aged 85 and over will make up 5.8 percent of the total population (almost four times the proportion in 2006) (Turcotte and Schellenberg 2007).

Today Canada, along with Japan, Sweden, Denmark, Norway, and the United States, has some of the highest life expectancies in the world. In Canada, in 2001, life expectancy at birth was 77 years for males and 82 years for women (Turcotte and Schellenberg 2007). This means that more Canadians than ever before will live to old age.

Birth Rates

The **birth rate** is the number of births per 1,000 women in a population. A decline in the birth rate primarily causes population aging. In the 1700s, for example, Quebec had one of the highest birth rates ever recorded and a young population. From 1700 to 1730, women averaged the birth of one child every two years until they reached age 30. Women who reached the age of 50 averaged giving birth to eight or nine children. In the middle of the 18th century, the average was 13 children per woman (Henripin 1972). During this time the birth rate ran two to six times higher than the death rate. Quebec's population grew twentyfold from 1608 to 1765, and by one and a half times again by 1851 (Kalbach and McVey 1979). Death rates in Quebec began to decline after 1780, but despite this, the province's birth rate was still high and the population stayed young (Henripin 1972; Kalbach and McVey 1979).

Frontier regions in Ontario also had high birth rates. McInnis (1977) and Henripin (1972) report rates similar to Quebec's in rural Ontario in the mid-19th century. A writer of the time reported that children "in Canada [are a man's] greatest blessing, and happy is that man who has a quiver full of them" (Philpot 1871, cited in Gagan 1983b). McInnis (1977, 202) says that Upper Canada at the time "had one of the highest birth rates in the world." Gagan (1983b) estimates that settled Ontario families in Peel County had eight to nine children. New immigrants to Canada before 1830 often had more.

Canada began its demographic transition around 1850 as the birth rate decreased. Henripin (1972) shows that the birth rate in Canada as a whole dropped by about 30 percent from 1851 to 1951 (with a sharp drop during the 1930s). Though the provinces all showed the same declining trend, their individual rates varied: The Quebec birth rate dropped least, by about 20 percent from 1851 to 1921; Ontario showed a sharp drop of about 50 percent during this same time; Manitoba between 1881 and 1921 showed a drop of more than 60 percent; and Saskatchewan showed a similar drop between 1901 and 1921 (Henripin 1972). This drop in the birth rate, more than any other demographic change, led to the aging of Canadian society.

Baby Boom and Baby Bust

Two phenomena affecting the birth rate, the **Baby Boom** and the **Baby Bust**, account for the greatest changes in Canadian population from 1951 to the present (see Exhibit 4.3).

From 1946 to 1965, Canada went through a Baby Boom. An explosion in the fertility rate and the birth rate explains this phenomenon. Beaujot and McQuillan (1982, 220–21) define the **fertility rate** as "the average number of children that would be born alive to a woman during her lifetime if she were to pass through all her childbearing years conforming to the age-specific fertility rates of a given year." Between 1941 and 1961, the total fertility rate rose from 2.83 to 3.84. The **age-specific birth rate** (the number of births in a given age group per 1,000 women in that age group) nearly doubled for 15- to 19-year-olds, going from 30.7 to 58.2 (Statistics Canada 1978, cited in Beaujot and McQuillan 1982). Women averaged more than 3.5 children each at the height of the Baby Boom (Statistics Canada 2007g). Total

births soared from 264,000 in 1941 to almost 476,000 in 1961 (Statistics Canada 1978, cited in Beaujot and McQuillan 1982).

The Baby Boom spanned a 20-year period. The first Baby Boomers (born in 1946) turned 60 in 2006. The youngest Boomers will turn 65 in 2031. At that time the leading-edge Boomers will be 85 years old. Wister (2005 citing Statistics Canada 2007d) says that in 2006 Baby Boomers made up one-third of the Canadian population.

Foot and Stoffman (1998, 25) say that "Canada's was the loudest baby boom in the industrialized world." Owram (1996, 5) says that after World War II "society seemed to revolve around babies … sometimes it seemed like everybody was pregnant or had a new baby." Foot and Stoffman (1998) trace the Baby Boom to two conditions: a good economy (people felt confident about the future) and a large number of immigrants (many of childbearing age). The Baby Boom reversed not only a general trend of decreased fertility rates that had begun in the 19th century but also a century-long trend in population aging (excluding the years 1911 to 1931) that began in the late 19th century.

After 1965, Canada went into a Baby Bust. Foot and Stoffman (1998) trace the Baby Bust to two trends: the use of the birth control pill and the increased participation of women in the labour force. During the Baby Bust, the total fertility rate dropped from 3.84 (children per woman) in 1961 to 2.81 in 1966, a rate below that of 1941. It dropped further to 1.49 in 2000 (Beaujot and McQuillan 1982; 1994; Denton and Spencer 2003). Canada's low fertility rate today falls below the level (2.1) needed to replace the population.

Low fertility led to a sharp drop in the number of young people in Canada. Between 1976 and 2002, for example, the population of people 0 to 14 years old decreased from 5.9 million to 5.8 million, which was a decrease from 26 percent of the population (in 1976) to 18 percent of the population (in 2002) (McKie 1993; Statistics Canada 1989; Statistics Canada 2003o). Statistics Canada projects a continuing decline in the proportion of the population made up of younger people in the years ahead. A medium-growth projection by Statistics Canada estimates that the younger population (under age 18) will fall to 19 percent of the population in 2041, while the older population will grow to 25 percent of the population (George et al. 1994; Health Canada 2001a; Lindsay 1999; McKie 1993).

This decrease in the birth rate, especially the sharp drop since the mid-1960s, sped the rate of population aging in Canada. Between 1961 and 2002, the population aged 65 and over rose by more than 5 percent, moving

● **Exhibit 4.3**

MEDIAN AGE* OF THE POPULATION, CANADA, 1881–2006
(EXCLUDING NEWFOUNDLAND)

Year	Median Age	Year	Median Age*
1881	20.1	1966	25.6
1891	21.4	1971	26.2
1901	22.7	1976	27.8
1911	23.8	1981	29.6
1921	23.9	1986	31.6
1931	24.7	1991	33.5
1941	27.0	1996	35.3
1951	27.7	2001	37.6
1961	26.3	2006	39.5
		2011	41.0 (projected)
		2056	46.9 (projected)

*Half the population is older and half is younger than the median age.

Canada's median age rose 17.5 years from 1881 to 2001. The table shows a jump of 2.3 years in the median age between 1931 and 1941. This reflects the sharp drop in the birth rate during the Depression years. The table also shows a rise in the median age until 1951, followed by a drop from 1952 to 1971. During these years, the rise in the birth rate (the Baby Boom) led to a decrease in the median age by 2.1 years to 25.6 years. In 1976, the median age rose again to above its 1951 high of 27.7. By 1986, more than half the population was over the age of 30. The aging of the Baby Boom cohorts will increase the median age in the years ahead. Statistics Canada projects a continued increase in the median age into the middle of this century.

Sources: Dominion Bureau of Statistics, 1964, *Census of Canada (1961 Census), Bulletin* 7: 1–4, Ottawa: Queen's Printer; Statistics Canada, 1968, *1966 Census of Canada,* Vol. 1 (1–11), Ottawa: Queen's Printer; Statistics Canada, 1973, *Census of Canada (1971 Census), Bulletin* 1: 2–3, Ottawa: Information Canada; Statistics Canada, 1978, cited in W.E. Kalbach and W.W. McVey, 1979, The Demographic Bases of Canadian Society, 2nd ed., Toronto: McGraw-Hill Ryerson, 161, Table 6:3; M.S. Devereaux, 1987, "Aging of the Canadian Population," *Canadian Social Trends,* Winter, 37–38; C. McKie, 1993, "Population Aging: Baby Boomers into the 21st Century," *Canadian Social Trends,* Summer, 2–6; and M.V. George et al., 1994, *Population Projections for Canada, Provinces and Territories 1993–2016,* Ottawa: Ministry of Industry, Science and Technology. Adapted from *Annual Demographic Statistics,* Cat. No. 91-213, and from Statistics Canada (2002a), 11 *Median Age, Canada, 1901–2011,* 11 http://www12.statcan.ca/english/census01/Products/Analytic/companion/age/ cdamedaget. cfm, accessed September 27, 2003, Statistics Canada. July 1, 2006. *The Daily.* Retrieved: December 26, 2007 – http://www.statcan.ca/Daily/English/061026/d061026b.htm; Statistics Canada. 2007. *Portrait of the Canadian Population in 2006, by Age and Sex, 2006.*

from 7.6 to 12.7 percent of Canada's population. The older population will increase sharply again in the early decades of this century when the Baby Boom generation moves into old age. We have only begun to study the experiences of the oldest people in our population (see Exhibit 4.4).

Will an increase in fertility in the years ahead reverse population aging? Statistics Canada considers this unlikely. The fertility rate of 1.5 children in 2006 would have to increase to 2.1 just to reach a replacement level. To give an idea of where the fertility rate stands today, the rate during the height of the Baby

● Exhibit 4.4

CANADA'S OLDEST SENIORS

Canada has more very old people (aged 80 and over) in its population than ever before. And demographers predict a growing number of very old people in the future. Few studies have looked at this age group. The National Advisory Council on Aging (NACA) talked with Canada's oldest seniors to learn something about their lives and how they see the world. The excerpts below show the varied perspectives very old people have on aging and on living in late old age.

It is very peculiar being over 100 ... and fun. I'm a rare breed, a museum piece. They bring people in to look at me. I would say that I have had a very good life. There have been bad times but I am happy now, although my health is slowly deteriorating. Last night, I went to hear my grand-daughter and her husband in a Gilbert and Sullivan musical. I was an actress and singer when I was young. They must get it from me. (101-year-old widow living in a long-term care facility)

You shouldn't be congratulated for living too long. It's a question of endurance.... Nothing works properly in my body, from teeth to toes.... Old age is a form of punishment. The more you go on, the more you endure. I hate every minute of it." (87-year-old single woman living in a long-term care facility)

I really mourn the loss of my friends. I miss most of all having someone to share news or encounters, reports of the day when I return from shopping or an outing. I sometimes find myself saying 'I must tell Mary about that,' and then I remember that she is no longer around. We used to be a close group of six and now I am the only one left. (87-year-old widow living in a seniors' housing complex).

I was born blind and have been living here for 40 years. Last year, I married a fellow resident who has cerebral palsy. I am happier than I have ever been in my life because I am so much in love. Life is good to me now. (80-year-old woman living in a long-term facility)

How do you think you will feel if you live to a very old age? Does living 100 or more years appeal to you? Do you think you might agree with some of the comments above? Which ones seem closest to your own imagined view of very old age?

Source: National Advisory Council on Aging, 1992, *The NACA Position on Canada's Oldest Seniors: Maintaining the Quality of Their Lives,* Ottawa: National Advisory Council on Aging. Courtesy of the National Advisory Council on Aging, Health Canada, 2000.

Boom, reached 3.9 children per woman (Statistics Canada 2007a).

Summary of Population Aging in Canada

Canada's demographic transition took place from before 1850 to the present in three stages. In the first stage, before 1850, Canada had both high death and high birth rates, and, in Ontario and the Maritimes, a high rate of immigration. These forces kept the average age of Canadians low. In Ontario in the mid-19th century, half the population over the age of 15 was made up of men under the age of 30 (Gagan 1983a). Statistics Canada data puts the **median age** of Canadians in 1901 at 22.7 (compared with a median age of 39.5 in 2006).

The second stage of the transition began after 1850 as major declines in birth and death rates occurred. This stage differed from the second stage in Europe's demographic transition, where death rates declined and birth rates stayed high for some time before they dropped to complete the transition. In Canada, both birth and death rates dropped (with some important fluctuations in birth rates) until the present. These changes transformed Canada from a young nation (under 4 percent aged 65 and over) in the late 1800s to an older nation (with about 7 percent of the population aged 65 and over) by 1950.

Today, in the third stage of the transition, Canada has low death rates, low birth rates, and an aging population. As this century progresses, Canada's population pyramid will change from that of a wide-based, triangular shape to a more rectangular one (see Exhibit 4.5).

● **Exhibit 4.5**

POPULATION PYRAMIDS BY AGE GROUP AND SEX, CANADA, 1991, 2011, 2031

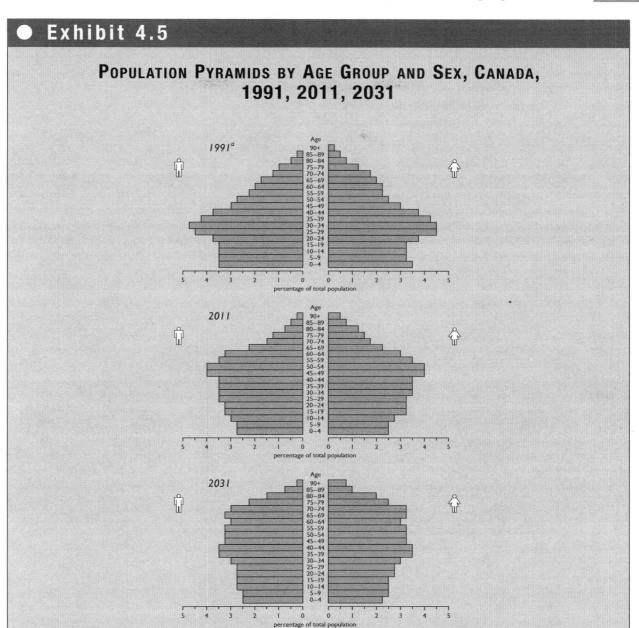

[a] Estimates based on 1991 census; standard projection as of January 17, 2000.

These pyramids show at least three important trends: the dramatic growth in size of the older age cohorts (aged 40+); a continued higher proportion of women compared with men in the oldest cohorts; and the movement of the baby boom cohorts into old age. The 2031 pyramid is top-heavy, with small younger age groups below a large older population.

Source: Adapted in part from the Statistics Canada publication "*Population Projections for Canada, Provinces and Territories, 1993–2016,*" Catalogue 91–520, 1993–2016.

AGING IN CANADA TODAY

Older people differ by age, sex, marital status, and health. They come from different ethnic backgrounds, have lived through varying historical events, and live in all parts of the country. These differences make older people one of the most heterogeneous age groups in Canada.

The Aging of the Older Population

The older population itself has grown older. Canada has seen a growth in its oldest-old population—people aged 100 and over. The 2006 census counted 4,635 Canadians aged 100 years old or older, up from 3,795 in 2001 (more than a 22 percent increase). Women outnumbered men in this group more than four to one. Statistics Canada says people in this group, born around 1906, had about a 1 percent chance of reaching age 100. Genetics, a good environment, a healthy lifestyle, and good luck account for the long lives of these elders (Statistics Canada 2007d). Statistics Canada (2007d) says that the number of people over age 100 could grow to 14,000 by 2031.

The oldest-old (85-and-over) population also makes up a larger share of the Canadian population than ever before. The oldest-old group more than doubled in size between 1981 and 2005. And their proportion in the population almost doubled—from 0.8 percent to 1.5 percent. This group will nearly double again to 800,000 people by the year 2021. And it will soar to 2.5 million in 2056 when the Baby Boom generation hits later old age (Turcotte and Schellenberg 2007). At that time the 85-and-over group will make up almost 5.8 percent of the total population (almost four times the proportion in 2005). Women in 2000 made up 70 percent of the Canadian population aged 85 and over (United Nations 2002). Longer life expectancy and larger numbers of people entering this age group account for this growth.

The increase in the oldest-old population will raise new issues, which will influence social policy and the use of resources in the future. For example, the oldest-old group, compared with people aged 65 to 74 (the young old), shows higher rates for institutionalization, disability, and poor health. The oldest-old population makes up only about 10 percent of all seniors but accounts for nearly half of all seniors in health-related institutions (Health Canada 2001b).

More recent research by Wister and Wanless (2007) on 90-year-olds in Canada report that this group has high rates of chronic illness and cognitive impairment. Eighty-five percent of 90-year-olds in this study suffered from some functional disability and the majority of the people had at least one chronic illness (also Hogan, Elby,

and Fung 1999). Compared to people under age 85, those aged 85 and over show a greater need for daily support. This group will need more institutional support, medical care, household maintenance, and community health care support in the future (Conference of Deputy Ministers of Health 1999).

At the same time that the oldest cohorts grow in size, the younger cohorts aged 65 and over will also get larger. Projections show more than a doubling in the population aged 65 to 74 between 1998 and 2041 (Lindsay 1999). This large number of older Canadians will make new demands on society. The young old will change retirement patterns by retiring early or by staying at work past age 65. This group will want more recreational and educational opportunities, and services such as job bureaus, schools, and counselling programs will also be needed to serve these people.

Programs for all types of older people will cost taxpayers more money. In 2000–02, for example, Canada spent $26.6 billion on its income security system (compared to $11 billion in 1984) (Human Resources Development Canada 2003a). More of this money went to older people than to any other age group. The single largest amount of this money went to the **Old Age Security** program (including the **Guaranteed Income Supplement** and the **Allowance**). If the proportion of older people more than doubles in the next 50 years as expected, will the public be willing to pay out even more of the country's income for older people? Or will the costs lead to resentment and a crisis in Canadian society? We will discuss these issues in more detail later in this chapter under the topic of dependency ratios.

Ethnicity

In 2001, people who had immigrated to Canada made up 28.4 percent of the older population. But immigrants made up only 21.3 percent of the 25- to 54-year-old age group in the same year. Compared to the proportion of immigrants in other age groups, immigrants made up a larger percentage of the older population. A large majority of immigrant seniors (70 percent) arrived in Canada before 1971. They moved to Canada to join their families, and this trend of family reunification continues today (Turcotte and Schellenberg 2007).

The 2001 census reports that most older immigrants (54 percent) came from Western Europe. Another large group (19.1 percent) of older immigrants came from Asia. About 5 percent of older immigrants came from the United States. Smaller groups (3 percent or less of the older immigrant population) came from Africa, Central and South America, and the Caribbean. Younger immigrants today (aged 25 to 64) tend to come from Asia, Africa, the Caribbean, and Central and South America (Turcotte and Schellenberg 2007). As these younger people age, they will create greater diversity among the older population.

About 1.3 million people in Canada in 2001 identified themselves as Aboriginal. This group has a relatively young population with a median age of 24.7 compared to a non-Aboriginal median age of 37.7 (Statistics Canada 2003a). The Aboriginal group has about 40,000 seniors. The Aboriginal senior population grew by 40 percent between 1996 and 2001 (about four times the rate of growth of the non-Aboriginal older population). Still, due to high fertility rates and the large number of younger Aboriginal people, seniors comprise only about 4 percent of the Aboriginal population. Projections show that Aboriginal elders will make up only about 6.5 percent of the Aboriginal population by 2017. At that time Canada as a whole will have 16.6 percent of its population over age 65(Statistics Canada 2005c).

A large proportion of older Aboriginal people (34 percent) live on reserves. Another 43 percent live in cities. Aboriginal elders continue to play an important role in some communities, serving as keepers of the group's tradition, history, culture, and language. They also pose a challenge to their communities due to Aboriginal elders' high rates of chronic illness, such as diabetes and high blood pressure (Turcotte and Schellenberg 2007). These illnesses require long-term care.

Most older people in Canada today speak either English or French. A small group of older immigrants, who learned a language other than English in their native countries, continue to use this language at home. For example, 4.5 percent of people aged 75 to 84 and 6.1 percent of people aged 85 and over could speak neither English nor French, and this proportion has increased since 1981 (Turcotte and Schellenberg 2007). The increase in numbers of immigrants from non-English speaking countries explains this change in language use. Compared to older immigrant men, older immigrant women tend to have less ability in English and French. Many of these women worked only in the home and spoke only their mother tongue.

Both the size of an ethnic group and the proportion of older people in the group determine the institutional supports that older people can expect from their ethnic group. A large group with a moderate proportion of its population aged 65 and over can provide a more complete community life for its elderly. A small group with a high proportion of older people may be able to offer little support. Turcotte (2006, 22) says, for example, that "large concentrations of individuals in one area with the same mother tongue may render the learning of another language less essential."

The concentration of the group (how close members live to one another), their location (urban or rural), the proportion of old-old to young-old, family size, and cultural values all affect the number of supports older people can draw on. People of Chinese, Greek, and Italian backgrounds, for example, tend to have large families, live in cities, and live with their children (Brotman 1998). Older members of these groups, compared to members of smaller groups, have more access to community resources and more family support in old age.

This brief look at ethnicity and aging shows that ethnic groups vary in their size, their location, their proportion of older people, and their institutional completeness, a term that refers to the amount of community support they offer their older members. For this reason, Driedger and Chappell (1987, 75) say that "ethnicity can have significant implications for care and supportiveness in old age." Ethnic diversity means that policies for older people from different types of groups (large, small, rural, or urban) will vary. Planners need to take ethnicity into account, along with socioeconomic status and physical mobility, when designing programs for older people. (See Chapter 7 for a more detailed discussion of ethnicity and aging.)

Geographic Mobility

Older people follow internal migration patterns similar to those of younger people, but they are less mobile (Lindsay 1999; Newbold 2007). Between 1996 and 2001, for example, 19.2 percent of non-institutionalized older people made a residential move. Only about 14 percent of home owners moved during those years compared to almost 36 percent of older tenants. Two-thirds of older movers move within their urban or rural setting.

The 1995 General Social Survey found that three-quarters of Canadians aged 60 and over who moved in the previous five years moved less than 50 kilometres. Many moved no more than 10 kilometres. Only 10 percent of older movers moved more than 200 kilometres. Many older movers simply moved from a larger home to an apartment in their community (Che-Alford and Stevenson 1998). Only a small percentage (1.2 percent) of older people move between provinces, so interprovincial moves have only a small impact on provincial older populations. British Columbia, for example, with the highest net migration of seniors, increased its number of seniors in 2005 by only 1,184 people (Turcotte and Schellenberg 2007).

Litwak and Longino (1987; also Newbold 2007) describe three stages of later life when people may choose to move. The first is the retirement stage, when freedom from the need to live near work allows people to move to a more pleasant climate and to have a more relaxed lifestyle. Migration researchers say that retirees often have "'remote thoughts' or daydreams about moving before they make a move. They also gather information about new locations that shape their decision to move" (Longino and Bradley, 2006, 77).

Studies in Canada, Great Britain, and the United States report that retirees tend to migrate to specific areas. Mobile older people tend to move to places with a mild climate often by a coast. They also look for places with a reasonable cost of living (Walters, 2002).

Some senior migrants move out of the country to the U.S. sunbelt. Others move to Canadian retirement sites like Niagara-on-the-Lake and Victoria. People in good health, with grown children, and with a good income in later life tend to make lifestyle-related moves (Hayward 2001). Statistics Canada reports that, compared to widowed, never married, or married seniors, separated and divorced seniors show the greatest likelihood of moving.

Northcott (1988) reports a peak in migration among older age groups around retirement age (60 to 69 years). This corresponds to Litwak and Longino's retirement stage. Many of these people moved within their communities. But some moved out of their locality, and they most often relocated to improve their quality of life. Alberta showed the greatest rates of gain in older migrants in 1997–98, followed by Ontario and New Brunswick. During this same period, Quebec and Saskatchewan showed the greatest net losses of older people due to migration (Health Canada 1999c; Lindsay 1999). British Columbia, the Northwest Territories, Yukon, Saskatchewan, Manitoba, Nova Scotia, P.E.I., and Newfoundland also showed losses during this period (Health Canada 1999c; Lindsay 1999). New Brunswick showed a small net gain in older migrants. Older people who move away in their middle years to find work may migrate back to their home province in their retirement (Moore and Pacey 2003; 2004).

Often, migrants have visited a place before. Some have even lived in the place for part of the year in the years before they move. People need to think about the community life, the culture, and the kinds of services they use (e.g., a library or a theatre) (see Exhibit 4.6).

Some migrants never move permanently. As many as 80 percent of seasonal migrants never settle permanently in their seasonal homes. This most often applies to Canadian snowbirds. These people live a lifestyle different from that of permanent migrants. When their health declines they make fewer and shorter visits to their seasonal location. Eventually they give up their seasonal visits.

In the second, or disability stage, physical limitation may lead the older person to move closer to children or others who can give them help. Statistics Canada reports that, compared to people with no disability, older people who had a long-term illness or disability showed a greater likelihood of moving (Turcotte and Schellenberg 2007). The likelihood of this type of move increases with age. Moore and Pacey (2004) say that migration due to disability may run counter to amenity migration. People return to locations where they can get care and support from family members.

The third stage is the severe disability stage, and it requires the older person to move to a nursing home or other institution.

Migration patterns show a flow of seniors in and out of geographical regions. But some trends do appear. Litwak and Longino's (1987) second and third stages of migration help explain these trends. Older people most often say that they move to buy a new home, to change the size of their home, to move to a less expensive home, or to move to a home with special features (Che-Alford and Stevenson 1998). Older people also say that they move to be near family or to care for a family member. People move to get more support as they age (Newbold 2007). Older people tend to move from farms to towns or cities, and most older movers relocate within their local area. Provinces, towns, and neighbourhoods with increased numbers of older people will face new challenges in the future (see Exhibit 4.7).

Increased Numbers and Proportions of Older Women

The death rates for older women have decreased faster than they have for older men through most of the last century. In 1931, the life expectancy for a 65-year-old woman was 13.7 years; in 1961, it was 16.1 years; and for 2003, it was 20.8 years (for a 65-year-old man it was only 13.0 years in 1931, 13.6 years in 1961, and 17.4 years in 2003) (Lindsay 1999; United Nations 2002; Turcotte and Schellenberg 2007). As a result of these changes, the proportion of older women in the population has grown.

Lindsay and Almey (2006, 265) say that women aged 65 and over "constitute one of the fastest growing segments of the female population in Canada." Between 1981 and 2004 this group increased by 72 percent to 2.3 million people. This has increased the proportion of older women in the female population and the proportion of women in the total older population. In 2004 women

● Exhibit 4.6

ENJOYING THE GOOD LIFE

NUMBER OF CENTENARIANS IN THE CANADIAN POPULATION, 1996, 2001 AND 2006

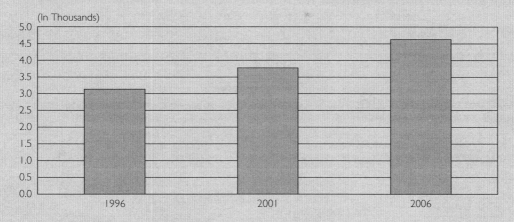

Source: Statistics Canada, censuses of population, 1996, 2001, and 2006.

Older Canadians who move after retirement often choose to live on the West Coast. The warm weather and the large number of older people with similar interests make this a good retirement spot. The cases described below fit the type of migration that Litwak and Longino (1987) call "amenity migration." This often begins when a couple vacation in a spot for a number of years. They then decide to settle there after retirement. Reporter James Deacon describes the amenities and social life that attracted the Perrigos and their neighbours to Qualicum Beach, British Columbia.

A brilliantly sunny morning in late July greeted Ladies' Day at the Qualicum Beach Memorial Golf Club. As the first groups finished their rounds, they gathered in the clubhouse to add up their scores. Nearly all of the women were in their 60s, and most had moved to the Vancouver Island community from somewhere else in Canada. One of the golfers, Beth Perrigo, 64, said that she first visited Qualicum Beach 13 years ago, while vacationing from Ottawa with her husband Howard and their two children. Perrigo said that she was strongly attracted by the town, which overlooks the Strait of Georgia 40 km north of Nanaimo. "We bought a lot and just sat on it," she says. In 1989, Howard Perrigo retired from his job with the federal government. The couple had already decided that they did not want to stay in Ottawa ("My husband got tired of shovelling snow.") The Perrigos

considered wintering in Florida, but in the end chose Qualicum Beach, attracted by the mild climate and relaxed lifestyle that has made the province the most popular retirement region in the country....

As in many retirement communities, Qualicum Beach's municipally owned golf course is a busy social centre. Sitting with Perrigo at a table overlooking the golf course and the strait beyond, Wilma Bleakley, 66, and Gladys Morton, 70, discussed the area's mild climate as being one of the main attractions for senior citizens. "There may be two weeks when we can't play golf," said Morton, who moved to Qualicum Beach from the central B.C. mining town of Hendrix Lake. "But that's about it."

Patricia and Conrad Nadeau lived in an ocean-view home in Lions Bay, 30 minutes northwest of Vancouver, but were lured to the Island by its weather and the abundance of recreational opportunities. Conrad Nadeau, a semi-retired insurance executive, and Patricia, a keen gardener, bought a two-bedroom condominium alongside Morningstar Golf Course, six km east of Qualicum Beach, and moved in eight months ago. Surveying her flourishing garden, which backs onto the golf course, Patricia Nadeau said: "I don't think we could do any better than this." Clearly, that judgment is shared by the thousands of retirement-aged Canadians who have responded to the attractions of British Columbia.

Source: James Deacon, *Maclean's* Magazine, August 24, 1992, p. 50. Reprinted with permission.

● **Exhibit 4.7**

POPULATION AGED 65 AND OVER 2005, PERCENT BY PROVINCE, 2005 AND 2031 (PROJECTED)

Province	2005 000s	% of total provincial population	
		2005	2031
Newfoundland and Labrador	67.7	13.1	29.5
Prince Edward Island	19.5	14.1	26.4
Nova Scotia	133.6	14.2	28.1
New Brunswick	104.7	13.9	28.6
Quebec	1,045.7	13.8	25.3
Ontario	1,608.7	12.8	22.1
Manitoba	158.6	13.5	21.7
Saskatchewan	147.1	14.8	24.9
Alberta	340.6	10.5	21.4
British Columbia	586.8	13.8	24.1
Yukon	2.2	6.9	19.7
NWT	2.0	4.7	15.1
Nunavut	0.8	2.6	5.7

This chart shows the number and proportion of older people in each province for 2005. It also shows a projection of the proportion of older people in each province in 2031.

Note that by 2031 all provinces will have higher proportions of older people. In many cases the proportion of older people in a province will double or nearly double. But population aging will occur unevenly across the country (Belanger et al. 2005a). The populations of the NWT and Nunavut will remain young in the future. Ontario, Manitoba, Albert, and Yukon will have more than one person in five aged 65 or over in 2031. British Columbia and Saskatchewan will have about one person in four aged 65 or over. But more than one person in four in Quebec and the Maritime provinces will be aged 65 or over.

Newfoundland and Labrador will have nearly a third of their populations aged 65 or over.

Communities with large increases in the proportion of older people will need to shift social and health care resources to serve this age group. But in some cases they have the fewest economic resources. Moore and Pacey (2004, S19) say that regional shifts in the size of older populations increases the risk "that the landscape of *have* and *have-not* communities will become even more pronounced" (emphasis in original).

Source: Adapted from M. Turcotte and G. Schellenberg, 2007, *A Portrait of Seniors 2006,* Ottawa: Statistics Canada, Ministry of Industry, Table 1.2, 29; Statistics Canada, 2005, Catalogue No. 89-519-XIE, *Populations Projections for Canada, Provinces and Territories, 2005*; Statistics Canada, 2005, *Estimates of Total Population, Canada, Provinces and Territories, Vital statistics—Birth and Death, 2005*; E.G. Moore, and M.A. Pacey, 2004, "Geographic Dimensions of Aging in Canada, 1991–2001," Canadian Journal on Aging *23* (Suppl. 1), S5–S21.

made up 57 percent of all older people and 69 percent of people aged 85 and over. Women aged 85 and over make up the fastest growing segment of the older female population.

Lindsay and Almey (2006) say that the number of senior women will increase even more rapidly in the future due to the aging of the Baby Boomers. Statistics Canada projects that by 2031 one woman in four will be a senior.

At the same time that the older female population increases, the male older population will also increase. The life expectancy of men has begun to catch up to that of women. At the beginning of the 20th century, there were 105 men for every 100 women aged 65 and over, and in the mid-1950s older men still outnumbered older women. But by the 1960s the pattern reversed. By 2000, there were 74.9 men for every 100 women aged 65 and over. Projections show that men will again begin to catch up to women in the future. Projections for 2050 show that the ratio of men to women aged 65 and over will increase to 78.6 men per 100 women. In that year, women will make up 54.5 percent of all people aged 65 and over (a decrease from 2004) (United Nations 2002; Lindsay and Almey 2006). For the 85-and-over group, the ratio of men to 100 women will decrease until 2011 (from 44 in 1991 to 39 in 2011). It will then rise to 42 in 2031 (Norland 1994). Changes in the lifestyles of women, including the stress of the workplace, in part account for these changes.

The large size of the older female population means that policies and programs for older people will have a greater impact on women than on men. Most women will live longer than men, so they will be affected by programs for older people for more years. Also, women in later old age, many of them widows, will need more support and services. This is especially true of health care, housing, and income supports. We will study these programs in detail in the chapters ahead. For now, we will look at the overall impact of population aging on Canada's economy (see Exhibit 4.8).

THE IMPACT OF POPULATION AGING

The Dependency Ratio and the Cost of an Aging Population

Concern about the increasing numbers of older people sometimes pits the old against the young. An editorial in the *Calgary Herald*, for example, told its readers to prepare for "an astonishing increase in the tax burden" due to an aging society (cited in Denton and Spencer 1999, 3). An editorial in *The Globe and Mail* (1993) calls the Baby Boom generation "a massive unfunded liability." "It's probable," the editorial goes on to say, "that those in the baby boom's wake will rebel at paying ... to subsidize the retirement of a generation that may well be better off than they are."

These sources assume a high dependence of older people on the young, and they suggest that the young will rebel against or resent the apparent burden of a large

older population. Gee and Gutman (2000) say that this fear has little basis in demographic fact. They call this extreme view "**apocalyptic demography**." And they say that it distorts the likely effects of population aging.

Gerontologists use a figure called the **overall dependency ratio** to gauge the burden that the old and the young place on people in middle age. Experts arrive at this ratio by adding the number of people under age 20 to the number of people aged 65 and over. They then compare this figure to the population aged 20 to 64:

$$\frac{\text{(Population aged 0 to 19)} + \text{(Population aged 65+)}}{\text{Population aged 20 to 64}}$$

(Some writers use ages 0 to 14 or 0 to 17 as the age span for the younger group.)

Denton, Feaver, and Spencer (1998) used the dependency ratio to look at dependency in Canada. They found that while the ratio of people aged 65 and over to those aged 20 to 64 will more than double from 1996 to 2041, the proportion of young people will decline. When they combined these projected changes in the young and old populations, they found that, compared to 1996, the first two decades of the 21st century will show a lower overall dependency ratio. Then, they say, the overall dependency ratio will increase. In spite of this increase, in 2041 (when the Baby Boom will have created large increases in the over-65 population) the overall dependency ratio may not be much higher than in 1971 (Denton, Feaver, and Spencer 1998; Denton and Spencer 2000). Denton, Feaver, and Spencer (1998, 103–104) conclude that Canada in the 21st century will still have an overall dependency ratio by historical standards."

Exhibit 4.9 shows dependency projections based on moderate demographic change. This box introduces the concept of the elderly and youth dependency ratios. The **elderly dependency ratio** refers to the number of people aged 65 and over divided by the population aged 20 to 64. The **youth dependency ratio** refers to the number of people aged 0 to 19 divided by the population aged 20 to 64. These ratios show how these two subgroups contribute to the total dependency ratio.

Denton, Feaver, and Spencer (1986, 86) say that figures such as these should reassure "those who are concerned about the possible inability of the economy to support its dependent population, young and old, in the decades ahead." But not everyone agrees with this conclusion.

The **crude dependency rates**, which are based solely on the number of people in each group, tell only part of the story; they do not address the economic burden of an older population.

● **Exhibit 4.8**

NUMBER OF MEN PER 100 WOMEN, AGE GROUP 65 AND OVER, CANADA, 1901–2001

Note that over time the ratio of men to women has decreased. For this reason many of the issues of later life have a greater effect on women than on men.

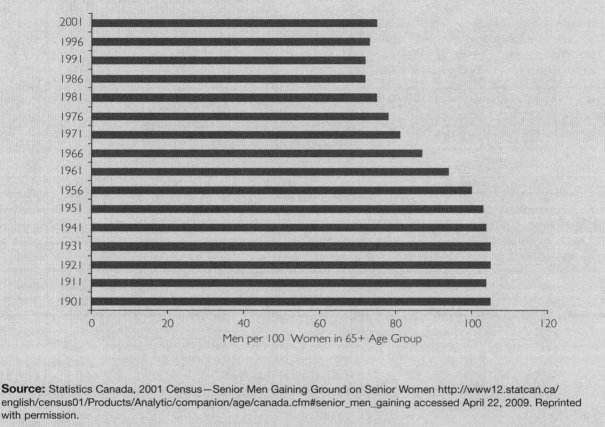

Men per 100 Women in 65+ Age Group

Source: Statistics Canada, 2001 Census—Senior Men Gaining Ground on Senior Women http://www12.statcan.ca/ english/census01/Products/Analytic/companion/age/canada.cfm#senior_men_gaining accessed April 22, 2009. Reprinted with permission.

Scarth (2003), for example, says that it costs more to serve an older population because health care for the old costs more than education for the young. Some studies (Robson, cited in Scarth 2003) say that Canada may need a 3 percent increase in its gross domestic product (GDP) to finance social security and other programs for older people in the future.

In a series of studies Denton and Spencer (1995; 1997; 1999) also project large increases in government expenditures in the future as Canada ages. They predict a steady increase in the total cost of health care, education, and social security between 1986 and 2041. Population aging accounts for most of this increase. They report, for example, that by 2011 social security costs (for the old) will surpass education costs (for the young) as a percentage of the GDP. Social security costs will triple between 1986 and 2041, while education costs will increase by about 10 percent. Likewise, health care costs will more than double between 1986 and 2041.

A report by the Canadian Council on Social Development (CCSD) (1999) says that 7 percent of total public health costs went to care for children under age 15 in the early 1990s. But 48 percent of total public health costs went to care for people aged 65 and over. The largest share

● Exhibit 4.9

DEPENDENCY RATES FOR CANADA, SELECTED YEARS FROM 1921 TO 2036

Year	Elderly Dependency (65+ / 20–64)	Youth Dependency (0–19 / 20–64)	Overall Dependency
1921	.09	.84	.94
1941	.12	.67	.79
1961	.15	.83	.98
1981	.16	.54	.71
2001	.21	.41	.62
2011	.23	.37	.60
2031	.43	.37	.80
2041	.46	.36	.82

These figures show a steady increase in the elderly dependency ratio over the years shown here. They also show a steady decrease in the youth dependency ratio (except for the sudden jump during the Baby Boom years around 1961). The overall dependency decreases through the early years of the 21st century. It then increases only to the 1941 level in the years after 2031. These figures suggest that an older population will not create an undue burden on Canadian society.

Note: Projections for the years from 1921 to 1961 assume modest increases in life expectancy of 0.8 years per five-year period, a total fertility rate of 1.8, and immigration of 250,000 gradually decreasing to 200,000 by 2011. Projections from 1981 onward assume a life expectancy increase of 6.5 years for men and 5.1 years for women, a fertility rate of 1.66, and an immigration rate of 200,000 per year.

Source: Adapted from the Statistics Canada publication "*Population Ageing and Elderly*," Catalogue 91-533, April 1993.

of health spending went to older people, and only their share grew between 1980–81 and 1994–95. Likewise, the amount spent on the Old Age Security and other income security programs increased nearly 50 percent during this period; Canada Pension Plan payments increased nearly 300 percent. The CCSD reports that spending on older people between 1980–81 and 1994–95 increased more rapidly than did their proportion in the population.

Burke (1991) says that in the years between 1980 and 2040, pension costs will rise more than any other expense, and he projects a 204 percent increase over this time. If this comes to pass, pensions will "account for 38% of social spending, up from just 24% in 1980" (7). At the same time, health care costs will increase by 118 percent and account for 33 percent of social spending

(compared with 29 percent in 1980). These trends would lead to an increase in social spending of 87 percent in Canada, which is high compared with predictions of 65 percent for the United States and 40 percent for Japan. It seems as if the apocalyptic demographers have a point when they warn about the crisis due to population aging. But not everyone agrees with these predictions.

Evans and his colleagues (2001, 162), in an article entitled "Apocalypse No," challenge the prediction of economic crisis. They agree that "'apocalypse' cannot be definitively ruled out." But they say that the data so far do not support the link between population aging and runaway health care costs.

Evans and his colleagues (2001) reviewed economic data from the British Columbia health care system. They studied acute hospital use, physicians' services, and drug use. They looked at the impact of population aging on the costs of these services. They found that, in spite of rising numbers of older people in British Columbia, the per capita use rate of hospitals declined from 1969 to the late 1990s. They found that in-patient days per capita decreased because of changes in health care practices over the 30-year period. Hospitals tended to send people home sooner and they increased same-day surgical care.

Evans and his colleagues go on to show that projections for the age 65 and over population in 1969 should have led to "truly hair-raising" costs—triple the 1969 cost by the end of the 20th century and another doubling for the next 25 years (169). In reality, the researchers show, acute care hospital use rates have decreased by half for the 65 and over population since 1969. This study shows the danger of projecting costs based on population growth figures alone.

A similar study of physician services and pharmaceutical use did reveal an increase in per capita costs. But the researchers show that increases in the number of physicians as well as the rising cost of drugs accounts for most of this change. For example, the total expenditure on drugs in British Columbia increased more than threefold between 1985 and 1999—an annual increase of 9 percent. Forces other than population aging, like the increased cost of new and expensive drugs, account for most of the rise in drug expenditures. Evans and his colleagues (2001, 181) say that "the evidence from British Columbia is quite clear.... Changes in the age structure of the overall population have not in the past been major contributors to trends in the per capita utilization of these three categories of health care services, and they will not be in the future" (176).

Researchers may disagree about the specific impact of an aging population on health and income resources. But nearly all of them agree that more health care and retirement income resources will go to serve older people and that this will cost more money. This shift in resources to the older population will force Canadians to make choices. Burke (1991, 8), for example, says that "Canadians will most likely have to choose between increasing tax rates and social security contributions or lower levels of social benefits." The next 50 years will see increased debate over this issue and some change in the allocation of health and income resources.

These reports on the future look gloomy. But dependency ratios tell only part of the story. Even small changes in Canada's economy and social norms, for example, could lead to large decreases in the effective dependency rate. The **effective dependency rate** is based on the real differences in the costs for older and younger age groups. Denton, Feaver, and Spencer (1986, 90) say that "non-demographic forces [e.g., changes in the demand for services, increases in per capita worker output, or changes in the federal government's commitment to fund programs] could easily be more important quantitatively than demographic ones in their effects on government expenditures."

Most projections, for example, assume a traditional retirement age of 65 (when people become entitled to Old Age Security payments). But government policy could change and this age could be raised. The United States has done this already by raising the age of full eligibility for Social Security benefits. Denton and Spencer (2002, 354) say that this would "both reduce pension costs and increase the ability of the economy to meet those costs." Also, the Canadian government has taken steps to increase Canada Pension Plan payments and to invest current CPP surpluses in income-generating markets. This is expected to keep the CPP solvent for many years to come without further raises in the cost to workers, although market declines in 2008–09 may undermine this plan if markets don't return to former levels. Canada can deal with the social "problem" of population aging by redefining pension eligibility and by creating sound policy today.

Dependency ratios also ignore the fact that people save in one part of their lives and use these savings later on (Denton and Spencer 2000). Today, many middle-aged workers have private pension plans and savings. And these have begun to play an important role in retirees' incomes. In the future, compared to pensioners today, retirees will have to rely more on their own resources when they reach old age. In the future, for example, more flexible retirement plans will allow some people to work full- or part-time after age 65. The Canada Pension Plan has changed its rules to make both early and late retirement more attractive. All these trends will change current dependency patterns and alter projected costs.

A stronger economy would also ease the dependency burden. Even a small improvement in the income of middle-aged people, compared with costs for services to the old, would significantly decrease the effective dependency rate. In a strong economy, higher costs for services to the elderly may not create a burden for the middle-aged.

Discussions of dependency ratios focus mostly to the costs of an older society. But an older population will also bring benefits, such as a lower crime rate and increased concern for fitness, diet, and disease prevention. These trends have already begun. Larger numbers of older people may also improve the economy. They will likely spend their savings on travel, restaurants, and professional services. These trends may reduce some of the cost of social resources and create a higher quality of life for people of all ages.

McDaniel (1986) says that dependency ratios lead to **demographic determinism**. Demographic determinism assumes that population dynamics determine the future of social relations and social institutions. McDaniel believes that social policies have the greatest effect on the dependence of older people (see also Denton and Spencer 2000). Cheal (2000) agrees and proposes ongoing changes in social policies to meet the needs of an aging society. Retirement policies today, for example, encourage retirement at age 65. Ironically, countries with the highest elderly dependency ratios encourage older people to leave the workforce early. They appear to encourage and may even demand economic dependency by the older population. Likewise, patients rarely choose the treatment for their illness. The cost of health care treatment depends on choices doctors make about treatment, on the cost of drugs, and on policies that support community care options.

Demographers need to study the connections between demographic facts, political realities, and social change. How much choice do countries have in how they will respond to demographic change? What determines the choices a country makes? Are there models of preferred adaptation to an aging population? Countries such as Sweden and Norway could serve as models for Canadian policy. Already, more than 15 percent of the populations of these countries are over age 65, and they have not faced crises as a result (United Nations Population Division 2002). Progressive programs have been put in place to serve older people, and citizens pay more in taxes to support them. These countries show that the transition to an older society can come about through planning, without social conflict and distress.

CONCLUSION

Canadian society has its own history, its own mix of ethnicity, age/sex ratios, economic institutions, and values. Canada also faces its own demographic issues. Canadians now expect to receive a public pension and they expect free health care in old age. Canadian discussions of societal aging often revolve around the costs of these two systems (Venne 2001). Will this generation demand an unaffordable level of social support as it ages? Will the Baby Boomers develop a broader view of their relationship to society and moderate their expectations? Will younger people step up and pay for services to Boomers as part of a social contract? After all, Boomers may claim that they paid into the system all their lives and expect services and programs that meet their needs. This intergenerational debate will continue in the years ahead.

Canada will face unknown political, economic, and social challenges in the years ahead and it will have to discover its own responses to population aging (Denton and Spencer 2003). An AARP (2007, 54) study of aging among the G7 nations (Japan, Germany, the United States, the United Kingdom, Italy, France, and Canada) ranked Canada among the nations that can achieve a good old age for its citizens. "Compared to the other G7 countries," the report concludes, "Canada, the U.K. and the U.S. have fewer demographic and labor market challenges and have a number of supportive policies in effect regarding the aging population. The combination of these factors makes these countries well-positioned for the future." The chapters that follow describe the conditions that support this optimistic view.

Friedland and Summer (1999, 5) say that Canadian "society can and will adjust [to an aging population] as it has done before. But adjustment will be easier if the challenges are addressed in a rational manner today." Preparation for the future will take planning, thought, and creative social action, and all of us will play a part in this societal transformation. The more we know about individual and population aging, the greater the chance that Canada will make a smooth transition to the future.

Summary

1. Canada has a younger population than most of the other developed nations. Thirteen percent of its population was aged 65 and over in 2001. Demographers project that this older population will more than double by 2041 and will equal almost 23 percent of the total population.

2. Canada went through a demographic transition between 1850 and 1950. During this time, immigration increased, the death rate decreased, and, most importantly, the birth rate decreased. Between 1850 and 1950, the older population grew from about 4 percent of the population to almost 8 percent.

3. Canada today has a diverse older population. Older people differ by ethnicity, sex, income, education, and marital status. They also differ by age. Longer life expectancy in old age has given rise to a wide range of age groups within the older population. Large increases in the oldest-old population will place new demands on health care and social service resources.

4. Ethnic groups vary in their size, location, proportion of older people, and the amount of community support they offer older people. Researchers and policy makers will have to take ethnicity, socioeconomic status, and physical mobility into account when designing programs for older people.

5. The growth of the older population (and the decrease in the younger population) has led some people to predict an economic crisis due to the large numbers of dependent older people. Gerontologists measure the dependence of young and old people on middle-aged people and call this measure the overall dependency ratio (or rate).

6. Experts look at dependency rates to project the future costs of an aging society. But the effect of future dependency rates will depend on a number of social conditions. A weak economy, low birth rates, low immigration rates, and a rise in costs of services for the old (compared with per capita income for the middle-aged) will increase the burden on middle-aged people.

A strong economy, higher birth rates, more immigration, and a rise in per capita income for middle-aged people (compared with costs in services for the old) will mean less burden on middle-aged workers. Changes in social values and retirement ages, as well as better preparation for old age by middle-aged people today, could also decrease the dependence of older people on the young.

7. Dependency rates focus on the costs of an aging society. But an aging society may have a lower crime rate, a lower accident rate, and more concern for lifelong health and fitness. These changes would decrease the waste of social and economic resources and improve the quality of life in Canada.

8. Canada can grow old without upheaval and conflict; most of the developed nations have done so. But the transition to an aging society will take planning, thought, and creative social action.

Study Questions

1. List the three demographic forces that caused Canada's population to age from the 1850s to the present. How did each force affect societal aging?

2. What developments helped increase the life expectancy of men and women in Canada during the past century?

3. What two factors account for the greatest changes in Canada's population from 1951 to the present? How did these factors affect Canada's population?

4. State three ways that an increase in the number of older people affects public policy.

5. How does ethnicity affect the care and support of older people?

6. Where in Canada do older people tend to live? Why?

7. Describe the changes that brought about the growth of the large older female population today. What implications does this increase have for older women? For social policy?

8. What do gerontologists mean by the "overall dependency ratio"? How do gerontologists calculate this ratio? How might a higher percentage of older people affect the economy in the future?

9. What steps can we take to help reduce the potential economic costs of an older population in the future?

Key Terms

age-specific birth rate   the number of births in a given age group per 1,000 women in that age group. (64)

allowance   an income security program for spouses of pensioners who receive only Old Age Security income. (68)

apocalyptic demography   the use of demographic facts (such as the aging of the population) to project the high cost of an aging population to predict that population aging will lead to economic and social crisis. (73)

Baby Boom   the sharp drop in the fertility rate from the mid-1960s on. (64)

Baby Bust   the sharp rise in the fertility rate in Canada from about 1946 to the early 1960s (precise dates vary). (64)

birth rate   the number of births per 1,000 women in a population. (63)

crude dependency rate   a rate based solely on the numbers of people in each age group. (73)

death rate   the number of deaths per 1,000 people in a population. (62)

demographic determinism   the assumption that population dynamics determine the future of social relations and social institutions (e.g., the amount of dependency of the old on the young). (77)

effective dependency rate   the rate based on differences between the costs for older and for younger age groups. (76)

elderly dependency ratio   the number of people aged 65 and over divided by the population aged 20 to 64. (73)

fertility rate   "the average number of children that would be born alive to a woman during her lifetime if she were to pass through all her childbearing years conforming to the age-specific fertility rates of a given year" (Beaujot and McQuillan 1982, 220–21). (64)

Guaranteed Income Supplement   an income security program for the poorest older people. (68)

infant mortality rate   the death rate of children less than a year old. (62)

median age   half the population is older and half is younger than the median age. (66)

Old Age Security   Canada's basic retirement income program, which supplements the income of nearly all of the country's older people. (68)

overall dependency ratio (or rate)   the combined total number of people under age 19 and people aged 65 and over to the number of people aged 20 to 64. (73)

youth dependency ratio   the number of people aged 0 to 19 divided by the population aged 20 to 64. (73)

Selected Readings

Bélanger, A. 2006. *Report on the Demographic Situation in Canada—2003 and 2004.* Ottawa: Statistics Canada, Minister of Industry. Catalogue No. 91-209-XIE.

   This volume is part of an annual series on demography in Canada. Each volume contains an overview of basic demographic facts, e.g., births, deaths, immigration. These studies provide a good overview of the latest demographic trends in Canada.

Turcotte, M., and G. Schellenberg. 2007. *A Portrait of Seniors 2006.* Ottawa: Statistics Canada, Ministry of Industry. Catalogue No. 89-519-XIE.

   This volume contains summary statistics (including charts and tables) on a wide range of topics related to seniors in Canada. Sections focus on topics such as health, wellness, and security; continuous learning, work, and participation in society; and supporting and caring in the community. Individual chapters report on indicators of health, leisure, immigration, income, education, etc. The authors provide analyses of the data. This book provides one of the best single sources of data and analyses of aging in Canada today.

Foot, David K., and Daniel Stoffman. 1998. Boom, Bust, and Echo 2000: Profiting from the Demographic Shift in the New Millennium. Toronto: Macfarlane Walter & Ross.

   An entertaining, informative, and readable study of how demography affects Canadian society. The authors begin with an overview of demographic changes in the later years of the 20th century. They then look at how these changes affect housing, health, the economy, recreation, and leisure, and use demographic facts to predict future social change.

Gee, E.M., and G.M. Gutman, (eds.). 2000. The Overselling of Population Aging: Apocalyptic Demography, Intergenerational Challenges, and Social Policy. Don Mills, ON: Oxford University Press.

   This collection of articles by Canadian researchers challenges the "alarmist" view of population aging. Chapters focus on topics such as aging families, hospital usage by older Canadians, intergenerational caregiving, retirement income, social policy, adult children returning home, and economics and women's pensions. This book demonstrates that in many ways older Canadians give more to the younger generations than they receive. It also argues that contrary to "much of the thinking on the subject that has gotten into the public consciousness … population aging should never be perceived as a 'crisis.'"

Statistics Canada. *Canadian Social Trends.* Cat. No. 11-008E. Ottawa: Minister of Supply and Services, Annual. http://dsp-psd.pwgsc.gc.ca/Collection-R/Statcan/11-008-XIE/11-008-XIE.html

   Statistics Canada publishes this journal four times a year. Articles report on data from recent government studies in a readable magazine format. Articles include charts and graphs that help interpret the statistics. Each issue contains useful and up-to-date information on topics such as demography, living arrangements, and aging in Canada. This is a good resource for professionals and students of aging.

Websites to Consult

Statistics Canada

http://www.statcan.gc.ca/start-debut-eng.html

   This site provides access to information gathered by Canada's national statistical agency. You can get information on daily statistical reports, summary statistics, or publications. It provides a vast storehouse of current and past information on Canadian society.

Healthy Living— Seniors (Health Canada)

http://www.hc-sc.gc.ca/hl-vs/seniors-aines/index-eng.php

This site provides information on health issues of interest to seniors. It serves as a portal to other websites on osteoarthritis, diet, exercise, etc.

Aging and Seniors (Public Health Agency of Canada)

http://www.phac-aspc.gc.ca/seniors-aines/index_pages/whatsnew_e.htm

This site offers information each month on new publications and information related to aging in Canada. Entries for 2007 include a guide to Age-Friendly Rural and Remote Communities. It also offers an archive of past monthly announcements and access to statistical data.

Chapter 5

Personal Health and Illness

© Paul Barton/CORBIS/MAGMA

INTRODUCTION

Jeanne Calment of Provence, France, died in 1997 at age 122 and 5 months. Before her death she was the oldest person in the world and the longest-lived person ever. To celebrate her 121st birthday, Mme. Calment released a four-song CD. The songs mixed rap and techno music with stories from her life (for example, she met Vincent Van Gogh in her childhood). Money she earned from the CD went to pay for a minibus for her nursing home (Mitchell 1996). When Mme. Calment died, Marie-Louise Meilleur, a French Canadian, became the oldest person in the world. Mme. Meilleur died in 1998, in a nursing home in Corbeil, Ontario. She was 117 years and 7 months old. At the time of her death, her 85-year-old son lived in the same nursing home.

How did these women live so long? For one thing, Mme. Calment stayed active throughout her life. She lived on her own in a second-floor apartment until age 110 and she rode a bicycle until age 100 (Glass 1995). Other centenarians also attribute their long life to an active lifestyle. Some say they enjoy regular sex, never worry, or drink a shot of whisky before bed. Mme. Meilleur was reported to be a vegetarian. One 100-year-old man claimed that he lived so long because he ate a pound of peanuts a day.

Scientific research supports some of these methods for longer life. Moderate drinkers live longer than teetotalers (although it is unclear why); a simple diet low in fat, salt, and sugar can decrease disease; and exercise leads to good health and possibly a longer life (Chernoff 2002). But even with good habits, a good diet, and a good environment, physiological aging takes place. These changes take place as part of normal aging. Older people on the covers of health and nutrition magazines beam good health, but they often have white hair, brown spots on their skin, and wrinkles, like older people all over the world.

Gerontologists distinguish between the **maximum life span** (the maximum number of years a member of a species can live) and **life expectancy** (the number of years at birth an average member of a population can expect to live). Scientists think that the maximum human life span of somewhere between 110 and 125 years has stayed the same for the past 100,000 years. Human life expectancy at birth, on the other hand, has increased in the past 2,000 years from an average of 22 years in ancient Rome to around 75 or 80 years today (Clarfield 2002). Women have gained more in life expectancy than men. A girl born today can expect to outlive her male peers by five to six years. Technology and biomedical science continue to extend life expectancy, and, if this trend continues, more and more people will live close to the maximum human life span. This means that more people will live to old age and more will live longer in old age than ever before.

The study of personal health and illness has two goals: to understand changes in the body that come with age and to apply this knowledge to extend and improve human life. This chapter will look at (1) what effects aging has on health, behaviour, and everyday life, (2) how older people cope with physical change, and (3) future changes in health and illness.

SENIORS' HEALTH STATUS

Researchers have asked two questions about the effects of physiological aging on the older person's well-being. First, do health problems increase with age? Second, does physiological aging limit the older person's activities?

Older Canadians live relatively healthy lives (see Exhibit 5.1). Nearly three-quarters (73.4 percent) of older Canadians view their own health as good, very good, or excellent. Even among people aged 85 and over, two-thirds of people (66.3 percent) report good to excellent health (Lindsay and Almey 2006). In an earlier study, Shields and Shooshtari (2001, 39) report that "the self-perceived health of people aged 75 or older did not differ significantly from that of 35- to 44-year olds."

The National Advisory Council on Aging ([NACA] 2006) publishes an annual report card on Canadian seniors. The report found that "Seniors assess their own physical and mental health in largely positive terms" (5). Three-quarters of seniors in 2005 considered their health good, very good, or excellent. The 2006 report describes improvements in the rate of heart disease between 2001 and 2006. Compared to the past, older Canadians enjoy longer life expectancy and expect to live more years in good health.

Still, the frequency of chronic diseases remains high. For example, the NACA report found increases in obesity and chronic diseases (arthritis or rheumatism, hypertension, and diabetes). Schultz and Kopec (2003, 41) say that Canada has moved through an "epidemiological transition." This means that Canadian society shows a decrease in acute and infectious diseases and an increase in chronic and degenerative disease. A longitudinal study conducted in Manitoba examined health status trends over a 14-year period (Menec et al. 2003). This research found improvements in health over time related to heart attack, stroke, cancer, and hip fractures. However, it also found significant increases in the prevalence of chronic illnesses such as diabetes and dementia.

Wister (2005) also reports a recent upturn in chronic illness in Canada for older cohorts. Men aged 65 to 69

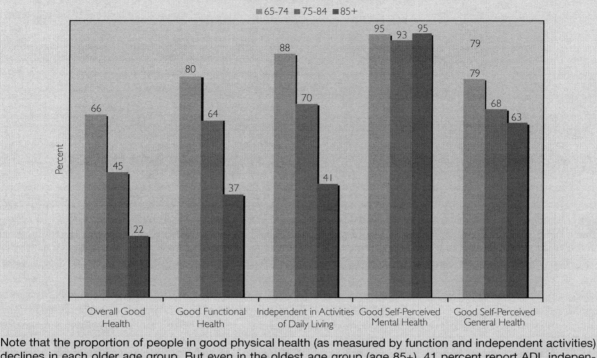

PERCENTAGE OF PEOPLE IN GOOD HEALTH, BY AGE GROUP, HOUSEHOLD POPULATION, AGED 65 AND OVER

■ 65-74 ■ 75-84 ■ 85+

Note that the proportion of people in good physical health (as measured by function and independent activities) declines in each older age group. But even in the oldest age group (age 85+), 41 percent report ADL independence and 63 percent report good general health. Note also that the proportion of people who report good self-perceived mental health stays stable across age groups. Nearly all the people in this study (95 percent), regardless of age, report good mental health.

Source: Statistics Canada. 2003 Community Health Survey, Shields, M. and Martel, L. *Health Reports*, 16, Supplement; Healthy Living Among Seniors.

reported an increase in chronic illness between 1978–79 and 2000–01. In this age group, 77.2 percent of men reported at least one chronic illness in 1978–79. This rate increased to 78.9 percent in 2000–01. Men aged 70 and over showed an increase in chronic illness in these years, from 79.4 percent to 86.2 percent. Women show a similar trend. In 1978–79 79.3 percent of women aged 65 to 69 reported a chronic illness. This figure jumped to 84.3 percent in 2000–01. In 1978–79 85.1 percent of women aged 70 and over reported a chronic illness. This figure jumped to 91.4 percent in 2000–01. Compared to

men, women showed higher rates of chronic illness at both points in time.

Martel and colleagues (2005) report on a study that looked at the health of Canadians aged 45 and over between 1994–95 and 2002–03. The study looked in on these people every two years. The following conditions predicted declines in health for older people in the study:

• Being older;

• Living with someone other than a spouse or alone;

- Low income;

- Chronic condition;

- Low education level (both younger and older participants;)

- Smoking, alcohol consumption, inactivity (among older participants in the study);

- Lack of coherent focus in life (meaninglessness); and

- Not seeing a doctor for checkups (among older participants in the study).

Martel and colleagues (2006, 5) say that "At all ages people with healthy behaviours were at less risk of losing their good health, and the difference became more pronounced with advancing age … From this result it can be hypothesized that the impacts of healthy habits are cumulative through time." (Martel et al., 2006, 5). These results show that people at any age can modify their behaviour and improve their health (see Exhibit 5.2).

Specific groups among the older population report high rates of chronic conditions. For example, women live longer than men, but they also experience poorer health in later life (Bélanger et al. 2002; Statistics Canada 2000a). Women report higher rates of hypertension, arthritis, and rheumatism than men. And they are more likely than men to have at least one chronic condition

---

● Exhibit 5.2

LIVING A GOOD AND LONG OLD AGE

The 2006 Canadian census reported there were 4,635 centenarians living in Canada, a 22 percent increase from the earlier census. Women centenarians outnumber men by about four to one. But what does living this long mean for quality of life in advanced old age? Florence Himes is one example of what it is like to live past the 100-year mark.

Florence Himes may be 108 but she has yet to slow down. She is so fast on her walker she is almost a blur as she negotiates the halls of New Horizons Tower, the not-for-profit Toronto seniors' residence she has called home for 20 years. She lives in the assisted-living area on the second floor, but is up and down the elevator several times daily. Who better, then, to take on a bunch of young whipper-snappers in the residence's 200-storey stair challenge in June 2003 to raise money for low-income seniors who want to live at New Horizons.

"I told them I thought I would win," she confides. "I wanted to win. [The home's administrator] Mr. [Ian] Logan was counting on me for the money."

As six runners ran a route up and down the building's stairs, Himes rode the elevator on a gold brocade chair. At every other floor, she was up, on her walker, out in the hallway and back inside the elevator again.

"I kept asking her if she wanted to stop. I'd say 'Had enough, Nanny?' and she would say no," says Cliff Himes, her 74-year-old stepson who rode along with her. "She never gives up."

An active lifestyle is not new to Himes. She's participated in a fundraising walk within the residence—and walked the farthest and raised the most money. For years she has made doilies to sell at the Christmas sale. At 105, she was off to see Niagara Falls, and she's never missed the residence's annual outing to see the fall colours.

"If there's something going on, she wants to be a part of it, she's always been like that," her stepson says.

Widowed three times, she's lived throughout Southern Ontario, in Montreal and in Manitoba, where her family emigrated from England when she was 14. She's worked on a farm, as a dressmaker and in a munitions factory during the Second World War. She also used to mix cement, hang wallpaper, lay tiles and do her own wiring around the house. Her son Ross, a doctor, died three years ago. …

How has she managed to live so long? "I don't worry," she says with a wide grin. "I do what I can about things and let the rest take care of itself."

What year will it be when you're 108 years old? If you live that long, what do you think you will be doing? What do you think aging will be like in that year and how will it feel to be an older person then?

Source: Catherine Dunphy. 2003. "Going Strong." *Toronto Star, Comfort Life.* Reprinted with permission of the author.

● Exhibit 5.3

PERCENTAGES OF SENIORS IN PRIVATE HOUSEHOLDS WHO REPORT SELECTED CHRONIC CONDITIONS, 2003

	Age					
	65–74		75–84		85+	
Health Problem	Men	Women	Men	Women	Men	Women
Arthritis/Rheumatism	35.0	52.1	41.7	56.9	42.0	60.0
High blood pressure	37.3	44.2	37.8	51.0	32.2	48.0
Heart disease	18.3	13.3	26.4	22.1	33.4	30.7
Diabetes	16.4	12.0	14.7	12.3	10.2	9.8
Chronic bronchitis	3.7	5.8	5.0	5.3	6.6	4.3
At least one chronic problem	85.8	91.4	89.2	94.0	92.1	92.7

The proportion of people who report health problems varies by age and gender. Compared to men, women in every older age group have higher rates of arthritis/rheumatism and high blood pressure. Compared to women, men have higher rates of heart disease, diabetes, and chronic bronchitis. Chronic health problems tend to increase with age for both men and women (with the exceptions of chronic bronchitis and diabetes).

Bélanger and his colleagues (2002) say that, compared to men, a higher proportion of women aged 45 and over report more disabling chronic diseases. Diabetes, arthritis, and physical inactivity decreased women's disability-free life expectancy. Diabetes, smoking, arthritis, and cancer led to the greatest decreases in men's disability-free life expectancy.

Source: Adapted from Colin Lindsay and M. Almey, 2006, "Senior Women" in *Women in Canada, 5th Edition. A Gender-based Statistical Report:* 265–90; and Statistics Canada, Social and Aboriginal Statistics Division. Catalogue No. 89-503-XIE. Ottawa: Minister of Industry: Table 11.8, 286.

(Lindsay and Almey 2006) (see Exhibit 5.3). Compared to men, older women also use more health care services, including more physician visits (Statistics Canada 2001c). Health service use may reflect the continuation of a pattern of health care use by women during their middle years and may also reflect a denial of health problems by men.

INCOME AND HEALTH

People with low education, people with low income, the unemployed, and unskilled workers are more likely to report poor health (Cairney 2000). People with low incomes report higher rates of chronic illnesses and activity limitations than do other seniors. Compared to other seniors, poor seniors say they engage in less

physical activity (Melzer et al. 2000; National Advisory Council 2001b). Health differences between people with low and high incomes show up at all ages in later life. But Prus (2004) discovered a widening gap in health between poorer and wealthier seniors as years went on. Poor nutrition, poor-quality housing, and lack of information all lead to poor health among low-income people. Poorer seniors risk a shorter life expectancy due to their poor health.

A person's lifestyle and behaviour, as well as poverty, can lead to poor health. For example, smoking, tranquilizer use, excessive alcohol consumption, and lack of physical activity among poorer people help explain their high rates of poor health (Cairney 2000). Low-income smokers reported the least intent to quit. This places their health at risk as they age.

LIMITS ON ACTIVITY DUE TO PHYSICAL DECLINE

Eighty-seven percent of older women and 92.7 percent of older men say they have one or more **chronic health problems** (Lindsay and Almey 2006). Chronic illness, which is any long-term illness such as arthritis, rheumatism, hypertension, diabetes, or heart disease, can lead to functional disability. **Functional disability** refers to a limitation on a person's ability to perform normal daily activities due to illness or injury. This measure focuses on the effects of illness on a person's everyday life.

Statistics Canada (2007f) conducted the Participation and Activity Limitation Survey (PALS) in 2006. This national survey assessed activity and disability rates. The study found that activity limitation due to disability increases with each older age group. Adults aged 15 to 64, for example, report an activity limitation rate of 11.5 percent. This rises to 43.4 percent for people over age 65. And for people age 75 and over, more than half the population (56.3 percent) reports an activity limitation.

The PALS also found that disability increases dramatically in later old age. The study found that the oldest age group (75 and over) has more than one and a half times the rate of disability of the 65 to 74 age group (33 percent vs. 56.3 percent). Compared to men, women in the 75-and-over age group have a higher disability rate (57.8 percent vs. 54 percent).

Chronic problems decrease the number of years people live without a disability (Bélanger et al. 2002). And this can decrease an older person's quality of life and subjective well-being (Clarke et al. 2000) (see Exhibit 5.4).

● **Exhibit 5.4**

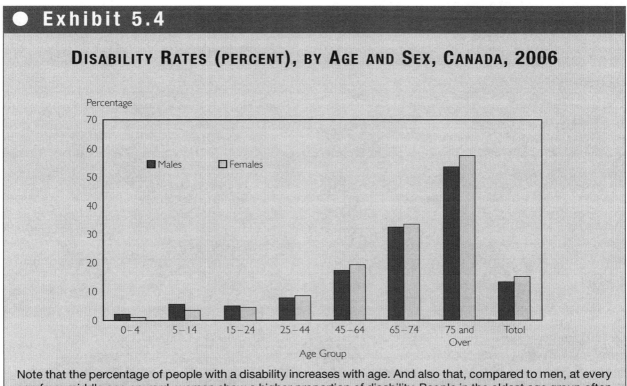

DISABILITY RATES (PERCENT), BY AGE AND SEX, CANADA, 2006

Note that the percentage of people with a disability increases with age. And also that, compared to men, at every age from middle age onward, women show a higher proportion of disability. People in the oldest age group often need help to maintain their independence.

Source: Statistics Canada — Social and Aboriginal Statistics Division. 2007. *Participation and Activity Limitation Survey 2006*: Tables 2006. Catalogue no. 89-628-XIE.

Statistics Canada (2003i) reports that almost one person in five aged 65 to 74 (18.5 percent) say that pain or discomfort limits some or most of their activities. This figure jumps to almost one person in four (23.8 percent) aged 75 and over. A higher proportion of women in each age group reports limitations due to pain or discomfort. Compared to men, women also tend to face activity limitations earlier in life and to live for more years with these limitations.

Disabilities impair some functions more than others. Disabled older adults most often say they have trouble with mobility (e.g., walking from room to room or standing for a long time). They also have trouble with agility (e.g., bending, dressing, or grasping things) and hearing.

The PALS found that people with the most severe disabilities needed the most help with assistive devices. But a large majority of older people (69 percent) felt they got all the help they needed with assistive devices. People who did not have the help they needed often cited the cost of equipment or insurance costs as the reason (Duclos and Langlois 2003; Statistics Canada, 2004d). Schultz and Kopec (2003) report that, even with help some older people have trouble with everyday functions. For example, 8 percent of older people could not see well enough to read, even with glasses. And 6 percent of older people said that, even with a hearing aid, they could not follow a conversation due to hearing loss.

Community services, such as modified vans with wheelchair lifts, can help with some functional problems. But many disabled seniors report that they could use more help. For example, older people at all ages report the need for help with everyday housework. And the proportion of people who need this type of help increases with age (from about one person in ten aged 65 to 74 who needs help to nearly one person in four aged 75 and over who needs help). After age 75 one person in ten needs help with personal care such as washing, eating, dressing, or taking medicine, and 13.2 percent of people aged 75 and over need help preparing meals (Lindsay and Almey 2006).

Gerontologists study the effects of functional disability on **activities of daily living (ADLs)** and **instrumental activities of daily living (IADLs)**. ADLs include bathing, moving from a bed or chair, dressing, getting to and using the toilet, eating, and walking. IADLs refer to home management activities such as using the phone, preparing meals, managing finances, shopping, and doing light housework. Limitations may range from a mild problem such as trouble using the phone to more serious problems such as the inability to eat unassisted or inability to use the toilet. The National Advisory Council on Aging (2006) *Report Card* found that in 2005 only

about 7 percent of seniors in the community needed help with ADLs though 22.4 percent needed help with IADLs. A drop in the ability to care for oneself signals a drop in quality of life and in the number of active years a person will live (Elgar, Worrall, and Knight 2002).

The Participation and Activity Limitation Survey asked people about their need for help with everyday activities—heavy and light housework, banking, transportation, etc. Half of older people in this study said they got help from family members, friends, and neighbours. And about half of these people got help from family members outside their household. Regardless of age, this study found "it is always family members who play the main role in providing help, whether they live with the respondent or not" (Statistics Canada 2003, 8). The study also found that about one-third of men and women aged 65 and over said they needed more help than they got. About half the older people (47 percent) cited the high cost of home modification as the reason they lacked this type of support.

The focus on health problems and disability in later life can give the impression that nearly all older people suffer from a decline in the quality of life. Stone (2003, 64; Statistics Canada 2007) says "it is not the case that all old people or even most old people reported having disabilities ... *more than half* do not report any disabilities." Also, for some seniors disability comes and goes in later life. Statistics Canada (2000a) reports that about 20 percent of older people developed a long-term activity limitation between 1994–95 and 1998–99. But about one-third of older people with long-term activity limitations (31 percent of men and 37 percent of women) overcame their limitation during this time.

The National Population Health Survey (NPHS) in 2002–03 found that "not all seniors who lose their health do so for good" (Shields and Martel 2006, 17). People who reported leisure physical activity, moderate alcohol use, normal body weight, and non-smoking had the highest odds of recovery. These findings show that activity limitation and dependency may last only a short time. People can recover from acute injuries such as a strained back, and treatment for chronic problems like arthritis can help a person function on their own.

Disability in later life deserves researchers' attention. First, older people with disabilities need informal and sometimes formal support to maintain a high quality of life. These seniors may rely on the health care system for service. An increase in the number of disabled seniors will increase costs and will affect the types of resources that the health care system needs to provide. Second, some older people cope well with their disability and some get their functioning back. This group can help us understand how to encourage and rehabilitate disabled seniors. Third, exercise and self-care can prevent, ease, or reverse disabilities. Studies show that even people with chronic illness can improve their functioning. Ferraro (2006) reports a growth in the use of technology and environmental modification as methods of self-care. But he notes that when a health condition becomes serious (e.g., something that might require surgery), people turn to conventional medicine. Most people will combine self-care methods with the drug therapies and approaches of modern medicine.

Manton and his colleagues (2006) look to improvements in basic medical science and medical care for future declines in disability. They foresee an important role for biomedical research and cellular and molecular understanding of chronic diseases. For example, gene therapy in the future may have a profound effect on health and illness in later life. Genes make up a part of the DNA in every cell; they hold the code for over 100,000 proteins that keep the body working. Gene therapy will allow researchers to replace a defective gene and reverse a state of illness or physical decline. Researchers would use recombinant DNA methods to (1) multiply the gene in a bacterial culture, (2) use a benign virus to place the gene in the host's cell, and (3) allow the gene to produce a needed protein. Scientists may use this technology in the future to cure immune system breakdown, Parkinson's disease, and cancer. In the meantime, a healthy diet, exercise, and self-care play an important role in disease prevention, reduction of symptoms, and in the promotion of well-being in later life.

COPING WITH PHYSICAL CHANGE

Most older people cope with declines in their health. They accept the health changes that come with age, adjust their expectations about their activities, and gradually make changes in their lives to cope with physical decline.

Moore, Rosenberg, and Fitzgibbon (1999) found that chronic conditions do not always turn into functional disability or the need for assistance with daily activities. Although over three-quarters of elderly persons have at least one chronic condition, less than one-half experience some functional disability. Even fewer, about one-fifth, require assistance with ADLs. Research shows that a large majority of older people lives without functional handicaps on certain activities. For example, only 6 percent of older men and 7 percent of older women in private households need help with activities such as bathing or dressing (Gilmour and Park,

2006). Even at age 85 or older, Gilmour and Park say, only 20 percent of men and 23 percent of women in the community depended on others for ADL help.

Evans and his colleagues (2001) say that healthy aging can slow the process of physical decline (see Exhibit 5.5). Older people compensate for declines in the senses, muscles, and organs as they age. Assistive devices can further help people cope with physical decline. Clarke and Colantonio (2005, 192) call assistive devices "a powerful tool to help older adults overcome functional limitations." For example, more than one-third of seniors with a hearing disability use a hearing aid. Eighty-two percent of seniors with a vision disability wear glasses. And an estimated 4.6 percent of seniors in the community use wheelchairs (Clarke and Colantonio 2005).

Sutton, Gignac, and Cott (2002) found that 92 percent of older adults with disabilities used a wide range of non-medical assistive devices and about two-thirds of them used a medical device. Most people used assistive devices for personal care and inhome mobility. Most often people used simple products to make life easier. One woman, for example, bought a cordless phone so she could carry it with her around the house. An older person may use the microwave oven as an assistive device. She can boil water by the cupful in the microwave to avoid lifting a heavy kettle.

A simple device such as a bathroom grab bar can prevent falls and injury. A national study of nearly 2,000 Canadian veterans found that 60 percent of them had a grab bar in the bathroom. And almost 80 percent had anti-slip mats in the tub or shower (Speechley et al. 2005). Edwards and her colleagues (2003) estimate that more grab bars in homes could save an estimated $210 million per year in health care costs.

Zimmer, Hickey, and Searle (1997) found that people with arthritic pain tended to cut back on activity (the greater the pain, the greater the tendency to quit activities). But a group of people, called "replacers," added more passive activities to replace activities they had quit. These people often were younger than "quitters." They also tended to have a spouse, a social network, and fewer mobility problems. These researchers say that professionals should encourage arthritis patients to take up new activities. People who replace their activities will live a higher quality of life.

Cott and Gignac (1999) found that people with activity limitations used many methods to cope with their illness. These included keeping a positive attitude toward life, cutting down on household chores, and relying on others for help. Although Litwin (2000) reports that disability negatively affects a person's sense of well-being, he also found that a supportive social

● **Exhibit 5.5**

A Love of Dance

Elizabeth Patterson, "on the doorstep of 70," shares her love of dance with audiences of all ages. Sharon Aschaiek describes Patterson's renewed life as a dancer and performer.

On the doorstep of 70, Patterson taught ballet for 38 years at her own school, the Oakville School of Dancing, and also worked as an examiner—a role that took her globetrotting to places such as Brazil, New Zealand, Malta, England and across Canada and the United States.

She retired 10 years ago and eventually moved to Village by the Arboretum, a Guelph, Ontario retirement community. But her first love has never been far off the radar screen.

A new interest in tap dancing led to lessons at the Oakville Senior Citizens' Recreation Centre, and before long she joined the Happy Tappers, a 19-member group that performed twice at the [RBC Seniors'] Jubilee [Concert] (an annual event sponsored by the Royal Bank of Canada).

She also began teaching tap at the Evergreen Seniors Centre in Guelph, and formed Evergreen Footlights, a dance troupe that performed its own colourful routine at the show.

But Patterson's biggest thrill came from her newest act—Two's Company, a contemporary dance piece she developed with a partner.

"It's light rock with a classical feel to it," says Patterson, who marked five years with the Jubilee this year. "You definitely know you've danced when you're done!"

Participating in the Jubilee year after year allows Patterson a chance to reconnect with old friends and to sustain her long-time love affair with dance. "I feel better when I dance. If I have a day where I'm not dancing, I can't say that I feel as good," she says. "It keep you in a good frame of mind and it keeps you healthy."

Source: Sharon Aschaiek. 2003. "Senior Idols: Annual Jubilee Puts Talent Front and centre." *Toronto Star, Comfort Life*, p. 22. Toronto-based Sharon Aschaiek (sharon@summitmediagroup.com) writes and edits for newspapers, magazines and websites.

network improves well-being. Support from family and friends—the quality of their relationships and the frequency of help—brought disabled older people the most satisfaction. Cott and Gignac (1999) found that married people relied on a spouse for help. People without a spouse sometimes hired a homemaker to help with housework or cooking. Community meal programs can help older people with severe disabilities to eat well. These programs also get people out of their homes and give them a chance to socialize with others.

Three responses to aging can decrease the effects of physiological decline: changes in the environment, improvements in technology, and changes in lifestyle.

Changes in the Environment

Sense thresholds, the points at which a person can begin to perceive a stimulus, begin to increase as early as age 30, and by age 60 most people notice changes in their senses. Turcotte and Schellenberg (2007) report that 3.4 percent of older people have a hearing problem even with a hearing aid and 2.1 percent have a vision problem even with corrective lenses. Hearing aids may not help a person follow a conversation because they amplify all sounds, even background noises. In one case, an elderly man with a hearing aid in a university class showed up to take the course a second time. Surprised, the professor asked him why. The man said that students talking behind him, a bus depot across the street, and a noisy heating system all made his hearing aid useless. Some days he left it at home or shut it off and tried to read the professor's lips. "I only got half of what you said last time," he told the professor. "So I've come back to get the rest." This man needed a quieter classroom.

Changes in the environment—including changes in the way other people speak to or treat an older person—can help that person cope with physical decline. Also, older adults can compensate for a disability by changing their environment. For example, older people who cannot walk stairs may choose to live in a one-floor, ground-level home. Nearly all older people say they would prefer to live in their own home and never move. But few people have a home that can easily adapt to their changing physical needs as they age. Many older people face a dilemma: live in unsuitable housing (e.g., a home with an inaccessible upstairs bedroom) or move and adjust to new housing.

New designs in household products can offer a higher quality of life to older residents. New products include a bathroom sink that stops scalding water from reaching the faucet, rubber flooring in the bathroom to prevent slips and falls, window shades with pinholes that let in light with less glare, and lamps that turn on and off with a touch at the base or a voice command. As the market grows, companies will respond by designing and producing more products for older people. New technology will increase a person's ability to live in his or her own home for life. For example, new technologies can allow family members to visit with each other online. A person in a nursing home can play a game of cards with a relative thousands of miles away.

Technology can also allow families to monitor an older relative's activity. Cutler (2006) says that technology can report any changes in a person's physical condition to a health care centre. With the parent's permission, some children have arranged to have a camera located in a parent's home. The camera monitors the older person's behaviour and through the Internet will alert the children about any changes that signal danger. For example, the family can program the camera to expect the older person to enter the kitchen in the morning. If this does not happen, the system can alert the children, who can then check for any problems. The older person can turn off the camera at any point. Technology can also detect wandering, can note when a door opens, and can track a person through GPS devices.

These technologies can help older people age in place (Hutlock, 2003). Some people appreciate this kind of support, although others find it intrusive. Melenhorst and colleagues (2004) find that older people will tolerate the intrusion if the technology improves their sense of safety and security.

Some architects and landscape designers have designed special gardens for nursing homes and day centres. Garden designs often include benches for residents and staff to sit with family or clients. A fountain may serve as a destination for short walks. An enclosed loop and coloured walkway can guide people who have cognitive impairment. These gardens can also allow clients or residents to care for some plants of their own.

Gigliotti and Jarrott (2005) started a horticulture therapy program in an adult day service for people with dementia. The day program provides a respite for family caregivers and allows dementia clients a chance to socialize and stay active. The researchers tested the effectiveness of gardening as an activity for dementia clients. Forty-eight clients (average age 80) took part in the study. The dementia clients spent half an hour once a week for nine weeks on horticulture therapy. The researchers compared the results of this program with traditional adult day service programs (exercise, games, crafts, puzzles). They found that, compared to the time they spent in traditional activities, clients spent more time engaged in horticulture therapy, less time doing nothing, and developed more positive relationships.

Designers find that an enclosed garden offers a safe setting for outdoor activity. The Gigliotti and Jarrott (2005) study shows that a gardening program suits the abilities and skills of dementia patients. Designers can create an environment that matches and enhances the decreased cognitive and physical abilities of the older clients or residents. Staff in one day centre used the garden for calm activities with Alzheimer's clients. A walk in the garden soothed agitated participants (Lovering et al. 2002). Staff members also used the garden for mild physical activity such as bocce and shuffleboard, and to hold group discussions. One staff member commented about the garden's effect on clients: "It's good for them, it's healthy for them. They enjoy it. I know that people benefit and are healthier from having just 20 minutes of sunlight a day" (423). The designers say that "specially designed outdoor spaces" can improve the quality of life of frail and confused older people (417) (see Exhibit 5.6).

Improvements in Technology

In the 18th century, Benjamin Franklin invented bifocals. He cut his glasses in half when he needed to watch the speakers' expressions at the French court. Today, technology helps older people cope with aging in dozens of ways. Some people wear electronic pacemakers to regulate their hearts; people with severe arthritis can have joint replacement surgery; and in some cases a person can have a childhood problem corrected in old age.

One woman lived her first 60 years with her hip bones outside their sockets. Her muscles and ligaments allowed her to walk, but she limped and tired quickly. As she aged her muscles weakened, and her doctor said she would have to spend the rest of her life in a wheelchair. She searched for and found a doctor who agreed to operate on both her hips. He warned her that the operation would endanger her life, but she decided to go ahead with the surgery. She now has both hips in place in their sockets and she stands two inches taller than in her youth.

Technological aids to older people range from the simple (e.g., a thick piece of rubber tubing that fits over a wooden spoon handle to help a person with arthritis or a weak grip) to the complex (e.g., a battery-powered tub seat that lowers a person into the tub, reclines at the push of a button, and uses an optional turntable to help the person into and out of the tub). Some aids are simple (e.g., rubber strips applied to the bottom of the bathtub

● Exhibit 5.6

A SMALL CHANGE CAN MAKE A BIG DIFFERENCE

The Public Health Agency of Canada (2009) pro-duced Canada's Physical Activity Guide to Healthy Active Living for Older Adults. *It encourages active living, makes suggestions on how to get active, and gives tips on activities that will lead to better health. The guide also provides a series of case studies to show what older people have done to live a more active life. Below we present one of these cases. It shows how a simple environmental change can open a person to a new and healthier lifestyle.*

Li is 65. She is a small woman and has never been very strong, but she has always loved gardening. She has become very depressed and bored after she retired from her job. She began to sleep a lot and rarely did any activity. She missed her yard since she moved to an apartment and did not know what to do with her time. …

Li's friends began to worry about her and found her a garden plot very close to the seniors' apartments where she was living. Li was thrilled and determined to make it the best garden on the block. Every day she is out there digging, weeding, planting, and trimming … and her energy level has improved. But what was she going to do in the winter?

One of the other gardeners told her about a mall-walking program and asked her to join it with her. Through her new friends she found out about a T'ai Chi class as well, and she loves it so much she now does it summer and winter.

Getting physically active changed Li's life. She has a whole group of new friends. Her spirits have lifted and she feels stronger and more secure.

Source: Adapted from Health Canada, 2003, *Canada's Physical Activity Guide to Healthy Active Living for Older Adults: Handbook*, Ottawa: Canada's Communications Group. Retrieved: January 18, 2008. http://www.phac-aspc.gc.ca/pau-uap/paguide/older/started.html.

to prevent slipping) and some are complex (e.g., a living room chair with a seat that lifts a person to a standing position when a button is pressed). People with visual impairment, for example, use simple technologies such as talking books and complex technologies such as computerized reading aids (Ryan et al. 2003). Koncelik (2003) reports that computers can now control hearing aids so that the aid adjusts the sound to the environment. The user can filter out high- or low-pitched sounds or reduce background noise. Improvements in technology make coping with disability easier. As prices on these innovations decrease, more people will benefit from their use.

In the future, older people may have access to more exotic aids. For example, computerized robots may help older people with daily chores or help bathe and feed people in nursing homes. Voice-activated robots will pick things up or move them around. Robots may also help patients do passive exercises, help them walk, or bring them something they need. Robots could free nursing home staff from unpleasant work and allow them more enjoyable time with residents. Voice-activated robots would give an immobilized person a feeling of control over their environment, thereby increasing their life satisfaction. Research will have to determine whether robots further dehumanize institutional settings, whether older people (or institutions) can afford complex machines, and whether people will use high-tech equipment if they have the choice (see Exhibit 5.7).

The Use of Computers to Enhance Everyday Life

Computers already allow a housebound older person to order groceries, get mail, or play Scrabble with a grandchild across the country. New technologies may make some disabilities less of a problem. Telebanking allows older people with a mobility problem to manage their finances from home. Computer websites allow people to get medical and health promotion information. People with disabilities use computers to communicate with one another, with family members, or with a caregiver support group.

Cutler (2006) says that few studies report the effects of online support groups. But early research shows that they have a good effect on health and well-being. One study looked at the effects of an Internet support group

● Exhibit 5.7

ROBO-SAPIENS RISING: SONY, HONDA AND OTHERS ARE SPENDING MILLIONS TO PUT A ROBOT IN YOUR HOME

In a retirement home, a robot offers its undivided attention to a silver-haired woman sharing stories about her grandkids. Meanwhile, at a hospital, another makes an elderly patient smile with a joke, before reminding him to take his medication. Think of them as high-tech granny and grandpa sitters, fully equipped with interactive webcams to help keep tabs on your favourite seniors. And while not as grand as science-fiction legend Isaac Asimov's robotic future, this is clearly on the way—and coming sooner than you think, courtesy of some of the biggest names in consumer electronics.

Driving this robotic revolution—in health care, especially—are global concerns about the greying of the population, a phenomenon already well advanced in Japan, where personal robots have suddenly become all the rage. Robots can now vacuum your house, watch for prowlers, page you at the airport and play with the kids. Advocates say it is only a short step from there to having them monitor shut-ins for signs of distress. This could allow frail seniors to live independently longer, and it may also bring them peace of mind. "By talking with the elderly," says Norihiro Hagita, whose Kyoto-based team of roboticists at ATR Intelligent Robotics and Communication

Laboratories is developing a prototype robot with a touch that feels almost human, "a robot can ease mental stress."

Recognizing a gold-mine when they see it, several of the world's largest electronics companies and car manufacturers—brand names such as Sony, Honda and Toshiba—are pouring hundreds of millions into a field once dominated by super geeks in university labs. And the race to fulfill one of the last great promises of the 20th century—an affordable robobuddy—is on in a big way. "People don't just want robots like the Roomba," the disc-shaped machine that whips around your home cleaning floors, says Mark Tilden, the Tokyo-based creator of Robosapien, a $119 toddler-sized device that sold 1.5 million units last Christmas. "People want their robots to be like Rosie from *The Jetsons*—a wise-cracking New Yorker with an apron."

Do you think older people will accept robotic helpers in their homes? What do you think it will take for people to see robots as just another helpful technological aid?

Source: John Intini, J. Robo-sapiens Rising. *Maclean's* Magazine, July 15, 2005. Reprinted with permission.

---

on Alzheimer's family caregivers. Caregivers in the group reported reduced strain. Spousal caregivers gained the most from this support (Bass et al., 1998). Other studies find that online support groups reduce depression and anxiety (Mahoney, et al., 2003).

Barriers still exist to widespread computer use by older people. For example, computer use demands physical skill (fine motor coordination to use the keyboard) and mental ability. Scialfa and Fernie (2006) say that computer use taxes verbal and spatial working memory. Computer users need to keep information about search paths and previous Web pages in mind as they browse and search. They also have to contend with pop-up ads and windows that intend to draw attention away from the person's main task. Multiple web page links,

information presented in hard-to-read fonts, and poorly organized websites can make computer use a challenge (at any age). A search on the Internet can quickly lead to confusion as the reader jumps from one link to another.

Today, the older population falls into two groups: those who feel comfortable using the latest technologies, and those who don't (Liu & Park, 2003). Brink (2001) reports that, compared to younger Canadians, fewer older Canadians use the Internet. Of all adult groups, for example, they showed the least use of online shopping. Barriers to use include the cost of a computer, lack of access to a computer, and lack of time and skills. Czaja and Lee (2006) say that lack of familiarity with computers, lack of training, and hard-to-use systems all present barriers to the use of computers by older people.

This could lead to a digital divide within the older population (Mundorf and colleagues 2006, 245). Some people will have access to electronic health information and social networks; others will not.

Computer manufacturers need to adjust their products to serve an older market. For example, some older adults find it difficult to use the mouse (Hendrix and Sakauye 2001), so touch pads may provide a better way for an older person to navigate onscreen. Simple techniques can encourage older people to use computer technology; many websites now have a button that users can click to increase font size. People with arthritis or visual disabilities should be able to adjust the keyboard and screen to suit their needs.

Makers of new information technology should keep systems simple, know and respond to the needs of older users, and offer help and training. For example, middle-aged and older adults show the best performance when a presentation uses black-on-white text. Older people may need more time and assistance to learn a software package. Research also shows that older people benefit by learning about computers in pairs.

Emerging technologies, like the use of mobile phones as information sources, open worlds of information and social supports to older users. Mobile phones now access the Internet, send instant messages, and download emails. But small screens, tiny words and pictures, and miniscule keyboards all challenge older eyes and fingers. New devices with touch screens and large icons help overcome some of these barriers. Future generations of older people will face new challenges and new options as new technologies emerge. Good design can reduce the lag between innovation and the use of technology by older users.

Assistive Devices

Assistive devices can help people stay active and live safely. But for aids to be useful, three things are necessary: (1) people have to know about them, (2) people have to understand their usefulness, and (3) products have to be affordable and accessible. Manufacturers, safety organizations, and the government need to set up norms and standards of safety and suitability for new products. Older people will reject devices that make them look different or dependent. For example, a person may use a motorized scooter to get around, but would not use a wheelchair. Product design has to overcome an older person's resistance to appearing dependent.

Current transportation technology helps solve many disabled seniors' problems. But sometimes the technology does not meet seniors' needs. Seniors report problems with boarding and leaving planes, long-distance buses, and trains. They also have problems with local transportation, finding it difficult to get to and wait at bus stops.

Some older people who need mobility, visual, and hearing aids do not have them. Seniors often report that they cannot afford the aids they need. Government programs cover the cost of some aids but not others. And government support differs from province to province. Clarke and Colantonia (2005) report that in 2005 only four provinces (Alberta, Saskatchewan, Ontario, and Quebec) had programs to help cover the cost of assistive devices like wheelchairs.

Zimmer and Myers (1997) studied older people's openness to wearing protective clothing. For example, would an older person wear padded underwear to protect against hip injuries? About a third of the sample said they would. Those at highest risk showed the greatest willingness to try such an aid. This type of study shows the value of market research using an older audience. Zimmer and Chappell (1999) found that people differed in their willingness to accept new technology; people who report the most concern about managing at home show the most receptivity to new technology.

Marketers need to price products within the reach of the average senior. Also, technology developers must understand what customers want, what features they prefer, and what they expect from the product. Wylde (1998) says that age alone cannot predict use of a device. She says that developers need to know the life stage, personality, health, and attitudes of potential customers.

McWilliam and her colleagues (2000) report that many people who need an assistive device do not use one; fear of embarrassment or perception of dependence may be the issue (Gignac, Cott, and Badley 2000). Aminzadeh and Edwards (2000) found that about one-third of cane users and almost two-thirds of non-users feel that a cane signifies the loss of independence and being "old." Those who used a cane tended to hold a more positive attitude about this aid. Over 85 percent of people in this study who used a cane said that it improved their functioning, made them feel safer, and prevented falls.

People can overcome negative views of assistive devices. If they do, a mobility aid can increase their autonomy and improve their quality of life (Sutton, Gignac, and Cott 2002). An assistive device can help reduce the need for medical care and can help older people stay in the community (Hoenig, Taylor, and Sloan 2003; Sutton, Gignac and Cott 2002). One U.S. study found that 80 percent of older people who used assistive devices and services said they depended less on others, while 50 percent avoided entry into a nursing home (National Council on Disability, cited in McWilliam et al. 2000). Shapiro and Havens (2000) propose that government programs provide financial aid and professional advice to people who need assistive devices. They also propose a loan program for people who need devices for only a short time. Studies need to look at how people use devices and the benefits they feel they gain from them.

It is also important to know the effects of health care aids on a person's social life. A simple self-administered blood sugar test, for example, can cut down on the cost of a nurse's visit. But this cost-saving initiative may remove an important social contact for the older person, who may prefer to see a nurse. Little is known about whether technology can have side effects such as social isolation. As well, technology can create dependence. Does an electric wheelchair help a woman who has trouble using a walker or does it put an end to her ability to walk? Researchers have begun to address these and other questions as they look at the impact of technology on older people's lives.

Changes in Lifestyle

Research finds that early life experiences influence health in later life (Hall 2007). For example, childhood abuse, poverty, or a parental divorce can lead to drug abuse, adult obesity, and even attempted suicide later in life. Low socioeconomic status (SES) also can lead to self-destructive behaviour. Compared to people with middle-class income and above, people with low-SES tend to smoke, remain physically inactive, and abuse alcohol and drugs (Ferraro, 2006). Also, compared to people with middle-class income and above, people with low income may have less access to health care programs and services. In spite of these trends, studies show that people in any socioeconomic bracket can improve their health through exercise, weight reduction, and ending risky behaviour (Clark, Stump, and Damush, 2003).

Costs of Smoking in Later Life

People can change their habits to cope with past abuse and biological aging. Smoking is one of the leading causes of serious disease and death for older Canadians (Health Canada 2002c; Little 2002). One-half of long-term smokers die from diseases related to their smoking. Smoking leads to decreased psychological well-being, poorer subjective health, and reduced levels of physical functioning (Health Canada, 2002c).

The economic burden of smoking is immense. In 2002, the cost was estimated at $15 billion annually in Canada (Health Canada, 2002c). The direct health care costs from tobacco use were estimated between $3 billion and $3.5 billion annually, with most of the costs spent on hospital care. Older people account for some of the highest costs. For this reason, Health Canada proposes

that smoking-cessation programs focus on older and middle-aged adults (Health Canada, 2002c).

Some research suggests that older people have begun to change their habits. Wister (2005) analyzed data from five Canadian national surveys. He found the lowest rates of smoking among the 65-and-over age groups for men and women. The proportion of male smokers aged 65 to 69, for example, dropped from 39.7 percent in 1978–79 to 16.0 percent in 2000–01. Over the same time, women 65 to 69 showed a decrease in the proportion smoking from 22.9 percent to 13.8 percent. Fortunately, former smokers (especially those who have been nonsmokers for 15 years or more) and people who never smoked are more likely to maintain health and to recover from loss of health (Shields and Martel, 2006). The same trends were found for those who engaged in regular leisure physical activity, had a normal body weight, and consumed alcohol occasionally or weekly. This suggests that there is a cumulative effect of healthy behaviours on seniors' ability to maintain their health and recover from illness (Shields and Martel, 2006).

Martel and colleagues (2005, 6) conducted a longitudinal study that compared people over five cycles of the National Population Health Survey (NPHS) in Canada. The study looked at health behaviours over an eight-year period from 1994–95 to 2002–03. They found that poor health habits like smoking and inactivity in middle age catch up with people as they age. Those who had poor health habits suffered from more chronic disease as they aged. The researchers conclude that "Seniors who started out in good health in 1994/95 were at a significantly higher risk of losing their health by 2002/03 if they smoked or quit in the last 10 years, had inactive leisure-time pursuits or were in a weight range that was not appropriate for their height." Martel and colleagues say these findings support "the hypothesis that the impacts of healthy habits are cumulative through time. This result reinforces the public health message that healthy habits are profitable throughout the life cycle" (6).

Diet and Exercise

Like smoking, overeating can increase a person's risk of heart disease and diabetes. Using figures from 1998, Health Canada researchers estimate that unhealthy eating leads to as much as $1.3 billion in direct health care costs. They estimate another $5.3 billion in indirect health care costs (Health Canada 2003 cited in Federal/Provincial/Territorial 2006) (see Exhibit 5.8).

Lack of physical activity adds to the problems caused by poor diet. Often what people see as unavoidable consequences of aging falls into the category of **hypokinesia**, or physical problems due to lack of movement. Statistics

● Exhibit 5.8

GOOD NUTRITION IN LATER LIFE

Most nutrition experts today have come to similar conclusions about eating habits that lead to good health in later life. They say that an adult past age 50, for example, needs between 2,000 and 3,000 calories per day (the exact number of calories needed depends on a person's weight, gender, unique metabolism, and activities). A woman generally needs fewer calories than a man.

Health Canada (2006, 2) says that "moderating the amount that you eat" is the key to weight management—and this includes portion control. Health Canada advises that people "avoid eating out in places where very large servings or 'all you can eat' are offered."

The trend toward bigger portions with the high sugar and fat content in popular foods in part explains North America's obesity crisis. For example, a meal at Burger King that includes a double beef burger Whopper, fries, a large Coke, and a Dutch apple pie for dessert provides 1,929 calories. That's about the entire daily caloric allowance for an adult woman, and these calories come mostly from processed sugar, refined starch, and fat.

By comparison, a balanced diet will contain about 40 percent complex carbohydrates, 30 percent low-fat protein, and 30 percent healthy fat (olive oil, fish oil, etc.). An older person will either have to eat less or exercise more (or both) to maintain an ideal weight. As people age they need to choose foods that give them a balanced diet and get the maximum nutrition from the optimum number of calories.

Canada (2000b) reports that seniors have the lowest rate of participation in vigorous leisure activity (such as jogging for 20 minutes). Only 19 percent of older men and 11 percent of older women said they engaged in this type of exercise. Older people also showed high rates of overweight and obesity. Two-fifths of men and one-third of women fall into the overweight category; 14 percent of men and 15 percent of women fall into the obese category (using the BMI or body mass index). Menec and colleagues (2005, 12) say that Canadian policy needs an "emphasis on prevention, such as reducing the prevalence of obesity, which is one risk factor for diabetes."

Wister (2005, 80) reports that obesity rates (a BMI of 30+) for men aged 60 to 64 nearly doubled between 1985 and 2000–01 (from 9.4 percent in 1985 to 17.7 percent in 2000–01). Women in this age group showed a similar trend; their rates of obesity increased from 9.7 percent in 1985 to 18.7 percent in 2000–01. Wister calls this rise in obesity "alarming given the relatively short interval under study." Men and women in their 40s and 50s show the highest rates of obesity (in some middle-age groups the obesity rate in men reached 20 percent). If these middle-aged people remain overweight as they age, they will face serious health problems in later life, which will also increase the cost to the Canadian health care system.

Katzmarzyk and colleagues (2000) estimate that in 1999 physical inactivity directly led to $2.1 billion in health care costs. This came to 2.5 percent of all health care costs that year. Even modest increases in activity levels could result in substantial cost savings. For example, a 10 percent reduction in the prevalence of physical inactivity has the potential to reduce direct health care expenditures by $150 million a year."

Lack of exercise causes overweight, decline in muscle and bone mass, and a loss of function. The National Advisory Council on Aging 2006 Report Card found that in 2005 55 percent of older men and 67 percent of older women reported inactivity. Both genders show an increase in inactivity compared to rates in 2001. Three quarters of women aged 75 and over reported inactivity in 2005. Health Canada (2002a says that inactivity levels could reach as high as 79 percent (based on standards of the Canadian Fitness and Lifestyle Research Institute).

Bélanger and his colleagues (2002) report that physical inactivity in women can shorten disability-free life expectancy by six years. The National Advisory Council on Aging (2006, 11) says that "… health problems are not the only reason for explaining physical inactivity among seniors. In many cases, physical activity is simply not incorporated into day-to-day living due to a lack of awareness of its importance in later life, or due to ageist attitudes that still negate its relevance."

Studies show that exercise can slow the aging process, improve health, and improve physical function

(Chernoff 2002; Lalive d'Epinay and Bickel 2003). Shields and Martel (2006) report that seniors who engaged in activity three or more times per week reported the best health. Sixty-seven percent of seniors who exercised three or more times a week reported good health. Among seniors who exercised infrequently, only 36 percent reported good health. The association between exercise and good health remained after the researchers compared people with like sociodemographic status and chronic conditions. Shields and Martel (2006, 18) end their report on an optimistic note. "It is always possible," they say, "to change or improve behaviour. … [This] may allow people to spend their senior years without being dependent on others, and with positive perceptions of their physical and mental health."

Researchers list dozens of benefits from exercise in later life. They include reduced body fat, greater muscle mass, greater strength, improved cardiac output, improved endocrine-metabolic function, lower blood pressure, decreased hypertension, decreased heart disease, and decreased osteoporosis (Adams 2003; Chernoff 2002). Gillis and Hirdes (1996) looked at findings from

Canada's General Social Survey. They found that greater activity led to a lower risk of psychological problems and better subjective health.

McWilliam and her colleagues (2000) support this conclusion. They reviewed five rigorous studies of exercise programs and found that "regular low intensity exercise" improves mental as well as physical function, and exercise leads to more functional independence (105). Gillis and Hirdes (1996) say that "there appear to be considerable gains in quality of life associated with moderate levels of physical activity compared with a sedentary lifestyle" (312). The Conference Board of Canada reports that a 1 percent increase in physical activity would result in a $10.2 million savings on health care related to ischemic heart disease. It would reduce the cost of care for adult-onset diabetes by $877,000 and for colon cancer by $407,000 (Health Canada 2002a).

Aldwin and colleagues (2006) say that aerobic exercise improves a whole range of physical conditions. It improves cardiac output, strengthens the heart muscle, lowers bad cholesterol, raises good cholesterol, and increases lung function. Aerobic exercise also improves

Swim Class

muscle strength, flexibility, walking, standing, and balance. Weight-bearing exercise increases muscle strength and balance. It also slows calcium loss from bones. People show improvements from exercise even late in life. These improvements lead to better functioning in their homes and greater independence.

Studies show that the more often a person exercises, the better his or her health. And moderate exercise offers almost as much benefit as vigorous exercise. Exercise can even buffer other risks created by smoking or by having high blood pressure. Sobczak (2002) reports that exercise can stop and in some cases reverse the trend toward loss of mobility and dependence that may come with age.

Kramer and colleagues (2006) report that exercise also improves mental ability. They report that older adults who exercise show improvements in mental tasks, and they

show the greatest improvement in highly complex tasks. Studies on animals find that exercise increases survival of neurons, growth of new neuronal interconnections, and the growth of new capillaries in the brain (Cotman and Berchtold, 2002 cited in Kramer et al. 2006).

Exercisers also show increases in gray matter volume and white matter links between the frontal lobes. Kramer and colleagues (2006, p.76) say that "the end result of exercise training then is a brain that is more plastic and adaptive to change and more able to survive the vagaries of the aging process. … These results suggest that even relatively short exercise interventions can begin to restore some of the losses in brain volume associated with normal aging" (see Exhibit 5.9).

Health promotion programs encourage a more active lifestyle. Chou and Wister (2005) studied the cues

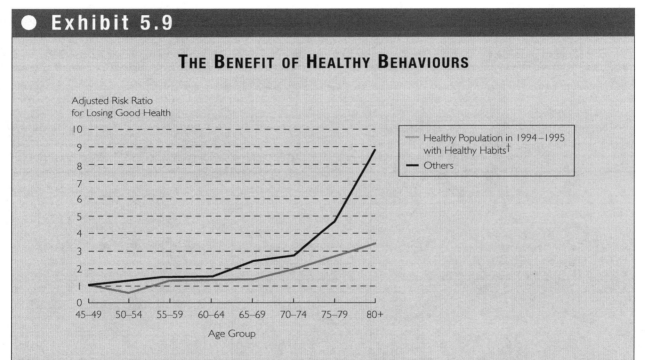

● Exhibit 5.9

THE BENEFIT OF HEALTHY BEHAVIOURS

Adjusted Risk Ratio for Losing Good Health

Legend:
- Healthy Population in 1994–1995 with Healthy Habits[†]
- Others

Age Group: 45–49, 50–54, 55–59, 60–64, 65–69, 70–74, 75–79, 80+

† Never smoked or quit for atleast 10 years, physically active in leisure time, normal weight range.

This chart shows the benefit of health behaviours (non-smokers, physically active, and normal weight) on the risk of losing good health. At every age after age 65 those who practise healthy behaviours show less risk of losing good health. Among the oldest age group (80+), compared to people with poor health habits, those with healthy behaviours show about one-third the risk of losing good health. This chart underscores the importance of healthy behaviours throughout life and the benefits that come from an active lifestyle.

Source: Laurent Martel, Alain Bélanger, Jean-Marie Berthelot and Yves Carrière, "Healthy Today, Healthy Tomorrow? Findings from the National Population Health Survey: Statistics Canada," *Healthy Aging,* Component of Statistics Canada Catalogue no. 82-618-MWE2005004. Reprinted with permission.

that led people to exercise. They found that, compared to people who did not read about their chronic illness, people who read about their illness had twice the likelihood of exercising. Also, knowledge of services, consultations with friends, and visits to a health professional all led to a higher probability of exercising. Chou and Wister say that "information translates into significant self-care action …" (405). The researchers say that health promotion programs should use reading material and other media to educate clients about exercise.

Programs for women, for example, should include education and counselling on exercise and other physical activities (Chernoff 2002). Studies find a dramatic decline in the percentage of women who report physically active and moderately active lifestyles after age 65. At the same time women report a significant increase in the rates of inactivity (Federal/Provincial/Territorial 2006). (Men tend to show this pattern of decline only after age 75).

These studies point the way to a new view of aging. Science cannot stop the aging process, but individuals can improve their environment and can delay chronic problems through lifestyle changes and exercise. Even institutionalized older people with many chronic conditions can benefit from an exercise program. Lazowski and his colleagues (1999) conducted a study of institutionalized seniors. They found that a program designed to improve strength, balance, and mobility led to significant improvements in mobility, balance, flexibility, and knee and hip strength. The researchers conclude that frail and incontinent seniors as well as those with mild dementia can benefit from a challenging exercise program. Chernoff (2002) says that improvements in dietary habits and physical activity can contribute to better health and greater longevity.

Stress Reduction

Many tension reduction techniques exist, from secular relaxation methods to meditation practices, to religious retreats. Studies show that regular practice of many of these methods can improve health and well-being in later life.

Cerpa (1989), for example, studied the blood sugar levels of people with type II diabetes. He compared subjects who practised a meditation-relaxation technique and those in a diabetes education program. He found that the meditating group showed significantly reduced blood sugar levels after participating in the program for six weeks. The control group showed no change in blood sugar levels. The findings support the idea that meditation-relaxation techniques can help control diabetes.

Alexander and colleagues (1989) conducted a controlled study of Transcendental Meditation, mindfulness training (a method of increasing awareness of reactions to the environment), and relaxation. They found that the meditation and mindfulness groups, compared to the relaxation and control groups, showed improved mental health, better cardiovascular function, and improved mental ability. These two groups also showed greater longevity. The entire meditation group and 87 percent of the mindfulness group survived after three years. Only two-thirds of the control group was still alive after three years.

A later study by Alexander and his colleagues (1996) further supports the value of meditation as a way to improve health in later life. This study looked at the effect of Transcendental Meditation on older African American men. The researchers found that meditation significantly decreased hypertension, obesity, and other risk factors for heart disease. Aldwin et al. (2006, 94; also Seeman et al, 2003) say that "this accords with the growing evidence of the beneficial effect of meditation practice on cardiovascular health." Idler (2006, 291) says that experimental and epidemiological studies show "direct biological pathways from religious states, particularly those induced by meditation, to health by way of cardiovascular, neuroendocrine, and immune function …"

Lindberg (2005) reviewed the literature on meditation, spirituality, and health in older persons. She reviewed 25 years' of research and found that overall meditation reduces anxiety and depression. It improves a person's physical, emotional, and spiritual health. And it helps a person cope with problems, challenges, and stress.

Disease prevention, health promotion, and stress management should play a role in planning for a successful age. These activities can reduce the risk of many chronic conditions of later life (anxiety, high blood pressure, and heart disease).

THE COMPRESSION OF MORBIDITY HYPOTHESIS

Canadians have a longer life expectancy today than ever before. Will this mean more years of health and activity with a short period of illness at the end? Or will it mean a slow decline in health with more years of disability? Will we wear out quickly like Oliver Wendell Holmes's "one hoss shay" that fell apart in a day? Or will we rust out over many years like an old Chevrolet? How many people will want to live 120 years, if they know that they will spend their last 30 years in a nursing home with dementia or paralysis due to a stroke?

Researchers have developed two concepts to measure the quality of life in old age. The first, **disability-free life** expectancy refers to the years of remaining life free of any disability. Researchers compare this to the total number of years of life expectancy. It gives an indication of the quality of life of a person's remaining years. A similar concept, **dependence-free life expectancy**, measures the number of years of remaining life that a person will live in a state free of dependence on others for daily tasks.

Statistics Canada reports that men aged 65 to 69 years old in 1996 can expect on average to live 16.3 more years and 12.7 of those years would be dependence-free (Martel and Bélanger 2000). They would spend 1.5 years in a state of moderate dependence (needing help with tasks such as shopping), 1.1 years in severe dependence (they would need an assistant to help with personal care), and 0.8 years in an institution. Women in that same age group in 1996 can expect on average to live another 20.2 years. They would live 13.5 years dependence-free, 2.7 years in moderate dependence, 1.6 years in severe dependence, and 2.1 years in an institution. In other words, a man can expect to live about a fifth of his remaining years with some dependence. A woman can expect to live about a third of her later life with some dependence.

These figures show that women live longer than men but may spend more of those years dependent on others for their well-being. Martel, Bélanger, and Berthelot (2002, 42) report that gender creates a "double-jeopardy" for women. "Elderly men," they say, "had lower odds than did elderly women of losing their independence. And if they experienced an episode of dependence, men had significantly higher odds of recovering." Health behaviour such as smoking and lack of exercise leads to chronic illness and dependence. Compared to non-smokers, smokers show the least likelihood of recovering from a state of dependence.

Both of these concepts (disability-free and dependence-free life expectancy) measure the quality of life in old age. As more people live more years in old age, researchers want to know whether people will live these added years in good health and independent or disabled and dependent on others. An active and independent older person will have a higher quality of life. This type of older population will also make less demand on the health care and social service systems.

About 30 years ago, Fries (1980; see also Fries and Crapo 1981) gave an optimistic answer to the question of what a longer life would mean. He predicted three things: first, more people would live a life that approached the hypothetically fixed life span of 110 to 120 years (see Exhibit 5.10); second, longer life would come about primarily through the reduction of chronic illnesses such as heart disease, cancer, and stroke; and third, severe chronic illness would occur for a short time near the end of life (the **compression of morbidity hypothesis**).

Exhibit 5.10 illustrates the rectangularization of the survival curve. This exhibit uses the example of Canadian women at three time periods. Note that cohorts born more recently die off at a slower rate than those born earlier. Also, note the decline in numbers at later ages for the most recent cohorts. This trend almost forms a right angle on the chart and produces a **rectangularization** or **squaring to the survival curve**. Researchers conclude from these curves that a finite life span exists and that modern populations have begun to approach this limit (Clarfield 2002; Martel and Bélanger 2000).

Fries believed that healthier habits, training, and health policies could compress morbidity. Recent research supports this belief. Studies find that higher socioeconomic status (Melzer et al. 2000), smoking reduction (Bronnum-Hansen and Juel 2001), and regular physical activity (Ferrucci et al. 1999) all lead to a relative compression of morbidity.

Fries (2006, 258) more recently reported on a 21-year-long longitudinal study at Stanford University. The study documents the benefit of vigorous exercise on postponement of disability. The study compared 537 members of a runners club aged 50 and over with 423 people of the same age in a control group. The exercise group "delayed the onset of disability *by over 12 years* compared with controls, far more than any associated differences in longevity" (emphasis in original).

Fries goes on to say that lifetime disability measured in exercisers comes to only one-third to one-half that of people who do not exercise. Fries cites at least five other major studies that support the compression of morbidity hypothesis. He concludes that "both cumulative morbidity and morbidity at the end of life are decreased in those with good health habits. Morbidity is postponed and compressed into fewer years in those with fewer health risks" (258). This research shows that people have control over their well-being in later life. Good health habits pay off in more disability-free years.

Fries also said that the variation in ability among seniors showed room for further compression of morbidity. In other words, if some people live morbidity-free lives into late old age, other people can follow this pattern. The potential for further improvement in well-being among older people has led some authors to study the phenomenon of successful aging. Martel and colleagues (2005, 6) conclude that "Healthy aging, which contributes to 'successful' aging, does not seem to be reserved to a small group of individuals with a well-kept secret: this study shows that through a combination of personal effort and public will, many people can make it."

● Exhibit 5.10

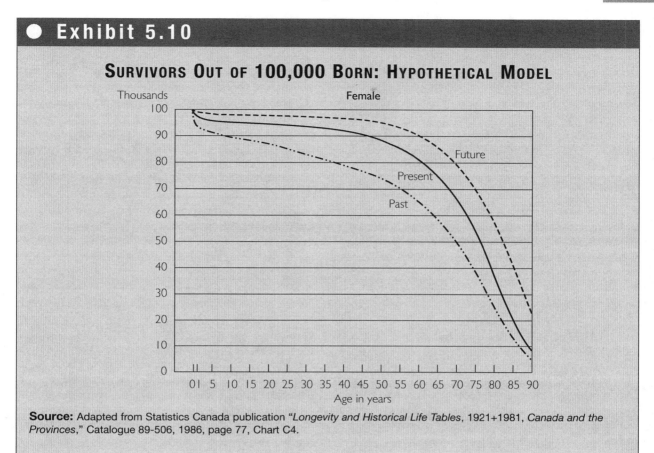

SURVIVORS OUT OF 100,000 BORN: HYPOTHETICAL MODEL

Source: Adapted from Statistics Canada publication *"Longevity and Historical Life Tables,* 1921+1981, *Canada and the Provinces,"* Catalogue 89-506, 1986, page 77, Chart C4.

SUCCESSFUL AGING

The Rowe and Kahn Model of Successful Aging

The focus by biologists on intrinsic processes has led to a more precise description of normal aging. But this research does not explain (nor does it try to explain) the differences in function among older people. It does not deal with the influence of the environment, lifestyles, and habits on physical functioning.

Rowe and Kahn (1995) understood the importance of these lifestyle and environmental influences. In a pioneering research study they developed a model of **successful aging**. They describe three signs of successful aging: (1) low chance of disease and disability; (2) high mental and physical functioning; and (3) active engagement in social relations and productive activity. They propose that scientists look at people with these traits. The people to be studied "demonstrate little or no loss in a constellation of physiologic functions … [and] would

be regarded as more broadly successful in physiologic terms" (Rowe and Kahn 1991, 22). The research would focus on understanding the reasons for these people's success.

The concept of successful aging may be of little use to biologists (because, they say, if people can avoid decline through lifestyle or environmental change, decline may not be part of true biological aging). But for the physiologist, the clinician, and others who work at improving life in old age, the focus on successful aging has value. Rowe and Kahn (1991) reviewed a variety of studies, including research on metabolism, osteoporosis, cognitive functioning, mortality, and well-being. They found that extrinsic influences such as diet, exercise, and social relations can inhibit and sometimes reverse functional decline.

Reker (2001–02) examined predictors of successful aging in a longitudinal study of community-dwelling and institutionalized older adults in Canada. This research looked at dimensions of Rowe and Kahn's model (physical health, cognitive competence, and social resources) as well as other more existential measures that included purpose in life, death acceptance, and religiousness. The research found that those who scored high on measures of successful aging when the study began showed similar signs of successful aging one year later. Social resources and having a purpose in life also predicted successful aging over time for both community-dwelling and institutionalized older adults. These results provide some support for Rowe and Kahn's model.

A study based on the Canadian Study of Health and Aging asked 2,783 Canadian seniors what they thought led to a long and healthy life (Bassett et al. 2007, 116–21). The study recorded seniors' responses in their own words and analyzed the results. The study found that most older people considered a good age their own responsibility. Even in the face of illness, they felt that they had the power to overcome their problems. People mentioned that a good and long life depended on a positive attitude ("take things as they come, don't worry"), self-care ("take care of yourself, don't take risks"), planning and financial control ("keep busy, work hard"), and individual autonomy ("if you can't do that [retain autonomy], it's the beginning of the end").

In general, respondents emphasized the importance of monitoring their health, staying active, and keeping busy. They also recognized the need to adjust to changes in health, ability, and circumstances as they aged. The researchers conclude that for this group "successful aging is about maintaining control and order in the face of decline" (124). These findings give insight into how older people themselves view successful aging, and how they attempt to make it a reality.

Some researchers suggest that we add positive spirituality as a separate dimension to Rowe and Kahn's model of successful aging (Crowther et al. 2002). Martel and colleagues (2005, 5) say that "in fact, among seniors, the chances of healthy aging were significantly enhanced by a related variable: a strong sense of coherence, that is, finding life meaningful, manageable and comprehensible. Because a high sense of coherence is significantly associated with healthy aging, a positive attitude towards life is desirable in order to stay healthy while aging."

These findings show that researchers need to use an interdisciplinary approach to the study of aging. Studies should include psychosocial as well as physiological measures of functioning, and researchers should look for links between the psychosocial and the physiological findings. Studies of successful aging show that we can learn from people who function best in each age group.

These people may hold the key to a longer life and a better old age for everyone in the future.

A Life Course Model of Successful Aging

Research shows that successful aging can take place at every age. But what can or should a person do to age successfully? Ashley Montague, ethologist and researcher, says "The goal in life is to die young—as late as possible" (1989, 5) Baby Boomers want to come into their 60s looking and feeling like 40 and into their 70s looking and feeling like 50. In order to do this seniors need to (1) preserve the health they've got, (2) do as little damage as possible to their bodies, and (3) strengthen what they can.

Most people agree that a healthy old age depends on personal action—diet, exercise, and self-care. But people enter later life with different chances of living a healthy old age. Aboriginal people at age 65, for example, have a life expectancy 4 years lower than the national average. In 2001 44 percent of off-reserve Aboriginal elders report fair or poor health compared to 30 percent of the general population. In this group 25 percent of senior woman and 20 percent of senior men had diabetes. The National Advisory Council on Aging (2006) *Report Card* says that on-reserve elders may also show a higher proportion of people with diabetes.

Low income in general leads to poorer health. Almost two-thirds of the highest income seniors (62 percent) reported good health. But only 41 percent of the lowest or lower-middle-income seniors reported good health. Some researchers trace health in old age to childhood and a lifetime of good or bad health. O'Rand (2006, 154–55), for example, says that poverty in early childhood leads to a "chain of life course 'insults.' … Early and sustained poverty has been shown repeatedly to predict higher rates of disability and mortality in later life." Studies now link cardiovascular diseases to childhood stress, illness, and poverty (Leon and Ben-Schlomo, 1997 cited in O'Rand, 2006).

Research on the "early origins" of disease takes a life course approach to health (Ferraro, 2006). Studies find that mothers who experience famine while pregnant have children who report ill health 50 years later. Other studies show long-term effects of mothers' health-damaging behaviour during pregnancy. Not everyone agrees that a clear link exists between fetal health and health in later life. But the literature does point to some connections between health in childhood and adulthood. Low birth weight, for example, raises the risk of obesity in adulthood. And obesity, in turn, raises the risk of diabetes. So low birth rate has an indirect, but potentially strong, influence on health in old age. Ferraro (2006, 241) says that only longitudinal studies can trace these detailed connections. These studies will make an "important contribution for both maternal and gerontological health."

Research on the early origins of disease show that people from poor families tend to engage in more health-destructive behaviour in later life. This includes smoking, alcohol abuse, drug abuse, and lack of exercise (Ferraro, 2006). Compared to middle-class children, children brought up in low-income households are exposed to these poor health habits. Ferraro (2006, 245 and 248) says that a childhood in a poor family may lead to "a cascade of risks. … A good start in life aids the chances for a good finish. … It is hard to overstate the influence of early disadvantages."

Socioeconomic differences mean that some older people will suffer from the effects of early health disadvantage. Other older people will build on the good health and income that they enjoyed throughout their lives. Life course studies of health make the case for public policies that improve health in childhood and middle age (e.g., health education, welfare programs, income security programs, childcare, and public health programs). Health promotion programs for poorer older people can also help. Exercise and weight loss programs, for example, can improve health, functional ability, and quality of life at every age. This makes health in later life a societal issue as well as a personal problem.

Will the Baby Boomers Age Successfully?

Will the Baby Boomers enter old age in better health than past generations, or will this large generation enter old age with chronic illnesses that bankrupt the Canadian health care system? Wister (2005) set out to answer these questions by looking at Boomers' health conditions and behaviours in midlife. He used five Canadian national health surveys to compare Boomers with past generations. These studies took place in 1978–79, 1985, 1990, 1994–95, and 2000–01. These studies allowed him to compare Boomers in 2000–01 (aged 35 to 54) with people the same age at earlier points in time.

His findings show a complex pattern of good and bad health behaviours and health conditions. Below we present some of the key findings from his study.

Lifestyle Improvements

- Boomers show a smoking rate "significantly lower than for persons of those exact ages in earlier periods."

The late 1970s and 1980s show the greatest decrease in smoking, possibly due to publicity about the negative effects of smoking. Compared to younger Boomers, older Boomers showed a larger drop in smoking.

- Boomers show a sharp improvement in exercise patterns. They showed a 40.9 percent drop in sedentary or infrequent exercising. By 2000–01 only 39.3 percent of boomers reported poor exercise habits (compared to 66.5 percent of this age group in 1978–79). This still leaves two out of five boomers with poor exercise habits. However, Wister says, on a positive note, "healthy exercise levels are at an all-time high" (122).

- Only 6.3 percent of mid-life Boomers reported heavy drinking in 2000–01. In 1978–79 13.8 percent of the same age group (35 to 54) reported heavy drinking.

Health Conditions

- Younger and older Boomers show decreases in arthritis compared to similar age groups in the past.

- Boomers show higher rates of chronic illness in 2000–01 compared to people of the same age in earlier studies. And "the increase is larger and more definitive for younger baby boomers than for older baby boomers" compared to people the same age in the past (126).

- Boomers show an increase in obesity compared to past cohorts of people in mid-life. In 2000–01, for example, Boomers had an obesity rate of 16.2 percent. But in 1985 people in this same age group had an obesity rate of only 8.2 percent. Wister notes that younger Boomers show the greatest "bulge in obesity rates" (123).

- Boomers show higher rates of hypertension than similar age groups in the past. Again, compared to older Boomers, younger Boomers show greater increases in hypertension.

- Baby Boomers show a 76.5 percent increase in diabetes compared to the same age group in 1978–79. Wister calls this "the most striking pattern in chronic illness in midlife" and an "alarming acceleration" (129).

Wister (2005, 180) notes one curious development in the health of the Baby Boomers. He cites Dr. Nicolas DiNubile, member of the American Academy of Orthopedic Surgeons, who calls this new health problem "*boomeritis*—the tendency for baby boomers to attempt to remain active but to overuse their bodies in doing so, resulting in musculoskeletal injury." Some boomers, it seems, work too hard at trying to stay young, and their aging bodies suffer injury from overuse and overwork.

Wister notes that in the United States MRIs and emergency room visits by Boomers have increased due to their overzealous workouts.

The findings from Wister's study show both improvements and decreases in health conditions among mid-life Boomers. Boomers show improvements in health habits and lifestyle but have higher rates of chronic illness than the same age group at earlier times. Wister points to a paradox: compared to midlife age groups in the past, Boomers report that they exercise more, but also show higher rates of obesity than former midlife groups. Wister suggests that changes in Canadian eating habits—more high-fat fast foods, more high-sugar soft drinks, and super-sized portions—lead to obesity. It appears that these eating habits cancel out the benefits of increased exercise.

The Boomer generation shows a complex pattern of both healthy and unhealthy lifestyle choices. This makes prediction of health in later life and health care system use "complex and unpredictable" (Wister 2005, 179). But the data clearly show that healthy behaviours earlier in life lead to better health and less chronic illness in old age.

Vaillant (2002), a supporter of successful aging, agrees. "The good news" he says, "is that most of us—if we start young and try hard—can voluntarily control our weight, our exercise, and our abuse of cigarettes and alcohol, at least by the time we are fifty. …Whether we live to a vigorous old age lies not so much in our stars or our genes as in ourselves" (Vaillant, 2002, 212–13). Schneider and Miles (2003, 1) say that, for adults, "behaviors and lifestyle account for a full 70 percent of how well you age."

The increase in the older population and the entry of the Baby Boom generation into later life make the study of successful aging more important than ever.

HEALTHY AGING: A CANADIAN PERSPECTIVE

Along with nonprofit organizations and researchers the Canadian government has turned its attention to healthy aging. Discussions on this topic have resulted in a Canadian vision of healthy aging. This definition takes a comprehensive view of health that includes physical, mental, social, and spiritual well-being. (Edwards and Mawani 2006). Healthy aging is "a lifelong process of optimizing opportunities for improving and preserving health and physical, social and mental wellness, independence, quality of life and enhancing successful life-course transitions" (Health Canada, 2002a).

The federal government sponsors national health promotion programs to support healthy aging. Programs offer exercise, fitness, and dietary advice. The Canadian

Health Network, for example, provides information through its website on active living, a healthy diet, and many other health promotion topics. The federal government also sponsors a home adaptation program. This program offers up to $3,500 in forgivable loans to people aged 65 and over who need to modify their homes to live comfortably (CMHC 2007). This program provides for installation of grab bars in bathrooms, handrails, and easy-to-reach storage cupboards.

The government provides support for healthy aging for at least two reasons. First, the people of Canada want to have programs that improve the lives of older people. Second, health promotion can delay and in some cases decrease the use of expensive health care services. For this reason everyone has an interest in supporting a good and healthy old age.

Wister (2005, 192) summarizes the literature on healthy aging. "One of the most simple but powerful messages [in the literature] is that infusing balance in one's lifestyle is pivotal to good health; that balancing stress and relaxation, activity, diet and eating habits, body and mind, individual responsibility, and awareness of barriers to changing health behaviours are all part of a healthy lifestyle. Such an approach is not automatic; it is learned and relearned through various interpersonal and institutional channels as we age."

CONCLUSION

People have tried to reverse or stop the process of aging at least since Ponce de Leon set out to find the fountain of youth. Drug companies have looked into the effects on aging of animal glands, sex hormones, and chemical therapies. Salons now offer Botox injections to erase facial wrinkles and other methods to create smoother-looking skin. These methods can make the skin softer or add water below the skin to temporarily smooth out wrinkles but do nothing to increase life expectancy or reverse aging.

Still, the search goes on. Scientists have explored many methods for increasing life span and extending youth. They have found that certain drugs, calorie-restricted diets, and lowered body temperatures (during hibernation) extend the lives of some animals in the laboratory.

Will any of these methods lead to a longer, healthier life for humans in the near future? Most biological researchers predict a slow increase in life expectancy in the next few years due to better health care, healthier lifestyles, and new medical technology. An end to cancer in Canada, for instance, could add a total of 12.9 years to the life expectancy of women who now have cancer. The estimated gain for men would be 11 years (Bélanger et al. 2002). The elimination of the most common causes of death would raise life expectancy for those born in 1981 to about 90 years for men and about 101 years for women (Statistics Canada 1989a). Nevertheless, these figures still do not approach the currently estimated human life span of 110 to 120 years.

Some scientists propose an even more optimistic scenario. Crews (1993, 288), for example, says that "the possibility of human life span extension is real and interventions that postpone human aging are a likely prospect." Rose (1993, 72), for example, says

> Given enough time and resource, there is no reason to doubt that eventually we will be able to postpone human aging, at least to some extent. … [T]here is the further possibility that increases in the human "health span" could likewise be open-ended. … [E]volutionarily postponed aging involves an enhancement in performance at later ages, not an extended period of debility. The long-term prospect, then, is more of an extension of youth than an increase in longevity, though the latter does occur.

Any of the following changes could increase the length of life and increase well-being in old age: the discovery and use of gene therapy, the use of human growth hormones, or genetic postponement of aging through natural selection. These changes would both extend the human life span and increase the number of healthy years people live.

But the technical ability to extend life may arrive before we have worked out the social effects of this change. For example, how would personal and social life differ if people lived on average for 120 years? How would this change our ideas about youth, middle age, and old age? Would retirement at age 65 make any sense? Could people afford to retire at that age and then live another 50 or more years? Would people adjust their life events (e.g., age of first marriage) and careers to meet this new condition?

Studies of people aged 100 years or older throughout the world give some clue about what a long-lived society would look like. Vogler (2006, p.47) says that centenarians serve as "a useful human model of disease-free or disease delayed aging." These studies report that long-lived people have good genes, a purpose in life, physical activity, independence, close family ties, friends, good hygiene, a simple balanced diet, low stress, good self-esteem, and religious faith (Wister and Wanless 2007). In other words, centenarians live balanced lives in supportive social settings.

These findings suggest that we should place the search for a full life where it belongs: within the power of each of us and the society we live in. We can and will extend life through scientific research and positive changes in our lifestyle and environments. But life extension will only put off the deeper question: Can we give meaning and purpose to those added years?

Summary

1. Chronic health problems increase with age. People with a low income have more health problems than those with a higher income.

2. Although women live longer than men, they also suffer from more chronic conditions and higher rates of disability. These conditions include hypertension, arthritis, and rheumatism.

3. Changes in health in turn lead to changes in a person's ability to function on his or her own. Declines in ability can lead to the need for help with activities of daily living.

4. Social and health care supports as well as a more supportive environment can help older people maintain their independence.

5. Technology can help people cope with declines in health. Simple objects such as spoons can be adapted for people with arthritis, computers can increase a person's contact with others, and in the future robots and computers may help people bathe, exercise, and perform daily tasks. Eyeglasses, hearing aids, and a supportive environment can make up for some losses in the senses.

6. The use of technology will improve the quality of life for people with disabilities. The Internet, well-designed household appliances, and robots in the future will make life richer, safer, and more comfortable for older people.

7. Older people today and in the future risk increased illness due to obesity. Obesity increases the risk of diabetes, heart disease, and other chronic and life-threatening illnesses. A sensible diet and exercise offer the best ways to combat this problem.

8. Stress reduction can play a role in creating a successful age. Methods include meditation, relaxation techniques, and spiritual retreats. Any or all of these methods can improve physical function and mental alertness.

9. Research shows that changes in smoking, diet, and exercise can slow the aging process. People can even improve their lung capacity and bone density through exercise. This can lead to a longer and healthier life.

10. The compression of morbidity hypothesis says that people will live longer and have more disability-free years in the future. Some research supports this hypothesis while other research suggests that a longer life may lead to more years of disability.

11. Many older people stay healthy and active as they age. They live without physical handicap and without special help. Studies of successful aging show that people can extend the number of years they live in good health. In the future, science may find a way for people to live past the current limits of the human life span.

12. A lifetime of inequality can lead to poor health in later life. The life course model of aging studies the connection between health early in life (as early as childhood) and health in old age. Those with good income and health earlier in life generally live a healthier old age.

13. Research on Baby Boomers finds that they engage in positive health behaviours and yet report more chronic health problems and obesity than past generations. It remains uncertain how these contradictory tendencies will influence Boomers' health in later life.

Study Questions

1. Describe the changes in health that often occur in later life. How does income affect health in old age? Do health changes differ for men and women?

2. What effects does physical decline have on activity in later life? What do older people need in order to maintain their independence? How can older people cope with physical change?

3. Describe three broad responses to physical aging that can improve or maintain physical well-being in later life. Discuss some of the problems that can limit useful responses to physical change. How could these problems be overcome?

4. State the compression of morbidity hypothesis. Briefly discuss research that supports and challenges this hypothesis.

5. Discuss Rowe and Kahn's model of successful aging. How can this research on successful aging expand our thinking about the potential for aging well in later life?

6. What scientific developments might extend the human life span in the future? What developments might expand the span of good health?

7. What are three models of successful aging? What does each of these models add to our understanding of later life?

8. What link do gerontologists find between health in youth and later life? What kind of studies would confirm this link?

Key Terms

activities of daily living (ADLs) activities performed daily, such as bathing, moving from a bed or chair, dressing, getting to and using the toilet, eating, and walking. (88)

chronic health problems　long-term illnesses such as arthritis, rheumatism, hypertension, diabetes, and heart disease. (87)

compression of morbidity hypothesis　the idea that severe chronic illness would occur for a short time near the end of life. (100)

dependence-free life expectancy　the number of years of remaining life that a person will live in a state free of dependence on others for daily tasks. (100)

disability-free life expectancy　the years of life remaining that are free of any disability. (99)

functional disability　a limitation in the performance of normal daily activities due to illness or injury. (87)

hypokinesia　physical problems due to lack of movement. (95)

instrumental activities of daily living (IADLs)　home management activities such as using the phone, cooking, shopping, managing finances, and doing light housework. (88)

life expectancy　the number of years at birth an average member of a population can expect to live. (83)

maximum life span　the maximum number of years a member of a species can live. (83)

rectangularization or **squaring to the survival curve**　the change over time in survival curves resulting in a right angle or square shape, leading researchers to conclude that a finite life span exists. (100)

successful aging　aging characterized by a low chance of disease and disability, high mental and physical functioning, and active engagement in social relations and productive activity. (101)

Selected Readings

Durdick, D., and S. Kwon (eds.). *Gerotechnology: Research and Practice in Technology and Aging.* New York: Springer, 2007.

　This book presents articles on how technology affects the lives of older people throughout the world. One section deals with the use of the Internet and its value as a source of information and communication. Another section describes how technology can improve home safety and make life easier for older people.

Haber, David. *Health Promotion and Aging: Practical Applications for Health Professionals*, 4th ed. New York: Springer, 2007.

　This book focuses on the U.S. context but it contains some good discussions of health promotion, doctor–patient collaboration, and health-related deceptions on the Internet. This book also discusses controversies over medical screenings, medical practice, and disease prevention. Chapters on exercise, nutrition, and obesity apply to Canada as well as the United States.

Masoro, Edward J., and Steven N. Austad, eds. *Handbook of the Biology of Aging* (6th ed.) Burlington, MA: Elsevier, 2006.

　This is a review of the latest findings in the field of biology and aging. Topics range from studies of cells to studies of physiological change in later life. Readers with little scientific background may find the chapters difficult to understand; still, this is an excellent resource for recent findings in the biology of aging.

National Advisory Council on Aging, ed. *Seniors and Technology.* Cat. No. 0-662-30932-4. Ottawa: Minister of Public Works and Government Services Canada, 2001.

This is a collection of well-written articles by gerontologists on topics related to seniors' use of technology. Articles range from a report on seniors' views of everyday technologies such as bank machines to a discussion of Internet and e-mail use. The essays show the attitudes of seniors toward new technologies (often ambivalent) and the benefits (such as reading assistance) that technology can bring to people as they age.

Websites to Consult

Active Living Coalition for Older Adults (ALCOA)

http://www.alcoa.ca/e/index.htm

The Active Living Coalition for Older Adults (ALCOA) strives to promote a society where older Canadians lead active lifestyles that contribute to their well-being.

Canadian Fitness and Lifestyle Research Institute (CFLRI)

http://www.cflri.ca

The CFLRI is a national research agency that works to educate Canadians about the importance of healthy, active lifestyles. Begun in September 1980, the institute receives grants from the Canadian government as well as other agencies. Its site provides data on health and wellness for people of all ages in Canada. It also offers access to publications related to fitness and health.

Inventory of Fall Prevention Initiatives in Canada—2005

http://www.phac-aspc.gc.ca/seniors-aines/pubs/fall_prevention_initiatives/fpi-on_e.htm#1

This site describes fall prevention programs throughout the country. Programs take place in universities and in a variety of health service units. The site gives the contact person and the website for each program. A good resource if you're researching falls prevention or want to learn more about a specific program in your part of the country.

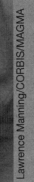

© Lawrence Manning/CORBIS/MAGMA

Chapter 6

The Psychology of Aging

INTRODUCTION

A few years ago, one of Canada's leading geriatric specialists gave a talk on memory to a group of seniors. He told the group that, in the absence of disease, changes in an older person's memory should cause no problems in everyday life. Young people and old people both forget things, he said, but older people notice it more because they expect memory loss to come with age. A man stood up at the end of the talk and said, "I respect your views, doctor. But I know my memory has gotten worse with age. What I want to know is what I can do about it."

This response fits with two things research has found out about older people and memory: first, a large proportion of older people believe they have memory problems and, second, memory failure upsets them, even if they forget something unimportant. People fear that memory loss could lead to a loss of independence (Park and Meade 2006). Some studies report that 40 percent of people aged 25 to 75 report memory problems at least once a week (Lachman 2000). McDougall (2000) says that people fear memory loss more than almost any other effect of aging.

Many people, older people included, accept the stereotype that cognitive decline is a normal part of aging. But recent research on memory, intelligence, and creativity questions this belief. Studies show that people can learn and grow intellectually in old age as well as in youth. On some measures, mental ability may decrease with age, but on other measures mental ability can improve. Dramatic declines in mental functioning are due to physiological disorders or distress, not to normal aging.

This chapter will look at (1) memory and intelligence in later life, (2) creativity, and (3) the psychological problems some older people face.

NORMAL CHANGES IN PSYCHOLOGICAL FUNCTIONING

The brain changes with age. The changes vary from person to person, but, in general, the brain shrinks in size, loses weight, and parts of the brain lose neurons (Albert and Killiany 2001; Vintners 2001). The brain also develops more abnormalities such as **neurofibrillary tangles**, which are neuronal fibres that wrap around one another. These tangles show up in healthy older brains and in greater numbers in cases of Alzheimer's disease (AD). Tangles appear to increase rapidly after age 70 (Vintners 2001). Albert and Killiany say that "changes in the brain are, at least in part, responsible for age-related declines in cognition" (163).

Still, research on the older brain shows that (1) changes in the brain take place gradually throughout life, (2) people lose more neurons in childhood than in healthy adulthood, (3) the nervous system has a remarkable ability to adapt to change, and (4) most neurons live through the entire life of the person and (5) the body creates new neurons even in later life. The stability and adaptability of the adult brain allow for continuity and growth at every age. Recent studies of learning, memory, and intelligence show the variety of changes that take place in mental functioning as people age.

LEARNING AND MEMORY

Psychologists define **memory** as the recall of information after learning has taken place. Most formal measurement of memory takes place in psychology laboratories. Psychologists in the field of aging have spent more time on the study of memory than on any other topic.

Psychologists show a strong interest in memory and aging for a number of reasons. First, popular stereotypes about aging and early psychological research on memory predict a decline in memory with age. If this is true, studies of memory can trace the causes of this decline. Second, psychologists can study memory in the laboratory under controlled conditions, making research on memory relatively easy. Third, studies of memory have produced testable models of how the mind works. These models attempt to explain complex processes such as learning, forgetting, and the storage and retrieval of information. Finally, the increasing numbers of people with Alzheimer's disease has led to greater public awareness (and fear) of memory loss. This has led researchers to look for the differences between normal and pathological changes in the brain in later life. Researchers, the public, and policymakers would all like to slow or reverse memory loss in old age. For all of these reasons, the study of memory dominates the study of psychological aging.

Researchers break the process of remembering into a series of steps. Most researchers today use an information-processing model to guide their work. The model includes the following steps: (1) a person perceives information, which psychologists call **sensory memory**; (2) the person acts on this information and transforms it in some way while the information sits in **short-term memory**; and (3) the person stores the information in **long-term memory**, the storehouse of knowledge that also includes the rules for applying knowledge.

Take the example of looking up and remembering a phone number. You open the phone book and see the number (sensory memory). You repeat it to yourself a few times as your eye moves from the phone book to the dial (short-term memory). You make a rhyme of the number so you can remember it later (long-term memory). The greatest mental work goes on when a person moves information into long-term memory.

Much of the research on memory and aging points to some decline in memory with age. What causes this decline? Research supports the idea of a "common cause" (Hoyer and Verhaeghen 2006, 219). Some studies point to declines in vision and hearing as the source of this decline. Hoyer and Verhaeghen (2006, 219) say that "sensory functioning is a strong late-life predictor of individual differences in cognitive function." Other studies show a decline with age in the functional integrity of the brain. Studies that look at processing speed link this general decline to decreased brain function.

Many studies show that older people take longer to learn new information, longer to search for it in memory, and longer to use it when they need it. For example, **latency** (the length of time a person takes to process information or make a response to a question) increases with age. Foisy (1995) reviewed 22 studies of word memory. He found that older people showed the greatest decline in memory on free-recall tests when they had the fewest cues from the environment. Older people showed the least decline in memory on recognition tests. Foisy says that free recall probably demands more processing resources; therefore, a decline in these resources with age would account for the findings.

Madden (2001, 289) says that "slowing is a fundamental dimension of age-related change in cognitive function." Such findings point to the link between decreased brain structure and function and mental ability (Kramer et al. 2006).

Park (2000) uses an analogy to explain changes in mental function in later life. Think of the older mind as a computer, he says, with a large store of memory in the hard drive, but with limited random access memory. This computer will have limited memory function and will process information slowly. The processing capacity cannot make efficient use of the large store of memory. "The computer works, but perhaps a little less efficiently than one would like" (5).

Hundreds of studies have tried to sort out the effects of age on memory. In particular, the research has focused on differences in learning (acquisition and recall) between younger and older subjects. Psychologists believe that acquisition and retrieval are closely related. How someone retrieves information (how they search for and find information in memory) depends on how

they acquired it (the methods they used to organize and store the information).

Laboratory Studies

Bäckman, Small, and Wahlin (2001) say that decline in memory occurs in both **non-episodic memory** (information oriented toward the present or the future with no reference to the time at which it was acquired, such as general knowledge of the world) and **episodic memory** (memory acquired at a specific time and place, such as the recall of words memorized from a list). Much of the laboratory research on memory looks at episodic memory, which depends largely on recollection (Hoyer and Verhaeghen, 2006). The decline in episodic memory begins earlier in adulthood than most people think and continues steadily with age (Bäckman et al. 2000). Episodic memory shows a greater decline with age than other types of memory.

Some laboratory studies have found deficits in memory in older people due to the way they learn and store information. Perfect and Dasgupta (1997) studied recall in younger and older subjects. They found that older adults recalled less than younger adults on psychological tests. They traced this difference to **encoding** (the process whereby a person puts new bits of information together with already stored information). The older adults said they could not think of encoding strategies or they used less elaborate encoding. Perfect and Dasgupta believe that encoding, rather than retrieval, accounts for the lower recall rate in older adults.

Speeded trials appear to increase the learning deficit. More than the young, older subjects miss verbal and pictorial items presented at a rapid rate. They miss late items in a list more than earlier ones, and they encode some items at the expense of others. Kramer and colleagues (2006, 59) say that slowed processing has a "cascading effect on information processing."

This research suggests that memory decline in older adults may be due in part to the use of inefficient processing techniques. Light (1990), for example, traces memory differences between older and younger people to deficits in the older person's **working memory**. Working memory stores recent information and also manipulates this information. In addition, it processes new information while temporarily storing other information (Hoyer and Verhaeghen, 2006).

First, studies of working memory find that older adults remember less well when irrelevant information comes between two things to be remembered (Light and Capps 1986). Second, older adults have more difficulty remembering and making sense of the information when the material they have to remember comes in a scrambled order (Light et al. 1982). Third, the ability to remember decreases when the load on working memory increases. For example, changes in topics place a greater load on working memory and lead to poorer memory in older people. When a topic changes, older people appear to forget relevant information. Decreased processing efficiency leads to poorer working memory in older people.

Kramer and colleagues (2006) report that older people have trouble ignoring irrelevant stimuli (information or sounds), and this leads to decreased mental performance. Gazzaley and colleagues (2005) studied the impact of irrelevant information on the working memory of healthy, well-educated younger and older people (aged 19 to 30 and 60 to 77 respectively). They presented the subjects with pictures of faces and outdoor scenes. They instructed groups to ignore the faces or the scenes or to take a passive approach. The researchers studied the brain activity of the two groups and found that people in the older group had trouble ignoring irrelevant stimuli (faces or scenes). This led to decreased short-term memory of relevant information. The researchers conclude that attention deficit may underlie some of the observed decline in memory. Bäckman and his colleagues (2000) say that this decline in working memory increases in late old age. Craik (2000, 82) says "it is clear that older adults have particular problems in situations where they must hold, manipulate, and integrate moderate amounts of information over short time spans."

Kramer and colleagues (2006, 59) say that processing speed "can often account for a large proportion of age-related variance across a wide assortment of tasks and environments." For example, he notes that due to decreased processing speed an earlier task slows a later activity (e.g., if someone needs to keep some figures in memory, this will inhibit later decision-making speed). Slower processing accounts for the loss of information from an earlier task as a person performs a more recent task (e.g., a person may forget figures held in memory while he or she tries to make a decision). Kramer and colleagues (2006, 59) say that processing speed "can often account for a large proportion of age-related variance across a wide assortment of tasks and environments."

But processing speed alone does not explain age-related changes in mental activity. Hartley (2006) reviewed the research on speed of processing and its effect on mental function in later life. He concludes that research does not support a single cause (like decreased speed of processing) as the explanation for age-related changes in mental function. At best, he says, a few causes might underlie the changes that psychologists find. These could include changes in executive functions (like switching between tasks or maintaining focus on a task), loss in working memory systems, changes in neurochemistry, or changes in the brain structure (decreases in white matter).

Physical Change as the Source of Mental Decline

Psychologists look at brain structure and function as a source of mental decline in later life. Cerella (1990, 201), for example, proposes that deficits in mental functioning (such as memory) may be "distributed throughout the information-processing system rather than being localized in particular stages." He proposes that breakdowns in the older person's neural network lead to slower processing of information. Each breakdown in the network requires the input to travel a greater distance. The older the person, the greater the neural decay and the slower the processing time. This not only explains the general slowing phenomenon, but also indicates why older people do less well on tests that emphasize speed. It also accounts for why older people may do as well as younger people on skilled tasks because these tasks use well-established neural networks. This model offers a simple explanation that replaces the many explanations related to specific tasks (such as storage and retrieval).

Recent work supports the idea that changes in the brain lead to cognitive decline. Kramer and colleagues (2006, 65) report losses of gray and white matter in the brain. They go on to say that losses in prefrontal gray matter correlate with reduced performance on "frontally mediated executive tasks." They conclude that changes in brain structure over time (e.g., atrophy of sections of the brain) predict declines in cognitive performance. Small (Columbia News 2008) reports changes in the hippocampus, a part of the brain that serves as a gatekeeper for information. The hippocampus processes information and creates long-term memory, and shows declines in function with age. Small and colleagues use MRI technology to map blood flow to the brain and pinpoint the exact location of functional decline. Hartley (2006, 191; also Salthouse and Caja, 2000) says that differences in processing speed may be due to "a general reduction in the functional intactness of the central nervous system."

Raz (2000) reviewed the research on the relationships between mental performance and neural activity in the brain. In a number of studies researchers asked older and younger adults to take a variety of memory tests (including some that required encoding). The researchers then compared the brain activity of older and younger subjects. They found that, compared to younger people, older people showed less activation or no activation in certain parts of the brain during these tests. Younger and older subjects' brain function also differed when they worked on harder verbal recall tasks. More work on brain function will attempt to describe the neural sources of memory changes that come with age (Prull, Gabrieli, and Bunge 2000).

Arnsten and colleagues (2008) at Yale University focus their research on the chemicals that influence brain function. They focus on the prefrontal cortex, the site of higher brain functions like memory. They report that the disruption of chemical pathways—particularly the function of catecholamines norepinephrine (NE) and dopamine (DA)—leads to declines in prefrontal cortex function. This leads to attention deficits and shows up as a decline in working memory.

Recent work reported from the Berlin Aging Study also points to physical change as a source of cognitive decline. Lindenberger and Baltes (1994; also Valentijn et al., 2005) propose that sensory decline serves as a measure of brain integrity and has a strong impact on all cognitive abilities. They found that declines in visual and auditory ability explained nearly all age-related declines on a series of psychological tests. Further research by this team controlled for education, social class, and income. They still found declines in cognition based on sensory decline. They say that this points to "a common factor or ensemble of factors"—the decrease in the brain's structural and functional integrity.

Researchers admit that current knowledge has just begun to trace the link between the brain's function and mental performance. The sixth edition of the *Handbook of the Psychology of Aging* (Birren and Schaie, 2006) contains reviews of the literature on brain function and mental performance. Psychologists have also studied genetics, cellular function, and brain physiology to understand mental performance. These studies show the growing interest among psychologists in the effects of biology and physiology on mental functioning.

The Limits of Laboratory Research on Memory

Other causes besides physical aging account for the differences in memory between older and younger people found in laboratory studies. Differences in educational background and verbal ability, for example, influence results in memory research. Cavanaugh (1983) studied the recall of TV show content and found that when subjects had low verbal ability, older people recalled less than younger people. But when younger subjects and older subjects both had high verbal ability, the study showed no difference between the scores of the two age groups.

Test conditions can also influence older subjects' performance on memory tests. Researchers report that a supportive context improved older subjects' ability to learn paired words. Supports can include guidance on how to encode information, prior knowledge of a topic, practice, or external cues to help learning (Carstensen et al., 2006; Zacks, Hasher, and Li 2000). The design of memory tests, their content, and the use of cross-sectional designs (that compare older and younger people at one point in time) may all lead to exaggerated findings of memory decline in older people.

Some studies show that an older person's fear of failure on memory tests leads to poor performance. Researchers call this "stereotype threat" (Hess, 2006). Rahhal and colleagues (2001), for example, found that test instructions that focus on memory make people aware of declines in mental ability, and this can lower a person's score. Hess (2006, 394) reports that "differences in performance were essentially eliminated" when test instructions said positive things about aging and memory.

Laboratory studies raise an important question: How well do the results of memory research predict an older person's ability to remember details in everyday life? The answer: not very well. Memory studies done under laboratory conditions have poor ecological validity (the transferability of knowledge from lab to life) (Park and Gutchess 2000). Older people rarely learn or recall well under pressure, and research shows that they remember best when they learn information relevant and useful to them.

The Contextual Approach

The **contextual view of memory** begins with the insight that many conditions influence memory, including "the physical, psychological, and social context in which the event was experienced, the knowledge, abilities, and characteristics the individual brings to the context, [and] the situation in which we ask for evidence of remembering" (Hultsch and Deutsch 1981, 153).

In his early work Charness (1981, 1985) reported on a study of younger and older chess players' problem-solving abilities. He found that older players had more difficulty than younger players at the same skill level in recalling positions accurately. He attributes this difficulty to older players' poorer retrieval ability. But when Charness evaluated game-playing performance, he found that skill level, not age, determined a player's ability. Older players did as well as younger players of the same skill level. "Given the retrieval deficits associated with aging," Charness asks, "why is there no deficit in molar [overall] problem-solving performance?" (1981, 34–35).

Mireles and Charness (2002) in a later study used a neural network model to measure chess performance in the laboratory. They found that in a chess recall task people with a larger knowledge base achieved more accuracy on the recall task. The researchers say that pre-existing knowledge can overcome the effects of systemic slowing due to neural noise.

More recent work by Phillips and colleagues (2006) supports these earlier studies. Phillips and her colleagues studied two groups of 39 subjects each. One group, aged 22 to 31, had a mean age of 24.8. The second group, aged 60 to 80, had a mean age of 69.5. The researchers asked each group to engage in two computerized tasks: one, a traditional laboratory task, entailed abstract planning, and the second, a planning task, entailed running a number of errands in a made-up situation with specific constraints. The researchers found, as expected, a decline in performance based on age for the abstract planning task. But the researchers found no relationship between age and performance on the more ecologically valid errand-planning task. The researchers conclude that a decrease in information processing speed and education account for the decrease in performance by the older subjects on the abstract task. They say that task-related knowledge and experience helped older subjects compensate for decreases in processing speed in the errand-planning exercise. In other words, in real-life situations older people draw on their experience and can perform as well as younger people.

Allen and colleagues (2006) report a number of studies that support a process-specific effect of aging on mental activity. They find that while complex problems lead to poorer performance by older workers, this applies to only some tasks. On tasks that have to do with word recognition, for example, older people do as well or better than younger people. These researchers report similar findings for math problems—probably because older people have a lifetime of experience with arithmetic. The researchers conclude that some mental processes decline with age while others remain stable. "Therefore," they say, "the aging process is not comprised simply of cognitive decline." Analyses of specific mental processes "opens the possibility for interventions to help older adults compensate in domains that do show age-related decline" (591).

Studies of prospective memory (the ability to remember something to be done in the future) find similar results. These studies find that older people can outperform younger people. For example, older people do better at remembering to carry out a task like mailing back a postcard or telephoning the researcher in the future. Hoyer and Verhaeghen (2006) say that after years of experience older people may use external devices to assist their memory. Park and Meade (2006) say that a person who needs to remember to take medication may chain that activity to another routine. For example, he or she may take the medication routinely at breakfast or just before bed. Liu and Park (2004) found that people who linked the process of monitoring their blood sugar level to breakfast, for example, increased the accuracy of their monitoring. Park and Meade say that studies of everyday memory need to take into account the person, the demands of the task (e.g., is it a new task or a routine task), and the environment.

In sum, research supports the idea that causes other than biological decline can influence mental performance in older people. Research shows that different types of older people (with more or less education or skill), under a variety of conditions (supportive or non-supportive context), and exposed to varying types of materials to learn (relevant or irrelevant), differ in their ability to perform mental tasks or to remember specific information. Dixon and Cohen (2001) say that **competence** (a person's skill at real-world tasks) can influence performance on mental tasks, and that competence can improve with age. They go on to say that older people often show more competence in real-world tasks than psychological tests measure. Competent older people draw on experience and use strategies (such as selecting only the information they need) to succeed in mental tasks (Smith 2006).

Some studies have looked directly at what older people remember about the world around them. These studies have found less of the memory deficit reported in laboratory research. Craik (2000; also Hoyer and Verhaeghen, 2006) reports that **semantic memory**, the store of factual information, shows little decline with age. For example, older and younger people show little difference in general-knowledge questions on IQ tests. The more repeated and familiar the knowledge, the better the older person's memory. Older people have a good memory for past personal events (Zacks, Hasher, and Li 2000). Hoyer and Verhaeghen (2006, 216) say that "older adults do not show a deficit on [vocabulary] tasks, but rather an advantage …" They go on to say that "vocabulary measures probably underestimate the breadth and depth of knowledge and development of word meanings and language accumulated through years of experience and use." Longitudinal studies support these findings. Only after age 90 do decreases in word knowledge appear. The more automatic the recall (for example, driving a car in a person's own neighbourhood), the better the older person will perform (Park and Gutchess 2000).

The ability to accumulate knowledge and draw on it increases through adulthood. Older people who maintain their cognitive abilities may put more effort into a task, they may call on a past skill, or they may develop a new skill. Carstensen and colleagues (2006, 344) say that "such expertise can even offset cognitive decline."

The research reported to date should end the stereotyping of older people as forgetful. Studies report compensation for decline, positive effects of physical exercise on memory, and benefits from training. Bugos and colleagues (2007), for example, found that sensory-motor training (learning to play the piano) led to significantly improved mental function. Other studies show that social engagement leads to improved mental ability (Stine-Morrow et al. 2007).

Research also shows that the use of memory aids (such as the use of a notebook) can significantly improve memory performance. Park (2000, 11) says that "environmental supports" lead to improved recall. For example, an older person will do better on a multiple-choice test (with all the possible answers displayed) than on a free-recall test with no cues. Supports reduce the amount of mental processing or resource use. And this leads to better recall.

Bäckman and his colleagues (2000) summarize the literature on memory and aging. They say that "no form of memory appears to be fully resistant to the negative influence of human aging. Thus, age-related deficits may be observed in tasks assessing implicit memory … semantic memory … primary memory … working memory … and episodic memory…. However it is important to note that the size of age-related deficits and the consistency with which such deficits are observed varies systematically across different forms of memory. Specifically, age deficits tend to be *large and robust for measures of episodic memory and working memory, smaller and more contingent on demand characteristics in tasks assessing implicit and semantic memory, and even smaller in primary memory tasks*" (501, emphasis added).

The researchers go on to say that memory in old age varies by individual (education level), lifestyle (social activity), and health. Some people show greater decreases in memory than do others. Also, research shows that older people have a reserve mental capacity. Studies show that people can improve memory performance by using memory cues and by training. Salthouse and Craik (2000) say that researchers should look at ways that older people can put off the declines that come with age and "optimize [their] mental capacities" (701).

INTELLIGENCE

The research on intelligence in old age parallels the research on memory. Early studies assumed that intelligence decreases in old age as the body declines. More recent research questions this simple connection between senescence and intelligence.

Psychologists use at least two definitions of **intelligence**. First, taking a global view, they refer to it as the "ability to negotiate environmental demands successfully" (Labouvie-Vief 1985, 506). Second, they take a pragmatic view, referring to it as "that which intelligence tests measure" (506) or what a person taking a test can do now. Psychologists most often use this second (more limited) definition when they conduct research on intelligence and aging.

Early research done in the 1930s reported a decline in intellectual ability after age 20 (Jones and Conrad 1933; Miles and Miles 1932; Wechsler 1939). These findings supported the idea that mental ability declines along with the body, and IQ tests build this expectation of decline into their design. They assume that older people will score less well than younger people, and they correct for supposed age declines in their formulas for calculating IQ. The Wechsler Adult Intelligence Scale (WAIS-R) manual uses this approach. It puts the peak of intelligence at between 20 and 34 years (Wechsler 1981) and assumes that each later age group will show a decline in scores.

The actual scores on WAIS-R scales reported by Wechsler (1981) support this assumption of decline with age, but they also show that decline does not take place uniformly. Scores on the WAIS-R Verbal Scale, for example, decreased steadily from a mean score of 61.42 at ages 25 to 34 to a mean of 51.50 at ages 70 to 74 (84 percent of the younger group's score). Scores on the Performance Scale dropped earlier and more sharply from 51.14 at ages 20 to 24 to a mean score of 30.62 at ages 70 to 74 (60 percent of the younger group's score) (Wechsler 1981, 26).

Other cross-sectional studies of intelligence show a similar pattern of decline in some abilities and less decline in others. Researchers argue over the meaning of these findings, disagreeing on at least three issues: (1) the concept of intelligence as a single structure, (2) the methods used to produce these findings, and (3) the potential for cognitive functioning in later life.

Intelligence as Multidimensional

Current research on intelligence supports a multidimensional view of intelligence. For example, the Performance Scale scores show a much greater decrease with age than the Verbal Scale scores (40 percent versus 16 percent). "This classic aging pattern, relative maintenance of function in verbal skills as compared to performance skills, has been seen many times with a variety of different populations" (Botwinick 1984, 254). A cross-sectional study by Park and colleagues (2002) showed the same results. The study found decreases in working memory, short-term memory, long-term memory, and processing speed in each older age group. But verbal knowledge showed stability across all age groups. People in their 80s, for example, showed scores on verbal knowledge similar to that of 50-year-olds and better than those of 20- and 30-year-olds. These findings support the idea that older people may lose some abilities, but remain stable or improve on others.

Horn and Cattell (1966, 1967) developed a model of intelligence, still in use today, that explains these results. They describe two types of intelligence—fluid intelligence and crystallized intelligence. **Fluid intelligence** refers to reasoning, abstracting, concept formation, and problem solving. It makes little use of knowledge gained through reading, schooling, or work. Fluid intelligence relies on how well the physical and nervous systems function. Performance tests that demand the use of fluid intelligence ask subjects to manipulate unfamiliar material in new ways mentally, and they sometimes require skill at manipulating objects physically. **Crystallized intelligence** refers to the use of stored information, acculturation, and learning Verbal tests, such as a test of vocabulary or historical events, demand the use of crystallized intelligence.

This two-part model helps explain the empirical results on intelligence. Numerical and verbal skill problems measure crystallized intelligence; spatial and reasoning questions measure fluid intelligence. Fluid intelligence may follow the decline of the biological system from the teen years on, while studies of crystallized intelligence show stable intelligence scores and even increases in scores with age (Park 2000; Kramer et al., 2006).

Longitudinal versus Cross-Sectional Methods

Like studies of memory, most studies of intelligence use a cross-sectional method to draw conclusions about age changes. These studies ignore the fact that older and younger cohorts differ on more variables than just age. Few studies of intelligence have looked at the variability among individuals (differences such as educational level, social class, personal experience) in their samples. Age cohorts differ in education, test-taking ability, and vocabulary. These characteristics depend on when people were born and what they have done in their lifetimes.

When intelligence tests are used to compare different age groups at one point in time, they can lead us to mistake cohort differences for differences due to aging. Schaie and Hofer (2001; also Hofer and Sliwinski, 2006) say that cross-sectional studies "provide a very poor basis for inference" about how age affects changes in an individual's mental functioning.

Longitudinal and sequential studies of intelligence try to overcome this problem by measuring the same groups of people at more than one point in time. Most longitudinal studies find less decline in intelligence with age than do cross-sectional studies. Schaie (1990, 114) studied one group over time and found that "virtually none of the individuals … showed universal decline on all abilities monitored, even by the eighties." By age 60, he reports, three-quarters of the people in the study maintained their ability over a seven-year period on four of five measures. Even at age 81, more than half the sample maintained its ability over a seven-year period. These findings support the idea that each person shows unique changes in mental ability with age. They also show that mental abilities change at different rates. Some abilities may decline steadily. Others stay stable over time. Mental stimulation may protect the brain from decline. Or it may help the brain compensate for losses in some abilities (Snowdon, 2001; Mobbs 2006). A sudden decline in ability may signal disease or trauma rather than an age-related decline (Hofer and Sliwinski, 2006).

Critics of these conclusions say that decline takes place over time whatever method researchers use. Longitudinal studies, for example, play down the effects of age on intelligence because people with low intelligence scores drop out of the studies, leaving more intelligent people at older ages. The longer the study and the greater the number of tests on the subjects who remain, the more the dropout factor affects the results.

The debate over the effects of age on intelligence continues in the literature. Future research will focus on the causes of differences in intelligence within different age groups and between different age cohorts.

Improvements in Cognitive Functioning in Later Life

The research on memory and intelligence shows variation in mental changes in later life. Different abilities change at different rates and older individuals differ in their mental abilities. Some older people perform as well as younger people on psychological tests, while other older people show a decline in ability. In their study of memory, Gazzaley and colleagues (2005, 1300) found that, compared to younger people, older people had trouble suppressing irrelevant information.

which impaired their memory. But, the researchers say, "Encouragingly, a subgroup of the older population with preserved suppression also demonstrated intact working memory performance, reflecting the variable impact of the aging process …" This suggests that older people can improve their memory through training.

Some research on intelligence explores ways to improve older people's intellectual functioning. Charness and Campbell (1988) tested young, middle-aged, and older people's mental calculation skills. They found that older adults gained skill in calculation in the same way that younger adults did. The older group showed "marked improvement" in their ability with practice (127). And they equalled the starting level of the youngest group before the end of the study. The researchers conclude that the older group's improvement "is testimony to the malleability of the human information processing system, even in old age" (1128). This research shows that older people can improve their performance on intelligence tests. Instruction in test-taking methods and in problem-solving strategies can improve the cognitive performance of older subjects. Schaie (2006) reports on a 14-year longitudinal study of intelligence in older people. The study found that 40 percent of the people in the study who took training showed a reversal in intellectual decline. Another 25 percent showed a reduction in decline. Many other people in the study showed stable performance.

A study done by Kramer and colleagues (2006) supports these findings. In a review of studies on cognitive training, they say that in some cases "older adults can achieve greater gains from formal cognitive training interventions than their younger counterparts." Meyer and Pollard (2006) taught older readers how to recognize the structure of a text and how to use the signals writers give to readers. In one case, a 66-year-old woman improved her recall by using these techniques. Meyer and Pollard (2006, 246) say "she more than doubled her ability to remember information from her reading." This woman went on to teach this strategy to others over the next six years. During that time "she maintained her mastery of the strategy and high level of text recall."

Studies show that people who have good health and who live in a challenging environment score better on intelligence tests than those who do not (Gold et al. 1995). People who read books and newspapers and who travel and talk with friends keep their minds fresh. Researchers now think of the individual as modifiable.

Baltes (1997, cited in Norris 1998, ii; also George, 2006), has developed a model of mental development in later life that he calls "**selective optimization and compensation**" (**SOC**). He says that people who age well select tasks that will likely lead to success. They keep up (or optimize) the skills they have, and they compensate for losses by gaining new skills.

The SOC model recognizes that aging brings change, but it also shows that people can adapt to changes and improve their mental ability as they age. Riediger and colleagues (2006, 296, 300) say that "people themselves influence their development within the range of available opportunities." They refer to this as "active life management."

Hoyer and Verhaeghen (2006) propose several methods for improving memory as a person ages. These include memory training, an enriched environment, and fitness training. The researchers report on a summary of 18 studies that show a strong effect of fitness training on the improvement of memory including speed of processing (Colcombe & Kramer, 2003). Aerobic conditioning, for example, leads to improvement in simple and complex mental tasks. Conditioning improves complex tasks the most (Kramer et al. 2006). Kramer and colleagues (2006) find that exercise leads to improvements in the brain that include neuronal survival, the growth of new connections between neurons, and the growth of new capillaries in the brain. "The end result of exercise training then is a brain that is more plastic and adaptive to change and more able to survive the vagaries of the aging process" (Kramer et al. 2006, 76).

New Models of Mental Ability in Later Life

Traditional models of aging tend to view life as a hill. The assume that ability increases over time, plateaus, then and declines. But, Schroots (1995) says, this view has begun to change.

First, research shows variability between individuals. In general, younger people outperform older people on memory and intelligence tests. But, on a given measure, some older people perform better than younger people. Second, research shows **plasticity** (the ability to change and adapt) for each individual. Each person has a reserve mental capacity. Researchers have found plasticity in brain function, in personality change, and in skill development. Training, practice, and education can enhance this ability to grow in later life

Dixon and Cohen (2001, 138) say that these findings offer a "cautiously optimistic perspective, with emphases on resilience and adaptation in late life." Baltes (1992, 1993) concludes that past research has taken too narrow a view of mental ability in old age. He says that certain types of cognitive processes, what he calls **cognitive mechanics** (the information-processing mechanisms that implement fluid intelligence), decline with age. Other types of cognitive processes, what he calls **cognitive pragmatics** (the culture- and knowledge-related applications of intelligence, similar to crystallized intelligence), improve with age (Li et al. 2004). Baltes says that knowledge and culture can enrich cognitive pragmatics throughout life.

Research on decision making supports this view. Marsiske and Margrett (2006, 317) say that older adults think beyond purely rational solutions to a problem. "In the real world … individuals also consider their own preferences, values, and feelings as well as those of their social partners and cultural context." For example, older adults used both emotional and action-oriented coping strategies in problem solving. The researchers say that this attention to the complexity of life shows a higher order of thinking than purely rational problem solving.

Baltes set out to explore the "new domain" of cognitive pragmatics in old age. To do this he set up the Berlin Aging Study. This project studied **wisdom** in later life. The project defines wisdom as "a highly valued and outstanding expert knowledge about dealing with fundamental—that is, existential—problems related to the meaning and conduct of life" (Kunzmann 2006, 1232). Older people who display wisdom appear more skilled in everyday life. Skills include "life planning, life management, and life review" (Dixon 2000, 32). (See Exhibits 6.1 and 6.2). Society could use this broad perspective and flexible thinking to redefine problems that escape rational and technical solutions. Baltes and his colleagues study wisdom by asking older people to solve real-life problems. One problem, for example, asked people to respond to a suicidal call from a friend. Another asks: "A 15-year-old girl want to get married right away. What could one consider and do?" (Kunzmann 2006).

Baltes and his colleagues found that expressions of wisdom could occur from the teen years onward. In a review of the research, Brugman (2006, 449) reports that "in most empirical studies thus far no age differences [between younger and older people] have been found." Some researchers propose that wisdom exists as a "potential" in later life, with only some people realizing this potential.

● **Exhibit 6.1**

SOME CRITERIA FOR WISDOM

Psychologist Paul Baltes compiled a list of five criteria for wisdom based on cognitive psychology and life-span theory. A person who had this knowledge would have "exceptional insight into life matters and good judgment and advice about difficult life problems."

1. Rich factual knowledge about life matters.

2. Rich procedural knowledge about life problems.

3. Life-span contextualism: Knowledge about the contexts of life and their temporal (developmental) relationships.

4. Relativism: Knowledge about differences in values and priorities.

5. Uncertainty: Knowledge about the relative indeterminacy and unpredictability of life and ways to manage.

Dr. Gene Cohen gives further insight into the wisdom that can develop with age. He calls the growth of wisdom in later life **"developmental intelligence."** He considers this an "advanced style of cognition." His concepts echo those of Baltes. Cohen describes three "styles" that characterize this type of thinking:

1. Relativistic thinking: an awareness that context can affect knowledge and understanding. An awareness that knowledge is not absolute.

2. Dualistic thinking: the ability to suspend judgment while trying to resolve contradictions. The ability to hold mutually exclusive ideas in the mind at the same time.

3. Systematic thinking: the ability to take a broad view of a situation or a system of knowledge.

Source: P.B. Baltes, J. Smith, U.M. Staudinger, and D. Sowarka, 1990, "Wisdom: One Facet of Successful Aging?" in M. Perlmutter, ed., *Late Life Potential,* 63–81, Washington, DC: Gerontological Society of America. Reprinted with permission of the Gerontological Society of America, 2000; G.D. Cohen, 2005, *The Mature Mind: The Positive Power of the Aging Brain,* New York: Basic Books, 36–37.

● Exhibit 6.2

WISDOM IN LATER LIFE

In Plato's Republic, Socrates, says that he likes to talk to older people because they have gone along a path that all of us will one day follow. So they have a unique perspective on life and aging; some might call it wisdom. Consider the following thoughts on aging by some thoughtful older people.

Art Blake, a retired judge from Jamaica, says that he recently attended the funeral of a friend. He flew back to Jamaica and went directly to the church from the airport. He reached the church before anyone else. "I watched as the people arrived," he says. "Many of them I knew from my childhood, we went to school and grew up together. These are all old people, I thought. Then I thought, I too must look like this. But I couldn't see it in myself. I shave everyday and I don't see my age. But I could see it in them ... The mind plays tricks on you."

Art serves as the legal adviser to an education program for older people and sits on the advisory board of a university certification program. "We want to be young," Art says. "We use creams to smooth out the wrinkles. But this is the most natural process. We cannot help but get old."

Bertrand Russell developed new interests as he aged. He began his career as a mathematician, moved on to philosophy, then in late old age he turned to political and social issues. At age 80, he said

The best way to overcome it [old age]—so at least it seems to me—is to make your interests gradually wider and more impersonal, until bit by bit the walls of the ego recede, and your life becomes increasingly merged in the universal life. An individual human existence should be like a river—small at first, narrowly contained within its banks, and rushing passionately past boulders and over waterfalls. Gradually the river grows wider, the banks recede, the waters flow more quietly, and in the end, without any visible break, they become merged in the sea and painlessly lose their individual being (quoted in Puner 1979, 270).

John Holt, an educator who wrote about children and their untapped potential, turned to reflect on education for adults later in his career. Holt took up the cello in late middle age. In his book *Never Too Late* (Holt 1978, 185), he wrote about his experience learning the instrument and about his own potential as a person:

If I could learn to play the cello well, as I thought I could, I could show by my own example that we all have greater powers than we think; that whatever we want to learn or learn to do, we probably can learn; that our lives and our possibilities are not determined and fixed by what happened to us when we were little, or by what experts say we can or cannot do.

The researchers conclude that wisdom develops in later life under certain conditions. A person's openness to experience, the presence of role models, and a time of societal transition all foster the development of wisdom. Academic knowledge does not automatically lead to wisdom as Baltes and his colleagues define it. But, Kunzmann (2006, 1233) says, "an interest in understanding and helping others, and social-emotional competencies such as empathic concern seem to be more important." Some research shows that people can express wisdom given the right conditions. One study had participants discuss a difficult life problem with a person they often confided in. This type of discussion significantly increased the participants' display of wisdom. These studies shows that "many adults have

the latent potential to perform better on wisdom tasks than they actually do." This research shows that practice, coaching, and training can bring out a person's latent abilities.

CREATIVITY

The bulk of research on psychology and aging has focused on changes in memory and intelligence with age. Comparatively few studies have looked at creativity in later life. The word "creativity," for example, does not appear in the subject index of the *Handbook of the Psychology of Aging* (Birren and Schaie 2006). At least three different measures of creativity exist in the literature. First, some studies measure creative achievement by evaluating the greatness of a work or by counting the number of creative works by an individual. Other studies use a more global definition of creativity: fulfillment to the individual and possibly even to others (though it might not reach worldwide or historical importance). Studies done from each point of view have looked at whether creativity declines with age.

Creativity as Measured by Great Works

Lehman (1953) conducted the classic work in this field. He studied the ages at which scientists, philosophers, mathematicians, painters, inventors, and other creative people produced their greatest works. He selected for his sample people who had already died (because someone still alive could still produce a great work). Lehman found that most past and present scientists produced their greatest creative work between the ages of 30 and 40. Most great writers produced their foremost work before the age of 45, and most poets produced theirs in their late 20s and early 30s. Painters peaked between ages 30 and 45. In most fields, Lehman found that achievement steadily decreased after age 45.

Lehman (1968) went on to study athletes, chess champions, orators, politicians, businessmen, and atomic scientists. He found that still-living atomic scientists, for example, showed a peak in achievement between ages 25 to 29 and a sharp drop in achievement from age 35 on. He also found that older atomic scientists (aged 60 to 64) made only one-tenth the number of contributions as the younger scientists (25- to 29-year-olds). Lehman found the same pattern for still-living astronomers, mathematicians, and botanists.

Lehman's research set off a wave of controversy. Dennis (1968), for example, challenged Lehman's conclusions about the decline in creativity with age. First, he said, Lehman's research combined people with different lengths of life. Fewer people live to old age, so there will be fewer people to create great works in later life. Lehman's findings, therefore, might reflect a demographic fact rather than a decline in creativity. Second, Dennis questioned Lehman's approach to the study of creativity. Lehman used the works of critics, historians, and experts to decide on the quality of his subjects' work. Dennis argued that experts may favour the early, groundbreaking work of great people and could find it harder to judge more recent work by a great master.

Dennis (1968) used a measure different from Lehman's to compensate for these errors. First, while Lehman studied the age when creators produced their greatest work, Dennis studied the creative output (the number of works produced) of 738 people. Second, he selected long-lived subjects, all of whom had lived past age 78, to control for the effects of mixed longevities.

Dennis measured the output of a variety of creative people: artists, scientists, scholars, and dancers. He found that each group produced the least amount of work in their 20s. In almost all fields, creativity (measured by output) peaked between ages 40 and 49, about 10 years later than Lehman's finding. Dennis, like Lehman, found that people in different fields peaked at different ages. Artists (dramatists, librettists, architects) peaked earliest and showed the sharpest decline in their 70s. Dennis found that scientists also experienced declines in middle age, but they showed a sharp decline only after age 60. Scholars showed little decline with age. They produced as much in their 70s as in their 40s, and they added to their former number of books by 25 percent between ages 70 and 79.

Dennis's work expands on Lehman's, rather than contradicting it. Dennis shows that differences in the peak age of creativity may depend as much on the social structure of a discipline as on a creative person's age. Scholars reach a peak later than artists and stay productive longer. Dennis explains that the arts, such as painting or composing, depend more on individual creativity, and an artist's output declines if he or she loses strength or becomes ill. Scholars and scientists can get younger colleagues (such as graduate students) to help them with their work, staying productive even if their strength declines (Dennis 1968).

Later studies by Simonton (1977) on great composers partly supported the idea that creativity declines with age. Simonton found that total productivity peaked between ages 45 and 49 and then declined. Total themes (musical ideas) in composers' works also decreased after ages 30 to 34, although they did not decrease to a point below the totals of the composer's younger years. Studies of Nobel Prize winners (Zuckerman 1977) and high-level chess players (Elo 1965) also report peaks in creativity for people in their mid-30s.

In a later study Simonton (1988, 1990) reviewed the research on creativity and aging. He concluded that in the last decade of a creative person's career, his or her productivity equals about half his or her peak output (given a normal life span). In general, Simonton (1990, 322) says, "if one plots creative output as a function of age, productivity tends to rise fairly rapidly to a definite peak and thereafter tends to decline gradually."

Does the quality of the work also decline with age? In other words, do the creative works of a person's later career decline in quality? Simonton (2006) says that creative people can produce great works at every age. Across an entire career he proposes a **constant-probability-of-success model.** This model states that the ratio of quality works to total works produced during a career stays the same at every stage of the career. An older person may produce fewer masterpieces but will also produce fewer mediocre works.

Why does creativity decline with age in some people? Simonton found that a decline in health, a decrease in energy, changes in a profession, and different goals and motivations later in life all explain the decline in creative output. But even with this general decline, creativity can continue into late old age. Sophocles, Michelangelo, Goethe, Picasso, Winston Churchill, Grandma Moses, and Georgia O'Keefe, to name just a few, all remained creative past the age of 80. Lehman reported many cases of creativity in old age. He found that 20 percent of atomic physicists made contributions to their field after age 65 (Lehman 1968, 100).

Simonton argued that most of the creative people he studied created their greatest works at younger ages. Still, they continued to contribute to society and culture as they aged. And some types of creativity, like comprehensive historical or philosophical studies, may be possible only in old age. It may take a historian a lifetime to amass the knowledge and gain the perspective needed to make a great contribution. Cohen (2005) notes that a historian at age 75, for example, could outshine a 25-year-old Rhodes history scholar when it comes to discussing or interpreting history. Arnold Toynbee, the great historian, at age 77, wrote that "an historian's work is of the kind in which time is a necessary condition for achievement." Simonton (2006, 270) concludes that past research "may underestimate the creativity of older individuals. The decline may be neither drastic nor inexorable."

Galenson (2006) provides another view of creativity in later life. Galenson's work helps explain why some creative people peak early in their careers while others show great creativity throughout their lives. Galenson focused on the work of modern artists and writers. He discovered two styles of creativity—experimental innovation and conceptual innovation. Each type of artist and writer approaches creative work differently. And these two approaches show up as creative excellence at different stages in the life cycle.

Experimental innovators in art, for example, focus on presenting visual perceptions. Impressionist artists like Monet and Cezanne fall into this type. They work in a tentative style and paint the same scene or object many times. They use their art to search for perfection in their work. They build their skill and knowledge throughout their careers, and their work improves slowly over time. Cezanne would paint a mountain over and over again in

© 2009 Jupiterimages Corporation

People can express their creativity at every age. Orchestra conductors, for example, can produce great work late in life. In some fields (music, philosophy, history) it may take a lifetime of experience and reflection to understand the depth of a subject.

search of a satisfying image. Cezanne said, about his art, "I seek in painting."

Galenson says that Cezanne arrived at his central creative challenge—creating Impressionism as a solid and timeless art—in his 30s. He then developed his art for the next 30 years. Wassily Kandinsky, another great 20th-century artist, who falls into the experimental camp, developed his best work in his 50s. Kandinsky says that "'only after many years of patient toil and strenuous thought, numerous painstaking attempts, and my constantly developing ability … did I arrive at the pictorial forms I use today …" (Galenson 2006, 29).

In contrast to experimentalists, conceptual innovators communicate a specific idea or emotion. They know the goal of each work precisely. They create detailed preparatory sketches and then produce a preconceived image. The great conceptual innovators break with tradition. They develop a new style or approach to art that appears suddenly. Conceptual innovators do not view their work as a search for truth through the production of the work. The conceptual innovator shows in a work of art what he or she has already found. Pablo Picasso, one of the great conceptual innovators said about his art, "I don't seek; I find." Picasso, like most of conceptual innovators, created his most important idea in his early years. In his case, he created cubism in his mid-20s.

Galenson shows that the artistic approach of the painter leads to different peak ages in his or her creative output. Experimenters (like Cezanne) peak later because of their approach—a slow, methodical search for their ideal visual presentation. Conceptual artists (like Picasso) produce great works early because they have the end already in mind and they produce sudden breaks with tradition.

"Cezanne's slow production and elaboration of his creative ideas led to a very late peak in the quality of his work, whereas Picasso's rapid production and development of his new ideas led to a very early peak" (Galenson 2006, 15).

Galenson extended his work to include sculptors, poets, novelists, and movie directors. Galenson (2006, 161) says, "the results are impressive, for this investigation [into other forms of creativity] is sufficient to show that some of the very most important figures in the modern history of these arts clearly fit the two categories described by the analysis, and that their careers clearly fit the life cycles predicted for their respective categories." Galenson admits that this simple theory doesn't capture the many variations in artistic approach. He notes, for example, that some artists show a more extreme version of each approach, others a more moderate version. He also finds that artists can change their approach as they arrive at their mature style. Galenson considers the link between artistic styles and the life cycle "not laws, but tendencies" (61). Still, his work shows that the production of great work has more to do with the artist's personality and approach to art than with the artist's age.

Creativity as Personal Expression

Creativity can refer to a great achievement or a form of personal expression. This last perspective treats creativity as a source of individual satisfaction regardless of how other people judge the works produced.

Research shows that when older people have more opportunity to express their creativity they show more creative behaviour. A program in Bergen, Norway, for example, offered courses in poetry writing and storytelling. About 45 people aged 67 to 90 took part in the program. They found that creative expression led to sharpened awareness, increased self-esteem, and good social relations in the classes (Aadlandsvik 2007).

Engelman (2000) led a creativity class for six years with a group of women at a senior centre. The class solved puzzles, engaged in brainstorming, and invented poems and stories. Engelman concludes that people at any age can display creativity and that the act of creation brings joy to older people's lives. A mental fitness program in Canada called "Fitness for Life" included a creative thinking module. Researchers compared baseline mental fitness scores with outcomes after an eight-week program. The researchers found that at the end of the program depression scores had declined while mental fitness and self-esteem scores had improved (Cusac k, Thompson, and Rogers 2003).

Cohen (2005) reports that creativity can improve the health of older adults. One study compared 150 older people involved in community-based arts programs with 150 people not in this kind of program. The arts groups met once a week for 35 weeks. Cohen and his co-researchers found that many of the people in the arts groups showed stable health over a two-year period, and some improved their health. The study found, that compared to the control group, people in the arts groups reported fewer doctor visits, better mental health, using fewer medications. The group members averaged 80 years old.

Cohen conducted another study of a professionally led choral group (Cohen et al. 2007). This program included 128 people with an average age of 79. The members of the group attended 30 practice sessions and gave 10 public concerts. The researchers used a control group to assess the effect of this program. The researchers found fewer doctor visits, less medication use, less depression, and better morale among the choral group members. Cohen (2005) says that challenging mental activity and the achievement of control and mastery led to better health and good mental function. Arts and creativity programs offer a good method of health promotion and a good way to improve the quality of older peoples' lives.

Not everyone can or wants to join a group to express their creativity. Some people take charge of their own learning. They transform their world in response to their own concerns, and, in the process, create something new. Older people have more opportunities than ever before to engage in creative, personally and socially rewarding activity (Solan 2007). This view of creativity makes later life a time of potential discovery and self-renewal rather than a time of decline (see Exhibit 6.3).

Exhibit 6.3

PORTRAITS OF THREE CREATIVE OLDER CANADIANS

Doris Finta

Doris Finta, 86, discovered a passion for art after she retired. She explains to Marg Langton of *The Hamilton Spectator* how this happened.

I retired at 63 and finished my degree the next year. I started in French, then English literature but I got seduced into art. Art ended up being the air I breathe.

I got my honours degree when I was 71. It was 50 years after I started university. I did a two-year project on [artist] Joyce Wieland. I got to know her quite well. I used to meet her at the art gallery [Art Gallery of Ontario]. We'd go up to the modern section and she'd know everybody....

Art is my life now, it gave me back joy—rich, rich possibilities. It's coloured everything.

I was a founding member of the Burlington Fine Arts Association. I'm still carrying on with an art appreciation program that I lead at the Burlington Art Centre. I'm doing printmaking, watercolours and drawing. I take summer courses in Haliburton.

My degree was a gate into a whole new world.

Helen Dougher

Helen Dougher, 89, began writing poetry at age 11. Suzanne Bourret profiled her for *The Hamilton Spectator*.

Helen Dougher ... has good friends but her closest friend is the poetry she writes. It keeps her company when she cannot sleep and it soothes and comforts her when she misses loved ones. Her reflective verses project lovely and vivid pictures of nature and the seasons, her favourite cats, the European cities she has visited, and thoughts about those close to her who have passed on.

When you read [her poetry], you find an intelligent, gentle soul who hears and sees from a different level and who shares her pictures of a different age and a quieter time. When her poetry is read, it smoothes away rough edges, it consoles and soothes the soul ...

She had her first poem printed in *Chatelaine* when she was 11 or 12 and was paid $3 ... She says, "I think people thought it was very queer to write poetry in a town like that [Dunnville, Ontario] in those days."

Dougher kept writing poetry through [out her life. She] joined the Tower Poetry Society in the early 1960s. It's a group that meets monthly to discuss their poetry at Carnegie Gallery in Dundas. Her first book of poetry, *This Golden Fire,* was published by the Tower Poetry Society Press in 1977. Her second book, *Homecoming,* was published in 1986 by Potlatch Publications. She did much of the distribution herself ... Her poetry ended up in schools and libraries across Canada and, once while vacationing in Providence, R.I., she found a copy of her verse at Brown University.

Elena Turroni

Elena Turroni, 90, began her career by teaching cooking and sewing at local high schools. She also made wedding cakes and cooked for family and friends. Her sister suggested that she start a small business. Over the years she became a well-known caterer and cookbook author. She told her story to Diane Ujfalussy of *The Hamilton Spectator.*

When you've made strawberry shortcake for Eleanor Roosevelt, have been asked to cook dinner for the Queen and rustled up grub for former prime minister John Diefenbaker, you get a pretty good idea you can cook. Elena Turroni has spent decades inventing and reinventing all kinds of recipes. She ran her own lucrative catering business in Welland for years and raised funds for charitable organizations through local cooking shows.

"I would cook what anyone asked me to. I did a lot of research at the library," Turroni said. "I read books on the cooking of most every country. I love to improvise. I find it challenging and rewarding to create different tastes or textures."

The influx of Italian immigrants in the '50s made the Turroni name synonymous with fine Italian catering. She would be called upon to cater Italian

(Continued)

● Exhibit 6.3 (cont.)

weddings and some Saturdays she would have anywhere from four to seven. "There was always a book and pencil in my hand. Even in bed, I had to have my book nearby in case I got an idea," she said.

She recalls creating fabulous fare for original parties—events on the beach, gardens and even an Indian party complete with dancers and women in saris ...

She is still involved in the community and coming up with new mouth-watering recipes. [She] will soon be releasing her fourth cookbook—*Italian Regional Cooking, Elena Turroni Turns 90* (and is still turning out cookbooks).

Source: M. Langton, "Seniority: In Their Own Words: Doris Finta, 86," *Hamilton Spectator,* September 23, 1999, D6; S. Bourret, "Poet Evokes Images of Times Past," *Hamilton Spectator,* February 15, 2000, E2; D. Ujfalussy, "Terrific Turroni Still Turning It Out," *Hamilton Spectator,* October 13, 1999, B4. Reprinted with permission of *The Welland Tribune.*

PSYCHOLOGICAL DISORDERS: ABNORMAL AGING

Studies of memory, intelligence, and creativity describe the normal changes that come with aging, but some people show abnormal changes as they age. They may suffer from psychological problems such as paranoia, anxiety neuroses, and schizophrenia. Experts call these functional disorders because they interfere with how a person functions. These problems have no clear organic cause, and some older people may have suffered from them throughout their lives. Other people suffer from organic disorders. At least two different types of organic disorders show up in old age. First, some people enter old age with an existing developmental disability (e.g., Down syndrome). Second, some people develop a disease of the brain or an illness such as Alzheimer's disease, Parkinson's disease, or stroke.

Organic Brain Disorders

Developmental Disability

Developmental disability refers to the effects of diseases such as Down syndrome. These illnesses usually begin at birth and affect a person's function in society throughout his or her life. Better treatment and medical care have led to longer life expectancies for people with developmental disabilities. Sparks and his colleagues (2000) report that average life expectancy for people with a developmental disability rose from 11 years in the 1930s to more than 50 years today. These advances have led to an increase in the number of people with such disabilities in later life. Salvatori and her colleagues

(1998) report that the number of older people (aged 55 and over) with developmental disabilities will double by 2028 to between 26,000 and 60,000. Many of these people now live in the community, a trend that will increase in the future.

People with developmental disabilities face unique issues as they age. First, they frequently age prematurely. In their 40s they may need to be supported as if they were an older person. Second, they rarely have children or a spouse to give them support. Third, they will rarely have a pension, savings, or other personal economic resources.

People with a developmental disability will rely heavily on social services and public support. But Salvatori and her colleagues (1998) say that social services and government policies often fail to serve their needs. Their relative youth (most need help before age 65) often makes them ineligible for programs open to older people. Also, current housing and recreation options for seniors often fail to meet the needs of a person with a developmental disability.

People with developmental disabilities need a wide choice of social support and housing options, including group home living and supported independent living. They also need special programs to support work, leisure, and retirement. These programs should focus on their individual needs and should promote social integration, autonomy, and economic independence.

Janicki and colleagues (2005) found that people with Down Syndrome, for example, placed greater hygiene and behaviour demands on staff in group homes. Sparks and his colleagues (2000) found a need for training among agencies that provided services to people with a developmental disability. Agencies that served clients with developmental disabilities reported that their staff needed training in general aging and dementia care. Service providers also felt the need for health and medical information. They "expressed concern about the lack of well trained medical specialists available to serve aging adults with DD" (215). Sparks and his colleagues propose a number of actions to serve adults with developmental disabilities better. These include better education for service providers, integration of adults with developmental disabilities into existing programs, and help for clients with developmental disabilities in finding recreation and activities in retirement. This relatively small but growing number of older people will pose new challenges to current policies and to current social services.

Cognitive Impairment in Later Life

Organic brain syndrome, senile dementia, and dementia are general terms used to describe a variety of organic brain disorders. Organic disorders lead to confusion, forgetfulness, and sometimes antisocial behaviour. Some individuals with these disorders wander, strike out, or resist help from their caregivers. Dementia cases create stress for both professional care providers and family caregivers. As more people live into late old age, dementia will occur in greater numbers.

Canada began its first nationwide study of dementia in 1990—the Canadian Study of Health and Aging (CaSHA), the largest of its kind. The study included more than 10,000 older people in five Canadian regions and included institutionalized seniors as well as people who live in the community. The study had four objectives: (1) to report on the prevalence of dementias among older Canadians; (2) to assess the risk of someone getting Alzheimer's-type dementia; (3) to describe patterns of care for dementia patients and to measure caregiver burden; and (4) to create a uniform database (Gauthier, McDowell, and Hill 1990; Martin-Matthews 2006). The study also included a number of add-on projects that focused on topics such as the genetic origins of Alzheimer's disease.

This study has provided the best estimate yet of the prevalence of dementia in Canada. For example, the researchers found that 253,000 people or 8 percent of people aged 65 or older in Canada in 1991 (the most current national data) had some form of dementia. The study found a dementia rate of 2.4 percent among people aged 65 to 74 and 34.5 percent among people aged 85 and over (cited in Tierney and Charles 2002; see also Conn 2002). Researchers project a threefold increase in the number of dementia cases by 2031 (double the rate of total population growth) (Burke et al. 1997). A

background paper for federal, provincial, and territorial officials (Federal/Provincial/Territorial 2006, 6) calls this "one of the greatest public health challenges of the coming generations" (see Exhibit 6.4).

Aminzadeh and colleagues (2004) studied residents of residential care facilities (RCF) in Ottawa. RCFs house people who can no longer live on their own but do not need nursing home care. The researchers found that two out of five people in these settings suffered from a cognitive impairment. In the future, residential care facilities, nursing homes, and hospitals will have to care for more and more cognitively impaired patients.

Slaughter and Bankes (2007) report that people in the community with Alzheimer's disease on average lose one functional ability every two months. People in the early stages of the disease will tend to lose Instrumental Activities of Daily Living (IADLs) like driving, banking, or cooking. People in the middle and later stages lose ADL abilities like bathing, dressing, or toileting. Slaughter and Bankes say that people with Alzheimer's disease may also suffer from other illnesses (e.g., an infection) or medical complications (e.g., drug interactions). This creates "excess disability"—disability that further decreases ADL ability.

Shapiro and Tate (1997) found that community-dwelling older people with dementia tend to use more formal services than healthy older people or people with other forms of cognitive impairment. They found that the health care system spends more than twice as much to care for dementia clients as for non-impaired older people. But Shapiro and Tate report that, compared to people with other cognitive impairments, people with dementia use less expensive services (such as home support and personal care services). This group and their caregivers also tended to use respite care more than any other group. Still, the CaSHA estimates that the cost of care for dementia patients in Canada comes to more than $3.9 billion per year (Tierney 1997). The cost for each community-dwelling dementia patient came to more than $8,000 per year and for each institutionalized dementia patient more than $28,000 per year (in the mid-1990s).

Biomedical research so far has not produced a method to treat Alzheimer's disease (the most common form of dementia). Physicians often cannot make a certain diagnosis of the disease's presence. They first try to rule out other causes of confusion and personality decline such as brain tumours, blood pressure problems, or hyperthyroidism. Caution prevents doctors from quickly reaching a conclusion of Alzheimer's because a patient might have a treatable illness or a problem such as overmedication or infection. Tierney and Charles (2002) report on the development of the Alzheimer

Exhibit 6.4

THE PREVALENCE OF DEMENTIA IN CANADA, 1991

Age	Dementia (%)	Alzheimer's (%)
65–74	2.4	1.0
85+	34.5	26.0
All 65+	8.0	5.1

The Canadian Study of Health and Aging reported the above estimates for the prevalence of dementia in Canada. "These Canadian estimates of the prevalence of dementia," the report says, "fall towards the upper end of the ranges in other studies, whereas the estimates for Alzheimer's disease fall in the middle of the ranges. This may suggest an unusual balance between Alzheimer's and other forms of dementia in the Canadian population."

Source: Adapted from Canadian Study of Health and Aging Working Group. Canadian Study of Health and Aging: study methods and prevalence of dementia. *Canadian Medical Association Journal*, 150:899–913, 1994.

Source: October 24, 2003, http://www.uottawa.ca/academic/med/epid/csha1.htm

Predictive Index. Physicians can use this index to assess people who have some memory loss. Research shows that 89 percent of the time the index can predict the onset of Alzheimer's disease within two years. This index and other new methods will lead to quicker diagnosis in the future (Standish et al. 2007). Early diagnosis helps families cope with the disease's progress. Research on early treatment may develop ways to slow or stop the progress of the disease.

Organic disorders pose problems for the affected individuals and their families. Family caregivers often feel despair because their care receiver does not recognize them anymore. This can add to their burden. A better understanding of memory loss might help these caregivers cope with their care receivers' illnesses.

Sainsbury and Coristine (1986, 99) studied patients with cognitive impairment. They found that patients often could not recognize a relative's picture, but these same patients could choose the relative's picture from a set of four pictures. The researchers said that even though a person loses "recognition memory," "affective memory" remains intact.

The researchers added that "the subject may be aware that he knows the visitor but not recall the relationship. Awareness of this fact in conjunction with the knowledge that severely impaired people can yet possess strong affective associations can be of considerable comfort to concerned relatives" (Sainsbury and Coristine 1986, 103).

People with Alzheimer's disease pose practical problems for their families (see Exhibit 6.5). Patients sometimes suffer from depression or may sleep all day and wander all night. Sometimes they leave home and lose their way. All these behaviours create stress for caregivers. In partnership with the Royal Canadian Mounted Police, the Alzheimer Society of Canada (2004) established the Safely Home—Alzheimer Wandering Registry, a national database of people with Alzheimer's disease. Police can use the database to help find and return a lost person home. In addition, the Ministry of the Solicitor General has funded the creation of a police handbook to advise police on how to deal with Alzheimer's patients (*Seniors Today* 1995).

Families often feel committed to care for their care receiver at home as long as possible. Smale and Dupuis (2003a, 2003b) conducted a study of dementia caregivers in Ontario. They found that caregivers most often reported that (among supports currently provided) they needed home health care, in-home respite care, and adult day-away programs. They also reported a need for support groups, homemaker services, and transportation services.

But when a care receiver's behaviour becomes too difficult to handle, even the best family supports and community care cannot relieve caregiver burden. Lévesque and her colleagues (2000) studied the use of services by caregivers in Quebec. They found that some family members with dementia resist day-care pro-

● Exhibit 6.5

THE STAGES OF DECLINE DUE TO ALZHEIMER'S DISEASE

Health and Welfare Canada (1984) has described the three stages that an Alzheimer's patient goes through. Some people may go through these stages in a few months; for others, it may take years. The changes that come with Alzheimer's disease begin slowly. Often family members recognize the first signs only when they look back over a year or two of caregiving.

Stage I: A person first shows changes in memory. He or she forgets the keys or a wallet more frequently. The person may also forget recent events or forget that he or she did a job around the house. The forgetfulness gets worse over time. The person forgets more often, takes longer to do simple jobs, or begins to recheck work already done.

One woman recalls that her husband, an engineering professor, would spend three or four hours writing a 50-minute lecture that used to take him an hour to write. Another woman recalls that she first became worried when her husband, a physician, lost his way home from work one night. He planned to stop at a patient's house for a short house call around 5 p.m. The patient lived only a few blocks away from their house, so his wife expected him home by 6 p.m. She began to worry at 8 p.m. when she still hadn't heard from him. An hour later he came in exhausted. He had spent the last three hours driving around their neighbourhood looking for their house.

Stage II: The second stage of the disease includes more memory decline, loss of speaking ability, and an end to normal daily activity. The ill person may wander at night, lose control of his or her bowel and bladder, and threaten others. One woman left a knife in her garden after she used it to weed the flowerbed. Her husband picked it up and stalked through the bushes into a neighbour's yard, saying to the neighbour, "I'm going to kill you." The neighbour ran inside and called the police. When the man's wife came outside to finish weeding, she found the police wrestling her husband into a squad car.

In another case, a man walked into a new car dealer and signed a contract for a $40,000 car. His wife found out only after the salesman called her to check on the financing. The owner of the dealership agreed to void the contract, but only after she pleaded and explained about her husband's illness.

This stage of the disease can put additional stress on the family. Caregivers—most often spouses or children of the ill person—can feel tense, trapped, and exhausted. Family members have to take on new roles: Wives become chauffeurs or nurses; children become parents or police; and husbands become homemakers (Novak and Guest 1985). Mace and Rabins (1981, 63) report one case of a burdened husband who had to bathe his wife. "She screams for help the whole time I am bathing her. She'll open the windows and yell, 'Help, I'm being robbed.'" One man confessed to Mace and Rabins, "There was a time when I considered getting a gun, killing my wife, and then killing myself" (179).

Stage III: The person in the last stage of Alzheimer's disease needs institutionalization and often 24-hour nursing care. The person can no longer speak or communicate. He or she may wander or move constantly unless restrained. Seizures may occur. Death occurs between two and nineteen years after the disease starts (Health and Welfare Canada 1984). Death often comes from an illness such as pneumonia or heart disease, but death certificates rarely mention Alzheimer's disease as a cause of death, making it impossible to know the exact number of deaths associated with Alzheimer's.

Not all Alzheimer's patients show all the above-mentioned symptoms. Some show other symptoms of confusion such as depression and crying. But these stages give a general picture of the disease. They also give only a faint idea of the stress that Alzheimer's disease puts on the primary caregiver.

grams and wouldn't cooperate with in-home helpers. This made it hard for family caregivers to get the day care or the attendant help they need. Family caregivers risk burnout unless they get some relief. One woman in Ontario, who cared for her husband with dementia, described her feelings.

"Many times I've locked myself in the bathroom, not because I was afraid of what [my husband] might do but just to get away from the constant barrage ... I'm very exhausted ... I'm on my own and I'm getting very down, I've done more crying in the past two years than I ever thought I had in me."

Another woman who cares for her husband says, "I haven't had any peace of mind or rest for years. [My doctor] said I had a high rate of burnout, caregiver burnout and he said you can't go on like this anymore" (Dupuis and Smale 2004).

Professional caregivers can also feel burdened by the demands of dementia patients. A study by Novak, Chappell, and Miles-Tapping (1990) found that nursing assistants who were distressed by patient behaviour felt most burdened. In the coming years, service workers will care for more and more clients with these illnesses and will need to understand the basis of the illness and how to treat these clients.

Several drugs on the market (Razadyne®, Exelon®, and Aricept®) may delay the decline in mental function for people with mild to moderate symptoms. The drugs may also help control behavioural symptoms (National Institute on Aging (NIA) (2009).

Research continues on drugs that may slow the progress of the disease in its mid to later stages. Some drugs (e.g., Namenda®) may allow patients to maintain daily functions, such as toileting, a little longer than without medication. This can ease the stress on caregivers. Drugs, such as sleeping pills and antidepressants, can also control some symptoms. But, at present, nothing can stop the progress of the disease.

Scientists continue to work on finding a cure for Alzheimer's disease. Vogler (2006) says, for example, that researchers have found three genes that influence early onset or familial Alzheimer's disease. Genetic research and new technologies may provide insight into the cure.

Functional Disorders

Functional disorders disrupt normal life. They include emotional upset, depression, and anxiety. Health and Welfare Canada (1991, cited in MacCourt et al. 2002) estimates that 25 percent of older people in Canada need mental health services. Studies report rates of mental disorder between 10 percent and 25 percent among institutionalized older people (Préville et al. 2002).

Still, the majority of community-dwelling older people today report generally good mental health. In 2002, the Canadian Community Health Survey (CCHS) asked a sample of 30,000 people aged 15 and over from across Canada to report on their mental health. The study found that, compared to the population aged 15 to 64, the group aged 65 and over reported about the same level of very good or excellent mental health (66 percent). Older people, compared to younger people, report the least contact with services and support associated with mental health. And only about 1 percent of

older people report having an unmet mental health care need (the lowest of any age group). They also reported the lowest rate of barriers to getting mental health care (Statistics Canada 2003c).

Depression

Depression refers to a state in which a person feels sad, helpless, irritable, and hopeless (Normand 2000). In general, studies have found that the risk of depression decreases in later life. People aged 65 and over have a lower risk than any other age group (Normand 2000). The CCHS found that only 1.8 percent of older people reported a major depressive disorder (Statistics Canada 2003c). Those aged 75 and over had a rate of major depression less than 1 percent. Andrew and Rockwood (2007) reviewed data from the Canadian Study of Health and Aging and found a 12.6 percent rate of psychiatric illness among community-dwelling older Canadians. Most of these people reported depression. About 1 percent reported both depression and another psychiatric illness. Other studies report similar rates of depression among older populations (Knight et al., 2006) (see Exhibit 6.6).

People with resources such as social skills, problem-solving ability, and emotional support from family and friends will less likely feel depressed (Antonucci 2001). A person who appraises a situation as non-threatening or who copes actively to improve situations will also show less depression.. This perspective shows that social as well as psychological conditions influence depression.

Social support buffers the effect of poor health and protects a person from feeling depressed. A study of depression among elderly Chinese Canadians supports this conclusion. Lai (2000) studied a sample of older Chinese people in Calgary. He found that 9.4 percent of his sample reported mild depression and 11.5 percent reported moderate to severe depression. This sample had higher rates of depression than did the general population of older people in Canada. He says that depressed Chinese elders often lack access to mental health supports. Their inability to speak English creates a barrier to support. Also Chinese elders may not understand the Western approach to mental health. We will look in more detail at the influence of social conditions on psychological well-being in Chapter 7.

Préville and his colleagues (2002) studied psychological distress in institutionalized and frail community-dwelling older people. They found that nearly 47 percent of their total sample showed psychological distress (three times the rate of the Quebec general older population).

● **Exhibit 6.6**

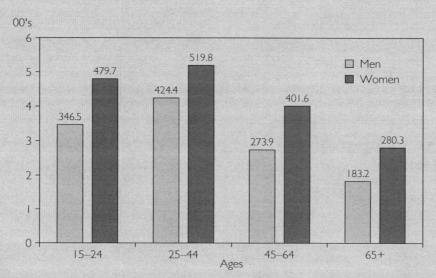

RATES OF HOSPITALIZATION FOR ONE OF SEVEN MENTAL ILLNESSES* IN GENERAL HOSPITALS PER 100,000 BY AGE AND SEX, CANADA, 1999/2000

Note that hospitalization due to mental illness (for functional disorders) decreases after age 44 for both men and women. The oldest age group shows the lowest rate of hospitalization for this type of mental illness.

*The seven diagnoses most responsible for hospitalization are anxiety disorders, bipolar disorders, schizophrenia, major depression, personality disorders, eating disorders, and attempted suicide.

Source: Adapted from Health Canada, 2002, *A Report on Mental Illnesses in Canada,* Ottawa: Health Canada Editorial Board, 18.

They found that, compared to institutionalized older people, frail older people who lived alone had more than twice the rate of psychological distress. Also, people with functional limitations reported more psychological distress.

Andrew and Rockwood (2007) found that the frailest older people showed the greatest tendency toward depression. The inability to get out and the loss of social supports can also lead to unhappiness or depression. Gilbart and Hirdes (2000) studied institutionalized older people in Ontario hospitals. They found that many of these residents reported sadness and some anxiety. And people with the least social engagement reported the least happiness.

People in the best health get the most out of social engagement; a decrease in social supports in later life puts the mental health of infirm and isolated older Canadians at risk. Gilbart and Hirdes (2000) say that care planning should take a holistic approach, including attention to patients' psychosocial as well as physical needs.

Treatment and Intervention

Mental health experts sometimes overlook the needs of older people. Eaton, Stones, and Rockwood (1986), for example, found that physicians often failed to detect cognitive impairment in older patients. Stones and colleagues (2006) say that 40 to 55 percent of people in long-term- care settings who have depressive symptoms fail to get treatment. Older people may experience depression without displaying sadness (a common symptom in younger people). For this reason health care workers may fail to diagnose it.

Doctors, during their medical school training, should receive more knowledge about the care and treatment of mental disorders in older people. Continuing medical education could also include this training. Doctors need to understand the causes and treatment of mental disorders in later life (MacCourt et al. 2002).

A range of treatments can help older people cope with psychological problems. An individual's characteristics (including age), the diagnosis criteria used, the older person's adaptation patterns, and the intervention setting (community or institution) all influence the choice of treatment. For example, some reversible organic brain syndromes can be treated with chemical therapies. Physicians can treat alcoholics in the early stages of Wernicke-Korsakoffs dementia (a neurological disease) with large doses of thiamine.

Many therapies exist for older people with functional problems (problems related to a person's personality or social life). Drug therapy, for example, can help older people cope with anxiety and depression. Stones and colleagues (2006) say that long-term care institutions often use drug therapy to treat depression. However, non-drug therapies can also help relieve depression and its symptoms. Behaviour therapy, for example, can help with insomnia and psychotherapy can help people with personality disorders (Gatz and Smyer 2001).

Katz (1999, cited in Gatz and Smyer 2001) says that problem solving, interpersonal therapy, and brief psychotherapy should form the first line of treatment for depression. Life review can help with adaptation to loss, and milieu therapy, where a person makes changes to his or her environment, can help a person deal with stress-related problems. Knight and colleagues (2006) report that, compared to psychosocial treatment (e.g., support groups or social activities), psychotherapeutic treatments (e.g., behaviour therapy or psychotherapy) proved more effective. Also, compared to group therapies, individual therapies proved more effective. Cognitive behavioural therapy (CBT) helps people think more positive thoughts and engage in more positive behaviour. This method shows some of the strongest effect in reducing depression.

A policy statement by the Canadian Association on Gerontology (MacCourt et al. 2002) points out the need for specialized training for health care providers and special services to meet the needs of older people. Special services include day programs, outpatient assessment units, and community outreach programs designed to serve psychogeriatric patients. The association's policy statement supports a social model of care, which addresses the social and environmental (as well as the psychological) needs of the older person. It also proposes a multidisciplinary response to these needs. Chapter 8 will discuss in more detail this general shift toward a comprehensive health care model.

The Loss of Competence

Psychological intervention can sometimes protect the older person from harm. It can also lead to making decisions for people who can no longer decide for themselves. A person with a cognitive impairment may lose the ability to understand his or her situation and make decisions. But when should another person step in to make decisions for someone else? Checkland and Silberfeld (1993) say that this should occur only after a careful assessment of a person's **competency**.

Saint-Arnaud (1993, 35) defines competency as the ability to "understand information relevant to the decision to be taken, weigh the pros and cons in terms of his/her goals and values" and to be "capable of communicating decisions" (see also Silberfeld 1994). Competency differs from **legal capacity**, "the exercise of rights by all citizens" (Saint-Arnaud 1993). Legal incapacity refers to the loss of civil rights when a person comes into protective care. In this case, someone else (a lawyer, family member, or the public trustee) has the legal right to make decisions for the older person. This guardian attempts to follow, to the extent that he or she knows them, the wishes of the person under care.

A professional (a physician, psychiatrist, or other recognized expert) formally decides a person's competency through an assessment. An assessment attempts to answer the question of whether a person should lose his or her legal rights based on his or her inability to make a decision. An assessment should ensure the same assessment standards for everyone and the absence of an assessor's bias. Also, assessment should take place more than once to monitor a person's present and future ability to make decisions. If a person has been assessed as being incompetent, that person's ability to make choices on his or her own behalf is removed. For this reason caution is urged in making the judgment.

Checkland and Silberfeld (1993) say that, even after an assessment of incompetence, others should intervene as little as possible. For example, they say that a person may have lost the ability to manage money, but may still have the ability to live at home. Thus, a person can have decision-specific capacities. The researchers propose that someone else make decisions for this person on financial issues, but the person keep the right to make the decision on where to live. The authors say that competency should rest both on mental ability and on what a person can do. For example, a person may thrive at home but not have the verbal skill to say how he or she does that.

Silberfeld (1994) says that a competency assessment should find this person competent. Also, any view of a person's decision-making ability should take into account that individual's past decisions, values, and track record (Silberfeld et al. 1996). Shidler (1998) says that in cases of decisions about life-prolonging treatment, the physician and the proxy (often a family member) should involve the older person as much as possible.

The issue of competency can often come up in cases of older people at risk. An older person may feel able to live on his or her own, although the individual's children may feel this puts the person at risk. Older people who want to live on their own may minimize risk and hope all goes well. But "caregivers, who fear the worst, can magnify the risk" (National Advisory Council on Aging 1993b, 3).

The National Advisory Council on Aging (1993b, 2) presents the following case:

> Mrs. X is an 86-year-old widow who has lived alone with the help of home support services for the past ten years. She is an insulin-dependent diabetic with a sweet tooth. During the past two years, she has become increasingly short of memory and confused. She often forgets to eat or eats junk food. Efforts to have her live with her only son and daughter-in-law several miles away have failed. The home care case manager is becoming uncomfortable because, even with the maximum level of home care available, Mrs. X is considered to be at risk. Following a fall, where she fractured her wrist, she was hospitalized. The son, in consultation with home care, decided to institutionalize his mother. Mrs. X is clearly unhappy in the nursing home, objecting to all aspects of her care and continually asking when she can go home.

Has the son acted in his mother's best interests or in his own? Family members may consult the family doctor for a competency assessment in order to carry out their own wishes. This assessment may go along with a desire to assume **legal guardianship** for the older person. But guardianship (where the court appoints someone to make decisions on the older person's behalf) also creates a risk. "Starting from assuredly good intentions [to keep the older person from harm], risk becomes part of an unconscious rhetoric for controlling elderly people" (Silberfeld 1992, 134).

Naglie and his colleagues (1995) point to the importance of careful competency assessment in an aging society. The label of incompetence removes a person's free choice, and experts should apply it with caution. Stelmach, Konnert, and Dobson (2001, 390) say that "competence is specific to one moment in time and one decision at a time, and therefore, does not refer to a … [person's] ability to make all decisions." Browne and his colleagues (2002) say that interference with a person's liberty should take the mildest form necessary to ensure the person's and his or her care receiver's safety. They propose that in health care facilities, for example, staff members should document problem behaviours in writing before placing limits on a person's freedom. Borovoy (1982, cited in National Advisory Council 1993a, 4) says that "when we are talking about the precious freedom to be left alone, then we should insist that it cannot be lost unless there are the most exacting criteria and the most scrupulous procedures."

CONCLUSION

Psychological well-being means more than coping with problems, stress, and loss. It means growth, learning, and a sense of purpose. The research on the psychology of aging shows that older people in good health stay alert, intelligent, and able to learn. They face stresses unique to later life, but they can get through these crises, often with the help of others. Sometimes the biggest block to older people's well-being comes from the prejudices and stereotypes other people have about old age. The research on the psychology of aging has begun to remove the basis for these stereotypes. Studies have begun to explore and describe the changes that take place in old age. They have begun to chart human potential in later life. More research and knowledge about old age and new cohorts of older people will teach us more about mental potential in later life.

Summary

1. Early research supported the myth that intellectual ability declines with age, but recent studies show more complex findings. For example, younger people perform better than older people on memory and intelligence tests in the lab. But the pace of testing, the types of questions asked, and the way older people learn can all affect the older person's performance.

2. In general, laboratory studies show that memory declines with age, although different types of memory show different amounts of decline. Recent research suggests that a decrease in working memory accounts for poorer

memory in older people. Education and background differences between older and younger people may account for some of the differences in performance in memory studies.

3. Test conditions may decrease older people's ability to remember in laboratory studies. Studies of memory in real-world (not laboratory) contexts show that older people can compensate for memory declines. Studies also show that, when compared, older people's recall of historical and social events showed little or no deficit compared to younger people.

4. Early studies used cross-sectional methods to study the effects of aging on intelligence. The results confused cohort differences with age changes. Longitudinal methods show declines in fluid intelligence (problem-solving skills) but little change in crystallized intelligence (skills based on acquired knowledge). Research also shows that older people can improve their scores on intelligence tests through training. Studies of fluid intelligence in later life show that some people show stable scores, and others showed decline. Training increased both types of intelligence in older individuals.

5. New models of intelligence have begun to look at human potential in later life. Researchers have begun to study wisdom—a person's good judgment and his or her expert knowledge about life. Older people have the potential to develop wisdom, but this remains a potential that each person needs to fulfill.

6. Studies of both the quality and quantity of creative production show a decline in creativity with age. Comparisons of older and younger people on psychological tests find greater creativity among younger subjects. All of these studies look at the production of creative work. However, reports of subjective creative development show that people can be creative and can learn to be creative at any age. Education, opportunity, and an interest in a subject can all lead to creativity in later life.

7. Creativity can expand in later life. Creativity improves well-being and gives a sense of purpose in life. Some creative work—in fields like history and literature—shows the benefits of lifelong experience. The age of greatest creative activity depends in part on the creative person's approach to his or her field. Some creative people explode on the scene with world-shattering innovations in their youth. Other creative people use their work to discover solutions to creative problems, often producing great work late in their careers.

8. The number of cases of organic brain disorders such as Alzheimer's disease will increase as more people live to late old age. These disorders place a heavy burden on families, and people with these diseases often need professional health care at the end of their lives.

9. Functional mental disorders (e.g., anxiety and depression) show up less often in old age than people commonly believe. Older people with these problems can benefit from drug therapies, psychotherapy, or milieu therapy.

10. Older people can lose competence to manage their lives due to organic or functional problems. Researchers, ethicists, and physicians work to clarify the concept of competency. They want to find a definition and assessment of competency that serves older people's needs and limits restrictions on their rights.

11. The research on the psychology of aging presents a balanced view of aging. Some mental faculties may decline, but others remain stable as long as a person is in good health. More research and knowledge about the process of aging will teach us more about mental potential in later life.

Study Questions

1. What approaches have psychologists taken to the study of memory in later life? State two findings that show up in most laboratory studies. How do laboratory and contextual studies of memory differ in what they conclude about memory in later life?

2. What do psychologists mean when they speak of intelligence as multidimensional? Describe the differences between fluid and crystallized intelligence.

3. Discuss the costs and benefits of longitudinal and cross-sectional studies of memory.

4. What are some of the newest theories about intelligence and aging?

5. State three ways in which psychologists measure creativity in later life. What does each of these measures find?

6. What do psychologists mean by organic disorders? Give some examples. What do they mean by functional disorders? Give some examples.

7. What treatments do psychologists propose for organic disorders? For functional disorders?

8. What issues does the loss of competence raise for the older person? For the person's physician? For the family? Discuss the tension that exists between older people's potential need for protection and their right to make decisions for themselves.

Key Terms

cognitive mechanics   information-processing mechanisms that implement fluid intelligence. (117)

cognitive pragmatics   culture- and knowledge-related applications of intelligence, similar to crystallized intelligence. (117)

competence   the real-world skill used to adapt or respond to a challenge. (114)

competency   the ability to understand information that applies to a decision, the ability to think about the consequences of the decision, and the ability to communicate a decision. (130)

constant-probability-of-success model   a model that states that the greater the number of creative works a person produces in a given period within a career, the more great works are produced. (121)

contextual view of memory   the idea that many conditions influence memory, including physical, psychological, and social contexts and the knowledge, abilities, and characteristics of the individual, as well as the situation in which the individual is asked to remember. (113)

crystallized intelligence   intelligence that depends on stored information, acculturation, and learning. (116)

depression   the emotional state of feeling sad, helpless, irritable, and hopeless. (128)

developmental disability   a significant impairment in mental ability present at birth or acquired in childhood or adolescence. (124)

developmental intelligence   the growth of wisdom in later life – an advanced style of cognition. (118)

encoding   the process whereby a person puts new bits of information together with already stored information. (111)

episodic memory   memory oriented toward the past, or acquired at specific time and place, as in learning in an experimental setting. (111)

fluid intelligence   reasoning, abstracting, concept formation, and problem solving, with little use for knowledge gained through reading, schooling, or work. (116)

intelligence   the "ability to negotiate environmental demands successfully" (Labouvie-Vief 1985, 506), "that which intelligence tests measure" (506), or what a person taking the test can do now. (115)

latency   the length of time it takes for a person to process information or respond to a question. (111)

legal capacity   the right of all citizens to take part in the legal process and to have civil rights. (130)

legal guardianship   process in which the court appoints someone to make decisions on another person's behalf. (131)

long-term memory   the storehouse of knowledge that also includes the rules for applying knowledge. (110)

memory   the recall of information after learning has taken place. (110)

neurofibrillary tangles   a sign of Alzheimer's disease in which neuronal fibres wrap around one another and fail to function properly. (110)

non-episodic memory   memory oriented toward the present or the future with no reference to the time at which the person stored the memory; includes learned skills through practice or a person's general knowledge of the world. (111)

plasticity   the ability to change and adapt. (117)

selective optimization and compensation (SOC)   people who age well select tasks that will likely lead to success. They keep up (or optimize) the skills they have, and they compensate for losses by gaining new skills. (117)

semantic memory   the store of factual information. (114)

sensory memory   information perceived through the senses and stored as memory. (110)

short-term memory   where information is stored temporarily while it is being processed or for a short time afterward. (110)

wisdom   "highly valued and outstanding expert knowledge ... related to the meaning and conduct of life" (Kunzmann 2006, 1232). (118)

working memory   where recent acquired information is manipulated and processed at the same time as it is being stored temporarily. (111)

Selected Readings

Ferlstein, Susan. "Expression and Quality of Life: A Vital Relationship for Elders." *Generations* Spring 2006.

   This journal devoted an entire issue to the topic of creative expression on later life. This topics receives little attention in the gerontology literature. This volume presents many examples of creative expression by older people. The references at the end of each article offer pathways to more information.

National Advisory Council on Aging. *Writings in Gerontology: Mental Health and Aging,* No. 18. Ottawa: Minister of Public Works and Government Services, 2002.

A collection of articles by experts in mental health and aging that discuss positive mental health as well as mental disorders. Articles also deal with groups that need special attention—gay and lesbian seniors, seniors in institutions, and people with dementia. Many of the articles review the literature on interventions and propose methods of treatment.

Park, D.C., and N. Schwarz, eds. *Cognitive Aging: A Primer.* Philadelphia: Taylor & Francis, 2001.

This book reviews research on mental activity in later life. Topics range from a report on the underlying mechanisms of mental activity, to a summary of research on memory, to applied topics like cognitive aging and health. A well-written book that tackles complex topics, it is a challenge to the beginning student, but useful for a more advanced look at these topics.

Weinberg, Janet Amalia. *Still Going Strong: Memoirs, Stories, and Poems about Great Older Women.* Binghamton, NY: The Haworth Press, 2006.

This is a collection of stories about and creative works by older women. The writings show the meaning of later life as seen through the eyes of the writers or people who admire them. The book expresses the fulfillment that many older women feel in later life.

Websites to Consult

The Seniors Mental Health Website

http://www.seniorsmentalhealth.ca

This site supports seniors' mental health through psychosocial interventions. The content of the website comes from the Seniors' Psychosocial Interest Group (SPIG). It evolved from a Population Health Fund project awarded to British Columbia Psychogeriatric Association (BCPGA) and developed to continue the work begun by BCPGA on a national level. The site offers information on best practices for working with older people.

Canadian Mental Health Association

http://www.cmha.ca

This site covers mental health issues for Canadians of all ages, and it also offers discussions and publications related specifically to seniors. Publications include a guide to mental health through home care and national guidelines for seniors' mental health. http://www.cmha.ca/bins/content_page.asp?cid=2-74 deals specifically with advice on seniors' mental health.

Creative Retirement Manitoba

http://www.crm.mb.ca/

Creative Retirement Manitoba (CRM) offers innovative programs for older people that stimulate mental activity and creativity. This organization started in 1981 as one of the first learning communities for seniors in Canada. Today CRM offers an array of courses and special programs. This site provides insight into the interests of older people today.

Chapter 7

The Social Psychology of Aging

© Ariel Skelley/CORBIS/MAGMA

INTRODUCTION

What is a good old age? What social forces shape adult development? What contexts and social conditions lead to good aging? These questions have guided research in the social psychology of aging for more than 50 years. Researchers have found that many patterns of good aging exist. Three cases follow that show the variety of forms a good old age can take.

Joe Willis, 70, worked as an engineer for an oil company until he retired. Now he spends January and February playing golf in Florida and spends the summer at his cottage in Muskoka. His company calls him back two or three times a year as a consultant, he serves on the board of directors of a seniors' centre, and he volunteers as a nursing home visitor. "I visit the old folks once a week," he says. "At Christmas I take them to a show or out shopping." Joe does not see himself as old. He works less now and has more leisure time, but he feels the same as before he retired. He stays active and involved, and has found new ways to give meaning to his life.

Birdie Caldwell's husband died 15 years ago. She moved out of their house and into a two-bedroom apartment a year after his death. She also went back to work as a secretary—work she had not done since her teens. Now, at age 65, she still lives on her own. She has two daughters who live less than an hour away by car. She visits them a few times a month and sometimes stays for the weekend. She travels, belongs to a bridge group, and enjoys her freedom.

Rose Reitman, 73, also lives by herself in her own apartment. Her husband died three years ago. She has a bad case of arthritis in her legs, which keeps her indoors most of the year. On warm days she walks a few blocks to the local shopping centre. Most of the time she watches TV, knits, or talks to friends on the phone. Rose feels content in her old age. She sometimes talks to 10 or 15 friends and relatives in a week. Nieces and nephews call her from all over the country on her birthday or on holidays. Her daughter lives two and a half hours away by car, and her son lives across the country. She has six grandchildren; their pictures cover her walls and tabletops.

Three different portraits of old age: Birdie stays active; Rose lives a quiet life without social demands; Joe has found new roles to replace ones he had lost. Each of these people shows a different response to the challenges of aging, but they all report high life satisfaction. These cases show only a few of the patterns of successful aging today.

This chapter will look at (1) theories of human development in later life, (2) the social structural conditions (such as membership in an ethnic community) that influence the experience of aging, and (3) some social-psychological problems that older people face in society today.

WHAT IS A GOOD OLD AGE?

Three social-psychological theories of aging—disengagement theory, activity theory, and continuity theory—each claim to describe the ideal way to grow old. Researchers have debated the merits of these theories since the 1960s, and references to them show up in the literature even today.

Disengagement Theory

Early work by Cumming and Henry (1961) describes old age as a time of disengagement—a time to withdraw from social roles and to decrease activity. They base **disengagement theory** on a study of 279 people aged 50 to 70 in Kansas City. The study focused on people in good health and with enough money to live comfortably. They found that in this sample social roles and emotional ties decreased with age.

Cumming and Henry (1961) describe disengagement as inevitable, universal, and satisfying to both the person and society. Disengagement, they say, serves an important psychological function: It allows older people to reduce their activity naturally as their strength declines. Disengagement also serves a useful social function: It allows older people to leave social roles before the final disengagement—death. This withdrawal creates a smooth transfer of power and responsibility from one generation to the next.

Almost as soon as disengagement theory appeared, critics attacked it on three fronts. First, disengagement theory supports the stereotype of old age as a time of weakness and decline. Second, the theory assumes that the old perform less well than the young and, therefore, supports the existence of mandatory retirement based on age, rather than on a person's ability to do the job. Third, the theory assumes that all older people respond to the world in the same way—that they all disengage from social roles. More recent research shows that many older people, especially those who have good health and a good income, stay active in later life.

Activity Theory

Neugarten, Havighurst, and Tobin (1968) put forward a second major theory of aging: **activity theory**. This theory is the reverse of disengagement theory. It holds that, as people lose social roles in old age, they stay happiest when they replace these roles with new ones. This theory, moreover, blames society for the process of disengagement. Modern society, it says, pushes older people out of social roles. The activity theory fits the North American view that happiness comes from work and activity.

Neugarten, Havighurst, and Tobin (1968) found three types of active people who reported high life satisfaction. One group started new activities to fill in for lost social roles. The researchers called them "reorganizers." Another group held on to their mid-life roles and stayed active. The researchers said these people were "holding on." A third group stayed active but narrowed the range of their activities, and this group the researchers described as "focused."

Lemon, Bengtson, and Peterson (1972b) set out to test activity theory. They asked 411 older people about their activities and their life satisfaction. The researchers found little relationship between the frequency of activities and life satisfaction. Only informal activities with friends predicted life satisfaction. The researchers say that "the data provide surprisingly little support for the implicit activity theory of aging" (31). Today, most gerontologists feel that both disengagement and activity theories provide too narrow a view of later life

Continuity Theory

A third theory of aging is that people feel most satisfied if they continue the roles and activities of their middle years (Atchley 1982). This theory, **continuity theory**, says that old age is a continuation of a person's past (rather than a break with it or a change in direction) and that people will choose the lifestyle in old age that is most like the pattern of life they lived in middle age. People will adapt to new situations by using successful patterns of behaviour from their past (Atchley 1999). Mildly active people in their younger years will prefer a mild level of activity in later life and will feel satisfied with this lifestyle. But active people will want to keep up their activity—although activity might take new forms in old age. Quirouette and Pushkar (1999) found that well-educated women plan to continue their activities. The women studied had a strong core identity and expected their abilities to continue into later life.

These three theories tell part of the truth about life satisfaction in later life, but each paints too simple a picture of old age. Some people disengage from some roles and have high life satisfaction; other people remain active and feel little life satisfaction. Life satisfaction, in part, depends on the kind of activity a person takes part in.

Smale and Dupuis (1993) say that older people find satisfaction in activities that have personal meaning. "It may not simply be hobbies and crafts which are related to well-being, but rather the opportunity they provide for freedom of choice, self-expression, and personal fulfillment" (Dupuis and Smale 1995, 84). In a study of older francophone Canadians, Bourque and colleagues (2005) found that, for women, social support from family, friends, and children led to high life satisfaction.

Leithman (2005) studied satisfaction among 146 Canadian men and women aged 50 and over. She found that anxiety and financial regret over money decisions led to lower life satisfaction for both men and women. Newall (2005) also found a link between regret (over things not done, the death of a loved one, and health behaviours) and lower life satisfaction. Life satisfaction depends on a person's attitude, expectations about life, and activities.

PERSONALITY DEVELOPMENT

Stage Theories

Some psychologists who study the individual in society focus on personality development. A number of researchers describe this development as a series of stages. Erik Erikson (1963), for instance, created one of the best-known stage models of the life cycle. McCrae and Costa (1990, 11–12) call it "the single most important theory of adult personality development." Erikson's model describes eight stages of ego development. At each stage, he says, the person faces a crisis with two possible outcomes. If a person gets through the crisis successfully, growth occurs. As a result, the person reaches a new stage of development. If not, the person experiences some psychopathology that inhibits further development.

The task of late adulthood, Erikson says, is "to be, through having been, to face not being" (1959, Appendix). Wisdom is the virtue of this last stage; it comes when the person achieves "**integrity**" and overcomes the threat of "despair and disgust" (1959, 98). Like other psychoanalytical thinkers, Erikson describes old age as a time of inwardness, a time when a person reflects on the past and brings closure to life. At this point, he says, a person with a healthy personality accepts his life as the product of his own actions within a particular culture. This last stage sums up the seven earlier stages, and when a person achieves integrity, Erikson says, it brings a wholeness to life. A person who displays integrity inspires the young to trust in the culture and to follow its prescriptions for action (Erikson 1982).

Some writers have expanded on Erikson's outline of middle and later life. Erikson began as a child psychologist, and his life-cycle model reflects his interest in children. In his classic paper "Growth and Crises of the Healthy Personality" (1950), for example, he spends

45 pages on the first 20 years of life and devotes only five pages to the next 50 to 60 years.

Peck ([1955] 1968) modified Erikson's model by adding more stages to it. Erikson's last stage, Peck said, "seems to be intended to represent in a global, nonspecific way all the psychological crises and crisis-solutions of the last forty or fifty years of life" (88) Peck divided this last stage of life into two periods—middle and old age. He found seven crises a person had to overcome within these periods. At each stage, the person gives up the narrow commitments—to the body, to people, to concepts, and, finally, to the self—that dominated earlier stages of life. Peck's work shows that middle and later life are complex and active periods of development.

Erikson, Peck, and others (Gould 1978; Levinson 1978) propose that a stage model of development best describes middle and later life. Each writer proposes an ideal pattern of aging and development, implying that those who follow it live a successful old age, while those who deviate from it face problems and frustrations as they age. Later studies question whether a set of universal stages exists. Surveys of large numbers of people have not found the stages these models predict. Lacy and Hendricks (1980), for example, looked for attitude changes predicted by Gould's work. They used data from a survey of more than 9,000 people, but could not find attitude shifts to support Gould's stages.

Braun and Sweet (1983–84) reviewed data from four large surveys to see if passages from one stage of life to another existed. They compared personality differences within and between age groups. Although they did find personality differences between age groups they also found that in studies done at different times and in different countries (the United States and Canada), the characteristics of each age stage differed. In addition, they found that after a passage around age 19, little developmental change took place in people's attitudes as they aged. These findings don't support the stage model of adult development. Dixon and Cohen (2001, 135) say that the research shows personality changes in adulthood. But it doesn't show "changes through particular sequences leading to specific endstates."

Butler (1975; also Novak 1985–86) has criticized the stage model of development for another reason. He challenges the idea that people in old age can only accept who they are and what they have been. "People are locked in by such a theory," he says. They may look healthy from Erikson's point of view, but they suffer because they are trapped by their work, marriage, or lifestyle. "Excessive or exaggerated identity," according to Butler, "seems clearly to be an obstacle to continued growth and development through life and to appreciation

of the future. Human beings need the freedom to live with change, to invent and reinvent themselves a number of times throughout their lives" (400–401). Blau (1973, 185) warns that adults can "become too well adjusted to society's expectation and insufficiently attuned to their own nature and needs" in old age.

Stage models create a simplistic picture of current conditions. Today, people divorce, remarry, have children, start businesses, leave careers, return to careers, and return to school at all ages in adulthood. Studies find many stages in the life cycle and different stages and patterns for men and women. These findings reflect the diversity of the life course in a time of social change (Ryff, Kwan, and Singer 2001).

SELF-DEVELOPMENT IN LATER LIFE

Breytspraak (1995, 93) defines the **self** as "the ability to be aware of one's own boundaries and individuality and to reflect upon these." The self can act as both subject and object.

Breytspraak (1995) says that two motives shape behaviour as people age. First, people try to view themselves positively and to present a good image of themselves to others. Second, people try to maintain their sense of self in the face of a changing social environment. This makes the self a dynamic process more than a state of being. The self constantly shapes interaction and interprets events to achieve these two goals. Researchers report that self-constructs may change throughout life. Compared to younger people, for example, older people have a more limited view of their future selves. They reported fewer hopes and fears for their future selves. And they tend to define themselves in relation to their current concerns, especially health (Blanchard-Fields and Abeles 1996).

Aging poses a number of challenges to the self. These challenges come from at least three sources: social attitudes toward older people, physical decline, and the loss of social roles. Ageism, for example, poses a challenge to everyone in later life; in our society a person must work to combat ageism. The self's sensitivity to others' perceptions can make experiencing this bias a painful experience. It can lower a person's self-esteem. A strong social support network will make it easier to resist and overcome ageism. For example, friends and family can give a person feelings of worth and importance that combat negative stereotypes.

Physical decline also challenges a person's sense of self (Chapman 2005). A person who derives self-esteem from playing sports may feel let down as his or her ability decreases with age. Losing the ability to drive can cause a profound blow to self-esteem because our culture links driving with maturity, adulthood, freedom, and self-efficacy. Even people with Alzheimer's disease, a radical loss of the self, resist giving up driving a car. Sports programs for older people, such as the Seniors Olympics or the Seniors Golf Tour, help people maintain their self-esteem in the face of physical decline. So do programs that refresh older people's driving skills.

Furthermore, role loss can rob a person of self-worth. Social roles give a person status, purpose, and a sense of achievement. Retirement, loss of a spouse, and the empty nest all challenge people's sense of self as they age. Most people cope with these role losses and find new sources of self-esteem. A retired teacher may find self-worth as a volunteer counsellor. A retired machinist may find self-esteem in a second career as a handyman. Sometimes these new roles lead to a more satisfying sense of self. The challenge of role loss demands that the older person search for new meaning in later life.

Ryff and her colleagues (1999) report that higher income and more education lead to greater feelings of well-being in later life. Wealthier, better-educated people feel more purpose in life and report more personal growth in old age. This summary of the literature shows the link between the self and social conditions such as income, education, and social class. Likewise, a person's culture plays a role in self-development. How does a person's culture view old age? What roles does the culture offer older people? Answers to these questions shape a person's sense of self in later life.

Ryff and Singer (1996, cited in Clarke et al. 2000) say that in modern society "opportunities for continued growth and development and for meaningful experience may be limited." Ryff, Kwan, and Singer (2001) call for more research on the effects of social integration on health in later life. Singer and Ryff (1999, cited in Ryff et al. 2001) found, for example, that people with a history of poverty showed less physical decline if they had strong social relationships.

SPIRITUALITY: THE SEARCH FOR MEANING IN LATER LIFE

Chapman (2005) says that identity in later life relies on a lifestory, and this story changes over time. A person in later life, having lived a story shaped by social obligations and external goals, may begin an inward journey. Tornstam (2005) refers to this as "gerotranscendence"—the self begins to expand its boundaries and reflect on the meaning of human life.

This search for fulfillment in later life can take many forms, including religious faith, attendance at religious services, and non-traditional spiritual beliefs. Some people see spirituality as the person's relationship to God (Moore et al. 2006). Moore and colleagues (2006) found that spirituality and faith in God gave people a sense of purpose and enthusiasm. Other people take a more philosophical view. Moberg (2001, 10) defines spirituality as a person's "ultimate concern, the basic value around which all other values are focused, the central philosophy of life."

Some people express their spirituality outside traditional religious channels. They may feel oneness with nature or a commitment to the betterment of all life. Some older people turn to Eastern and Western meditation practices to feel a sense of wholeness. Yoga and tai chi exercises can create a sense of unity within oneself and with the environment. Studies show that spiritual practices such as these can lead to better health, improved social relations, and high life satisfaction (Chan 2003).

Richard and colleagues (2005, 23) studied the quality of later life in urban environments by interviewing older people in Montreal as part of a national study. About half of the groups in their study mentioned spirituality or religion as an important part of aging well. Some people linked quality of life to traditional religious belief. One person said, "I have peace of mind … Because I'm a religious person." Another took a broader view of spirituality. "I'm not really religious," he said, "in the sense of belonging fully to a particular church, although I'm a Catholic. I find interest and solace in the general attitude to the development of the universe …" One woman said, "I don't think I could be a survivor without faith. And I talk about spirituality, not religion, because sometimes religion doesn't provide the answers for everyone." These responses illustrate that faith and belief mean different things to different people.

The diversity of Canadian life, with its many ethnic and cultural groups, leads to many different religious and spiritual perspectives. Most Canadians claim Christianity as their religious belief. Forty-four percent of adult Canadians claim Roman Catholicism as their form of Christianity and 30 percent claim Protestantism (Statistics Canada 2003s). Other faiths include Judaism, other Christian faiths, Islam, Bahai, Buddhism, Hinduism, Sikhism, Confucianism, and Taoism.

Canadian spiritual life in the past often centred on the church or synagogue. Religion gave people a common set of values, a community of like-minded people, and a meaning to life. Many older people today still feel a strong connection to their religious community and have a strong religious faith (Clark 2000).

Compared with other age groups, older Canadians report the highest rate of attendance at religious services (Clark 2000, 2003). Thirty-seven percent of seniors report that they engage in religious activity at least once a week (Lindsay 1999). Older age groups have kept up their religious attendance while younger age groups show a decrease in attendance.

A greater proportion of older women, compared with older men, report activity in their faith community. Older women stay active in their religious community even after widowhood, but widowers show a drop in attendance at services (Clark 2000). Compared to younger people, seniors, also report the largest financial contributions to their place of worship. Moberg (1997, cited in Schulz-Hipp 2001, 87) says that older people show the strongest religious belief "on almost all measures" and that "this has remained the same year after year when similar questions are asked."

Clark and Schellenberg (2006) created a religiosity index to measure the strength of religious practice and belief among Canadians. This index measures four dimensions of religion: affiliation, attendance, personal practice, and importance of religion. A person could score between 1 and 13 on this index. A person with no affiliation scored zero. Forty-four percent of people aged 60 and over scored between 11 and 13 (the highest grouping) on this index—twice the proportion of people aged 15 to 29 and one and a half times the proportion of 45- to 59-year-olds.

Older people face some barriers to religious attendance as they get older. Illness, disability, and transportation problems often limit religious attendance as a person ages. But even with these challenges, 62 percent of people aged 60 and over say religion remains very important to them, and 58 percent say they maintain a weekly private religious practice (Clark and Schellenberg 2006).

This commitment to religion may partly reflect the past experiences of older people. In the past, religion played a bigger role in people's lives than it does today. The commitment to religion may also reflect the role that faith can play as health, income, and social supports decline in late old age. Coping methods included prayer, faith in God, and support from clergy and the faith community. Religious belief can help a person find meaning in the face of despair.

Fry (2000) studied religiosity and spirituality in a community and an institutional sample of older people in Alberta. The study found that religious participation and spiritual practices predicted greater feelings of well-being. Religiosity and spirituality had more influence on well-being than measures of social resources or physical health.

Religious leaders and caregivers can help older people live their faith. It's important that professionals understand and respect the religious traditions of the people they serve. Clergy can help a religious community provide support to older members, and they can help older members take part in their religious communities. Support can take the form of arranging outreach religious services or car pools to places of worship.

Spiritual practices, whether formal religious services or quiet reflection on the past, can bring fullness to later life. McFadden (1996) says that researchers and practitioners need to learn more about the many expressions of religion and spirituality in later life. They can then apply this understanding to improve the quality of later life.

LIFE-SPAN DEVELOPMENTAL PERSPECTIVE

The **life-span developmental perspective** sees the individual as continually changing from birth to death (Baltes and Goulet 1970). Unlike stage models, it does not describe an end point or goal of development (such as integrity or ego transcendence). Instead, the life-span developmental model treats crisis and change as a constant part of life. "At the very moment when completion seems to be achieved," Riegel (1976, 697) says, "new questions and doubts arise in the individual and in society."

The life-span developmental model views development as a **dialectical process**. Through this process, the individual changes in response to societal demands and society changes in response to individual action and adaptation (Riegel 1975). Life-span developmental theorists find many patterns and stages of aging. They say that people's personalities differ, as do their coping styles and the resources they use in dealing with the world.

McDonald, Donahue, and Moore (2000), for example, describe the responses people make to unemployment in later life. They found at least two responses to layoffs in later life. Some people still saw themselves as workers and looked for new jobs. Other people defined the layoff as early retirement (see Ryff, Kwan, and Singer 2001). The path chosen by a person depended in part on the individual's pension benefits, the timing of the job loss, and the person's attitude. One early retiree said, "Oh, we were gearing down. We figured we'd retire at 60, so it was three years earlier." A less happy worker could barely contain his anger. He said, "Well, when I … after all the time and never received the interviews and no answer back, I … made up my mind, that's it.

Like, that's me finished for the rest of my life for working" (McDonald, Donahue, and Moore 2000, 75).

The life-span developmental model proposes that older people, like these former workers, give meaning to the events that shape their lives. Some people accept events and build them into their life plan. Other people resist change and fight to hold onto their former selves. The life-span developmental perspective also says that older people can reshape society. For example, some older people have formed job bureaus. These agencies, often run by seniors, help retirees find work that suits their interests and abilities.

Older peoples' responses to aging differ by gender, age cohort, and social class. All of these differences create varied patterns of aging. The life-span developmental model turns the researchers' attention to the social context to explain the differences in the time of onset, direction, and duration of development in later life.

PERSONALITY AND SOCIAL CONTEXT

Life-span developmental researchers study three types of environmental effects: (1) **non-normative events** (unexpected events such as illnesses, layoffs, and accidents); (2) **normative history-graded events** (historical events that shape a person's life, such as the Great Depression of the 1930s or World War II); and (3) **normative age-graded events** (socially sanctioned events that occur most often at a certain age like marriage or retirement).

Non-Normative Events

Sociologists define norms as shared rules or guidelines that prescribe correct behaviour under certain conditions. Every society has age norms that prescribe how a person of a certain age should act. University students, for example, can travel across the country with backpacks each summer, see Europe on Eurail passes, and sleep in railway stations or open fields. People accept this behaviour from the young, and they even expect students to take time off to travel. Social scientists call this a normative life event.

People can also go through non-normative events, including accidents, sudden changes in health, or the death of a child. Social psychologists call these events non-normative because society does not prescribe that everyone experience them and because people cannot plan for them.

Non-normative events or life crises can lead to shock and fear. Novak (1985) studied the response to life events in a sample of 25 healthy, middle-

class, community-dwelling older people in Winnipeg. These people all scored high on a standard test of self-actualization (a measure of personality development). Most of them had gone through at least one major non-normative event—early retirement, loss of a spouse, or an illness.

Novak (1985) reports that these non-normative events had a common pattern. First, a person faced a problem or moment of crisis—a "challenge." These challenges included loss of a spouse, early retirement, or illness. Second, individuals "accepted" the challenge and interpreted it as a demand for some response. Third, they responded to or "affirmed" their lives in spite of the challenge. This response allowed them to enter a new phase of life beyond the roles and responsibilities of middle age.

These people were studied after they had passed through the life event. Did they succeed in affirming their lives because of their self-actualizing, integrated personalities, or did the life events they faced lead them to a new integrated stage of adulthood? Longitudinal research of healthy active older people can help answer these questions.

History-Graded Events

Non-normative events describe sudden changes in a person's personal life, but history-graded events change the lives of many age cohorts. The term "cohort," as stated in an earlier chapter, describes a group of people born at the same point or within the same period (usually five or ten years) of time.

Older people who were between the ages of 75 and 85 in 2005, for example, were born between 1920 and 1930. These people share the experiences of World War II and the Great Depression. If you talk to one of them about their past, you will almost always hear stories about the Depression and the war. These historic events left their mark on this cohort, shaping their family lives, work lives, and values.

Tindale (1980) studied a group of poor older men in a large Canadian city. Most of them had lived through the Depression as teenagers. They rode the rails as hobos, and picked tobacco or fruit for 25 cents an hour. They had little education and few family ties. Their later lives showed the effects of their past. "They were poor before the depression," Tindale says, "poorer still during it, and only a little less poor after it" (1980, 91). In later life these men lived alone on government pensions. They ate and slept in the downtown missions and Salvation Army shelters. They never had much, and they did not expect much at the time of the study.

The cohort born between 1945 and 1955 (55- to 65-year-olds in 2010), for example, expect different things from life and from society than do other age cohorts, based on their experiences. These people belong to one of the largest cohorts in Canadian history. Canada built elementary schools for them when they were children in the 1950s and 1960s, universities for them in the 1960s and 1970s, and the private sector built housing for them in the 1980s. They have lived through a relatively peaceful, affluent time in Canada's history, and they expect more from society than do older age groups.

As cohorts age (and members die), cohorts replace one another in society's age structure. Riley, Johnson, and Foner (1972) call this "cohort flow." As cohorts flow through the age structure, they change the size of particular age groups (e.g., the size of the group 20 to 30 years old differed in 1940 and 1970 and 2010). New cohorts also bring new experiences with them as they age. The oldest cohorts today, for example, have less education than younger ones. In 1990, for example, 62.7 percent of people aged 65 and older had less than a high school education. By 2004 this figure had dropped to 46.6 percent. The higher educational attainment of younger cohorts explains this change. These cohorts enter later life with more postsecondary diploma and university education, improving the average education level for seniors. Future cohorts will enter later life with even more education (Turcotte and Schellenberg 2007). They may demand new educational opportunities as they age.

The model of aging used by Riley, Johnson, and Foner omits a few important concepts about aging and age grading. Historical events, for example, also get filtered through the age stratification system, the system of age grades a society uses (e.g., child, adolescent, young adult). The 1920–30 cohort went through the Great Depression of the 1930s in childhood and adolescence. The Depression affected their health (due to poor diet) and their educational opportunities (some had to work at an early age to help support their families). The Depression also affected the cohort born between 1930 and 1940, but it had a different effect on these people. They lived through the Depression as infants and children. Some of them may not remember the Depression at all; others may simply have accepted the hard times as "the way things are."

Gerontologists use the term "generation" to describe people who share an awareness of their common historical or cultural experiences, but who may come from different age cohorts. The Baby Boom generation spans cohorts born between 1945 and the early 1960s; they all lived under the threat of nuclear war, they lived through the turbulent political times of the 1960s, and they lived through a relatively affluent time in Canadian history.

Braun and Sweet (1983–84) found that a "generational event" theory of personality better explained the differences between age groups than did a theory of life stages. **Generational event theory** says that attitudes form for a generation in their teens. (See Exhibit 7.1). People who grow up at the same time in the same society share the same attitudes. These attitudes stay fairly stable throughout life. This may be because people respond in the same ways to life's demands, others expect the same responses of them, and people choose their friends and contacts to support a stable sense of self.

These studies all show the effect of social and historical events on individual personality. Like non-normative events, history-graded events happen without warning, and sometimes the changes they bring about do not show up until years later. Society also shapes personality growth more directly through normative age grading.

Normative Age-Graded Events

Anthropologists report that all societies move people through a series of age grades. Age grades define certain rights and responsibilities for their members. They give order to the life course and help people judge their own development.

Males of the Nandi tribe in Kenya, for example, belong to one of seven age groups—two for boys, one for warriors, and four for elders. These groups give males their status and allow them to play certain roles at given times in their lives. Likewise, pre-industrial societies recognized three stages of life—infancy-childhood, mature adulthood, and old age.

Industrialized society today includes the stages of infancy, childhood, adolescence, young adulthood, middle age, and old age. Some writers have now added a new stage, the "Third Age," after middle age but before late old age (the "fourth age") begins. This new stage makes sense in a society where people can expect to live in good health for 10 or 15 years after age 65.

Neugarten, Moore, and Lowe (1968) say that people internalize the age-grade system and know the proper time for a life event to occur. A Canadian middle-class girl who falls in love today at the age of 14 will feel it is too early to marry. A woman graduate student in her early 20s may also feel it is too early to settle down. A single woman in her late 40s who wants to get married may feel it is too late.

Someone for whom major life events come early or late—a teenaged mother or a newlywed octogenarian—may feel out of sync with the age-status system. Gerontologists call this **age-status asynchronization**.

● Exhibit 7.1

GENERATIONAL DIFFERENCES IN THE WORKPLACE TODAY

Supervisor (age 50): It's 8:15.

Nick (age 23): Uh-huh.

S: You're 15 minutes late.

N: Uh-huh.

S: We start here at 8 o'clock ...

N: Well, I get my work done. So what's the difference when I get here or when I leave? Sometimes I stay late, when everyone else is gone.

S: Just try to be on time from now on.

Nick (to his friends later): Can you believe it? He got on my case over 15 minutes. Fifteen lousy minutes. What's the difference when I get in or leave as long as I get my work done? What a drag. I wish I worked for Google or Yahoo! They provide snacks and sodas all day and a volleyball court.

This dialogue took place between workers from two different generations. Each has a different view of work, time, responsibility, and achievement. A number of books and studies attempt to explain generational differences in the workplace today. Lynne C. Lancaster and David Stillman, in their book, *When Generations Collide* describe the uneasy coexistence of four generations in the workplace today.

The table below summarizes their findings:

The age difference between the young worker and the older supervisor in the dialogue above in part explains the difference in their view of punctuality. But historical events (the Internet, new forms of virtual communication, tele-commuting) have created a younger generation with different views of everyday life.

Lancaster and Stillman (2002, 32) say, "... we need to look at how each generation shares a common history and how, having lived through certain events and conditions each generation has adopted its own personality." The authors say that these generation-based personalities mingle and sometimes clash in the workplace (and perhaps in family and social life as well). We tend to think of personality as innate and unique to each individual. But this analysis suggests that historical and social events shape the personalities of entire generations.

What do you think of this analysis? Do you see examples of generational differences at school, at home, at work? Do you agree with the descriptions of each generation given above? Does this analysis provide some insight into how people relate to one another today?

Does this approach apply to minority group members? To people who grew up in another country and migrated to Canada? Do men and women show these tendencies equally? Does this theory confuse differences due to age (e.g., the views of young people compared to those of older people) with differences due to generational or historical events (e.g., the influence of technology on younger people's view on life)?

Generations	Birth Years	Events	Values	Personality
Traditionalists	1900–1945	WWI, Great Depression, WWII	Save for rainy day, God fearing, hardworking, patriotic	loyal
The Baby Boom	1946–1964	Postwar peacetime affluence, television	Idealistic, questioning authority, competitive, "Me Generation"	optimistic
Gen X	1965–1979	Media explosion: cable TV, VCR/DVDs, electronic games, Internet, two-career families	"Show me the money," resourceful, independent	skeptical
Millennials or Gen Y	1980–2000	Cell phones, IM, Facebook, virtual communities	Practical, technologically aware and skilled, confident to take action, appreciate diversity	realistic

Sources: Lynne C. Lancaster and David Stillman. 2002. *When Generations Collide*. New York: HarperCollins.

People can be on time in certain ways and late or early in others. They can feel on time when they choose to marry, but late in advancing in their profession. Research shows that occupation, ethnic background, and social class affect the timing of life events.

For example, Canadian women with less education tend to marry earlier and have children earlier (Kobayashi et al. 2001). Today many highly educated young women put off marriage and child-rearing in order to start their careers. Women also go through different life events than men. Men typically start a career in their early 20s and stay in the labour force until retirement. But a woman may enter a new phase of life in her late 40s. At that time her last child leaves home, menopause occurs, and she may re-enter the labour market and begin a new career.

Social groups regulate their members' life cycles. Groups expect certain behaviour from their members, and members rely on these expectations to guide their actions. Members also observe the transition times of others and get a sense for when changes should occur. These normal transition times and expected behaviours differ by historical period. In the past, for example, women fit a traditional model of the life course. Today, women show more diverse life course patterns (Kobayashi et al. 2001). For example, more women than ever before have children before they marry. This reflects an increased acceptance of common-law partnerships or single parenthood.

The literature on the life course shows that researchers have increased their interest in life events, life transitions, and life trajectories. This increased interest may reflect recent changes in the timing and sequencing of life events. Women show more diverse patterns of development than ever before. Changing social values, birth control, new career options, more education, and the need for two earners in a family account for this change. This has led to a more flexible life course for women.

The life-span developmental model accepts the idea that maturation and psychological change affect human development, but it says that a more complete picture of human development requires knowledge of a person's life events and social context. It shows that society and history play important parts in shaping individual development.

ETHNICITY AND SOCIAL SUPPORTS

The National Advisory Council on Aging (2005) defines and "ethnocultural minority senior" as

1. someone whose race, ethnicity, religion, or culture differs from mainstream Canadians. A person who belongs to a visible minority may face discrimination

and prejudice in addition to the challenges that come with aging.

2. someone who has immigrated to Canada and aged here. Gee and colleagues (2004) report that people aged 65 and over make up nearly one-fifth (19.4 percent) of the immigrant population in Canada. Almost all of these older immigrants (93.8 percent) have lived in Canada 10 years or more.

3. someone who immigrated to Canada in later life. Recent immigrants to Canada face unique challenges as they age. More recent immigrants, compared to Canadian-born older people, had significantly poorer health. Compared to Canadian-born older people, recent older immigrants had a 1.5 times greater chance of activity limitation and poorer overall functional health. The inability to speak an official language keeps them from getting health care they need, and low income can lead to poor diet and unhealthy living conditions.

A person's immigration history, cultural background, language, and country of origin all affect how he or she will adjust to aging.

Sociologists define an ethnic group as a group of people who see themselves as being alike because of their common ancestry and who are seen as being alike by others (Hughes and Hughes 1952). Culture and ethnicity form a backdrop for psychological development in old age. Ethnic culture gives meaning to life events and can buffer life crises. The size and age composition of an ethnic community also determine the number of social supports a person has available in old age.

Canadian studies on ethnicity and aging show that older people from different ethnic groups (including those from British and French backgrounds) experience old age differently. Kobayashi (2000), for example, says that in 1996, 90 percent of Chinese elders in Canada were born in China, while only 15 percent of Japanese elders in Canada were born in Japan. For this reason, compared to Japanese elders, Chinese elders may have less access to a Canadian government pension. Newly arrived Chinese elders may also rely on family supports because they don't speak English or French (Pacey 2002). Even within one group, differences exist. Group members can differ by gender, social class, geography, religion, and political beliefs. Some group members have lived in Canada for many years, others have just arrived.

Most of the Canadian research so far has explored three theories that attempt to explain the ethnic elders' experiences: levelling theory, buffer theory, and multiple jeopardy theory.

Levelling Theory

According to **levelling theory**, aging levels ethnic differences. A decline in health or loss of a spouse will lead all older people (regardless of their ethnicity) to depend more on their families and on social services for help. These changes outweigh cultural differences in family structure or differences in cultural values of parent–child relations.

Rosenthal (1983) found support for the levelling theory of aging and ethnicity. She studied Anglo- and non-Anglo-Canadian older people in Ontario (Anglo-Canadians here are people who report a British background). Modernization theory predicts that Anglo-Canadian families will show weaker family ties compared with non-Anglo-Canadians and that non-Anglos will show more traditional family structures and more support for older people. Rosenthal (1983, 1986a) did not find support for this theory. Instead, she found that older Anglo-Canadians and non-Anglo-Canadians in her study reported similar family structures, similar views of family life, and similar family relations. She did find that slightly more non-Anglo-Canadians lived with their middle-aged children, but this difference disappeared in older age groups. Rosenthal (1983, 14) says "there is a strong suggestion that age levels these differences [between groups]."

Buffer Theory

Buffer theory says that ethnic identity buffers people from role loss as they age. A number of studies have found support for the buffer theory of aging and ethnicity. Kobayashi (2000), for example, studied third-generation Japanese adult children and their parents. A large majority of the adult children felt a commitment to support their parents. Children provided emotional, financial, and service support.

Thomas (2001) reports that nearly half of all older recent immigrants (48 percent) lived with their families. This helped buffer the challenges of aging, such as culture shock, language differences, death of a spouse, or poor health. Many of these recent immigrants came from Asia (Chui et al. 2007). Their cultural values make living with their children a desirable option. Pacey (2002) found that Chinese seniors between the ages of 80 and 85, compared to non-Chinese seniors, showed nearly four times the likelihood of living with their children. This buffered the effects of lower income and their inability to speak English or French.

Chappell (2005) studied Chinese seniors (aged 55 and over) in seven cities across Canada. She found that people with a strong connection to their ethnic roots felt life had improved since age 55. These people took part in traditional cultural activities, visited China, immigrated to Canada to reunite with their families, and believed in ancestor worship. Participation in Chinese culture buffered the challenges that came with aging. Chappell says that people who get involved in traditional Chinese culture "report improvements in social relationships and community participation … Their traditional culture would appear to be an important factor in a positive experience in old age" (84, 87).

Fuller-Thomson (2005) found that a high percentage of Aboriginal grandparents cared for their grandchildren in "skipped-generation" households (where only members of the grandparent and grandchild generations lived together). Though Aboriginal people make up only 2.8 percent of the Canadian population, they made up more than 17 percent of skipped-generation households. In part this reflects the traditional role of grandparents in Aboriginal culture, in which grandparents pass on the native way of life to their grandchildren. It also reflects the crises in some Aboriginal families where drug abuse, alcohol abuse, and imprisonment require the grandparents to step in as surrogate parents. The role of surrogate parent puts stress on Aboriginal elders who may have health problems and a spouse to care for. But the close tie to their grandchildren gives the Aboriginal elder a vital role in family and community life today.

Frideres (1994, cited in Wister and Moore 1998, 105) says that many Aboriginal elders face a "double alienation." They stand outside mainstream Canadian society and they have lost their role in their own communities. However, some programs work to reverse this trend. Vanderburgh (1988) reports that, in Ontario, the Ojibwa Cultural Foundation began an elders' program to revive the Aboriginal elders' role as mentors. The program arranges for elders to teach language skills, crafts, and healing methods to the young, and, with other programs, encourages elders to speak with authority at public gatherings about their experience. The mandate to speak with authority and play a guiding role in community life, rather than chronological age, is what defines elderhood. An Aboriginal person who achieves this status has a buffer against the stress of aging. Working for a higher cultural purpose can buffer people from the threat of meaninglessness that sometimes comes with old age and death.

Multiple Jeopardy Theory

Multiple jeopardy theory says that aging makes life worse for members of an ethnic group. Minority members have low status to begin with, and they often have low incomes too. Aging may add to their troubles.

Moore (1995) found support for the multiple jeopardy theory. She compared Aboriginal and non-Aboriginal older people. She found that Aboriginal men tended to have higher unemployment rates and lower incomes than non-Aboriginal men. Compared with non-Aboriginals, Aboriginal men and women, had about one and a half times the proportion of people with low incomes. Low income leads to poor health and poor housing. Wister and Moore (1998) report that Aboriginal elders often lack opportunities for work and have poor preventive health care services. Compared to the total Canadian population aged 45 and over, older Aboriginal people (aged 45 and over) have higher rates of diabetes, arthritis, heart disease, stroke, and other chronic illnesses (Prus and Lin 2005). Older Aboriginal people also have higher rates of disability, and studies estimate that older Aboriginal people have a hospitalization rate twice that of the national average (Wister and Moore 1998). These findings show that older Aboriginal people face multiple jeopardy. Older people in visible minorities show similar characteristics and also face multiple jeopardy (Chard 1995).

Older members of Asian, African, and Latin American ethnic groups show some of the lowest economic well-being on measures of labour force activity, retirement income, and investment income (Wanner and McDonald 1986). Lai and colleagues (2007) found that, compared to seniors born in Canada, older Chinese immigrants reported lower levels of physical and mental health. Visible minority elderly make up a large proportion of older immigrants. As they age they will add to the diversity of the older population and to the challenges that older people face.

The National Advisory Council on Aging (2005) reports that senior immigrant men earned on average 8.5 percent less than senior men born in Canada. Immigrant senior women had on average incomes 9.2 percent below Canadian-born women seniors. Immigrant senior men and women also had higher poverty rates than Canadian-born seniors.

The National Advisory Council on Aging (2005, 10) gives the following examples of how older minority members can face double jeopardy in their contact with the health care system.

Mrs. T. is a senior who immigrated to Canada from Vietnam as a young woman. She married and stayed at home to raise children while her husband worked outside the home. As is often common, her children adopted a Western way of life and when her husband got sick, she could not get the help she needed from her adult children. So, Mrs. T. made most of the hospital visits alone. At the hospital, she tried to communicate what she believed her husband needed but, due to her limited English, found that she could not make herself understood, yet the hospital never provided her with interpretation services. Mrs. T. believes that her husband's death could have been made easier were it not for the language barrier.

Mr. P. has recently undergone a surgical procedure and is currently in the hospital. After a short period of time, the staff have labelled him "a non-compliant" patient because he continues to get out of bed even though he was clearly instructed not to do so in order to heal. What the staff don't know is that, as a Muslim, Mr. P. is meeting his religious obligation to face Mecca, bow, and pray five times a day.

Gee and colleagues (2004, S68) say that "health care policies must begin to address the differential needs of immigrant adults by age group." The older immigrant, for example, "may have increased need for services, due to poor health status." Specific subgroups, like older immigrants from China, Taiwan, or India, may need dietary advice due to the rapid change in their diet after immigration. A subgroup that offers a strong ethnic community to immigrants may buffer the shock of immigration. Immigrants from less service-rich communities risk health care problems due to culture shock.

Marmen and Delisle (2003) found that French-speaking seniors outside Quebec face challenges similar to those of immigrants. Those who speak only French face problems when they need health care services. In provinces like Nova Scotia and New Brunswick older people who speak only French tend to live outside large urban centres in fringe or rural settings. In remote areas of New Brunswick, for example, 45 percent of the French-speaking senior population spoke only French. But French-speaking health care practitioners tend to work in urban centres.

Marmen and Delisle (2003, 26) say that seniors who speak only French and who live in rural areas may find health services in French "problematic." They conclude that to meet the needs of French-speaking seniors "healthcare providers ... have to be conveniently located for patients to be able to take advantage of their services" (Marmen and Delisle 2003, 27). This example shows that French Canadians can face issues similar to those of ethnic minorities when they lack community and language supports (see Exhibit 7.2).

The Challenge of Aging among Aboriginal Peoples: A Case Study of Multiple Jeopardy

Compared to the rest of Canada, Aboriginal communities have a younger age structure. The median age of Aboriginal people in Canada was 24.7 in 2001 (compared

● Exhibit 7.2

OVERCOMING BARRIERS: TELLING IT LIKE IT IS

Elvira Herrera, of the Centre for Spanish Speaking People in Toronto, composed the letter below. Five seniors in the centre's English as a Second Language program contributed to the letter. The letter shows the tensions that can exist in families that sponsor the immigration of older members in Canada. In particular, the letter points to the language barrier that keeps older immigrants from living a normal life. The letter ends on a note of hope for a better life in their new country.

My dear family:

How happy I felt coming to Canada to live with you! I thought all my dreams would come true: Enjoying the company of my children, watching my grandchildren grow up, learning English, having a job, making new friends. ... Look at me now. ...

Oh! if you knew how many times I have tried to write this letter, my dear son, my dear daughter, my beloved grandchildren. But I preferred to hide my feelings in order not to make you suffer, too. Did you ever think of the consequences when you sponsored me to come to this country? Then I could have thought twice before deciding to make this enormous change in my life. Now it's too late. I don't have my house, my friends, my independence, I don't have money I can spend freely, and I think I'm also losing my family!

Please do not think I don't value your efforts. I know you have to work hard and don't have much time for housekeeping or taking care of your children. But I did not know you wanted such help from me. It's my pleasure to babysit my grandchildren from time to time, but I didn't think this would be a daily obligation. When I told you that I wanted to learn English so I could go out by myself and feel more secure, your answer was, "Mama, you are very old, you cannot learn English. Beside that, I need you here." For years, I didn't venture to ask again. I thought the least I could do was help you, since I was already a burden on the family. But, to tell you the truth, I cannot stand it anymore! I couldn't even go to church on Sundays, if your husband was tired or not in a mood to drive me there, because you were afraid that I could get lost if I went by bus.

You came to this country very young. You have already adapted to the culture and customs here. For me, as a senior, the process is very difficult. I cannot even communicate with my grandchildren because they haven't learned to respect the old ones. When I ask the eldest to go with me to a store, he refuses, because he doesn't want anyone to know that we speak Spanish. He's ashamed to go out with his grandma. I feel so lonely and frustrated. ... When I lived in my homeland I used to go everywhere, saying hello to everybody, solving problems, helping people, receiving friends in my home. Now, when your friends come over, I prefer to go to the basement and cry silently in my room, because your friends aren't mine and I do not feel welcome to join you. You don't seem to care about talking in English, although you know I don't understand. And I don't have the confidence to invite over some people I have met at church. This is not my house. I just have a dark little room in the basement. ...

However, things are going to change now. A friend opened my eyes. She asked me, "Why don't you go to school? Why don't you have coffee with us when we invite you? Why do you seem so sad?"

I know you were very surprised when I told you about my registration in a seniors' English class. I know you were mad at me because I wouldn't have lunch ready for the family, or be home to babysit your daughter until you returned from work. But dear one, I need to have a life, too. I can help you. As your mother, I am willing to do that. But you know I need my own activities and friends, too. I know now that I'm capable of learning English, although you laugh at me and try to convince me not to go back to classes because I'm "wasting my time." Now I ride the bus, I have joined a seniors' club and I don't need anyone to take me to church. Certainly I am old, but I have rediscovered the valuable person inside me. I hope you'll understand.

I want to lead my own life, a life worth living, as long as I am alive. Let me live.

Your loving mother.

Source: "Growing Older, Growing Bolder," *The Moment* 21 (1994): II. Courtesy of Jack Costello, director of the Jesuit Centre for Social Faith and Justice.

to 37.1 for the total Canadian population). But Statistics Canada projects an increase in median age to 27.8 years for Aboriginal peoples by 2017 (compared to 41.3 years for Canada as a whole). This means more than a doubling of the Aboriginal elder population from 42,400 in 2001 to 92,500 in 2017. The proportion of elders in Aboriginal communities will remain relatively small at under 7 percent, but Aboriginal peoples will have to meet the needs of a larger older population in their communities (Statistics Canada 2005c).

Buffer theory says that a culture can buffer the effects of physical decline and loss that come with age. Aboriginal culture, under the best conditions, buffers elders from some of the effects of aging. But Aboriginal culture cannot always buffer people from the lifelong inequalities, poverty, and health conditions that lead to problems in old age. Margaret Labillois (1994), elder and former Micmac chief, describes the decline in status of older Aboriginal people in her own lifetime. "When I was growing up," she says, "elders were always respected for their knowledge and their experience. They were our teachers, our books, our education, our baby-sitters, our story tellers, and our special helpers—in short, a way of life. … Today elders are no longer elders, but just old people" (15; see also d'Anglure 1994). Many Aboriginal older people today live in poverty. For example, half the elders in the Northwest Territories and Nunavut have so little income that they receive the Guaranteed Income Supplement. And many other elders qualify for the GIS but have not applied (National Advisory Council on Aging 2004).

Aboriginal seniors have few housing options on reserves. The cost of housing can put home ownership outside the reach of all but the wealthiest person; in Nunavut near Quebec, a typical single-family home costs $196,823. This is three times the cost of a similar home elsewhere in the province (National Advisory Council on Aging 2004). Older people who live off-reserve may live in poor-quality housing.

Modernization accounts for part of this decline in status of Aboriginal older people. Because young people receive formal education and the mass media provides so much information, older people's knowledge seems obsolete. But ageism and racism throughout life also account for the decline in Aboriginal elders' well-being. Chipperfield and Havens (1992), for example, studied Aboriginal elders' own sense of respect at two points in time. They found that in both the mid-1970s and mid-1980s Aboriginal elders gave themselves the lowest rating of respect of any ethnic group in Manitoba.

Aboriginal older people suffer from more health problems than non-Aboriginals. In the Northwest Territories, for example, elders have high rates of respiratory disease, diabetes, and lung cancer (National Advisory Council on Aging 2004). Elders also spend twice the average length of time with a disability in life, compared with non-Aboriginals. Poor nutrition, poor living conditions, and poverty throughout life lead to poor health in Aboriginals in old age (Armstrong-Esther 1994). Unfortunately, many Aboriginal communities lack a complete hospital, and some lack a nursing home or health counsellors to help people cope with diseases such as diabetes.

Professional care providers may assume that Aboriginal older people get the support they need from their families. But some people question the Aboriginal family's ability to care for an older member. The National Advisory Council on Aging (2004, 3), for example, says that support can sometimes disguise exploitation: "A senior who qualifies for subsidized housing may soon find other family members moving in. Whether this is an act of support or a situation of abuse is not always clear."

A recent revival of interest in Aboriginal culture and tradition has restored some older people to the status of elder (National Advisory Council on Aging 2004). In Nunavut, elders attend monthly meetings to express their views. They share their concerns and ideas with younger community members. The meetings spun off a series of camps where young people learn from the elders. The young people learn traditional skills and find links to their heritage. This suggests that Aboriginal elders may still play a useful role in their culture.

Limitations of Ethnicity and Aging Theories

Each of the theories discussed gives some clues about how ethnicity affects social and psychological well-being as a person ages. But each theory has its limits. Levelling theory, for example, may hold true only for people in late old age. At that point, almost everyone turns to government-run services such as home care or institutions for help. Buffer theory describes aging in a culture that holds the old in high esteem. But an ethnic group with a different belief system, or a group with few members in Canada, may find that ethnicity does not buffer the effects of aging.

For example, Hall (1993) studied 16 elderly Vietnamese immigrants in Lethbridge, Alberta (most of them women who lived with their adult children). They reported dissatisfaction with their living arrangements. They also said they felt isolated and rarely met with other relatives. Hall found that for many of them, life in

Canada meant boredom, a lack of social contacts, and clashes with children and grandchildren.

The case of Aboriginal people in Canada also calls into question buffer theory. Compared with non-Aboriginal people, Aboriginal elders have a lower life expectancy, less formal education, and lower income, and they are more likely to live in poor-quality housing. Blandford and Chappell (1990) found that older Aboriginal people reported lower life satisfaction and more loneliness than non-Aboriginal people. This example again shows that membership in an ethnic group may not buffer aging; social-psychological well-being in later life also depends on objective conditions such as health and social supports.

What can we conclude about the effects of ethnicity on aging from these theories and research reports? What seems certain is that the effects of ethnicity on aging depend on many things other than membership in an ethnic group. The age distribution of the ethnic group's population (the ratio of younger to older people in the group), the geographic closeness of the group (how easily members can pool their resources), the degree of assimilation of the group into Canadian society (how well members can use available resources), and the time of immigration (recent immigrants have less access to public pension funds and less time to save for retirement) all influence the experience of aging for ethnic elders. These conditions differ for each ethnic group, so that "ethnicity" or membership in an ethnic group can mean many things.

Eastern and Southern European ethnic groups, for example, can differ as much from one another as they do from a British ethnic group. This observation also applies to immigrants from Asian countries such as China, Japan, or Vietnam. Asian immigrants come from different societies and have different cultural traditions and religious beliefs. Also, some older immigrants have lived in Canada for many years, and others arrived only a few years ago. Studies of ethnicity need to specify the social and economic conditions of the groups under study.

The next section discusses a model for understanding the social causes of individual problems in later life. It also describes some of the ways social breakdown can be avoided or reversed in the case of immigrant seniors.

THE SOCIAL ROOTS OF PROBLEMS IN OLD AGE

Studies of how history and culture influence aging show that successful aging, maladjustment,

and psychopathology can have social roots. Some maladjustment in later life comes about because society gives older people fewer guides to define correct behaviour than it gives the young. In the case of seniors newly arrived from another country, for example, the norms of Canadian culture may not fit their understanding of old age.

Researchers say that older people in modern societies occupy a tenuous status—a status or position in the social structure that does not have a role associated with it. A retiree occupies a status—that of a retired person—but does not have a role to play in society, since retirees are expected not to work, and nothing else is expected of them. The loss of roles in later life, through retirement, children growing up, or arrival in a new culture, excludes older people from taking part in society. It also signals a problem some older people have today: finding meaning in later life.

Loneliness

Perlman (2004) reviewed studies of loneliness among older people in four countries (Wales, the Netherlands, Finland, and Canada). He found evidence of loneliness among older people in each country. He reports that "loneliness appears to be present everywhere researchers look for it." "Others have found it in virtually all parts of the world (e.g., Africa, the Middle East, Japan)" (185). Why do people feel lonely? Does the person who lives alone feel lonely? Can a person with a large family feel lonely? Researchers have explored these questions.

Gerontologists distinguish between social isolation and loneliness. **Social isolation** refers to the decrease in social contacts that often comes with age (Hall and Havens 2002; de Jong Gierveld and Havens 2004). Widowhood, the deaths of friends, or children moving away can lead to social isolation. Havens and Hall (2001; Havens et al. 2004) studied isolation rates among older Manitobans. They found that 16 percent of older men and women described themselves as extremely isolated, and another 69 percent as very isolated.

Loneliness comes about when people feel a "relational deficit" or a gap between the number of relationships desired and the number they have (Sermat 1978). Loneliness refers to dissatisfaction with the quantity or the quality of social relationships (Hall and Havens 2002). An isolated person may or may not feel lonely, and a person may feel lonely despite having many social contacts. For example, a widow may play an active part in her bridge club, but she may feel lonely because she misses the company of her husband. Hall and Havens

(2002, citing Holmen et al. 1992) say that some older people who live with their children or with siblings report high levels of loneliness. Hall and Havens (2002) found that, in Manitoba, 45 percent of people aged 72 and over reported strong feelings of loneliness. The oldest group in the study (aged 90+) reported the most loneliness. Other Canadian studies report loneliness rates between 20 and 80 percent (Havens et al. 2004).

Researchers find that a drop in the number of social contacts and a feeling of loneliness often go together (Hall and Havens 2002). The death of family members, retirement, or a move to a new home can put a person at risk of loneliness. For example, people who live in an institution risk loneliness. Ryan (1998) studied hospitalized older people and found that people who reported decreased social contacts with family and friends reported more loneliness. Delisle (1988; also Havens et al. 2004) found that single older people, those without children, people in poor health or bed-ridden, people with poor education, introverts, timid people, or those with low self-esteem face the greatest risk of feeling lonely. People with disabilities may also feel lonely; they may find it difficult to go places and socialize with others. De Jong Gierveld and Havens (2004) refer to this as social loneliness, the lack of belongingness. They contrast this with emotional loneliness, the absence of an intimate figure in one's life, e.g., a partner or best friend.

The Fredericton 80+ Study looked at healthy people aged 80 and over in rural New Brunswick (Miedema and Tatemichi 2003). About one-third of the people in this study said they felt lonely sometimes or regularly. Women made up the majority of these cases. The researchers found that living alone and feeling dissatisfied with child contact best predicted feelings of loneliness. Dissatisfaction with child contact can feel especially distressing. De Jong Gierveld and Havens (2004, 111) say that "communication within the family and maintaining continuity across life phases" helps a person feel linked to others.

Havens and colleagues (2004) studied data on loneliness from the 1996 Aging in Manitoba study. The study found that nearly half of the sample of rural and urban seniors reported both isolation and loneliness. The researchers found differences in rural and urban sub-samples. They found that living alone and a decline in physical health led to feelings of isolation for both groups. But living alone predicted loneliness only for the urban group.

The researchers say that professional service workers and policy makers can influence feelings of loneliness. Programs that keep older people integrated into their communities can decrease loneliness; older people who get involved in planning for their communities feel important and worthwhile, which can reduce loneliness. Likewise, housing options can support socialization, and good transportation can help older people maintain and build relationships.

Most studies agree that a good old age means more than the acceptance of loss or isolation. The research suggests two ways to combat loneliness.

First, older people should maintain their social contacts with friends and neighbours. A project in England, for example, arranged for volunteers to visit frail and isolated older people. The older people reported satisfaction with the visits, and some friendships grew beyond the original program (Andrews et al. 2003). Moen and her colleagues (2000; also de Jong Gierveld and Havens 2004) say that church work and volunteering can decrease loneliness and isolation. French and her colleagues (2000, 69) found that helping others gave older people a purpose in life. As one woman told the researchers, "if there's nothing to get up for in the morning, what's the use of getting up? What's the use of living?" The prevention of loneliness should include broader changes in society that would help older people stay involved in social life.

Programs that promote social participation also reduce loneliness. Cohen and his colleagues (2006) created a choral group that practised and performed in public. The researchers compared this group to a control group. They found that the choral program led to better health and reduced loneliness. A lunch program that brought people together to learn about health issues also reduced feelings of loneliness (Sorrell 2006).

Second, older people need a supportive social setting to grow old in. Modern life can break up families and communities. Social resources can help older people keep in contact with their social network: better transportation, well-designed housing, and more recreational facilities can help older people combat loneliness. They give older people a choice of activities and a stronger sense of control over their lives.

Some institutions have used animal-assisted therapy (visits by a pet to a long-term- care facility) to combat loneliness (Banks and Banks 2003). The researchers found that visits of 30 minutes once a week reduced loneliness for patients who enjoyed the presence of animals. A controlled study found a significant decrease in loneliness among the group that received visits from a pet (Banks and Banks 2002).

Technology can also help older people combat loneliness. Cellphones and the Internet can help people to stay in touch with relatives and friends. A study of "cybersenior empowerment" (McMellon and Schiffman 2002) found that the Internet can help older people combat loneliness. The researchers conducted a survey of Internet use by a sample of older people. They found that nearly all of the people in the study who used the Internet (91 percent) used it to keep in touch with friends through e-mail. People in this study with physical limits or those who lived in social isolation felt more in control of their lives.

Older people run the risk of loneliness as they age. Some people adapt to social isolation and enjoy being alone, but others prefer a more active and engaged social life. Some people have large networks of friends and family; others may grow lonely as family and friendship circles shrink over time. Awareness of the potential for loneliness can help family members and social service providers meet seniors' needs.

Suicide

Men aged 65 to 69 had a suicide rate of 14.5 per 100,000 population in 2004, men aged 75 to 79 had a rate of 19.3, and men aged 85 to 89 and over had a rate of 26.8. These figures show that the suicide rate for men increases with age. Also, men aged 85 to 89 and over had the highest rate of suicide among all age groups. Compared to men, women had much lower suicide rates at all ages. Women aged 65 to 69 had a rate of 6.4 per 100,000, women aged 75 to 79 had a rate of 3.5, and women aged 85 to 89 had a rate of 4.4. In contrast to those of men, women's rates show a decline in older age groups (Statistics Canada 2008f).

Why do people commit suicide in old age? French sociologist Emile Durkheim (1951) proposed that a lack of social integration led to high rates of suicide in modern society. Normlessness or anomie, a lack of connection between the person and society, puts a person at risk. Current research on suicide in later life supports this view; older people often lose the contacts and links that prevent suicide. Researchers rank "death of a spouse" as the most negative life event. Retirement, the deaths of friends, and a move to a nursing home also weaken the older person's social network. As this network shrinks, the person may lose a sense of purpose and meaning, which increases the risk of suicide. Mireault and de Man (1996) report that people tend

to think about suicide if they live alone or in a nursing home, abuse alcohol, or feel dissatisfied with their health and their social supports. Older people who commit suicide often felt depressed. Men may face a higher risk than women if they lose a spouse or lose their social network as they age.

The National Advisory Council on Aging (2003, 3) says that "the consistently higher suicide rates for men aged 85 and older … is a longstanding problem that has not yet drawn the attention needed." Studies (Richardson, Lowenstein, and Weissberg 1989, cited in Health Canada 1994, 22) report that "in the month before committing suicide, three-quarters of elderly suicides visited their physicians, and during the week before, one-third visited their physicians." More awareness by physicians of the signs and symptoms of suicide might prevent some deaths. Also, older people should have better access to psychiatric services, should they need them. The media should make people more aware of the signs of potential suicide in older people.

CONCLUSION

Older Canadians face a number of threats to their social-psychological well-being. But, in general, they report high life satisfaction. They know about the problems of old age, such as loss of a spouse, illness, and physical decline, but they also see many good things about old age. Connidis (1983b) found that older people enjoyed their personal freedom and the chance to do the things they want to do. These advantages, she found, outweigh the problems that come with age. Northcott (1982) found similar results in a study of 440 people in Edmonton. "The elderly," he says, "are more likely than the nonelderly to report no area of life as a major source of pressure and the older the respondent the less pressure reported from all areas of life except health. As pressure falls, satisfaction tends to rise. … In short, the picture one gets of old age is that it is a period of relatively low pressure and relatively high satisfaction, though not without its problems." Each stage of life has its good and bad points, but "old age," he concludes, "looks far more attractive than stereotypes suggest" (77).

Summary

1. Social psychologists describe at least three models of good aging: disengagement, activity, and continuity. Research shows that each of these patterns can lead to high life satisfaction.

2. Men and women adapt differently to aging, but most older Canadians of both sexes report high life satisfaction. They report that they feel less pressure and enjoy more personal freedom in old age.

3. Theories of personality development state that people go through a series of predictable stages as they age. Erikson described three stages for middle and old age; other theorists describe more stages. Some studies question the universality of these stages, but nearly all researchers and theorists see later life as a time of challenge and change.

4. The life-span developmental perspective sees crisis and change as an essential part of life from birth to death. This view states that, as people age, they make choices in response to social demands. This perspective allows for many patterns of aging.

5. Self-development takes place throughout life. At least two motives shape development: the desire to present a good image of oneself and the desire to maintain a sense of self in the face of change. People face a number of challenges to the self in later life, including ageism, physical decline, and role loss.

6. Spiritual development can also take place in later life, although many older people today come into old age with strong religious beliefs. The diversity of Canadian society ensures a diversity of beliefs among older Canadians; some people express their spirituality outside traditional religious faiths.

7. Life events shape human development. These include non-normative events, normative history-graded events, and normative age-graded events. Studies of history-graded and age-graded events show the effects of social structures on personal development.

8. An ethnic group's culture and structure both shape the experience of aging. The group's values, beliefs, and degree of assimilation in part determine how young people treat older members. The group's structure, size, geographic closeness, and age structure also determine the treatment of older members.

9. Members of different ethnic groups will need different forms of social support. Proper support can reverse or avoid social breakdown and lead to a high quality of life. Policy makers need to keep ethnic differences in mind when they plan programs for older people.

10. The way society treats older people can lead to personal problems like loneliness, suicide, and the breakdown of competence. Social psychologists trace these problems to the lack of social supports for older people today.

Study Questions

1. Name and briefly state three of the major social psychological theories of aging.

2. Name and briefly describe the last stage of adult development in Erikson's theory of the life cycle. State some of the criticisms of stage models of adult development.

3. What are three challenges that face the self in later life? How can individuals cope with these challenges?

4. What role does religion play in many older people's lives? How and why might religiosity in later life change in the future?

5. Name and describe three types of environmental effects that influence people throughout life.

6. What three theories attempt to explain ethnic elders' experiences? Explain these theories in detail.

7. Briefly describe the social breakdown and reconstruction syndromes. What role does society play in each of these processes? Why can someone's ethnicity put that person at risk of social breakdown?

8. Discuss the sources of loneliness in later life and state at least two ways to combat the condition.

9. What does current research tell us about older people and suicide? How do suicide rates differ between older men and women? What might account for the differences in rates between older men and women?

Key Terms

activity theory   a theory that people need to stay active to live a satisfying old age by replacing old activities with new ones as they age. (137)

age-status asynchronization   the discomfort a person can feel when some life events happen later or earlier than for other people. (143)

buffer theory   a theory that membership in an ethnic group buffers the effects of aging. (146)

continuity theory   a theory that people age best when they continue to do the things they have always done. (138)

dialectical process   the process of the individual changing in response to societal demands and society changing in response to the individual's action and adaptation. (141)

disengagement theory   the theory that people naturally disengage from activity as they age. (137)

generational event theory   the theory that attitudes form for a generation in their teens, so people who grow up at the same time in the same society share the same attitudes, which stay fairly stable throughout life. (143)

integrity   the state of fulfillment and self-knowledge achieved in a good old age, according to Erikson. (138)

levelling theory   the theory that aging levels out the differences among people in different ethnic groups. (146)

life-span developmental perspective   the view of the individual as continually changing from birth to death, with crisis and change considered a constant part of life. (141)

loneliness   an emotional state that occurs when a person feels a "relational deficit" or a gap between the number of relationships desired and the actual number that exist; also refers to a dissatisfaction with the quality of social relationships. (150)

multiple jeopardy theory   the theory that membership in an ethnic group increases a person's troubles in later life. (146)

non-normative events   unexpected events such as illnesses, layoffs, and accidents. (142)

normative age-graded events   socially sanctioned events that occur most often at a certain age, such as marriage or retirement. (142)

normative history-graded events   historical events that shape a person's life, such as the Great Depression of the 1930s, the invention of the personal computer, or the terrorist attacks of September 11, 2001. (142)

self   "the ability to be aware of one's own boundaries and individuality and to reflect upon these" (Breytspraak 1995, 93). (139)

social isolation   the decrease in social contacts that often comes with age; the death of a spouse, the deaths of friends, and children moving away can all lead to social isolation. (150)

Selected Readings

The Research Policy Initiative (RPI). *A Life-Course Approach to Social Policy Analysis. (A Discussion Paper).* 2004. http://policyresearch.gc.ca/doclib/DP_LC_Social%20Policy%20Analysis_200412_e.pdf, accessed May 13, 2009.

   This framework builds on sociological literature on the life course. It shows how the life course theory may be used to understand the roles of people in relation to different social institutions, and how it can inform social policy. It views the resources between an individual and the main institutions of society as a two-way flow. Individuals have their own resources but can also draw on social resources like home care support or a national pension plan.

Ryff, Carol D., and Victor W. Marshall (Eds.). *The Self and Society in Aging Processes.* New York: Springer, 1999.

   A collection of articles by authors from Canada and other countries who link the individual experiences of aging to the larger society. The book includes theoretical and empirical studies on identity and adaptation, social class and self-concept, and retirement. A challenging book for the person new to gerontology, but a good resource for a more in-depth study of social-psychological issues.

Schaie, K. Warner, N. Krause, and Alan Booth (Eds.). *Religious Influences on Health and Well-Being in the Elderly.* New York: Springer, 2004.

   This edited volume looks at the ways that religious practices, organizations, and institutions affect the health and well-being of older people. It includes discussions of how religion helps people cope with stress. It also looks at how social class, race, and gender influence religious belief and practice.

Websites to Consult

National Indian and Inuit Community Health Representatives Organization (NIICHRO)

http://www.niichro.com/2004/

   This site reports on topics related to Aboriginal people. Among other resources, it presents results of a survey of Aboriginal communities. The survey provides data on what works in programs for Aboriginal frail elderly. The study found that such programs should help people deal with isolation, boost self-esteem, retain culture, encourage interaction, and support family caregivers.

St. Christopher's Health Action Theatre by Seniors (HATS)

http://www.stchrishouse.org/older-adults/health-action-theatre

This site presents information on a theatre group in Toronto. The group includes Portuguese- and Vietnamese-speaking senior actors. The troupe created 27 non-verbal short plays on health-related topics including caregiving, heart health, nutrition, substance abuse, and communication with health providers. The HATS program was effective in reaching St. Christopher's senior immigrant communities.

Canadian Association of Retired Persons (Canadian Association for the 50+)

http://www.carp.ca/

CARP takes an advocacy role and supports issues to improve the lives of seniors. The website contains summaries of news events related to seniors living in Canada, as well as travel information for seniors.

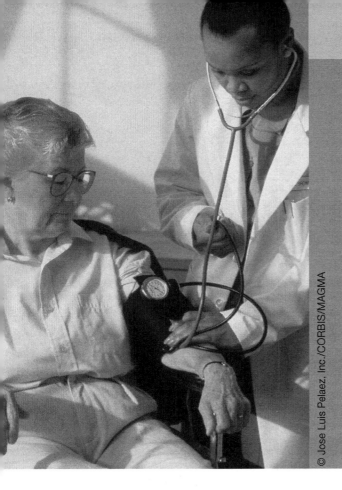

Chapter

8

Health Care

© Jose Luis Pelaez, Inc./CORBIS/MAGMA

INTRODUCTION

Mrs. Granovetter, 72, lives by herself in a three-room apartment. Until six years ago, she worked as a supervisor in a nursing home, but poor health forced her to quit. She says she has an aortic aneurysm that "looks like a bicycle tire with a bubble in it." She also has arthritis, and her joints get so stiff during the night that, she says, it sometimes takes her until noon to get out of bed. Still, she manages to live on her own. Her daughter, who lives on the other side of town, calls her every day; she talks to or visits with her next-door neighbour daily, and she can still drive. A few times a week, she drives to a nearby shopping centre to sit and watch the people go by. She knows just where to park and how far she has to walk to the nearest bench. Last year, her children took her on a trip to England. She says they didn't get to walk through the castles, but they toured around in the car and she saw the countryside. With help from family and friends, Mrs. Granovetter stays active and enjoys life.

Like Mrs. Granovetter, a majority of older women suffer from arthritis and almost a quarter of them have heart trouble. And, like her, most of them cope well with some help, and they say they have good health. Even among people aged 75 and over, nearly three-quarters of those who live outside institutions report good to excellent health (Turcotte and Schellenberg 2007). A Canadian policy statement defines health as "a resource which gives people the ability to manage and even to change their surroundings" (Epp 1986, 3). By this definition, more than 90 percent of people aged 65 and over have enough good health that they can live on their own in the community.

Health care refers to the support needed for people to maintain optimum health. The health care needs of Canada's older population range from health promotion to health maintenance, to long-term chronic care.

This chapter looks at (1) the structure and function of the health care system today, (2) how the present system fits the needs of older people, and (3) how the system is changing to meet the needs of an aging society.

THREE MODELS OF HEALTH CARE

Social scientists use models to simplify and describe complex social systems. A model does not perfectly represent the system, but it describes the system's basic structures, functions, and values. Three models of health care have shaped the development of the health care

system in Canada: the medical model, the social model, and the health promotion model.

The Medical Model

The **medical model** focuses on the treatment of diseases and injuries. Treatment most often takes place in the physician's office, in a hospital, or in other health care institutions. The medical model favours surgery, drug therapy, and rehabilitation through physical therapies. Within this model, "medical care and treatment are defined primarily as technical problems, and the goals of medicine are viewed in terms of technical criteria, such as validity, diagnosis, precision of disease-related treatment, symptom relief and termination of disease process" (Chappell, Strain, and Blandford 1986, 101). Physicians control both the organization of health care and the work of other health care professionals. They learn this approach to medicine in medical school and often get little training in other forms of health care such as counselling or long-term community care. Canada's health insurance system supports the medical model. It funnels most health care dollars to doctors and hospitals, and it places the medical profession at the centre of the health care system.

The Social Model

The **social model** sees medical care as only one part of a complete health care system. This model sees personal and family counselling, home care, and adult day-care programs as part of the health care system. This model of health care tries to keep older people in their own homes. Care often takes place in the community—in a person's home, at a drop-in centre, or in a counsellor's office. In this model, the doctor works as part of a health care team that includes nurses, physiotherapists, counsellors, social workers, and other professionals. The social model has grown in importance as more older people need continuing care or long-term care.

Long-term care (LTC) serves people with functional disabilities and few informal supports. Long-term care is "a combination of medical, nursing, custodial, social, and community services designed to help people who have disabilities or chronic care needs, including dementia. Services may be provided in the person's home, in the community, in assisted living facilities or in nursing homes" (Family Caregiving Alliance 2009). LTC supports people who have functional problems and gives people as much autonomy as possible. LTC often takes place in the community as an attempt to keep people out of institutions. Home care, for example, offers a range of services that allow people to stay in their homes. Services include Meals on Wheels, homemaker visits, volunteer visits, and physiotherapy.

Béland and Shapiro (1994) reviewed provincial reports on long-term care. They found a number of policies common to nearly all provinces: (1) decentralized decision making; (2) a coordinated, single-point-of-entry system; (3) a shift from institutional to community services; (4) integration of health and social services; and (5) a continuum of care that includes institutional and community care. The Canadian health care system has begun to shift from the medical to the social model of care. (See Exhibit 8.1).

● Exhibit 8.1

THE MEDICAL MODEL AND THE SOCIAL MODEL IN LONG-TERM CARE

Medical Model	Social Model
Patient	Resident, consumer
Acute patients	Chronic clients
Physicians and hospitals	Community settings and home
Patient fits organization	Organization fits client, changes to fit client if necessary
Rigid system boundaries	Open system boundaries
High priority to short-term need	High priority to long-term need
Serves long-term care if it has excess capacity	Serves long-term care first
Diagnosis/treatment/cure model	Assessment of functional capacity, service needs identified, services delivered
Organizationally inflexible	Organizationally flexible and creative
Institutional care	Community-based and home care
Excludes people in the community	Includes community members and may include institution
Institution-centred	Person-centred
Makes little use of informal network	Includes informal support
Medical/physical assessment	Multidimensional assessment (physical, psychological, social needs)
Meets patients' medical needs	Helps clients meet their own needs
Patient accepts professional treatment	Client plays role in developing treatment plan
Professional has most power in relationship	Client and professional share power
Hierarchical organization	Flat organization, team approach
Expensive resources	Lower-cost resources
Major share of health care budget	Small share of health care budget

The table above presents an ideal type of these two health care models. Each has a role to play in the Canadian health care system. These two approaches see and treat the older person differently. Some critics believe that the system today relies too heavily on the medical model, and that an older population needs more services based on social model principles. Many programs exist as a hybrid between the two approaches. For example, a physician may oversee a team that provides a multidimensional health assessment. Or a hospital may work closely with a community care program to move a person back into the community.

Source: Adapted from B. Havens, 1995, "Long-Term Care Diversity within the Care Continuum," *Canadian Journal on Aging* 14(2): 245–62. Reprinted with permission from the *Canadian Journal on Aging*.

The Health Promotion Model

The **health promotion model** focuses on prevention and self-care. It aims to prevent disease through lifestyle change, increased knowledge about healthy behaviour, and environmental improvement. Programs that promote fitness and those that warn about the dangers of smoking or excessive drinking follow this model. The model also includes actions that most people do not associate directly with health care, such as workplace safety regulations, seatbelt legislation, and pollution control for factories.

Each of these models plays a part in the Canadian health care system today. The social model has gained acceptance as a possible alternative to institutionalization. The health promotion model may save the health care system money in the long run by keeping people healthier longer. Recent decreases in heart disease, for example, may have come about through health promotion programs that encourage low-fat diets and discourage smoking. A review of the health promotion literature found that educational and group activity interventions decreased social isolation and loneliness (Cattan et al. 2005). Still, the medical model dominates the system today. Canadians spend more money (much of it through taxes and health insurance programs) on physicians and hospital care than on any other kind of health care.

CHALLENGES TO THE HEALTH CARE SYSTEM TODAY

In 1957, the Canadian government put in place a hospital insurance system that covered the entire population. In 1968, the government insured physician services, and by 1972 all provinces belonged to a national medical insurance program. The provincial and federal governments shared the costs for this system of health care, with the federal government matching provincial contributions to the program dollar for dollar. The *Canada Health Act* of 1984 described the principles of the Canadian health care system (Canada 1984): (1) universal coverage; (2) access to services; (3) portability (people could get the benefits in their new location when they moved); (4) comprehensive services that include outpatient and hospital care; and (5) administration of the system by a non-profit public agency.

Sullivan and Baranek (2002) state a core value of the Canadian health care system. They say that "all citizens in Canada ... are entitled to the same quality, timeliness, and level of medically required service, based on their health care needs and not their ability to pay" (5). This system compares favourably with the U.S. system, where no national system of health care exists. Compared to Americans, Canadians have lower mortality rates, better

cancer survival rates, and lower rates of obesity, hypertension, diabetes, and respiratory disease. Canadians tend to use health care services and to get the services they need when they need them (Armstrong et al. 2006). The National Forum on Health said that "the vast majority of Canadians [in the study it conducted] were immensely proud of the type of health care system that has been built in Canada. They had an abiding sense of fairness and equality" (cited in Conference of Deputy Ministers of Health 1999, 135) (see Exhibit 8.1).

But the Canadian national health care system faces some new challenges. For example, current health care reforms have shifted care from institutions to the community. This policy has decreased institutionalization, but it has placed more burden on women, families, and communities. Funding has not always followed this shift to community care.

Also, waiting times for services have increased, leading to some loss of confidence in the system (Wilson and Rosenberg 2004). In one international study, Canadians and people in the United Kingdom most often complained about waiting times (Chen and Hou 2002; Chen et al. 2002). The proportion of the public who rated Canada's health care system as excellent or very good fell from 61 percent in 1991 to 25 percent in February 2000 (Angus Reid 2000, cited in Sullivan and Baranek 2002). And only 62 percent of Canadians in 1999 believed that the health care system met the needs of all the people in their province (Chen et al. 2002). Recent data reflect an "increasing concern about the state of the health care system" (Chen et al. 2002, 18). McDaniel (2003) reports, as an example, that "74 per cent of Albertans overall think that the government should make a significant reinvestment in Alberta's health care system."

The need for long-term care will grow in the future as the population ages. Increases in the prevalence of Alzheimer's disease, for example, will lead to more use of community and institutional care. Although most provinces provide some long-term care insurance, the current system does not fully insure LTC. Users often have to pay for programs such as adult day care or homemaker services. Also, the system emphasizes medical and institutional care, the two most expensive types of services (Shapiro 2003). The health care system will need to consider expanding its scope to include long-term care in the community.

HEALTH CARE COSTS IN AN AGING SOCIETY

The Canadian system has moved toward community-based health care services in the past few years. For example,

● Exhibit 8.2

THE CANADIAN AND AMERICAN HEALTH CARE SYSTEMS: A COMPARISON

Canadians value their health care system. It stands as a point of national pride and it embodies many of the values Canadians hold dear—fairness, equality, and service for the good of all. Americans have a much less positive view of their system. The United States looks at the Canadian system with both envy (at the universality of service and relatively low cost) and curiosity (How can a "socialist" system of medicine exist in such an otherwise decent country?). The Canadian system seems to have the edge on the American health care system. Below we present a brief comparison of the two systems:

- **Attitudes:** A CBS/New York Times poll of Americans (2007) found that nine out of 10 Americans think the U.S. health care system needs at least fundamental changes, including 36% who think it needs "a complete overhaul." Only 14 percent of Canadians in a Commonwealth Fund study (Schoen and Osborn 2007) felt that their system needed "a complete overhaul." Canadians expressed most dissatisfaction with wait times to get to see a doctor or get treatment.

    In an earlier study (Barer et al. 1992) 93 percent of older Canadians said they felt "very satisfied" with their most recent hospital stay compared to 68 percent of older Americans.

- **Universality of Coverage:** The Canadian health care system covers all older people without cost to the individual. The system allows no private insurance (except for extras such as single-room hospital coverage) and charges no user fees or co-payments. Medicare in the United States does not cover everyone, it covers only some hospital or physician services, and it requires co-payments. About three-quarters of the older population in the United States buy supplementary health insurance. A study of the U.S. health care system found that cost posed the greatest barrier to care (National Union 2006). "More than seven times as many U.S. residents reported going without needed care due to cost as Canadians (7.0% of U.S. respondents vs. 0.8% of Canadians). Uninsured U.S. residents were particularly vulnerable; 30.4% reported having an unmet health need due to cost."

- **Cost of the System:** The Canadian system (although more comprehensive) costs less than the U.S. system. Canada insures 100 percent of its population; the U.S. insures only 84 percent. Administrative costs by insurers account for the greatest difference in expenses between the two countries. About 26 of every 100 insurance premium dollars for private insurance go to administrative costs and profit in the United States; Canada's universal system spends only 1 percent of its total budget on administrative overhead. In short, Canada's universal health program costs less to administer than the fragmented U.S. system of state and private providers (Barer et al. 1992).

- **Coverage:** Health care coverage in Canada improves when a person turns age 65. All provinces provide free or low-cost pharmaceutical services for older people. Provinces all have long-term institutional and community care programs, although some user payments exist for some LTC programs. However, these programs link costs to a person's retirement benefits. Medicare in the United States covers only hospital and medical care. States may offer some long-term institutional care or community care but most use a means test (based on income) to decide a person's eligibility for a program. Medicaid covers nursing home stays only for poor older people. Access to Medicaid support can require that a family spend all of its non-housing assets, and this can reduce a family to poverty.

- **Cost to the Individual:** Feeley (2006) reports that, after accounting for cost-of-living differences, yearly out-of-pocket-costs for health care for Americans came to almost double the amount spent by Canadians ($793 versus $448). For the older person, the U.S. system of Medicare Part A involves a complex calculation of user costs for hospital stays. Older people who want more coverage also subscribe to Medicare Part B (98 percent of older people choose this option). People pay a monthly premium, a deductible of US$200 for services and at least 20 percent of physicians' charges beyond the deductible. Most older Americans buy additional and costly insurance to cover

(Continued)

● Exhibit 8.2 (cont.)

these extra Medicare costs. Older people in the United States now spend as much of their own income on health care as before the institution of Medicare (Wiener and Illston 1996).

- **Catastrophic Illness Protection:** The Canadian system protects older people from financial ruin due to catastrophic illness (such as Alzheimer's disease). Hospital, medical, long-term care, and pharmaceutical services come either free or at a low cost to Canadian seniors. Barer and his colleagues (1992, 151) say that, "in marked contrast, elderly Americans without comprehensive private health insurance face potential economic ruin from hospital, medical, and pharmaceutical costs ... [To get coverage beyond Medicare] "they must first deplete both income and assets to pay such costs." Wiener and Illston (1996, 439) say that in the United States "long-term care still imposes a substantial financial burden that can be financially crippling." This system can put at risk a lifetime of savings, home ownership, and the hope of leaving a legacy to one's children. The middle-class person, neither rich nor poor, can suffer the greatest loss under this system.

The Canadian health care system provides an umbrella of care for individuals and families. It provides a sense of security for older people and reduces the fear of illness that can come with age.

The U.S. system consists of a patchwork of private and public insurance systems. The quality and amount of insured service depends on one's ability to pay for acute and long-term care. People who buy private LTC insurance, for example, will get only the amount of service (number of days at a specific rate) that they pay for. This system can place older people and their families at financial risk. The system requires that individuals look out for their own interests, buy the most insurance they can afford, and hope for the best.

Dr. David Himmestein, Associate Professor of Medicine at Harvard, co-authored a major study that compared the U.S. and Canadian health care systems. His findings support the Canadian approach to health care. The study, he said, raises "serious questions about what we're getting for the $2.1 trillion we're spending on health care this year [in the U.S.]. We pay almost twice what Canada does for care, more than $6,000 for every American, yet Canadians are healthier, and live 2 to 3 years longer" (National Union 2006).

Source: Adapted from M.L. Barer et al., 1992, "On Being Old and Sick: The Burden of Health Care for the Elderly in Canada and the United States," *Journal of Health Politics, Policy and Law* 17(4): 163–82. Copyright © 1992 Duke University Press. All rights reserved. Used by permission of the publisher.

the number of hospital beds in Canada declined from about 177,000 beds in 1992 to about 109,000 in 2004 (OECD 2007). Canada had about 6,000 other health care facilities (including nursing homes) and 62,307 physicians in 2006 (up from 31,000 in 1970) (Statistics Canada 1999; Canadian Institute for Health Information 2008).

The decrease in hospital beds has reduced the number of overnight admissions and the average length of a hospital stay (Statistics Canada 2003l) This has lowered the cost of hospital care. Finlayson and colleagues (2005) looked at hospital stays in more detail by studying hospital stays for older people in Manitoba between 1985 and 2000. They

found "a substantial and consistent decrease" in use of hospitals for inpatient stays during the 16 years of the study. They found 53 percent fewer long-stay days and 25 percent fewer short-stay days during this time.

They say that this trend began before the decrease in hospital beds. They suggest that patterns of practice in the health care system (e.g., more home care), in part, account for these changes. Also improvements in technology (e.g., better diagnostic tools) may have led to a decrease in hospital stays. These findings show that changes in the health care system can lead to decreases in hospital use and decreases in the cost of hospital care.

But the decrease in beds can lead to longer waits for hospital services (due to fewer hospital beds) (Rosenberg and James 2000; Shapiro and Havens 2000). This change in hospital practices (e.g., earlier discharges) leads to more need for home care funding.

In 2003, Canada spent $121 billion or $3,800 per person on health care. This came to 9.3 percent of its gross domestic product (GDP) in 2001, up from 7.3 percent in 1981(Statistics Canada 2004c). Nearly 70 percent of health care funding came from public sources (the federal and provincial governments), while private health expenditures accounted for about 30 percent of the total. Hospital and other institution costs came to $32.4 billion in 2001. Hospitals accounted for 30.6 percent of total health care costs in 2001 (Canadian Institute for Health Information 2003).

Although the proportion of health care dollars spent on hospitals fell during the 1990s, both private and public spending on health care increased each year during the 1990s and early 2000s. From 1997 to 2002, for example, private and public health care expenses rose by more than 43 percent (Statistics Canada 2004c).

These facts show both the strengths and weaknesses of the health care system today. Canadian medical and hospital insurance matched the most complete coverage in the world, with almost 100 percent of Canadians covered. Older people, for example, receive free hospital and surgical care as well as free access to a range of programs that include chiropractic and optometric services. Also, all Canadians have access to some form of public support for pharmaceuticals. Public programs pay for about half of Canada's $8 billion drug costs (Sullivan and Mustard 2001). But Canada also ranks among the nations with the greatest per capita expenditures for health care (Commission on the Future of Health Care in Canada 2002; Rosenberg 2000).

Policy makers and government officials express concern about the rising cost of health care. Will an older population lead to a crisis in health care spending? The cost of Canada's medical care system grows each year and Denton and Spencer (1995) project that health care expenses will more than double between 1986 and 2041. In part, these higher costs are explained by the fact there are more older people in the population. But many research studies now show that population change alone does not account for the growth in health care use or expenses (Watson et al. 2005a; Evans et al. 2001).

Denton and his colleagues (2001) studied physician services in Ontario. They projected increases in costs over the next four decades. They found that population aging did lead to increased costs in the future, but had only a moderate effect by past standards. General population increases had a greater effect than population aging on doctor costs over the next four decades. The researchers also say that changes in technology, medical knowledge, and doctors' treatment choices will affect costs.

Evans and his colleagues (2001) studied the link between population aging and health care use (see Exhibit 8.3). They looked at acute inpatient hospital days, physician services, and drug use. In each case, they report that population aging has little effect on the rates of use or on costs. For example, drug use by older people increased by 147 percent (per capita) from 1985 to 1999, but the increased number of older people accounts for only 2 percent of this increase. Instead the researchers found that increases in specific costs for specific treatments account for over three-quarters of the rise in costs.

They trace most of this increase to shifts in doctors' choice of more expensive drugs. The researchers conclude that "demographic trends *by themselves* are likely to explain some, but only a small part, of future trends in health care use and costs, and in and of themselves will require little, if any, increase in the share of national resources devoted to health care" (Evans et al. 2001, 166). Evans and his colleagues say that nondemographic conditions account for most of the increases in health care costs.

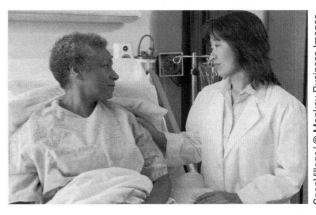

SnapVillage/ © Monkey Business Images

Hospitals will serve a higher proportion of older people in the future. A strong community care system can lead to earlier discharges and fewer days in the hospital for older patients.

● **Exhibit 8.3**

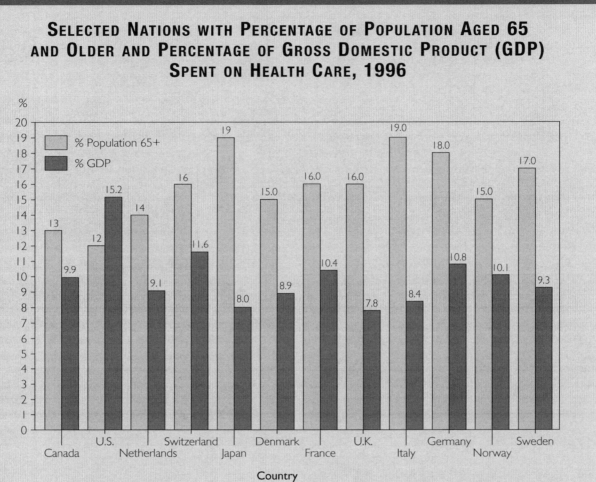

SELECTED NATIONS WITH PERCENTAGE OF POPULATION AGED 65 AND OLDER AND PERCENTAGE OF GROSS DOMESTIC PRODUCT (GDP) SPENT ON HEALTH CARE, 1996

The percentage of GDP spent on health care bears no direct relationship to the proportion of older people in a country. This table shows that the proportion of older people in a country does not explain high health care costs. Canada, for example, has the youngest population among the developed nations presented here, but ranks among the top six nations in spending. Public policies that encourage or discourage health care use affect how much money gets spent on health care in a country. So do doctors' treatment decisions and the increased use of high-tech medical treatment.

Source: M. W. Rosenberg (2000), The Effects of Population Ageing on the Canadian Health Care System, Tables 6 and 8. Social and Economic Dimensions of an Aging Population Research Program (SEDAP), Paper No. 14. Hamilton, ON: McMaster University.

A study by Carrière (2000) supports this conclusion. Carrière projected hospital use in the future based on past trends. He found that population aging does not affect the total number of days that Canadians stayed in hospitals per year. But population aging does lead to an increased proportion of older hospital patients. It could also lead to a large majority of hospital beds occupied by older patients in the future. Carrière says that in the future we will need different types of care to serve older patients.

This will require more training in geriatric care for doctors, nurses, and staff. For example, Canada had 144 geriatricians in 2000. But the population needed as many as 481. The country had about 200 in 2006, but the country needed as many as 538. Canada has 0.44 geriatricians per 100,000 population, but the Royal College of Physicians in England set a standard of 2 per 100,000 (nearly five times the Canadian level) (National Advisory Council 2003). Canada needs more specialists who can provide care that suits the needs of older people.

Increased drug costs, more doctors, rising costs for complex treatments, unionization of hospital workers, and more tests to diagnose disease account for most of the increases in the cost of health care. Drug-related illnesses also add to the cost of medical care (Tamblyn and Perrault 2000). Kozyrskyj (2003, 26; also Metge et al. 2005) says that "almost 50 per cent of drugs prescribed for the elderly have been reported to be either inappropriate or unnecessary. Drug-related problems in the elderly not uncommonly lead to hospitalization." These practices drive up the cost of drugs and of health care in general.

Some critics of the system today question whether older people need more done to them; others wonder whether older people need done to them what currently gets done. Some question whether the medical model fits the needs of an aging society. They argue that for the same cost Canadians could buy care that more closely fits their needs. "As a society," Chappell, Strain, and Blandford (1986, 112) say, "we have not yet dealt with the issue—especially during old age—'When is health care servicing inappropriate or too much?'"

THE HEALTH CARE SYSTEM AND OLDER PEOPLE'S HEALTH CARE NEEDS

By any standards, older people have more health problems than younger people and use more health care services. Lindsay (1999; also Roterman 2006) reports that seniors, compared to younger people, see specialists and general practitioners more often. They also have more hospital separations[1] than younger people and they spend more days in the hospital during each stay. Hospital use increases with age from middle age on. Women aged 75 and over have a hospital separation rate more than two and a half times the rate of women

aged 45 to 64. They spent 23.1 days in the hospital on average during each stay, compared with 9.2 days for the 45- to 64-year-old group. Men aged 75 and over had a rate almost four and a half times the rate of men aged 45 to 64. They spent 17.1 days in the hospital on average during each visit, compared with 8.6 days on average for each stay for the 45- to 64-year-old group. The older the person, the longer the stay.

Roterman (2006, 40) says that "seniors make up just 13% of the Canadian population, but account for a third of all acute-care hospitalizations and almost half of all hospital days." Also, compared to younger people, older people show more repeat admissions. The more chronic conditions a person has, the greater the likelihood that they will spend time in a hospital. Likewise, seniors who suffered an injury or reported "fair" or "poor" health showed a greater chance of hospitalization.

Barer and his colleagues (1986) studied the reasons older people use more health care services today than in the past. They wanted to find out whether this increase in costs reflects changes in the diseases older people have today, or whether it reflects the way the system cares for older patients. If the costs reflect older people's increased need for treatment, population aging could lead to a sharp increase in health care costs. But if changes reflect the way the system operates, new approaches to treatment could contain costs. Barer and his colleagues found that little data existed to test the first possibility (that older people have different diseases or more diseases today than in the past). They do suggest that the way the system responds to older people's needs leads them to make heavier use of the medical care system today than in the past.

Studying consultation visits to specialists, Black and her colleagues (1995) analyzed Manitoba data to see why older people use more health care now than in the past. They found that a decrease in the health of older people accounted for only a tiny increase in consultation visits (one-tenth of 1 percent). Instead, they traced an increase in consultations to doctors' increased tendency to make referrals. This practice, they say, accounts for at least half of added visits to specialists by older people. They go on to say that people in good health account for at least one-third of this increase in visits to specialists. These findings have led researchers to link physicians' choice of treatment to health service use.

Chappell, Strain, and Blandford (1986, 100) report that physicians "control approximately 80 percent of health care costs." Only a quarter of this percentage goes directly to physicians; the rest goes to hospital use (half of all health care costs), drugs, tests, and other medical expenses. Doctors control these expenses through the

---

1. "Hospital separations" refers to the discharge or death of an inpatient; a person discharged more than once in a year counts as more than one separation.

decisions they make about treatments and through their reliance on high technology in hospital settings.

Shapiro and Roos (1986, 165) say that hospital-based care uses "about 60 percent of all health care dollars," but they determined that individual need cannot explain older people's pattern of hospital use. Looking at physicians' "hospitalization style," Shapiro and Roos found that patients of hospital-prone doctors spent, on average, twice as much time in the hospital as patients of non-hospital-prone doctors. These doctors also accounted for 73 percent of high users who had repeated hospital stays. Some researchers propose that fewer doctors would lead to lower health care costs (Evans et al. 2001). Other researchers suggest that doctors need more knowledge about how to care for older people. As well, more appropriate care might lower health care costs.

Drug Use by Older Canadians

Drugs serve as a basic tool in the medical response to health issues in later life. Appropriate use of prescription and over-the-counter drugs can help older people maintain or improve their health and well-being. However, the misuse of drugs can create or intensify existing health problems (Bergob 2004). Most drug use among older Canadians is by prescription, typically medications for the heart or blood pressure. Compared to younger people, older people use more prescription drugs; older people represent approximately 12 percent of the Canadian population, yet they use 20 to 30 percent of all prescription drugs. Prescription drug use is higher among older women than older men and tends to increase with advancing age for older women. Drug use tends to decline for older men as they age.

While most older Canadians report good to excellent health, in 2003 nine in ten seniors reported taking at least one type of medication during the past month. On average seniors reported three different types of medication (Roterman 2006). Multiple-drug use is more common among older women than older men. More than a quarter (27 percent) of older women reported taking at least five types of medication (only 16 percent of senior men reported this pattern). And, as with prescription drug use overall, multiple-drug use tends to increase with advanced age for women but decrease for men. Older people in fair or poor health tend to use more than one drug (Roterman 2006). This applies particularly to those who report greater stress in their lives and to those without family or friends to provide social support (Bergob 2004).

In a Quebec study that examined the use of mood-altering prescription drugs among young adults (those age 18 to 64) and older adults (those 65 years of age and

older), 22 percent of the older adults used this type of drug compared to 5 percent of younger adults (Préville et al. 2001). Women and those with lower incomes were more likely to use these medications than were men or those with a higher income. A Montreal study found that older people who used mood-altering drugs were more likely than non-users to report feelings of loneliness and to feel they lacked social support (Perodeau and du Fort 2000).

The proportion of older Canadians who use mood-altering prescription drugs to treat depression has risen from 9.3 percent in 1993 to 11.5 percent in 1997 (Mamdani et al. 2000). This represents a cost increase of 150 percent, from $10.8 million to $27 million in that period. Part of this increase (about 20 percent) is a result of population shifts and an increase in the use of antidepressants among the older population. However, a more significant factor, accounting for approximately 60 percent of the increase, is related to changes in prescribing practices, with a greater use of more expensive antidepressant medications.

In a study that examined the over-the-counter drug use of older adults (Amoako, Richardson-Campbell, and Kennedy-Malone 2003), 90 percent of older adults used pain medicine, two-thirds took high blood pressure medication, more than one-half used caffeine daily, and about 10 percent used alcohol. The researchers caution that older adults may be unaware of the potential adverse effects that could result from combining these substances.

A study that examined the nature and extent of medications stored in the homes of older Canadians found the number of medications ranged from 3 to 48, with an average of 20 medications per home (Poirier and Barbeau 1999). About one-half of the medications were prescription medications, while the others were over-the-counter drugs. Approximately one-quarter of these medications were past their expiration date. This raises concerns related to the effectiveness and safety of expired medications in the homes of older Canadians.

The large number of medications in each home also raises the problem of adverse drug reactions due to the misuse or inappropriate combining of medications. Health professionals, family members, and older adults themselves can help ensure the proper use of prescription drugs. Older people who use more than one drug or who have more than one physician face the risk of adverse reactions (Bergob 2004). Older people should inform their various health care providers about the number of drugs and the type of drugs they're taking.

The present and future cost of prescription drugs for older adults is a concern for individuals and for society as the population continues to age. Luffman (2005) reports that the people in the highest 25 percent of those who spent money on prescriptions drugs accounted for 72 percent of all expenditures. Seniors made up 43 percent of this group. Many of these people live on government transfers or other social assistance programs. Senior households report that more than a quarter of their health care expenses (27.3 percent) go to pay for prescription drugs. For seniors living alone (among the poorest older people) drug costs jump to 29 percent of health care expenses. Because of this potential financial burden all provinces have some drug reimbursement plan for seniors. Still, older people report higher-than-average expenses and out-of-pocket costs.

Some researchers believe that, as younger Canadians move into later life, their use of prescription drugs may be different than today's older people's. Bergob (2004, 6) says that "increased public awareness and adoption of lifestyles and behaviours that promote good health may result in tomorrow's seniors being healthier and less dependent on medical interventions." On the other hand, drugs play an increasing role in the treatment and management of chronic conditions in later life. New drugs (such as those that control arthritis pain or blood pressure) promise to extend years of active living. Longer life expectancy will mean that many people in the future will rely on drug therapy to maintain and extend their disability-free years. For this reason the cost of prescription drugs will remain a policy issue for years to come.

INSTITUTIONAL CARE

The proportion of seniors who live in an institution (primarily a nursing home or hospital) increases with age. In 2001 about 2 percent of people aged 65 to 74 lived in institutions (mostly nursing homes and hospitals). This figure jumps to 32 percent for people aged 85 and over. Most of these seniors were women (Turcotte and Schellenberg 2007). Institutionalization rates vary from province to province. Canada's national rate of institutionalization of seniors was 7 percent in 2001. This is higher than that of the United States (4.6 percent) and of the United Kingdom (4.1 percent), but lower than other developed countries such as Holland (11 percent) (Health Canada 1999b; Kinsella and Velkoff 2001; National Advisory Council 1996).

The *Canada Health Act* does not cover nursing home care. So older people have to cover the cost themselves. The cost of nursing home care varies by province and territory; the National Advisory Council on Aging (2005) reports that out-of-pocket costs average $18 per day in Yukon (in 2004); $74 per day in Nova Scotia (in

2005); and $137 per day in New Brunswick (2005). The National Advisory Council (2005, n.p.) says "The New Brunswick income/asset definition [which determines a person's out-of-pocket fee]—the most severe in the country—can result in the family of a resident being depleted of almost all their assets" in order to pay for long-term care in an institution. The National Advisory Council on Aging calls for federal funding of long-term care institutions and funding for health care services in these institutions.

Some institutions house only older people. These facilities go by a variety of names: special care facilities, residential care facilities, and personal care homes. The term "nursing home," as it is used here, refers to any institution that is not a hospital and offers medical care for chronically ill older people. The proportion of older people who live in an institution has declined since the early 1980s. For example, among seniors aged 85 and over the rate dropped from 38 percent in 1981 to 32 percent in 2001. Nursing homes today mostly serve the oldest-old people aged 85 and over. Better health of older people and more community care explain the decrease in nursing home living (National Advisory Council 2005).

Each province has its own system for classifying institutionalized patients. The government allocates funds to institutions based on the level of care needed by each patient. Most provinces define four levels of nursing home care. In Manitoba, people in levels three and four need 3.5 hours of nursing care per day and need help with at least two basic activities of daily living such as bathing, dressing, and eating. People in level two need 2 to 3.5 hours of nursing care per day and need moderate care and help with at least one basic activity of daily living. People in level one need 0.5 to 2 hours of nursing care per day and need personal help only to wash or attend activities (Frohlich et al. 2002).

A detailed analysis of institution admission calculated the odds of entering an institution given certain conditions in a person's life. Shapiro and Tate (1988b, 238) found that people in Manitoba with specific characteristics—age 85 or over, living without a spouse, "recent hospital admission, living in retirement housing, having one or more [problems with activities of daily living] … and having a mental impairment"—had more than a three-in-five chance of entering an institution within two and a half years. Montgomery, Kirshen, and Roos (1988) report that the chance of residing in a nursing home increases dramatically over the four years before a person's death. Trottier and her colleagues (2000) found that health problems such as Alzheimer's disease, urinary incontinence, and stroke led to institutionalization.

These people required higher levels of care than younger residents (Frohlich et al. 2002).

When a person enters an institution he or she faces added stress. Institutionalization can lead to decreased well-being and even death for older residents. Bravo and her colleagues (1999, cited in Dubois, Bravo, and Charpentier 2001) studied institutions in Quebec. They found that in 25 percent of the institutions at least one person received below-standard care. This occurred most often in smaller institutions (40 people or less), where up to 20 percent of older people got below-standard care. Although the researchers found that only a few homes reached these high percentages of below-standard care, in these cases the older people suffered from a low quality of life.

Shapiro and Tate (1988a) found high mortality rates right after admission to a nursing home. They suggest that clinical instability or relocation may account for this high rate (see also Hirdes and Brown 1996). Also, the sickest older people enter institutions. This, in part, accounts for the high death rate for new patients. Still, Chappell and Penning (1979) found that, after matching for levels of health, people in institutionalized settings showed lower well-being than those in the community.

Most people, including government leaders, doctors, nursing home staff, and older people themselves, agree that we should keep older people out of institutions when we can. Provinces use community care programs to keep people in the community as long as possible. A study by Frohlich and colleagues (2002) in Manitoba, for example, found that overall rates of nursing home residence decreased from 1989/90 to 1999/2000.

Still, institutions play a useful role in the continuum of health care services. LTC institutions can reduce or delay hospitalization and this reduces the cost to the health care system. Sometimes people need to live in a nursing home. Kelly, Knox, and Gekoski (1998) asked middle-aged and older women whether they would choose a nursing home setting for themselves or someone else with severe cognitive or physical problems. They found that women chose institutional care most often if the older person lived alone or had little informal support. Only one-third of the people in this study had negative views of institutional care.

People with Alzheimer's disease may also benefit from institutional care. Institutions can have design features (such as circular hallways, colour-coded walls, or a secure garden) that make life easier for people with memory problems (Lovering et al. 2002). Canada's long winters, the great distances between some older people and hospitals, the need for constant care, few informal supports, and poverty sometimes make institutional life the only way for people to get the care they need.

Quality of Care in Institutions

Brillon (1992) notes that some provinces have no special laws to protect the rights of older people in nursing homes, and some institutions have no clear policies that protect residents' rights. Poirier (1992) proposes three types of rights that institutions should protect: the right to take care of one's own things, the right to have respect for one's rights, and the right to manage one's own life. This last right poses some of the greatest problems. An institution has to serve the collective good as well as ensure the right to manage one's own life. For example, the institution may infringe on the right to privacy as staff enter and leave patients' rooms or to provide personal care.

The Canadian Healthcare Association (CHA) (2004 cited in National Advisory Council 2005) produced a critique of the facility-based long-term care system. It cited as issues (1) lack of public funding and affordability of institutional care; (2) lack of quality care and lack of accountability by providers; (3) lack of dignity and choice in institutions; and (4) lack of respect for volunteers and families.

MacLean and Bonar (1983; see also National Advisory Council 2005) say that institutions can and should make life in the institution as much like life outside as possible. They call this the **normalization principle**.

First, people should feel the normal rhythm of the day, week, and year. They should get dressed each day, have a weekly routine, and celebrate holidays, birthdays, and anniversaries. Institutions should also include programs that keep residents active. This can include outdoor as well as indoor activities. A garden, for example, can provide a safe environment for outdoor programs (Heath and Gifford 2001; Lovering et al. 2002). Activity can increase the quality and length of patients' lives.

Second, people should receive a normal amount of respect. Sometimes staff members forget that patients have a right to decide things for themselves. Staff should treat the older patient as an adult. They should avoid using baby talk, talking down to the person, or making decisions without consulting the patient. People show high levels of psychological adjustment when the institution offers freedom of choice (O'Connor and Vallerand 1994).

MacLean and Bonar (1983) say that staff should treat the older patient as an adult. They should avoid using baby talk, talking down to the person, or making decisions without consulting the patient. Penning and Chappell (1982) found that older residents who felt they had freedom and the ability to make choices showed improved mental health. People showed high levels of psychological adjustment when the institution offered freedom of choice (O'Connor and Vallerand 1994).

Third, people should lead as normal a social life as possible. This can include day outings, camping trips, and garden boxes for outdoor activity (Cott and Fox 2001). Gilbart and Hirdes (2000) found that most residents in the institutions they studied faced the risk of feeling sad or anxious, but people who engaged in social activity and had a good relationship with a key person in their lives reported the most happiness. The Index of Social Engagement used in this study contained items on activity participation and involvement in facility life. The researchers say that social engagement was "the most important variable for explaining variation in well-being among residents" (62).

Normalization should also include sexual contact and sexual intimacy if a person has a willing partner. Institutions often allow married couples to live together. This can improve a person's quality of life. An 87-year-old man says that when his wife had a stroke she spent a year in a hospital. "I lived alone and was terribly depressed," he says. "When we both got accepted here [in a nursing home] I was really glad to be with her again. At least I'm not lonely for her anymore" (National Advisory Council 1993c, 24).

People should also have access to their money, and they should have their own pictures, small pieces of furniture, or pets to make the institution more like their home. A normalized institution expects patients to socialize and to do as much for themselves as they can.

A normalized environment should also include a weekly staff meeting. Meetings allow staff members to talk about problem patients and help them to channel frustration into methods for helping patients function better. Devine (1980) found that normalizing encourages nursing staff "to become leaders and teachers of the residents" instead of just caretakers. She found that staff stopped stereotyping older people as senile and useless because it worked against the goals of the program.

Models of Quality Care

Some groups have special needs. People with a strong ethnic identity can benefit from a setting that supports their culture. Wister and Moore (1998) describe a number of institutional settings for Aboriginal elders that attempt to normalize the environment. The North

Thompson Band in British Columbia, for example, offers a public lunch in its senior health care facility on the Chu Chua reserve. This lunch draws other elders from the community as well as family and friends. This creates community involvement in the life of the home. Tsawaayuus (Rainbow Gardens) in Port Alberni houses both Aboriginal and non-Aboriginal elders. The setting provides Aboriginal elders with Aboriginal cultural activities and foods, and employs Aboriginal workers. Both of these programs attempt to buffer the effects of isolation caused by institutionalization.

The Residence Yvon-Brunet in Montreal takes the rights of its residents seriously. It abides by a "Charter of Rights and Freedoms of the Elderly." The document lists 31 rights that ensure respect for residents. The residence also has an ombudsman who reports to the director general. The ombudsman ensures that patients' quality of life takes precedence over staff routines. The director general puts the residence's philosophy and practice into a simple statement. You can't have "two categories of elderly people—those who live in an institution, and those who are free!" (National Advisory Council 2005, 4).

The Simon K.Y. Lee Seniors Care Home in Vancouver serves Chinese community elders. Residents can speak their own language because the home respects and supports Chinese culture. It provides contact for residents with plants, animals, and children to allow residents as much control over their lives and environment as possible (National Advisory Council 2005).

The Simon K.Y. Lee home expresses many of the values of a new philosophy in institutional care—"the Eden Alternative." Dr. William Thomas founded the Eden Alternative in 1991. It works to de-institutionalize nursing homes and other long-term care institutions. The organization has trained over 15,000 Eden Associates. Over 300 Eden Alternative homes now exist in the United States, Canada, Europe, and Australia. The Eden Alternative teaches that "where elders live must be habitats for human beings, not sterile medical institutions." Eden Alternative institutions "are dedicated to eliminating the plagues of Loneliness, Helplessness, and Boredom that make life intolerable in most of today's long-term care facilities" (Eden Alternative 2008).

The Sherbrooke Community Centre in Saskatoon became the first Eden Alternative home in Western Canada. The centre has its own radio station and its own aviary. The bird sanctuary holds budgies, lovebirds, and canaries so that residents can enjoy the bird song. The centre organizes residents into the "Village," eleven special care homes with nine or ten residents per home. The village has street signs, house fronts, and numbers on each house, although all exist inside the institution. Homes in the village often have pets, and residents can decorate their rooms as they choose. Some homes within the village specialize in support for a specific need. For example, a home may house people with Alzheimer's disease. Staff members at the centre do a variety of tasks from cooking to personal care, to recreation, which tends to de-bureaucratize the institution. Staff members see residents in a variety of settings and roles (rather than as patients), which humanizes the relationship between residents and staff. The centre works to keep the environment as much like living in a normal community as possible (National Advisory Council 2005).

Nursing homes and other institutions will never take the place of a person's own home or apartment, but the changes suggested here show that a nursing home can be made more comfortable and homelike (see Exhibit 8.4).

THE NEED FOR CHANGE

Canada's commitment to the medical model accounts for much of the increase in health care costs today. In 2001, for example, the largest contributors to health care expenditures were hospitals (30.6 percent), physicians (13.2 percent), and drugs (15.7 percent) (Canadian Institute for Health Information 2003).

Some signs suggest that change in the system has begun. British Columbia, for example, created several programs to control the rising cost of drugs. One program gave patients a 10-day trial of a new drug (rather than a 90-day supply) to cut down on the cost of wasted

---

● **Exhibit 8.4**

HOW TO MAKE VISITS COUNT

A person with an older relative or friend in an institution may come to dread visiting day. If the relative has a cognitive impairment or few verbal skills, a well-meaning visitor can find the visit unpleasant and disturbing. Below, Pat Gibbs, consultant to the Ministry of Health in British Columbia, gives some helpful advice on how to make the most of a visit.

Q: My husband is glad to see me when I visit him at the Extended Care Unit, where he has lived for the past two years since I could no longer look after him at home. But he doesn't talk or respond much, and I run out of things to say. Sometimes it's hard to come up with ideas to pass the time during our visits.

A: You have raised a concern that many other caregivers share. Perhaps some of these suggestions might help.

- Bring in photograph albums from home—many pleasant hours can be spent in reminiscing using old photographs.
- Bring in a small tape deck and cassette tapes of music that the two of you enjoyed, and spend a visit listening to music together.

- Include other residents, room-mates, or visitors in social interaction during the visit. For example, if you turn on the T.V. so that your husband can watch a game, invite someone else to join in. This may facilitate your husband's forming relationships with others in the Extended Care Unit.
- Simple grooming activities are relaxing, do not require conversation, provide the soothing contact of touch, and may be things that the staff have limited time to do for your husband, such as a manicure, or even a massage!
- Try reading out loud—clips of interest from the newspaper, or letters from relatives. Some letters can be read more than once—it doesn't have to be a new one each time.
- Capitalize on all the amenities and resources that the facility has to offer. If possible, change the location of your visits from time to time. Take your husband in his wheelchair down to the chapel, the library corner, the lounge for tea, out to the courtyard for fresh air.
- Incorporate special events going on at the residence into your visiting time with your spouse, such as a family barbecue, or happy hour.
- If appropriate, bring in a pet from home.

Source: P. Gibbs, 1996, "How to Make Visits Count," *BC Caregiver News* 1(5): 4. Reprinted with permission.

medicines. Another program targets drug fraud and medication abuse. It links pharmacies throughout the province via computer so pharmacists can review a person's entire drug use pattern to ensure the best treatment. A third program attempts to cap the cost of expensive medications by proposing preferred (less expensive) brands of the drug.

In 1997, Alberta's health minister called for a review of the province's long-term care system. The government set out a plan to reduce costs and to give responsibility for health services to regional health authorities (RHAs). The plan also called for decreases in acute hospital beds and increases in community care. Saunders and his colleagues (2001) report that in part this plan succeeded. During the 1990s, Alberta's acute hospital stays decreased and use of home care and doctors' services increased. But the plan did not reduce costs. Also, the researchers say that their report didn't study the quality of care that patients received. New systems and policies try to contain costs, but continued reliance on doctors, hospitals, drugs, and expensive treatments will drive up the costs of medical care in the future.

Shapiro (1992) says that nursing homes rely too heavily on the medical model. They hire costly registered nurses to give care when most patients need help with activities of daily living (such as bathing). "Except for residents who require specialized resources," she says, "even the heaviest care residents are in this category because their heavy dependency on others is primarily for ADL [activities of daily living] help or for supervision due to their cognitive impairment" (208). Reliance on the medical model also sometimes leads to inappropriate care for the older patients in the community.

These and other issues led the federal government to review the national health care system. In April 2001, Prime Minister Jean Chrétien commissioned a study of Canada's health care system. He appointed Roy Romanow, Queen's Counsellor, to chair the Commission on the Future of Health Care in Canada. The prime minister charged the commission to study the current system and propose reforms to meet Canada's future health care needs. The commission met with citizens and groups across the country, held televised forums, and received reports from researchers. The commission handed down its report (often called the **Romanow Report**) in November 2002 (Commission on the Future of Health Care in Canada [Commission] 2002). It contained 47 proposals for change. This forms what the report calls a "roadmap for a collective journey by Canadians to reform and renew their health care system." Many of these proposals respond to the needs of older

people. Below is a sample of the recommendations that speak to older people's needs.

Recommendation 1: A new Canadian Health Covenant should be established as a common declaration of Canadians' and their governments' commitment to a universally accessible, publicly funded health care system (Commission 2002, 247).

Recommendation 5: The *Canada Health Act* should be modernized and strengthened by:

- Confirming the principles of public administration, universality, and accessibility, updating the principles of portability and comprehensiveness, and establishing a new principle of accountability;
- Expanding insured health services beyond hospital and physician services to immediately include targeted home care services followed by prescription drugs in the longer term;
- Clarifying coverage in terms of diagnostic services;
- Including an effective dispute resolution process;
- Establishing a dedicated health transfer directly connected to the principles and conditions of the *Canada Health Act* (Commission 2002, 248).

Recommendation 7: On a short-term basis, the federal government should provide targeted funding for the next two years to establish:

- a new Rural and Remote Access Fund,
- a new Diagnostic Services Fund,
- a Primary Health Care Transfer,
- a Home Care Transfer, and
- a Catastrophic Drug Transfer (Commission 2002, 248–49).

Recommendation 26: Provincial and territorial governments should take immediate action to manage wait lists more effectively by implementing centralized approaches, setting standardized criteria, and providing clear information to patients on how long they can expect to wait (Commission 2002, 251).

Recommendation 34: The proposed new Home Care Transfer should be used to support expansion of the *Canada Health Act* to include medically necessary home care services in the following areas:

- Home mental health case management and intervention services should immediately be included in the scope of medically necessary services covered under the Canada Health Act.

- Home care services for post-acute patients, including coverage for medication management and rehabilitation services, should be included under the Canada Health Act.

- Palliative home care services to support people in their last six months of life should also be included under the *Canada Health Act* (Commission 2002, 252).

Recommendation 35: Human Resources Development Canada, in conjunction with Health Canada, should be directed to develop proposals to provide direct support to informal caregivers to allow them to spend time away from work to provide necessary home care assistance at critical times (Commission 2002, 252).

The report concludes by stating that "the immediate priorities must be to strengthen medicare's legislative and institutional foundations, to stabilize funding, and to address the critical concerns that are eroding Canadians' confidence in the system" (Commission 2002, 254). These changes will take place over time; the implementation plan extends to 2020.

The Canadian Geriatrics Society's response to the Romanow Report proposes an increase in the number of physicians who choose to specialize in geriatrics. It also proposes more geriatric expertise for general practice physicians (MacKnight et al. 2003). This group also calls for more home care services for those with chronic illness, more assistance to family caregivers, and an increase in qualified staff in long-term care facilities. The changes proposed in the Romanow Report and responses to this report will improve the health care system overall, but the implementation of these changes will depend on the government's ability to fund these reforms.

LONG-TERM CARE: NEW APPROACHES TO COMMUNITY CARE

The *Canada Health Act* of 1984, the basis of Canada's health care system, ensures hospital and physician care for all Canadians. One important benefit of the system is that it protects acute and chronically ill older people from financial ruin in case of a long-term illness. Still the system focuses on institutional and acute medical care. Older people who need other types of long-term care, including homemaker help, Meals on Wheels, or transportation, must often turn to the social welfare system for help. These programs and services fall between health care and social service, and the availability of these services varies by province and region.

Some communities have a wide range of services, others have few. Havens (1995c, 84) says that "community based long term care is both less universal and less uniform across the country than any other form of health care." This kind of care gets less funding from the federal government.

An aging population needs a system that responds to older peoples' unique needs. This means blending medical care with social and community supports. It means rethinking the meaning of health care. To meet these needs, the federal and provincial governments have begun to consider an insured national home care program. Home care looks like a way to cut health care costs and provide quality services to older people. Most provinces have begun to shift health care services away from institutions.

This change has led to an overall decrease in hospital beds, a move from short-stay to long-stay beds in hospitals, and hospital and nursing home bed closures in some provinces (Saunders et al. 2001). It has also meant fewer doctors in some provinces and more review of doctors' practices. Finally, it has meant the growth of community care services. Mitchell and colleagues (2005) report more than a doubling of home care public costs in Canada during the 1990s from $1 billion to over $2 billion. During the 1990s Manitoba, for example, experienced a 34 percent increase in home care users and a 121 percent increase in expenses. Researchers estimate that people privately spend another $500 million on home care (Sullivan and Baranek 2002).

The greatest increases in the use of home care were by older women and people who live alone. Also, people with chronic conditions and a need for ADL support tend to use home care services (Wilkins and Beaudet 2000; Mitchell et al., 2007). Home care use rises dramatically with age. People aged 85 and over, for example, show a usage rate five to six times greater than people aged 65 to 69 (Coyte 2000, cited in Sullivan and Baranek 2002). Peterson and colleagues (2005) found that some people use home care after a discharge from the hospital. These people often lack informal supports that would allow them to live at leave the hospital and live at home on their own (Peterson et al. 2005). Others used home care before nursing home admission to give them support while they waited for placement. Finally, some people used home care before death (Mitchell et al. 2005). Nursing and housekeeping were used more than any other home care services.

New Brunswick has a single-point-of-entry community care program, which allows access to all community social and health care services from one point in the system. This program serves older people throughout the province. Manitoba has had a similar system for many years. Other provinces also use this approach.

Ontario expanded its commitment to community-based LTC in the late 1990s. The government set up 43 **Community Care Access Centres (CCACs)** across the province. Volunteer boards run these centres. They buy services from providers that compete for contracts. CCACs award contracts based on quality and price. For-profit and not-for-profit organizations (such as the Victorian Order of Nurses) compete for the contracts. This system creates managed competition of community care. Williams and his colleagues (1999) point out a number of challenges this system will face. How will CCACs decide the quality of a service? Who will service providers account to for the quality of their service? How much should CCACs monitor quality? The CCACs will feel increasing pressure as the population ages and as budgets remain capped. However, this system has moved community care to a prominent place in the health care system.

Quebec has also set up a community health network. Its network has 161 **Centres locaux de services communautaires (CLSCs).** These centres combine the work of professionals and volunteers to deliver home care services. The system tries to direct health needs away from hospitals and toward community care. Quebec has also regionalized the hospital sector, decentralizing authority. "The basic purposes of regionalization are to minimize the duplication of services and facilities, to increase access to services, to permit the establishment of efficient referral channels and mechanisms, and to allow communities to become more involved in decision making over their priorities and program development" (Manga 1993, 197).

The use of regional health boards or councils has spread to other provinces. Regional boards manage and finance institutional and community health care services. They control costs in a time when the federal government has cut funds to the provinces and are thus responsible for tough decisions about where to cut services. Some of these boards or councils have seniors on advisory committees or the boards consult with local seniors' groups.

Critics of these boards fear that administrators and health care professionals will have most of the power on the boards. Also, community control may lead to unequal access to services and varied standards of service. Skinner and Rosenberg (2002), for example, say that rural communities often have smaller tax bases due to aging populations, which can lead to lower levels of health care service. Supporters of regional boards say they are familiar with local needs and can work for the best interests of the community, but health care experts disagree about the value of the boards.

Many provinces intend to shift health services from institutions to community care. But in many cases the development of community care lags behind hospital bed closings. Morris and his colleagues (2000) point out that community care has grown more technical and demands more knowledge of medical practice as older people leave hospitals sooner. A lack of funding puts more pressure on community services. And in some cases community care simply means more stress for an elderly spouse or an overworked child caregiver—usually a woman (Saunders et al. 2001). Some critics of health care reform say that it covers up the government's plan to have family members take on more health care work (Montigny 1997). If the government underfunds community care the system puts more burden on women, who are usually the primary caregivers; and this will leave poor older people without health care resources. (See Exhibit 8.5).

The National Advisory Council says that too little community care leads to poor care for patients after they leave the hospital. A study in Saskatchewan, for example, found that 60 percent of people discharged from the hospital with home care needs did not get formal services (Saskatchewan Health 1998, cited in National Advisory Council 2000b). The National Advisory Council goes on to say that unmet needs for home care exist throughout Canada. Older people in rural settings, for example, sometimes find themselves without ongoing care. Shapiro and Havens (2000) say that poor discharge planning can lead to a person's re-admission with worse health problems.

Wells (1997) found that hospital staff often began the discharge planning process early in the person's treatment—too early for the patient or the family to make a good discharge planning decision. Also, she found that discharge plans often reflected the hospital's concern for shorter stays, rather than the clinical condition of the older person. Patients were sometimes left out of the decision-making process, leading to their dissatisfaction with the decision. Wells points out that this policy also raises ethical questions as health care professionals face a conflict between the hospital's goals and the patient's best interests.

Typical Community Care Programs

The social model of health care looks for ways to keep people out of institutions. A health care system based on the social model of care would provide community care for chronic illnesses and ADL needs. Community

● **Exhibit 8.5**

BASIC COMPONENTS OF A SOUND CONTINUING CARE SYSTEM

The Federal/Provincial/Territorial Subcommittee on Continuing Care (1992, 25; also 2001 cited in Home Care Sector 2003) proposed a list of "major categories of services and settings" that make up the long-term care system. The list below presents the programs most often used by older people. It gives a flavour of the mix of services, some medical and some social. This mix can cause confusion for people who need long-term care. Many providers offer these services (government, not-for-profit, for-profit); provincial health insurance pays for some services, and other services charge a user fee. Case managers can help make sense of this system and can ensure people get the services they need.

Meals on Wheels

Meals on Wheels delivers hot, nutritious meals to a person's home. Volunteers deliver the meals. These programs supplement diet to maintain health.

Adult Day Care

Adult day care provides personal help, health care services, and recreation in a group setting. People attend for half or full days.

Homemaker Services

Non-professionals help with personal care or house-keeping. Services may include help with bathing, cleaning, and cooking.

Home Nursing Care

A nurse visits someone's home to provide care. This service may cover day and evening care

seven days a week and usually requires a doctor's referral.

Community Physiotherapy and Occupational Therapy

Physiotherapy and occupational therapists provide direct treatment and advice on illness prevention, arrange for equipment for home use, and teach family members how to help clients.

Assessment and Treatment Centres and Day Hospitals

Short-term services are available for diagnosing and treating health problems, including physical and psychological assessments, usually in an acute-care hospital.

Nursing Home Care

A nursing home provides institutional care for people who cannot remain at home because of health problems. Nursing homes provide long-term care for chronically ill people.

Chronic Hospital Care

An institution that provides special care for people with a chronic illness and functional limits and who do not need all the services of an acute-care hospital.

Other Services

Other services include programs that provide people with assistive devices, nutrition counselling, and social workers' services.

Source: Copyright © Minister of Public Works and Government Services Canada, 2000.

care programs include hospitals, nursing homes, doctors' services, and community-based services such as geriatric day hospitals, adult day care, and home care.

The programs discussed below, beginning with geriatric day hospitals, form a **continuum of care**—from more institutional contact to little or no institutional contact. They show how the Canadian health care system has applied some of the principles of the social model of health care to meet older people's needs.

Keep three points in mind as you read about these programs. First, the same people who run the programs have done some of the evaluations of programs presented here, and this could bias their reports. Second, few evaluations use control groups to see what would have happened to a similar group if they had not used this kind of program. A program that claims to save money by keeping people out of institutions should compare its costs to service for a similar group of people who were in an institution. Third, evaluation studies often report short-term changes, which makes it difficult to judge the long-term effects of a program.

Even with these shortcomings, however, evaluations and reports often provide the only available information about new programs. They give some idea of what these programs do and how well they work.

Geriatric Day Hospitals

Geriatric day hospitals offer a full range of hospital services to people who live in the community. A day hospital will assess an older person's needs and plan a rehabilitation and care program. Services include physical checkups, drug monitoring, dental clinics, diagnosis, treatment, and rehabilitation. Day hospitals can also keep an eye on older patients at risk in the community and ease older acute-care patients back into the community when they leave the hospital.

In a Quebec study, Desrosiers and colleagues (2004) found that day hospitals can improve patients' physical and emotional well-being. Patients with walking problems and with a history of falling showed little improvement, but people with stroke or neurological disease and those with musculoskeletal disorders or amputations did the best. People with cognitive disorders and psychological problems also improved. Patients who improved showed gains in mental function and IADL activity, and reported a greater sense of well-being. The day centres also led to improvements in caregivers' feelings of burden. The study found that nearly all improvements lasted up to three months after discharge.

A study of a geriatric day hospital program in London, Ontario, by Crilly and colleagues (2005, 308) expanded on the Quebec study. They found that 146 of 151 patients in the program improved while in the program. But a study of these patients from 6 to 18 months after discharge found that nearly 2 in 5 (39 percent) reported deteriorated health. The researchers then compared those who deteriorated with those who maintained their health. They found that the more independent patients—those with less risk of falling, those who live alone, those who got around without an assistive device—tended to maintain their health gains. The frailer older person who lived with someone else and who needed support from the formal care system tended to decline. The researchers suggest that frailer, more dependent day hospital patients after discharge "may need ongoing input from the system in the form of continued therapy." The researchers say that the health care system must integrate geriatric day hospitals into the continuum of care. This needs to include "active

intervention in the home after 'discharge'" especially for frail patients.

Will geriatric day hospitals save the system money? Only if they can keep people out of nursing homes and in the community. The studies above suggest that they can play this role for many older people who need rehabilitation. The studies also show that people can maintain the benefits they get through day hospital care after they leave the program. But some people may need more intensive and ongoing help in their homes. More research on the effects of geriatric day hospital services will improve their ability to keep people in their homes.

Adult Day Care

Adult day-care programs provide support in the community for people who cannot stay in their homes without it. These programs include hot meals, recreation programs, and a chance for the older person to socialize. The programs also give family caregivers time off to rest, shop, and maintain their own social life. Adult day care offers fewer medical services and more social and recreational services than day hospitals. Some provinces require that people pay for day-care services themselves, while other provinces include the service as part of the provincial health program (Weeks and Roberto 2002).

As yet, research has not shown a conclusive improvement of function or a reduction in the use of other services due to adult day care (or day hospital care) alone (Baumgarten et al. 2002; Lucas 2006). However, studies do report an increase in participants' well-being and their satisfaction with the service. A study in Quebec found that two-thirds of adult day-care clients said they felt less lonely and half said they felt less anxious and depressed (Baumgarten et al. 2002).

Home Care

Home care is one of the most important parts of a comprehensive health care system. Chappell (1999, i) calls it "a cornerstone of a comprehensive, appropriate health care system for seniors." Home care includes medical care, such as a visiting nurse; housework; personal care; and meal delivery. A federal government report describes three goals of home care: (1) substitution for more costly care in institutions; (2) maintaining a person at home at a lower cost to the system; and (3) prevention of functional breakdown that could lead to institutionalization (FPT Subcommittee 1990).

In 1977, the Canadian federal government started the Extended Health Care Services program to support provincial home care programs. Home care programs differ from province to province, but all the provinces and territories in Canada have some public home care and nursing services. Some provinces have extensive home care programs that include Meals on Wheels, home repair services, laundry and cleaning help, emergency alert services, friendly visitors, nutrition counselling, and transportation.

Chan and Kenny (2001) say that all provincial home care programs assess clients, coordinate services, and manage cases. Case coordinators in Manitoba, for example, use an assessment interview to identify client needs. They then set up a system of supports to help the older person stay in his or her home. Ontario provides case managers to assess a person's needs and link them with public and private services. Case managers set up personalized care plans and try to protect clients from decreases in care services (Aronson 2002; Aronson and Sinding 2000). Hall and Cotye (2001) found that older people (aged 75 and over) and people in poor health who needed help with IADL tended to use home care the most. McWilliam and her colleagues (2000) say that in-home assessments and care management lead to more physical independence for seniors at home.

Paré (2000, cited in National Advisory Council 2000d) reports on a Montreal program called SIPA (a French-language acronym for integrated care for seniors). This program uses hospitals and long-term care settings to serve frail seniors in the community. It offers nursing services around the clock. Paré reports a 50 percent drop in LTC admission rates and fewer seniors in hospital beds waiting for care.

Private for-profit and nonprofit home care agencies also exist. They most often provide help with housework, some nursing care, and palliative care. A wide range of older people use home support and personal care services to maintain themselves in the community. People with dementia and other kinds of cognitive impairment use more home care services than any other group of older people.

In 2003, 15 percent of community-dwelling seniors (11.7 percent of men and 17.6 percent of women) received home care in Canada. The larger number of women in late old age, compared to the number of men, in part, explains the heavier reliance of women on home care. Roterman (2006, 42) says that "the services included nursing care, other health care, personal care, everyday housework, meal preparation or delivery, shopping and respite care. Sources of care were formal providers, such as nurses and homemakers, and/or informal providers such as family, friends, or neighbours." The older the person and the more chronic conditions a person reported, the greater the likelihood that the person would receive home care. People in poor health, people formerly hospitalized, and people with activity limitation tended to use home care. People who lived alone also showed a greater tendency to use home care. Home care helps to keep older infirm people out of hospitals and institutions (see Exhibit 8.6).

In the past, home care played a relatively small role in the Canadian health care system. A government study of home care in 1990, for example, said that "home care remains a minor component of the health budget" (FPT Subcommittee 1990). A policy statement by the Canadian Association on Gerontology said that in 1997–98 Canada spent $2.1 billion on public home care. This came to only 4 percent of the total spent on public health care (Chappell 1999).

But home care programs have grown in recent years. Hollander and Chappell (2002) say that public spending on home care in Canada grew by 11 percent per year from 1990–91 to 1997–98. Ontario, for example, increased its home care budget more than fivefold from $177.4 million in 1984 to more than $1 billion in 1999 (Hall and Coyte 2001). Hollander and Chappell (2002, 1) say that "the amount of spending on home care by private individuals needing care, and their families, is not known at this time but may be substantial."

Krueger and his colleagues (2000) studied the health care needs of seniors in the community. Seniors reported the following five needs in this order: caregiver support, community long-term care, services for people with dementia, palliative care, and cancer patient care. People considered community long-term care the single most important health issue for the next five to ten years.

Until recently, governments funded home care in the belief that it lowered overall health care costs. A national study of home care costs in Canada supports this belief. This study took place across Canada in a number of sites. The British Columbia sub-study compared home care to institutional costs. Hollander (2001; 2003) found that home care clients cost from one-half to three-quarters as much as institutional clients (depending on the level of care needed).

The study goes on to report that the more stable the person's type and level of care, the better the savings to the system. Home care costs came to less than institutional costs even when the study included informal caregivers' costs. The amount of savings depends on whether the study assumed a cost for informal caregivers equal to a professional caregivers' wage or equal to a minimum wage (Hollander and Chappell 2002).

The more hours of home care used, the closer costs approach those of institutional care. At 120 hours of home care, for example, the costs equal those of an institution (Hollander and Chappell 2002). An increase in the number of oldest-old people (85 and over), who

● Exhibit 8.6

HOME CARE USE AND TYPE

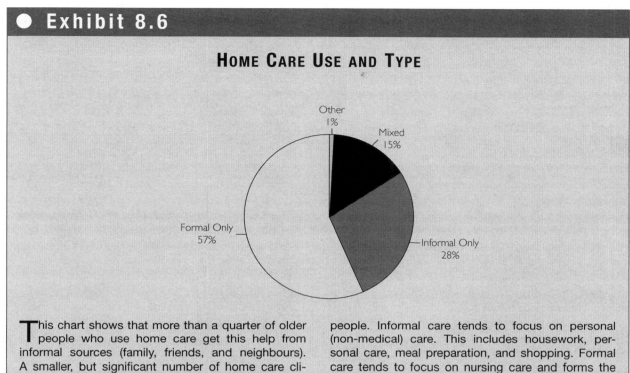

Other
1%

Mixed
15%

Formal Only
57%

Informal Only
28%

This chart shows that more than a quarter of older people who use home care get this help from informal sources (family, friends, and neighbours). A smaller, but significant number of home care clients (15 percent) use both informal and formal care. Informal care (whether alone or mixed) makes up a large percentage of all home care provided to older people. Informal care tends to focus on personal (non-medical) care. This includes housework, personal care, meal preparation, and shopping. Formal care tends to focus on nursing care and forms the basis of the home care system. These figures show that informal and formal care supports complement one another to meet the needs of older people.

Source: 2003 Canadian Community Health Survey, Statistics Canada. Health Reports. Supplement, 2005, Catalogue 82-003-SIE, vol. 16, page 42, chart 6.

have the most health problems and the most functional decline, will increase the use of home care in the future (Finlayson and Havens 2001). This will create more demand for home care and will increase the need for home care funding.

A move to increase home care will require a change in the funding priorities of the health care system. The Romanow Report proposes such a change (Commission 2002). It proposes federal funding for home care and makes home care a legitimate program within the national health care system. This may slow the shift of home care costs from the government to the family (Aronson 2002). But the report proposes to support home care only for mental health care, post-acute care, and palliative care. This recommendation needs to broaden its definition of home care to include the social services that older people want and use.

Policy discussion should now turn to the integration and coordination of all continuing care services

(including long-term care and case management). A study by Tourigny and colleagues (2004) supports this view. They studied an integrated health care delivery system in the Bois-Francs ISD (integrated service delivery) network in Quebec. The system used single point of entry and case management to coordinate service. The program coordinated all services in the area including health promotion and prevention, treatment, rehabilitation, long-term care, and palliative care. The network serves all frail older people in the Bois-Francs area. These people have ADL and IADL needs and lack informal supports. The study compared the health of people in the ISD network with people in the nearby area of Drummondville, who had no integrated service program.

The study found that the ISD group had a significantly lower risk of institutionalization during the three-year study, and showed a decrease in the desire for institutionalization. This shows that the seniors in the ISD group, after the first two years of the study, felt that they received services that met their needs. Seniors in this group also maintained their benefits during the first part of the study. Those in poorest health had the greatest likelihood of not deteriorating further. In addition, caregivers in the ISD group showed a significant decrease in caregiver burden.

Hollander and Chappell (2002) say that "[I]ntegration and coordination will make it easier to substitute home care services for residential services and acute care services." They say that a coordinated and integrated system will provide the most appropriate care for the lowest cost. The Quebec study did not find a significant decrease in health service use in the ISD group; both groups used hospital services, drugs, emergency room use, and physician services at about the same rate. But the Bois-Francs ISD focused on social interventions; all of the case managers had social work training. Clients in this program had to turn to hospitals and medical services to meet their health care needs. A program that included nurses or other health care professionals might reduce the cost of health service use. This suggests that ISD programs include health care professionals as well as social workers on the assessment and case management teams.

Roterman (2006, 44) concludes a review of health care system use by older people with the following summary. "In relation to their numbers in the population, seniors are heavy users of health care services. This is largely a reflection of the decline in health that often accompanies advancing age." Chronic illness, injury, poor self-perceived health all lead toward more health care use—including visits to doctors, hospitalization, drug use, and home care use. The health care system has changed over the years to accommodate the needs of Canada's aging population. Though the medical model still dominates the health care system, the system has increased the use of home care and other community-based services.

Further improvements in health care for older people will focus on health promotion and self-care. New generations of older people will come into later life in reasonably good health, live longer than older people in the past, and benefit from programs that help them maintain good health into late old age.

HEALTH PROMOTION

So far, this chapter has focused on illness rather than health, but there is no other way to talk about the health care system. We call it a health care system,

but it is actually a sickness treatment system. It serves people who are already sick, and it focuses on curing disease. This approach has its limits. Hospitals, doctors, nursing homes, and home care do not prevent disease; they treat illness after it occurs. The health promotion model puts health in a social context. The World Health Organization ([WHO] 1984, 101) defines health promotion as "the process of enabling people to increase control over, and to improve their own health.... [It is] a mediating strategy between people and their environments, synthesizing personal choice and social responsibility in health to create a healthier future."

Canada's interest in health promotion predates this WHO definition by a decade. In 1974, Marc Lalonde, then the federal minister of health, discussed this and other approaches to Canada's health care system in a report called *A New Perspective on the Health of Canadians* (Lalonde 1974). There he proposed the concept of the **health field**. The health field includes the usual health services, but within it the health care system is one way—not the only way, or even the best way—to improve health. In addition to traditional medical services, the health field also includes improvements in human biology (through basic research), improvements in lifestyle, and improvements in the environment as ways to better health.

Research, for example, shows that low income and low levels of education lead to poor health (Buckley et al. 2005). People with higher incomes have access to better housing, food, and private health care. Low income also creates stress and leads to unhealthy behaviours (e.g., smoking, excessive drinking, and lack of exercise). Likewise, studies of the environment have linked pollution to poor health. These studies support the idea that health promotion must deal with the environment, society, and personal habits.

This model makes sense in Canada today. Studies show that the large majority of older people remain healthy and active to an advanced age. The 2003 Canadian Community Health Survey, a study of community-dwelling older people in Canada, found that among respondents only 6.8 percent of the 65-and-over population and only 8.4 percent of the 75-and-over population reported poor health. The large majority of older people aged 65 and over (73.4 percent) reported good to excellent health. Even among those aged 75 and over, 67.9 percent reported good to excellent health (Turcotte and Schellenberg 2007).

The National Advisory Council (2000a, citing Rachlis 2000) reports on a program in Edmonton called CHOICE (Comprehensive Home Option of Integrated

Care for the Elderly). This program promotes good nutrition, exercise, and contact with others. CHOICE staff members go to clients' homes, help people get ready for a day at the CHOICE centre, and help clients home again at night. The centre provides medical, dental, and foot care, as well as rehabilitation aid. Health professionals monitor clients who have chronic conditions to prevent further illness. The centre serves healthy meals and provides activities.

Health Canada now has an Internet site called Health Promotion Online (HPO) that offers health promotion information. Developed by Health Canada's Health Promotion and Programs Branch (HPPB), HPO gives older people and health professionals the resources they need in an easy-to-use website. Resources include information on the latest health issues and approaches to healthy living (http://consumerinformation.ca/app/oca/ccig/abstract.do?abstractNo=HC000031&language=eng also http://www.phac-aspc.gc.ca/hp-ps/index-eng.php)

The Future of Health Promotion

Older people can benefit from improvements in health promotion. Some older people already engage in self-care. They take vitamins, eat breakfast every day, and engage in regular exercise. Improvements in self-care can improve an older person's quality of life. McWilliam and her colleagues (2000) found, for example, that low-intensity aerobic exercise improves physical and mental well-being. A more educated older population may have a better understanding of how to prevent illness and an even greater interest in health promotion.

But will the government support changes in social structures, policies, and the allocation of funds? Wister (2005) reports that support for health promotion programs remains uncertain. In 1971 the federal government started a health promotion program called ParticipAction, promoting it through a nationwide media campaign. In 1995, Wister says, "89% of Canadians were aware of the agency and 65% stated that it had influenced their exercise behaviour" (185). Between 1971 and 2000 the program cost a total of $21 million—less than $1 million per year. The program also drew over $40 million in private-sector funding. Yet, starting in the mid-1990s Health Canada cut the ParticipAction budget—in 1999/2000 from $1 million to only $200,000.

The government closed the program at the end of 2001. Then in 2007 a newly installed federal government reinstated the program with a $5 million budget for two years to help cope with rising obesity rates and declining activity among Canadians. The program will promote active living, advocate for government policies that promote wellness, and collect data on healthy lifestyles. This example shows the uncertainty in funding that health promotion programs face. It also shows the marginal role that governments assign to health promotion within the health care system.

Still, Health Canada continues to support health promotion activity. For example, Health Canada produces guides to help people live an active lifestyle. The handbook for *Healthy Active Living for Older Adults* prescribes daily and weekly amounts of exercise to maintain good health. In 2002 the Canadian government set out to develop an "Integrated Pan-Canadian Healthy Living Strategy" (Wister 2005, 186). This strategy focuses on reducing obesity through healthy diet and encouraging physical activity. This approach makes sense, given the findings that show increases in obesity and the importance of exercise. But, Wister notes, the strategy fails to target smoking reduction as a key to healthy later life. Also, the first phase of the strategy targets children, youth, and Aboriginal peoples; later life gets less attention. Recent decisions by the federal government show only weak support for health promotion in later life.

The Challenge to Health Promotion Programs

Glor (1991) reports two problems faced by health promotion programs. First, no agreement on quantitative measures of health exists. Second, few programs produce a measurable effect on health where scientists have tried to measure it. Shapiro and Havens (2000) say that some programs continue even when they show little effect, while other programs that show promise end for lack of funds. These authors call for better decisions about funding based on careful evaluations.

Still, disease prevention and health promotion have caught on in Canada among seniors. A report on Canada's Health Promotion Survey found that, compared with younger people, seniors less often skipped breakfast, smoked cigarettes, drank alcohol, or used illicit drugs. In 2003 nearly half of all seniors (48 percent) said they ate five or more servings of fruit or vegetables each day. Only 39 percent of 25- to 54 year-olds reported this kind of healthy diet (Turcotte and Schellenberg 2007). Also, compared with younger drivers, a smaller proportion of older drivers said they drink and drive, and a larger proportion of older drivers said they used seatbelts (Health and Welfare Canada 1988). Some of these health promotion behaviours reflect the values and lifestyles that seniors have brought with them into old age. But in other cases, as in the use of seatbelts, seniors have responded well to health promotion policies.

Ward-Griffin and Ploeg (1997) used critical feminist theory to assess health promotion programs today. They found that these programs focus too much on the individual and the body. Instead, they say, health promotion programs should focus on the economic and social conditions that limit an older woman's health promotion options. For example, many older women live in or near poverty. Also, many older women spend time and energy as caregivers. These conditions put limits on health promotion choices. Ward-Griffin and Ploeg propose that health promotion move beyond fitness and diet programs focused on the body to programs that improve income, housing, and equal opportunity for women at all ages.

ISSUES FOR THE FUTURE

Provincial and territorial long-term care systems differ across the country. The provinces and territories often agree on the same values and principles of LTC, but each has its own commitment to services, its own policies on access to care, and its own funding arrangements.

This means that the principle of universality that underlies acute health care does not apply as well to LTC (Havens 1995, 1995c). First, clients often must pay for long-term care. Government health benefits may not cover day hospital, respite, or homemaker costs. This can leave the poorest older people without help. Second, long-term care can lack coordination. This makes it hard for people to find the help they need. Third, many people fall through the cracks. They may not know about services or may not have access to a service (for example, a religious-based service may serve only people who share that faith). Health professionals refer to this as the **care gap**—the difference between what care could or should be and what usual care is. The care gap leads to missed clinical benefits and higher costs for payers.

The health care system of the future will need to respond to these problems in the LTC system. Three areas of the present system will have to be revised to meet older people's needs: the availability of services, access to services, and coordination of services.

Availability

The ability to stay in the community depends in part on the availability of services that support a person at home. Some provinces or parts of provinces have a continuum of care—from home care to acute hospital care—for older people. Other parts of the country, such as many rural areas, offer only a few home care options.

Rural areas also show a decline in the number of physicians, bed closures to save money, longer wait times, and less access to medical technologies. This leads to poorer health care services for rural seniors (Denton and Kusch 2006). Conde and McDonald (2007) studied health service use in rural areas for people aged 55 and over. They found that, compared to people in urban centres, rural people tended to see a general practitioner, a specialist, or a dentist less often. The researchers expressed concern over this finding because regular checkups with a GP or dentist can prevent serious health problems.

Skinner and Rosenberg (2002) say that government policies now make local communities responsible for managing health care. This has led rural areas to rely on informal and volunteer home care programs, but the aging of rural populations puts pressure on these informal services. These communities have more older people and fewer young people to provide volunteer services.

One rural community care worker described the workings of the Meals on Wheels program in her community. She arranges with a local restaurant to pick up a half-dozen to a dozen meals each day at noon, then she delivers them during her lunch hour to people on her caseload. She marvels at the good luck of city-based community workers, who can refer their clients to existing Meals on Wheels programs. Rural parts of Canada will need more community programs in the future.

Accessibility

A program is accessible if an older person can get to it and make use of it. Better access requires better transportation and more home-based care for very old seniors. Also, specific groups need help gaining access to health care services.

Denton and Kusch (2006) report that new immigrants and seniors from ethnic groups may need special help to get services. Unique dietary requirements, cultural differences, and food preferences can limit ethnic group members' use of community services. Culturally sensitive professionals can help overcome some of these barriers. Sometimes people do not take advantage of the programs that exist; Ma and Chi (2005) found that many Chinese-Canadian elders did not know about services in their community. They also faced a language barrier when it came to using services. Better information for seniors not fluent in English would provide them more access to services. Older people would also benefit from multilingual workers trained to work in multicultural settings.

Evans (1996) says that the Canadian health care system sometimes intentionally limits access to care. He says that the system makes services scarce and delays treatment in order to control costs. Using waiting lists to ration services for older people makes it harder for older people to get the treatment they need when they need it. In the case of life-threatening illnesses such as heart disease, waiting lists may risk a person's life (Pringle 1998). In the case of less-threatening illnesses, such as a hip replacement, a person may wait in pain for a year or more. Pringle says that if the Canadian system is going to use waiting lists, they should function predictably. Today, she says, a person's wait may depend on the number of other people on the list, the surgeon's judgment about the urgency of treatment, or how the surgeon's secretary manages the list. This barrier to care has led to a decline in satisfaction with health care among Canadians.

Chen and colleagues (2002, 20) say that "[people in poor health] are more likely than others to recognize the deficiencies in the delivery of … services." The concern about access grew to a point where Canada's first ministers addressed the issue. In September 2000 they restated that the health care system must ensure access in a reasonable time, and a range of services anywhere in the country. The system should meet peoples' needs regardless of their ability to pay (De Coster et al. 2005).

Coordination

The health care system needs better coordination and integration. This need will increase with the growth of community care, because community programs decentralize care. They bring together nurses, social workers, and therapists, who often work for different agencies and whose views on how to care for a client will vary.

The National Advisory Council on Aging (1995, 13) says that a **single-point-of-entry model** best coordinates services for older people. It improves "flexibility, continuity and quality of care for clients." It also controls costs. A single-point-of-entry model gives personalized help to each client. A staff from a single agency assesses clients' needs, coordinates service delivery, and monitors clients' progress. The staff member may arrange for meal delivery, a visiting nurse, and homemaker help in one case. In another case, the staff member may arrange for respite care and day-hospital use. Many provinces, including Manitoba, Alberta, and New Brunswick, already use this approach. The National Advisory Council on Aging supports further development of single-point-of-entry systems throughout the country.

Coordination avoids overlap between services, and integration unites health and social services into one system. The principle of universality in the *Canada*

Health Act ensures that everyone has access to the same services. A more coordinated system will also save time and may save money. Hébert and colleagues (2001) looked at the costs of care for disabled older people. They found that home care was more expensive than intermediate facility care when they took informal caregiver costs into account. For a very disabled person, home care was more expensive than nursing home care. Hébert and his colleagues propose an increase in the number of intermediate-care facilities, which would best serve older people with disabilities who had little informal support.

This study shows the need to provide careful and ongoing assessment of an older person's needs. This will keep costs down and will provide care that best suits the older person. The National Advisory Council on Aging sums this up: "health reform means more than controlling costs to achieve an affordable health care system. It means providing appropriate and effective care that is responsive to the changing needs of Canadians" (National Advisory Council on Aging 1995, 20). Responding to older people's needs should be at the core of a reformed health care system.

CONCLUSION

The changes taking place today suggest that the health care system will look different in the future. Government concerns with efficiency and costs have led to proposals for reform. Health care professionals have proposed a shift from a biomedical model to a social, community-based model of health care. Closer study of older people's health care needs will allow the system to fine-tune programs and treatments. The critique of the medical model and growing interest in social models of health care will lead to more community-based services. Also, as the population ages, more people will show an interest in disease prevention and health promotion. More comprehensive models of health care, such as the social and health promotion models, will lead to better health care for older people as well as better health at all ages.

Closer studies of older people's health care needs will allow the system to fine-tune programs and treatments. The critique of the medical model and growing interest in social models of health care will lead to more community-based services. Also, as the population ages, more people will show an interest in disease prevention and health promotion. More comprehensive models of health care, such as the social and health promotion models, will lead to better health care for older people as well as better health at all ages.

Summary

1. Health care needs for the elderly range from maintenance programs for the well elderly to long-term institutional care for those who have severe health problems.

2. Three models of health care exist in Canada today: the medical model, the social model, and the health promotion model. The medical model that dominates the health care system today is concerned with the treatment of illness.

3. The Canadian health care system consists of five basic principles: universal coverage, access to services, portability, comprehensive services, and administration by a nonprofit public agency. The provincial and federal governments share the cost of this system.

4. Canada has one of the most comprehensive health care systems in the world, but it spends proportionately more of its gross national product on health care than do some countries with more comprehensive systems.

5. Research shows that the commitment to the medical model may account for higher than necessary health care costs. Complex medical procedures, increased salaries for medical personnel, and high institutional costs all lead to increasing health care costs.

6. Canada has one of the highest rates of institutionalization in the world. Institutions serve the needs of many older people, and programs exist that can improve the quality of life of institutionalized patients. But sometimes people enter institutions because they cannot get the support they need to stay in the community.

7. The Romanow Report on the Canadian health care system proposes reform to the system. The report repeated Canada's commitment to its universal medical care system. It also rejected the use of user fees. Some reforms, such as support for palliative care and long-term care, will improve care for older people. Other reform proposals, such as the limitation of home care to post-acute, mental health, and palliative care patients, need expansion to include seniors' needs.

8. The social model of health care supports a continuum of services from institutional care to home care. It calls for health care programs that help older people stay in their own homes. These programs include geriatric day hospitals, adult day-care programs, and home care.

9. Home care programs tailor services to fit the needs of the older person. They provide families with help to relieve caregiver burden. These programs may or may not save money, but they do achieve allow people to stay in their homes as long as they can.

10. The health promotion model of health care supports healthy lifestyles and a better environment. It takes a broad view of health care that recognizes a need for changes in the workplace and improvements in socio-economic status.

11. The government will have to deal with three service issues in order to meet the needs of an aging population: availability of services, accessibility of services, and coordination of services.

12. The health care system will change in the future, and evolve to meet the needs of older people. This will include more community-based care and more health promotion programs. The system has already begun to make some of these changes.

Study Questions

1. List and describe the three major approaches to health care that exist in Canada today.

2. Explain why the cost of health care in Canada grows each year. How might the government control costs?

3. Discuss three ways in which doctors directly help keep the cost of health care high. How can doctors take steps to lower these costs?

4. Describe the normalization principle. How can institutions use this principle to provide higher-quality care for patients?

5. How does the government propose to restructure the current health care system? How will this provide better service to an aging society?

6. Describe at least two alternative health care programs that exist today.

7. Explain two of the major approaches to health promotion and give an example of each.

8. Discuss three types of improvements in health care that would improve service to older people.

Key Terms

adult day-care programs programs that provide noninstitutional support for people who are otherwise unable to remain in the community. (175)

care gap the difference between what care could or should be and what usual care is. The care gap leads to missed clinical benefits and higher costs for payers. (180)

Centres locaux de services communautaires (CLSCs) Quebec's local centres for community services combine the work of professionals and volunteers to deliver home care services and direct health needs away from hospitals toward community care. (173)

Community Care Access Centres (CCACs) Ontario's system of volunteer-run community care centres that provide a single point of entry into the health care system and services such as the Victorian Order of Nurses. (173)

continuum of care the array of services that range from institutional care to little or no institutional contact. (174)

geriatric day hospital a hospital program that offers a full range of hospital services to older people who live in the community, and that assesses individuals' needs before setting up a health care plan. (175)

health care the support needed for people to maintain optimum health. The health care needs of Canada's older population range from health promotion to health maintenance, to long-term chronic care. (158)

health field the realm of health services, including the health care system, traditional medical services, improvements in human biology, improvements in lifestyle, and improvements in environment, as envisioned by former federal Minister of Health Marc Lalonde. (178)

health promotion model a health care model that focuses on self-care and preventing disease through lifestyle change, increased knowledge about healthy behaviour, and environmental improvement. (160)

home care a range of social and medical services designed to help people live independently in the community. (175)

long-term care social and medical services, including formal services, home or institutional care, and family care, for people who have functional limitations. (158)

medical model a health care model that favours surgery, drug therapy, and rehabilitation through physical therapies with a focus on the treatment of diseases and injuries, usually in the physician's office, a hospital, or other health care institutions. (158)

normalization principle the idea that institutions can and should make life in the institution as much like life outside as possible. (168)

Romanow Report the 2002 Canadian federal government report of the Commission on the Future of Health Care in Canada, led by Roy Romanow, which underscores Canada's commitment to its health care system and makes several proposals for improving the delivery of health care to seniors. (171)

single-point-of-entry model   a single agency that assesses clients' needs, coordinates service delivery from multiple sources, and monitor clients' progress. (181)

social model   a health care model that includes personal and family counselling, home care, and adult day-care programs as part of the health care system, and that tries to keep older people in their own homes. (158)

Selected Readings

Béland, François, and Evelyn Shapiro. "Policy Issues in Care for the Elderly in Canada." *Canadian Journal on Aging* 14(2), 1995.

> This special issue of *Canadian Journal on Aging* contains writings on issues in Canadian health care. Articles range from a discussion of population aging and its impact on health care costs to the role of long-term care in the continuum of care. The collection attempts to answer many questions about the future of the health care system by looking in detail at the use of the system today.

Cousins, S. O., and T. Horne, (Eds.) *Active Living among Older Adults: Health Benefits and Outcomes.* Philadelphia: Brunner/Mazel, 1999.

> This book summarizes a large body of literature on physical activity in later life. The authors find that most studies look at exercise and fitness programs. The book shows that during the 1990s researchers and practitioners came to value physical activity for older adults. They also began to promote less-intense activities preferred by older people (such as yoga and walking). This is a good summary that shows the benefits of activity in later life.

Haber, David, *Health Promotion and Aging,* 4th ed. New York: Springer, 2007.

> This book emphasizes the active role that older people can play in shaping the care they receive. Haber promotes collaboration between the older person and the health care professional. He promotes the idea that health professionals should serve as health educators. The book contains thorough information on exercise, nutrition, weight management, and health education, as well as resource lists and health education material.

Websites to Consult

Canadian Institutes of Health Research (CIHR)—Institute of Aging (IA)

http://www.cihr-irsc.gc.ca/e/8671.html

> The Institute of Aging, one of thirteen CIHR "virtual" institutes, is a government initiative that funds researchers across Canada working in the field of aging. This includes research on the causes, prevention, and treatment of aging-related diseases, health services and health policy, and many other areas of health and aging research. The IA website provides information on the types of funding opportunities available to researchers, current and recent multidisciplinary research projects, and relevant publications and other resources.

Canadian Health Network—Seniors

http://www.phac-aspc.gc.ca/sh-sa-eng.php?rd=senior_agee_eng

> This Public Health Agency of Canada site has a section for seniors, which contains information on self-care, sexual activity, and other topics of interest. This site also links to reports on health issues. Some of the general links contain information (e.g., on fitness) that applies to health promotion in later life and seniors' well-being.

Health Canada

http://www.hc-sc.gc.ca/hl-vs/seniors-aines/index-eng.php

> This site offers tips on healthy living for seniors. It includes links to sites on osteoarthritis, vision impairment, reports on topics such as falls, and resources such as a CD on end-of-life care.

© Kindra Clineff/Index Stock Imagery

Chapter

9

Finances and Economics

INTRODUCTION

Jack Bruckner, aged 65, took early retirement two years ago. He gets a pension from his job and an Old Age Security cheque each month. His wife, Betty, 59, never worked outside the home, so she receives no pension.

They live in a small government-subsidized apartment. Last spring, Jack and Betty decided to travel east. Jack knew their old car would never make the trip, so he went to the bank for a car loan. "I never thought they'd give me a loan," he says. "I went in thinking they'd just laugh at the idea. But the bank manager looked at my pension income and approved the loan. I can't believe it—I never thought, with the little we make, that we'd be able to buy a new car."

Like many older people, Jack and Betty do not have much, but they feel satisfied with what they have.

Both of them lived through lean times when they first got married. They worry less about money now than in the past, and, Jack says, when Betty gets her pension from the federal government in a few years, their financial worries will be over.

Canada's pension system can take most of the credit for the Bruckners' financial well-being. The income of older people adjusted for inflation increased faster than that of younger people (aged 15 to 64) from the early 1980s to the present. Lindsay and Almey (2006) says that between 1981 and 2003 the average annual income of women aged 65 and over increased by 32 percent (compared to 2 percent for younger women). Over the same period, older men showed an increase in income of 24 percent. Younger men showed an income increase of only 2 percent (see Exhibit 9.1).

● Exhibit 9.1

INCIDENCE OF LOW INCOME, BY AGE GROUP, CANADA 1980–2003

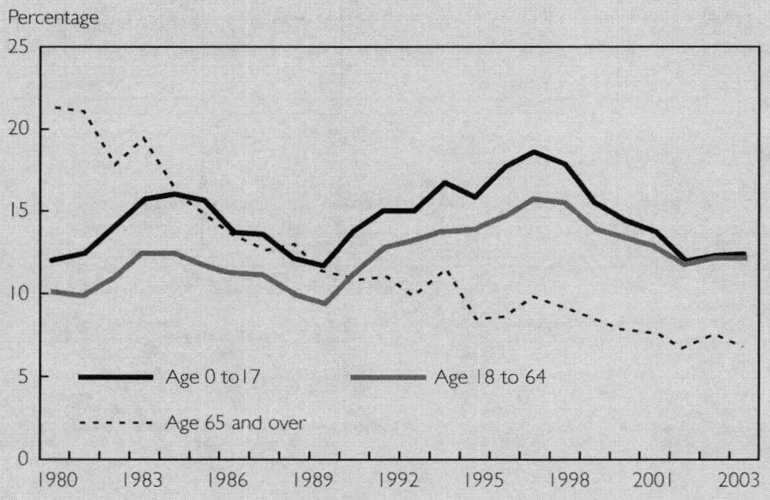

This graph shows the general downward trend in the poverty rate for all older people. By the early 1990s seniors' low income rate had dropped below all other age groups. It continued to decline to 2003. Relative to other age groups, older people as a group show the lowest rate of poverty. The decrease in poverty rates holds for all groups of older people. But senior women who live alone show the highest rates of poverty among older people.

Source: Martin Turcotte and Grant Schellenberg. 2007. A Portrait of Seniors in Canada 2006. Statistics Canada. p. 68.

A study by the OECD (2001) found that by the 1990s Canada had the highest rate of income replacement for retirees of all nine developed countries studied. The study found that between the 1970s and the 1990s the income of low-income older people increased more than for any other country in the sample. Also, among these countries, Canada's seniors had the highest rate of investment income. Mo and colleagues (2006) say that the Canadian retirement income system encourages investment throughout a person's working life. This leads to more diversified income in retirement it accounts for the relatively high incomes of Canada's seniors today.

Myles (2000, 288) concludes that Canada has one of the best income security systems in the world and one of the lowest rates of seniors' low income among the developed nations. Yet he calls the cost of the public system "modest by international standards." "In short," Myles says, "like Baby Bear's porridge, Canada seems to have gotten it 'just right' when measured against these international benchmarks."

The strong financial condition of older people shows up in their relations with their children. Dependency ratios, for example, assume that older people depend on the young for support. However, studies of inter-generational family transfers show just the opposite. Ploeg and colleagues (2004, S137) studied the financial relations between 138 people aged 55 and over and their family members. The researchers report that "overall, participants provided significant financial assistance to their children and grandchildren." These older people provided support for a variety of expenses including the purchase of a home, a car, wedding expenses, and education.

Most of these funds went to children, but some went to grandchildren (often for education). The researchers found that older parents felt "very moti-vated to provide financial support" to their younger family members. Findings from this and other studies show that money tends to flow from the older to the younger generation. This suggests that many older people can meet their own financial needs and still assist their children and grandchildren. Ploeg and colleagues (2004, S142) conclude that older parents "wanted to help out of love and commitment to family but, perhaps most importantly, because they were financially able to provide this assistance."

Studies and reports like these show that, as a group, older people have better incomes than many people imagine. For example, the poverty rate for seniors has decreased since the early 1980s (Lindsay and Almey 2006). Seniors now have a rate lower than other age groups in the population. Also, poorer seniors, compared

to other age groups, tend to spend less time in poverty. Statistics Canada reports that between 1996 and 2001 14 percent of seniors lived below the low-income cut off (LICO) at some time; however, 25 percent of the entire Canadian population lived below the LICO at some time during that period. Also, senior households, compared to other types of households, show less **depth of poverty**—the distance between their income and the poverty line (National Advisory Council, 2005).

Still, the retirement income system has its flaws, some of them serious. While income has risen in the past few years for older people in general, certain groups still have incomes below the poverty line in old age. Older people from lower-income backgrounds, people who cannot speak English or French, people without much education, and people who live in small towns all tend to have lower than average incomes. Very old people, women, and unattached individuals (a term used by Statistics Canada to describe a "person living alone or in a household where he/she is not related to other house-hold members") often live below the poverty line. Older women, compared with older men, also show a greater depth of poverty and a smaller proportion of people living well above the poverty line. In 2002, for example, unattached women aged 65 and over had after tax pov-erty rates of 19 percent while men in this age group had a 15 percent after-tax poverty rate. In contrast, the after-tax poverty rate for older women who lived in a family was just 2 percent (Lindsay and Almey 2006).

Even reports of average family incomes show that, compared to middle-aged people, older people live on lower incomes. For people who earned an average wage before retirement, the Old Age Security (OAS) will make up about 14 percent of their pre-retirement income. The Canada Pension Plan (CPP) will make up another 25 percent. Therefore, the average wage earner will have to find other means to make up lost income in retirement or live on a lower income. People who earn above the average wage will need to make up even more income in order to maintain their standard of living, and those on fixed pensions (i.e., not indexed to the cost of living) get poorer every year because of inflation. Most people, except the very rich and the very poor, will feel a drop in their income when they retire.

Many individuals and groups, including the federal and provincial governments, the National Council of Women, and the Royal Canadian Legion, have suggested changes to Canada's pension system. Their concerns led to the **great pension debate** in the 1980s and more recently to a debate over the **universality** of Canada's public pension system. The results of these debates have begun to influence the retirement income system in Canada and will influence the pensions of future retirees.

This chapter looks at (1) the structure of the Canadian pension system and how it works, (2) the flaws in the system and suggestions for pension reform, and (3) the future of Canada's retirement income system.

HISTORICAL DEVELOPMENTS IN CANADA'S PENSION SYSTEM

Until the 1920s, Canadian pension policy reflected the "market ethos" (Bryden 1974, 19). According to this thinking, individuals should take responsibility for themselves in old age and those who need help should get it from their families. Bryden reports that city life and industrialization in Canada made this ethos hard to practice. The *Labour Gazette*, for example, stated in 1924 that "high rents, [and] overcrowding in houses, make it difficult for the poor to provide for their aged parents. It has been the experience of social agencies that many of the old men and women in their districts are suffering from the lack of the necessities of life" (*Labour Gazette* 1924, cited in Bryden 1974, 42).

The federal government decided to act to relieve the poverty among older people. A House of Commons committee issued a report in 1925 that called for a $20 monthly pension to people aged 70 or older who passed a residence requirement and a means test (a test of financial need). The committee proposed that the federal government and the provinces should each pay half the cost of pension benefits. The plan did not require pensioners to pay anything into the program. The committee saw the program as a supplement to income more than as a pension. The *Old Age Pension Act* became law in 1927, and all the provinces and the Northwest Territories agreed to the plan by 1936. This plan, for the first time, defined pensions as a right due to all older Canadians. Snell (1993) shows that men, compared with women, had greater access to these pensions. For example, a woman with a younger, employed husband could have her claim rejected because the state expected her husband to support her. Snell traces this type of discrimination to the state's assumption about male dominance in families.

In 1951, the federal government passed the *Old Age Security Act* and the *Old Age Assistance Act* to replace the *Old Age Pension Act*. The *Old Age Security Act* set up a pension plan run solely by the federal government. The new plan paid up to $40 a month at age 70 without a means test. The federal government increased this pension to $55 a month in 1961. The *Old Age Assistance Act*

set up a means-tested pension for people between 65 and 69 years old who could demonstrate financial need. The provinces and the federal government shared the cost for this program. The plan required no contributions and paid the same pension to all poorer pensioners, including homemakers.

These early programs supplemented the incomes of older people (by offering basic income security). The federal government kept payments low so people would have an incentive to provide for their own old age.). In the 1960s, the federal government broadened the pension system by setting up the Guaranteed Income Supplement program to supplement Old Age Security. This program was designed to help the poorest older people. In 1966, the federal government and the government of Quebec started the Canada and Quebec Pension Plans. Today, all wage earners in Canada pay part of their incomes into these plans.

By the 1970s, Canada had two types of programs in place: **income security programs** (the Old Age Security and the Guaranteed Income Supplement) and **income maintenance programs** (the Canada and Quebec Pension Plans). These programs form the basis of the Canadian pension system today. The federal government designed the first type of program to help people meet their basic needs in retirement and the second type to help people maintain their pre-retirement income and lifestyle.

By 1999, federal government transfers (the Old Age Security and the Guaranteed Income Supplement and other transfers paid for from tax revenues) and the Canada Pension Plan accounted for 47 percent of older Canadians' retirement incomes (Statistics Canada 2003c). Federal government transfers and the CPP have made up increasing proportions of seniors' income over the years. Also by the 1990s seniors began to get more of their income from occupational pensions and other sources than ever before. These trends led to an overall increase in seniors' income.

A report by Mo and colleagues (2006) describes the diversification of seniors' income sources from the 1980s to the early 2000s. They found that, in particular, seniors got more of their funds from government and private pensions than ever before. Income from private pensions, for example, grew from 18 percent of the average senior's income in 1990 to 29 percent in 1999 (Li 2006 citing Maser 2003). The researchers say that this diversification of income sources occurred among people in all income levels (not just wealthy people).

The maturation of public and private pension plans in Canada best explains this shift in income sources (Baldwin 2006). The maturation of workplace pension plans also played a role in increasing older peoples' incomes. Studies show that the more diverse a person's income sources, the better off that person becomes financially. This movement away from government transfers and toward public and private pension income characterizes the Canada pension system's evolution from the 1980s onward. "Thus, on the average," Mo and colleagues say (2006, 14), "the low-income elderly counted traditionally on a lower number of income sources to ensure their standard of living; but the situation has improved in recent years."

The diversification has also happened among older women living alone. Twenty years ago, this group depended mainly on governmental transfers and on investment income. As they diversified their sources of income, they relied more on private pensions. These pensions will pay less compared to those of men. Public and private pensions still reflect inequalities in the labour market in lifetime work opportunities. Still, private pensions helped older women move out of poverty (especially single women who live alone) (Stone 2006).

In sum, Mo and colleagues say (2006, 18), "the elderly count today on improved balance among various sources of income." Any decline in work income or investment income among older people (for example, due to an economic downturn, such as the one in 2008–09) increases the importance of government and private sources of income—in particular, government transfers and pensions. This makes the study of the Canadian pension system vital to an understanding old age today.

THE CANADIAN RETIREMENT INCOME SYSTEM TODAY

Canada's complex system of pension plans and programs, along with earnings from work, should create a decent old age for all Canadians, but it does not (see Exhibit 9.2). Some older people still suffer a sharp loss in income and a shocking change in lifestyle when they retire. Almost every tier and subsection of the Canadian pension system needs improvement to address this problem.

● Exhibit 9.2

SOURCE OF INCOME FOR PEOPLE AGED 65 AND OVER IN CANADA, 2003

Source	Men	Women
Private pensions	40.5	26.3
OAS/GIS/SPA	18.4	31.7
CPP/QPP	20.2	20.5
Investments	8.8	12.6
Employment	8.1	4.3
Other income*	4.0	4.6
Total	100.0	100.0

*Other sources of income, such as provincial and territorial tax credits, GST and HST tax credits, and other government transfers.

Note that men get more of their income from private pensions. Compared to women, men have higher incomes throughout their work lives, they typically have unbroken work records, and they work for companies and in positions that provide a private pension. Women rely more heavily on government pensions programs (OAS/GIS/SPA). Compared to men, women typically have lower incomes in retirement.

Source: Created from M. Turcotte and G. Schellenberg, 2007, *A Portrait of Seniors 2006*. Ottawa: Statistics Canada, Ministry of Industry. Catalogue No. 89-519-XIE. Table 2.2.3, p. 94. Based on Statistics Canada, Survey of Consumer Finances; Survey of Labour and Income Dynamics.

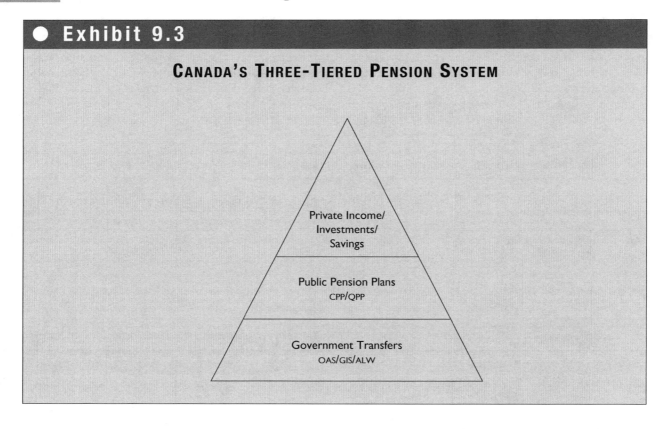

CANADA'S THREE-TIERED PENSION SYSTEM

Private Income/
Investments/
Savings

Public Pension Plans
CPP/QPP

Government Transfers
OAS/GIS/ALW

The following discussion will look at the structure and the limits of the Canadian pension system today.

Tier One: Government Transfers

Canada has a three-tiered pension system shaped like a pyramid (see Exhibits 9.2 and 9.3). The Old Age Security (OAS), the Guaranteed Income Supplement (GIS), and the Allowance (ALW)—called federal government transfer programs—make up the first tier. Nearly all Canadians aged 65 or over, rich or poor, get the same OAS pension ($516.96 maximum per month for April–June 2009). But people who earned over $66,335 in 2009 had to repay their OAS at a rate of 15 percent of their income over this amount. So someone with a net income of $107.692 or more repaid his or her entire OAS benefit (Service Canada 2009).

The Guaranteed Income Supplement (GIS) goes to people with a low income or no income other than the Old Age Security (OAS). Poon (2005) reports that families who get the GIS, for example, have about half the income of non-GIS families. And unattached people who got the GIS had one-sixth the total assets of non-GIS unattached people. Allowance (ALW) payments go to spouses or common-law partners or survivors of OAS pensioners. The ALW helps survivors aged 60 to 64 and

couples with only one income. People do not directly contribute to OAS, GIS, or ALW pension funds; the federal government pays them out of tax revenue. The GIS and ALW accounted for about 23 percent of government transfer costs in 2000 (Maser and Begin 2003).

The federal government estimates that it spent more than $36.2 billion on government transfers (OAS, GIS, and Allowance) in 2009–2010 (up from $11 billion in 1984) (Service Canada 2009). This first tier of programs (OAS/GIS/ALW) in 2003 accounted for 18.4 percent of the incomes of older men and 31.7 percent of the incomes of older women (Turcotte and Schellenberg 2007). These programs protect older people's incomes—especially those of the very poor—from falling below a specified level.

Not surprisingly, poorer people depend on transfers most. These transfers (OAS/GIS/ALW) reduce low-income rates and also decrease income inequality (Myles 2000). Older women rely more heavily on government transfers. Men received more of their income from private pensions (40.5 percent for older men compared to only 26.3 percent for older women). These figures reflect the different work careers of older men and women in the past and today (Turcotte and Schellenberg 2007).

In the period April–June 2009, the OAS went to 4.5 million Canadians. The federal government indexes

OAS payments to the consumer price index or cost of living, and adjusts the rate four times a year. But the high cost of the program (over $26 billion in 2009) makes it an obvious target for federal government cutbacks.

The GIS goes to the poorest seniors. In January 2009 1.6 million OAS pensioners (35 percent) received full or partial GIS (Services Canada 2009). GIS benefits in 2009 went to single older people who received less than $15,672 that year from sources other than the OAS and GIS. It also went to a spouse or common-law partner of an OAS pensioner in 2009 with a (non-OAS and non-GIS) income of $20,688 or less. The federal government does not tax the GIS, and it indexes GIS payments to the consumer price index, so that they go up quarterly as the cost of living rises.

A person (or a couple) gets either full or partial GIS payments based on a yearly income test. In the second quarter of 2009, a single person could receive a maximum GIS of $652.51 per month, while a partner of an OAS recipient could get a maximum GIS of $430.90 per month (Services Canada 2009). Single pensioners, more often than married pensioners, have incomes low enough to need the GIS. Women, many of them widows, make up about 65 percent of all people poor enough to get the GIS (National Advisory Council 2005).

The federal government added the Spouse's Allowance (SPA) program (now called the Allowance (ALW) to the first tier of the system in 1975. The ALW goes to a low-income pensioner's spouse who is aged 60 to 64 years old. It pays an amount equal to the OAS and the maximum GIS at the married rate. This couple gets the same transfer payments as a poor couple with both spouses aged 65 and over. If the GIS pensioner dies, the spouse continues to receive payments. When the survivor reaches age 65, the federal government stops ALW payments and the person then gets an OAS/GIS pension.

The vast majority of ALW payments go to women. All widows or widowers aged 60 to 64 with low income (below $21,120 in the period April–June 2009) can get the ALW. In January 2009, for example, about 93,000 older Canadians got the ALW. The estimate for total Allowance payments in 2009–2010 came to $552 million (Service Canada 2009). Without GIS and ALW benefits, almost half (47 percent) of all older Canadians would live below the poverty line. However, the ALW, like the GIS, fails to bring the poorest recipients above the poverty line for a large city (Human Resources Development Canada 2003b).

Newfoundland, Ontario, Manitoba, Saskatchewan, Alberta, British Columbia, Yukon, the Northwest Territories, and Nunavut also have provincial or territorial supplement plans to help the poorest seniors (Statistics Canada 2003c). More than 300,000 seniors get provincial or territorial supplements, with benefits totalling about $250 million per year. Most provinces and territories do not index payments to the cost of living, but some provinces increase the amounts from time to time (National Council of Welfare 1999). All provinces also reduce taxes for older property owners or give rent rebates to seniors. These programs play a further role in keeping very old people and even people with occupational pensions at a decent income level.

The National Council of Welfare reviewed the federal government transfer system and concluded that the system keeps many older people out of poverty. Still, the Council says, "it is clear that the government programs that make up the first level of Canada's retirement income system are not generous enough to keep all pensioners out of poverty" (National Council of Welfare 1996, 16). In 2009, for example, the OAS and GIS together guaranteed a single older person a yearly income of $14,033. But this leaves many seniors who live in an urban centre of 30,000 people or more below the national low income cut-offs (LICOs). This means that a large proportion of single seniors (most of them unattached women) live in poverty even with government transfers (Statistics Canada 2008) (see Exhibit 9.4).

Some policies weaken the universality of the OAS pension. In 1977, the federal government introduced new residence requirements for government pensions. Until 1977, an older person who had lived in Canada for at least 10 years qualified for an old age pension. After 1977, a person earned one-fortieth of his or her pension for each year in Canada after age 18, and anyone with fewer than 10 years in Canada received no benefits. Many immigrants to Canada will now get less than a full OAS when they turn 65, and others will have to manage without government transfers (National Advisory Council on Aging 2006). This policy will erode the universality of the old age pension system.

Another policy has further weakened the universality of the OAS. The federal budget speech of April 1989 introduced a **clawback** of OAS benefits from wealthier seniors. The effect is that seniors who had a net income in retirement of more than $66,335 per year (in 2009) had to pay back a portion of their OAS pension for every dollar they receive in income over this amount (Service Canada 2009). This measure has turned the OAS into a means-tested pension plan. Myles and Street (1995, 346) conclude that the "OAS will gradually lose its status as the first tier of the retirement pension system and, along with GIS, become part of the social assistance program for low income seniors."

● Exhibit 9.4

THE CANADA PENSION SYSTEM

Pension	Maximum Benefits per Month (April–June 2009)
Old Age Security	$516.96 (single)
Requirements and program details: 65 years or over; residence requirement; Canadian citizen or legal resident; noncontributory; indexed quarterly.	
Guaranteed Income Supplement	$652.51 (single)
	$947.86 (couple, married, or common-law with one OAS pensioner)
Requirements and program details: income below $15,672 per year; noncontributory; indexed quarterly.	
Allowance	$947.86
Requirements and program details: equal to the sum of OAS and maximum GIS at married/common-law rate; partner of OAS pensioner who gets GIS; partner between 60 and 64; must satisfy other OAS requirements; noncontributory; indexed quarterly.	
Widowed Partner's Allowance	$1,050.68
Requirements and program details: paid to any low-income widow or widower (60 to 64 years old); noncontributory; indexed quarterly.	
Canada Pension Plan Retirement Pension (max.)	$908.75 (monthly, 2009
Requirements and program details: 9.9% of income paid into plan; half by worker, half by employer (minus a basic exemption of $3500). Up to Year's Maximum Pensionable Earnings (YMPE)—$46,300; indexed yearly.	
Canada Pension Plan Survivor Benefits	$545.25 (CPP 2009, partner 65 and over)
	$506.38 (CPP 2009, partner under 65)
Canada Pension Plan Death Benefit	$2500 (CPP, max. lump sum, 2009
Program details: paid to estate of deceased contributor.	
Canada Pension Plan Disability Benefit	$1,105.99 (max. 2009)
Program details: paid to contributors with severe and prolonged disability.	
Canada Pension Plan Children and Orphan Benefits	$213.00 (CPP 2009)
Program details: paid to each child or orphan of contributor.	

Source: Figures from Service Canada, *Income Security Programs Information Card*, http://www.hrsdc.gc.ca/eng/isp/statistics/rates/aprjun09.shtml accessed May 16, 2009.

Tier Two: The Canada Pension Plan and the Quebec Pension Plan

The Canada Pension Plan (CPP) and the Quebec Pension Plan (QPP) form the pension system's second, smaller tier. Virtually 90 percent of the labour force between ages 18 and 70, their employers, and self-employed people paid about $30 billion into the plans in 2001–02 (Human Resources Development Canada 2003a). The CPP/QPP paid a maximum retirement benefit in 2009 of $908.75 per month. It paid over $21 billion in 2009 to 3.6 million retirees.

The CPP allows a province to opt out of the plan. Quebec chose to do so and set up its own plan. The QPP differs from the CPP in a few details, but in most ways it mirrors it. This text will use the term "CPP" to refer to both plans.

The CPP does two things. First, it ensures that workers have some pension beyond the OAS/GIS/ALW when they retire, and, second, it saves the federal government money in GIS and ALW payments in the future. The CPP combines two types of pension plans: a savings plan and a transfer plan. It works like a **savings plan** because each worker pays a percentage of his or her salary into it each month. In 2000, for instance, the law required workers to pay 4.95 percent of their wages into the plan; their employers paid a matching amount. Self-employed people paid 9.9 percent of their incomes into the plan. The government expects that investment of the surplus in the plan will allow it to freeze the contribution rate at 9.9 percent until at least 2014. The payments are credited to individual workers and, when they retire, their pension will depend on how much they paid into the plan.

The CPP also works like a **transfer plan** because the money paid in today does not go into a private account for each person; instead, it goes to pay the pensions of retired plan members today. Pension experts also call this a pay-as-you-go plan. Today's workers will receive their CPP pensions from workers' contributions in the future. This type of plan does not require that a person spend many years saving for a pension, but it does require that each younger generation pay for the pensions of the older generation.

The CPP does some things well.

First, it protects people from inflation. Personal savings can decrease in value over time, but the CPP promises that a person will get a pension in the future geared to the cost of living at that time.

Second, the CPP covers almost all workers, so most workers will enter retirement with some CPP benefits.

Third, the plan is **portable**, which means it moves with workers when they change jobs. In a fluid job market, in which people change jobs often, this can mean the difference between having a pension or not.

Fourth, the plan locks in both workers' and employers' contributions from the start. This is called **vesting**. Workers get credit for their total payments (their own and their employer's contributions) even if they move from one employer to another.

Fifth, the CPP promises to pay workers up to 25 percent of their preretirement pensionable earnings (to a maximum of 25 percent of the year's average industrial wage) for life.

Sixth, the plan applies the same rules to men and women. Women pay in at the same rates as men, and the plan entitles them to the same benefits. Some occupational plans (also called employer plans or registered pension plans—RPPs) base benefits on different mortality tables for men and women, so women in some plans get smaller payments because on average they live longer than men.

Seventh, all CPP members get survivor and disability benefits, a vital point because in Canada women often outlive their husbands and many women today have no pensions of their own.

Eighth, the CPP calculates a person's pension by adjusting pensionable earnings from past years to bring them up to current wage levels. This adjusts for the fact that inflation makes earlier wage levels a poor basis for calculating a pension today and makes the CPP better than occupational plans that use lifetime earnings to calculate pension payments.

Ninth, the CPP allows contributors to choose early or late retirement. A contributor can receive benefits as early as age 60 or as late as age 70. The CPP decreases or increases by 6 percent per year for each year a person begins receiving benefits before or after his or her 65th birthday. A person who retires at age 60 would receive 70 percent of his or her normal CPP pension. The retiree will get this lower rate even after the age of 65. A person who retires at age 70 will get a 30 percent larger pension than he or she would have received at age 65.

Tenth, and not least, the federal government indexes the CPP to the cost of living. It goes up as the cost of living increases, so people do not fall behind each year as they do with a fixed-income pension.

The CPP now pays benefits to more older people than ever before. In 1967, it paid benefits to less than one-half of 1 percent of older people, but in 2003 the CPP retirement benefit went to 85.8 percent of women and 95.8 percent of men aged 65 and over (Statistics Canada 2003c; Turcotte and Schellenberg 2007). The number of people who receive CPP pensions, the size of their pensions, and the total paid out in CPP pensions will all increase in the years ahead.

Still, the CPP has its limits. For instance, it does not help people maintain their preretirement income—the second goal of the Canadian pension system. For many older people today—those who never worked for a wage—the CPP offers no help at all, and some people who get the CPP find that it does not pay enough. In 2007, for example, the OAS/GIS and CPP paid a maximum of $24,000 to a single person. This kept a person only about $7,000 per year above the LICO for a single person in a city of 500,000 or more (Canadian Council on Social Development 2008). Recipients who receive less than the maximum CPP can fall below the poverty line.

These low CPP payments do not replace much of the average person's income. Also, the plan pays low survivor benefits. The CPP paid a survivor aged 65 or over $10,905 per year for the maximum survivor benefit plus the CPP pension in 2009 (Service Canada 2009). And the poorest older people, who receive the GIS, lose $1 of their benefits for each $2 they receive from the CPP. As a result of these low rates, most people who rely on the OAS/GIS and CPP face a drop in living standards when they retire. People need private pensions or savings to maintain their preretirement lifestyles.

The Challenge to the CPP in the Future

Even at the plan's low benefit rate, the CPP could face financial problems in the future. For example, today Canada has five workers to pay the pension of each CPP retiree. By 2030, this will drop to three workers. Also, an increase in the older population accounts for only about a third of the higher projected increase in CPP costs. About 45 percent of the projected increase in future costs comes from higher payouts for disability and enriched benefits. Higher-than-expected payouts of disability pensions would threaten the CPP reserve fund. This potential danger led to a variety of proposed reforms in the late 1990s. These included cutting back benefits, better administration of the program, and investment in the stock market. (Battle 1997; Lam, et al. 1996; Robson 1996). Some people at that time proposed raising the retirement age or limiting cost-of-living increases (Brown 1995; Freeman 1994; Gee 1995a).

The government has adopted some of these measures. First, the government responded to this challenge by raising contribution rates (to a total of 9.9 percent of a person's wage). The government expects that this rate increase will be enough to sustain the CPP into the foreseeable future. Second, in 1998 the Canadian government created the CPP Investment Board to manage CPP surplus revenues. The Board accounts to Parliament and to federal and provincial finance ministers for its actions; however, the Board operates independently of the CPP and at arm's length from the governments. The Board began investing current surplus funds in the financial markets in 1998. The Board invests in a variety of financial instruments and markets. These include emerging market equities, real estate, and utilities. The report notes a downturn in investment returns in 2008 during the world-wide recession. But it emphasizes its commitment to long-term strategy and growth. The Board's *2008 Annual Report* describes the Board's plan to increase international investment in order to boost returns (CPP Investment Board 2009).

CPP Investment Board President and CEO David Denison called the reforms of the 1990s "a bold and visionary achievement that has become a model for pension reform around the world." The CPP Investment Board invests in publicly traded stocks, private equities, real estate, and inflation-linked bonds. The CPP Fund, Denison went on to say, grew from "a legacy portfolio of more than $35 billion in government securities to what is now a broadly diversified portfolio of more than $121 billion invested on behalf of 17 million working and retired Canadians" (Reuters 2007). Future returns and the investment success of the Board will depend on the performance of the stock market and the economy in general.

Prus (2000; 2002) underscores the importance of the CPP in the Canadian pension system. He found that income inequality dropped in later life because of the help poorer seniors got from public pensions (CPP and OAS/GIS). Myles (2000, 305) supports this view. He says that even "small proportional increases from all public income sources, including CPP/QPP], tend to reduce inequality." More people than ever before, at every income level, will rely on the CPP to meet their financial needs in later life.

Tier Three: Private Pensions, Savings, and Work

Private income makes up the third tier of the Canadian pension system. The OAS/GIS and CPP alone cannot provide a comfortable income for most older people. These sources together still don't lift all seniors out of poverty (National Council of Welfare 2006), and they don't amount to a comfortable income for a middle-class person or family.

Other income received in retirement includes earnings, rent subsidies, and tax exemptions. In 2003, employment income accounted for 8.1 percent of the incomes of men aged 65 and over and 4.3 percent of the incomes of older women (Turcotte and Schellenberg 2007). Also, many organizations offer subsidies to seniors for their goods and services, such as reduced prices on theatre tickets or reduced bus fares for older people. These indirect subsidies add to older people's average total income. In addition, seniors benefit from subsidized health care costs and home care services. Nevertheless, these sources of income cannot make up for the loss of earnings after retirement. Workers need private pensions and savings to make up the difference between federal government pensions and subsidies, and their preretirement income.

Maser and Begin (2003) report that 5.3 million workers belonged to occupational pension plans in 2000. In that year pensioners in total received $21 billion in pension income. This made up almost a third of seniors' total income (up from 12 percent in 1981). Nearly all public-sector workers (87 percent) (such as government workers, teachers, nurses, people who work for a Crown corporation) belonged to a plan, compared to 28 percent of private-sector workers (people who work for privately owned companies) (Schembari 2003). More than half of all older people had occupational pension income in 2000. Li (2006) estimates that the Canadian government provided tax subsidies to occupational pension plans worth $8.7 billion in 2000.

Most pension plans pay 2 percent of a person's salary times the number of years of service. The majority of occupational pension plan members (60 percent) say their plan indexes their income to the cost of living (National Advisory Council 2006). Men more often than women benefit from pension income; two-thirds of men compared to only one half of women receive occupational pension income. Occupational pension benefits also make up more of a man's income. In 2003 occupational income made up 40.5 percent of the income of males aged 65 and over, but only 26.3 percent of the income of females aged 65 and over (Turcotte and Schellenberg 2007). Upper-income workers tended to get the most benefit from these pensions in retirement. For example, occupational pensions made up about half the income of those who earned between $40,000 and $80,000 per year. But occupational pensions made up less than 10 percent of the income of people who earned under $20,000. Poorer people relied on public pensions for most (77 percent) of their income (Li 2006).

Schulz (2001) says that the high cost of running pension plans and reporting on them has led some employers to cancel them. Some companies in the United States, in industries such as airlines, steel, or coal have declared bankruptcy and have ended their pension plans completely. In Canada and the U.S., pension underfunding puts many workers' pensions at risk (Jametti 2007). The bankruptcy of Air Canada in 1993 uncovered this problem in Canada. The airline underfunded its pension plan (it did not have enough money in reserve to cover pension obligations to workers). The company's declaration of bankruptcy left Air Canada workers without assurance that they would receive their expected pensions. The unions consented to labour savings while the company continued to fund its pension plan. But the issue of pension security for workers arose again in 2009 when Air Canada again faced bankruptcy. Workers again had to fight to retain their pension funds. This case points to the uncertainty of pension funding in specific industries. To date in Canada, only Ontario has put a government-based pension insurance program in place.

Defined Benefit and Defined Contribution Pension Plans

Employers who want to cut costs and avoid the worry of underfunding, have changed the type of pension plan they offer. They moved from **defined benefit pension plans** to **defined contribution pension plans**. A defined benefit plan states how much an employee can expect to earn in retirement based on a formula that takes into account years of service and highest salary. The company guarantees the benefit based on this formula. A defined contribution plan states how much a person will pay in (often matched to some degree by the company). This plan defines the contribution but does not guarantee the outcome. The employee must invest the money, and the outcome in retirement will depend on how well the employee's investments do over time.

Today, nearly all occupational pension plans in Canada are defined benefit plans (Li 2006). These 7,000 plans enroll 4.8 million workers (mostly unionized workers, public-sector employees, and executives). Experts who have studied the occupational pension system in Canada today express worry about the solvency of these plans. Longer life expectancy, early retirements, low interest rates, and lower stock prices put these programs under stress (Selody 2007 cited in Hering and Kpessa 2007; also Baldwin 2006). Hering and Kpessa (2007, 1) say that by one estimate at the end of 2005 "there were significant funding shortfalls in about three quarters of the traditional defined benefit pension plans that fall under federal jurisdiction in Canada."

Bob Baldwin, former director of social and economic policy, Canada Labour Congress (cited in Hering and Kpessa 2007), makes an even bleaker assessment. He says that in Ontario underfunded defined benefit plans increased from 58 percent of all plans in 2001 to 83 percent in 2004. The bankruptcy of Air Canada, for example, led to the discovery of a $1.2 billion shortfall in its pension plan. The company had no means to repay the plan; at one point it suggested a 10-year timeline for repaying the shortfall. This provided little comfort to workers on the verge of retirement. Eventually the unions agree to reduce labour costs while the airline continued to meet its pension obligations. Pension underfunding puts the retirement security of current and future retirees at risk.

Workers with a pension in the private sector often belong to a defined contribution plan. Many companies (large and small) now opt for defined contribution plans for a number of reasons. First, they find it hard to plan for the costs of defined benefit plans. A company has to make complex and uncertain predictions about workers' life expectancies and about financial markets in the future. Many companies today, in the automobile and airline industries for example, find it hard to compete because of their pension obligations.

Second, the government regulates defined benefit plans, which gives companies fewer options in how they design and fund these plans. Finally, some companies say that employees prefer defined contribution plans. The programs vest immediately and workers know exactly how much they have in their accounts. Workers who switch jobs may also like these plans. The savings in the plan goes with the worker when he or she moves from one company to another.

But defined contribution plans load investment risk on the worker. And research shows that most people have little financial knowledge and cannot make informed investment decisions (Schulz and Borowski 2006). In some cases, for example, workers have invested all of their money in their own company's stock. This will leave them with no job and no pension if the company closes. Also, workers who manage their own funds may choose riskier investments than they should late in their careers. Many people near retirement lost large amounts of money in the 2000–2002 stock market crash. Some had to postpone retirement to make up for these losses. The stock market and housing declines of 2008 had a similar effect. These shocks in the market demonstrate the risks that individual investments face in an ever-changing economy.

Schulz and Borowski (2006, 368; also Conroy et al. 2006) conclude that "DC [defined contribution] plans place major risk management burdens on financially unsophisticated individuals." They go on to say that "adequate education in financial affairs is difficult, if not impossible to find (assuming most people would be willing to take the time to learn)." Gross (2006, 10) says that "it's hard not to conclude that defined benefit pensions are under assault." This movement away from DB to DC plans (though gradual in Canada) will have an effect on retiree benefits in the years to come.

Most older people rely on savings to make up lost preretirement income. And Canadians tend to prepare well for old age. For example, over one-third of people say they have consulted a financial adviser (Townson 2006b). Investment income in Canada in 2003 made up 8.8 percent of the income of males aged 65 and over and 12.6 percent of that of females aged 65 and over. These sources ranked as the fourth major source of income for males and females (Turcotte and Schellenberg 2007).

Registered Retirement Savings Plans

The federal government has encouraged more savings through **registered retirement savings plans (RRSPs)**. An RRSP is a government plan that allows people to save money for their future pension without paying income tax on it until they withdraw it in retirement. This defers the taxes to a time when they have a lower income and a lower tax rate. Statistics Canada (2003s) reports that

since 1995 Canadians have invested more in RRSPs than in registered (occupational) pension plans (RPPs). The maximum contribution to an RRSP for 2008 is set at $20,000 (Canada Revenue Agency 2008). Individuals who belong to a private pension plan can contribute to an RRSP up to this maximum after adjusting for their contribution to their private pension plan. The number of RRSP members grew from 206,000 in 1969 (2.3 percent of tax filers) to 6.3 million in 1999 (40 percent of the labour force) (Maser and Begin 2003). Li (2006) estimates that the federal government spent $9.1 billion to subsidize Registered Retirement Savings Plans (RRSPs) in 2000.

Data from a comprehensive study of wealth in Canada in 2005 reported that 60 percent of all families and unattached individuals held a total of $343 billion in RRSP savings (Wannell 2006). These accounts had a median value of $25,000. Statistics Canada (2006a) reports that in 2004 about 5.6 million people, 38 percent of all people aged 25 to 64 who filed their taxes, contributed to an RRSP. Their contributions came to $25.2 billion in 2004.

But not every person or family shares equally in the benefits of RRSP savings. Older workers (aged 55 to 64) and those in the highest income brackets contributed most to RRSPs (Palameta 2001). Statistics Canada (2006a) reports that in 2004 only 3 percent of people aged 25 to 64 with incomes under $10,000 contributed to an RRSP. But in that year 76 percent of tax filers who had incomes of $80,000 and over made a contribution. This group made the highest average contribution of any income bracket—$9,512 per person. People who earned $85,000 per year or more in 2005 reported RRSP accounts on average of $80,000. "This differs sharply," Pyper (2008, 6) says, "from families with lower incomes (less than $36,500) where only 35% of families held RRSPs, with a median value of just $10,000." The wealthiest tax filers also got the highest tax benefit from their contribution due to their high tax rate.

The higher a person's tax bracket, the more they receive through tax deductions when contributing to an RRSP. For instance, a tax filer in the highest tax bracket got a tax saving of $447 for an RRSP contribution of $1,000. But a filer in the lowest bracket got a tax saving of only $255 for a $1,000 contribution. The richer person's higher tax rate leads to more tax savings. So, people with more money do better than poorer people under the current system. And wealthier Canadians take more advantage of the system. Morissette and Ostrovsky (2007) report that in 2004 the top income earners' savings in RRSPs and RPPs came to 9.2 times more than the average savings of the lowest income earners. Any future increase in the limits for RRSP contributions would make them even more attractive to middle- and upper-income earners.

The people with the lowest incomes have the least money to save in RRSPs. But these people also gain less than high income earners through RRSP savings. This program may even cost them money. For example, low income people pay little or no tax and so gain little or no tax benefit from the RRSP program. Also, if they do pay into an RRSP, when they withdraw money from the RRSP in their retirement, they may lose income. If they receive OAS/GIS funds or other benefits like subsidized housing, the added income from an RRSP account could lead to a reduction in government funds (Wannell 2006). This makes RRSPs most attractive to the relatively well off (see Exhibit 9.5)

Private Pensions—Registered Pension Plans (RPPs)

How well does the private pension and savings tier of the retirement income system help most people cope with retirement? Not very well, on three counts. First, private pension coverage is low: in 2001 only 5.5 million employees or 40 percent of all workers had a Registered Pension Plan (RPP) through their work. This is a decrease from 45 percent in 1991. Coverage dropped for men by 8 percent to 41 percent. It dropped for women from 41 percent to 39 percent between 1991 and 2001 (Morissette and Zhang 2004; also Morissette and Ostrovsky 2007).

Less unionization, pressure on companies to lower costs, and more workers in low-paid industries all account for this decrease.

These figures include workers in the public sector and workers in the private sector. But where most public-sector employees have an RPP, relatively few private-sector employees do. The Policy Research Institute (2005) reports that only about 30 percent of private-sector workers in Canada have an RPP. Most of these people work for firms with 1,000 or more employees; smaller firms tend not to offer an RPP. Also, the rate of plan membership for men and women differs in each sector. Women made up more than half (57 percent) of public pension plan members at the end of 2000. But men outnumber women in private-sector RPPs by nearly two to one (Maser and Begin 2003). In other words, relatively few women in the private sector belong to an RPP.

Research points to another problem with the private pension system. Many people don't know whether they have an RPP or not. Morissette and Zhang (2004, 12) found that 4 percent of all full-time permanent employees (390,000 people) "thought they had a retirement plan but didn't." Among recent immigrants (people who arrived in Canada after 1990), 27 percent reported having an employer-sponsored pension plan, but didn't. These workers cannot accurately plan for retirement. Workers need a clearer understanding of their pension savings.

In 2003 less than 50 percent of seniors received income from a private pension plan (National Advisory

● Exhibit 9.5

RRSP Contributors, by Selected Income Class, 1999 All Tax Filers

Income Class	Percentage of Tax Filers	Average Contribution
Under $10,000	3	$1,050
$10,000–$19,999	13	1,670
$20,000–$29,000	31	2,250
$30,000–$39,999	46	3,000
$40,000–$59,999	59	4,120
$60,000–$79,999	70	5,830
$80,000 and over	72	9,920
Total	29	4,090

This table shows a clear pattern. The higher the income bracket, the greater the proportion of people who paid into an RRSP. Also, the higher the income bracket, the larger the amounts of money that people in that income bracket paid into a plan. The average contribution for people who earned $80,000 and over came to more than nine times the amount on average contributed by people who earned less than $10,000 a year. Increases in contribution limits will increase the use of RRSPs by wealthier Canadians and will increase the gap between the contributions of the rich and the poor. The poorest Canadians cannot afford to save in an RRSP.

Source: Adapted K. Maser and J. Begin, 2003, *Canada's Retirement Income Programs: A Statistical Overview (1990–2000),* Cat. No. 74-507, Table 4-7, Statistics Canada, 90. Reprinted with permission.

Council 2006). People who work part-time, who do seasonal work, and who work for small businesses and at low-paying jobs rarely have an RPP. These workers will need to rely on public pensions and savings. But even people with an RPP can't count on this for a large part of their retirement income. Statistics Canada reports that in 1999 the average annual income from occupational plans came to $14,593 for men and only $8,452 for women (Maser and Begin 2003). In sum, "occupational pension plans play an important, but limited role in providing retirement income to Canadians" (National Council of Welfare 1999, 42).

Also, the poorest people have the least chance to get a private pension. In 1996, only 4 percent of people with incomes under $10,000 per year belonged to an RPP that they paid into. On average, these people paid only $253 into their plans. On the other hand, 49 percent of people with incomes more than $50,000 paid into occupational plans in that year. They paid on average $3,121 into their plans. According to the National Council on Welfare (1999, 39), "it seems unlikely that occupational pension plans will ever be an important

source of retirement income to people in low-wage jobs. Coverage by contributory pension plans increases sharply as incomes rise."

Second, in 1997, 74 percent of public-sector RPP members had some inflation protection. But only 17 percent of private-sector RPPs had some inflation protection (National Council of Welfare 1999). In an inflationary economy, people on a fixed pension—even a good one—become poorer as they age. At 3 percent inflation, a pension will lose about 25 percent of its value over 10 years and nearly half its value after 20 years. Those in the private sector (even workers with defined benefit plans) face the loss of income due to inflation. Workers in the private sector with defined contribution plans face an even greater risk. They depend on market conditions and low inflation rates in order to maintain their income (see Exhibit 9.6).

An example shows the impact of declining income over time. Robert O'Connor worked as a registrar at a university for 26 years. He and his wife planned for retirement. "We took steps to reduce economic problems as far as we could," he says. "We paid off our mortgage,

● Exhibit 9.6

PURCHASING POWER OF A DOLLAR'S VALUE AT THE END OF EACH DECADE (FOR NON-INDEXED PENSIONS) 1950S THROUGH 1990S, CANADA

Decade	Purchasing power remaining
1950s	87%
1960s	77%
1970s	44%
1980s	58%
1990s	84%

This table shows the potentially devastating effect of inflation on a fixed-income retiree's pension. It shows the percentage of a person's income left at the end of each decade (if the person had no inflation protection for his or her pension).

People who lived through several decades of high inflation (e.g., 1970–1990) would see a compounding effect of inflation on their income. For example, their pension would have only 44 percent of its 1970 buying power in 1980. The 1980 amount would be further reduced to 58 percent of its buying power by 1990. In other words, $100 in pension funds in 1970 would buy only $44 worth of goods in 1980—and only about $25 worth of goods in 1990.

This could reduce a middle-income retiree in 1970 to poverty or near poverty by 1990. This person would have aged 20 years in that time, probably be a woman, and have almost no chance of working to make up the loss of real income. For this reason the lack of inflation protection for most pension plans puts all but the wealthiest retirees at risk as they age.

Source: B. Baldwin, 2006, "A Shaky Third Pillar: The Vulnerability of Retirement Incomes," in L. O. Stone (Ed.), New Frontiers of Research on Retirement (383–406), Ottawa: Minister of Industry. Statistics Canada. Catalogue no. 75-511-XIE, p. 393 Table 20.2. Author's calculations based on Statistics Canada CANSIM data reported in Canadian Institute of Actuaries, "Economic Statistics, 19 to 20."

we bought a new car—anything so we could go into retirement as well equipped as we could."

Still, a drop in their living standard came as soon as he retired. "When I was working, I'd say to my wife, 'Well, come on, where will we go for dinner?' Now we don't go out to eat as much. And when we do go, it's more likely we go to a Sizzler's Steak House with a discount coupon than to our favourite restaurant.

"We don't talk much about it. But we've faced a lowering of our social standards. We can't say, 'Let's go back now and look at Scotland.' We say, 'Let's renew our subscription to *Britain in Pictures.*'

"One of the problems when you retire is to build up a small nest egg, but even relatively fortunate people like myself often watch it disappear. Six weeks ago we had to put a roof on our house—$5,000. Last week our washing machine broke down. There we had to dip into our bank account. The time is coming when it's not imprudent to contemplate almost the virtual exhaustion of our savings" (personal communication with author).

Schulz (2001) reports that in retirement a one-worker couple would need between 68 and 82 percent of their preretirement income to maintain their standard of living. And "only 6 percent to 8 percent of new retired workers replaced at least two-thirds of their *highest* earnings" (Schulz, 2001, 152). Single people, minority group members, and women do less well.

Third, only a small percentage of people who belong to occupational pension plans ever collect a full pension. Two things account for this. First, few plans in the past had early vesting. Early vesting locks both the employer's and the employee's payments in the plan soon after employment begins. Second, most plans lack portability. When workers leave a company today, most of them get either a deferred pension (if their money is vested and locked in) or they get their own (but not their employer's) pension contributions back—sometimes with no interest. The employer's share stays in the fund when workers get their pension contributions back, so a person who changes jobs loses half of his or her pension savings and has to start again. Even if the whole labour force belongs to occupational pension plans at any time, as long as workers change jobs often (as they do today), only workers with fully vested contributions will ever collect a full pension.

An expansion of private pensions to more workers would provide a better income for more older people. Unfortunately, pension plan expansion seems unlikely at present. Many companies have cut back on pension programs or have shifted to defined contribution plans. This will put more responsibility for retirement savings

Rapid changes in the economy make planning for retirement a challenge. Here, a couple puzzles over how to meet their expenses. Retirees on a fixed income may need to adjust their spending as they age.

on individual workers, and it will increase the risk of low retirement incomes for many people. At the least, the government needs to provide oversight of private pensions. This helps ensure that those people who pay into a company pension plans will get a pension when they retire.

INEQUALITY IN LATER LIFE

Older people differ by social class, gender, marital status, urban or rural environment, ethnicity, date of immigration to Canada, and a variety of other characteristics. These characteristics all shape a person's income and economic condition in later life.

The political economy perspective looks at the structural reasons for inequality in old age. It points to education and former occupational status as forces that determine income in later life. A person with a high level of education and a high-status occupation stands the best chance of a high income in retirement. These people also stand the best chance of maintaining their status after retirement. Older people who have access to work, investments, and occupational pensions will have higher incomes. These benefits go to people with higher levels of education and higher job status.

Some groups face more financial problems than others in old age. Membership in a non-European ethnic group leads to lower income in retirement. Asian, African, or Latin American ethnic group members tend to retire later and have less chance of getting OAS, GIS, or CPP benefits. Minority seniors also have less chance of getting an occupational pension and thus have lower incomes. Trends in public pension policies also lead to lower incomes for immigrants (Mo et al., 2006). Veall (2007 cited in Hering and Kpessa 2007) reports that recent immigrants have some of the highest poverty rates among older people in Canada. He reports that non-immigrant seniors have a low-income rate of about 5 percent. But immigrant seniors have a low-income rate of more than 70 percent.

Chard (2000) reports that, compared to older men or other older women, older visible-minority women have the lowest incomes. Brotman (1998) reports that older people who belong to a visible ethnic minority and Aboriginal older people had the highest rates of poverty among the seven groups she studied. She goes on to say that Chinese and black older people had a rate of poverty one and a half times the rate of senior poverty. Racial discrimination throughout life, through job discrimination and lower than average incomes, in part accounts for these high levels of poverty.

Women and Pensions

Cheal (2002, 11) says, "The increasing average income of older people obscures the fact that not all older Canadians are well-off, especially some older women." In 2004, for example, senior women had a mean before-tax income 67 percent that of senior men. Men earned on average $32,500, women earned $21,400—a $10,800 gap. The low-income rate of all older women before taxes was 19.1 percent in 2003, almost double the poverty rate of elderly men (10.2 percent) (Veall 2007). In 2004 unattached women made up 60 percent of low-income seniors. Separated and divorced older women, compared to widows, show the highest rates of poverty.

Why do women have such low incomes in old age?

First, traditional expectations about women and work lead women to have different work patterns than men. Women often leave a first job to raise children. Due to family responsibilities, they spend longer than men between jobs, and they tend to work at each job for a shorter time than men.

The traditional expectation that women will place family before career leads to part-time work. This keeps women from getting high salaries and from storing up pension credits (Street and Connidis 2001; Denton and Boos 2007). When women work outside the home, they often take part-time, low-paying jobs. Many working women say they cannot find a full-time job, and Denton and Boos (2007) report that more women than men work fewer than 30 hours per week. In 2002, for example, women accounted for nearly three-quarters of part-time permanent employees (Vosko et al. 2003).

Vosko and colleagues (2003) call these "precarious jobs." People in these jobs (most of them women) risk job loss, have little control of working conditions, rarely belong to a union, and have low wages. Part-time workers rarely get pension benefits. For this reason, compared to a man, a woman can work for her entire adult life and still have no pension savings.

Second, the structure of public and private occupational pension plans discriminates against women— sometimes in hidden ways. In 1999, 54.6 percent of women worked outside the home (up from 42 percent in 1976) (Maser and Begin 2003). This should lead to more and better occupational pensions for women. But women often work for smaller, non-unionized companies with no occupational pension plans, and, as mentioned above, they also tend to work part-time. Even among union members, compared to women, a higher proportion of men have employer pensions (19 percent versus 15 percent) (Denton and Boos 2007). This means that, compared to women, men will tend to have more diverse sources of income, including employment pension income, in retirement.

Moen and Spencer (2006, p.134) say that a person's work career shapes his or her opportunities and choices in retirement. "Health insurance, pensions, unemployment insurance, disability insurance, and Social Security all rest on the edifice of the male lock-step life course." To the extent that a woman's life course differs from this model, women face a disadvantage in retirement.

Third, women in general are paid less than men and hold lower-status jobs (Denton and Boos 2007). Women more often than men work in low-wage jobs that are defined as unskilled and offer little chance for advancement. Women tend to work in sales, service, administration, and health occupations. Men tend to work in management, applied and natural sciences, trades and transportation, and manufacturing. Statistics Canada (2003b) reported on earnings for all men and women (in full-and part-time work) in 2001. It found that women earned only 64.2 percent of men's incomes (a figure almost unchanged since 1992).

Only 39.3 percent of women in paid labour in 2000 belonged to an occupational pension plan (compared with 41.8 percent of men), and most of these women work for government or for Crown corporations. In private industry, a smaller percentage of women belonged to a pension plan (Maser and Begin 2003).

Even within relatively low-paying fields, women find themselves in the poorest-paying jobs. For instance, women tend to work as salaried clerks. Men tend to sell expensive products such as cars or appliances; these jobs often pay a commission in addition to a base salary. Women work in service jobs such as waitress, hairdresser, or child-care worker. Men tend to work at services such as police officer, security guard, or soldier. Even when women work at the same job as men, they often get lower pay (see Exhibit 9.7).

Low pay means that, compared to men, women pay a smaller amount into the CPP. This results in a smaller

CPP pension when they retire. Women received only 56 percent of the average CPP benefits received by men in 1999. In that year, most women received less than 60 percent and many received less than 40 percent of the maximum CPP. In that same year, most men received between 80 percent and 100 percent of the maximum CPP. Low incomes and short careers at paid labour explain this gap (National Council of Welfare 1999). A study of younger retired workers (i.e., those aged 65 to 69), for example, found that women received an average annual pension of $3,588. Men in this age group received on average $6,396 or 56 percent more than women (National Council on Welfare 1999).

The work histories of women lead to lower income in later life and lower overall wealth. A study by Denton and Boos (2007) found that work and family roles led to lower asset buildup throughout life. The researchers found that women aged 45 and over had a net worth only 64 percent that of men. Women, they say, "have about two-thirds the non-financial assets (including the value of their home) than men do, they have less than

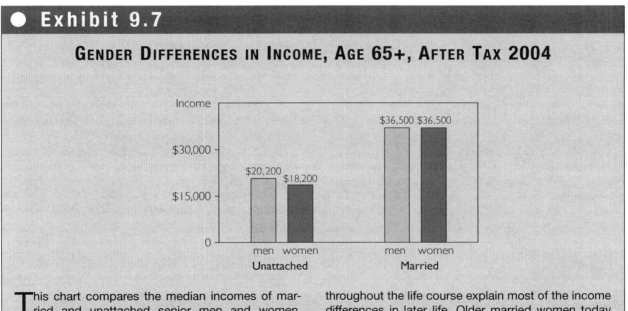

● Exhibit 9.7

GENDER DIFFERENCES IN INCOME, AGE 65+, AFTER TAX 2004

This chart compares the median incomes of married and unattached senior men and women. Unattached seniors have about half the income of married men and women. Unattached men had incomes slightly higher than those of unattached women. Gender differences in income and work opportunities throughout the life course explain most of the income differences in later life. Older married women today also tend to have low incomes, but benefit from their husbands' pension plans. Unfortunately, these plans decrease in value (sometimes by half) or pay nothing at all if the woman becomes a widow.

Source: Adapted from Statistics Canada, 2003, "Gender Differences in Low Income," No. 15, http://www.hc-sc.gc.ca/seniors-aines/pubs/factoids/2001/no15_e.htm, accessed on August 10, 2004. From A Portrait of Seniors in Canada, 3rd ed., Cat. No. 89-519, October 1999. Reprinted with permission.

half the financial assets (including the value of their pensions and other financial assets)" (12). This leaves older women without a safety net of savings and resources.

Divorced and separated women, compared to married women, have less income and wealth in retirement. In addition, women tend to live an average of five years longer than men, meaning that, compared to men, women will have to make their smaller assets last for a longer time. Denton and Boos (2007, 17) say that the long-term consequences of inequality in the labour force "are that the majority of women will fail to build up the financial assets to provide good incomes for their retirement."

The National Council of Welfare sums up these findings: "[Women] become the prime victims of the built-in injustices of our labour market, which excludes women from the best positions, pays them less than they are worth and segregates them into a narrow range of low-wage occupations with few fringe benefits and limited chances for advancement" (National Council of Welfare 1990b, 2).

Widows

Widows make up the largest group among women 65 and over, and, of all women, they benefit least from Canada's pension system. This shows up in the statistics on low-income seniors. Statistics Canada reports that in 2004 unattached women (most of them widows) made up 60 percent of low-income seniors. A comment by the National Council of Welfare more than 40 years ago still holds today: "After fifty years or so of unpaid, faithful service a woman's only reward is likely to be poverty" (1979, 32).

Bernard and Li (2006) found that 72 percent of widows suffered a loss of income after the death of their spouse. And widowhood on average led to a steady decline in income in the five years after the death of the spouse. After five years widows had an income 15 percent lower than in the year before the spouse's death, and 8.7 percent of widows lived below the government's low income line. By contrast, compared to the year before widowhood, widowers (men), on average had a higher income five years after the spouse's death, and only 5.1 percent of widowers fell below the low income line. After five years, widows entered poverty at twice the rate of widowers. These findings show the dependence of older women on their husbands' earnings and pensions. Senior widows today often have little or no employer pension of their own.

If her husband has an employer pension plan, a widow may find that the plan reduces the benefits when her husband dies. For example, only about half of private pension plans in 1997 paid a lump-sum survivor pension to the surviving spouse of a retired worker. Another 26 percent paid a survivor pension of only 50 to 60 percent of the plan member's pension. Nine percent of plans offer only a refund of contributions to the surviving spouse of a retired worker. Many private-sector plans provide for only five years of survivor payments (National Council of Welfare 1999). Even when a survivor plan exists, sometimes a woman gets nothing because her spouse opted for higher benefits in retirement while he was alive. "A woman who loses her husband when she is 65 and lives until age 85 could be in dire straits for the last 15 years of her life" (National Council of Welfare 1989, 39).

In addition to these reduced payments in retirement, only 69 percent of members of public-sector plans and 27 percent of members of private-sector plans provided a survivor pension if the plan member dies before retirement. Many plans refund only the worker's contributions with interest if a plan member dies before retirement. Some plans return nothing to the surviving spouse.

Private-sector pensions put widows at risk of poverty and the public pension system also lets widows down. The CPP sets the benefits for a surviving spouse aged 65 and over at 60 percent of the deceased spouse's pension. The maximum amount payable came to $6,543 a year in 2009.

Davies and Denton (2002) report a similar outcome for an older woman who experiences a divorce or separation. Divorced and separated older women have the lowest incomes among seniors. They rely for almost 40 percent of their income on the OAS/GIS system. Davies and Denton (2002, 487) speak of the "grave economic situation of women who have experienced a divorce or separation late in life."

Women and Pensions in the Future

Women coming into old age in the future, compared to older women today, will have better incomes. More women today work during their middle years, and women between ages 35 and 54 have the highest earnings for women (Lindsay 2000a). Women today who leave work to raise a family tend to return to work more quickly than women did in the past. Women with higher education tend to have fewer interruptions in work. Women have also begun to enter male-dominated occupations and more of them belong to private pension plans (Connelly and MacDonald 1990; Statistics Canada 1996). Many of these women will get their own CPP pensions in the future. Maser and Begin (2003) report that 44.2 percent of women contributed to the CPP in 1990. This figure rose to 45.5 percent in 1999. Also, the average contribution of women to the CPP rose from 37.3 percent of the total to 39.9 percent. In other words, more women now contribute to the CPP and with higher contributions than ever before. Smith and her colleagues (2000) say that the CPP/QPP accounts for most of the rise in income for older women. This especially applies to women aged 60 to 75.

More women today than in the past pay into RRSPs. In 1999, 2.77 million women paid into an RRSP (compared to only 1.9 million in 1991). Nevertheless, the large majority of women have no RRSPs. And those who do, compared with men, pay less into their RRSPs (Maser and Begin 2003). McDonald (1997) also reports that women have few chances to find work in later life.

Denton and Boos (2007, 19) say that current trends will lead older women in the future to have financial supports more similar to those of men. But, they say, "we should not be lulled into a false sense of optimism." In 2003, for example, women aged 55 to 64 earned from all sources just over half the income of men in that age group. Women aged 35 to 54 earned in total around 60 percent of men in that age group. This inequality in younger age groups will means that even in the future women will receive a lower proportion of the maximum CPP than men (Lindsay and Almey 2006). Homemakers will have no employer pensions; they will get no CPP pension of their own; and if their husband's pension plan pays no survivor benefits, they will get no pension at all.

The system needs reform to meet the needs of older women. McDonald and Robb (2004, 14–15) say that "the current pension system does not mirror the complexity of women's lives in terms of their multiple transitions in and out of the labour force, their institutionalized lower earnings, their unpaid work and the changes in individual and family life styles." Women and men need better occupational pension plans, and women need better survivor and homemaker benefits and more help from the OAS/GIS/ALW. By proposing some changes to the system, the federal government sparked what some people call the great pension debate in the early 1980s. The debate was about whether a public pension plan such as the CPP or whether private pension plans would best serve Canadians. More recent debates have been concerned with universality of the OAS and ensuring the solvency of the CPP.

PENSION REFORM

Canada has debated pension reform since the early 1980s. A series of conferences, task forces, and papers

at that time all proposed changes in the pension system (Government of Canada 1982; House of Commons Canada 1983), and some changes did indeed take place. By the late 1980s, for example, all provinces except British Columbia and Prince Edward Island had some legislation covering occupational pensions. Also, new rules have improved the public pension plan system. What follows are some of the highlights of these reforms.

First, the federal government income security system has made three important improvements over the years: (1) improvements in GIS have led to decreased poverty rates for single older people; (2) as of 1985, all widows and widowers with low incomes get the ALW; and (3) the federal government continues to index the OAS to the rate of inflation, although it has not increased the OAS to bring it closer to the average industrial wage (AIW).

Second, beginning in June 1984, the CPP also allowed women and men to deduct the years they spent child rearing from their pensionable years (until 1984 these years counted as zero income and lowered a person's average lifetime salary). People who take time off to care for their children can now deduct from their work record 15 percent of the years with the lowest earnings. Also, the CPP now provides for **credit splitting** if spouses divorce. Each spouse gets an equal share of the credits accumulated during their time together. This provision, however, includes a hitch: it requires an application for credit splitting.

Third, in May 1985 the federal government announced changes in the *Canada Pension Benefits Standards Act*. These changes set minimum standards for one million federal government workers and workers in federal government industries such as Crown corporations. The federal government asked the provinces and territories to change their rules to meet the new standards:

1. locked-in vesting mandatory after two years in an occupational plan;

2. improved portability by transfer of vested pensions to locked-in RRSPs;

3. the right of all full-time workers to join a private plan after two years of work; all part-time workers must have the right to join if they have earned at least 35 percent of the yearly maximum pensionable earnings ($43,700 in 2007);

4. payment of survivor benefits worth at least 60 percent of the amount the couple would have received had the contributor lived; these benefits will continue if the survivor remarries;

5. division of pension credits and payments 50–50 if a couple divorces, unless the couple or the courts choose a different option.

Fourth, the federal government and the provinces agreed that all occupational plans will provide a joint life/last survivor benefit. A spouse will receive at least 60 percent of the occupational pension the couple would have received if both had lived (Maser and Begin 2003). The pension continues even if the survivor remarries. This provision has one drawback: Both spouses must agree to lower pension payments in the present. If the couple chooses a higher pension today, they forgo survivor benefits in the future.

These changes fix some of the inequities in the system. The poorest older people on the GIS benefitted from these changes, and so did widows and women who work part-time. But the federal government will still have to tackle some tough issues in the future. These include homemakers' pensions, the rising cost of indexed OAS pensions, and **indexation** of private pension plans. Women face many disadvantages in old age that current pension reform only partly addresses. "The whole income-security debate," Neysmith (1984, 18–19) writes, "has been defined in terms of pensions that are related to one's track record in the paid-labour force [and] occupationally based pensions by definition cannot meet the needs of most women." Canadian society will need to deal with this larger issue through broader reforms that will have to include increasing opportunities for women in the labour force.

THE FUTURE COST OF REFORM

Changes in private and public pension plans will mean one thing: Pensions will cost more money. CPP rates have increased to 9.9 percent of workers' earnings (from 3.6 percent in 1986). Better occupational plans will also cost more. So will better survivor benefits. In 2001, Canada's chief actuary reported that current reforms will lead to a sustainable CPP system in the future (Health Canada 2002a). The chief actuary predicted that assets will grow in the coming years and they will absorb future economic and demographic changes. But as Canadian society ages, more people will begin to draw pensions, and younger people will have to pay for most of these costs.

How will people feel about these changes? Will younger people revolt at the high cost of pensions for the older generation? The state of Canada's economy will partly determine how younger people will feel about pension costs. A strong economy and low inflation will make it easier to pay more for pensions; an increased cost of living and low wages will make it harder. A weaker economy could lead younger people to balk at the high cost.

The vision of economic crisis in the future has led to many reform proposals. One plan would privatize the Canada Pension Plan. Under this proposal, each person would invest CPP funds in private-sector assets, manage his or her own fund, and receive the accumulated money. This plan could serve all Canadians much as the CPP does today. But this approach has many drawbacks: each worker would bear the risk of a poor investment or of inflation, the plan would include no death or disability benefits, and women would lose child-rearing drop-out provisions. Furthermore, based on the experience of other systems, the cost of managing a privatized plan would run about 10 times that of the CPP. Still, some people believe that privatization would solve many future pension plan problems.

Other proposals fit more easily into the current system. They include a later age for retirement. Myles (2002, 325) says that "keeping current and future generations in the labour force longer (i.e., later retirement) is widely seen as the most painless and cost-effective cure for the expected impact of population aging." He goes on to say that a small increase in the retirement age has a large impact on the cost of retirement benefits. For example, a 10-month increase in the retirement age would lead to a 10 percent cut in the cost of benefits to the system. Workers who delayed retirement would take no money from the national pension system, add to national wealth through their work, and increase government tax revenues.

Myles predicts more labour demand for older workers and better pay in the future. The retirement of the Baby Boom generation will leave a skill shortage in many industries, so healthier and better-educated workers may choose to stay at work longer. The federal government recognized older workers' interest in staying at work and in 2006 allocated $70 million over two years to start the "Targeted Initiative for Older Workers (TIOW)." This program helps older workers who live in vulnerable communities to stay at work and to "remain active and productive participants in the labour market" (*The Latest* 2008). The government has added $90 million to this program to extend the program to March 2012. Work opportunities will help many older people maintain their standard of living in retirement.

Policies in Canada have also put a higher tax on Old Age Security benefits so that wealthier seniors keep less of their payments. Battle (1997) says that the OAS has already evolved from a universal program to a means-tested plan (by taxing back OAS payments from wealthier Canadians). This change fits a trend in government policy (including health care policy) to limit programs to people most in need. Myles and Teichroew (1991, 91) project a "withering away" of the OAS and more emphasis on public support through the GIS in the future.

The clawback of OAS payments to the wealthy begins to achieve what Myles and Teichroew (1991, 85) call "the main project of both the Liberal and Conservative parties throughout the 1980s—to make the welfare state more efficient by targeting scarce transfer dollars to those most in need." These policies also support the trend to shift responsibility for financial well-being in later life from the state to the individual. Such trends will place more pressure on middle-class Canadians to look after their own well-being in old age. The government provides some incentive for this move toward self-support.

A federal government newsletter called *The Latest for Seniors* reports that "Budget 2008 provides the most important federally driven personal finance innovation since the introduction of the Registered Retirement Savings Plan (RRSP): the Tax Free Savings Account (TFSA)" (*The Latest* 2008). **Tax-free savings accounts** allow Canadians age 18 or over to put up to $5,000 a year into a TFSA account. These dollars will be allowed to grow tax free and will not be taxed when taken out. The government will index this amount to inflation and these funds, when taken out, will not influence eligibility for any other government programs. The program includes other regulations that make the program flexible (e.g., funds can move from a deceased spouse's account to that of the surviving spouse). The government hopes the new vehicle will encourage more people to save more for their retirement. Still, this program will probably serve middle-class and wealthier Canadians best; poor people will have less money to invest in this program.

Canada has developed and maintained a stable and reliable pension system. It needs improvement, but the public has not called for radical change to the system. Béland and Myles (2003) give four reasons for the stability of the current system. First, Canada spends a relatively modest amount on public pensions (OAS/GIS/ALW). Second, the general revenue rather than payroll taxes supports most of the public pension system. Third, the government has other programs that it can target for spending cuts—for example, health care and postsecondary education. Fourth, most of the money spent on public pensions goes to poorer seniors. This approach has broad public acceptance.

Some years ago Myles (1982) offered two more reasons that Canadians will continue to support a strong public pension system in the future. First, he says, without state support the young would have to help care for their parents themselves, and younger people will prefer to pool their risks through a central pension system. Second, he says, middle-aged people, because they will be old soon themselves, have a self-interest in supporting a strong pension and social security system for the elderly.

In the end, a strong publicly supported pension system—given the longer life expectancy today—makes sense for everyone. As long as taxpayers see this they will continue to support improvements in Canada's retirement income system.

CONCLUSION

Pension policies over the past 20 years, including the most recent changes in pension laws, have created a dual pension system. First, the public system in the form of the OAS and GIS will support the most needy older people. Myles and Teichroew (1991, 99) call this system "a welfare state for women" that mostly serves people who work outside the labour market. Second, the private system in the form of RRSPs, TFSAs, and registered pension plans (RPPs) helps maintain the lifestyles of middle- and upper-income earners in retirement. This second system serves government workers, "organized workers and the predominantly male occupations of employed professionals and managers" (99). The CPP falls somewhere between these two systems. The government oversees the program, but it benefits people who have worked in the labour force.

The shift in policy to self-reliance for middle-income earners may not produce the end product that the government wants. Current and future policies encourage middle-aged, middle- and upper-income earners to save more money in RRSPs and TFSAs. This practice costs the government money in lost taxes and may counteract some of the savings made by cutting OAS payments to middle- and upper-income retirees (Myles and Street 1995). Myles and Street conclude that a larger retired population will cost society more money one way or another. Policies simply shift the cost of a retired population from one group to another (from young taxpayers to retirees who have to live on their own resources).

A new view of retirement could help solve this problem. Some studies project a shortage of young workers in Canada in the future (McDonald and Chen

1995). This shortage could create potential jobs for older workers and reduce the cost of retirement pensions to the state. Also, recent declines in the stock market have reduced pension savings for many people. This will lead some people to delay retirement.

Still, most older workers have shown little interest in staying at work. Retirement rates have increased and people tend to leave work as early as they can. All of this suggests that Canadian society will continue to debate and reshape its pension program in the years ahead.

Summary

1. Canada's pension system has a sound structure, but the current system needs improvement. Some people— very old women, people from lower-income brackets, people with low levels of education, widows, and homemakers—all run a higher than average risk of poverty in old age.

2. Canada has a three-tiered system: the OAS, GIS, and ALW make up tier one, the CPP and QPP make up tier two, and private pensions and savings make up tier three.

3. The Canadian retirement system has two goals: (1) to keep all older people out of poverty; and (2) to replace preretirement income. At present, it meets neither goal for many Canadians.

4. Poorer Canadians, the people who need private savings the most in retirement, have the least chance of having any. Private pension plans cover fewer than half of Canadian workers. The CPP at best replaces only 25 percent of a person's income up to the average industrial wage, and the OAS/GIS/ALW leave the poorest older people in poverty.

5. Compared with men, women face a higher risk of poverty in old age, because unequal coverage by pension plans, lower-paying jobs, and different work patterns due to child rearing often leave women with lower pensions.

6. Widows run a high risk of poverty in old age. The CPP pays a relatively small survivor pension, and private pension plans offer only about a 60 percent pension to survivors.

7. The federal government has recently made changes to the system. Reforms include higher GIS/ALW payments, a more secure CPP pension system, rules that encourage RRSP and TSFA contributions, and rules that strengthen private pension plans.

8. In 1998 the Canadian government created the CPP Investment Board to manage CPP surplus revenues. In 1999, for example, the Board invested nearly $2 billion in the financial markets (Maser and Begin 2003). Although this entails some risk, good management of these funds has added to the CPP's ability to meet future demands.

9. Many employers have moved from offering defined benefit pension plans to offering defined contribution pension plans. A defined benefit plan makes the employer responsible for a specific pension for each retiree; a defined contribution plan states how much a worker will pay into the program, but does not guarantee a specific income in retirement. This trend has shifted pension risk from the employer to the worker.

10. Proposed reforms to the CPP and to private plans try to ensure that more Canadians, including homemakers, get pension coverage. Better public and private pensions for these people may reduce the costs of federal government transfers in the future. This will save the government money and give more people a better income in retirement.

11. The government will probably reduce its role in providing pensions to middle-income workers in the future. Individuals, families, and the private sector will have to provide income for people over the poverty line.

12. Canadians will pay for pension reforms as long as people support the notion that everyone—young and old—gains from a strong pension system.

Study Questions

1. Name and describe the parts of Canada's three-tiered retirement income system.
2. Explain how the Canada Pension Plan funds pensions today.
3. List two strengths and two weaknesses of the private pension system. Why does the private system fail to help most people in retirement?
4. Present the social-structural causes of financial inequality in old age. What groups face the most financial problems as they age? Why?
5. Explain the difference between a defined benefit and a defined contribution pension plan. How do they differ? And how does each type of plan affect a workers' retirement pension?
6. How has the Canadian government changed the public pension system to provide better coverage for older Canadians? How will reforms affect middle-class Canadians? How will they affect poorer Canadians?
7. What changes have writers proposed in the current public pension system to provide better retirement incomes for older people in the future?

Key Terms

clawback   required repayment of Old Age Security benefits from wealthier seniors to the government. (191)

credit splitting   a plan by which each spouse of a divorcing couple gets an equal share of pension credits accumulated during their time together. (203)

defined benefit pension plan   a defined benefit plan states how much an employee can expect to earn in retirement based on a formula that takes into account years of service and highest salary. The company guarantees the benefit based on this formula. (195)

defined contribution pension plan   a defined contribution plan states how much a person will pay in (often matched to some degree by the company). This plan defines the contribution but does not guarantee the outcome. The outcome in retirement will depend on how well the employee's investments do over time. (195)

depth of poverty   the distance between a person's income and the poverty line. (187)

great pension debate   the debate in the 1980s over how to fund public pensions for older Canadians in the future. (187)

income maintenance programs   income supplement programs such as the Canada and Quebec Pension Plans that help people maintain their preretirement income and lifestyle. (188)

income security programs   income supplement programs such as the Old Age Security and the Guaranteed Income Supplement that help people meet their basic needs in retirement. (188)

indexation   a method of increasing pensions linked to increases in the cost of living. (204)

portable   a pension that moves with workers when they change jobs. (193)

registered retirement savings plans (RRSPs)   a government plan that allows people to save money for their future pension without paying income tax on the money protected within the RRSP. The pension is taxed when it is withdrawn in retirement. The taxes are deferred to a time when the person has a lower income and is in a lower tax rate. (196)

savings plan   a payment plan to which each person contributes a percentage of his or her salary each month. In the case of the CPP/QPP, the payments are credited to individual workers; when they retire, their pension will depend on how much they paid into the plan. (193)

tax-free savings accounts (TFSAs)   a program that allows Canadians age 18 or over to put up to $5000 a year into a savings account. These dollars will be allowed to grow tax free and will not be taxed when taken out. (205)

transfer plan   (also called a pay-as-you-go plan) money paid into the plan goes to pay the pensions of retired plan members today. The CPP/QPP also works like a transfer plan. (193)

universality   the idea that everyone in Canada has a right to a public pension regardless of his or her income. (187)

vesting   workers with a fully vested pension have credit for their total pension contributions (their own and their employer's contributions) even if they move from one employer to another. (193)

Selected Readings

Denton, F.T., D. Fretz, and B.G. Spencer, eds. *Independence and Economic Security in Old Age.* Vancouver: UBC Press, 2000.

> This book looks at the relationship between economics, health, and independence in later life in Canada. It includes articles on income and savings, retirement, women, and the future economic well-being of older people. The articles contain many original analyses of Canadian data. The book also contains comparisons of Canada with other countries. This book serves as a good source of current information on economics and aging.

Ginn, J., D. Street, and S. Arber, eds., *Women, Work, and Pensions: International Issues and Prospects.* Buckingham: Open University Press, 2001.

> This book takes a critical look at women, work, and pensions in several countries, including Canada. It allows for a rare cross-cultural comparison of aging policies related to older women.

National Advisory Council on Aging (NACA). 2005. *Seniors on the Margins: Aging in Poverty in Canada.* Ottawa: Minister of Public Works and Government Services Canada. Cat No.: H88-5/3-2005.

> This report focuses on the poorest seniors, the causes of their poverty, and suggested remedies for their condition. The report advocates for a pension and economic system that keeps all older people out of poverty.

Websites to Consult

Human Resources and Social Development Canada

http://www.hrsdc.gc.ca/en/gateways/nav/top_nav/program/isp.shtml

This site gives up-to-date information on Canada's government pension programs. It also provides a retirement income calculator and access to personal retirement information. It is a good source for details on pension benefits.

Canadian Council on Social Development

http://www.ccsd.ca/home.htm

The Canadian Council on Social Development (CCSD) is a nongovernmental, not-for-profit organization that develops and promotes progressive social policies. The website includes data and information on the workforce, poverty, and inequality in Canada. It reports on the condition of older people in the context of wider social issues and includes access to reports on these and related issues.

National Council of Welfare

http://www.ncwcnbes.net

The National Council of Welfare (NCW) is an arm's-length advisory body to the Minister of Human Resources and Social Development on matters of concern to low-income Canadians. The site provides information on income and poverty in Canada and reports on older people in the context of the larger issue of poverty and income needs.

Chapter
10
Retirement and Work

© Bob Winsett/Index Stock Imagery

INTRODUCTION

Claude Rioux retired six months after his 65th birthday. He had worked as a warehouseman for an electronic supply company. Claude never thought much about retirement in his middle years. A year or two before he retired, he began to feel he had nothing in common with his fellow workers. Most of his friends had retired, and most of his new co-workers had just left high school. They talked about girls and motorcycles and listened to loud music. He had always liked work, but he began to enjoy it less each day. After he turned 65, his boss came by to ask if he had any retirement plans. Another time, the boss called him into his office and asked him when he planned to leave. "I said I didn't know," Claude says. "Why give him the satisfaction of thinking he could push me out? Hell, I still do a good job. Better than some of the kids who work here now. Oh, I planned to leave in January, but I wouldn't tell him. I thought, 'I'll leave when I'm good and ready.'"

No one forced Claude to retire and he left work just about on schedule. He had little reason to keep working past age 65—he had a small pension from work as well as his Canada Pension Plan (CPP) and Old Age Security (OAS), and he planned to open a small electronics repair shop at home. He stayed on until January only to show that no one could push him around.

Statistics Canada reports that only a small proportion of men and women work past age 65. In 2004, only 21.8 percent of men and 11.0 percent of women aged 65 to 69 continued to work in the labour force. By age 70 and over the proportion of workers dropped to 6.9 percent for men and only 1.9 percent for women (Turcotte and Schellenberg 2007). These figures show that retirement has become a normative life event. With longer life expectancy today, some people will spend a quarter or more of their adult life in retirement.

Gerontologists view retirement today from two points of view: first, as a social institution and, second, as a process of personal adjustment. This chapter will look at retirement from each of these perspectives. It will look at (1) the origin and role of retirement in modern society, (2) the forces that lead a person to retire, and (3) the effects of social structures and social class on retirement options.

RETIREMENT AS A SOCIAL INSTITUTION

The Origins of Retirement

Myles (1984) traces our idea of old age today to two developments. The first is the **retirement principle**—the idea that a person leaves work at a fixed age, regardless of mental or physical ability. The second is the **retirement wage**—a pension paid by the state to support older people. Myles says that a new group of people grew out of these two developments: "a population of elders still fit for production who do not engage in economic activity" (7).

Employers and employees have both supported the retirement principle in North America. Industry supported it for two reasons. First, retirement allowed companies to retire older, skilled workers and hire younger, less-skilled workers at lower wages; and, second, companies, using a philosophy of "scientific management," sought to speed up production and get more out of their workers. Unions offered to have workers work faster if companies reduced the workday, but a faster pace of work made it hard for older workers to compete with younger workers. Retirement gave older workers a graceful way to leave work.

The Canadian government supported the retirement principle for a number of reasons. Canada's first civil service commissioner, Adam Shortt said in 1922 that "retirement relieves the government of the embarrassment and extravagance of retaining the services of officers who have outlived their usefulness; creates a proper flow of promotions; renders the service more mobile; deters efficient workers from leaving the public service for private employment [and] in general tends to promote efficiency in every way" (quoted in Bolger, 1980, 8, cited in Myles 1984, 13).

Canada introduced the *Old Age Pension Act* in 1927 to promote the goals outlined above and to solve a social problem created by retired workers. Matthews and Tindale (1987) give three reasons for this act. First, more people lived to old age; second, many old people lived in poverty; and, third, employers needed to reduce unemployment and increase productivity. The *Old Age Pension Act* encouraged retirement. It provided a basic income to the poorest older people, and it opened up jobs for the young.

Unions in North America wanted companies to use seniority (first hired, last fired) as a method for deciding layoffs or cutbacks. Seniority gave workers a right to a job, and it gave the oldest workers the most job security. But companies resisted the seniority system because older workers cost them more and seniority rights made it hard for them to fire inefficient older workers. Retirement served both unions and employers: it limited seniority rights to people under the age of retirement and allowed companies to let older workers go. The unions traded the older worker's right to a job for job security in middle age. Snell (1996, 6) says that the new "mandatory, continuing unemployment [program that emerged] would be known by the euphemism 'retirement.'"

Still, compared with today, few people retired in the past. First, in Canada many people worked on farms or in small businesses, types of work with no retirement age. Second, and most important, a lack of retirement income kept most people working as long as they could. Only with the increase in public pensions and social supports for older people after World War II did retirement spread.

The U.S. Social Security program led the way for this change. The United States designed Social Security in 1935 as a way to get people to retire (Myles 1984, 16). Until then, governments had given social assistance to older people, but this assistance, like Canada's early old age assistance program, gave only the poorest older people a small amount of money to help them survive. The U.S. government based the program on the English poor law notion of "less eligibility." This rule held that assistance should relieve poverty, but should come to less than the lowest working wage.

In time, Social Security, and later Canada's public pension system, set a new goal for public pensions. They promised to make up for a retiree's lost income. "By 1980, the institution of retirement had been consolidated and old age had become a period in the life cycle defined and sustained by the welfare state" (Myles 1984, 21).

Government now plays the major role in guaranteeing pensions to older retirees. Public pensions and transfer payments act as a deferred wage because people pay into the programs through taxes and payments to the CPP and the Quebec Pension Plan (QPP) while they work. In Canada, though, the amount a person gets does not depend only on how much he or she paid in. People today get "a share of the social product over and above any claims they may have possessed in their capacity as wage earners" (Myles 1984, 29). Myles calls this a **citizen's wage**. This wage makes retirement a time of economic security and freedom for many older people (see Exhibit 10.1).

With government help, retirement has become an option for many more people than ever before (Milligan and Schrile 2006). Shultz (2001) shows that if people want to replace 60 to 70 percent of their preretirement income, they would need to save about 20 percent of their earnings *each and every year*" (105, emphasis in original). Most people could not or would not save at this rate, and without public pension plans, a large proportion of older people would live in or near poverty. Public pension plans ensure that everyone will have income security in old age.

WHY DO PEOPLE RETIRE?

A number of personal conditions lead people to choose retirement. These include a person's expected pension income, early retirement incentives, loss of a job, health, a spouse's decision to retire, and family responsibilities (Pyper 2006; Turcotte and Schellenberg 2007). Social forces can also lead a person to choose retirement. These forces include (1) mandatory retirement rules, (2) better pensions that start at age 65, and (3) a more positive societal attitude toward retirement.

The Debate over Mandatory Retirement

No federal law in Canada forces a person to retire at age 65, and no statute requires a worker to leave work at a certain age. The federal public service ended mandatory retirement in 1986. As of 2006, Yukon, Manitoba, Ontario, Quebec, and New Brunswick did not allow mandatory retirement. Ibbott and colleagues (2006) report that all national political parties except the New Democratic Party propose the abolition of mandatory retirement. Still, two-thirds of collective agreements had mandatory retirement clauses at the close of the last century, and mandatory retirement rules affect half of all workers (Goodman 1999).

The debate over mandatory retirement concerns two principles: (1) that of individual equality and justice, and (2) that of group rights (Guppy 1989). The first principle says that society should prohibit discrimination against a person on the basis of race, religion, gender, or age. The Croll Commission report, *Retirement without Tears*, used this principle in its argument against mandatory retirement, which, it said, violates the older worker's human rights (Senate of Canada 1979).

"Discriminating against people in employment because they are no longer young," the report says, "[is] clearly objectionable on social grounds. [It is] no more justifiable than discrimination because of religion" (128). The Canadian Association of Retired Persons uses this argument to fight mandatory retirement (MacAuley 2005 cited in Ibbott et al. 2006).

The second principle says that all adults have the right to a fair share of social opportunities. Employment equity regulations are based on this principle. The mandatory-retirement debate often focuses on specific issues like the need for older workers to allow younger workers a chance to work. But beneath this and other issues lurk the conflicting principles of individual versus group rights.

● Exhibit 10.1

LABOUR FORCE PARTICIPATION RATES, BY SEX AND AGE GROUP, 1976–2004

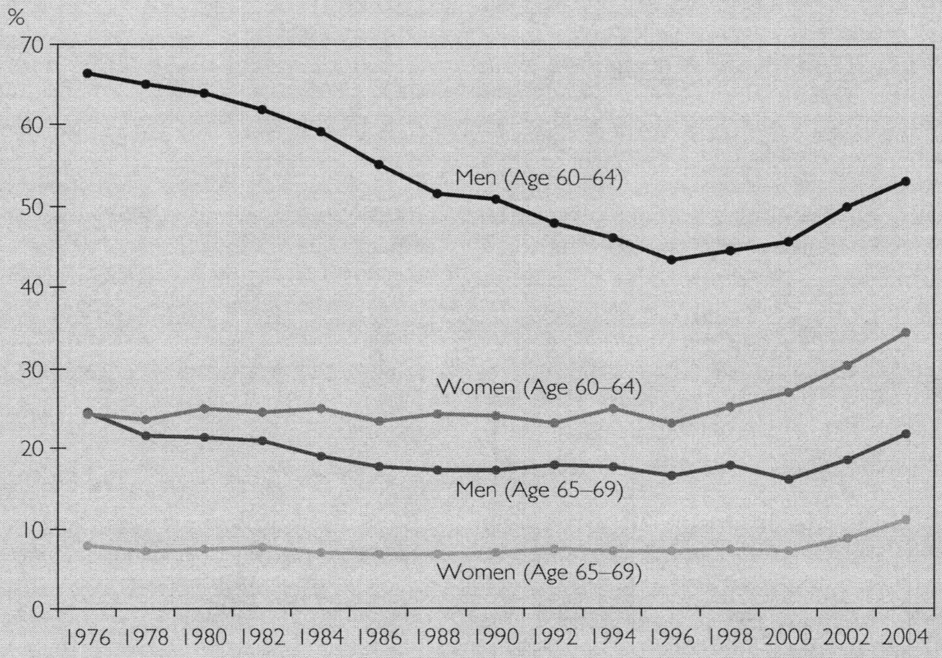

Note that labour force participation for men and women show different patterns over this 28-year period. Labour force participation for men aged 60 to 64 declined until the mid-1990s, then started to rise by 2000. By 2004 the proportion of men aged 60 to 64 in the labour force was higher than at any time in almost two decades. Labour force participation for men aged 65 to 69 in 2004 reached the highest point in 26 years. These figures indicate a trend toward greater labour force participation for older men.

Labour force participation for women aged 60 to 64 remained relatively stable at around one-quarter of women in this age group in the labour force for most of the period shown here. But the proportion of women aged 60 to 64 in the labour force grew to more than one in three by 2004. Women aged 65 to 69 show a similar pattern of stable participation until the early 2000s. By 2004 one woman in 10 in this age group took part in the labour force. This points to a tendency for older women to enter the work force later in life or to remain at work longer.

What accounts for the increase in labour force participation by older men and women? Some older workers say they enjoy work and don't want to retire. More often people enter the work force in later life or stay at work longer because they need the income. A widow, for example, may find that her deceased husband's pension no longer provides enough support. A projected labour shortage in the future may lead to more hiring of older workers in some professions, which may further increase labour force participation of older men and women.

Source: Adapted from Turcotte and Schellenberg 2006, 130. Statistics Canada, Labour Force Survey. Catalogue 89-519-XWE.

The Canadian *Charter of Rights and Freedoms* appears to outlaw mandatory retirement based on age. The *Charter* states in Section 15(1) that "every individual is equal before and under the law and has the right to the equal protection and equal benefit of the law without discrimination and, in particular, without discrimination based on race, national or ethnic origin, colour, religion, sex, age or mental or physical ability" (cited in Guppy 1989). But the *Charter* contains other sections that make this passage unclear. For example, it does not regulate private conduct, so it may not apply to private-sector retirement agreements. Also, the *Charter* protects the good of society from individual freedoms. Guppy concludes that "the Charter does not offer a clear formula to follow in deciding the future of mandatory retirement" (175).

In cases through the 1990s the Supreme Court of Canada supported mandatory retirement. As late as 2008 the Supreme Court continued to support this position in limited contexts. In a 4 to 3 decision, the Court upheld mandatory retirement in New Brunswick in cases where an employer has a bona fide retirement pension plan. The *Human Rights Act* in New Brunswick allows this exception. The New Brunswick Human Rights Commission appealed this exception. Its chair, Gordon Porter, expressed disappointment at the ruling. He says that "Mandatory retirement is clearly age discrimination. A person who wants to continue to work should be allowed to do so. It is a question of fairness, and it makes economic sense."

Gordon then points to a change that will take place in Canada in 2009. By 2009, he said, "mandatory retirement will have been abolished throughout Canada, except at the federal level. Only Newfoundland and New Brunswick retain an exception that explicitly allows mandatory retirement for employees who receive a pension from their employer." (New Brunswick 2008).

The near end of mandatory retirement comes at an opportune time. Canada may need its older workers to remain on the job. Statistics Canada (2003t) reports that the fields of education and health care will soon feel the "retirement crunch." About half the workforce in education will reach retirement age in 12 years, and half the managers in education will reach retirement age in nine years. MacGregor (2005, 29) says that universities "present a spectacular example" of this retirement wave." The Association of Universities and Colleges of Canada (Tibbetts 2007) says that as many as one half the country's 40,000 professors may retire and need to be replaced in the next decade. Health care has a little more breathing room. About half the health care labour force will reach retirement age in 20 years. Statistics Canada

goes on to say that the forestry, mining, oil and gas, and utility industries will face a wave of retirement in the next two decades.

A shortage of managers throughout the workforce may also develop in the near future. Robson (2001) warns that employers and the government may need to revise policies that now encourage (or force) older workers to retire. Canada could keep older people in the workforce by retraining workers for service-sector jobs and by increasing educational opportunities. This would allow older people to stay on at more administrative and management jobs.

At present, few opportunities exist for older worker retraining. Underhill (2006) reports that in 2002, compared to younger workers, fewer older workers in Canada took part in job-related training. Only Ontario and Manitoba have training programs for unemployed older workers; the federal government has no policy on training older workers and no training program targeted to them. This will have to change if Canada wants to keep older workers productive and in the labour force.

Employers in the future may find that they have to entice older workers to stay at work. Tindale (1991, 19; see also Gee 1995) says that while "mandatory retirement will not disappear with a bang, by means of precedent-setting judicial decisions, it may well disappear with a whimper of attrition as the labour force shortage grows."

Will an end to mandatory retirement solve the projected Canadian labour shortage? In an analysis of six countries including Canada, Cooke (2006) doesn't think so. He says that "despite references to population aging in the mandatory retirement debates in Canada, there is little evidence that banning mandatory retirement has had an effect on labour force participation in other countries" (392). Ontario Ministry of Labour (2006) figures agree. For example, the ministry estimates that the end to mandatory retirement in that province will add only about 4,000 older workers (out of about 100,000 retirees) per year to the labour force.

Employers may still favour the release of older workers even in the face of a labour shortage. First, Cooke (2006) says, employers view older workers as more expensive and less effective than younger workers. They believe this "despite anti-discrimination laws and evidence that older workers are indeed capable of learning new tasks and tend to have higher loyalty and less absenteeism" (396). Firms that want to retire older workers will do so through "voluntary buy-outs" even where states make mandatory retirement illegal.

Second, Cooke notes that mandatory retirement does not at present affect all workers. Ibbott and colleagues

(2006) report that only about half of Canadian workers have mandatory retirement clauses in their work contracts. And only between 12 and 21 percent (depending on the study) report that mandatory retirement triggered their decision to leave work. Of those who expect to leave work due to mandatory retirement, only 18 percent of men and 3 percent of women say they want to keep working. So, an end to mandatory retirement will affect only part of the labour force and will change the retirement plans of few workers.

Third, "there are powerful incentives for older workers to leave the labour force, including public and private pensions" (392). Cooke notes, based on the experience in other countries, "retirement is desirable for many … Those who can afford to retire because of private pensions or other income may well continue to do so, while those who cannot may look for other routes of exit from paid work" (2006, 396). Wannell (2007b) reports that people who retire early (in their 50s) generally leave high-paying jobs. Their retirement income on average comes to about two-thirds of their preretirement income, about the amount the pension experts consider necessary to maintain a preretirement standard of living.

Hicks (2002, 46 in Schellenberg 2004, 5) says "… that there is an entrenched culture of early retirement in Canada." In other words, as long as public and private pensions offer incentives to retire at age 65 or sooner, an end to mandatory retirement will have little effect on keeping older people at work. "Some people apparently would like to go on working beyond age 65," Townson says (2006a, 149), "but most are retiring before then."

Townson (2006a, 226 citing Policy Research Initiative 2004) goes on to say that "innumerable surveys have shown that people do not want to work longer if it can be avoided. They might be willing to do so in a job that they liked, but a good many people don't seem to like the jobs they are doing. As one focus group participant [in a Policy Research Initiative study] put it, 'I love to work. It's just that I hate my job.' … Reminding these participants that Canadians were living longer and healthier lives, and thus more able to work past retirement, 'had little impact on their view.'"

Fourth, several barriers exist that keep retirees from working. Some pension programs (the GIS for example) claw back a share of retiree earnings. In other cases added income may increase a person's tax rate. These rules make work unattractive to many people (Wannell 2007a).

Fifth, inflexible work arrangements give older workers little incentive to stay at work. Canada's Policy Research Initiative (2005) reports, for example, that one in five retirees would have remained at work if they could have found part-time work or work with flexible hours. But most employers find it difficult to arrange part-time or flexible work for retirees (Cooke 2006).

Clearly people retire for many reasons. And an end to mandatory retirement may not change current patterns of retirement. Still, an end to mandatory retirement gives older adults the right to remain in their current jobs if they choose.

Age Discrimination in the Workplace

Employers who discriminate on the basis of age will not admit it; only the number of formal complaints lodged by workers gives a glimpse of the problem. Still, Rix (2006, 3; also Cooke 2006) says, "Age continues to work against many older jobseekers, as evidenced by the average length of time it takes them to find work, the wage loss many experience upon reemployment, and the size of court awards to victims of discrimination."

An AARP (2002) survey in the United States found that two-thirds of middle-aged workers believed that age discrimination exists in the workplace. They said they felt concerned about their ability to reenter the workforce or to get promotions as they aged. Sixty percent of these workers said they believed that employers let older workers go first when they cut staff. Almost one person in 10 believed their firm had passed them up for a promotion. Six percent of said their firm fired them or forced them out of work due to their age, and 15 percent said they failed to get hired for a job due to their age.

An AARP–sponsored (2007, 59) study of seven developed nations found that "age discrimination in hiring practices continues to be a serious concern around the world. The level of confidence among workers age 50+ in their ability to find new jobs is much lower than for workers below age 50. Age discrimination is viewed as the single largest barrier to finding jobs for workers over age 50." In this study, 72 percent of Canadians aged 50 and over felt that age discrimination would create a barrier to them finding a new job. Twenty-eight percent of people aged 50 and over said they had experienced age discrimination. Sixty-percent of these people said they experienced age discrimination when looking for a job, and over 35 percent reported age discrimination in promotion decisions.

A number of experimental studies document age discrimination in the workplace. Townson (2006a, 192) says that "it is widely recognized that age is a barrier for individuals trying to get a job." Studies find that "younger job applicants were favored over older applicants who were identical in all respects save age" (Rix 2004, 15). Lahey (2005, cited in Rix 2006), for example, sent out résumés for equally experienced older and younger workers. She found that the people presented as younger in their resumes had a 40 percent greater chance of getting called for an interview.

A number of companies in developed countries address age discrimination in the workplace. Deutsche Bank developed a task force on age diversity with senior managers in the lead, and the National Health Service in the United Kingdom conducts training on the value of older workers and promotes intergenerational mentoring (AARP 2007). Danny Green, human resources director of Merck Frost in Quebec says, "Frankly, it's good business for government and employers to make it easier for over-50 employees to continue working. It's a win-win all around—it adds to the GDP of the country" (AARP 2007). These companies and others recognize the experience and dedication that many older workers bring to their jobs and that a company must take a proactive stance to overcome age discrimination in the workplace.

Better Pensions

Better pension plans today make retirement more attractive than ever before. First, some workers with good pension plans may have more disposable income in retirement than if they keep on working; taxes and the cost of commuting, clothes, lunches, and other work-related expenses may make work an more expensive option.

Second, most private pension plans begin to pay full benefits at age 65. These plans provide workers with a strong incentive to retire at 65.

Third, OAS payments start at age 65, as do Guaranteed Income Supplement (GIS) payments, and CPP/QPP payments. A person who works past age 65 will still get these benefits, but will lose a large portion of them through higher taxes. The GIS program, for example, reduces the GIS by $1 for each $2 a person earns (after an exemption of the first $3,500 earned); a person who earns a provincial supplement loses the other $1 from his or her supplement benefits. Government policies such as these can result in a large "**taxback**" on the poorest people (*The Latest* 2008). Also, the taxback takes money from the older person's income next year for money earned this year. This means that low-income older people who work risk losing next year's income supplements (as well as their salary) if they get sick or lose their job. These rules create a strong incentive for retirement.

Better pensions and incentives to leave work have increased the trend in early and on-time retirement in the past few decades. In addition, increased leisure and recreational opportunities have changed social attitudes toward retirement (Ekerdt and Sergeant 2006).

Early Retirement

Statistics Canada (2003t) reports that 43 percent of Canadian retirees retired before age 60, 31 percent retired between aged 60 and 64, 19 percent between ages 65 and 69, and 7 percent after age 70. This means that nearly three-quarters of retirees left work before age 65. In 2001, Canadian men on average retired at age 62 and women at age 59.

Three types of workers tend to take early retirement: workers in poor health, women who retire for personal reasons, and those who expect a good income in retirement (Statistics Canada 2001e; Turcotte and Schellenberg 2005).

First, compared to healthy workers, unhealthy workers tend to retire at an earlier age (McDonald and Donahue 2000). A study by Au and colleagues (2004; also Pyper 2006) found that about one-quarter of retirees aged 55 and over said they left work for health reasons. Unhealthy workers tend to have lower education, come from lower-status occupations, and lack a private pension. Au and colleagues (2004) say that more generous disability insurance programs today make it easier for workers to retire early if they have a health problem.

Retirement due to poor health affected men and women differently. Women who retired due to poor health did not show a drop in income. The researchers say that for these women, the "starting point on the income ladder is so low to begin with and their work patterns so limited, none of their work history much matters when it comes to retirement income. It is marriage that has the largest and most positive effect on women's household retirement income" (McDonald and Donahue 2000, 516). But men who retired due to poor health faced significant drops in income. They often had no private pension or investment income, and they often got few transfer dollars. McDonald and Donahue ask whether the government ought to make special pension arrangements for this large group of older retirees.

Second, in Canada, more women than men retire early for personal reasons. In 2004, for example, only 1.9 percent of women aged 70 and over worked for pay compared to 6.9 percent of men in that age group. Many women retire because their spouse has retired. And, because women often marry older men, they retire at an earlier age on average than men. Also, women, more often than men, retire because of the ill health of a spouse or a family member. The 2002 General Social Survey in Canada found that 12 percent of women, compared to 6 percent of men, retired to care for a family member (cited in McDonald 2006b).

A Statistics Canada study found that family responsibilities ranked third as the most common reason for women to retire (Turcotte and Schellenberg 2007; also Zimmerman et al. 2000). This item barely ranked at all for men. McDonald, Donahue, and Moore (1998, cited in McDonald 2006b) found that women who retired to give care often worked in marginal jobs, worked irregular schedules, and took voluntary absences. They also tended to have lower personal incomes and were less likely to get benefits from any pension plan or from investments. These findings show the effects of family and personal pressures on women's decisions to retire. These findings also caution against using data based on male retirement patterns to draw conclusions about retirement for women.

Workers in the public sector, for example, retired on average three and a half years earlier than those in the private sector. Self-employed workers tended to retire later than other workers. These figures support the idea that good pension benefits encourage early retirement. As Burtless and Quinn (2001, 385 cited in Myles 2006) conclude, the "simplest and probably most powerful explanation for earlier retirement is rising wealth." As workers' wealth increased, they tended to buy more years of retirement. Schellenberg (2004) found that older workers who stay at work do so because they need the money.

Some private pension plans encourage people to choose early retirement. Many large companies, the government, and universities sponsor early retirement plans. Early retirement allows companies to hire less costly young workers or to leave jobs empty after a retiree leaves. Bell Canada, which had an average retirement age of 55 in the early 1990s, used retirement to trim its labour force. Almost all retirees in that period left the company before age 65 through an incentive program that encouraged early retirement (Marshall 1995).

Robertson (2000) studied the reasons older people left work with an incentive package. Reasons included timing, the financial incentive, and changes in corporate culture. The early retirement package helped workers make up their minds to leave. One woman said, "I had planned to retire at 60 … and I thought, well, at 59 they're offering a package that would probably equal my year's salary … And if I hadn't taken it, I may have been still sitting there today working … it kind of made my mind up for me" (70). Another worker said, "they came and offered me over a year's wages to leave … which I thought was just fantastic … And I said, well, okay. Thirty-eight years. And I thought, that's long enough" (70).

Schulz (1991) says that retirement policies in developed countries serve as a way to adjust the labour supply. These programs "intentionally … discourage people from working" (303). Companies use retirement as a buffer against economic change. McGoldrick and Cooper (1988) found that managers referred to incentive programs as voluntary, but workers more often saw them as coercive. Marshall (1995, 46) calls this the "retirement incentive game." Management tries to offer the fewest incentives possible to produce the desired effect: downsizing. The worker needs to make a decision: take the offer, wait for a better one, or risk a layoff. Marshall says that playing this game requires that workers know the cost of taking the plan, the benefits of early retirement, and their own life expectancy. No one wants to retire and then live in poverty for another 20 years (see Exhibit 10.2).

Statistics Canada (2001e) says that in the 1990s many public-sector industries encouraged workers to take early retirement. Between 1997 and 2000, for example, 63 percent of public-sector employees retired before age 60 (twice the rate of the private sector) (Kieran 2001). Canada's *Public Service Superannuation Act* allows public service workers to retire as early as age 55 with 30 years' service. This made age 55 the most popular age for public-sector employees. Private-sector employees tended to stay on until age 65. Some private-sector pension plans in Canada allow early retirement on a reduced pension. Some private plans even include a special rule allowing early retirement on an unreduced pension after a certain number of years of service or for age plus service.

Changes in the CPP in 1987 also encourage a more flexible retirement age. The plan now allows payments to begin as early as age 60 or as late as age 70. People who retire early get decreases in their basic pension equal to 0.5 percent for each month between the date the pension begins and the month after their 65th birthday. Retirees cannot earn more than the current maximum annual CPP pension at age 65. Those who retire after age 70 receive an increase of 0.5 percent on their basic pension for every month between the date the pension begins and the month after their 65th birthday.

Results from the 2002 General Social Survey (GSS) in Canada show an increase in flexible thinking about retirement (Statistics Canada 2003f). Almost two-thirds of workers aged 45 to 59 said they will have adequate or more than adequate income when they retire (Schellenberg 2004). Not surprisingly, given their feeling of financial security, more than one worker in five (22 percent) aged 45 to 59 said they planned to retire early (before age 60). Another 45 percent said they planned to retire between age 60 and 64 or at age 65. Only 3 percent said they planned to stay at work after age 65.

PLANNED RETIREMENT AGE OF EMPLOYED PERSONS AGED 45 YEARS AND OLDER AND AGED 16 TO 44

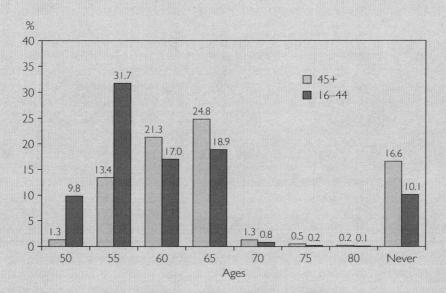

This graph shows the preference for early retirement among both younger and older workers. The largest proportion of older workers choose age 65, probably because their pension plans provide incentives to retire at that age. The largest proportion of younger workers plan to retire at age 55. The graph shows a shift in the planned retirement age to younger ages for all workers, reflecting the options available through private and public early retirement programs. Note also that 16.6 percent of older workers and 10.1 percent of younger workers said they never planned to retire. Workers make choices based on their personal circumstances—expected income in retirement, savings, and health.

Source: Adapted in part from the Statistics Canada "*General Social Survey*, cycle 9: education, work and retirement (1994) – Custom tabulation service," Catalogue 12C0013, April 2003. Reprinted with permission.

These findings show that many older workers (about 44 percent) plan on early retirement—before age 65. Relatively few workers plan to work past age 65. These findings support trends toward early retirement that began in the late 1970s.

McDonald and Chen (1995, 87) see a "seemingly unwilling labour force engaged in a stampede to early retirement." The Policy Research Initiative (PRI) (2005, 25) reviewed research on retirement expectations of workers aged 45 to 59. The PRI concludes that "the desire to retire early indicates that withdrawal from the labour force, or at least from dependence on one's current job, is a high valued expectation." Schellenberg (2004) calls this a "culture of early retirement." Sheppard (1991, 293; also AARP 2007) believes that early retirement "may increasingly become a valued end in itself, a life goal." The desire to leave work, and the existence of public and private pensions, make retirement an attractive option for more people than ever before.

Still many Canadians cannot afford to retire. A large proportion of people, 31 percent, said they either didn't know when they would retire or that they would never retire. These last two groups represent about 1.4 million Canadians. Many of them will have to work to maintain their standard of living. This makes retirement a personal choice, one that depends in part on a person's experience in the workplace.

The GSS found, for example, that poorer people, people without pension plans, and recent immigrants showed the greatest likelihood to report that they would never retire. Schellenberg (2004) reports that 45 percent of people who immigrated to Canada since 1980 say they have inadequate resources to retire, compared to only 29 percent of Canadian-born workers who said they had inadequate resources. Women more often than men expected to have low incomes in retirement. Widowed, separated, or divorced people also reported concerns about low income in retirement. McDonald, Donahue, and Moore (2000a) studied widows and found that they tend to retire later than married women. They often have low incomes, which affects their retirement options. They plan less for retirement, have less information about retirement, and save less for retirement.

ALTERNATIVES TO A FIXED RETIREMENT AGE

McDonald (2006b, 146) says that "retirement no longer represents an abrupt transition from work to non-work: it can be gradual, it can involve multiple exits, it is multi-layered with other life events and it may never happen." Hardy (2006) says that only about half of retirees today experience retirement as a once-in-a-lifetime break with their past. Many workers, she says, "retire from one job and begin collecting pension benefits as they search for new jobs" (Hardy, 2006, 207). Wannell (2007a, 19) says that people with private pension plans "are increasingly finding their way back into paid jobs in their 60s." Today many retirees cycle in and out of the retirement— sometimes more than once. A TD Waterhouse study (TD Bank 2005 cited in Townson 2006a) found that one-third of the people in the survey planned to work full- or part-time after age 65. Three-quarters of the people who said they would stay at work said they would do so out of choice. Women, more often than men, said they would stay at work because they had to. Novelli and Workman (2006, 88) say that "Workers who retire in phases, or steps, are more likely to have a positive view of work and may stay in the workforce longer."

The National Advisory Council on Aging (2000b, 5) reports a "blurring of the line between work and retirement." Marshall and colleagues (2001, 379) report on a study of workers at Bell Canada in Ontario. They found that many retirees return to work in "**bridge jobs.**" They work at something new after they retire from their mid-life career. For example, 46.5 percent of the men and 25.3 percent of the women worked for pay after retiring. Options for retirees today include flexible retirement, part-time work, and second careers. (See Exhibit 10.3 and 10.4).

Flexible Retirement

Atchley (1985, 192) predicts that in the future, "the small proportion [of people who do] not want to retire can expect to find it increasingly easier to stay on as long as they can still do the job." Some of these workers may choose **flexible retirement**, an option that allows them to slowly cut back the number of hours they work each week.

Older Canadians tend to work if they have occupations that allow for choice in their retirement age and if they can work at their own pace. People in religious professions, for example, make up the highest proportion of people employed after age 65. Also, many older male workers who continued working tended to work in manufacturing, construction, and transportation industries (Lindsay 1999; Townson 2006a). Kieran (2001) says that farmers (who are mostly self-employed) may need to work in order to earn money and to run the family business. People who find meaning in work and consider their work important also tend to work after retirement. This applies best to older men who work in managerial jobs, members of the clergy, and university professors. Job sharing can serve as an alternative to either retirement or full-time work by spreading the available work for a position over a number of workers. Paris (1989) reports that in a Canadian study 19 percent of 375 companies offered formal job-sharing programs. Another 10 percent of these companies said they allowed informal job sharing. This option, which fits a trend in the labour force toward more temporary jobs, would allow workers to work part-time in their current positions and might entice some older workers to stay on after retirement age. Job sharing can benefit employers by giving them more flexibility in responding to labour demands. It also opens opportunities for people who want part-time or temporary work. In 2004, for example, about one in four men and one in five women aged 65 and over in the labour force worked at a temporary job (Turcotte and Schellenberg 2007).

People who choose partial retirement often choose to work because it provides them with a sense of purpose. They may work at a special project for their former employer, as a consultant, or as a part-time employee. A study conducted for the HSBC (2006, 7), found that some Canadians "see retirement as a new chapter of life, a time for personal challenges (including work and careers) and taking risks."

Exhibit 10.3

PREFERRED RETIREMENT OPTIONS

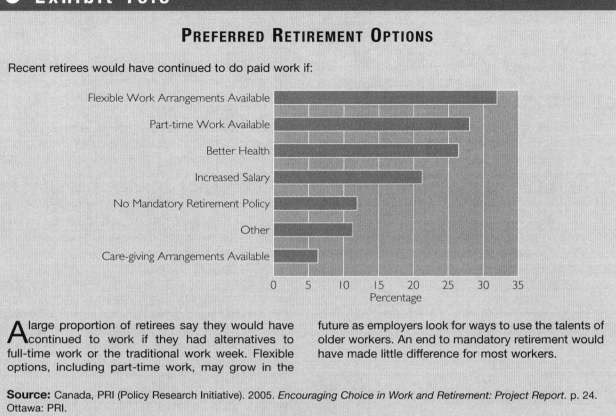

Recent retirees would have continued to do paid work if:

A large proportion of retirees say they would have continued to work if they had alternatives to full-time work or the traditional work week. Flexible options, including part-time work, may grow in the future as employers look for ways to use the talents of older workers. An end to mandatory retirement would have made little difference for most workers.

Source: Canada, PRI (Policy Research Initiative). 2005. *Encouraging Choice in Work and Retirement: Project Report*. p. 24. Ottawa: PRI.

Walt Jamieson, historian and professor emeritus, took on a major research project several years after he retired; his university called on him to update the university's official history. Walt published a book based on his work that now serves as the best recent history of the campus. This past year the school's Continuing Education unit asked Walt to create a history of continuing education for the university's 150th anniversary. Walt spent a year visiting libraries, interviewing staff members, and tracking down historical documents.

Walt's study came out as a companion book to the university history. Walt says, "The project gave me a reason to get up in the morning. I thoroughly enjoyed engagement with the Dean of the unit and his staff. It was one of the best years of my retirement" (personal communication with author). The project led to publicity, requests for public lectures, and a new interest in Walt's university history. He's now begun a new research project that will explore the lives of early female graduates.

Walt has clearly retired. He works at his own pace from his home, and employs his wife as a research assistant. He stays involved in academic life through projects that use his expertise and both he and his institution benefit from this engagement.

Townson (2006a, 182) says that "more and more people … seem to be interested in phasing into retirement gradually…" Schellenberg and colleagues (2005) found that people in good health, professionals, managers, and technicians showed the greatest likelihood of returning to work. They found that more than half (55 percent) of retirees who returned to work after retirement gave reasons other than money. More than one in five (22 percent) said they didn't like retirement. Another 19 percent said they enjoyed the satisfaction of working. This interest in flexible retirement has begun to spread throughout the workforce.

For example, a 2003 study (Desjardins Financial Security 2004) found that 61 percent of Canadians aged 40 and over planned a phased retirement.

● Exhibit 10.4

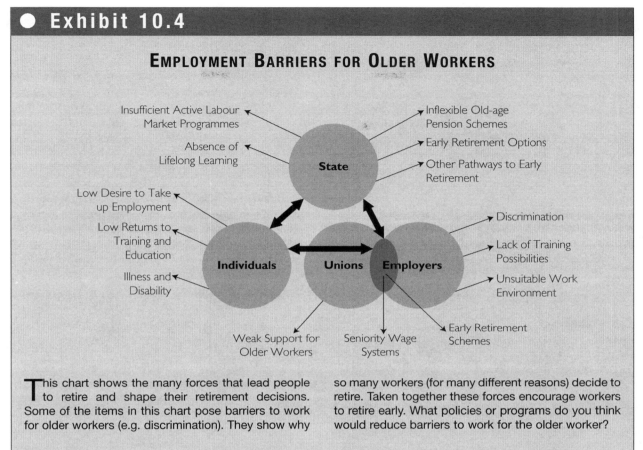

EMPLOYMENT BARRIERS FOR OLDER WORKERS

Insufficient Active Labour Market Programmes

Absence of Lifelong Learning

Inflexible Old-age Pension Schemes

Early Retirement Options

Other Pathways to Early Retirement

State

Low Desire to Take up Employment

Low Returns to Training and Education

Illness and Disability

Individuals

Unions

Employers

Discrimination

Lack of Training Possibilities

Unsuitable Work Environment

Weak Support for Older Workers

Seniority Wage Systems

Early Retirement Schemes

This chart shows the many forces that lead people to retire and shape their retirement decisions. Some of the items in this chart pose barriers to work for older workers (e.g. discrimination). They show why so many workers (for many different reasons) decide to retire. Taken together these forces encourage workers to retire early. What policies or programs do you think would reduce barriers to work for the older worker?

Source: Canada, PRI (Policy Research Initiative). 2005. *Encouraging Choice in Work and Retirement: Project Report*. p. 26. Ottawa: PRI.

They planned to become self-employed and to work fewer hours. These people wanted to stay active and wanted extra income to maintain their standard of living. "It seems almost inevitable," Townson (2006a, 187) says, "that interest in phased retirement will grow as the population ages."

Part-Time Work

A 1998 study found that 46 percent of Canadians expected to work after retirement (Ekos Research Associates 1998, cited in Goodman 1999). Retired men who work often do so for fewer hours per day than before retirement. In 2004, 36.5 percent of employed men and 63.3 percent of employed women aged 65 and over worked part-time (Turcotte and Schellenberg 2007). The trend toward part-time work in retirement has increased in recent years. Between 1976 and 2004 older men showed an increase of 34 percent in part-time labour force participation and older women an increase of 46 percent.

Professionals and people on the margin of the economy show the greatest tendency to take up part-time work. Many of these people retired due to mandatory retirement or because they could not find a full-time job. Part-time bridge jobs can ease a worker's move to full retirement. Examples of bridge jobs include security guard, hardware store salesperson, and department store clerk. These jobs pay less than the retiree's former salary and the work often has little to do with their former career job. But workers take these jobs to stay active and to earn extra money.

Some people (women without pensions or widows) want to work part-time because they need the money.

© istockphoto.com/Savas Keskiner

Some people choose to work past the traditional retirement age. Some stay at work because they need the income; others want to stay engaged in meaningful activity. Professionals often find it easiest to delay retirement.

Others like to work because it gives them a chance to meet new people. Sometimes people who retired because of bad health find that their health improves enough that they can manage a part-time job.

Some workers turn to part-time work because they cannot find full-time jobs. Dubé and Dionne (2005, 10) studied unemployment among older workers. They found that, compared to younger workers (aged 26 to 45), "the oldest unemployed (56 and over) were 39% less likely to find a job." In 1997, for example, about 20 percent of unemployed men aged 55 and over and 22 percent of unemployed women in this age group had been out of work for more than a year. This comes to about twice the rate for younger people (McDonald, Donahue, and Moore 2000b, citing Statistics Canada 1998). Prager (2003, 157) reports that many older workers who lose their jobs risk "permanent layoffs."

Rowe and Nguyen (2003) say that at age 65, the chance of finding a full-time job in their profession nears zero. The older the person, the more difficulty he or she will have finding work. Foot and Gibson (1993, 64) believe that unemployment among older workers will remain "an important policy issue" in the years ahead.

Gibson and colleagues (1993) studied employers' views of older workers. They found several barriers to older workers' re-employment. Employers felt that older workers lacked the skills to do the job, cost more to employ, and had a harder time fitting into the company's culture. McDaniel (2003) says that employers feel that older workers lack the ability to learn new technical skills. Also, employers feel that older workers show less willingness to change, compared to younger workers. McDonald and colleagues (2000b) also report sexual discrimination (against women) and racism as causes of unemployment among older workers.

Older Canadian workers with a record of unemployment tend to get "discouraged out" of the job market (McDonald, Donahue, and Moore 2000b). Some workers who lose their jobs may not find work that suits them, so they give up looking and retire early (McMullin and Marshall 1999).

Part-time work can help workers cope with job loss. Statistics Canada (2003q) reports that 27 percent of people aged 45 and over said they worked part-time because of business conditions or because they could not find full-time work. McDaniel (2003) says that part-time bridge jobs can help a person transition to a new career in retirement. A study of Canadian workers (AARP 2007) found that 30 percent of the workers who planned to work in retirement planned to do so part-time, for a different employer, in a different type of work.

McDonald, Donahue, and Moore (2000b) say that unemployed older people can benefit from counselling. The counsellor can encourage an older person to improve his or her job skills, go back to school, look for part-time work, or work as a volunteer in order to get a new job. The researchers also report retirees' need for social support from family and self-help groups. The government also provides some support. Nine "Experienced Workers Employment Bureaux" throughout Canada help retired workers find part-time work or other working arrangements that suit their needs. The government, foundations, and local agencies fund these offices, which provide counselling and job search services.

Moen and her colleagues (2000) found that work after retirement led to greater life satisfaction for men but lower life satisfaction for women. Older men may choose to work for personal fulfillment, but older women may have to work to pay their bills.

Second Careers

Some people retire to a **second career**. Job bureaus for seniors report that former teachers want to work as cabinetmakers, former accountants want to work as painters, and former homemakers want to work in an office or a retail store. These people work at second careers for more than the money; a second career allows them to develop skills they could not use when they worked full-time.

A study conducted by Towers Perrin on behalf of AARP (2007) asked a random sample of 565 Canadian workers why they would work in retirement. Nearly half of the respondents (45 percent) said they would work for the extra money. Nearly as many (42 percent) said they would work to stay mentally active. And a quarter of the respondents said they planned to work to stay physically active, stay productive, and have something interesting to do. This supports the idea that many older workers see work in retirement as a form of self-development.

Tournier (1972, 129) calls a second career a "**free career**." A second career, he says, differs from leisure and from the kind of work a person does in middle age. "It has a goal, a mission, and that implies organization, loyalty, and even priority over other more selfish pleasures—not in the line of duty, since professional obligations are not involved, but for the love of people. It is, therefore, not an escape, but a presence in the world" (130). A second career, Tournier says, grows out of interests that lie dormant or undeveloped in middle age. A saleswoman at a large department store, for example, spent her weekends cooking traditional Ukrainian food for her family. When she retired from work, she served as a volunteer kitchen director at her local senior centre. The work gave her a sense of purpose and allowed her to use her talents in a new way.

Tournier (1972, 136) also calls a second career a "personal career" because "one has to formulate one's own aim, choose one's own method of work, set one's own daily task and assert one's identity in one's work."

An organization called Civic Ventures in the United States has developed the idea of a second career further. Civic Ventures sponsors the Experience Corps, a program that recruits older people to serve as tutors and mentors in schools. Civic Ventures also helps community groups develop projects served by older volunteers. It gives awards to older social entrepreneurs to encourage their work and it helps people prepare for new careers in their **third age**.

Marc Freedman (2007), CEO of Civic Ventures, supports what he calls "encore careers." An encore career has the following features: first it takes place after a mid-life career ends. Second, it could last as long as 10 or 20 years and accomplishes something important. Third, it pays a salary and offers benefits. Fourth, it allows a person to give back to society (Ruffenach 2007). Freedman says many Baby Boomers will want to work at something meaningful. "They are searching for a calling in the second half of life." As an example, consider "someone who—after spending 30 years as a money manager—decides in his or her 60s to become a math teacher or to launch a second career with an environmental organization" (Ruffenach 2007, n.p.) This work won't pay as much as a person's mid-life job. But, Freedman (2007, 5) says, an encore career swaps "income for impact."

Freedman foresees a time when Baby Boomer retirees would take a one- or two-year sabbatical at the end of their mid-life career. They would travel, fix up their homes, take up a hobby—the things that people expect to do in retirement. Then they would re-engage in an encore career. Some people would train for this new career; others would use the skills and experience they gathered in their first career.

Ed Speedling went from being a health care executive to serving as an advocate for the homeless. "When I walked into St. John's [a homeless shelter]," he says," it was love at first sight. It was really the fulfillment of a deep desire to work with the poor, to align myself with people who are vulnerable …" As his encore career evolved, Ed went on to do other work with the homeless. He's worked on the streets talking with homeless people and helping them get the services they need. He's also used his first-career skills in the boardroom, advising organization executives. Freedman (2007, 5) uses this case to show the power of what he calls "the 'experience economy.'"

The encore career allows society to reap a "windfall of talent" (Freedman 2007, 22). Members of the biggest generation can throw their weight into solving some of society's biggest problems. Canadian researchers Stone and Harvey (2001, 267–68) agree with Freedman. The interest in "status-enhancing work opportunities in the voluntary-organization sector," they say, could expand choices for people in their retirement years. They go on to say that, "an increased supply of such opportunities would contribute to the strengthening of civil society."

Could meaningful work also lead to better health and longevity? A number of studies point in this direction. Researchers at Johns Hopkins University Medical Centers, for example, studied seniors who tutored elementary school students in reading. Half the people in the study worked 15 hours a week in Baltimore helping students learn to read. The other half of the group did not work at all. The researchers found improved "'physical, cognitive, and social activity'" in the tutor group. The study found decreases on these measures in the control group (Freedman 2007, 82). This study and others suggest that work in later life can lead to good health, longer life, and successful aging.

Disrupted Careers

Many older workers who leave the workforce today do so involuntarily. Corporate downsizing and globalization have led companies to retire or lay off older workers (He, Colantonio, and Marshall 2003). Rowe and Nguyen (2003) studied cohorts of workers as they lost and gained jobs from age 50 to 65. They found that only 51 percent of men and 30 percent of women said that they had retired from their job by age 65; the large majority of job losses (84 percent for men and 88 percent for women) came from other sources—layoffs, illness, or family needs. About a quarter of the workers in this study, who appeared to retire between ages 50 and 65, went on to take new jobs. The researchers say that only about 20 percent of men and 10 percent of women fit the traditional model of retirement (work at a single job until age 65 and then retire).

McDonald and colleagues (2000) report that among people aged 55 to 64 who retired, 68 percent of men and 66 percent of women said they retired unexpectedly. These researchers found that unexpected early retirement led to low incomes in retirement. Those who retired because their company laid them off had the lowest incomes in retirement. These younger retirees cannot qualify for government pensions and they experience a "retirement gap" that leaves them with low incomes (289). Turcotte and Schellenberg (2007, 123 citing Schellenberg, Turcotte, and Ram, 2005) say that "generally speaking, involuntarily retirement is associated with less positive outcomes for retirees, such as lower enjoyment of life in retirement."

A study of involuntary retirement found that people with low incomes showed the greatest likelihood of post-retirement depression (Gallo et al., 2006). McDonald and colleagues (2000b, 78–79) report the effects of low income in retirement. One retiree said, "I've never been as poor, having worked all these years, as I am today." Another retiree said, "I'm coping, I'm coping. But I have to dip into my RRSP. I cannot survive on what I receive … and now I'm planning to move out of my apartment to look for cheaper accommodation."

Some workers will adapt to this new world of retirement by working part-time or starting second careers. Other workers will try to find new jobs. They will often have to work in lower-status jobs, at low pay, and they may face further job disruptions. Researchers have just begun to study this new pattern of retirement. Marshall and colleagues (2001) see later life work disruption as a shift away from a stable work career that leads to retirement. "Retirement is taking on new meanings for men and women: It is not a discrete event marking secession of paid employment, nor is it a stable state following exit from the paid employment. Rather, it is a process that varies in its timing and duration" (180).

WOMEN AND RETIREMENT

McDonald (2002) says that the concept of retirement rarely applied to women in the past. Retirement occurs when a person leaves the paid workforce; but, until recently, relatively few women had a work career that led to retirement. McDonald (2002; 2006b) reports that in 1931, for example, only about 20 percent of women worked in the paid labor force (compared to about 61.6 percent in 2003). But even with more women in the labour force, women follow different career paths than men. Some take up careers after raising a family; others work during their child-rearing years; many single women show unbroken work records. McDonald (2006c, 153) calls women's' retirement "amorphous and fluid."

In 2004, for example, "forty per cent of women's jobs compared with about 29% of men's jobs … were considered 'non-standard'" (Stone 2006, 22–23; Townson 2006c, 348). Non-standard jobs include part-time work, seasonal work, and self-employment (Kapsalis and Tourigny 2004). This variation in the type of work women do makes it hard to describe a typical pattern of retirement. "The male model of retirement," McDonald (2006a, 130–31) says, "with its emphasis on individual, rational choice, founded on a one-job, continuous work history with pension trade-offs, made no sense for women because it was lopsided. The model ignored gender differences in work and the fact that the majority of men and women live or have lived in some type of family arrangement."

Few studies have looked at how women adjust to retirement or at what retirement means to them. In the past researchers treated women's retirement as a non-event. Szinovacz (1982) says that until 1975 the annual meetings of the Gerontological Society of America contained almost no discussion of women's retirement. McDonald (2006a) says that the first text on families and retirement came out in 1992. And Denton and Kusch (2006, 8) say, even in 2006, "We know little about women's retirement in Canada …" The studies that have focused on women show diverse patterns among women subjects and large differences between women and men. Atchley (1982, 165) concludes that "women's retirement is indeed a separate issue compared to men's."

McDonald (2006b) says women's lives remain bound up with family obligations and traditional gender roles. For this reason "women's retirement has always been different from men's and will continue to be different for the foreseeable future, despite arguments to the contrary." For one thing, women's multiple entries and exits from the labour force will lead to smaller pensions. So will their "concentration in non-standard and part-time work, their under-representation in unions, their over-representation in the services sector and the continued distribution of their occupations in female employment" (McDonald 2006b, 157; Kapsalis and Tourigny 2004).

Marshall (1995) says that older working women are more likely than older men to say they do not know when they will retire. One woman said, "If we've had children and had to stay at home for periods of time, we don't have pensions that we can live on. … If and when we retire, the pension I've earned you couldn't live on" (Marshall 1995, 38–39). A woman in another study (McFadgen and Zimmerman 1995, 108) said, "It is hard to plan for retirement if you don't have the means to support yourself."

A woman who relies on her husband's pension may fall into poverty if she faces widowhood, divorce, or separation in later life. A divorced woman aged 68 told Denton and her colleagues (2004, S80), "I assumed I would be in my house until I died and the house was going to be paid for when my husband retired so I thought we were … that was going to be our life. We were going to be all set you know, not have to worry about anything." She now lives on a yearly income of less than $20,000. In general Denton and her colleagues (2004, S81) found that women with fewer resources could plan less for retirement. They "were required to 'take life as it comes', living as best they could day to day."

Berger and Denton (2004) interviewed 28 women aged 59 to 92 (mean age 72) to learn about their work histories. They found that a woman's work patterns shaped their ability to plan for retirement. Women with continuous work records had good financial knowledge and planned financially for later life. They also had employer pension plans and a Canada Pension Plan pension. But few women in the study had unbroken work records. The women in this sample spent an average of 14 years out of work to care for their children. This created financial challenges for them in later life.

Women with broken work records had low financial knowledge and low financial preparedness. They rarely had a company pension plan. And in general they had fewer financial resources. They relied on public pensions like the OAS and GIS. The researchers say that "this suggests that women who disrupt their careers are in great need of financial assistance from the government…" (S108). Women without an occupational pension risk poverty in later life.

McDonald (2006b, 158) says "the pension system today, with its emphasis on job tenure in a life-long career, excludes many Canadians who do not match this profile. Specifically, pension policy barely recognizes the burden of institutionalized lower earnings for women or the costs of their unpaid work, and ignores the multiple job changes that women have experienced in the last ten years." Pension policies need to reflect the unique work lives of women in Canada. Until they do, older women will face inequality and often poverty in old age even if they spend much of their lives in the labour force.

Szinovacz (2006; also Schellenberg et al. 2006) says that retirement studies need to look at the family context to understand women's retirement decisions. Schellenberg and Ostrovsky (2008, 5) report that about fifty percent of two-earner couples say they would prefer to retire together. But "age differences, health conditions, pension eligibility, job loss and career aspirations" often make this difficult. In 2001, for example, less than a third of two-earner couples (29 percent) retired within two years of each other. Many conditions influenced the decision to retire jointly. But if a husband retires due to illness or if a wife has her own pension the likelihood of joint retirement decreases.

As more women spend more years at work, the likelihood of joint retirement decreases. Future studies of women and retirement need to look at how other family relationships influence women's retirement decisions. For example, researchers need to look at how life changes in other family members (sickness of a spouse or parent, marriage of children, or widowhood) affect women's' careers and retirement patterns.

McDonald (2006a, 135–36) sums up the need for more research and a new view of women and retirement. "It would seem, therefore," she says, "that the time has come for scholars to go back to the drawing board and address the lack of theoretical progress about gender, families and retirement. At minimum, a life course perspective with revised definitions of retirement that include gender/family/work linkages would be valuable in reflecting the experiences of people and would lead to policies that would have a better chance for success."

THE PERSONAL EXPERIENCE OF RETIREMENT

Cohen (2005, 144) conducted in-depth interviews with retirees. He says that if people plan for retirement at all, they tend to do financial planning. Few people plan for "how you will be socially engaged, how you will spend your time, what larger goals you want to pursue, and how you can take full advantage of the extra time available in this phase of life."

Crowley (in Crowley and Lodge 2004, 29–97) describes the social pressure he felt when he retired from work:

> "It occurs to me," he says, "that my greatest fear then was not that I would fall apart – although I worried plenty about that. It was that I would be useless and idle and bored. And ashamed because I was not doing anything. When I first retired and found myself walking along the streets of New York at midday with nothing to do, I felt as if I'd just walked out of a porno movie. I didn't want my friends to see me, because they'd know I had no job, that I wasn't *doing* anything. I felt that weird guilt for a long time. In retrospect, that was silly, but I think a lot of men see retirement that way. We can't bear the idea of doing nothing, but we don't know what to do."

Both Cohen and Crowley point out the importance of planning for social engagement in retirement. Denton and colleagues (2004) studied how people planned for retirement. They conducted qualitative interviews with 51 men and women aged 45 and over. They found that a small group of people (about 20 percent of their sample) did little planning. These people lived from day to day and hoped for the best. Widowed, divorced, and separated women made up a large proportion of these "day-to-dayers." Compared to people who planned for later life, they had lower incomes and fewer choices in later life.

The majority of people in this study planned for later life. They made financial plans, intentionally led healthy lifestyles, and planned for social engagement. These people had a positive view of life and felt in control of their future. The planners "envisioned a life-style of their choice and actively sought, through planning and preparation, to achieve their goals" (S79). The researchers say that people with more education and resources see later life as a time of leisure, enjoyment, recreation, and activity.

Ekerdt (1986), in a classic essay, says that many retirees subscribe to what he calls "the busy ethic." This ethic values an active life. People who subscribe to this ethic often carry electronic organizers and have telephone answering machines so they won't miss messages.

Ekerdt says that the busy ethic helps retirees ease into retirement and allows retirees to maintain the same values they held while working—engagement in community affairs, an active social life, and self-development. Retirees legitimate their retirement through "involvement and engagement … [the busy ethic] esteems leisure that is earnest, occupied, and filled with activity" (Ekerdt 1986, 239–40). The busy ethic domesticates or tames retirement. It supports energetic activity and healthful lifestyles, two long-standing North American values. The busy ethic keeps retirement and retirees in the mainstream of life.

Cohen (2005, 138) adds a caution to enthusiasm for the busy ethic. "No one," he says, "should feel pressured to be more active than they want to be." But people can do more than just stay busy. People in retirement have a chance to choose what interests and motivates them. They can plunge into activities with energy and purpose.

Corbett (2007) created the concept of the "life portfolio." A life portfolio consists of a person's commitments to specific activities and relationships. These include family, community service, spiritual development, recreation, and, in some cases, work. Imagine these items placed in a pie chart. The size of each slice will depend on a person's commitment to each activity, group, or individual. A retiree decides how much time and energy he or she will commit to the segments of their portfolio. A portfolio approach gives a person control over his or future. And it encourages action.

Corbett (2007, 107) gives an example of an exercise that helps people create their life portfolio. "Think about the dreams, talents, projects, achievements, loves inside of you that would be unexpressed or unrealized if your life ended today. If, at the end of the day you are still alive, and you have done this exercise faithfully, you have the first draft of a portfolio plan." Corbett also encourages people to write a personal mission statement. This statement helps people define what they care most about. From there they can set goals and begin to take action.

Cohen (2005) emphasizes balancing active with quiet activity, social with personal time, short-term and long-term projects and commitments. Like the review of a financial portfolio, the social portfolio needs periodic review. If a social activity like a volunteer position ends, a person may want to substitute something new. Part-time work may offer a more satisfying social outlet.

This social portfolio demands reflection—awareness of one's total life experience—and a structure or context for thinking about and anticipating the future. A person may serve as a volunteer on a nonprofit board starting before retirement, knowing that he or she will retire in a year or so. The continuing board membership will provide a social outlet that will substitute for the social relations that exist at work.

CONCLUSION

Moen and Spencer (2006, 140) say that today a person must make "intentional choices … about employment, retirement, civic engagement, caregiving, and other behaviors, roles, and relationships." Changes in pension plans (e.g., from defined benefit to defined contribution plans), flexible retirement options, and better health in later life all lead to more choices for the retiree.

Many people will still follow the traditional path from work to a life of leisure. But people in later life today take diverse paths in retirement (Stone 2006). Longer life expectancy and better health of retirees today have created a new stage of life beyond the middle years of work, but different from the traditional model of retirement. Taylor (1995, 18) says that "retirement as we know

it—ten or twenty years of fun, partly at public expense, as a reward for showing up at work during our adult lives—is doomed. The happy coincidence of generous governments and the postwar economic and population boom that made it possible has come undone."

Today the traditional model of retirement exists alongside many other patterns of work and post-work life in what researchers call the Third Age. This stage, beyond a person's main career, now includes many roles and relationships. Moen and Spencer (2006, 132) refer to these activities as "second acts." People explore many options in this post-career period. Guillemard (2006, 49) says that "we are witnessing a real revolution in the social organization of time." She says that the traditional three-stage view of the life cycle—childhood, work, and retirement—"is falling apart." Instead people live more complex lives—they may work, return to school, retire, re-enter the workforce, gain more training, engage in volunteer work, etc. This new model of later life blurs traditional lines between life stages and it challenges the traditional meaning and experience of later life.

Summary

1. Most people want to retire, and they retire as early as they can if they have a good pension.

2. Some people want to continue working, and they have challenged compulsory retirement rules in court. The Supreme Court of Canada has supported compulsory retirement, except in provinces that prohibit it. But changes in public sentiment and the future need for older workers point to the end of mandatory retirement in Canada in the future.

3. Arguments against mandatory retirement suggest that most workers want to work past age 65, but studies show that if their health is poor or a good income awaits them, most people will leave work before age 65. People now accept retirement as a reward they have earned for years of work, and they want to collect that reward as soon as they can.

4. Canadians now have more choice about when they retire and what pattern of retirement they will follow. Some people take full retirement at age 65, others work part-time, and still others start second careers and encore careers. Some older workers take the option of flexible retirement. They may retire for a while, then return to work—and they may do this more than once. Social conditions (such as the economy, the availability of jobs, or a person's occupation) affect a person's retirement options.

5. A good income gives retirees the most options and the best chance to plan for and enjoy retirement. Professionals and people with good private pensions or savings have the most options. People need to plan for a good retirement, and this should go beyond financial planning to include a "life portfolio."

6. The larger number of women in the labour force will lead to new theories of retirement and new research approaches. Women have different work careers than men, and often face social-structural barriers (such as low pay and broken work records) that lead to low incomes and few retirement options.

7. Canadian society may need to find ways to keep older workers on the job in order to avoid a labour shortage. Changes to government pension plans will encourage people to stay at work longer, and more flexible work opportunities may attract older workers.

8. Retirement research in the past has focused on how individuals cope with retirement. A broader view of retirement links individual behaviour to social and economic inequities in society. More research needs to be done on the effects of gender, educational background, and socioeconomic status on retirement.

Study Questions

1. List the two perspectives that gerontologists use to study retirement.
2. Explain how the retirement principle and the retirement wage give rise to the social institution called retirement.
3. What conditions lead people to choose retirement?
4. Explain the two principles involved in the debate over mandatory retirement.
5. Why does the practice of mandatory retirement affect only a small number of people?
6. What developments have made early retirement possible for older people today?
7. Describe two alternatives to a fixed retirement age.
8. What social groups stand the most chance of being satisfied with retirement? What social groups usually opt to continue working past the normal retirement age?
9. Discuss the different effects of social and economic structures on men and women. How do social structures discriminate against women and lead to fewer options for women in retirement?
10. What social forces will shape retirement in the future?

Key Terms

bridge job   a job that a worker takes on the path to retirement (often in work outside the individual's former career). (219)

citizen's wage   a government pension tied to age. (212)

flexible retirement   an option that allows workers to slowly cut back the number of hours they work each week. (219)

free career   a second career in a field that allows a person to explore previously dormant or undeveloped interests. (223)

retirement principle   the idea that a person leaves work at a fixed age, regardless of mental or physical ability. (211)

retirement wage   a pension paid by the state to support all older people. (211)

second career   work that allows people to develop skills they did not use in their preretirement career. (223)

taxback   taxes paid on earnings by recipients of the Guaranteed Income Supplement and provincial supplements, which can amount to a 100 percent reduction in supplement payments for the poorest older people who work. (216)

third age the period of life after the period of work and child rearing in the middle years but before frailty and dependence set in (the fourth age). A period of life created by longer life expectancy and a longer period of good health in later life. (223)

Selected Readings

Denton, F.T., D. Fretz, and B.G. Spencer (eds.). 2000. *Independence and Economic Security in Old Age.* Vancouver: UBC Press.

This collection contains articles on issues and trends in retirement. Articles look at unexpected retirement, the role of the economy in retirement decisions, and options to traditional retirement.

McMullin, J. A. and Cooke, M. 2004. *Labour Force Ageing and Skill Shortages in Canada and Ontario.* Work Network Project W-092. London, Ontario: Canadian Policy Research Networks.

This study looks at the demographics for different industries and jobs. It assesses the impact of workforce aging on the needs of industry for skilled workers. The study focuses on case studies in Ontario of nursing, information technology, manufacturing skilled trades, and biotechnology. The study results do not support the projected future Canadian skill shortage due to population aging. The study identifies certain fields where labour shortages could occur (e.g., nursing). The study proposes policy responses to future labour market needs.

Stone, L.O. (Ed.) 2006. *New Frontiers of Research on Retirement.* Ottawa: Minister of Industry. Statistics Canada. Catalogue no. 75-511-XIE.

This collection features articles on retirement by Canadian and international experts. Authors cover topics from the history of retirement to current social policies, to the impact of family life on work and retirement. A number of the articles look at the effects of gender and family commitments on work and retirement. It provides an excellent and extensive overview of the issues related to retirement in Canada.

Websites to Consult

HR for Employers

http://www.hrmanagement.gc.ca/gol/hrmanagement/site.nsf/en/hr11197.html#Agencies

This site offers information to employers and older workers about job opportunities, and lists job bureaux for older workers. The site explains why employers should hire older workers and provides tips on how to attract older workers. The site provides links to other websites and information related to older workers and the labour force.

Experienced Workers Employment Bureaux in Canada

Bureaux d'emploi des travailleur(euse)s âgé(e)s à travers le Canada

http://www.crm.mb.ca/job-bureau/index.html

This site contains links to job bureaux throughout the country. These offices help older workers find jobs. Some sites collect information from employers so that workers can match their skills with job demands.

Seniors' Info—Ontario Government

http://www.seniorsinfo.ca/en/categories/604

This site provides information on work and volunteering. It contains links to information on mandatory retirement, employment opportunities (including access to a national job bank), and business ownership. The site gives good examples of work opportunities for retirees.

Seniors & Baby Boomers Markets Worldwide

http://www.thematuremarket.com/SeniorStrategic/contacts.php

This site offers information to seniors about a wide range of topics, including retirement, throughout the world. The site also provides information on conferences internationally. This is one of the few sites that covers this topic from a global perspective.

© Ariel Skelley/CORBIS/MAGMA

Chapter 11

Housing and Transportation

INTRODUCTION

Beatrice, 78, and her husband Wes, 83, live in their own home—a one-storey brick house on a quiet residential street. They have lived in this same house for more than 50 years—all of their married life. They raised two children here, a son who now lives on his own in the same city and a daughter who lives about three hours away with her husband and two children. Although Wes has some difficulty getting around, he continues to drive—but only in good weather and only short distances. Bea and Wes live close to a grocery store, a drugstore, and their doctor's office, and a short walk from the bus. In good weather, Bea walks for exercise around her neighbourhood. On summer evenings, she and Wes sit on their front porch, watching children play and talking to neighbours out for their evening stroll. Bea and Wes are known to everyone on the street. But now their children have become concerned about them remaining in their house. At a recent family gathering, their son and daughter brought up the issue of Bea and Wes selling their house and moving in with them. "Mom, dad," their son said, "sis and I have been thinking. You don't need a house this big anymore. It requires too much upkeep. You have stairs to climb to get to the basement laundry room. And you have the yard to mow in the summer and the driveway to shovel in the winter. It is too much for you now. Why not move in with us? You could live half of the year with each of us so you wouldn't have to worry about being a burden on anyone."

"We knew what they were planning," Bea says. "So we were ready. 'This is our house and our home,' I told them, 'We own it. We paid for it. We are happy and comfortable here. And this is where we're going to stay, for as long as we possibly can.'"

Beatrice and Wes's house gives them more than just a place to live; it gives meaning to their life. It connects them to friends on the street, and to a lifetime of memories. The wall over the TV, for example, holds vacation pictures from trips they took over the years—as a couple, and as a family. In the dining room, the bookshelves Wes built are filled with pictures of their children and grandchildren and their collection of travel souvenirs. Their home connects them to a life—and a neighbourhood—that is familiar, secure, and comfortable.

A home allows older people like Beatrice and Wes to feel more independent. Home also means security, comfort, and familiarity (Shenk et al. 2004; Stevens-Ratchford and Diaz 2003). It is a place that offers privacy and control, and where personal routines and important celebrations become part of the fabric of daily life. For many older people, home is intricately tied to treasured possessions and cherished memories of an earlier life—children growing up or the early years of marriage. This is often particularly true in widowhood. "I just love it here … I have almost anything I want here," one widowed woman said of the house she and her husband had built together years before (Shenk et al. 2004, 165). For another widowed woman her long-time home "contains many memories and much love" (167).

Not all older people need or want to live in a single-family house. Some older people live in apartments; others live with their children; still others live in supportive or enriched housing (where they can get help with meals and cleaning); and some live in garden suites (portable, self-contained dwellings built beside a family member's permanent home). The kind of housing that an older person needs and can afford depends on their health, marital status, income, and ability.

A single-family house, for example, presents the most challenges. It demands good health, knowledge about home repairs, and enough income to pay for heat and taxes. An apartment requires less know-how and fewer worries about heating costs, (and usually fewer or no stairs to climb). People who are too frail to prepare their own meals can live in assisted living apartments with meals served in a common dining room (CMHC 2005b). A nursing home cares for people too ill to care for themselves.

Canada's housing system today allows older people many choices about where to live. Housing options include private houses, apartments, retirement communities, and long-term care homes. All these housing options have a place in the housing market. Yet, not all older people have equal access to these choices—either financially or geographically. A study by the Canada Mortgage and Housing Corporation (CMHC 2005a) found that almost 30 percent of senior households lived in "below standard" housing—housing that lacked adequate physical condition, suitable size, and affordability.

In a multi-city Canadian study, older people identified housing and transportation as two of the issues important to their quality of life (Bryant et al. 2004). Seniors in the study expressed concern about the lack of housing options for older people. They felt older people should be able to choose where, and how, they want to live. Affordable housing was central to their concerns. They also identified the need for good public transportation. Transportation links the older person to services and social activities.

This chapter will look at (1) the housing options available to older people, (2) the programs and policies that exist in Canada to help older people meet their housing needs, and (3) transportation systems

© iStockphoto.com/stu99

Owning a home requires the most ability to manage the environment. Home repairs and maintenance require know-how and physical strength. For this reason, couples tend to live in single-family homes. Widowed and single older women opt for a less-demanding housing option like apartment living.

that enable older people to keep in touch with their community and use the resources available to them.

AN ECOLOGICAL MODEL OF HOUSING

Lawton and Nahemow (1973) created an **ecological model** that describes the relationship between the older person and his or her environment. Their model describes the interrelation of two variables: individual capability (competence) and the demands of the environment (**environmental press**). Lawton and Nahemow define capability as "the aggregate of a person's abilities, including health, psychological adjustment, and intelligence." They define environmental demand as

"environmental forces that, combined with need, lead a person to make a response" (659).

People feel the most comfort when their capability matches the demands of the environment and they can fulfill their needs. Too great or too little environmental demand leads to a decreased feeling of well-being and a maladaptive response (Young et al. 2006). A healthy person in a hospital bed, for example, will feel bored and lethargic because the environment demands too little. A person recovering from a stroke may feel fatigued after a 10-minute conversation because the conversation demands too much. The Lawton–Nahemow model says that people try to find a comfortable fit between what they can do and what they need to do to meet their needs (see Exhibit 11.1).

Parmelee and Lawton (1990) propose an updated version of the person–environment model. This revised model redefines the competence dimension as "autonomy" and redefines the environmental press dimension as "security." An autonomous person (one with high competence) can pursue goals with his or her own resources. This person has freedom of choice and action. If a person has some disability, a secure environment (one with little press) can help that person achieve his or her goals. A secure environment offers dependable physical and social resources. Autonomy and security "form a dialectic that lies at the heart of person–environment relations in late life" (466). An increase in security—for example, a move to a nursing home—puts limits on a person's autonomy. Likewise, greater autonomy, such as driving a car, entails some risk.

Housing and transportation should maximize autonomy but provide enough security for a feeling of comfort. Loss of a spouse, changes in a person's informal supports, and illness may all lead to changes in a person's autonomy. And this in turn may lead to changes in housing needs. Some people will need help in order to feel secure. Help can include home maintenance, financial aid, and changes that adapt the environment to fit the person's level of autonomy. Housing options offer different balances between autonomy and security. The most suitable choice will depend on the older person's ability, which will also change over time.

The current approach to housing for older people in Canada focuses on **aging in place** (CMHC 2008a; 2008b). This policy attempts to provide older people with environmental, social, and economic supports so they can stay in their own homes as they age. Older people, especially those in cities, express a desire to age in place. Older people who live in suburban settings find it more difficult to age in place unless they have access to social services. Planners may need to provide

● Exhibit 11.1

THE LAWTON-NAHEMOW ECOLOGICAL MODEL

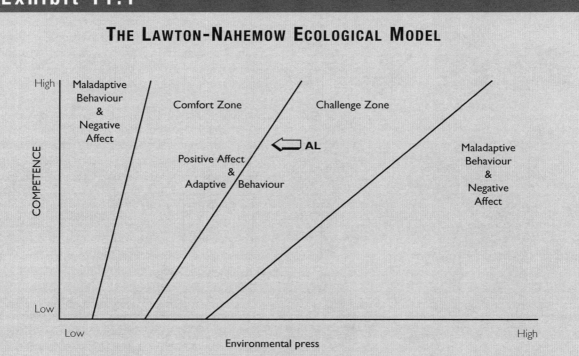

The ecological model states that "when a person of a given level of competence behaves in an environment of a given press level," the result could be placed on a chart like the one shown (Lawton 1980, 11). The chart shows the results of the fit between a person's competence and environmental press in terms of the person's behaviour and affect (feeling). The model shows that varied combinations of competence and press can lead to adaptive behaviour and positive affect. Likewise, the model shows that improvement in person–environment fit can take place on two dimensions: the person can move to or create a less-demanding environment; the person can improve his or her competence; or the person can do both.

The exhibit also illustrates the following points:

1. The mid-point of the chart (AL) represents average press at a given level of competence. To the immediate left of the mid-point is the "comfort zone" where a person feels most at ease.

2. As press increases, adaptation takes place until the press goes beyond the person's ability to adapt (the right diagonal).

3. If the environmental press decreases below the adaptation level, a person will feel bored and anxious (the left diagonal).

4. The "challenge zone" represents the points where press encourages the maximum use of a person's ability.

5. The greater the competence, the greater the adaptive ability; the lower the competence, the lower the adaptive ability.

6. No matter how high the level of competence, at some level of press the person will lose the ability to adapt. And no matter how low the level of competence, the person still has some adaptive ability.

7. A person with low competence can be easily upset by even a small increase in press. But a person with low competence can benefit from even a small improvement in the environment (Lawton 1980).

Source: M.P. Lawton and L. Nahemow, 1973, "Ecology and the Aging Process," in C. Eisdorfer and M.P. Lawton, eds., *Psychology of Adult Development and Aging.* Washington: American Psychological Association. Copyright © 1973 by the American Psychological Association. Reprinted with permission. Courtesy of Lu Nahemow.

special transportation and services for suburban seniors (CMHC 2008a).

This chapter uses the ecological model to look at the housing and transportation options that exist for older people. An ideal housing system would allow people to match their ability to the environment's demands. It would help them to stay where they are as long as they want to stay there, and it would allow a smooth movement from one setting to another when a change in a person's ability or needs makes a move necessary.

LIVING ARRANGEMENTS

An older person's living arrangement can influence their quality of life and well-being. Living arrangements refer to the type of household a person lives in.[1] These arrangements can include living in an institution, living with a spouse, with grown children, with relatives or non-relatives, or alone. Older Canadians live in all of these arrangements, but the proportion of people in each type of accommodation differs by age and gender.

According to the 2001 Census, most older Canadians (93 percent) live in a private dwelling in the community (Turcotte and Schellenberg 2007). Most of these people live in houses (69 percent); some live in apartment buildings (29 percent); and a few live in mobile homes (1 percent) (Clark 2005). These numbers shift somewhat with increased age. For example, for those 85 years of age and older, the percentage who live in houses decreases (to 58 percent) while the proportion who live in apartments increases (to 41 percent). This pattern shows that "selling the family home seems to be the exception rather than the rule for most seniors" (Clark 2005, 3). And when a person does move from a house to an apartment the move tends to come late in life.

Married or common-law couples who live without children make up almost half (45 percent) of all senior households. Those who live alone make up 27 percent of senior households. Eighteen percent of seniors live with their children or grandchildren (with or without their spouse). Seniors who live in institutions (primarily nursing homes) make up about 7 percent of the senior population. The remaining 3 percent of older adults live with other relatives or non-relatives. Three-generation households make up only 3 percent of all households in Canada (Che-Alford and Hamm 1999). Many

three-generation households are immigrant households. In a study of older South Asian immigrants in Edmonton, compared to older men, unmarried older women tended to live in a three-generation household (Ng et al. 2007).

Older people who live with adult children do so for reasons related to their own needs or the needs of their children. For example, some older people move in with their children to get support and assistance. This can take place after their spouse's death, the loss of their driver's license, or because of declining health. In other cases, older people live with their children to provide care to a grandchild, or to help an adult child make ends meet (Clark 2005). The 2001 Census finds that more than half (53 percent) of all older people who live with their children serve as the sole financial support for the family. In only about one-quarter of households does the adult child provide the sole financial support. This challenges the notion that older people who live with their children depend on them for financial support.

Turcotte and Schellenberg (2007) report that in 2001, 81 percent of men aged 65 to 74 lived with family members (a spouse and/or children and grandchildren) compared to about 66 percent of women in this age group. Among people aged 85 and over, these figures drop to 52 percent of men and only about 23 percent of women who live with family members. Of men aged 65 to 74 in 2001, 14 percent lived alone compared to 28 percent of women in this age group. For those 85 and over, 23 percent of men and 39 percent of women lived alone. About 3 percent of men and women aged 65 to 74 lived with people other than a spouse or children. These figures show that a man will typically live in a family setting throughout his life, but a woman will likely live alone at some point in her later years. This means that men and women have different housing needs as they age.

In 2001, about 7 percent of older people (age 65 and older) lived in long-term care institutions or **collective dwellings** (typically nursing homes and health care facilities). But with increasing age, the proportion of older people in institutions increases significantly, particularly for women. So, while about 2 percent of both men and women aged 65 to 74 live in institutions, this rises to about 6 percent of men and almost 10 percent of women aged 75 to 84, and climbs to 22 percent of men and 35 percent of women among those 85 years of age or older (Turcotte and Schellenberg 2007).

The Decision to Live Alone

The 2006 Census reports that seniors make up 34 percent of all Canadians who live alone (Rea et al. 2008). And the proportion of older people who live alone

---

1. Statistics Canada defines a household as "a person or group of persons who occupy the same dwelling and do not have a usual place of residence elsewhere in Canada" (Statistics Canada 2008a).

increases with age: 22 percent of those aged 65 to 74, 33 percent of those aged 75 to 84, and 34 percent at age 85 or older. Between 1971 and 2001, it was the 85-and-over group that showed the greatest increase in the tendency to live alone (Clark 2002). And for all age categories, the percentage of women who live alone is about double that of men (see Exhibit 11.2).

Women aged 75 to 84 show the greatest tendency to live alone (National Advisory Council on Aging 2006). This, in part, reflects their higher income compared to women in the past and their ability to live independently. Clark (2005, 3) says "that privacy and independence are 'purchased' by those who can afford to do so." Still, for many older people who live alone, the situation is not so positive. For example, 38 percent of seniors who live alone report trouble affording their housing. Other people who live alone report health problems and isolation. The National Advisory Council on Aging (National Advisory Council on Aging 2006) reports that, compared to people who live with a spouse or children, older people who live alone are less likely to be happy. The National Advisory Council on Aging says that seniors who live alone spend more time alone and tend to have low income.

Three things explain this trend toward women living alone. First, women tend to outlive men, leaving many women widowed in old age. In 2001, for example, only 11 percent of senior men, compared to 42 percent of senior women, were widowed. And, compared to widowed men, fewer widowed women remarry (Turcotte and Schellenberg 2007). Second, better government pension plans and subsidized housing make living alone in a private household a viable option for more women today. Older women who live alone make up the largest group in subsidized housing (Blakeney 1992). Community-based health care supports also make it possible for older women with health problems to stay in their own homes, rather than move to a nursing home.

Third, a change in attitudes and values explains this trend. Most older people say they would rather not live with their children (Stevens-Ratchford and Diaz 2003); they prefer the privacy and independence that come with living alone. Bess (1999a) reports that widowed women who live alone benefit from having the support of children and grandchildren living nearby. They also benefit from close connections to friends and neighbours. But most children and their elderly parents today share what Rosenmayr and Kockeis (1963) call "**intimacy at a distance**." Parents and children visit each other, help each other, and keep in touch by phone and e-mail, but most do not live together.

Lin (2005) examined the influence of culture on living arrangements preferences of older Chinese Canadians. Of the 2,053 older respondents in Lin's study, about half said they preferred to live with adult children and half said they did not. Canadian-born Chinese elders in this study tended to prefer living on their own. This group also tended to have a western religion, a higher level of education, and to live alone. They also had a lower level of identification with traditional Chinese cultural values.

Those who preferred to live with their adult children had a higher level of dependence on others for their activities of daily living. However, there was no significant difference between the two groups in physical and mental health, or number of reported illnesses. The study shows that a person's link to traditional culture influences his or her preference for living with adult children. Ng and his colleagues (2007) report a similar finding among South Asian immigrants. This group held to traditional cultural beliefs and practices and tended to live in extended families.

One of the most dramatic changes in living arrangements over the past several decades in Canada has been the increase in the proportion of older people, particularly women, who live alone (Clark 2005; Turcotte and Schellenberg 2007). Wister and Gutman (1997) reported that between 1961 and 1991, the proportion of older women who lived alone more than doubled.

Béland (1987) found that the number of older people in Quebec who lived alone more than tripled between 1956 and 1976, going from 5.6 percent to 19.1 percent. This change corresponded to a drop in the proportion of older people who lived with family members. Béland said that a decrease in the number of children an older person might move in with may account for this trend. He also linked the increase in people living alone to the norms of independence and autonomy.

Hamilton and Brehaut (1992, 8–11) studied 75 single older women in Prince Edward Island who lived alone. These women reported their desire for independence. "I mean, if you're independent," one woman said, "you want to stay independent." Many of the women in this study also reported that they relied on family and friends to support them in their independence. "I feel quite independent," one woman said, "and that's due to my own family's care."

A study at about the same time by Doyle (1994) in British Columbia also found that older women who lived alone enjoyed their freedom. More than 88 percent of these women said that living alone allowed them to do what they want, when they want. Doyle says that these women had cared for others throughout their lives and now enjoyed caring only for themselves, feeling "it's my turn now!" (43).

● Exhibit 11.2

PERCENTAGE OF SENIORS IN SELECTED LIVING ARRANGEMENTS, BY AGE GROUP AND SEX, CANADA, 2001

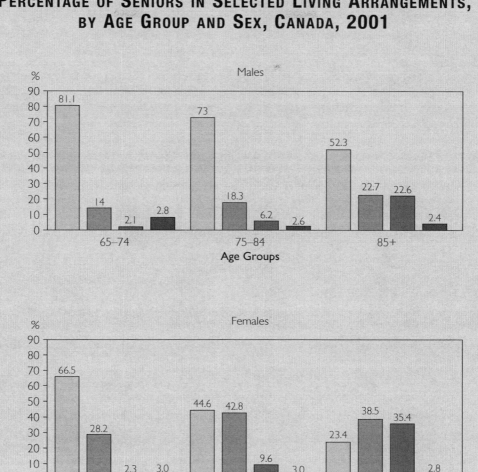

Note that the vast majority of older Canadians live in private households. Most live with family members (spouse or children and grandchildren) or on their own. And, in all age groups, more men than women live with a spouse. The percentage of women who live alone in all age groups is about double that of men. Few older people under the age of 85 live in institutions. However, the numbers increase significantly for those 85 and older, particularly for women.

Source: Adapted from M. Turcotte and G. Schellenberg, 2006, *A Portrait of Seniors in Canada,* Table 4.1.2, p. 191. Statistics Canada Cat. No. 89-519. Reprinted with permission from Statistics Canada.

This trend toward more older people, particularly women, living alone has policy implications. The Canada Mortgage and Housing Corporation (CMHC) says a person has **core housing need** if the housing is too small or in poor repair, or if the household spends more than 30 percent of its total income on housing (CMHC 2005a). CMHC (2002a) reports that 38 percent of women aged 65 and over who live alone have core housing need. This figure jumps to 55 percent of senior women who live alone in rented housing. CMHC says that "the incidence of core housing need for these female-led households was higher than that for male-led households. The central difficulty in female one-person households appears to be income, as the household incomes of each of these groups were well below the average for all comparable households" (7).

Unmarried older people also have smaller support networks than married people, and they rely more on formal health care services (such as home care) than do married couples (Connidis 2001). Those who live alone may also neglect their health. In a U.S. study, Sharkey and Schoenberg (2002) found that older women who lived alone were at an increased risk for poor nutrition.

More single older people living alone will increase the demand for suitable apartment housing and better public transportation. Many older people who live alone will need housing alternatives such as supportive housing and home-sharing programs.

TYPES OF HOUSING

Single-Family Houses

The 2006 Census reports that the majority of Canadian families with a head aged 65 or older owned their own home (Rea, MacKay, and LeVasseur 2008). And a majority (60 percent) of older homeowners live mortgage free (Chawla and Wannell 2004). Even among the oldest old (those 85 and older), more than half (53 percent) own their own homes mortgage free (Turcotte and Schellenberg 2007). Most homeowners want to stay in their own homes after they retire (Lin 2005).

Home ownership differs across the country. Of all the provinces and territories, the Northwest Territories has the lowest proportion of seniors who own homes: 34 percent of those aged 65 to 74, and 42 percent of people aged 75 and over. Compared with the other provinces, Newfoundland has the highest proportion of homeowners among its seniors. Eighty-eight percent of people aged 65 to 74 and 83 percent of people aged 75 and over own their own homes. Seniors have a higher

proportion of condominium ownership than any other age group. Almost 9 percent of seniors lived in condominiums compared to 5 percent of people aged 45 to 64. People who live alone or couples without children find condominiums a good housing option because they offer an affordable alternative to a single-family home (CMHC 2005a; Lo 1996).

Most older homeowners take good care of their houses. Only about 6 percent of families with a head aged 65 and over say their houses need major repairs. About 83 percent say their houses need only regular maintenance (Lindsay 1999).

Older men, more often than older women, tend to live in single-family houses. A woman often has to move out of a single-family home as she ages. First, when her husband dies she may have less money to spend on housing. Increased heating costs, maintenance, and taxes can all force a woman to sell her home and move into an apartment. "If I had the money, I would gladly stay here for the rest of my days," a woman in Prince Edward Island said, "but now that he's gone it's going to be a burden" (Hamilton and Brehaut 1992, 19). Another woman told Hamilton and Brehaut (1992, 21): "I don't heat all the house in the winter. I close all but one bedroom in the winter time and the bathroom. And I don't heat my dining room ... because your oil is so expensive and can't heat it all."

Second, older women give up their homes because they tend to know less about how to care for a home. Older women say they lack knowledge about repairs, lack experience hiring trades people, and can't afford to hire people to do the work (Hamilton and Brehaut 1992).

Even though the majority of people prefer to age in place, they do perceive barriers to growing old in their own home. Wagnild (2001) asked 776 older Americans (ages 55 to 93) about aging in place. Almost 70 percent of the people in the study wanted to grow old in their current home for the following reasons: (1) feelings of independence and control, (2) feelings of safety and security, (3) being near family, and (4) feeling familiar with their surroundings. They reported the following barriers to aging in place: (1) illness (2) inability to maintain the property, and (3) inadequate finances. And although the intention of most respondents was to stay in their own home as they aged, many people had not made plans to achieve this goal.

The Canadian government has studied ways to help older people age in place. For example, CMHC (2006a) explored the option of converting single-family housing into multiple units to allow seniors to rent out part of their home and remain in place for more years. CMHC (2008b, 2008b) has also explored strategies for making physical adaptations to seniors' single-family houses.

Some seniors move to a smaller home. Between 1999 and 2001, 43 percent of older people who moved did so to a smaller home (Lin 2005). Compared to people under age 65, seniors tend to downsize when they move. They also tend to move from a house to an apartment or condominium. Older seniors (those 85 and over) tend to favour apartments over houses. Lin (2005) says that "older seniors may trade their houses for apartments to reduce home maintenance costs or the amount of work it takes to keep up a home with a driveway, backyard and all their associated chores" (25).

When older people move from their home to a smaller house or apartment, they sometimes hire a professional organizer to help them downsize their possessions (see Exhibit 11.3). But most often it is family members, typically adult children, who get involved in the management and disposal of family possessions. Ekerdt and Sergeant (2006) found that, compared to the parents, adult children felt less attached to their parents' possessions and less concerned with their disposal. Some adult children could not say what had become of many things.

Typically, as part of the disbanding process, the adult children divide the items that their parents have to leave behind. Meaningful objects go to family members, some items are sold or donated; others are thrown away. Family photographs were among the most cherished of the family possessions and these most often moved with the parents (Ekerdt and Sergeant 2006).

Tax and Home Maintenance Programs

Older homeowners without mortgages live rent free, so they should have the most financial assets and they should have the least trouble paying for housing; however, many older people have trouble maintaining their homes. They own large, older houses—most of them single-family, detached—that cost a high proportion of the owner's income to heat and maintain.

The federal government and the provinces help older homeowners through grants, loans, and tax rebates. British Columbia, for example, allows seniors who have lived in the province for at least one year to defer payment of property taxes until they sell their home. At that time, they pay the outstanding taxes with interest (at below-market rates) from the money they get for their home.

The federal government's **Residential Rehabilitation Assistance Program (RRAP)** offers loans to homeowners of up to $16,000 for people who live in southern Canada and $24,000 for people who live in far northern areas. Landlords can receive between $24,000 and $36,000 depending on a house's location. These loans help home-owners and landlords improve run-down housing. The government will forgive these loans if an owner remains in the home during the "loan forgiveness period" (which can be up to five years), and if a landlord does not increase rent after repairs have been completed (CMHC 2009). This program also provides forgivable loans to convert existing housing into self-contained units. These suites provide housing for low-income seniors or adults with disabilities.

The government also grants forgivable loans to landlords and homeowners to adapt a building to seniors' needs. The loans cover costs up to $3,500. Improvements include additional handrails, lever handles on doors, bathtub grab bars and seats, walk-in showers, and easy-to-reach storage areas. CMHC (2009) calls this the Home Adaptations for Seniors' Independence (HASI) program. The National Advisory Council on Aging (2002b) proposes that the federal government increase this amount to $25,000 (part loan and part grant) to encourage the development of more housing for seniors.

Some provinces also sponsor home repair programs that offer low-interest and forgivable loans to low-income older people. Many provinces also offer older people a rebate or tax credit on school property tax. Programs tend to focus on the neediest cases and on people with health or safety needs. Alternative types of home ownership are also available that can help make housing more affordable for seniors in Canada (see Exhibit 11.4).

Programs focus on the neediest cases and on people with health or safety needs. Dunn (1997) reported that during the 1990s the federal government capped growth on social housing costs. It also reduced its commitment to new housing, including RRAP programs. These cuts limited housing supports at a time when the number of older people in the community continued to grow. However, in 2001, the federal government increased its funding to some select housing initiatives, including RRAP and other repair and renovation programs (Dupuis 2003). And between 2001 and 2007, government funding for renovation programs, including the Residential Rehabilitation Assistance Program (RRAP) and the Home Adaptations for Seniors Independence Program (HASI), increased each year (CMHC 2008e).

Home Adaptation

Studies show that the proportion of people with disabilities increases with age. Most older people in private households report some limitations in mobility (walking and carrying) and agility (bending and stretching).

● **Exhibit 11.3**

HELPING MOM AND DAD TAKE THE PLUNGE: "THEY SAY, 'IT'S TOO BIG OF A JOB. MAYBE I SHOULD JUST DIE HERE.'"

As a home-stager in Toronto's thriving real estate market for several years, Marsha Silverberg was accustomed to uncovering gracious houses hidden behind the accumulations of a lifetime: the little boys' hockey skates dating back to Bobby Orr's playing days, layers of nearly fossilized wallpaper, and complete sets of treasured china.

But at the centre of it all, she often found, was an apprehensive senior reluctant to leave the house.

For the most part, Ms. Silverberg was not daunted by the piles of detritus or outmoded decorating. "I saw past all that and focused on the senior citizens themselves."

More recently, she has focused her home-staging business, Richmond Hill-based Marsha's Helping Hand, on a specialized portion of the real estate market. She works with elderly people who are making the move to a smaller house, condominium, retirement residence or nursing home. "I noticed a common link—they were frightened and over-whelmed," she says of the homeowners she has encountered. "Their emotions were not their own."

In some cases, the elderly client has children too busy to help, or has recently lost a husband or wife. To them, the house represents their comfort and security, their identity and history.

She becomes the organizer, the shrink and the physical labourer.

Ms. Silverberg is a baby boomer herself, so she understands, she says, that people of her generation are all too busy with their own lives to spend that much time with their parents.

"I'm the daughter or daughter-in-law they don't have."

She says the elderly feel defeated by the prospect of sorting through all of their belongings. Just pushing the hangers aside to sort through clothes in the closet may take more effort than some are able to muster.

They don't know how to choose which items or pieces of furniture to take to the new space, and they worry that possessions will be broken in the move.

"It's a U-Haul of a whole lifetime that has to go somewhere." …

"We live in a world of decluttering. When I go in, I'm not really passing things on. Nobody wants it."

Ms. Silverberg is adept at sizing up the new dwelling, which could be a smaller house or—in about 90 per cent of cases—a retirement home. She can quickly decide which pieces of furniture will fit and be the most useful.

Once the merchandise is sorted, she enlists the homeowner's help in holding a contents sale or calls in dealers to buy up the vintage furniture and pieces.

"They come in and offer money so [the home-owners] get a little bit excited," she says. "I get them really involved in the project. I try to boost their morale."

Consignment shops will often buy the clothing—especially the very expensive pieces she finds hidden away in closets.

"There are many, many specialized vintage places that love to get their hands on this stuff."

Ms. Silverberg gets into the basements and attics herself—often donning gloves and a mask to sort through every box and cupboard.

Photos, tea pots, tea cups and sentimental gifts are often the possessions that hold the greatest resonance. "I know how to listen for their favourite things. I make sure it's sitting right where they see it as soon as they walk in."

Source: Carolyn Leitch. *The Globe and Mail,* October 19, 2007, G1. Reprinted with permission.

Because climbing stairs can become difficult, some people close off the upstairs of their home and live only in the downstairs rooms (Hamilton and Brehaut 1992). Others move to housing with only one floor (CMHC 2008a). People who want to age in place may need to adapt their current housing to support independent living. In the mid-1990s, Fox (1995) reviewed findings from the Canadian Health and Disability Survey of people aged 55 and over. She found that about 38 percent of disabled older people needed at least one design change to their homes. People with higher incomes had a greater likelihood of making this change.

● **Exhibit 11.4**

ALTERNATIVE TYPES OF HOUSING

The Canada Mortgage and Housing Corporation (CMHC) studied five alternative types of ownership for seniors' housing—life leases, equity co-ops, leaseholds, shared equity, and cohousing. These alternatives can help make housing for seniors more affordable. A CMHC report describes each of these options.

Life Leases. A life lease allows a person to live in a dwelling for life in exchange for an entrance fee (a one-time payment, usually about 30 percent of the total cost of the unit). Residents also pay a monthly payment to cover project maintenance and operating costs (CMHC 2008f). Nonprofit community groups such as service clubs often sponsor life-lease projects. These groups often help with the ongoing management and operation of the project.

Life-lease projects admit people aged 55 and over. The first projects opened in Manitoba and Saskatchewan in the 1980s. About 200 life-lease projects exist in Canada today, most of them in Ontario and Manitoba (Mancer 2003). No life-lease projects exist east of Ontario. The Manitoba government has enacted legislation that protects the investment of seniors in life-lease housing. Other provinces, such as British Columbia, apply other real estate legislation to life-lease projects. Life-lease projects allow residents to recover all or part of their payment when they leave the project.

Equity Co-ops. Members finance an equity co-op housing development. They use no government subsidies to finance their project. This type of housing began in the late 1980s. Eighteen equity co-ops exist in Canada—all of them in B.C., Alberta, and Quebec. Two-thirds of these equity co-ops serve the 55-and-over housing market. This housing option works best where each owner has responsibility for his or her unit only (a condominium arrangement). That way, if one member defaults, the other members are not responsible for the debt. This arrangement has encouraged the development of equity co-ops in Alberta and Quebec.

Leaseholds. A leasehold gives a tenant rights to the use of the property, but the landlord holds ownership of the property. The property goes back to the landlord when the lease ends. Local governments often use the leasehold option to develop affordable housing for groups such as seniors. The land still belongs to the government, so that it can redefine the use of the land in the future. Private-sector retirement communities also use the leasehold method. Leaseholds can lower housing costs because the landlord pays for and owns the land. The tenant then gets higher-quality housing for a lower cost (but has to give up the housing at the end of the lease).

Shared Equity. Shared equity offers another form of co-op housing. It provides affordable housing to lower-income seniors. These programs often take place in the inner city. Buyers can earn equity in their homes over a period of time. They can get this equity through a good payment record and by taking part in managing their project. CMHC says that co-op members report extreme satisfaction with this type of housing. This stable housing option has allowed some people to move from social assistance to employment.

Cohousing. Cohousing refers to Collaborative Housing. People in this type of housing have their own self-contained unit, but share common areas such as a kitchen, laundry room, and guest rooms for visitors. Only five of these projects exist in Canada—four in B.C. and one in Ontario. People who choose this option report satisfaction with their choice.

Most people in these alternate types of housing say they feel very satisfied with their choice. They especially felt a strong sense of community. In some cases the housing alternative allows them to own a home even though they may have a low income.

Source: Adapted from Canada Mortgage and Housing Corporation, 2003, "Alternate Tenure Arrangements," *Socio-Economic Highlight*, 65, http://www.cmhc-schl.gc.ca/publications/en/rh-pr/socio/socio065.pdf, accessed May 7, 2009. Reprinted with the consent of CMHC. All other uses and reproductions of this material are expressly prohibited.

Sorcinelli and her colleagues (2007) asked community-dwelling seniors to evaluate a home hazard checklist, *The Safe Living Guide: A Guide to Home Safety for Seniors* (Health Canada 2003). This checklist alerts seniors to potential safety risks in their home and encourages them to take an active role in locating and correcting the problems. The checklist includes items such as (1) seeing that there is an outside entrance-way light, (2) checking that all major appliances are grounded with three-pronged plugs, (3) being sure there is a smoke detector on every floor of the house, and (4) seeing there is a telephone in the basement. The seniors said that the checklist helped them identify hazards around their home. They also felt the checklist would increase seniors' awareness of home safety risks.

CMHC says that private and nonprofit housing companies have responded to older people's needs. Housing adaptation can take many forms. **Universal design**, for example, aims to serve people of all ages. Designers use lever door handles, low-threshold tubs, and temperature limits on hot water tanks to make life easier for older people. These features also meet the needs of children and people with disabilities. Companies use two strategies to adapt homes for older people (CMHC 2008b, 1): "first, adding assistive devices and other technical equipment and second, modifying rooms and areas such as hallways and entrances."

Geneviève Vachon and Carole Després at the École d'architecture of the Université Laval examined the home adaptation needs of frail older people in Quebec City (CMHC 2008b). They found that the most common modifications involved redesigning bathrooms and kitchens. Bathroom adaptations included adding a walk-in shower, installing grab bars, and widening the door entry. Kitchen modifications included lowering counters and cabinets for better access, and putting easy-to-grasp handles on shelves and drawers. Other adaptations improved outside access (such as installing an outside platform lift for better access to the yard) and improved movement inside the home (by widening doorways between rooms).

The older people surveyed said the home modifications made them feel safer in their homes and less confined indoors. They particularly appreciated the bathroom adaptations. The changes allowed them to maintain their dignity and privacy. All of the people in this study said the house modifications improved their comfort and quality of life. The growing desire of older people to age in place will increase the demand for housing adaptations. Housing adaptations will allow people to remain in their homes – safely, comfortably, and independently – for as long as possible (CMHC 2008a).

Life-span housing, an approach begun in Norway, puts all essential rooms (the living room, dining room, kitchen, and bathroom) on the ground floor. The United States calls it "universal housing" and the United Kingdom refers to it as "Lifetime Homes." Canada uses the term "**FlexHousing**" (CMHC 2008g). This type of housing has no thresholds or steps, provides easy access to all rooms of the house, and can

adapt to the needs of a person in a wheelchair. Details include easy-to-reach light switches and sockets, accessible furniture, non-slip flooring, and kitchen cabinets and appliances that can move up and down as needed on a wall bracket.

FlexHousing is based on four principles: adaptability, accessibility, affordability, and healthy housing (energy and resource efficiency) (CMHC 2003d). Older people can stay in their homes longer because a FlexHouse adapts to the older person's needs at a reasonable cost. The home can change again to meet the needs of a younger family when the older person sells the home.

Reverse Mortgages

Some older homeowners are asset rich but cash poor. A person may have $150,000 in equity in his or her home but be unable to pay the gas or water bill. A reverse mortgage allows older homeowners to draw on between 20 to 30 percent of the equity in their home (CMHC 2008h). They can use this money for daily expenses, home repairs, or other needs. Usually the loan and interest on the loan do not have to be repaid until the homeowner sells the house or dies.

Several types of reverse mortgages exist. The most common plan is called the **Reverse Annuity Mortgage (RAM)**. In this plan an older person uses the house to secure a loan from a bank. The person then buys a lifetime annuity from an insurance company with the loan. The insurance company pays the bank interest on the loan and pays the older person a set amount to live on for life. The older person can stay in the home as long as he or she wants. The bank takes over the house when the last survivor of a couple dies. This plan has at least one major limitation; the interest payments to the bank will increase if interest rates rise, thus reducing the older person's income.

Not everyone will benefit from a reverse mortgage. In one model, for example, a reverse mortgage can add interest charges of 25 to 40 percent to the original loan. A $55,000 loan could pay a 70-year-old single man almost $6,000 per year as an annuity (a yearly payment for life). This would amount to about $90,000 over 15 years. But at 11 percent interest, the RAM over 15 years would produce a debt of just over $274,000. The loan company would deduct this money from the sale of the house. In other words, the RAM would cost $274,000 less the $90,000 paid out, or about $184,000.

Some people will agree to this cost, choosing to have more money now. Other people will find the cost too high and may want to leave the full value of their home to their children. Many financial advisers believe that reverse mortgages should be used as a last resort. People need to fully understand the benefits and the costs of RAMs so that they can make informed decisions.

Apartment Living

Apartment living tends to follow a U-shaped path over time. Adults aged 25 and under tend to rent apartments. Then the rental rate drops in middle age and rises again in later life (after age 60 or so) (CHMC 2006b). CHMC (2002c) reports that in 1996, 42 percent of seniors who lived in senior-led households lived in multiple dwellings (including apartments, semi-detached houses, row houses, and apartments in duplexes). This figure increases to 48 percent among people aged 75 and over.

The 2001 Census reports that about 30 percent of seniors live in apartment buildings (Clark 2005). About 9 percent of men and 18 percent of women aged 65 to 74 and about 14 percent of men and 25 percent of women aged 75 and over live in high-rise apartment buildings (i.e., five or more storeys) (Lin 2005; Wister and Gutman 1997). Older people often choose to move into an apartment when they can no longer care for a house, or when they need improved accessibility because of mobility limitations (Clark 2005).

People with good incomes can choose from a wide range of apartments: a high-rise or a low-rise, a two-bedroom suite with a balcony and a view, or an apartment near a bus route and shopping. A relatively new housing option, the "**mingle apartment**," exists in large urban centres like Edmonton and Toronto. This type of dwelling provides "two, independent, two-bedroom suites that share a common entry, kitchen and combined living and dining area" (CMHC 2008a, 6). Mingle apartments offer older people independence and privacy, in a shared living environment.

Some older renters, however, have fewer options. Many people move to rental housing because they have low incomes. CHMC (2002c) reports that seniors who rented their housing made up 64 percent of senior-led households with core housing need. And renters make up 70 percent of senior-led households that report affordability need (CHMC 2005a). Lo and Gauthier (1995) say that 85 percent of older people with affordability problems received government payments as their main source of income, showing that many older people need rent support to ease the burden of housing costs.

Most of the provinces, along with the federal government, offer aid to renters in low-income housing. These programs keep a person's rent at or below 30 percent of his or her income. Some provinces offer **shelter allowances** to older people. British Columbia,

for example, sponsors a program called Shelter Aid for Elderly Renters (SAFER). The program provides help with rent to low- and middle-income seniors age 60 and older (National Advisory Council on Aging 2002b, also see BC Housing 2008). Shelter allowances subsidize the person, not the housing project. They allow older people to choose their own apartment from those available in the marketplace. This policy frees people from having to move into government housing. As of April 2008, SAFER subsidies had been paid to more than 15,000 senior renters in British Columbia.

Supportive and Enriched Housing

Most provinces have built supportive housing. Some years ago, Ontario took the lead in supportive housing for older people in need. CMHC (2005b, 1) defines **supportive housing** as "a range of housing options designed to accommodate the needs of seniors through design features, housing management, and access to support services." Supportive housing encompasses many and varied types of housing. Supportive housing provides a secure, safe, and home-like environment. It offers support services (i.e. housekeeping, meals, etc.), and social and recreational activities (Health Canada 2006). Both the public, nonprofit organizations, and the private sector can provide supportive housing.

One end of the "supportive housing" continuum gives people more social and health care support than they get in a normal apartment building. These dwellings suit people who need minimal to moderate support services such as Meals on Wheels, housekeeping, laundry, monitoring, and emergency response. These support services allow the older person to live independently (Ontario Ministry of Health and Long-Term Care 2004).

The term "**enriched housing**" can apply to many types of housing. In Canada, it ranges from converted hotels that offer rooms and hot meals for single men to campus-like settings with high- and low-rise housing and many levels of health care. Sometimes enrichment means only a lounge with a television set in an apartment building. More elaborate enriched housing includes lounges, shops, and, in some cases, clinics. Some buildings employ activity workers and program planners who show films and organize exercise programs and field trips for residents. Most enriched housing also includes communal facilities such as a dining room and laundry rooms. This type of housing provides social support services, safety, and a sense of community (CMHC 2005a). Even something as simple as being able to see a natural landscape from the apartment window has health benefits for older people (i.e., lowering blood pressure and heart rate) (Tang and Brown 2005).

At the other end of the "supportive housing" continuum are housing options and services designed for those with more significant care needs. This type of housing is often referred to as **assisted living**. It provides personal care services to frail seniors to help them live independently in the community. This type of supportive housing is well suited to older seniors (aged 75 and over) with moderate to severe disabilities (National Advisory Council on Aging 2002b). Support for tenants with dementia, for example, may include social services (provided by local agencies) and education for staff and other tenants (Schiff and Gnaedinger 1997). Assisted living can help some seniors stay out of nursing homes (Health Canada 2006).

Supportive housing can take many forms, from bungalows to high-rise apartments. CMHC says that supportive housing should have five characteristics: (1) it should look and feel residential; (2) the physical environment should support seniors' needs; (3) it should offer access to needed services; (4) management should have a progressive philosophy; and (5) it should offer choice at a reasonable cost (Davis et al. 2000; Health Canada 2006). The goal of supportive housing is "to provide Canadian seniors with an intermediate housing alternative, between living alone without supports (staying at home) and the heavily regulated environment of institutional care" (CMHC 2005b, 1).

One tenant in Sydney, Nova Scotia, said about her supportive housing unit, "It's like home. I have my own bedroom and furniture. My family doesn't have to worry." A resident in a Montreal high-rise complex said, "Everyone helps each other even if it means going to the corner store to buy a loaf of bread for someone" (Davis et al. 2000, 24–25).

Alberta has a system of lodges run by senior citizen foundations (Alberta Seniors and Community Supports 2008). These lodges house from 15 to 122 people. A person in a lodge has his or her own living space, but shares space for meals and recreation. Residents may also share bathroom space. Lodges do not provide nursing care but do provide meals, laundry services, and housekeeping to residents. Lodge residents get home care services as they would if they lived in a single-family home or apartment. As a protection for low-income residents, lodge management must ensure that every older resident (65 years of age and older) has at least $265 of disposable income remaining each month, after paying lodge rent, to use for personal needs. Lodges provide older people with the freedom to live on their own and the supports they need to cope with decreased abilities.

Critics of enriched housing say that it can lead to early dependency by giving people too many services and that it attracts sick or less-able people. But studies have found more benefits than drawbacks to this kind of housing. Early work by Lawton (1976) found that people in enriched housing reported high morale and high life satisfaction. He said that proper planning discourages dependence. In some cases, enriched housing can even foster independence, because it allows individuals to live on their own rather than in institutions. For example, an alarm system for each apartment gives people a sense of security and can save a person's life in an emergency. And something as simple as "I'm okay" signs for door knobs in apartment buildings encourages neighbourliness. Enriched housing offers an important alternative to people who need support but who do not need the high levels of care given in a nursing home or hospital.

For all its benefits, enriched housing can lead to unique problems. For example, the average age of residents increases over time as residents age in place. Some buildings that began with a mixture of age groups among residents 10 or 15 years ago now house a markedly older group, whose average age is 80 or older. This may compromise the self-government that exists in these buildings. Enriched housing complexes could become high-rise nursing homes over time.

Wister and Gutman (1997, 31) reported that the government built many apartment buildings during the 1960s and 1970s for "shelter only." These buildings contained mostly bachelor apartments with few amenities. Today, these buildings contain many very old and frail people. The emphasis on community care tends to keep them in the community, but these buildings and their apartments no longer suit tenants' needs. And many of these buildings lack space to allow for communal kitchens and other amenities. Wister and Gutman (1997, 32) said, "It is unrealistic to think that a project can offer only shelter." These buildings should also provide support services and flexible design.

Apartment housing comes in many packages: high-rise, low-rise, public, private, age-segregated, age-integrated, without services, or enriched with services. Older people need this variety because their needs and abilities differ. They also need tax rebates, shelter allowances, and subsidized housing so that they can freely choose the housing that best suits their needs. Appropriate housing design can also help people stay in their apartments or homes even if they lose some abilities.

Well-designed apartment buildings include space for meetings, lounges, coffee shops, places of worship, greenhouses, beauty parlours, and exercise rooms. Apartment housing in the past often ignored these needs, but some new buildings now include extra public space. They also include recreation and entertainment programs that help people use the space. Apartment residents also benefit from easy access to public transportation and downtown services.

Housing in Rural Communities

Seniors living in rural communities have special housing needs. About 23 percent of older people in Canada live in rural settings and another 8 percent in small towns or communities (Turcotte and Schellenberg 2007). The populations of many rural communities is aging (CMHC 2003a), and these communities have an increased need for affordable housing with services and amenities. Compared to urban senior households, rural senior households tend to have lower-than-average incomes (CMHC 2003a). And while they have slightly lower costs for housing, they face higher home maintenance, utility, and transportation costs. Rural areas also vary in their proximity to urban centres, and in the availability of adequate housing and social services (for example, health care services and home care support).

While most older people in rural communities (82 percent) own their own home (CMHC 2003a), the small number of older people in these communities limits the variety of housing options available. For example, few rental options exist in rural settings (CMHC 2003a), and older people who rent their homes often face severe affordability problems. While rural communities often have support programs and services for frail older people, they lack a range of options for older people who have varied needs for supports.

Zimmer and Chappell (1997) studied urban and rural older people in Manitoba. They found that both groups of older people valued three types of neighbourhood amenities: necessities (e.g., bank or food nearby); social interaction (e.g., friend or senior centre nearby); and life enrichment (e.g., park or library nearby). Rural older people, more often than urban older people, ranked social interaction as very important.

Keating (1991) reviewed the literature on rural older people in Canada. She found that, compared with all older people, rural seniors tended to live in older homes, had fewer services such as hot and cold running water and an indoor toilet, and faced high maintenance costs. At about the same time, Joseph and Martin-Matthews (1993) reported that rural households often lacked housing basics such as piped water or amenities such as freezers and cars. The poorer the province, the more likely rural older people lived in poor conditions. Elders on Aboriginal reserves had some of the poorest facilities.

Keating concluded that "rural elders are ... badly served. By all objective measures, rural elders have fewer amenities in their near environments than do their urban counterparts" (Keating 1991, 47).

A more recent report on the housing needs of low-income seniors in rural communities (CMHC 2003a; 2003b) finds little improvement in their condition. Many rural dwellings need repair, seniors have limited choice of rental housing, and supportive housing has long waiting lists. Aboriginal seniors in the rural North, in particular, face high costs, overcrowding, isolation, and an acute lack of housing options. The report concludes that in rural areas "the shortage of affordable, quality housing for low-income [senior] households is a major challenge" (CMHC 2003b, 5).

ALTERNATIVE IDEAS IN HOUSING

Garden Suites

In the early 1980s, Connidis (1983a, 361, 363) asked 400 older people in an Ontario community a simple question: "If circumstances were to change and you had to choose between living with a child or in a facility for seniors, which would you prefer?" She found an "overwhelming tendency to choose a facility for seniors rather than living with children." And still today, most older people do not want to move in with their children. The design of modern houses may explain part of the reason that most older people do not choose to live with their adult children; most modern houses have no room for another kitchen, bedroom, or bathroom to accommodate an aging parent.

In Australia, the state of Victoria created a housing option for older people that overcomes the problems of modern house design. They call this alternative a **granny flat**. It consists of a portable modular cottage for a parent. The government arranges to move the cottage onto a son's or daughter's property, then the government connects the flat to the electricity, sewer, water, and telephone services of the house. When the older person dies or moves to a nursing home, or if the family moves, the government takes the cottage away. This plan allows children to care for their parents as long as they can.

Canada developed a version of the granny flat known as the **garden suite**. These units allow older Canadians to live near, but not with, their children (CMHC 2008c). In Canada, a garden suite most often exists as a separate building on the child's property, although some families convert a garage to serve as a garden suite. This building sits in the backyard and uses the utilities attached to the child's home. A recent CMHC survey (2008a) found that 23 percent of older homeowners (55 years of age and older) would consider installing a garden suite on their property or creating an additional suite in their home to accommodate a family member. More than half of all older Canadians (44 percent of those 55 and older) would consider living in such accommodations.

There are pros and cons to creating garden suites (CMHC 2008c). Garden suites cost relatively little; they allow the older person to live independently in the community, with informal support nearby. They also allow an older homeowner to sell his or her house and free up money for living expenses. Garden suites may work best in rural areas where seniors have fewer housing options.

Garden suites need to overcome some barriers before they will gain general acceptance. Some locations put families through a lengthy approval process, and neighbours may object to a garden suite located in the backyard next door. Finally, homes with little land make installation a challenge.

Garden suites will suit only families where the adult children own a home with the space to locate the building. And when a family does agree to set up a flat, the family—parents and children—need to talk about what they expect from one another. Still, garden suites offer a unique option to older people and their families.

Garden suites and other innovative housing arrangements will lead to new social interdependencies and new challenges to family relations. What will happen if the older person's child separates from or divorces his or her spouse? Or what if the adult child moves to another city? Studies of these options will have to show that they make social as well as financial sense, and trial projects can answer only some of these questions; longer-term studies will show whether garden suites can work in Canada.

HOMELESSNESS

Homeless older people stand at the far end of the housing continuum. They often live on the street and use shelters for night-time rest and some meals. Some homeless people live in rural communities, although homelessness in rural areas is less visible than in urban centres (CMHC 2003a). Researchers consider homeless people over age 50 as seniors. Homelessness creates stress and leads to a poor diet and untreated health problems.

A CMHC report (2003b, 1) says that "homelessness results in premature aging, with those at 50 looking and acting 10 to 20 years older." Homelessness also leads to lower life expectancy.

In 2002–03, two researchers studied homeless older people in Quebec, Ontario, Manitoba, British Columbia, and Yukon for CMHC (CMHC 2003b). They found that people aged 50 and over make up 20 to 30 percent of homeless people who use shelters. Many of these people suffer from alcoholism and drug addiction. They also show a high rate of dementia, stroke, heart conditions, and incontinence. The researchers say that drug addiction leads to other problems such as hepatitis C, HIV/ AIDS, and brain damage.

In a review of the literature, McDonald and her colleagues (2007) report that more older men than older women are homeless. Compared to women, older men become homeless earlier in life, and so spend more years living on the street. Compared to younger homeless people, older homeless people tend to be more socially isolated and to have minimal contact with their families. They also tend to have poorer physical and mental health than the older population in general, higher rates of alcohol abuse, and multiple health problems.

In a study of 68 older homeless adults in Toronto, McDonald and her colleagues (2007) compared recent homeless older people (those homeless after the age of 50) with those who were homeless over a longer time (homeless before the age of 50). They found that (1) compared to women, more men were homeless; (2) more women than men became homeless after the age of 50, and (3) more than half of the homeless people were immigrants to Canada. The long-term homeless, on average, became homeless at age 38; the recent homeless at age 57.

The recent homeless identified their friends as their social support while the long-term homeless were more likely to name social service providers as their social contacts. Further, compared to the recently homeless, long-term homeless older people found ways to reduce their presence on the street. This included using more social services and shelters. Recently homeless older people used fewer services and noted barriers to health care service use. "It seems fairly clear," McDonald and her colleagues say, "that the housing issues vary between the two sub-groups and require different approaches. Certainly, affordable housing is needed to address homelessness in general, but we would argue that interventions to find housing for the recent older homeless should be swift and immediate and would be one of the first priorities of intervention in order to prevent entrenchment in street life" (40).

Shelters for the homeless often don't meet the needs of older homeless people. For example, shelters cannot offer help with activities of daily living or the need for bed rest. Also, many shelters cannot meet the needs of people with mobility problems. But the limited number of nursing home and hospital beds leaves shelters as the only option. Many homeless older people also have antisocial behaviour (such as poor hygiene and the use of foul language) that makes it hard to move them to other care settings.

Supportive housing and assisted living programs sometimes serve homeless seniors. These programs provide a room, meal services, recreation, and health care programs. They do not offer 24-hour nursing care. Many professionals who serve older people say that downtown locations would serve this type of senior best. A downtown setting puts them close to day-care programs, food services, and health care centres. These settings would support healthy aging, reduce harm, and provide client-centred care.

CMHC (2003b) presents a case study of a shelter that supports the needs of homeless seniors. Fairway Woods serves homeless older people in a 32-apartment housing project. The project, in suburban Langford, British Columbia, near Victoria serves as a model of successful supportive housing for homeless seniors (CMHC 2007). In 2006–07, a study of the Fairway Woods site found that 75 percent of the tenants were men, most between the ages of 55 and 64. Tenants at Fairway Woods had previously lived in shelters, a detoxification facility, substandard housing, and other social housing projects. Most of the tenants had multiple physical and mental health problems and addictions.

The majority of the tenants rated their quality of life as good, and their living arrangements as good or excellent. Prior to living at Fairway Woods, many of the tenants said they felt "anxious," "angry," "isolated," and "stuck" most of the time. Since coming to Fairway Woods, they felt they lived more stable lives. While their problems had not all gone, they felt "relieved," "more secure," and "more confident." They also felt better able to cope with life (CMHC 2007, 4). Tenants noted that Fairway Woods provided a quiet, predictable, socially supportive, and convenient setting. It provided meals where tenants ate together each day and easy access to shops and services. Residents also appreciated the support given by full-time staff. One tenant said, "I'm living happily every after." Another said, "Many have had rough lives; now we're in smoother waters" (CMHC 2007, 4).

TRANSPORTATION

A home has to suit an older person's abilities and meet his or her needs, but a house or an apartment can become a prison if the older person cannot get to services, friends, and recreation. The National Council on Aging (2006, 46) says that "the ability to drive a vehicle, and/or the availability of other transportation alternatives are critical for seniors to have access to services, recreation and to enjoy social contact." The National Advisory Council on Aging sees available transportation as key to health and well-being in later life.

Older people themselves identify transportation as one of the primary issues that affects their quality of life (Bryant et al. 2004). They feel that good public transportation can help seniors avoid loneliness and isolation. Those who live alone, the recently widowed, and people with chronic health problems all benefit from good public transportation. Older people with mobility problems require good public transportation to access needed services.

Public Transportation

Only a few studies have looked at the transportation needs and use patterns of older people in Canada (Dupuis et al. 2007, Turcotte 2006). Most of these studies report that the majority of older people have access to private or public transportation. In 2005, 95 percent of women aged 65 to 74, and 98 percent of men the same age had access to a vehicle or to public transportation. Even among seniors age 85 and older, 86 percent have access to a car or public transit.

Those who own a car and have a driver's license, or who can afford to take taxis, have an easier time meeting their transportation needs (Turcotte 2006). People who rely on family or friends for transport often feel they cannot meet their transportation needs (Cvitkovich and Wister 2001).

Public transportation does not meet the needs of many seniors—particularly older women and those who live alone. Compared to older men, older women tend to be more disadvantaged in their access to both private and public transportation. Dupuis and her colleagues (2007) find that older women are three times more likely than older men to have unmet transportation needs. Older women in poor health and with few financial resources report the most transportation problems.

Rural and urban seniors have different transportation problems. Seniors in cities see good public transportation as a necessary link to social networks and recreational activities (Bryant et al. 2004). Seniors in cities need convenient and safe bus stops and subway stations. They also need barrier-free transportation (e.g., buses without high steps, wheelchair access on trains, etc.).

People in the suburbs face other problems. Rigid bus routes and schedules make it hard for older people in the suburbs to travel. In the winter, long waits for buses, icy sidewalks, or snow mounds at bus stops keep people housebound. Rural areas often lack public transportation (Turcotte 2006).

People in rural areas rely heavily on cars and trucks. Small towns often lack other forms of transport and people often live far from friends and shopping. Statistics Canada reports that almost 20 percent of rural seniors live more than a half-hour from a grocery or convenience store; only 5 percent of urban seniors live this far from shopping. Sixty percent of rural and small-town seniors drive their own vehicles compared to 46 percent of urban seniors. Although more rural seniors own a vehicle and drive, those without a car are particularly vulnerable to mobility problems and social isolation. Turcotte (2006) says that older people in rural areas without a car "are particularly at risk for social isolation, as well as difficulty in accessing community and medical services" (48).

Access to transportation also varies in Canada by region. British Columbia provides some of the best transportation to seniors; only 3 percent of seniors there report lack of access to transportation. The Atlantic Provinces do less well in providing transport for seniors. There, 9 percent of seniors say they lack access to a household vehicle or public transportation (Turcotte 2006). Enman and Rogers (2002) found that in Atlantic Canada a lack of transportation programs and professional care increases depression and decreases the older person's ability to get help.

Hamilton and Brehaut (1992) interviewed women in Prince Edward Island who lived in rural settings. These women complained about the lack of public transportation and about their dependence on others. One woman in a small town said, "I don't like the idea that you got to bum somebody to take you uptown now. As long as I had my eyesight I could walk. It's just down and up around the corner. But now I can't walk and in order to go to get your medications, to get your cheques cashed ... you got to get somebody to take you." Another woman said, "I got no way of going anywhere. I gotta wait 'til some of the rest of them is ready to come and take me. It's too far off the main highway" (51–52). The researchers say that people who had their own transportation reported a higher quality of life.

Hodge and McKay (1992) observed that many small towns lack public transportation such as buses or taxis, but when seniors have access to public transit in a small town they seldom use it. When older people in five small British Columbia towns were asked about their use of the local bus service, only 22 percent of the seniors used the bus regularly and only 37 percent used it once a week or more. People in the study said the bus did not run on weekends or in the evening, it needed advance booking, and they had to wait a long time for the bus. People in these towns said they would prefer a fixed bus route or a dial-a-bus option.

People in rural areas need more options. First, town planners can place seniors' housing close to downtown in small towns. Seniors could then walk to the services and shops they need. Second, in small towns transportation programs might include volunteer-run shuttle buses or car pools for seniors. Hodge and McKay (1992) found that about a quarter of older people in towns without buses said they would consider using a taxi voucher system (where a service agency pays the taxi fare for the senior). About a fifth said they preferred a shared taxi ride or a mobility club (a volunteer group in which older people provide rides to other seniors).

In cities, most seniors do not need special transportation services; instead they need improvements to existing services. Ninety percent of the transportation disadvantaged said they could use services that already exist if the services changed slightly. Suggested changes include well-lit subway stations, buses that adjust their step height to suit passengers when they enter and leave, and clearer signage. These modifications would help people of all ages.

A report by CMHC (2008a) says that transportation routes and time schedules best suit the needs of younger, employed people. Also, older people express concerns about the safety of public transit. The National Advisory Council on Aging (2006) reported that 55 percent of older women in Canada felt unsafe using public transportation at night. Better lighting at bus stops and in subway stations would also help seniors feel safer when travelling at night. Seniors would benefit from flexible schedules during off-peak hours, door-to-door options with multiple stops, and a "stopping-when-hailed" system outside busy hours and on routes with light traffic.

Finlayson and Kaufert (2002) studied the community mobility patterns of older women. They found that even in a city with good public transportation older people can feel limited in their mobility. For example, older women perceived buses and transfer points as risky. These women mentioned their fear of confrontation with beggars, vagrants, and teenage gangs. This led them to cope by carrying extra change for beggars or avoiding travel at night. Some women also mentioned their fear of falling on ice or snow. The researchers say that "community mobility is dependent to some degree on risk perception, and ... this perception is closely associated with time of day and weather" (82). Limits to mobility (whether due to lack of transport or fear of trouble) can reduce an older person's independence. One woman described her view of mobility independence:

> Woman: "Well, really a car is independence to me. And independence is important to me because independence is power."
>
> M.F. "How is independence power?"
>
> Woman: "Because then you do what you want to do. It's doing what you want to do, when you want to do it. And that's power. It's the power to move around when you want to." (82)

Private Transportation

Older people, like younger people, prefer auto travel to other forms of transportation. Compared to older women, older men tend to have a driver's license and access to a car (Turcotte 2006). In 2003, 67 percent of Canadians aged 65 and older had a driver's license (86 percent of men and 52 percent of women). This was a 2 percent increase since 2000 for older women and seniors overall (National Advisory Council on Aging 2006). In 2003, 92 percent of senior couples owned a vehicle (up from 84 percent in 1999). In that same year, vehicle ownership also increased for older people living alone from 70 to 72 percent for older men, and from 41 to 50 percent for older women. These findings show "that the new generation of seniors, especially women, are enjoying greater mobility than before" (National Advisory Council on Aging 2006, 50).

Among older age groups, more men drive and have access to a car (Turcotte 2006). Among drivers 75 to 84 years of age, for example, 83 percent of men, compared to only 45 percent of women, drove a car. And for those 85 years of age and older, 66 percent of men and 33 percent of women had both a driver's license and access to a car. This gender gap is expected to narrow as the Baby Boomers enter later life because men and women in this generation have a lifetime affection for the private car.

The increase in senior drivers raises some new transportation issues. For example, Statistics Canada's 1996 Family Expenditure Survey found that urban seniors spent between 8 percent and 12 percent of their total budget on their cars (Bess 1999b). Rural seniors spent about 17 percent of their total budget on their cars. Older people who drive have to include the rising cost of auto insurance and maintenance in their budgets. Further, older people in high-rises and downtown apartments will need parking spaces for their cars. Finally, older people have health problems that may affect their driving. For example, about 16 percent of people between the ages of 65 and 69 have pain severe enough to potentially interfere with their driving. Arthritis and rheumatism may limit a person's ability to steer and respond to emergencies. Research shows that some older people take multiple medications that may interfere with their driving ability (Bess 1999b).

Many older people take their health condition into account when they drive. They may drive less often, avoid night driving, and stay off highways. Lord and Luxembourg (2006, 103) found that some older drivers modify their driving routes, or do their shopping closer to home—"favoring accessibility and proximity over quality of goods and services."

The decision to stop driving is difficult for older people. The transition to a "life after driving" (Adler and Rottunda 2006) is also difficult for seniors' families. They often have to convince the older family member that driving is unsafe. Rudman and her colleagues (2006) found that senior drivers (aged 65 and older) and pre-senior drivers (aged 55 to 64) wanted to continue driving for as long as possible (Rudman et al. 2006). For many older people, the loss of their driver's license is significantly linked to a loss of independence.

As one respondent said about giving up driving, "[i]t's a sign that you're growing old and you're going downhill" (Rudman et al. 2006, 68). Another respondent said, "[Y]our vehicle is your magic carpet ride to getting out there in the world. And without it, you're kind of imprisoned in your own home" (69).

People want to continue driving even into late old age, but the risk of accidents increases with age. Some people stop driving before functional problems lead to an accident or injury, but others do not. In their review of the literature, Rudman and her colleagues (2006) report that when distance driven is taken into account, drivers age 65 and older have the highest crash rates compared to all other age groups. And compared with younger or middle-aged drivers, older drivers (aged 65 to 75) stand a greater chance of a serious or fatal injury. Compared to drivers aged 30 to 59, drivers aged 80 and older have death rates 13 times higher per mile driven.

This has led the Canada Safety Council to set up a program called the "**55 Alive Mature Driving Program.**" This program helps seniors improve their driving skills and teaches them how aging affects driving.

Some people have suggested special driver's licenses for daytime-only drivers and non-highway driving. Charness (1993) says that smart cars (with automatic guidance systems), head-up instrument displays projected on the windshield, and night vision technology make driving easier. Transport Canada has sponsored research to test infrared monitors and audio warning systems in cars, which may help older drivers keep track of other cars, traffic lights, and pedestrians (Blackwell 2002). Research is required to see whether they also reduce accidents.

The rising number of older people with Alzheimer's disease also poses problems. The Alzheimer Society of Canada (1990, cited in National Advisory Council 1993d) reports that 30 percent of people with Alzheimer's disease still drive. More than three-quarters of these drivers said they had no problem with driving. And over one-quarter of their caregivers thought they had no problem. Still, the Alzheimer Society reports that, over a five-year period, 47 percent of these drivers had an accident. Families often agonize over when to stop a person with dementia from driving. Doctors play a key role in helping a family to make this decision. The Dementia Network of Ottawa produces a Driving and Dementia Toolkit that helps doctors assess a person's ability to drive if he or she has some dementia. It also provides doctors with information about referral centres and other help for families (Byszewski 2002).

Some provinces monitor the ability of older drivers. Ontario requires that drivers aged 80 and over take written and road tests each year. Alberta requires drivers aged 75 and over to produce a medical report that says they can drive. Drivers have to renew this medical clearance at age 80 and every two years after that.

An aging population raises new issues about the right to drive. For example, some studies show that accident rates increase with age (especially past age 74) (Daigneault, Joly, and Frigon 2002). But this same research shows that age alone cannot predict a person's driving ability. Millar (1999, 68) says that "decisions about licensing people with age-related disorders should be based on functional measures rather than on diagnostic labels. Older drivers are not a homogeneous group, and there does not appear to be a predictable pattern of risk." Regular testing of the older person's abilities (past age 75) can help keep unsafe drivers off the road. Education and training can improve older

drivers' abilities. And technology can make roads and cars safer for drivers of all ages. Policies and practices need to balance safety concerns and the older person's need for mobility (National Advisory Council on Aging 2002–03).

New Transportation Needs and Programs

Transportation needs for older people in the future will go beyond current use patterns. New programs may rely on technological change and on new forms of social organization. Older people will run some of these programs themselves. One program in Edmonton, referred to as a **transportation brokerage**, matches passengers with services that meet their needs. In Moncton and the Acadian peninsula, a **mobility club** helps people in small towns and rural areas. This club formed a nonprofit, self-help transport service. People with cars call in to tell a dispatcher about trips they plan to make in the next week or so. People who need rides call a day before they have to take a trip. A dispatcher matches riders with drivers. Drivers also volunteer for up to one emergency trip per month. Joseph and Martin-Matthews (1993) see volunteer programs as a response to decreases in government support and expect there will be more reliance on volunteer transportation programs in the future. Rural communities may need to combine a number of options to serve their older people.

Mercado and his colleagues (2007) say that Canada needs an improved transit system to prepare for the increased number of older drivers in the future. They say that "an improved transit system now will allow the next waves of elderly population to make an easy transition from car driving and perhaps encourage them to cease driving earlier than they do at present" (17).

THE FUTURE OF HOUSING AND TRANSPORTATION

Given the choice, older people say they want to live in their own homes for as long as possible. But low income, poor health, and a lack of support often make community living difficult. Older people see the loss of ability as the greatest threat to their independence and to their personal growth.

New technology will improve housing for older people and allow more people to age in place. New technologies include low-tech solutions such as countertops that can move up and down to suit the user and barrier-free floor plans. More sophisticated technologies include robotic arms that respond to a user's voice. They can take food out of a cupboard, pour a drink, or put food on the table. Other countries have developed electronic homes with electric door-openers and locks, remote-control window shades, and voice-activated appliances. Some of these devices already exist in Canadian homes and may become standard in the future.

Studies of supports for older people suggest ways to improve housing and transportation. For example, often different providers deliver housing, transportation, and social and health care services to older people. Different policies govern these systems, and they sometimes lack coordination. Seniors would benefit from an integration of these systems (CMHC 2008a). Kelley and MacLean (1997) say that, compared to city dwellers, rural older people face greater challenges in meeting their home maintenance and transportation needs. These researchers propose increased case management services to help older people get and manage resources. "The overall aim should be accessible, welcoming, enriching and sustainable communities for all" (CMHC 2008a,10).

What will the future of Canadian housing for seniors look like? No one can say for sure, but current trends suggest some new developments in seniors' housing. First, members of the Baby Boom generation will redefine seniors' housing needs as they enter old age. This group, unlike past generations of seniors, will enter old age with pensions and housing equity. They have already surprised housing pundits; people expected Baby Boomers to downsize their housing (to condominiums and townhouses) as they aged. But many of them have taken the equity from their mid-life homes and bought bigger homes. Likewise, many have bought vacation homes that may serve as their retirement homes in the future. Baby Boomers often buy new homes, which may create a demand for new construction (CMHC 2002b).

Second, as this group ages, people may eventually move into condos and townhouses. This could lead to a decline in the need for single-family housing, affecting different parts of the country differently. The Prairies or the Maritime provinces, for example, may see a decrease in their younger populations, with fewer young people available to buy the homes of downsizing Boomers.

Third, new types of housing options have begun to emerge. FlexHousing, for example, provides a multigenerational option. An older couple or person could help finance the home and would live in the home (in a separate apartment) with his or her adult children. Other options such as a prefabricated apartment that fits into a garage may offer another option to multi-generational living.

CONCLUSION

People can cope with environmental demands in several ways as they age. They can maintain or improve their abilities (through self-help or rehabilitation) or can change their environment (by modifying their homes, moving, or getting help through changes in social policy). Younger seniors, couples, and widowed men and women tend to live in their own houses and apartments. As people age, they often need more support to maintain their independence. However, with some help most older people can live high-quality lives in their own homes and apartments into late old age.

Summary

1. Research on housing and transportation shows that older people enjoy old age most when they feel in control of their environment. People can maintain this control by changing their environment (for example, moving to an apartment from a single-family home or modifying their existing home so they can remain there).

2. A good match between a person's ability and environmental demand leads to high life satisfaction. An ideal housing system offers older people a range of housing choices because people's needs differ. People should be able to move from one type of housing to another—from a house to an apartment, or from an apartment to enriched housing—as their needs change, or they should be able to get support to help them stay where they are.

3. Most older people want to stay in the kind of housing they now occupy and "age in place." Government policies and programs—such as rent subsidies, tax rebates, and repair loans—help older people stay where they

are. Other programs—such as loan guarantees, new building programs, and shelter allowances—allow older people to move to the kind of housing that suits their needs.

4. Canada offers older people a wide range of housing options. These include single-family homes, apartments and condominiums, congregate housing, retirement communities, and long-term care homes. New types of housing—like garden suites and multigenerational housing—will increase seniors' housing options in the future.

5. More older people than ever before, especially women, live alone. Fewer older people live with family members. For some older people, living alone reflects their financial ability to live independently. But for others, living alone means trouble affording their housing, and social isolation. People who live alone may need more formal supports to live on their own as they age. This could put more pressure on formal services in the future.

6. Both urban and rural older people value three types of amenities: necessities, social interaction, and life enrichment. Rural older people ranked social interaction as very important. Compared with urban older people, rural older people have the poorest facilities and fewest amenities available.

7. Homeless older people often live on the street and use shelters for overnight rest and meals. Homelessness leads to a poor diet, untreated health problems, premature aging, and shorter life expectancy.

8. Good transportation links older people to their communities—to services, recreation, and friends. But both urban and rural transportation systems need improvement. Most older people in cities could use the transportation that exists if it were modified to suit their needs. Poor lighting in subways, snow along bus routes, and rigid schedules make urban transportation systems unsuitable for many older people.

9. Rural seniors often have no available transportation, but new programs in rural settings include bus services shared by a number of small towns, volunteer bus services, and people who pool their resources to help one another get around. Older people in rural settings have begun to set up the transportation services they need.

10. Older people, like younger people, prefer auto travel to other forms of transportation. Older men are more likely than older women to have a driver's license and a car. Older people resist giving up their driver's license. They link the loss of a driver's license to a loss of independence.

11. Good housing and transportation lead to increased life satisfaction for older people. An environment that fits the person's abilities helps keep the person safe, satisfied, active, and in touch with their community.

Study Questions

1. Describe the ecological model of housing. When does a person feel the most comfortable according to this model?

2. Explain "aging in place." Describe some housing strategies and actions that help older people age in place.

3. Define the term "living arrangement." What types of living arrangements are available to older Canadians?

4. Why do many older women opt to live alone rather than with other family members? What conditions make this trend possible?

5. Explain the different types of housing available to older people today. What kind of people are likely to live in each type of housing?

6. What types of housing designs do seniors prefer? Why? What are the benefits of appropriately designed houses for seniors?

7. List and describe some of the new alternative types of housing that older people can choose to live in today.

8. Explain some of the different housing and transportation needs of rural seniors, compared to seniors living in urban centres.

9. Describe the major transportation issues raised by an increase in senior drivers.

10. Describe two programs now available to help older people meet their transportation needs.

Key Terms

aging in place   the situation of older people living into late old age in the same place they lived in their middle years. (233)

assisted living   housing that provides personal care services and other supports to frail seniors to help them stay living independently in the community. (244)

collective dwellings   dwellings that include health care facilities and long-term care institutions. (235)

core housing need   a person has core housing need if the housing is too small or in poor repair, or if the household spends more than 30 percent of its total income on housing (CMHC 2005a). (238)

ecological model   the Lawton–Nahemow model of interaction between the individual and the environment that holds that a person's ability and the demands of the environment influence that person's life satisfaction and ability to function. (233)

enriched housing   housing that provides services such as meals and cleaning services to help people live on their own. (243)

environmental press   the demands of the environment on a person. (233)

55 Alive Mature Driving Program   a program that helps seniors improve their driving skills and teaches them how aging affects driving. (250)

FlexHousing   a housing concept that designers and builders use to make future changes in housing easy and affordable in order to meet the changing needs of people as they age. (242)

garden suite   a separate building on an adult child's property or part of their house made into a self-contained unit for an elderly relative. Also known as a granny flat. (245)

granny flat   part of a house made into a self-contained unit for an elderly relative, or a small, portable cottage or dwelling erected in the garden of an adult child's house. Also known as a garden suite. (245)

intimacy at a distance   the desire of many older people to live near, but not with, their children. (236)

mingle apartment   a dwelling that contains two 2-bedroom suites with a common entrance, kitchen, and combined living and dining area. (243)

mobility club   a volunteer group of older people who provide rides to other seniors. (250)

Residential Rehabilitation Assistance Program (RRAP)   a federal government program offering loans to low-income people to help them improve run-down housing. (239)

Reverse Annuity Mortgage (RAM)   a type of reverse mortgage whereby a person buys a life annuity and gets an income while living in the home and the mortgage company takes over the house when the person dies. (242)

shelter allowances   government allowances that subsidize the person, not the housing project, and allow older people to choose their own apartment. (243)

supportive housing   housing for people who need minimal to moderate care and use services such as home-making, personal care, and social support programs. (243)

transportation brokerage   a program that matches passengers with transportation services that meet their needs. (250)

universal design   housing adaptations that serve people of all ages. Designers use lever door handles, low-threshold tubs, and temperature limits on hot water tanks to improve living for older people, as well as children and those with disabilities. (242)

Selected Readings

Hodge, Gerald. 2008. *The Geography of Aging: Preparing Communities for the Surge in Seniors.* Georgetown, ON: McGill-Queen's University Press, 2008.

> The author examines current and future distributions of seniors in Canada. He assesses the impact population aging will have on housing, transportation, and community services in both urban and rural areas. The book is divided into four parts: (1) where Canada's seniors live, (2) how seniors use community space, (3) future seniors and their communities, and (4) preparing communities for the seniors' surge. This book will be of interest to undergraduate and graduate students, as well as gerontologists, community planners, service providers, policy makers, and caregivers.

Scheidt, Rick J. and Paul G. Windley. eds. *Physical Environments and Aging: Critical Contributions of M. Powell Lawton to Theory and Practice.* Binghamton, NY: The Haworth Press, 2003.

> This edited book honours the work of M. Powell Lawton and his conceptual and theoretical contributions to aging and the environment. The articles highlight Lawton's influence on research, theory, and current thinking on housing.

Pastalan, Leon A. and Benyamin Schwarz. eds. *Housing Choices and Well-Being of Older Adults: Proper Fit.* Binghamton, NY: The Haworth Press, 2001.

> The articles in this edited book cover topics and issues related to the well-being of older people in many different environments. Articles report on independent living in the community to life in long-term care homes. Topics include growing old at home, environmental supports for maintaining independent living, and life-span environmental design. Students, researchers, and anyone else interested in housing and well-being for older adults will find this book of interest.

Websites to Consult

Canada Mortgage and Housing Corporation (CMHC)
http://www.cmhc-schl.gc.ca

CMHC is Canada's national housing agency. Established in 1946 to deal with Canada's postwar housing shortage, this government-owned agency is now a major national institution. It is "Canada's premier provider of mortgage loan insurance, mortgage-backed securities, housing policy and programs, and housing research." This website provides information on a range of housing topics and issues, including information for seniors on buying or renting a house, maintaining or renovating a home, and financial assistance programs. The site also includes research articles and reports on topics like home adaptations for seniors and regulations for building a garden suite.

CanDRIVE (Canadian Driving Research Initiative for Vehicular Safety in the Elderly)

http://www.candrive.ca

Initiated in 2002, the Canadian Driving Research Initiative for Vehicular Safety in the Elderly (CanDRIVE) is an interdisciplinary health-related research program. It seeks to improve the health, safety and quality of life of Canada's older drivers. For example, the program develops screening tools to identify unsafe older drivers. The website contains information for older drivers and their families, physician resources including pamphlets with tips for discussing the issue of driving with older people, and research publications on driving safety and the elderly.

Seniors Canada: Working for Seniors

http://www.seniors.gc.ca/h.4m.2@.jsp?lang=eng

This government of Canada website provides a wide range of information for and about seniors, including information on housing and transportation. Housing material includes information on home adaptations, home maintenance, subsidized and supportive housing, and numerous other programs and services. Transportation information includes how to get a disabled parking permit, transportation services that are available in each region of Canada, and resources for older drivers.

© Peter Poby/CORBIS/MAGMA

Chapter 12

Leisure, Recreation, and Service

INTRODUCTION

Dan Kreske worked as an insurance agent until he retired. He had a good income from his investments, savings, and Canada Pension Plan. He heard about free university classes and started to attend. Now he goes to class two or three afternoons a week (depending on the courses offered). He has also renewed his interest in athletics. He played golf all through his working years, and he jogged and swam, but in retirement he found he had more time to develop his ability. Recently, he competed at Lake Placid, New York, in the Masters Division of the North American Speed Skating Championships. He made two third- and two fourth-place finishes and won 10 points for his team. "I lost to guys 25 years younger than I am—it was one of the greatest thrills of my life," he says.

Many older people like Dan Kreske continue to develop established skills and talents in retirement. Other older people discover new interests when they retire, or they discover a talent for poetry, acting, or art. Still others turn to community service, or they may start to do volunteer work in a hospital or senior centre part-time.

Seniors today have more opportunities for self-development and community service than ever before, and many of them have a great desire to develop themselves and give to others as they age. For many older people, the years after retirement become a time of search, discovery, and fulfillment. This chapter will review some of the programs and activities that help seniors live a satisfying old age. This chapter will look at (1) how seniors today spend their time, (2) new personal development programs for seniors (recreation, fitness, and education), and (3) seniors' community involvement.

WHAT DO OLDER PEOPLE DO?

A number of studies in Canada (Stobert, Dosman, and Keating, 2006; Turcotte and Schellenberg 2007) have looked at what older people do every day. Mostly they show that, in the absence of work, older people use their time for unpaid work (e.g. housework and shopping), personal care, leisure, and recreation. Older people use their free time to engage in a variety of social activities, including participation in political or charitable organizations, or in neighbourhood, community, and school groups. They also eat in restaurants, take walks, and visit family and friends.

In retirement older men and women spend extra time sleeping and resting as well as increased time on leisure activities (including more time watching TV and reading). Older men and women say they spend seven to eight hours a day on leisure activities (Stobert, Dosman, and Keating, 2006). About half of older people (over 2 million seniors) say they take part in a religious activity at least once a month (Turcotte and Schellenberg 2007). But research shows that compared with younger people, they spend more of their time on solitary activities and at home. Statistics Canada's General Social Survey in 2005 found that, compared to people aged 35 to 44, people aged 65 and over spent an extra two hours per day on personal care (including sleep) (Stobert, Dosman, and Keating, 2006).

The 2005 General Social Survey also reported that, compared to people aged 55 to 64, men and women aged 65 and over spent more time watching television and reading. Men and women aged 65 and over on average, spent about one hour a day reading and more than three hours per day watching TV. An older person may watch a morning talk show over breakfast, eat supper with the evening news, and go to sleep after the national news. Some people schedule their days around afternoon soap operas.

Stobert and colleagues (2006) report on two broad types of leisure activity: passive leisure and active leisure. Passive leisure includes watching television, listening to the radio, or taking a pleasure drive. Active leisure includes reading, going to a movie, playing cards, using the Internet, socializing with friends, and physical recreation. Men and women aged 65 to 74 spend about four hours a day on active leisure. Men in this age group spend 3.7 hours a day on passive leisure and women in this age group spend 3.1 hours a day on passive leisure. Even people aged 75 and over spend about the same amount of time on active as on passive leisure. These findings show "that older Canadians remained engaged in a wide variety of activities well into later life" (24) (see Exhibit 12.1).

Stobert and colleagues (2006, 24) found that health and life satisfaction played a role in the older person's choice of leisure activities. "Healthy individuals," the researchers say, "spent more on paid work, unpaid work and active leisure. ... Less healthy and less satisfied men and women for all age groups consistently spent the most time on passive leisure."

How have activity patterns for older people changed over time? Are older people more active today than in the past? Victorino and Gauthier (2005) report on four time-use surveys between 1981 and 1998. They studied paid work, housework, active pursuits, passive leisure, and personal activities. They found that over this 17-year period paid work decreased for men and women with age. By 1998, men aged 65 and over on average worked only 0.7 hours per day at paid work. In that year older women on

● Exhibit 12.1

AVERAGE HOURS PER DAY SPENT ON MAIN ACTIVITIES, BY AGE GROUP

	Day	Unpaid work	Paid work	Leisure	Personal care
			Mean		
Women					
Age group of the respondent					
65 to 74 years of age	24.0	4.7	0.3	7.7	11.3
75 to 84 years of age	24.0	3.8	0.0	7.9	12.2
85 years of age and over	24.0	2.5	0.0	7.8	13.7
Average 65 years of age and over	24.0	4.2	0.2	7.7	11.8
Men					
Age group of the respondent					
65 to 74 years of age	24.0	3.6	0.7	8.2	11.5
75 to 84 years of age	24.0	3.9	0.2	8.1	11.9
85 years of age and over	24.0	1.5	0.0	8.6	13.7
Average 65 years of age and over	24.0	3.6	0.5	8.2	11.7

This table compares the activities of older people at different ages. Note that neither men nor women spend much time on paid work. At every age personal care and leisure activity dominate the older person's schedule. Also note that unpaid work drops off for both men and women aged 85 and over (this includes housework, shopping, and care for others). Leisure activity remains relatively stable at all ages, even amongst the oldest old (where it increases slightly for men).

Note that personal care increases with each older age group. It takes the place of unpaid work as a person ages. In late old age people have less energy to give to unpaid work and need to use their resources for the demands of personal care. This table shows that people shift priorities and time allocation to meet their changing needs as they age.

Source: J. Frederick and J. Fast, 2004, Days of Our Lives: Time Use and *Transitions over the Life Course 1998. Living Longer, Living Better*, Statistics Canada. Ottawa: Minister of Industry. Catalogue no. 89-584-MIE—No. 6. ISBN: 0-662-37001-5, p. 32.

average did paid work less than 0.5 hours per day. Older men engaged in housework about 3 hours per day, older women about 4 hours per day in 1998. The figures on housework stayed fairly stable over the 1981–98 period.

This study found that older people increased their active pursuits between 1981 and 1998. Men less than 75 years old and women of all ages reported more active pursuits. Active pursuits include sports and fitness as well as volunteering and reading. A further look at each of these pursuits found that men and women differed in their activities during this time frame. Men in all age

groups spent about the same amount of time over this time period on sports and fitness (about a half hour per day). But women showed an increase in their sport and fitness activity over this time, increasing their activity from 0.1 hours in 1981 to 0.4 hours in 1998 (nearly the same amount of time spent by men).

Older men and women volunteered at about the same number of hours (about 0.2 hours per day) over this time period. But the proportion of people who volunteered significantly increased from 2.7 to 8.2 percent. Finally the amount of out-of-home leisure (going to a movie or travel) almost doubled to nearly an hour per day for men and women under age 75. Older people spent very little time on education or childcare.

Watching television—a passive leisure pursuit—stayed fairly stable for older men and women during this time. Older men and women spent between 3 and 4 hours per day watching television. Other passive leisure pursuits (like listening to the radio) tended to decrease for older men and women.

Older men and women (compared to people aged 45 to 54) tended to spend one to two hours more of their time each day on personal care (bathing, dressing, and rest). Among seniors, the older the age group, the more time spent on personal care. The researchers say that this may reflect the time needed for older people with health limitations to care for themselves.

The researchers conclude that between 1981 and 1998 older people showed a significant increase in more active living. Men aged 65 to 74 tended to show only a slight change in active living, but all other age groups of older men and women showed increases in active pursuits. The researchers say that older people appear to have reallocated their time to more active leisure. "These trends," they say, "are encouraging, as studies have shown that engaging in moderate levels of physical and cognitive activities (e.g., reading) can have beneficial effects on physical and mental health and quality of life …" (54).

Research on leisure activities show that older people spend a large part of their day alone. Men aged 65 and over in 1998 said they spent on average 6.5 hours a day alone. Women in that year said they spent 8 hours alone. Widowed seniors spent on average over 10 hours a day alone (about twice as much time alone as married people) (Clark 2002). Seniors also spend a lot of time indoors with friends and relatives (Horgas, Wilms, and Baltes 1998). When older people do take part in outdoor activity, the activities usually demand little exertion (such as walking or gardening).

Compared to younger age groups, seniors spend more of their time resting during the day. Lefrançois and his colleagues (2001) studied the leisure activities of 224 people aged 80 to 85 in Quebec. They found that this older age group engaged in few physical or intellectual activities. They most often engaged in emotional, spiritual, and social activities. A decrease in their physical condition during the year of the study had the greatest negative effect on their activities. Decline in instrumental activities of daily living affected all types of activities (not just physical activities). The researchers found that people substituted less-demanding activities as their ability declined.

Strain and her colleagues (2002) conducted a longitudinal study of seniors' leisure activity by studying 380 people aged 60 to 85 in Manitoba. Two-thirds were women and two-thirds were married. The researchers looked at whether a person continued or dropped an activity between the years 1985 and 1993. In 1985, they found the most participation in watching television (99.5 percent), reading (95.8 percent), and shopping (93.2 percent). They found the least participation in church services/activities (66.1 percent), playing cards (64.7 percent), and going to the theatre/movies/spectator sports (58.9 percent). They found that over the eight-year period of the study nearly all people in the study continued to watch television (93.1 percent) and read (91.2 percent). More than half (55.4 percent) of those who went to the theatre, movies, or a spectator sport had stopped that activity.

Strain and her colleagues (2002, 220) found that "being younger, having more education, rating their own health as excellent/good, and having no ADL/IADL limitations in 1985 were associated with a greater likelihood of continuing more activities." People who maintained their health and who remained married also showed the greatest likelihood of continuing their activities. This study supports the findings of other research (Lefrançois et al. 2001).

Strain and her colleagues say that a change in functional ability over time has a strong impact on whether a person continues to participate in leisure activities. People tend to reduce their participation in activities as physical function declines. They may choose new activities that better fit their ability or they may focus on fewer activities. Still, the National Advisory Council on Aging (NACA) (2006) says "… health problems are not the only reason for explaining physical inactivity among seniors. In many cases, physical activity is simply not incorporated into day-to-day living due to a lack of awareness of its importance in later life, or due to ageist attitudes that still negate its relevance." (p.11)

Social conditions can influence a person's activity. Menec (2003) studied older people over a six-year period. She found that people who took part in solitary activities (such as reading or handiwork) or in social activities (such as visiting friends) reported feeling happy and interested in life. Those who took part in social activities showed decreased mortality rates and less functional decline.

Seniors are travelling within Canada more often today than they did in the past. In 1997, seniors made an average of just under three trips per person within Canada—this is almost a full trip more per person than in the early 1980s. Furthermore, seniors made an average of 0.6 international trips per person in 1999 (Health Canada 2001c). Lehto and colleagues (2001) found that older travellers look forward to good weather, new foods, and shopping for local crafts. The researchers found that travellers fit into three clusters—eco-tourists, female enthusiasts who want to meet people, and people on a budget who want relaxation.

A VARIETY OF ACTIVITY PATTERNS

Older people as a group show some common approaches to the use of their time. They often engage in socially satisfying, nondemanding, nonstrenuous activities. This appears to support the disengagement theory of aging.

Other research questions this pessimistic conclusion. Studies show different activity preferences among different types of seniors. Income, region, and social status all influence what an older person chooses to do. Those with low income and little education and those with high income and a university degree show the lowest involvement in popular culture activities (such as watching TV, listening to music, going to movies, engaging in crafts, and reading newspapers). People with middle incomes and either a high-school diploma or some secondary education show the most involvement in popular culture activities. People with university degrees tend to read more books than other groups (McPherson and Kozlik 1987). "Even within the same age cohort life chances and lifestyles vary because of differences in social status" (115).

Edwards and Mawani (2006) say that older people's activities varied by season. Not surprisingly, cold weather in winter and hot, humid weather in summer lead to decreases in outdoor activities. Canadian winters, in particular, keep older people indoors and inactive.

Mall-walking programs can overcome this barrier. A mall provides a safe, well-lit, and comfortable setting for exercise. The West Edmonton Mall, for example, provides over 6 kilometres of walking space and lays out a walking course for mall walkers. A mall-walking program at the Londonderry Mall in Edmonton has 800 members. Hosler (2007) says that members of one program socialize and get discounts at stores in the mall. This kind of program lowers barriers to physical activity and encourages social contact. Doyle-Baker (2007) conducted a study of 39 mall walkers in Calgary. Participants' ages ranged from 46 to 83 (average age 66.4). Participants in the study improved their walking distance, body mass index, and perceived exertion over time.

Other studies in Canada show that, compared with seniors in Eastern Canada, those in the West report more physical activity and more involvement in sports. The Canadian Fitness and Lifestyle Research Institute (CFLRI 2004) found the highest rate of physical inactivity in Prince Edward Island (59 percent) and the lowest rate in British Columbia (42 percent). Social context can also influence an older person's activities. Witcher (2006) spoke about leisure with older people on Fogo Island, Newfoundland and Labrador. These people considered leisure activity acceptable only after a person completed all of his or her work. Interviewees thought that at their age they could get little health benefit from leisure physical activity. One participant told the researchers, "… we know no matter what we do we're going to get frail …" (Witcher et al. 2006, 18).

Witcher (2006) says that health promotion approaches in this community need to recognize the value the local culture places on keeping busy. This means engaging in productive activity (e.g., woodworking or picking berries). Walking for its own sake or for health benefit gets little support here. This community reflects the values of simpler societies, where each member must contribute to the economic life of the community. Witcher proposes that health promotion programs work within this context. For example, an older person who chops wood gains the benefit of the activity and also the support of the local culture. Witcher (2006, 3) says that activity programs need to understand "how the larger context can affect older adults' participation in leisure-time physical activity …"

Studies also show that gender influences activity level. Zuzanek and Box (1988) report that women, more than men, say they take part in visiting, religious activities, reading, bingo, sewing, and shopping. Men, more than women, say they take part in sports, outdoor activity, gardening, visiting pubs, do-it-yourself projects, and auto repairs (see Exhibit 12.2).

Strain and her colleagues (2002) found that the loss of a spouse (more common for women than for men) led to a decrease in activity over time. "By late life only a small minority of women are active at a health-maintaining level" (Cousins and Keating 1995, 340–41). Cousins (1995, 74; also Edwards and Mawani 2006) refers to "the almost universal withdrawal of North American women over their life-course" from vigorous, health-promoting activity. Later work by Cousins (2000) found that older women (aged 70 and older) had "sensational" negative views of strength and flexibility training. For example, they thought that strength training would lead to serious injury and illness. Cousins says these women felt frail due to inactivity, lacked experience with exercise, and accepted age and gender stereotyping.

This same difference between men and women shows up in sport participation. Corbeil (1995) reports that at all ages men are more active than women in sports. The low participation in sports by women may reflect the fact that fewer women than men have spouses with whom to share sports activity.

Low participation in sports by women may also point to the lack of past opportunities for women to participate in sports. A study by Curtis, McTeer, and White (1999) found that participation in high-school sports predicted sport participation in adulthood. They found that women participated less in high-school sports and less in sports in later life. Low participation in sports reflects a lifelong trend for these women.

The difference in activity level between men and women may disappear in the future. Longer life expectancy means that couples will live together and stay active together longer. This could lead to more active lifestyles. Also, more options for an active lifestyle exist today. For example, the growth of fitness clubs and health promotion programs will give women more opportunities to live physically active lives. Cousins (1996) reports that the most active women today believe they have social reinforcement for their activity and have the skill to take part. And Lalive d'Epinay and Bickel (2003, 161) report a change in traditional patterns of sport and exercise participation "from one in which sports and physical exercise were a mostly male, urban, and upper- (middle-) class activity, to a more generalized, democratic pattern."

This research shows that health, education, income, and social status all shape leisure in retirement. Also, age cohorts may develop leisure subcultures. Older cohorts today may prefer more passive leisure, while younger cohorts live a more active old age. Each cohort will have its preferred way of spending leisure time, in part, based on members' past experience.

● **Exhibit 12.2**

SENIOR BODY BUILDERS FLAUNT IT

When Tom Heffner sashays on stage, no one notices that his skin is so weathered and his hair so white that he could almost pass as the Man from Glad.

Stripped down to a Speedo, Mr. Heffner is more like He-Man—all eyes are on his massive fake 'n' baked chest, corrugated abs and thighs the size of a girl's waist.

At age 62, Mr. Heffner qualifies for most seniors' discounts. But instead of perfecting his golf swing, the drafting supervisor for the City of Winnipeg spends about three hours training almost every day for bodybuilding competitions. He bench presses 220 pounds, down from 405 pounds at age 55, and leg presses 540 pounds.

Later this month, he will strut his stuff at the world championships held by the International Federation of Body Building and Fitness in Budapest. "I go out there, I do my best and I show what I've got," says Mr. Heffner, who will do his routine to music by Enya.

In the past five years, a growing number of baby boomers have transformed themselves into incredible hulks. Many are goal-oriented professionals who are determined to defy the aging effects of gravity without resorting to steroids.

Unlike many younger bodybuilders, they often have ample time and disposable income to devote to training and coaching services, which can cost up to $300 a week. And their competitive drive is so strong that amateur bodybuilding associations are bending over backward to accommodate musclemen in their 60s, 70s and even 80s.

Last year, the Canadian BodyBuilding Federation followed the international federation's lead by adding a grandmaster category for competitors 60 and up. The grandmaster men's and master men's (50 to 59) are the fastest-growing categories, says Melanie Horton, vice-president of the Ontario Physique Association. "They're typically the largest classes in the national shows," she says.

As contemporaries of 60-year-old Arnold Schwarzenegger—the ultimate manly man—boomer beefcakes say health and appearance are key motivators for their intense bodybuilding regimens.

"People as they get older sag a little more and it helps you tighten up your body," says Bill Friedman, a 60-year-old corporate lawyer and competitive bodybuilder in Toronto.

He began training six years ago, whittling his soft middle-aged form into a sinewy sculpture of veined masculinity.

"Your skin feels like Saran Wrap around your body," he says. "It's a good feeling." …

Source: Barton, Adriana. 2007. *The Globe and Mail*, November 1. Reprinted with permission from The Globe and Mail.

EXPANDING LEISURE ACTIVITY

What theory of aging best describes leisure activity in later life? Most of the research on aging and leisure supports the continuity theory of aging. Cousins (1993) studied older women who take part in exercise programs and found continuity in their pattern of fitness activity; these women often report that they behaved as "tomboys" as young girls. Cousins (1995) found that childhood encouragement in sports led to social support for exercise in later life. Also, women who developed physical skill and mastery in childhood maintained positive beliefs about their physical ability later in life (Cousins 1997). Studies find that people often keep the leisure preferences in retirement that they had in middle age (Corbeil 1995). People who enjoyed athletic activity, socializing, or travelling will continue to do these things

Active people tend to stay active, though they may engage in less-strenuous activities. Here a man plays bocce in a competitive group. A community of active people encourages an active lifestyle.

© 2009 Jupiterimages Corporation

when they retire (unless something such as poor health prevents them).

A study by McGuire, Dottavio, and O'Leary (1987) suggests that we need at least two theories to account for older people's leisure patterns: continuity theory and the life-span developmental perspective. These researchers looked at data from a nationwide recreation survey in the United States and found two patterns of leisure involvement in older adults. One pattern fits the continuity theory of aging. People who fit this pattern were called **contractors**. This group had stopped at least one outdoor activity in the past year and had not learned any new activity since age 65. A second pattern fits the life-span developmental perspective. The researchers called the people who fit this pattern **expanders**. This group had not stopped any activities in the past year and had added at least one new outdoor activity since age 65.

The study found that contractors continued the same activities they learned in childhood. Expanders, on the other hand, continued to add activities throughout life. The researchers could not predict group membership by the use of income, age, race, or gender, and concluded that leisure service providers should create many options for older adults today. At least one type of older person, the expander, will take advantage of these new opportunities. Cousins and Keating (1995) support this view. They found that women remain active throughout life by starting new activities at turning points in their life cycles.

Can people learn to make better use of their leisure time? Zuzanek and Box (1988) found that people restructure their time after retirement. They maintain some activities, but they also trade old activities for new ones. Fast and Frederick (2004, 14) report that "women and men in later stages of the life course spent about 3 hours more on leisure activities (both active and passive) than those in prime employment and childbearing stages. This pattern is consistent with much of the literature on the time use of older adults. ..." These findings show that people can change and expand their repertoire of activities, and they can develop new interests as they age.

Leisure education can help people find new ways to enjoy life in retirement. Searle and his colleagues (1995, 1998) report that leisure education leads to increased leisure control, more **leisure competence** (the ability to make use of leisure time), less boredom, and increased self-esteem.

Research supports the relationship between leisure activity participation and improved physical and psychological well-being. Participation in leisure activities contributes to psychological well-being throughout life. Dupuis and Smale (1995, 84) conclude that "involvement in activities that promote creativity, self-expression, and a sense of accomplishment may be most strongly related to the re-establishment of a sense of purpose and/or self-worth" (see Exhibit 12.3).

NEW ACTIVITIES IN OLD AGE

Fitness and Health

Some decline in physical function is due to aging (for example, the slowdown in cell metabolism or a decrease in lung elasticity). Research shows that aerobic capacity and peak performance decline with age even in trained athletes (Young et al. 2008). But researchers still do not know how much of this decline is due to aging and how much is due to past health problems, past habits, and underuse of the body. Studies of fitness training show that exercise can slow and even reverse some of this decline (Aldwin, Spiro, and Park 2006; Young et al. 2008).

A decrease in physical activity accounts for some (and in some cases most) of the decline in physical func-tion that comes with age. Kraus and Raab (1961) call this the **hypokinetic disease**. They say that the lack of activity can lead to mental and physical problems, while increases in activity can prevent or reverse these problems (see Exhibit 12.4).

Many studies find clear signs of improvement in physical and mental well-being as a result of exercise. Lalive d'Epinay and Bickel (2003) report on a study of exercise and well-being among young-old (aged 64 to 74) men and women. They found that long-term exercisers and new exercisers reported greater feelings of well-being (less depression and better self-reported health) than those who quit or did not exercise. They found that those who quit exercising had the lowest well-being scores. Exercise can also lead to improvements in memory, intelligence, and cognitive speed (Kramer et al. 2006). McAuley and colleagues (2005) studied 174 people aged 60 to 75. The researchers exposed them to aerobic exercise activity and stretching/toning activity.

● Exhibit 12.3

TWO-WHEEL ADVENTURES BROOK NO COMPLAINTS

Continuity theory says that people will continue in later life the activities that they enjoyed in their middle years. The article below shows that older people can get great satisfaction from continuing their leisure interests into retirement. They may also bring a unique blend of enthusiasm and ease to their activities.

The repartee comes fast and furiously when members of The Geritols pack their motorcycles and meet for a coffee in a different part of Victoria every day. The loose-knit group of 38 biking enthusiasts, an offshoot of the Victoria Motorcycle Club, range in age from 60 to 85.

The group shares more than a passion for motorcycles. They also share a love of travel, a keen sense of humour, and an appreciation of the camaraderie that comes with shared interests.

Each year they take three or four road trips around the Pacific Northwest and many also take part in three motorcycle enduros west of Sooke on 2400 acres of land that Timber West lets them use. In this context, the enduros are a type of off-road orienteering on trail bikes.

The road trips are often spiced up with practical jokes, such as the time one member videotaped Bonge Noesgaard in the bath for the souvenir travelogue and another put a For Sale sign on Les Blow's bike and sat back to watch his consternation when people kept coming up to him with offers to buy his bike.

... There has been the odd brush with the law. "We've never been stopped for speeding, but we did get hauled in for riding on the shoulder near Tacoma once," says Noesgaard. "The first thing we did was take our hats off so the officer could see how old we were.

"Then we asked him if it was true that we would get steak three times a week in jail. When he told us it was just bread and water, we said, 'No thanks, we'd rather pay the fine.' By the time we got finished we had him feeling guilty for stopping us and he didn't give us a fine."...

Listening to their good-natured banter, it's easy to see what keeps this group of bikers coming back for more. They welcome new members to their kafee-klatsches and riding adventures. There's just one rule.

"We don't like to hear complaints. We like riders who take things as they come," says Noesgaard.

Source: "Two-Wheel Adventurers Brook No Complaints," Fifty Plus, *Victoria Times Colonist* advertising feature, October 5, 1999. Reprinted courtesy of *Victoria Times Colonist.*

● Exhibit 12.4

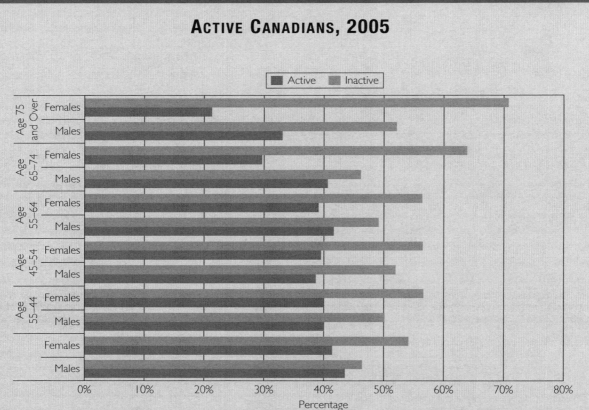

ACTIVE CANADIANS, 2005

Note: "Achive" = physicaly achive and moderately active.

This chart shows that the percentage of active people decreases in each older age group after age 55 to 64. At every age from age 55 onward, compared to women, men show a higher rate of engagement in physical activity. The rate of inactivity among older women increases dramatically from age 55 onward. By age 75 and over more than 70 percent of women are inactive.

Male rates of activity remain relatively stable (about 40 percent) until age 74. But even after age 75 more than one-third of men remain active. The decrease in activity with age among older women in part reflects declines in health and mobility. But these declines also reflect lifestyle choices that in turn may lead to less mobility and poorer health. Activity declines in the oldest cohorts of women may also reflect their experience throughout the life course. In the past, compared to men, women less often engaged in recreational activity and sports. The oldest women may have the least experience with and appreciation of recreational activity.

Source: Statistics Canada (2005b). Data from the Canadian Community Health Survey, Cycle 3.1. Reproduced from Edwards, P, and Mawani, A. (2006). *Healthy Aging in Canada: A New Vision, A Vital Investment From Evidence to Action*. A Background Paper Prepared for the Federal, Provincial and Territorial Committee of Officials (Seniors). Retrieved: November 9, 2008 – http://www.phac-aspc.gc.ca/seniors-aines/pubs/haging_newvision/pdf/vision-rpt_e.pdf, p. 25. Statistics Canada, CANSIM database table number 105-0433.

They found that after six months these groups showed increases in well-being and self-efficacy. Fillitt and colleagues (2002) reviewed the literature on the effect of exercise on mental ability in later life. They concluded that exercise, including leisure activities, can help maintain mental ability and prevent mental decline.

An **active leisure lifestyle** does at least two things: it directly benefits health and helps to buffer the influence of life events and illness. Other studies support this view. Aldwin and colleagues (2006) report that physical activity reduces the incidence of diabetes, lowers cholesterol, and increases bone density. Kramer and colleagues (2006) report that aerobic exercise improves memory, intelligence, and cognitive speed.

These benefits in turn lead to better functioning in daily life for older people. Coleman and Iso-Ahola (1993) report that leisure produces self-determination and social support that buffers stress. Edwards and Mawani (2006) say that engaging in physical activity with others creates social connections and builds social networks (see Exhibit 12.5).

● **Exhibit 12.5**

WHAT A SENIOR MOMENT. CANUCK MARATHON MAN, 74, SMOKES HIS RIVAL, 71

More than 50 minutes after Jimmy Muindi sweeps smoothly to victory in the Rotterdam Marathon, in an impressive time of 2:07:50, the cold and rain of an April day by the North Sea have scattered his welcoming party. The city's smiling mayor, Burgemeester Ivo Opstelten, last seen presenting flowers to the top three finishers—Kenyans to a man—is nowhere to be seen. Nor are the jostling photographers who fought to capture the final sprint. Now the halt, the lame, the crumpled over with dry heaves or diarrhea, and the just plain also-ran, stagger across the finish line. Then, as the clock ticks ominously closer to three hours—the cut-off point for *serious* marathoners—Ed Whitlock hoves into view.

At 2:58:40, Canada's unlikeliest star athlete—all five feet, seven inches and 112 lb. of him—crosses the line, sporting his ancient running shoes, shock of white hair and a huge grin. Whitlock, 74, from the Toronto suburb of Milton, is the only man over 70 ever to have broken the three-hour mark. Now he's done it again, for the third time, in the most prestigious race he's ever run. What's more, he's crushed his only serious rival for the over-70 crown, Rotterdam hometown hero Joop Ruter, 71, who arrives 14 minutes later. Back comes Burgemeester Opstelten, with a fresh bunch of flowers, along with an entire Dutch TV crew and several photographers.

Whitlock is a star entry in one of the world's Top 10 marathons—in another first for over-70 runners, organizers paid his way to Rotterdam and reserved an elite starting position for him ahead of the 11,000 ordinary racers. When he finishes, the PA system goes back into operation, trumpeting Whitlock's age and time. "I'm still recovering—it was a tough last k," a disconcertingly relaxed Whitlock tells the media. "I left Joop after about four kilometres. Then I spent much of the race in a large crowd, trying to hide from the wind; I'm a bit of a parasite that way. I was aiming for 2:57, so I lost a minute somewhere," he concludes, a flicker of displeasure momentarily dimming his smile. "But a good result anyway." ...

Whitlock takes no supplements or vitamins, refuses to stretch before races, trains by running in circles around a local cemetery after a breakfast of tea and bread, and hasn't had a regular physical in 30 years. So that late start in marathon life—which presumably has limited the wear and tear on his body—is observers' best explanation for his success. Whitlock's having none of it, though. "I've been a serious runner my whole life." He will allow for the luck of good genes—his mother died at 91, and an uncle recently passed away at 108. The real answer likely has more to do with his mind. Hours after the marathon, Whitlock declares, "It would have been a disgrace if I had lost to Joop. *I'm* the one with the record time, *he's* the one who should be intimidated by it. Obviously I have a competitive streak, but I'd have been very upset if I felt people had any reason to think I hadn't run well."

As for the future, there's the anticipated rematch with Ruter at September's Toronto Waterfront Marathon. Shrugging off age and possible injury, Whitlock's sure it will take place. "Joop said he'd come, and so did I. Besides, I said I'd take him to Niagara Falls."

Source: Brian Bethune. "What a senior moment. Canuck marathon man, 74, smokes his rival, 71." Maclean's, Apr 22, 2005. Retrieved: November 4, 2008. Reprinted with permission.

Fitness and Well-Being

Fitness programs can improve the psychological well-being of older people as well as their health (Lalive d'Epinay and Bickel 2003). Godbey and Burnett-Wolle (2007) report that older people take part in active leisure as much for the social as the physical benefits. Fitness often comes as a byproduct of enjoyable interaction.

Bravo and her colleagues (1996a; see also Estabrooks and Carron 2000) found that people in a group exercise program outperformed those in a home-based program. Other fitness programs show similar results. Mittelman et al. (1989) studied 33 seniors who bicycled from Victoria, British Columbia, to St. John's, Newfoundland. The group bicycled six days a week, averaging about 90 kilometres per seven-hour day, and made the trip in 100 days. The researchers studied the seniors at three points: before they started, at the midpoint of the trip, and two days before the end of the tour. (Eleven seniors dropped out during the tour.) The seniors filled out questionnaires that asked about their background (age, marital status, etc.), health, exercise habits, expectations for the trip, psychosocial condition, and anxiety. The researchers also gathered data on the seniors' physical condition (weight, height, etc.), strength, heart rate, blood pressure, blood chemistry, and food intake.

The study found that the seniors increased their flexibility during the tour, showed improved cardiovascular response to work, and had blood samples that suggested bone-mineral turnover (a sign of bone mass growth or maintenance). Eighty-five percent of the seniors who completed the tour rated it as enjoyable or extremely enjoyable. About one-quarter of the group reported that they felt stronger and felt increased well-being. Members also reported increased self-confidence, better fitness, and a sense of accomplishment. The researchers conclude that "bicycle touring has a generally positive effect on the initially fit senior citizen" (Mittelman et al. 1989, 154).

The Challenge to Fitness Programs

All fitness programs for older people face two hurdles: getting older people involved and keeping them involved. Chen and Millar (2001), for example, found that compared to younger people seniors showed the least tendency to start moderate physical activity, the least tendency to maintain moderate physical activity, and the greatest tendency to stop moderate physical activity.

The continuity theory of aging supports this view. It says that in old age people will tend to do the things they have always done or try to find substitutes for

This 73-year-old Canadian competes in Master athlete running and jumping events. Master's games give older Canadians a chance to participate in sports and to demonstrate their skill.

these activities. This, in part, explains the lower participation rates of women in sports. O'Brien and Vertinsky (1991) say that women in the past took part in sports to a lesser degree than men from adolescence on. Older women also avoid exercise and exertion. The stereotyping that labelled sport as male activities in the past helps explain this decrease in female physical activity with age.

Other factors that lead to decreased activity for women in old age include arthritis, chronic heart disease, caregiving demands, cost, and fears about injury (O'Brien and Vertinsky 1991). Wister and Romeder (2002) say that people with a chronic illness (such as arthritis or hypertension) can benefit from an exercise program. But their illness (for instance, pain or stiffness due to arthritis) may make it hard for them to join or stay with a program. The researchers suggest that program directors take disease symptoms into account when planning a program. They say that "programs should be fun and easy" (532). Also, programs should include self-care and self-help education.

Zimmer and colleagues (1997) found that many people with arthritis quit activities due to their illness, but they also found that some people—those with a strong social network, more education, and fewer mobility problems—replaced lost activities with new ones. The researchers say that, given support, older people with chronic illness can find substitute leisure activities and maintain an active life.

Leaders need to choose programs that fit seniors' approach to exercise. Myers and Gonda (1986) say that seniors can improve their physical condition with mild exercise. "Walking, dancing or swimming can also be used to enhance aerobic capacity and may be more appropriate for older adults than such activities as jogging-running, skating or cross-country skiing" (177). Less-strenuous programs fit the needs of more seniors today and encourage people to attend the programs more often.

Cousins and Burgess (1992) describe a number of ways to attract sedentary seniors to activity programs. First, they say, program leaders must minimize risk. Risks include injury, extreme fatigue, and, in some cases, sudden death. But programs also present a psychological risk, including fear of embarrassment, ridicule, and failure. People may fail to meet their own or others' expectations. This attitude can even be found in former athletes who set unrealistic goals for themselves.

Second, program leaders must be aware of diversity. Older people vary in their health, ability, and commitment to activity. Cousins (2001) found that women in one study differed in their views on the value of physical activity. Active people saw the benefits in better health and better physical function. Semi-active people had doubts about the value of activity. Inactive women felt committed to an inactive lifestyle. These women felt that keeping busy with other activities such as volunteer work better met their needs.

Professionals who work with older people need to listen to people who join a program. Good communication between a program leader and participants creates the most successful program. Program leaders can then set individual goals for clients, with realistic expectations. Education, income, gender, and personal background influence people's knowledge about exercise and their attitude toward it. Older people need varied types of programs to suit their varied needs and interests (Grant 2002).

Third, program leaders must make programs enjoyable and rewarding. Tudor-Locke and her colleagues (2000) studied frail older people in a home exercise programs. They found that some of these people became bored with the program. Bocksnick and Hall (1994) studied recreation programs in six nursing homes and found that half the residents who took part in the programs felt that they merely filled and killed time. Residents also said they felt pressure to take part in activities. Program leaders had a more positive view of the programs. To avoid this kind of discrepancy, leaders need to keep in close touch with what members define as an enjoyable and rewarding program. Older people need to play an active role in planning, assessing, and developing activity programs. This builds commitment to the program and leads to ongoing participation (see Exhibit 12.6).

Programs should give people a chance to socialize before and after classes. Rhodes, Martin, and Taunton (2001) studied women in a strength-training program over six months. They found that a feeling of improved ability as well as social support helped people stay in the program for the first three months. After that, they tended to stay with the program if they felt that they improved their ability. Leaders of exercise programs need to use varied methods to help people stay in the programs. A country-line dancing program can provide as much aerobic effect as a walking routine, and older women, for example, may find line dancing more fun (Gordon et al. 2001).

SENIOR CENTRES

Most cities and towns across Canada have senior centres, which form the closest thing to a nationwide recreation system for older people. People drop in to their local centre, meet other seniors, play cards, take classes, and in some cases get medical help. About 20 percent of older Canadians say they have used a senior centre (Strain 2001). Few studies have looked at who uses senior centres and why they use them.

Strain (2001) conducted one of the few Canadian studies of senior centres. She found that centres tend to serve rural low-income women who live alone and have a friendship network. Further analysis showed that centres served people with few limitations on their instrumental activities of daily living (IADLs). About one-third of the people in the study (30 percent) said they visited a centre five or fewer times in the past six months. About one-fifth (21 percent) said they visited a centre 48 or more times in that same period. Compared

● Exhibit 12.6

GRANDMA'S LEAP OF FAITH (FROM A PLANE)

One week after her 85th birthday, Olive Thompson was soaring with the eagles. While her grandchildren watched from the ground, she threw herself from an aircraft, falling a few hundred metres before her parachute snapped open.

"It was a feeling like nothing else in the world," she said, after her first experience with skydiving.

"I think it could become quite addictive. I've already booked next year's jump."

There could be a difference next year. She's thinking of going solo.

"I wanted my first jump to be solo but the training is quite vigorous. They make you jump from a picnic table about 20 times and I wasn't sure my knees were up to it."

In last week's dive, she was hitched to Scott Borghese, an instructor at the Borghese Parachute Centre in Simcoe.

With the plane three kilometres above the ground, she put on her helmet, pulled down the goggles and took the plunge.

"I'm not sure how long the free fall lasted, but it wasn't long enough. It was such a spectacular sight. I could see all the way to Port Dover and the line of cars crawling along the highway."

She even managed a smile for the photographer who joined her leap of faith.

"I wasn't the least bit nervous. Maybe that's because I'm at peace with my world. I have a wonderful family and I've had a wonderful life. If anything went wrong, it couldn't have happened at a better time."

She won $20,000 in a lottery last Christmas and decided to treat herself to a new stove and a parachute jump.

"I thought skydiving would be a great way to celebrate my birthday ... certainly more exciting than sitting around the house drinking tea."

Source: Mike Hanley, 1999, "Grandma's Leap of Faith (from a Plane)," *Hamilton Spectator*, July 7, A12. Reprinted with permission of *The Hamilton Spectator*.

to those who lived with others, people who lived alone tended to make more visits to a centre.

Strain (2001) says that senior centres attract a relatively small proportion of older people (about one in five). Her research shows that centres meet the needs of some seniors more than others. Strain says that in rural settings senior centres "may reflect a broad community appeal and acceptance of the senior center/drop-in centre as a meeting place" (486).

In small communities, the centre sometimes offers the only opportunity for social contact. Some centres offer social and health care services as well as recreation. The Regina Native Elders Incorporated runs a centre that offers Meals on Wheels, crafts, and health checkups. Other Aboriginal people's centres offer help with letter writing, filling out forms, and transportation to activities.

In Manitoba, senior centres belong under the auspices of Support Services to Seniors, a collection of programs within the Manitoba Regional Health Authority. The government has identified centres as a core health service. Centres create and develop resources to help older people stay active and independent in their communities

(Manitoba Regional Health 2008). The government calls centres "a community focal point."

In Winnipeg, a nonprofit agency called Age and Opportunity (A&O) runs five full-service centres as part of Manitoba's system of centres. A&O centres offer programs such as bingo, billiards, and folk dancing; financial and personal counselling; as well as foot care clinics, flu clinics, and blood pressure checks. The staff and the members of A&O centres share the work. While the staff ensures that the centres have programs for counselling, education, health clinics, and so on, the members decide on recreation programs, fundraising, and centre maintenance. Each centre has a unique program that reflects members' interests and needs. At one centre, classes might include English as a second language, at another conversational French. Centres also offer lunch and supper. Seniors at A&O centres also give to their communities; members plan programs and help prepare meals, sing in centre choirs, and visit local schools to perform for tudents.

In the United States, Wagner (1995) describes two models of senior centre membership: the social service agency model and the social club model. The first type offers services to frail older people in poor health; people attend for lunches and for health maintenance services. Healthier seniors use the centre as a voluntary organization or social club. In her longitudinal study, Strain (2001) found that young-old seniors had begun to use senior centres but fewer than 10 percent of older people joined a centre over the four years of the study. This finding highlights the challenge that senior centres face from other recreational programs.

Education programs at universities and colleges now attract many seniors who might once have been satisfied with the programs at a senior centre. Also, more mobile, younger seniors may prefer to attend an art gallery or fitness program across town that meets their needs better. This leaves less-well, less-mobile older people to use neighbourhood centres. People who see the senior centre as a voluntary organization take a less-active role in leadership and tend to use the centres for a shorter time. A concentration of less-healthy seniors in the senior centre of the future may move centres more toward the social service agency model.

Ouellette (1986) studied the recreation preferences of French and English senior citizens' club members in New Brunswick. The findings from this study suggest that Canadian senior centres need to take into account members' sociodemographic and ethnic background. Ouellette found that marital status, gender, and ethnicity all influence leisure enjoyment and participation. The French-Canadian women in this study, for example, said they enjoyed spiritual activities more than physical ones, while the English-Canadian men said they enjoyed mass media activities more (e.g., television, radio) and spiritual activities less.

Ouellette traces the difference in spiritual interest to gender, as well as to traditional cultural differences between the French and English. He says that leisure education and counselling need to take gender and ethnicity into account. He concludes that "there is some justification to develop and offer programs or services that would differ in orientation and/or content" for particular ethnic groups (226). Senior centres will need to take ethnicity into account as they alter their programs to fit the needs of a changing older population.

Morgan (2007) summarizes the current and future role of senior centres: "Senior centers are constantly evolving from *social centers* to *service centers* to *community centers* and even becoming *entrepreneurial centers* in order to adjust to the changing needs of the seniors they serve." The success of centres in the future will depend on leaders' ability to listen to people in their communities. They can then create "facilities,

programs, services and activities that meet the needs of this dynamic market."

EDUCATION

Most schools today serve the same basic function they did a century and a half ago, when they first began: teaching children to become adults and preparing young people for specific jobs in society. This system offers little to the older person, who is already an adult and retired from a job.

Compared to younger learners, older people have less interest in credentials and want shorter, more focused programs (see Exhibit 12.7). Older people most often take education programs for personal growth rather than career development. The National Center on Education Statistics (2007) in the United States studied the educational needs and preferences of older adults. The Center found that about one-quarter of people aged 55 to 64 (27 percent) continued to take work-related courses; 21 percent took personal interest courses, and only 2 percent took part-time degree or diploma courses.

The 65-and-over group showed even less interest in degree or diploma programs; only 0.3 percent took part in this type of education, and only 5 percent of this older group took work-related courses. But 19 percent took personal interest courses. Older people enjoy convenient programs that suit their schedule, income, and learning styles (Robinson et al. 2007).

Chené (1994) studied the meaning of learning in later life through interviews with 55 older people in Quebec. These people came from seven learning contexts, including a senior centre, a dance course, and a volunteer training program. Older learners emphasized the family spirit, friendship, and sense of belonging they experienced through their learning group. One group member said, "It is a group where one comes regularly. There is a spirit of ... almost a family spirit. You know, we get to know each other, and I like it very much." Another member says that classes give her a purpose in life. "When you wake up in the morning, you say to yourself: 'Oh good, this morning we have a class' ... because our children are all gone, and life is sometimes very empty" (770–71). Chené's work shows that older people value the social contacts as well as the knowledge that comes from learning in later life.

Traditional theories of aging, such as disengagement theory and activity theory, cannot explain older adults' interest in education. The growth of education programs for seniors today shows that seniors

● Exhibit 12.7

EDUCATIONAL ATTAINMENT OF WOMEN AND MEN, BY AGE, 2001

People aged

Educational attainment	20 to 24 Women	Men	25 to 44 Women	Men	45 to 64 Women	Men	65 and over Women	Men
Less than high school graduation	13.4	19.2	15.9	19.5	29.6	28.3	59.7	54.2
High school graduate	12.7	17.2	14.3	13.3	17.5	12.7	12.9	8.9
Trades certificate/diploma	6.9	9.4	9.8	16.2	8.7	17.0	5.2	13.4
Some postsecondary	29.4	29.1	11.0	10.9	8.0	7.6	6.2	5.2
Postsecondary certificate/ diploma	23.7	16.8	26.2	19.3	21.4	15.0	11.4	7.7
University degree	13.8	8.4	22.8	20.8	14.7	19.4	4.6	10.6
Total	100.0	100.0	100.0	100.0	100.0	100.0	100.0	100.0
Total population (000s)	963.3	980.5	4,607.9	4,439.2	3,680.0	3,561.2	2,032.8	1,592.1

Source: *Statistics Canada, 2001 Census of Canada.*

Note that, compared to older age groups, men and women aged 25 to 44 have the highest rates of postsecondary education. They also have the highest rate of university completion (22.8 percent for women and 20.8 percent for men). People with higher levels of education tend to want more education in their later years, which will increase the future demand for education in later life and probably lead to new forms of education.

Source: Lindsay, C. and Almey, M. (2006). *Women in Canada: A Gender-based Statistical Report.* Fifth Edition. Statistics Canada. Social and Aboriginal Statistics Division. Ottawa: Minister of Industry, p. 99. Catalogue 89-503-XIE.

stay engaged. Although some older people enroll in formal university and college classes, many older people engage in less formal kinds of education, such as programs at senior centres and community clubs. Few seniors take up middle-aged types of education that lead to degrees and credentials as activity theory predicts they would.

Continuity theory gives one explanation for older people's choice of education; it says that a lifetime of experiences leads a person to certain choices in later life. For example, people with many years of formal schooling will tend to return to school in old age. Also, people who have enjoyed learning as a form of leisure will opt for this type of learning experience. This observation fits with some of the facts about aging and education today.

For example, older people with higher levels of education tend to return to school. But continuity theory cannot account for the older person who attends university for the first time in retirement, or for the person who takes up a new interest in theatre, film, or music in later life.

The life-span developmental perspective or the life course approach offer a more satisfying theory of why older people keep learning. These perspectives say that growth and change take place at every stage of life, and that people grow and change along many dimensions. For example, a woman may have severe arthritis that keeps her housebound but she can still learn and grow intellectually. These perspectives emphasize the uniqueness of later adult life stages and the need for a flexible educational system to serve older people.

This view fits with current theories of lifelong learning. Adult educators say that the needs of older learners differ from those of younger learners. Older learners most often come back to school for personal development and to find meaning in later life. A study by the American Council on Education (cited in Robinson et al. 2007, 14) found that many older adults "are driven to study a subject area that they previously never had the opportunity to learn … Older adults who have already earned degrees in technical fields, such as engineering and nursing, often take advantage of new opportunities to study liberal arts and other related interests. Older learners ask: Is the knowledge useful? Does it help me make better sense of my life and the world around me? Does it help me live more fully and enjoy my life more?"

Schools will have to change their ideas about education and educational settings to meet the older student's needs. Myles and Boyd (1982, 271) describe the experience of an older person who walks onto a university campus today.

> Mrs. Smith arrives … and finds classes dispersed over a large campus with limited facilities for getting around. The principles of credentialism which lead to the organization of academic activity around exams and the accumulation of credits are of little relevance to her. When she attempts to relax in a recreation area she is subjected to loud music which she finds noxious … In effect, what Mrs. Smith is encountering is a social institution designed and organized for the young.

To meet the needs of older learners like Mrs. Smith, universities will have to give older students more options about class times, subject choices, and testing methods. They will also have to increase the kinds of social supports—such as counselling or pre-registration assistance—that they give to older students. Some of these changes have begun, and others will take place as more older people come back to school.

Many universities have begun to adapt their programs to older learners. Some offer free tuition and special classes for seniors. They give library cards to seniors and involve them in the planning and design of senior education programs. Teachers learn that they need to change their teaching style to fit older students' learning styles. Studies on learning and memory show that older people take more time to learn something new, and that anxiety, fatigue, and a lack of practice at school tasks make it harder for older people to succeed.

Also, older people will drop out of a program if they cannot link what they learn to what they already know. Instructors need to take more time to present material, allow time for students to ask questions or state their views, and match the pace of their instruction to students' abilities. The use of appropriate teaching methods along with more flexible schedules and open enrollment will encourage more older students to take secondary or postsecondary courses. Distance education methods open education to older people who live far from a school or find it hard to get to class. Delivery methods such as Internet-based programs and homebound learning will increase educational opportunities for older people.

Lifelong learning has become a part of Canadian society. Already, more people go to school for more years than ever before. Younger age groups have more education; Statistics Canada says that in 2001 only 5 percent of women and 11 percent of men aged 65 and over had a university degree, compared with 23 percent of women and 21 percent of men aged 25 to 44 (Lindsay and Almey 2006). This increase in education for younger people will lead to more demand for education in later life. These new generations of older students will require new educational models and new programs to meet their needs.

One of those needs has just begun to surface. A growing number of middle-aged people say they intend to work past the normal retirement age. Some will want to change their career in later life. The typical four-year degree or two-year community college program may not suit these students. They want education programs that get them back in the workforce quickly. Robinson and colleagues (2007) say "Older adults with an interest in new careers … want options that quickly transition them to new opportunities. Consequently, many want prior learning assessment, accelerated program formats, improved career counseling, and job placement." Schools will have to rethink their schedules, the location of their classes, and their admissions processes to meet the needs of this growing older population.

In addition, employers may use education as a way to keep older workers on the job; a shrinking labour pool may make this a good investment. In addition to employer support for job training, some older workers will take learning in their own hands. In 2002, about one-quarter (23.1 percent) of older workers (aged 55 to 64) said they engaged in self-directed learning. More than three-quarters of these workers consulted books or other written materials, and more than half used the Internet or computer software to develop job skills. More older workers in the future may turn to online educational resources to upgrade their skills or develop new ones.

Robinson and colleagues (2007) say that too little information exists today on the interests of older learners and their participation in postsecondary education. Turcotte and Schellenberg (2007, 111) say that in Canada, "Information on [the educational activity of] workers aged 65 or older is not available." The meaning and purpose of education change in later life. Researchers need to both understand the many reasons that people want to continue learning in later life and study the new channels of education that attract seniors today.

Educational Alternatives

Elderhostel

As more older people continue their education, new programs like **Elderhostel** will emerge to meet their needs (see Exhibit 12.8). Elderhostel is the largest education and travel program in the world for people aged 55 and over. About 200,000 older people enroll each year in 10,000 Elderhostel courses in 90 countries (Elderhostel 2003). Elderhostel combines formal learning with the European concept of hostelling (travelling from place to place and staying in inexpensive, safe lodgings).

Classic Elderhostel programs take place on a university campus. Most programs last one week—from Sunday afternoon until the following Saturday morning. A one-week program typically includes three courses. Elderhostel programs also take place in cities, national parks, and famous locations. Students may stay at a downtown hotel, a retreat house, or other simple lodgings (including safari tents when appropriate). Course choices include such options as whitewater rafting trips, touring Venice, and African safaris. The program also offers "homestay programs," where students live with a host family in another country. These programs give hostellers a chance to travel, meet new people, and learn things in a variety of settings they might not otherwise see.

Elderhostel has expanded beyond its traditional format to include active outdoor programs, service programs, shipboard programs, and intergenerational programs (for grandparents and grandchildren). International programs usually last two to three weeks. A two-week program in Peru, for example, looks at pre-Columbian culture and includes a visit to Machu Picchu. Experts give lectures during the program and students enjoy time in the capital city of Lima. A month-long program in Australia uses train travel to see the country. Students learn about the ecology of the country, sample Australian wine at a local vineyard, learn about current social issues, and visit Sydney Harbour and the Opera House.

● Exhibit 12.8

ELDERHOSTEL

A few samples from the Elderhostel online catalogue for 2009 will show why this program has grown so quickly:

- **Canadian Odyssey: A Tale of Three Cities: Quebec and Ontario.** Discover the beauty and significance of three of eastern Canada's most important cities: Ottawa, the capital; Montreal, the Paris of North America; and Quebec City, the last walled city on the continent. Uncover cultural treasures and landmarks. Step back in time as you explore the halls of grand cathedrals, chateaus and museums. And participate in lively discussions with local experts on the history, government and art of this truly unique country.
- **The Enchanted Wilderness of Coastal BC — Wildlife Viewing.** Famous for two hundred resident Orca, transient Mink and Humpback whales, bears and birds, majestic scenery and rich ecology, Vancouver Island and the Johnstone Straits offer visitors premier marine, freshwater and terrestrial wildlife viewing and outdoor learning. Come and experience bald eagles, otters and mink roaming the intertidal flats of large mainland rivers, sea lions feeding on herring and orca whales breaching and spy hopping.
- **Spectacular Newfoundland Coast to Coast.** Known to locals as "the Rock," the main island of Newfoundland and Labrador sports a rugged coast and picturesque peninsulas where some of the world's rarest land formations can be seen alongside the traces of four centuries of human settlement. Traverse the island from coast to coast to discover the true character of Newfoundland.

Elderhostel also offers international programs to England, Indonesia, Hungary, and many other countries.

Source: Adapted from Elderhostel: Adventures in Lifelong Learning, 2008. http://www.elderhostel.org, accessed November 2, 2008. Reprinted with permission.

Elderhostel began in 1975 in the United States. The University of New Brunswick offered the first course in Canada in 1980, and Canadian programs expanded quickly.

Today a program called "Routes to Learning Canada" (formerly Elderhostel Canada) offers programs similar to those of Elderhostel. Routes to Learning emphasizes environmental and cultural awareness, and programs take place throughout the country and abroad. They range from the strenuous to the sedate. One offered a 10-day Fraser River expedition in Voyageur canoes, encouraging grandchildren to attend with their grandparents. Another program offered a weekend at the opera in Toronto, and took members backstage to learn about the staging and choreography involved in an opera performance.

Routes to Learning partners with a company called Cross Cultural Solutions to offer volunteer opportunities abroad to fit Baby Boomers' desire for adventure travel and meaningful activity in retirement.

Arsenault (1997) studied 154 older adults at 10 Elderhostel sites in Canada. She found that Elderhostel programs met the needs of at least six types of older learners. "Activity-oriented people" joined because they liked the field trips, "geographical gurus" take the program to learn about a specific part of the country, "experimenters"

want to explore new ways of learning, "adventurers" will try anything new, "content-committed" attend to explore a special interest, and "opportunists" attend to get reduced travel costs (see exhibits 12.9 and 12.10).

Institutes for Learning in Retirement or Lifelong Learning Institutes

Institutes for Learning in Retirement (ILRs), also called Institutes for Lifelong Learning (ILLs), have met with success at a number of Canadian universities. These programs offer a variety of formats from lectures to seminars, to travel courses. Some programs charge a membership fee and a course registration fee. Others do not. In most cases older people decide together on the topics they will study; the ILR model uses peer teachers and group self-management.

These programs have grown rapidly in number throughout North America over the past few years. The New School for Social Research in New York started the first ILR in 1962 (Beck et al. 1991). Elderhostel has set up a network of Life Long Learning Institutes (the Elderhostel Institute Network—EIN) throughout North America, which continues to expand. By 1997, the network had 200 affiliate members and offered over 4,000 courses each term. ILR courses have no grades or tests,

---

● **Exhibit 12.9**

A Comparison of Second and Third Age Learning

Second Age Learning	Third Age Learning
Work	Leisure
Professional	Amateur
Workforce development/training	Self-development
Social capital	Personal enrichment
Society subsidized	Individual pays
First career	Second career
Have to know	Want to know
Schooling	Education
Social purpose	Individual purpose
Career preparation	Learning for its own sake

These lists present an ideal type of education at two stages in life (youth/middle adulthood and early old age). Education at each stage of life meets different social and individual needs.

Can you think of examples like those above that define education at each of these life stages?

● Exhibit 12.10

A PERSONAL ODYSSEY: AN EDUCATIONAL ADVENTURE

More older people than ever before now take adventure travel holidays, combining travel, learning new skills or information, and some physical challenge. Adventure travel programs range from whitewater raft expeditions to mountain-climbing treks. Rod Dawson describes an educational program that challenged him physically and emotionally.

Once more to dip my paddle and spin the world beneath my keel. A nine-day Canadian Outward Bound Wilderness School canoe trip, 100 miles northeast of Thunder Bay. Be there such a thing as heaven, it will surely include lakes, rivers, forest trails and campfires from northern Ontario.

A million reasons not to go.

At age 66 would I be able to keep up? I didn't feel old—on the other hand—neither did I feel young. Three major surgeries for cancer had taken a lot of the zip and vinegar out of me. I feared walking that lonesome road to another year—a year that might not be there for me. Maybe I can do it? Maybe I can't?

In the end I went because in my heart I really wanted at least one more trip.

We were all to meet at the airport in Thunder Bay. I opted to travel by bus from Belleville. When two other Outward Bounders boarded the bus in Toronto I knew I wasn't the only economy traveller. We shared a taxi from the bus depot to the airport.

Outward Bound policy states: "It is best that no one in your group has any preconceived ideas about your capabilities, therefore we do not allow spouses or partners to be in the same brigade." There are a few rules with Outward Bound. No alcohol, no smoking and no exclusive relationships. The expectation is that members will come with an open mind. The goal is to build confidence and self-esteem. A self-affirming experience, not a survival school. ...

Monday morning. We were scheduled for cold water immersion experience and this was September. We were taught canoe strokes and canoe over canoe rescue.

Then off to the Upper Kopka River, our first portage and my moment of truth. I asked to carry the first portage. If I could do this I could handle my share of the trip. When I put the canoe down at the water's edge I knew I had crossed my Rubicon.

Our canoe expedition had begun. Thirteen people, six canoes, five tents and all of our equipment. We travelled and worked together as a group, yet I think for everyone it was a very unique personal experience.

Wednesday. Just before dinner, we were dropped off for our "solo." Each participant was given a plastic tarp, rope, food, matches, sleeping bag and mattress to spend 24 hours alone on an isolated piece of shore. A steady drizzle kept me close to shelter and fire. Without watch or sun to mark the time the solitude was magnificent. Wrapped in a garment of morning mist, time marched forward with an immeasurable cadence and before I was ready 24 hours had passed.

It is said that adult participants in Outward Bound are often at a transition point in their life, reaching an age plateau, leaving an old job, ending a relationship or wondering about the wheres and whys of life. I had no grand expectations, I went only to canoe. But something happened.

On the solo and while paddling the next day, I met myself, my regrets, my hopes, my fears. It was Friday afternoon, paddling bow in the lead canoe I dipped my cup into the lake, drank, looked around and breathed deeply. One year ago this very day I lay in a hospital bed, alive because of surgeons' skills and a frightening array of painful medical technology. The contrast between then and now was so overwhelming that tears ran down my cheeks.

Source: Rod Dawson, "A Personal Odyssey," Maturity, January/February, 26–27. Reprinted with permission of Rod Dawson. Publisher: Maturity Magazine, CYN Investments Ltd.

and often take the form of study groups where students teach one another. Students in the ILRs, some of them retired professionals, often lead the classes. But they may teach subjects far from their specialties. A retired engineer might lead a course in Shakespeare, or a professor of adult education might teach a course on French cuisine.

Elderhostel estimates that about 500 ILRs affiliated with universities existed in North America in 2007, with another 300 to 500 education programs with high academic standards outside universities.

Members of ILRs generally take two or three courses per term, with most programs offering two or three terms per year. Over 60,000 people belong to network-affiliated ILRs (Elderhostel, 2004b). "It is quite clear," Elderhostel says, "that the future of the learning in retirement movement is very secure and will continue to grow, well into the 21st century" (Elderhostel, 2007b).

Unique Canadian institutes have also developed across the country. Grant McEwan Community College in Alberta, for example, developed a Minerva Senior Studies Institute (2003) that today provides learning opportunities for older adults over age 50. The institute sponsors a theatre program called the "Minerva Theatre Group," and also offers courses on topics such as history, art, and computing, as well as a "Walk-About" series of local tours.

McGill University has one of the largest and most active institutes in the country. The McGill Institute for Learning in Retirement (MILR) uses peer learning in small groups. Member volunteers, many of the whom come from executive, management, and leadership positions, act as moderators. The members and moderators plan about 30 nine-week courses on academic topics that interest group members. Courses have included an "A Comparative Study of a Rumanian Shtetl and a French-Canadian Parish in the 1930s," "Poetry: The Voice of Love," "Jazz Around the World," and a current-events course in French. A seniors' council coordinates the program with the support of the McGill University Centre for Continuing Education.

Clark and her colleagues (1997) studied the McGill students' satisfaction with peer learning. They interviewed 315 students enrolled in the program and 106 people who had not attended for at least a year. The responses showed a high degree of satisfaction with peer learning. Students said that the quality of the experience depended on the ability of the moderator and the participation of fellow students. Students also said they wanted to take part in planning programs as well as in attending them.

Institutes generally accept members aged 55 and over, and can take many forms. Some piggyback on already existing university classes. Some ILRs offer a unique set of courses that can include travel-study programs to China, history courses, or courses on foot massage and health maintenance.

Each institute has its own culture. Members in some ILRs teach the classes; in other cases an ILR may bring in an expert teacher. Where ILR members teach, the program provides them with an outlet for their intellectual curiosity and talent. It provides the class with insights from a fellow member and someone from their generation. This builds esteem for the teacher and creates respect from the students. Sometimes students in the ILR teach subjects far from their specialties; a retired chemical engineer, for example, may lead a class on mythologies of the Middle East, or a dentist may lead a study group on opera.

Students will follow a gifted teacher from class to class, telling friends and bringing them along to the lectures or presentations. Groups and courses often grow through this word-of-mouth and the enthusiasm of the members.

An ILR often feels like a club. Members know one another, have serious discussions, and feel committed to their institute. Often they lunch together before or after classes. Institutes create a social bond that enriches people beyond their classroom instruction. Lamb and Brady (2005, 215) studied members of Osher Lifelong Learning Institutes (OLLIs) in the United States. Members reported four benefits to the programs: "intellectual stimulation, participation in a supportive community; opportunities for enhancing self-esteem; and opportunities for spiritual renewal."

Research on social relations in ILRs shows the value and importance of these kinds of relationships in later life. Sociologists refer to these relations as **weak social ties**. These differ from the intimacy of family and friendship ties. Family and friends tend to come from the same social and economic background. But weak social ties like those in an ILR link people from diverse backgrounds. Weak ties expose a person to new views and opinions.

Krause (2006, 190) says that "weak social ties may be an important source of informational support. Having a wider range of views may help older people select the best coping responses during difficult times … weak ties provide a context in which a person may experiment with new ideas and new behaviors with relatively low levels of accountability." Weak ties between ILR members make for stimulating classroom discussion.

Bea Carruthers, a 73-year-old widow, grew up in an Episcopalian family. Her straight posture and short gray hair make her look like a model of conservative values. When she talks about what she's learning in her ILR, she speaks mostly of her studies in massage, yoga, and holistic health.

"I've done deep breathing, of course," she says. "Tai Chi and yoga, foot massage and meditation—a little bit of everything. I'm very keen on exercise for older people."

"My friends think I'm a bit crazy. My sister, who's 82, and a couple of her friends have been introduced to foot massage. But my own friends won't let me touch them."

The ILR freed Bea from her friends' opinions. The classes provided her with an alternative support group, and allowed her to experiment with new philosophies and new methods of self-care. Krause (2006, 190) says that the weak social ties that someone like Bea finds in her classes provide "anonymity, low accountability, and diversity of views … [and] cannot be found elsewhere." Life course changes like retirement can remove a person from the weak social ties they enjoyed at work. Education programs can replace this important source of social support.

These programs do not appeal to everyone. Lamb and Brady (2005), for example, report that women make up between 66 and 75 percent of the students in ILRs. Programs in Australia and in Europe show the same pattern. Women in these programs often have more education and higher incomes than people who do not attend programs. This leaves open the question of why men tend not to join ILRs and raises the question of what educational options appeal to men in the third age.

ILR students gain knowledge, but people in university-affiliated programs often give back to the university as much as they get. Some programs attract politicians, physicians, and business leaders. Some ILR students mentor undergraduates and may give lectures in required university courses. Members of other programs donate time to help the libraries at their institutions, or host dinners for foreign students.

Studies show that the benefits of learning in the Third Age go beyond learning new facts or information. Lifelong learning also increases a person's confidence and the ability to do new things. Mehrotra (2003) calls this the "can-do factor." People feel more confident and more competent as they learn.

Cohen (2005, p.179) reports on a study of older people in community arts programs. He says that "gaining a sense of mastery in one area can lead to feelings of empowerment that spread to other spheres of life, leading to more confidence, a willingness to take risks, and the energy for trying new things." People in these programs, compared to a control group, remained more socially involved a year into the study. Like the members of ILRs, the people in the arts programs supported one another socially. They felt a sense of belonging that enhanced their well-being.

Baby Boomers in ILRs will challenge educators by bringing bring fresh interests and new ideas to the classroom. But some criticize these programs. They say that programs such as Elderhostel or ILRs segregate older people and offer less mental challenge than university courses. Van der Veen (1990), for example, calls for "inter-age universities" that serve mixed age groups. These universities would take into account the special needs of older adults, but would mix older people with younger people in classes. In age-mixed settings, older learners create role models for younger students.

Will education programs in the future serve older people with little education and low income? How will they serve people who failed in school or who dislike formal education? How will future programs meet the needs of minority elders who may speak little English? Will these groups miss out on opportunities for personal growth through education as they age? Educators in the future will need to address these and many other educational needs of a diverse older population.

THE USE OF TECHNOLOGY IN THE EDUCATION OF OLDER PEOPLE

Older people in the future will come into later life with more education than past groups of seniors, and they will want to keep up with the world around them. For example, the use of computers in education for older adults will expand in the years ahead. Already some seniors show a strong interest in the use of computer technology (see Exhibit 12.11).

Still, a generation gap exists in computer use. Among the oldest-old people (aged 75 and older), for example, only one person in 20 had used the Internet, and older people felt less need for access to the Internet outside their homes. By contrast, nearly all people (90 percent) aged 15 to 17 said they used the Internet in 2000. Older people who use the Internet tend to use e-mail to stay in contact with family, for financial management, to get information on goods and services, and to get the news (Statistics Canada 2001d).

The use of the Internet among seniors will continue to grow. Studies of frail and institutionalized older people, for example, found that with some training these people began to search the Internet, use e-mail, and play computer games (Malcolm et al. 2001; Namazi and Mclintic 2003). Older women (aged 65 to 74) in one study reported that use of the computer made them feel less isolated from their families and better informed about health issues (Malcolm et al. 2001). Nearly all studies point to the need for instruction and support as older people learn this new technology. Hendrix and Sakauye (2001; see also Larkin-Lieffers 2000) say that trainers should set up a nonthreatening environment and give people time to practice.

Computer clubs for seniors have sprung up around the country. Johnston (1999) surveyed 170 seniors (between aged 51 and 81) who belonged to Canadian computer clubs. These members most often used their computers for word processing and to search for information from

Exhibit 12.11

PERCENTAGE OF WOMEN AND MEN AGED 15 AND OVER WHO REPORTED USING THE INTERNET IN THE PREVIOUS 12 MONTHS, 2003

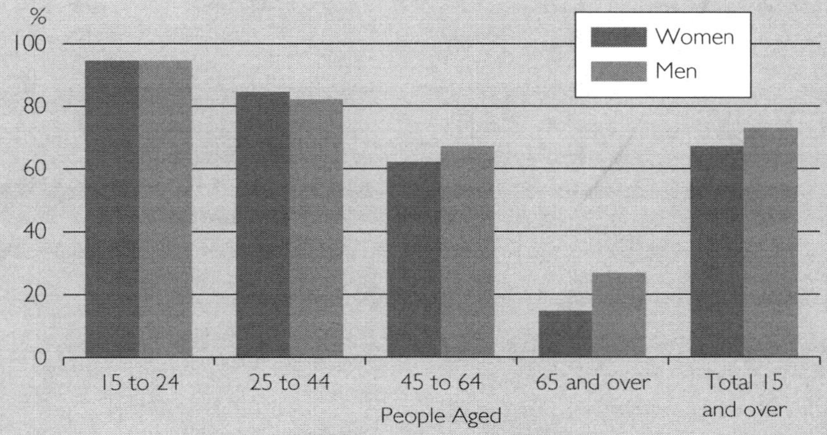

In 2003, only 14 percent of older women (aged 65 and over) used the Internet, compared to 27 percent of older men. But older women show some of the greatest increases in Internet use of any age group. Among younger age groups, men and women report about the same use of the Internet. As younger age groups enter later life they will bring their knowledge of computers with them, which will likely close the technology gap between young and old that exists today.

Source: Lindsay and Almey, 2006, *Women in Canada: A Gender-based Statistical Report*. Fifth Edition. Statistics Canada. Social and Aboriginal Statistics Division. Ottawa: Minister of Industry. Catalogue 89-503-XIE.

bulletin boards and on the Internet. They got the most satisfaction from using their knowledge to help others, sharing their knowledge face-to-face, and keeping up to date. Only 30 percent of these seniors said they often or very often used their computers to communicate with family and friends. These findings differ from studies of frail or institutionalized older people (see above).

Cutler (2006) warns of a "digital divide" in the older population. People with more education and a better income will have access to and familiarity with computers. They will feel more comfortable using computers and will take advantage of the latest educational opportunities. Those with less education and income may get left out of this lifelong learning opportunity.

The decreasing cost of computers and the prevalence of computers in the workplace may help close the digital divide. Those with more formal education may use

computers to take formal courses and training (a pattern that exists today in face-to-face instruction). Those with less formal education may use the Internet to gain information or to communicate with friends and relatives.

Seniors in the future will make even more use of the Internet. But seniors may have problems viewing the computer screen, reading small font sizes, and using a mouse. Education programs and improvements in technology will make computer use easier in the future.

Future cohorts of older people will enter old age computer literate. Many of them will use computers to surf the Internet for sites including everything from online pharmacies, health advice, and online shopping. Housebound seniors will find these services especially useful. As well, the use of e-mail, chat rooms, and discussion groups will open new social outlets for all older people.

COMMUNITY SERVICE THROUGH VOLUNTEER WORK

Exercise, recreation, and education lead to increased life satisfaction for older people. So does community service work or volunteer work. O'Brien and Conger (1991) report that active older women take great satisfaction in their ability to help others. "It is possible that the giving of social support may be as important to the integrity of today's aging women as is the taking" (86).

Hall and colleagues (2006) found that Canadians engage in at least four type of community service: charitable giving, volunteering through an organization, helping others directly, and membership in an organization. Nearly everyone in this national study (96 percent) said they participated in at least one of these activities in a year.

This study found that seniors tended to make larger than average donations to charitable causes (almost twice the amount of 25- to 34-year-olds' donations). The study rated 31 percent of people aged 65 and over top donors (those who gave $325 or more). Compared to older people, a higher proportion of younger people volunteered, but, on average, seniors spent more hours volunteering. Older people also stay active in organizations. More than one-quarter of people aged 65 and over in this study (28 percent) reported participating in an organization once a week or more. Another quarter (26 percent) participated at least once a month.

Turcotte and Schellenberg (2007, 170) say that volunteering "is not only a way of contributing to their communities and to society, but also an effective way to meet people and to avoid social isolation." They go on to say that volunteering provides people with a sense of purpose and psychological well-being. Benefits of volunteering include decreased depression, improved mental health, and improved life satisfaction (Musick and Wilson 2003). (Cullinane (2006) says that civic engagement also enhance the older person's health. Civic engagement can take the form of paid work, but many older people use their time to volunteer for causes they consider important.

Citing the 2004 Canada Survey of Giving, Volunteering and Participating (CSGVP), Turcotte and Schellenberg (2007) report that senior volunteers give more time to volunteering than any other age group. For example, senior volunteers between the ages of 65 and 74 averaged 250 hours of volunteer work each year. Volunteers aged 25 to 54 averaged about 100 hours less. Robb and her colleagues (1999) say that unpaid informal and formal help given by seniors amounts to over $4.5 billion per year.

Turcotte and Schellenberg (2007) report that, compared to younger people, more seniors (aged 65 to 74)

belong to service clubs or fraternal organizations (e.g., Lions, Rotary, etc.). For example, only about 4 percent of adults between the ages of 25 and 34 belong to this type of organization compared to 16 percent of seniors. About twice as many senior men as senior women belong to these groups (21 percent of men compared to 11 percent of women). People at every educational level and every age show about the same rate of membership in these voluntary associations (between 10 percent and 14 percent).

Gottlieb (2002) reports that about one-third of older volunteers provide support to others through programs like friendly visiting; about 27 percent help with meal delivery. The rate of volunteering increases with increases in education and with religious activity. Compared to people aged 65 to 74 who did not complete high school, university-educated seniors in this age group report twice the rate of volunteering (57 percent to 24 percent). Likewise, people aged 65 to 74 who attend religious services weekly report twice the rate of volunteering compared to less-religious people in this age group (56 percent to 27 percent). These results show that people connected to a social network tend also to volunteer. Only a small proportion of people without close friends (5 percent) volunteer. Volunteering creates another social link for the active older person. A Canadian national survey on volunteering found that one-quarter of the respondents said they "did not volunteer more because no one had asked them" (Hall et al. 2006, 11).

A study by Gottlieb (2002) found that agencies faced new challenges as they relied more and more on volunteers. Gottlieb studied 19 not-for-profit agencies in Ontario that relied on volunteers to carry out some of the agencies' work. Agencies reported three types of problems they faced when they used volunteers. First, clients today make heavier demands on volunteers than in the past. Staff members have to take more time to supervise these volunteers and volunteers find the work stressful.

Second, agencies have trouble recruiting volunteers, and older volunteers themselves often need help due to physical disabilities and lack of social support. Older volunteers also prefer short-term commitments and specific types of work. Third, agencies worried about the risk of sending volunteers to meet clients without supervision. They worried about volunteers' physical safety and their psychological well-being.

Gottlieb asks whether agencies expect too much from volunteers. Today, he says, "the twin challenges are to find ways of increasing the societal contributions made by older volunteers, and reciprocally, the contribution that volunteering makes to the health and well-being of Canada's older adults" (8).

Senior volunteers can have a global as well as a local impact. The federal government sponsors a program called **Canadian Executive Service Organization (CESO)** (pronounced "kesso"), begun in 1967. It recruits experienced volunteers and assigns them to work in underdeveloped countries in Africa, Asia, the Caribbean, and Central and South America. The program also works with Aboriginal groups in Canada. Volunteers, many of whom are retired people between the ages of 60 and 70, give technical and management advice to businesses, undertake feasibility studies, and help train workers and managers. The program now has 3,500 volunteer advisers in 22 underdeveloped countries and 16 new market economies in central Europe (CESO 2003) (see Exhibit 12.12).

● Exhibit 12.12

CANADIAN EXECUTIVE SERVICE ORGANIZATION: PAT AND DAVE REDEFINE RETIREMENT

TORONTO—Volunteering with the Canadian Executive Service Organization (CESO) gave Toronto couple Pat and David Evershed an opportunity to do something they had never done before—work professionally together.

Despite the fact that they both have degrees in social work, their areas of expertise are different. "It was interesting; we bring similar skills to a project, but we have different strengths," says David, 69.

"We have the ability to discuss things together. And even though we weren't used to it, we could play things off one another," adds Pat, 65. "We have an understanding of each other's work." ...

David began his career as a Family Services social worker before moving into management positions. "My father was a farmer and I was expected to be the same, but I knew that it wasn't the job for me. I wanted to work with people," he says.

Pat was a Justice of the Peace in Newmarket. She saw a need for qualified counsellors within the Family Court system and decided to go to night school to obtain her social work degree.

Both have been CESO VAs [Volunteer Advisers] since 1999.

"When David encouraged me to put in my application to become a VA I didn't think that I had any skills that CESO would need. I was surprised to be the first one to get an assignment," says Pat.

Together, they travelled on their first CESO assignment to Peru where they worked on a national program that serves victims of family violence.

"David was going to come with me as a spouse but I knew that his organizational expertise would be an asset, so he was put on the assignment as well," says Pat.

The Eversheds were also sent to Armenia where they worked on separate assignments, but both made a connection with the people. David helped two NGOs [non-government organizations] improve their management structure. Pat helped to establish a Family Court and worked on another project involving women's programs.

"The people were so wonderful. I will never forget the conditions and poverty they had to overcome," recalls Pat.

David agrees but notes: "They had a spirit and a generosity that I find gives me a lift. We really got to know the people. In Armenia they like learning about your family and they make you a part of theirs. It's an added bonus to be treated that way."

The Eversheds' work with CESO did cause some concern amongst family members.

They have four children and 11 grandchildren. "Our kids were upset because we weren't playing the role of the grandparent," adds David. "I think they are gradually getting used to our travels."

The Eversheds enjoy travelling together, because as David puts it: "It's just more fun!"

However, David has completed two assignments in Armenia by himself and Pat says she would travel without David "but only if it is to a place I know, or a big city."

Both believe that volunteering with CESO is important[:] "you get to use your skills where they are valued."

Not wanting to waste their retirement years sitting around the house, the Eversheds decided that they would also volunteer at the CESO Operations Centre in Toronto. Both work with Roster Services.

"I like working with people. I love going to new places. I have a real fear of having nothing to do. I'm not ready for the rocking chair," David says.

Source: Adapted from CESO News Release, November 20, 2003. Reprinted with permission.

Volunteering, whether at a local school or in a foreign country, can give an older person a sense of purpose in life. Turcotte and Schellenberg (2007) say that older people in the future will have more education and better health, increasing the number of potential volunteers. Canadian society needs to match the talents of these seniors with suitable volunteer opportunities.

CONCLUSION

In later life people need varied activities to fulfill the ideals of physical, social, and spiritual well-being. A wide range of leisure options creates the best condition for successful aging.

Today, a **structural lag** can exist between the changing lives of older people and the opportunity to live a good old age. For example, many older people say they would like to volunteer more, but cannot find suitable volunteer positions. Likewise, agencies sometimes have trouble using the talents of senior volunteers.

Many of the newest programs and activities respond to this mismatch or imbalance. Senior athlete programs, lifelong learning institutes, and innovative volunteer programs all respond to the growing leisure, recreation, and education needs of older people today. More affluence, a better-educated older population, and the desire for a meaningful retirement will call for more creative responses to leisure in the future. New generations of older people will define old age as a time of personal growth and community enrichment.

Summary

1. Older people spend a great deal of their time on passive media-related activities such as reading the newspaper and watching television. Older people often spend their time alone, but they also enjoy spending time with others.

2. Income, lifestyle, gender, and health influence what people do and how active they remain in old age. Older people in good health have shown one of the highest rates of increase in sports and exercise activities in the past few years.

3. Physical functions do decline with age, but fitness training can reverse some physical decline. Fitness training can also lead to a better self-image, more social contacts, and increased happiness.

4. Older people will join and stay in fitness programs if they have control over program content and feel relaxed and unthreatened by competition. An increasing number of older people now value fitness and exercise.

5. An active leisure lifestyle provides physical, psychological, and social benefits in later life. This leads to better functioning and greater life satisfaction.

6. Senior centres across the country offer education, counselling, and recreation for older people. They form the closest thing to a network of recreational programs in Canada. Centre activities will need to change in the future to meet the needs of younger, more active seniors.

7. People with many years of schooling will keep on learning as they age. Universities often sponsor special programs for seniors. Programs such as Elderhostel and Creative Retirement Manitoba offer alternatives to traditional schooling and are designed to fit older people's interests and learning styles.

8. Computer technology has attracted the interest of many older people. The Internet, for example, has provided new sources of information to both active and housebound older people. It has begun to change the way in which older people have access to new ideas, information, and people.

9. Many older people volunteer to help others, and studies show that volunteers report an increase in life satisfaction. More older people might offer their skills and services to the community if they had the opportunity.

Study Questions

1. How do most older people spend their time in retirement, according to studies on leisure activities? What activities do retired people enjoy most?

2. How and why do the lifestyles of older people vary in retirement? What conditions influence how active a person remains in old age?

3. Research suggests that two theories account for older people's leisure patterns. Name these theories and describe how they account for leisure choices in retirement.

4. Describe some of the programs and services available that can help older people stay active. What special needs must recreational planners consider when they design programs for older people?

5. List some of the physical and psychological benefits of regular exercise and fitness programs for seniors.

6. How can recreational planners attract sedentary seniors to activity programs?

7. What services do senior centres provide for older people? What other types of programs compete with senior centres for older people's participation?

8. Why do older people attend educational programs? What types of courses do they prefer when they go back to school?

9. How will universities and colleges have to modify their programs if they want to attract older students?

10. List and describe the major educational alternatives that are available to older people today. How has home computer use benefited older people?

11. Summarize the major types of activities that lead to increased life satisfaction in later life. Why does volunteer work, in particular, lead to high life satisfaction?

Key Terms

active leisure lifestyle   a type of lifestyle that directly benefits health and helps to buffer the influence of life events and illness by regular participation in physical activities. (264)

Canadian Executive Service Organization (CESO)   a federal government program that recruits volunteers, many of whom are retired executives, to serve as advisers and mentors in underdeveloped countries or with Aboriginal groups in Canada. (279)

contractors   people who have stopped at least one outdoor activity in the past year and have not learned any new activity since age 65, in keeping with the continuity theory of aging. (262)

Elderhostel   a not-for-profit company that promotes lifelong learning by organizing educational and cultural tours aimed at people in their 50s and older (originally based on a combination of university life and the European concept of hostelling). (272)

expanders   people who have not stopped any activities in the past year and have added at least one new outdoor activity since age 65, in keeping with the life-span development theory of aging. (262)

hypokinetic disease   the idea that the lack of activity can lead to mental and physical problems, while increases in activity can prevent or reverse these problems. (263)

Institutes for Learning in Retirement (ILRs) or **Lifelong Learning Institutes (LLIs)** programs that offer older people a variety of educational formats from lectures to seminars, to travel courses, with topics usually decided upon by the group. (273)

leisure competence the ability to make use of leisure time for life satisfaction. (262)

structural lag a mismatch between changes in the aging process (e.g., better health for older people, more active lifestyles) and the roles and places in the social structure that can meet the needs of this new older person. (280)

weak social ties these differ from the intimacy of family and friendship ties. Weak social ties link people from diverse backgrounds and expose a person to new views and opinions. (275)

Selected Readings

Cusack, S.A., and W.J.A. Thompson. *Leadership for Older Adults: Aging with Purpose and Passion.* New York: Brunner/Mazel, 1999.

This is one of the few books that looks at the potential for leadership through senior centre participation. The authors promote a dynamic model of later life, in which the older person takes charge of the organization and creates an empowering environment. The authors describe leadership styles and opportunities in later life. They also propose practical tips on how to develop leadership within seniors' organizations.

O'Brien Cousins S. (2005). "Ageism and Active Living: Recognizing Social Barriers to Older Adult Participation." *Research Update,* 10, (April). http://www.alcoa.ca/research_u_docs/2005_04apr_en_update.pdf, accessed May 4, 2009.

This issue of *Research Update*, a publication of the Active Living Coalition for Older Adults, discusses ageism in plain language and relates it to fitness and active living. The author shows how negative views of aging lead to decreased interest in and enthusiasm for exercise and physical activity. It provides a good reminder of the effects of ageism on a person's health and well-being.

Volunteer Canada and the Canadian Centre for Philanthropy (2004). *The Giving and Volunteering of Seniors. NSGVP 2000. FactSheet.* New Edition Released 2004: Imagine Canada. http://www.nsgvp.org, accessed May 17, 2009.

This study reports on a national survey of seniors in Canada. It provides data on seniors' patterns of giving and their volunteer activities. It is a good overview of two ways that seniors make a significant contribution to Canadian society, and presents the barriers that keep older people from volunteering.

Websites to Consult

Eldertreks

http://www.eldertreks.com

Eldertreks claims it is "the world's first adventure travel company designed exclusively for people 50 and over." Started in 1987, the company offers "off-the-beaten-path, and small-group adventures by both land and sea in over 80 countries." These trips focus on adventure, culture, and nature. They include wildlife safaris in Tanzania, tours by camel in Mongolia, and hiking in Patagonia.

World on Wheelz

http://www.worldonwheelz.com

World on Wheelz offers travel programs specifically for wheelchair users, slow walkers, seniors with special needs, and people who face mobility challenges. This organization serves a niche market that will grow in the years ahead as the older population grows larger and ages.

Routes to Learning Canada

http://www.routestolearning.ca/ProgramListing.aspx?CategoryName=Volunteer%20

AbroadRoutes to Learning Canada partners with a company called Cross Cultural Solutions (CCS), a global leader in international volunteering, to provide short-term volunteer opportunities for older travellers. Volunteers work in communities abroad along with local people. The program also includes instruction about the local culture and customs, some language training, and off-site tours.

Creative Retirement Manitoba

http://www.crm.mb.ca/index.html

Creative Retirement Manitoba (CRM) was one of the first senior learning organizations in Canada. It offers a wide range of courses that include travel tours, a science lecture series, and a new immigrant computer literacy program. CRM also sponsors a computer club and special-interest computer groups. CRM operates as an independent, nonprofit seniors' education centre in Winnipeg. It has won the Sharing the Flame award, a national program of the Canadian Council on Learning and the Conference Board of Canada.

Chapter 13

Family Life and Social Support

© Paul Barton/CORBIS/MAGMA

INTRODUCTION

Families have changed. Rising divorce rates, blended households, and high residential mobility all point to major changes in the structure of the modern family. Add to this the fact that people live longer and more older people live alone than ever before, and you might think that families have abandoned their aging members. Thirty years ago, gerontologist Ethel Shanas (1979) called this the "hydraheaded myth" of family breakdown. Yet, people continue to believe this myth today, even though studies show over and over again that it is not true.

Research shows that older people keep in contact with their families, that they turn to family members for help when they need it, and that they themselves provide support to family members (Connidis 2001; Townsend-Batten 2002; Turcotte and Schellenberg 2007). It is estimated that 75 to 90 percent of informal support received by older adults comes from family (Guberman and Maheu 2002). After spouses, children are the most important source of social support for older family members.

Today, most older people, even widowed older women, prefer to see their children but not to live with them. Better incomes, more housing options, and more accessible health services allow more older people to choose independent living than ever before. This chapter looks at family life and social support in old age.

Part One looks at three topics related to family life: (1) marital status (including marriage, widowhood, divorce, remarriage, and lifelong singlehood), (2) sexuality and aging, and (3) gay and lesbian older adults.

Part Two of this chapter examines four topics related to social support: (1) older people as a source of support, including their role as grandparents, (2) informal support older people receive from family members and friends, (3) family caregivers, and (4) abuse against older people.

PART ONE: FAMILY LIFE

MARITAL STATUS IN LATER LIFE

The life course perspective takes a dynamic view of family life and social relations. It shows how events and conditions that occur early in life affect roles and relationships in later life (Price, McKenry, and Murphy 2000). This perspective sees family life as a scene of both stability and change. For example, some people marry young and stay married to the same spouse throughout their lives. They experience the continuity of marriage. But many of these same people experience changes in their sex lives, in their

relationship with their spouse, and in the development of new roles within their marriage. Gerontologists view some of these changes, such as grandparenthood or widowhood, as normative or expected life events. Other changes, such as divorce, are less predictable and affect fewer people. Changes in marital status often lead to change in a person's social status and a change in that individual's social network. The following sections focus on life events and issues related to marital status in later life: marriage, common-law unions, divorce, remarriage, lifelong singlehood, and widowhood.

Marriage

Nearly all Canadians will marry at least once in their lifetime. In 2001, just over 80 percent of Canadians aged 25 and older and 90 percent of men and women aged 50 to 69 had married at least once (Statistics Canada 2001b; Clark and Crompton 2006). More than 60 percent of those who marry stay married to the same person to celebrate their 30th wedding anniversary (Clark and Crompton 2006).

In 2001, 68 percent of Canadians aged 65 to 74 were married or lived in a common-law relationship. Men are more likely than women to be married in later life (Turcotte and Schellenberg 2007). Older women are more likely to be widowed. The chart in Exhibit 13.2 shows the marital status of older Canadians by gender and age group. For the "oldest old" (those 85 years of age or older), 38 percent of men live with their spouse compared to only 7 percent of women.

Married older adults have some advantages over their unmarried peers. First, older married couples tend to have more financial resources than older unmarried people. Compared to older people who are unmarried, older couples tend to be younger, and often one or both members of the couple are working. Even among people the same age, married couples have more money (Turcotte and Schellenberg 2007). This may be because they had a higher lifetime income than unmarried people, more savings, and a family home.

Second, compared to older people who live alone or in other living arrangements, older married people report higher life satisfaction, greater well-being, and greater happiness (Proulx, Helms, and Buehler 2007; Turcotte and Schellenberg 2007). Older couples say they are generally satisfied with each other, particularly when both members of the couple are retired (Chalmers and Milan 2005). Women who work outside the home when their spouse has retired tend to report lower marital satisfaction than retired women with a retired spouse.

Satisfaction in marriage tends to be higher for those recently married and those in long-term marriages.

It tends to be lower among those in their child-rearing years. Researchers talk about this as the "U-curve" of marital satisfaction—higher satisfaction at both ends of the marriage continuum, with a dip in the middle years. Older spouses, particularly men, are more likely than younger couples to feel increased satisfaction with their marriage over time. In general, the older the person, the more likely he or she is to report positive feelings about his or her marriage (Chalmers and Milan 2005). Affection and companionship, rather than emotional intensity, often become more important in later-life marriage. And even those in late old age have the desire to marry (see Exhibit 13.1).

Increased satisfaction in long-term marriage may be due in part to children growing up and moving away from home. These "empty nest" couples often enjoy a new freedom in later life. They tend to spend more time together, and to disagree less about issues such as parenting and household chores (Shiota and Levenson 2007). They live adult-centred lives that allow them to travel, visit with friends, share work at home, and do things together. Researchers report increased marital satisfaction for many couples in the "empty nest" stage. This is often a time for couples to focus more of their time and energy on themselves and each other.

Third, research shows that married people tend to adjust better than nonmarried people to aging. A good marriage gives the couple intimacy, mutual support, and high life satisfaction. It also provides a sense of security and emotional stability (Fitzpatrick and Wampler 2000). Marriage is linked to longer life and better health, especially for men (Brockmann and Klein 2004; Statistics Canada 2003x). Married partners monitor each other's health. Marriage also helps reduce emotional loneliness (Dykstra and de Jong Gierveld 2004) and provides social support.

People who report a close relationship in their marriage also report reduced depression and anxiety, and higher self-esteem (Mancini and Bonanno 2006). Mancini and Bonanno (2006, 606) say "that marital closeness is a vital resource in old age." Married people also stand the best chance of staying out of nursing

© 2009 Jupiterimages Corporation

Most couples in long-term marriages report high life satisfaction. With the kids grown and out of the house, married couples can enjoy their time together. This married couple displays the fulfillment that many older couples report.

● Exhibit 13.1

NEVER TOO OLD FOR LOVE

The following excerpt shows that people can find love at any age. It also shows Canadians' desire to marry even late in life.

Sherman Browning, a 90-year-old bachelor, and Jean Goodbrand, 89, are getting married today at Trillium Villa Nursing Home, where both are residents.

Sherman Browning's fiancée thinks he's the cat's pajamas.

In fact, Jean Goodbrand, 89, is so in love with her 90-year-old husband-to-be that she invited all the residents at Trillium Villa Nursing Home to watch them tie the knot today.

"A diamond in the rough, that's what Sherman is," Goodbrand said in the Villa's library Tuesday. ...

When asked why he finally decided to get hitched, [Browning] said, "I'm getting married because I love her. Ninety years is not really a long time. If you think back, it's nothing. Time doesn't wait for nobody.". ...

The couple is looking forward to married life.

"I think we'll get along fine," said Goodbrand. "He's got a lot of good points."

Source: Excerpted from Dawn Cuthbertson, 2003, "Never Too Old for Love," *Sarnia Observer*, December 20, A1–2. Reprinted with permission.

homes if they get sick, because they have someone to care for them. Marriage ideally gives a person a live-in support system. Older married couples tend to rely more on each other than on outside social relations. They also report a greater likelihood than nonmarried older adults of having sexual relations.

Although high marital satisfaction is common among older couples, individuals also face challenges and disappointments in later-life marriages. Henry and his colleagues (2005) interviewed 105 older couples, who had been married an average of 42 years. The couples talked about difficulties, disagreements, and disappointments they dealt with in their marriage over the past few years. The three most common issues were (1) leisure activities, (2) intimacy, and (3) financial matters.

Leisure issues involved a lack of sharing or interest in the other spouse's hobbies and activities; travel disagreements (for example, one spouse wanting to travel, the other wanting to stay home, or a difference in the desired destination); or disappointment with the lack of "quality time" together.

Intimacy challenges included both physical and emotional issues. There were "roadblocks to physical intimacy" for some couples because of changes in sexual desire or disagreements over sexual practices. Emotional intimacy challenges tended to centre on communication problems—a spouse's lack of communication or that person's negative style of communication.

Disagreements over spending habits tended to be the most common financial issue identified by these married people. Typically this involved either a spouse not wanting to spend money or spending too much money.

Some couples in Henry and colleagues' (2005) study felt their relationship did not have any problems (the fourth most common theme), or at least, as one wife said: "Not enough of anything to count" (252). Other less common problems included personality differences, intergenerational relationships, personal habits, health problems, and work/retirement issues. Men and women reported about the same number of challenges in their marriage. But men and women reported different challenges. Compared to men, women more often reported health issues. Men more often reported financial issues. Men, more often than women, reported no problems with their marriage.

Couples in happy marriages were more likely to report fewer problems (or no problems) than were those in unhappy marriages. The authors state that the number of problems older couples face may not be as important as the types of problems husbands and wives identify. For example, they found that disagreements over household concerns (where to live and home repairs) and health problems (often related to a spouse's declining health and caregiving) showed up more often in unhappy marriages.

Research shows that the positive benefits of marriage apply only to good marriages. Constant bickering and dissatisfaction in a marriage can lead to depression and illness (Choi and Marks 2008). Studies need to look at the quality of a marriage to understand its impact on well-being (Henry, Miller, and Giarrusso 2005).

Common-Law Unions

The number of people in Canada choosing to live in common-law relationships has increased over the past two decades, and is one of the most significant demographic changes in the past 20 years (Turcotte and Shellenberg 2007). In 2006, 16 percent of all Canadian couples lived in common-law unions, compared to only 6 percent in 1981. More younger people than older people choose this form of relationship. But increasing numbers of older people choose to live together and not marry.

In 2006, 2.7 percent of all Canadians aged 65 and older were in a common-law relationship. This represents more than 106,000 Canadian seniors (Statistics Canada 2008a). Between 2001 and 2006, common-law unions increased 77 percent among 60- to 64-year-olds—the fastest growth among all age groups. So while common-law unions continue to be more prevalent among younger people, older age groups have been experiencing the most rapid growth in this type of relationship, particularly among people aged 40 and over (Martel and Caron-Malenfan 2008).

What explains the increase in common-law unions among the older population? First, many Baby Boomers live in common-law unions. The aging Boomers have contributed to increases across all marital groups—including common-law unions—simply due to the number of people in their age cohorts. Second, common-law unions have become more socially accepted among older people. Third, many cohabiting older couples entered these common-law unions at younger ages (perhaps in their 20s or 30s) and simply "aged in place" in those relationships. Fourth, people who experience separation, divorce, or widowhood often opt for cohabitation over remarriage. These older people desire a close and intimate relationship, but not necessarily one within marriage (Leigh 2000; Statistics Canada 2003k).

In the United States in the mid-1990s, Chevan (1996) conducted one of the first studies of cohabitation among the older population. He found that more older men than women cohabited (these older men tended to live with younger women). Fewer available partners for older women may explain this fact. He reported that poor men and women showed the greatest tendency to cohabit. Living together (outside marriage) may make good economic sense for the poorest older people.

More recent research by King and Scott (2005) compares the quality, purpose, and meaning of cohabitation for older and younger adults. They found a number of differences between these two age groups. First, compared to younger couples, older cohabiting couples report higher relationship quality, higher levels of fairness, fewer disagreements, and higher levels of happiness. Second, older couples report that they spend more time alone together, and they feel more confident that their relationship will last. Third, and consistent with earlier research, older couples saw cohabitation as an alternative to marriage. Younger couples saw cohabitation as a prelude to marriage and an opportunity to assess their compatibility before marriage. Researchers expect that the number of older adults who form common-law unions will increase in the future as more Baby Boomers enter old age.

Older adults now and in the future will have greater choice in the type of intimate relationships they form (Cooney and Dunne 2001). For example, today many unmarried couples live in long-term committed relationships while they maintain separate households. These non-resident couples are known as **LAT (living apart together) couples**. In 2001, 8 percent of Canadians 20 years of age or older lived in such relationships. Eleven percent of people in these relationships were 50 years of age or older (Milan and Peters 2003). A LAT arrangement offers some older adults a way to have their own home and independence, but still have an intimate and committed partner (Ghazanfaceeon Karlsson 2005).

Compared to older men, older women more often choose a LAT relationship (Borell and Ghazanfareeon Karlsson 2003). Often the motives for choosing a LAT relationship, particularly for women, revolve around autonomy—the importance of having a home of one's own, and the freedom from duties typically involved in a marriage. For many of these women, having their own home gives them the freedom "to segment their social relations in time and space" (Ghazanfaceeon Karlsson 2005, 81). They can have independent relationships with their children, grandchildren, and friends at some times and meet with family and friends as a couple at other times. LAT relationships among older people add to the diversity of modern family life.

Divorce

Divorce rates in Canada have increased significantly since the early 1970s following the liberalization of divorce laws, particularly the 1986 amendment to the *Divorce Act*. Statistics Canada (2003j, 2004b) reports that 38 percent of married couples can expect to divorce before celebrating their 30th anniversary.

Between 1981 and 2001, divorce among older Canadians tripled, from 1.7 percent to 5.1 percent. In 2001, about 5 percent of men and 6 percent of women age 65 and older reported that they were divorced (Turcotte and Schellenberg 2007). Women aged 55 to 64 years of age showed an especially high increase in the divorce rate. Their rate rose from less than 4 percent in 1981 to over 11 percent in 2001. For this age group of women, "divorced" now ranks second (after married/common-law) as the most common marital status.

Research also shows that more men and women are divorcing later in life (Statistics Canada 2004b), representing a shift toward greater acceptance of divorce among older people. Researchers project an increase in the number of divorced older people in the future as younger cohorts, many of whom will already be divorced, enter later life (McDonald and Robb 2004).

The reasons for late-life divorce are often different than for divorce at younger ages. For younger couples, interpersonal disputes often lead to divorce. Late-life couples often divorce because the marriage can no longer support the changing roles, needs, or desires of the individuals (Wu and Schimmele 2007). Other reasons for divorce are similar for younger and older couples. They include problems of abuse, alcohol or drug addiction, and infidelity. Most people who divorce in middle or later life do not remarry, but more divorced older men than women remarry.

Divorce in later life often means economic insecurity, particularly for women. McDonald and Robb (2004) compared the incomes of groups of "unattached" older women in Canada (separated, divorced, widowed, and ever single). They found that separated and divorced women had the lowest incomes. Davies and Denton (2002) compared the economic well-being of older women who divorced in middle or later life with divorced men and with women and men who remained married. They found that being divorced, for both men and women, meant greater economic hardship. But women, compared to divorced men or married people, more often lived below the poverty line. This study supports other Canadian research that finds very high rates of poverty among older unmarried women (McDonald, Donahue, and Moore 2000; Myles 2000). And because these older women are unlikely to remarry, they often feel the economic effects of divorce for many years.

Divorce also affects a person's social life. For example, divorced older people tend to have smaller social networks than married or widowed older people (Connidis 2001). Divorced older men have the smallest social networks, the weakest ties to their families, and the lowest life satisfaction of any marital group. They are also less likely to receive support from their adult children (Lin 2008). Divorce can lead to disruption in family celebrations such as Thanksgiving and Christmas and the need to renegotiate or re-create family rituals and traditions. Divorced older parents may also no longer have the financial resources to provide assistance to their adult children (Downs, Coleman, and Ganong 2000).

Longer life expectancies in the future could increase the number of marriages that last 50 years or more, but researchers also predict a higher divorce rate and more divorced older people in the future. This will make the economic well-being, mental health, and family life of divorced older people an ongoing concern.

Remarriage

Remarriage in later life is relatively uncommon (Connidis 2006). It is also more likely to occur for men than for women, and for divorced older adults than for the widowed (Calasanti and Kiecolt 2007). The motivations to remarry in later life include loneliness (especially for men), and financial security (particularly for women) (Calasanti and Kiecolt 2007). Widowed women are often disinclined to remarry because of the loss of freedom, increased domestic chores, and potential spousal care in the future (Davidson 2001).

Hurd Clarke (2005) asked women to compare their first marriages with their remarriage experiences. She found that most of the women reported a happy or happier second marriage. Some women whose first marriage had ended in divorce said they wished their second marriage had been their first. Many women reported a greater compatibility with their second partner, and a more equitable division of labour. Some talked about how the second marriage had "undone" some of the hurt and disappointment of the first marriage. For widowed women whose first marriage had been happy, the second marriage "complemented" the first. These women said their first and second marriages had fulfilled different needs. Whereas romance and sexual fulfillment had been important in their first marriage (at a young age), companionship was a more central component of their later-life marriage.

Hurd Clarke (2005) identifies a number of factors that might contribute to the satisfying second-marriage experience for these older women. First, the greater maturity of these women and the insights they gained from their first marriage helped them select a more compatible partner. Second, without child-rearing responsibilities (and in the case of retirees, work commitments), these couples had more time to invest in their relationship. They could also share domestic chores. Many of these women felt greater sexual freedom with their second or third husbands (Hurd Clarke 2006). This may be due, in part, to their increased confidence to express their sexual needs and desires—a confidence "acquired through age and experience" (138).

Lifelong Singlehood

A small proportion (about 5 percent) of older Canadians have never married (5.3 percent of older men and 5.5 percent of older women), down from just over 8 percent in 1981 (Turcotte and Schellenberg 2007). The proportion of older singles also increases with age, from 5.2 percent for people aged 65 to 74 to 6.7 percent for people aged 85 and over (Turcotte and Schellenberg 2007). This may reflect the different social and historical conditions that people in each of these older age groups lived through (Baumbusch 2004). Singles have made unique adaptations to aging. They play vital and supportive roles in the lives of siblings, older parents, and others, and form friendships and other social relationships to provide themselves with supporters, confidants, and companions.

Little research exists on the lives and social relationships of lifelong single older people. Older singles often face the stereotypes of aging as well as those associated with people who are seen as "unmarriageable." One common and enduring belief is that older never married people are lonely, socially isolated, and disconnected from family. But most older singles, particularly single women, develop strong and diverse social networks and have active ties with siblings, friends, and other family members (McDill, Hall, and Turell 2006).

In some of the earliest work on singlehood, Stein (1981) developed four categories of singles based on whether people viewed their singlehood as voluntary or involuntary, and as temporary or stable. Those who see their singlehood as voluntary, whether short-term or permanent, have made a conscious choice to stay single. Research shows that people who choose singlehood feel more life satisfaction, less loneliness, and greater well-being than those who feel their single status is involuntary.

Research that examines the singlehood experience of never married women over the age of 40 (McDill, Hall, and Turell 2006) found that the majority of women in their study (65 percent) felt no societal sanctions related to their single status. Many also said they had not married because they had not met the right person, not because of some personal shortcomings. These women were satisfied with their lives, and felt particularly positive about the freedom their single status afforded them. They saw themselves as part of a "unique social stratum" (46).

Overall, never married older people report that they lead active lives and feel happy, are in good health, and feel satisfied with their standard of living. In general, single women are more satisfied with their lives than single men. And they report greater feelings of mastery over their environment, something that is linked to greater well-being (Keith 2003). Older single women see their independence, their ability to control their own finances, and their freedom to arrange their own social activities, as benefits of singlehood (Baumbusch 2004). While older single people report more loneliness than married seniors, single people, particularly single women, tend to feel less lonely than divorced and widowed older people. Single women also report less "single strain" (fewer chronic stressors associated with being single) (Pudrovska et al. 2006). The never married older women in Baumbusch's (2004) study identified the lack of spousal and filial companionship, intimacy, and informal care as disadvantages of singlehood. They feel regret at the absence of children and grandchildren. However, overall, they are satisfied with their single status.

Never married older people, compared to married and widowed older people, tend to rely more on siblings and friends for social support (Campbell, Connidis, and Davies 1999). They also have strong relationships with parents, aunts, uncles, nieces, and nephews. Never married older people, especially women, report good emotional support and good help in everyday life (Connidis 2001). Still, never married older people lack spousal and child support in later life, so they may use more formal supports than married older people.

Researchers project an increase in the proportion of older single people as Baby Boomers enter later life. As they age, these singles may play a significant role in helping to change societal attitudes about permanent singlehood. Future studies should look at the coping strategies that never married people use to maintain their high quality of life.

Widowhood

In 2001, there were just over 1.2 million widowed Canadians aged 65 and older (*The Daily*, July 22, 2004). This came to almost 30 percent of all older Canadians—11 percent of men and 42 percent of women (Turcotte and Schellenberg 2007). Rates of widowhood increase with age for both men and women, but women have a higher rate of widowhood at all ages. For people aged 65 to 74, 7 percent of men compared to 28 percent of women are widowed. For those aged 85 or older, 33 percent of men are widowed compared to 77 percent of women (see Exhibit 13.2). This means that most older men, particularly those younger than

● Exhibit 13.2

MARITAL STATUS OF OLDER CANADIANS BY AGE AND SEX, 2001

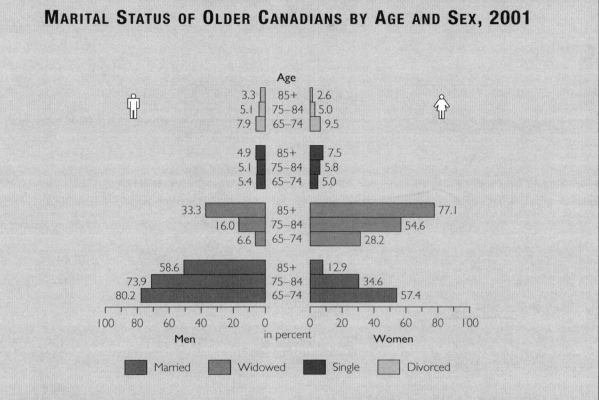

Married **Widowed** **Single** **Divorced**

Note that a higher proportion of men than women are married at every age presented here. Note also that the difference in rates of marriages between men and women increases with age. Almost 60 percent of men age 85 and over are married compared with only 13 percent of the oldest women. Widowhood rates for men and women differ as well. Very few men compared with more than one-quarter of women are widowed at ages 65 to 74. By age 85 and over, women have more than double the proportion of widowed compared with men. Why this difference in widowhood rates? First, wives tend to outlive their husbands. Second, compared to women, men show a greater tendency to remarry after the death of a spouse.

Source: Adapted from the Statistics Canada publication by Turcotte and Schellenberg, 2007, *A Portrait of Seniors in Canada*, 4th ed., Table 4.1.3, p. 192. Cat. No. 85-519 XIE. Reprinted with permission from Statistics Canada.

age 85, can expect to end their lives with a spouse. Older women, particularly those aged 75 and older, are more likely to live their final years in widowhood. Seventy-five percent of widowed women 65 years of age or older live alone (Bess 1999b).

Widows outnumber widowers for three reasons: (1) women live longer than men; (2) women marry older men; and (3) men, more than women, tend to remarry after widowhood. Older widowed men are seven times more likely than older widowed women to remarry (Cohen 1999). Matthews (1987) called widowhood an "expectable life event"—one that creates a great deal of stress. For example, many widows report that widowhood stripped them of their identity. In the late 1990s, van den Hoonaard (1997) called this "identity foreclosure". It signals the end of a woman's former identity (as a wife) and the need to build a new identity (Cicirelli 2002).

MacDougall (1998, 1–2), a widow, says that "part of the pain has to do with our sense of self; without our life-long partner, it becomes necessary to redefine our place in the world. When one has been part of a couple for a very long time, the adjustment can seem impossible." Some widowed women do find or re-establish meaning in their lives through holding on to memories of their role as wife and mother. They continue personal rituals and routines as mother and homemaker, and keep their attachment to their marital home and possessions (Shenk, Kuwahara, and Zablotsky 2004). As one widowed woman explained: "I do a lot of things [the same], you get into the habit over 50 years of marriage … I think it sort of keeps you connected" (Shenk et al. 2004, 167).

Gender and Widowhood

Most studies of widowhood in the past focused on women, but recent studies look at how widowhood affects each gender (Bennett 2007; Lee and DeMaris 2007). Studies of family supports, friendship, and **confidants** (someone in whom one confides) show that, compared to a married person, a widowed person is less likely to have a confidant (Ha 2008). However, support from children, friends, and other relatives tends to increase after widowhood.

Research finds that widowed women have more social supports than widowed men. Most older men spent their lives focused on their careers, while older women spent their lives focused on relationships. As a result, women have more close social ties than men in old age. Because men have fewer supports than women, they more often experience loneliness after their spouse dies. They may also experience a decline in their social functioning and mental health status. Chipperfield and Havens (2001) say that while life satisfaction declines for both men and women following the death of a spouse, men show a greater decline. Social support holds the key to life satisfaction for widowers. Carr (2004a), for example, reports that widowed men with strong social support (from friends and others) fare as well as widowed women in their adjustment to widowhood.

Women, more often than men, say they have close relationships with family and friends besides their spouses. They often name these friends, relatives, and children as their confidants, and they keep up these relationships when their husband dies (Campbell, Connidis, and Davies 1999). A widower loses a wife, a companion, and his link to other family and social ties. This may explain why many men seek another partner soon after they lose a spouse. Carr's research (2004b) finds that widowed men who have high levels of social support from friends are no more likely than widowed women to express a desire to repartner.

Research shows that widowed men, compared to women, find it harder to make new friends or to join self-help groups. Studies show that widowers suffer from isolation and loneliness after the loss of their spouse (Calasanti and Kiecolt 2007). This in part reflects their low involvement in relationships outside marriage over the life course. Some men may even experience elevated levels of depression *before* widowhood, because they anticipate the loss of their spouse. Women do not show this tendency (Lee and De Maris 2007). Compared with women, widowers run a higher risk of suicide. Men also have a higher risk of dying within the six months following the death of their spouse (Lee, Willetts, and Seccombe 1998).

Moore and Stratton (2002) found that, in spite of these challenges, some older widowed men bounce back from widowhood. The men in their study re-established a meaningful life after the loss of their spouse. Many of them found companionship and became involved in social activities. Research shows that social supports and family roles buffer the stress of widowhood for both men and women.

Men typically name their spouse as their confidant. But women more often have confidants other than their spouse (Calasanti and Kiecolt 2007). Widows, for example, often chose a sister or friend as a confidant (Campbell, Connidis, and Davies 1999). Campbell and her colleagues (1999) found that siblings, particularly sisters, provide emotional support to their widowed sisters. Sisters also serve as confidants and companions, especially if they live nearby. Siblings of both sexes can connect individuals to their past while being a source of support in the present. Confidants can contribute to good morale and lessen anxiety, tension, and depression.

Relatively few widows remarry. This, in part, reflects the larger number of eligible women compared with older men (Carr 2004b). Those who do remarry say they want companionship and the feeling that they add to another person's happiness. Those who remarry tend to be younger, worry less about finances, and have a higher household income than widowed women who remain single (Moorman, Booth, and Fingerman 2006). Wilcox and her colleagues (2003) report improved mental health and reduced depression in widowed women following their remarriage.

Many older widows report an interest in men, but not necessarily an interest in remarriage (Moorman et. al. 2006). Many report negative attitudes toward remarriage and an increased enjoyment in their independence. Older women may want to avoid the role of caregiver in a new marriage, or even having to arrange their lives around a new partner. Van den Hoonard

(2002) studied widowed women in New Brunswick. The women in this study felt disinclined to remarry because they felt they would always compare a new partner to their previous—and "best possible"— husband.

Research finds that women stay socially active in mother and grandmother roles after their husbands die. Many women also hold onto their wife role (Shenk et al. 2004). They remain committed to being a wife—or to the memory of being a wife—many years after the death of their husband. Van den Hoonaard (1999) says that the opportunity for widowed women to talk about the last days of their husbands' lives can give them comfort. These stories can also act as bridges on their journey from being a wife to being a widow.

Older women's longer life expectancy and the tendency to remain widowed lead to many of the problems that older women face. These often include financial difficulties. Inflation, for example, will eat away at a survivor's pension, if the widow has one. A widow may have to move from her home if her health declines (Bess 1999b). And she runs a greater risk of institutionalization than a married person because she will lack spousal support if she gets sick. Widowhood, in spite of good social supports, can put a woman at greater risk as she ages. Supportive relationships with family and friends help widowed women deal with the challenges they face.

Carr (2004a) reports that a woman's experience in marriage predicts how she will adjust to widowhood. For example, widowed women who had been emotionally dependent on their husbands (linked, in Carr's study, to low self-esteem) appeared to experience enhanced self-esteem through their ability to survive the loss of their spouse—"an event that had earlier seemed insurmountable" (232). Widowed women who had been dependent on their spouse for managing the finances and home maintenance tasks (tasks that are seen as traditionally male), experienced an increase in sense of purpose and self-confidence when they took on these responsibilities. To better understand the widowhood experience for both men and women, researchers need to examine multiple dimensions of their lives (Hatch 2000), including age, gender, race/ethnicity, social class, financial status, and social support.

SEXUALITY AND AGING

In the mid-1990s, Stones and Stones (1996) began their book *Sex May Be Wasted on the Young* with a discussion of ageism and sexuality. Young people in their teens and 20s, they said, thought of their grandparents as "way past

it ... The idea of their own relatives making love with passion evoked reactions from giggles at the improbable to horror at the unimaginable" (Stones and Stones 1996, x).

A decade and a half after the Stoneses' study, people still hold ageist stereotypes about sexuality in later life. Yet, studies show that these beliefs have little basis in fact. For example, most older people have an interest in sex throughout life and, given good health and a partner, older people can (and do) have sexual relations into late old age (AARP 2005; Elliott and Umberson 2008; Gott and Hinchliff 2003a). Older people who experience barriers to sexual activity—due to the lack of a partner or poor health—tend to place less importance on sex.

Researchers at Duke University conducted one of the earliest studies of sexuality in later life. This study, the Duke Longitudinal Study of Aging, began in the 1960s and included data on 254 people between the ages of 60 and 94 (see Pfeiffer, Verwoerdt, and Wang 1968; Verwoerdt, Pfeiffer, and Wang 1969). In that study, cross-sectional analysis showed a drop in sexual interest and activity with age, but longitudinal data showed many patterns of sexual change. About 20 percent of the men showed an increase in sexual interest and activity with age.

More current research (Gott and Hinchliff 2003a) finds that sex becomes more pleasurable and of greater importance to some people as they grow older. Masters and Johnson (1970), in their classic study, reported that men stopped having sex because of boredom, interest in outside activities, fatigue, drinking too much, poor health, or fear of failure. More recent research finds that the best predictors of men's continued sexual activity are good physical health, a healthy and interested partner, and level of sexual activity earlier in life (AARP 2005).

Women tend to stop having sexual relations earlier than men. This reflects the higher rates of widowhood for women in old age. Research shows that whether a woman maintains an active sex life or not depends on good health and the presence of an active sexual partner (Gott and Hinchliff 2003a; 2003b). Being married is key to older women's continued sexual activity. Jacoby (1999, 41) referred to a "partner gap" that disadvantages women and increases with age. Widowhood or a husband's decision to stop having sex often puts an end to a woman's sexual activity.

Current studies find that sexual activity in old age depends most on a person's pattern of sexual activity in the past. Men and women who have a partner and who enjoyed sex in the past will continue to enjoy it as they age (AARP 2005; Willert and Semans 2000). Sexual activity leads to high life satisfaction and good health.

Many older couples say that sex is more satisfying now than when they were younger. They feel more experienced, more relaxed, and enjoy the closeness with their partner. Sex is "a way of expressing love for a partner, helping maintain their relationship, as well as for giving them pleasure and improving self-confidence" (Gott and Hinchliff 2003a, 1625).

Sexual expression often evolves with age to include other forms of intimacy beyond just sexual intercourse, such as touching, hugging, and holding hands (Cooley 2002; Hurd Clarke 2006). Emotional closeness and companionship often take on greater importance for older couples. Older people can have a satisfying marriage without an active sex life. But research supports the idea that continued sexual activity can lead to happiness and well-being for older couples (AARP 2005).

A qualitative study by Elliott and Umberson (2008) explores how mid-life and older married people experience and negotiate sex in long-term marriages. The married men and women in their study both saw sex as integral to a good marriage—"as a barometer of the health of their own marriage" (396). However, many couples experienced conflict around sex, often related to gender differences in desired frequency—typically husbands wanting to have sex more often than their wives. Couples often tried to "change their sexual selves"—to show greater or lesser interest in sex to better match their spouse's desires. This negotiation of their sexual relationship was done to reduce marital conflict, enhance marital intimacy, improve a spouse's self-esteem, or all three. Elliott and Umberson (2008) call this "emotion work."

Thomas (1982) expressed it well and with humour, more than 25 years ago, when he compared sexuality in later life to eating popcorn: "It is not harmful, nor is it essential, but it is one of the pleasures of life." Twenty years after Thomas wrote those words, Cooley (2002, 2) echoed his message: "while expressing our sexuality isn't as essential for survival as food or water, it fulfils a need for affection and belonging. This in turn has a positive impact on our self-esteem and quality of life."

Adaptations in Sexuality Due to Aging

Sexually active older people have to adjust to changes in their bodies as they age. As he ages, a man takes longer to get an erection, takes longer to feel ready for intercourse again, and may have shorter, less intense orgasms. A woman may find that her vagina loses elasticity and opens less fully, and that she may have shorter orgasms (Calasanti and Slevin 2001). Older couples may need to use vaginal lubrication. Many books and videos exist that can help couples explore ways to adapt to these changes (Cooley 2002).

People can accept many changes as they get older—changes in strength, the senses, and athletic ability. But a change in sexual function can often damage a person's self-concept and psychological well-being. Sexual performance remains an integral part of what it means to be "manly" or "womanly" in our society. Many older men equate sex with sexual intercourse and, therefore, see their ability to "perform" as central to sexual activity as well as their own sense of self (Gott and Hinchliff 2003b). Impotence can significantly challenge a man's self-identity, particularly for men in the young-old age group (those in their 60s). For older men (in their 70s and 80s), erectile dysfunction is more likely to be seen as part of normal aging and, therefore, less challenging to their masculinity. For some men, erectile dysfunction may be a "trigger to self-defining as old" (Gott and Hinchliff 2003b, 73).

Women do not appear to have a comparable sexually related trigger that self-defines them as "old." In fact, many women feel growing older is sexually liberating. Today women have greater access to information on female sexuality and sexual aids. They also feel free from concerns about getting pregnant. Gott and Hinchliff (2003b, 73) say that "older age brought changes in the meaning of sex for women, with a shift in focus from reproduction to their own pleasure." Some older women see sexual intercourse as "the icing on the cake" (Hurd Clake 2006, 136). They emphasize cuddling and companionship more. As one remarried older woman said, "what is important is that we cuddle up ... and then if there is sex on top of it, that's extra good".

Almost 35 years ago, Butler and Lewis (1976) first talked about a **second language of sex** that could overcome the negative feelings that come with changes in sexual functioning. This language focuses on responsiveness, caring, and affection. Sometimes a couple will need medical help or counselling to cope with changes in sexual performance (Cooley 2002). This can take the form of a medical checkup, information about changes in the body with age, or sex therapy. Lifestyle changes can also improve sexual desire and functioning. This includes reduced alcohol consumption and smoking, good nutrition, and increased exercise. Studies show that older people can (and many do) make these adjustments as they age.

Drugs (such as Viagra) now exist to restore or enhance sexual performance in older men. The American Association of Retired Persons (AARP) conducted a study of sexual behaviour (AARP 2005) and found that 26 percent of men aged 60 to 69 reported taking medicine, hormones, or other treatment to enhance sexual performance, compared to 9 percent of same-age women. Many men who use Viagra, as well as their female partners, say it increases their sexual enjoyment (Vares et al. 2007).

The success of Viagra and similar products in the marketplace will no doubt lead to new forms of drug therapy. This option and a greater interest in sexual activity among Baby Boomers will lead to more active sex lives among older adults in the future.

Gay and Lesbian Older Adults

Most studies of sexuality in later life have focused on married or single heterosexuals. Few studies report on older gay and lesbian adults (Connidis 2003). Do these people face unique challenges as they age? Do older gays and lesbians adapt better or less well than heterosexuals to sexual changes with age? Like heterosexuals, many older gays and lesbians have committed and enduring relationships and close ties to family and friends (O'Brien and Goldberg 2005). Heaphy and his colleagues (2004) found that 40 percent of older gay men and 60 percent of older lesbians in their study were in couple relationships. These numbers are comparable to those found in other research (Patterson 2000). Typically, the younger the individual, the more likely he or she will be in a relationship.

The 2006 Canadian Census (Statistics Canada 2007; 2008) reported that close to 91,000 Canadians live in same-sex unions, or just over 45,000 couples. Seniors (those aged 65 or older) make up about 4 percent of people in same-sex couples.

Lee (1987) conducted the first study of gay aging men in Canada. He found that men who had partners in the past—a wife, lovers, or a combination of both—reported high life satisfaction even if they now lived alone. Lee found that gay men with a partner tend to report high life satisfaction, but he also reported that having a lover in later life "is not easy to achieve" (Lee 1987, 147; see also Heaphy et al. 2004).

Lee also found that men who preferred other gay men as friends, those who knew an older gay man as a role model, and those involved in a gay social life showed higher life satisfaction. Lee's findings showed that older gay men get satisfaction from many of the same things as heterosexual men—companionship, sexual fulfillment, and friendship. They also have unique sources of satisfaction and face unique challenges as they age. Lee's study showed that gay men can adapt to the changes that come with age and that, as he said, "it is possible to achieve happiness alone or by sharing life with a lover, even one found late in life" (151).

Current research supports Lee's findings. Many gays and lesbians have strong, committed relationships, and active social networks (O'Brien and Goldberg 2005).

Research suggests that older gay men and lesbians are concerned about the same things as many other older people—health, finances, body changes, loss of friends, and loneliness (Allen and Wilcox 2000). For example, having a committed partner increases life satisfaction and decreases loneliness for older gay men and lesbians. But some concerns of older gay and lesbian adults grow out of the stigma associated with their sexual orientation, including worrying about discrimination in health care, housing, long-term care, and rejection by children or grandchildren (McFarland and Sanders 2003).

One theme appears in nearly all the studies of homosexuality in later life. Societal attitudes toward homosexuality have shaped and continue to shape the lives of gay and lesbian older people. The double social stigma of being gay and being old may increase the challenges that older gays and lesbians face in later life (Connidis 2003). For example, societal homophobia has led many gay and lesbian older people to hide their homosexuality (Heaphy et al. 2004). They fear that exposure might cost them their jobs or their sense of belonging in their local communities.

Friend (1996) proposed that gays' and lesbians' adaptations to a hostile society may improve their ability to cope with the challenges of aging. First, he said that gays and lesbians have experience in constructing a positive image of themselves in spite of negative social definitions. This may help them construct a positive image of themselves as they age. Second, gays and lesbians have experience in creating supportive relationships, which may help them create the support networks they need as they age. Third, many gays and lesbians have experience with political advocacy and will be better able to defend their rights as they age (O'Brien and Goldberg 2005). This activist experience may help aging gays and lesbians get the social supports they need in later life (Brotman, Ryan, and Cormier 2002).

Like older heterosexual adults, older gays and lesbians need a broad range of social supports and services. Yet many mistrust the health and social service systems because of past discrimination, or a fear they will face discrimination (Richard and Brown 2006). Researchers report that gays and lesbians can best meet these needs by planning and implementing programs for their community. This includes participation in nonheterosexual clubs, groups, or organized networks (Heaphy et al. 2003). Informal supports also play a significant role in later life. Older lesbians and gays who are reluctant to use formal services may need to create their own informal support networks (Richard and Brown 2006). However, this reluctance can place an added burden on their caregivers (Brotman et al. 2007).

A long-term relationship with a committed partner provides both gay men and lesbians with companionship, acceptance, and support. Ties to other family members and friends also provide support. Many gay men and lesbians feel that if they needed care, their partner, along with formal care services, would be their care providers (Heaphy et al. 2004). Few expected care from their children, siblings, friends, or other relatives. However, many older gays and lesbians fear that their partner's role would not be recognized by service providers (McFarland and Sanders 2003).

Research on homosexuality in later life has only begun, and a number of research topics still need study. These include the longitudinal study of aging gay and lesbian couples (O'Brien and Goldberg 2000), ethnic and cultural diversity among gays and lesbians (McFarland and Sanders 2003; Patterson 2000), the special concerns of older gays and lesbians (Allen and Wilcox 2000), and caregiving for older gays and lesbians (Brotman et al. 2007). Researchers also need to study the relationships between gay older parents and their adult children and grandchildren (Connidis 2001). Studies of gay and lesbian aging show that societal influences and past experiences shape a person's life in old age. They also show that sexuality plays an important part in homosexual as well as heterosexual aging.

PART TWO: SOCIAL SUPPORT

Social support refers to help and assistance we give to and receive from others. Older people benefit from the support they receive from family members and friends in the form of emotional support, companionship, help with household chores, and a range of other help. But older people also give help to family members through financial assistance, emotional support, and help with childcare. They also provide a home for unmarried, divorced, or unemployed adult children. Part Two of this chapter looks at (1) older people as a source of support, including their role as grandparents; (2) informal support given to older people from family members and friends; (3) family caregivers; and (4) abuse against older people.

OLDER PEOPLE AS A SOURCE OF SUPPORT

Most of the writing on older people in families focuses on their needs and on what other people do for them. But older people also give help to their families (Keefe and Fancey 2002). Very early work by Shanas (1967) found that, contrary to the belief that older parents are passive recipients of their children's support, reciprocal help was given in the form of household chores, financial aid, and assistance during illness and other crisis situations. These findings remain true today. Older parents also provided childcare assistance. Research finds that reciprocity within supportive relationships leads to well-being and higher morale.

Robb and her colleagues (1999) found that, compared to younger people, older people provide more informal unpaid help to their families. Older people give at least three kinds of support. First, they help their spouses and children with health care and daily chores; second, they give their children financial support; and third, they give emotional support to and serve as role models for younger family members.

Daily Help Given by Older People

Contrary to what many people believe, younger seniors (under age 75) tend to provide more assistance to younger relatives than they receive (Turcotte and Schellenberg 2007). Research shows that older people give varied forms of help to younger people. For example, older people help others with housework or yard work, most often their children, or a friend or neighbour. Also, older people provide child care help with grandchildren. Some older parents provide daily and lifelong care to children with disabilities (Joffres 2002).

Many parents also share their home with adult children, who delay leaving home or return home in adulthood (Beaupré, Turcotte, and Milan 2006a; 2006b). Adult children who live with older parents often do so because they have no spouse, attend school, or have no job. The number of adult children (those in their 20s and 30s) who live with parents has increased since the 1980s (Boyd and Norris 1999). What accounts for this change? First, more children remain home longer into adulthood. Some delay leaving home in order to finish school. Others remain home after they get their first job in order to save money. Second, **boomerang children** return to their parents' home after having moved out at an earlier point in time. Turcotte (2006) found that more than 30 percent of Canadian parents whose youngest child was between the ages of 20 and 34 had at least one of their children living at home. In one-quarter of these families, these children were "boomerang kids."

Stone, Rosenthal, and Connidis (1998; Government of Canada 1999) studied different kinds of help given by older parents to their children. These included financial support, childcare, and help with daily chores. The researchers found that overall support from older parents to adult children peaks between ages 55 and 64, with 47 percent of these parents saying that they give help. Still, a quarter of parents aged 65 to 74 give medium or high levels of help. And even at age 75 and older, nearly one-fifth (18 percent) of parents say they give some help to their children.

These researchers say that older parents aged 45 to 74 probably give most of their support as unpaid work such as childcare. Later in life (age 75 and over), parents may offer more financial support as their own physical ability declines. These researchers suggest that parents give the most support to the children they feel have the most need. The authors find that the give and take of support remains relatively balanced between parents and children until around age 70. Then children begin to give more help than they receive.

These researchers and others (Connidis 2001; Turcotte and Schellenberg 2007) find that although support within families flows both ways, over a lifetime parents give more support than they receive. Furthermore, older people provide important support to their children throughout their later years. Stone, Rosenthal, and Connidis (1998, 24) said that "if we had included the monetary value of services provided informally by one generation to another we would increase markedly the relative size of the figure for flows that benefit the young." Older people also pass on possessions (see Exhibit 13.3), money, and property to younger generations through inheritance bequests.

Research finds differences in the types of help that older men and women provide to others (Turcotte and Schellenberg 2007). Men are more likely to help with home maintenance, outside chores, and transportation. They also tend to help with practical advice. Older women are more likely to provide emotional support or childcare. Older people, compared to those

---

● Exhibit 13.3

PASSING ON CHERISHED POSSESSIONS: THE MEANING OF FAMILY INHERITANCE

Many older people wonder how to pass on their family possessions. They know that family members can argue over small things. And they want to avoid a family feud. Dr. Lori Campbell and colleagues wondered how and why people decided to pass on their heirlooms. They asked 50 older men and women about their decisions.

Mrs. G, a twice-widowed 68-year-old woman, has three children, three step-children, six grandchildren, and four step-grandchildren. After her husband passed away, she started to think about leaving things to her heirs. She decided on a simple method. She says, "I have a book and I said, 'sign up for what you want.' And I listed all my stuff and Dave's stuff in there. So they've signed their names."

Mr. W, 82, and his wife of 56 years, have seven children and 17 grandchildren. He fears that his wife will die first and he will have to divide up their possessions. He says, "I was going to invite all the children to come for a week and put everything on the table and say, 'right, who wants what? Draw a number and take it in turns to pick something.'"

Objects collected through a lifetime take on a new meaning for people in late old age. These objects serve as links between the generations and as physical signs of "family continuity." Mrs. S explains this view.

Mrs. S: "Photographs or letters and things like that I find are really important. ... and teacups and things like that."

Interviewer: "And why are they important to you?"

Mrs. S: "'Cause I think it's continuity. It's looking at your family ... looking back at who they were, so that you can let your own kids know that this is where you came from."

What do you think is the best way for older people to pass on their possessions? Have you seen this done in your family? If so, what was the method used? If not, do you know of families where this was done successfully? Unsuccessfully? How do you think you will handle this process in old age?

Source: L.D. Campbell, J. Ploeg, C.L. Kemp, and C. Rosenthal, 2007, Who Gets Grandma's Silver Tea Service?: The Passing on of Cherished Family Possessions. Paper presented at the 36th Annual Scientific and Educational Meeting of the Canadian Association on Gerontology, Calgary, Alberta, November 1–3, 2007 (and additional unpublished data from the Campbell et al. Family Inheritance Study).

who are younger (those 25 to 54 years of age), are also more likely to provide help to a neighbour. These findings show that most older people live interdependently with family, neighbours, and friends. They give and receive help with practical activities and finances. They exchange emotional support throughout their lives.

Financial Support

Older people give younger members of their family financial support. The amount and kind of support given differs by social class and ethnic group, but studies show that even middle-aged people think of their parents as givers. Studies show that older adults give more money to their children than they get from them (Ploeg et al. 2004; Stone, Rosenthal, and Connidis 1998). Older people report that they get pleasure and satisfaction from giving money to younger family members (Bass and Caro 1996).

Ploeg and her colleagues (2004) found that most parents give financial assistance to their children because of the love and commitment they feel toward individual children and to their family overall. Some parents gave money as an early inheritance, when children could benefit from it most, and when they themselves could enjoy the experience of giving. Many parents saw their financial support as a way to help adult children "build" their lives as they began their careers or families. Others gave to help children "rebuild" their lives after difficult life events such as a divorce, illness, or the loss of a job. These parents saw a financial need and had the financial resources to help.

Emotional Support and Being a Role Model

Research shows that adult children rely on their parents as role models throughout their lives. Many adult children turn to their parents for emotional support and help during and after a divorce. Parents can also act as role models for their adult children as they experience important later-life transitions such as grandparenthood, widowhood, and retirement (Connidis 2001). Older family members derive great satisfaction from the help they give to their children and to other younger family members.

Rosenthal, Marshall, and Synge (1980) found that older people played many roles in their families. These included the "occupational sponsor" (the person who helps others find jobs or get started in business), the "comforter" (the person to whom people turn for personal advice and support), the "ambassador" (the person who represents the family at ceremonies), the "head of the family" (the person who makes choices that others go along with), and the "**kin keeper**" (the person who keeps family members in touch with one another). Women generally occupy the kin keeper role. Families with kin keepers tend to get together more often. Men in families with kin keepers benefit by having stronger ties to their siblings.

Older parents bring their families together on special occasions, which increases contact among family members. Older women often serve as advisers and confidants to their widowed daughters. Older men often give financial help to their children and grandchildren. Family roles can give meaning and purpose to an older person's life. Research finds that older people have the highest emotional well-being when they give as well as receive support. Reciprocity makes older people feel useful, independent, and worthwhile. Older people's supportive roles can strengthen intergenerational ties and create more fulfilling relationships between parents and their children, as well as their grandchildren.

Grandparenting

Grandparenthood is a common experience for older Canadians (Kemp 2003). More people will take on the grandparent role today than ever before, and many of them will assume this role in late mid-life. In 2001, there were about 5.7 million grandparents in Canada (Turcotte and Schellenberg 2007). According to the 2001 General Social Survey (GSS), 65 percent of Canadian women and 53 percent of Canadian men aged 55 to 64 are grandparents (Milan and Hamm 2003). Four out of five Canadians aged 75 and older have grandchildren. The average age of grandparents in Canada is 65.

Women make up 80 percent of grandparents, reflecting the fact that more women live into old age than men. On average, grandparents have between four and five grandchildren. And most grandparents have regular contact with at least one grandchild. Researchers expect the number of grandchildren per grandparent to decrease in the future as couples have fewer children (Kemp 2003).

Hagestad (1985, 48) calls grandparents "demographic pioneers." With increased longevity, many grandparents will live to see their grandchildren grow into adults with children of their own. Grandparents now play complex roles in the lives of their grandchildren. Some grandparents feel that they do enough by simply being present, but others play a more active role as family arbitrators, watchdogs, or family historians. Grandparents often look out for the well-being of younger relatives, help them when they can, and create links between family members. The grandparent role offers older people one of the most satisfying and enjoyable ways to give to other family members (Kemp 2005).

Some grandparents involve themselves in the daily lives and care of their grandchildren. In 2006, almost 4 percent of children in Canada aged 14 and under lived in multigenerational households with at least three generations (grandparents, parents, and grandchildren) (Milan and Hamm 2003; Statistics Canada 2008a). A small number of grandparents live with grandchildren without the presence of the middle generation. In 2006, about 1 percent of all grandparents or 12 percent of grandparents in shared households raised their children's children without the middle generation being present (Statistics Canada 2008a). Researchers call these arrangements **skip-generation households.**

Grandparents often care for their grandchildren because their own children can't provide the care. This can occur because of divorce or separation, mental health difficulties, substance abuse, or the death of an adult child (Waldrop and Weber 2001). Grandparents feel rewarded when they raise their grandchildren, but they also face challenges. These can include worries about their own health, problems with social isolation, and financial difficulties (Roe and Minkler 1998). At a period when older people expect more time and freedom in their retirement years, these grandparents take on unanticipated childcare responsibilities, often with high-risk grandchildren (Minkler 1999a). Caring full-time for a grandchild can create a close emotional bond, particularly for grandmothers (Bowers and Myers 1999), but it can also increase grandparents' stress (Sands and Goldberg-Glen 2000).

Research shows that grandchildren value their grandparents. Grandparents provide adult grandchildren with a view into the past—to their childhood, their family history, and historical events. As one 29-year-old grandson said of his relationship with his grandparents: "it is very important for knowing your roots and for family history and for knowing where you came from … It's like a key" (Kemp 2005, 168). Grandchildren feel respect for their grandparents. They admire their strength and resilience in surviving the hardships and struggles of their younger years. Grandchildren also worry about the present-day health challenges their grandparents face (Boon and Shaw 2007b).

An eight-year-old in a Quebec study (Grand'Maison and Lefebvre 1996, 83) said that he enjoyed visiting the garden at his grandfather's house. "He shows me things. He has lots of imagination, and he's very clever. We look at the mushrooms and imagine what kind of shapes they look like." A 12-year-old girl says, "I really love my grandparents. If I skip a week seeing them,

I miss them. They've looked after me so many times. … My grandmother is a terrific teacher. … She taught me about cooking and I can make great muffins. With my grandfather, I learned about using tools and about the value of work well done" (Grand'Maison and Lefebvre 1996, 88).

The grandparent–grandchild relationship has become more common in the lives of adult grandchildren. The majority of young adults in Canada have at least one living grandparent (70 percent of adults in their 20s and 32 percent of adults in their 30s) (Kemp 2003). Holladay and colleagues (1998) studied granddaughters in their teens and early 20s. The researchers found that sharing activities and going through family crises (such as a death or illness) led granddaughters to feel close to their maternal grandmothers. Boon and Brussoni (1998) found that undergraduates who had the closest relationship with their own grandparent saw the grandparent role as loving and supportive. Life course transitions within the family, such as divorce or death, can often bring grandparents and adult grandchildren closer together. With people living longer, adult grandchildren have the opportunity to get to know their grandparents as "real people" and as friends (Kemp 2005).

Kornhaber (2002) lists nearly a dozen grandparent roles today. A grandparent can play some or all of them. They include ancestor, buddy, hero, historian, mentor, nurturer, role model, spiritual guide, student, teacher, and wizard. This last role may surprise you. Kornhaber says that societies in the past have often ascribed magical powers to elders, and a modern grandparent can draw on this role to engage grandchildren in fantasy play. Kornhaber cites the case of a little girl who had an imaginary friend. Her grandparents set a place at the table for this friend when their granddaughter came to visit.

Grandparents can introduce grandchildren to the wonders of the natural world by taking hikes or going camping in natural surroundings. Grandparents can have fun and don't have to abide by the rational rules that parents sometimes need to enforce. Grandparents and grandchildren can provide support and enjoyment for one another.

Holladay et al. (1997) found that parental attitudes influenced teenaged granddaughters' feelings of closeness to their grandmothers. An absence of criticism of the grandmother by the parent and parents' comments on the importance of the grandmother led to greater feelings of closeness. Older grandchildren have closer ties with their grandparents if they see the relationship between their parents and grandparents as close (King and Elder 1997).

© 2009 Jupiterimages Corporation

Longer life expectancy and better health in later life will mean that several generations will live together for many years. Some people will live to see their great-grandchildren grow to adulthood.

Gender can also influence the quality of the relationship, with closer ties in general for female family members. For example, grandchildren tend to be closer to their maternal grandparents (Chan and Elder 2000). Grandparents are closer to granddaughters than to grandsons, and grandmothers have closer and more active ties with both granddaughters and grandsons than do grandfathers (Fingerman 2001). What a grandparent makes of the grandparent role also depends on the older person's gender, age, marital status, geographic proximity, and relationship with his or her adult children. Proximity can influence emotional closeness in grandfather–grandchild relationships (Roberto et al. 2001) but living nearby does not guarantee a close bond.

Some researchers say that the importance of grandfathers has been underestimated (Mann 2007). Roberto and her colleagues (2001) studied male views of grandparenting. Some men in that study felt that grandfathers should take a "hands-off" approach to caring for or disciplining their grandchildren.

But other grandfathers felt that they should play an active role in the lives of grandchildren. "[These latter grandfathers] revealed that it is not enough to just *be* a grandfather; one must also *do*, in an active and involved way" (Roberto et al. 2001, 422). Some researchers believe that "new norms of grandfatherhood" exist that focus on nurturing and mentoring (Mann 2007).

Research findings suggest that aging and decreased activity may lead to decreases in grandparents' influence on their grandchildren. Some of the grandparents in an early study by Cherlin and Furstenberg (1985), for example, used "selective investment" to focus their energy on some of their closer or more personable grandchildren. In general, research shows that while the bond between adult grandchildren and their grandparents remains high across the life course, the relationship involves continuity and change over time. This can mean continued closeness over time (Hodgson 1995), closer ties with grandmothers and less close ties to grandfathers (Mills 1999), or a gradual decline over time with some increased closeness in the grandparents' later years (Silverstein and Long 1998). For both generations, the tie is often seen as "an unconditional latent reserve of support" or a "safety net" of support, should it be needed (Kemp 2005, 173).

Research by Kemp (2004) looks at the expectations grandparents and grandchildren have of themselves and each other within what she terms these "grand" roles. Kemp finds that while the roles and relationships are diverse, grandparents and grandchildren do have expectations related to behaviour and responsibilities within the relationship. For example, both grandparents and grandchildren feel that grandparents should provide love, support, encouragement, and assistance to grandchildren, but should not interfere in their lives unless asked for help or advice. As one grandmother says, "I think being a grandparent is to listen and not to criticize" (11). A granddaughter says "grandparents are just supposed to be there when you need them and they always are ... they don't give advice unless you ask for it" (15). Grandparents were also seen as role models, teachers, and sources of family history and lived experience.

Grandchildren felt they should be respectful to grandparents and give them their time and attention. They felt an obligation to "give back" to grandparents for all the love and support grandparents had given to the family. This came in the form of spending time with grandparents and doing things to make grandparents proud of their accomplishments. Grandparents also hoped that their grandchildren would spend time with them and be an important part of their lives. However, for both grandchildren and grandparents, independence was important. Grandchildren sought to *establish* their own independence while grandparents wanted to *maintain* their independence. Some grandparents and adult grandchildren develop friendships over time (Kemp 2004, 2005).

Studies show that feelings between grandparents and grandchildren depend on the relationship between the grandparents and the parents (Monserud 2008). The closer the relationship between the parent and grandparent, the closer the tie between grandparents and grandchildren. The quality of the grandparents' relationship with their children-in-law may be of particular importance in influencing the quality of the grandparent–grandchild tie (Fingerman 2004).

In the late 1980s, Gladstone (1989) studied 110 grandparents in nonintact Canadian families (where parents had split up). He found that adult children and children-in-law act as mediators between grandchildren and grandparents. They can obstruct or arrange visits. Children-in-law can inhibit contact by keeping the former spouse from seeing children. This would, in turn, keep the grandparent from seeing the children. Contact with grandchildren of divorced or separated children depends on the grandparent's relationship to the former child-in-law, whether the child or the child-in-law has custody of the grandchild, and geographical closeness. More recent work in the late 1990s by Hilton and Macari (1997) found that, compared to paternal grandparents, maternal grandparents stay more involved in the grandparent role when their daughter gains custody of her children. The reverse takes place when a son gains custody of his children. Kruk (1995) found that denial of access by a child-in-law (often in the case of divorce) accounted for most cases of loss of contact for grandparents.

Gladstone (1989) concluded in his study that grandparents often need to negotiate relationships with their children and children-in-law in broken marriages to enhance contact with their grandchildren. This can present a challenge to the grandparent when emotions erupt during separations and divorces. Family practitioners can help to enhance grandparent–grandchild relationships during these times. Kruk (1995) said that family therapists should include grandparents in their work with post-divorce couples to recognize the grandparents' role in the post-divorce family and allow them to support their grandchildren during this stressful time.

A self-help group with chapters across the country called **GRAND (Grandparents Requesting Access and Dignity)** helps grandparents who cannot get access to their grandchildren. The group, started in 1983, provides education and support, and lobbies for changes in laws to protect grandparents' access to their grandchildren. After GRAND collected 10,000 names on a petition to change the *Divorce Act*, members presented the petition to the House of Commons. The petition asks that the act include a statement such as the one in the Quebec Civil Code that says "in no case may a father or mother, without serious cause, place obstacles between the child and grandparents." This petition, however, was not successful. The federal *Divorce Act* does allow for access applications from people other than parents, but does not explicitly identify grandparents (Goldberg 2003).

Kruk (1995) reported that grandparents who used legal means to get access to grandchildren had success. One Toronto lawyer reported that he handled 40 cases for grandparents between 1992 and 1995. He won every case and got the grandparents custody or access (Davis 1996). However, not all access cases are successful. In March 2001, in *Chapman v. Chapman*, the Ontario Court of Appeal decided in favour of the parents and their right to limit the grandmother's access to their children (Goldberg 2003). The parents had a poor relationship with the grandmother and felt she had a negative influence on their two children. The Ontario Court of Appeal ruled that competent parents are presumed to act in the best interests of their children and should therefore decide who can see and spend time with their children.

Grandparents who go to court risk increasing the tension with their children or children-in-law (Gearon 2003). Kruk (1995) said that legislative support for grandparent rights would decrease the need for legal action. Today, grandparents have to show the courts why they should have access to their grandchildren and that denying access would be harmful to grandchildren (Goldberg 2003). A change in the law would guarantee grandparents' rights of access. In 2006, Manitoba put in place a provincial "Grand Relations" strategy to help grandparents and families resolve grandchild access and guardianship issues. The strategy helps families avoid the financial and emotional costs of court hearings (Province of Manitoba 2008). Grandparent advisors are appointed to help families negotiate the best solution to grandchild access disputes. Families are also provided with information about options and services that are available, and how to enhance relationships within families in the best interest of grandchildren.

INFORMAL SUPPORTS FOR OLDER PEOPLE

Life course events and sociocultural conditions influence the quality of life in old age, but they do not determine it. Older people can and do respond actively to the changes that aging brings. Their response depends on their personality, past experience, and social resources, including social supports. This section will look at the social supports that help older people cope with aging and improve their quality of life and well-being.

Snell (1990) studied the legal history of family support in Canada in the 1920s and 1930s. The laws of the time held families responsible for caring for their older members. The *Criminal Code* today still requires children to provide their parents with the basic necessities of life if the parents cannot provide for themselves. All provinces also have legislation that requires a child to support needy parents, but the law seldom comes into play. For example, even though the *Parents Maintenance Act* has been a legal statute in Ontario since 1921, only a few times have parents sued adult children for support (Parsons and Tindale 2001).

Researchers study two types of social support: formal and informal. The 2002 GSS reports that one million older Canadians who live in the community need support due to a chronic health problem (Cranswick 2003; Cranswick and Thomas 2005). This assistance comes from informal support, formal support, or a combination of both.

Informal support refers to the unpaid help given by friends, neighbours, and family. Informal support includes everyday help such as rides to the doctor or to a shopping centre, help with house cleaning or yard work, or just a visit from a neighbour. Informal supporters can also help an older person cope with a personal crisis, adjust to a change in health, or locate a formal service.

In 2002, more than two million Canadians age 45 and older (one in five Canadians in this age group) reported providing some type of care or assistance to an older family member or friend (Cranswick 2003). Women provide the majority of informal support. Older care recipients are also more likely to be women.

The term **formal support** refers to help given by professional caregivers such as doctors, nurses, and social workers as well as paid homemakers and other health care services. People pay for formal supports either from their own resources or through their taxes. Studies find that few older people who need help with daily chores or health care use only formal care. More often people use both the formal and informal support systems. Keating and her colleagues (1997, 24) call this a "caring partnership." They say that social policies now favour this mix of informal and formal care. Studies show that people usually turn to the formal system only after the informal system no longer meets their needs. Formal care use also tends to increase with age (see Exhibit 13.4). Penning (2002) finds that even those who make extensive use of formal care services still rely on their informal care network.

Today, most older people get voluntary informal support from their families. Cranswick and Thomas (2005) report that just under half (45 percent) of older people in the community who receive assistance get all their help from family and friends. The rest (55 percent) receive both informal and formal support. Keating and her colleagues (1999) found that of the older people who receive help with household tasks, 90 percent receive informal assistance; 10 percent receive paid help.

Informal caregivers also provide about two-thirds of all care. People continue to get support, especially from the nuclear family, even after they face a health care crisis. Informal supports can also buffer stress from life events such as widowhood or illness. A greater proportion of older women, compared with older men, get

● **Exhibit 13.4**

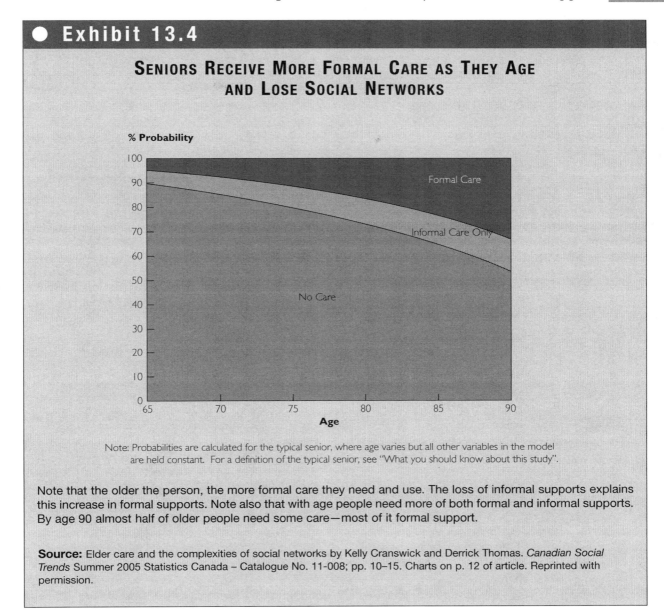

SENIORS RECEIVE MORE FORMAL CARE AS THEY AGE
AND LOSE SOCIAL NETWORKS

% Probability

Formal Care

Informal Care Only

No Care

Age

Note: Probabilities are calculated for the typical senior, where age varies but all other variables in the model are held constant. For a definition of the typical senior, see "What you should know about this study".

Note that the older the person, the more formal care they need and use. The loss of informal supports explains this increase in formal supports. Note also that with age people need more of both formal and informal supports. By age 90 almost half of older people need some care—most of it formal support.

Source: Elder care and the complexities of social networks by Kelly Cranswick and Derrick Thomas. *Canadian Social Trends* Summer 2005 Statistics Canada – Catalogue No. 11-008; pp. 10–15. Charts on p. 12 of article. Reprinted with permission.

emotional support from children or friends (Campbell, Connidis, and Davies 1999). Older men, compared with older women, have smaller support networks.

Stone (1988, 14) found that the availability of **primary potential support groups** changed as people aged. He defined this type of group as family and close friends who give help to the older person and who can expect help from the older person. Stone reported that about one-third of people aged 65 to 79 lived with a spouse and had family and friendship ties. Men more often than women had this kind of support group structure. Past the age of 80, community-dwelling older adults tended to live alone, but they still had links outside their household to children, close friends, and other relatives. Women more often than men had this kind of support group structure. Very old people in institutions had smaller support structures or none at all.

Caregiving networks vary significantly in size, proximity, and composition—by gender, relationship, and age (Fast et al. 2004). These network characteristics explain variations in the types and amounts of care older people get. Older adults may not get enough care when they have small networks, networks with mostly male nonrelatives, and networks with members who live far away. Research also finds that social networks and living arrangements can influence the informal and formal support that older people receive. Cranswick and Thomas (2005) say that "the size, quality and proximity of people's social networks are arguably among the things that determine whether seniors receive formal care delivered by professionals, rely on informal care provided by family and friends or, indeed, receive no care at all" (10). Overall, very few older people who live in the community are without some close supportive ties.

Recent studies have looked at how older people choose their informal supporters out of their potential group of supporters. Studies have also looked at the tasks informal supporters perform. Four models describe the way people use informal supports: the task specificity model, the hierarchical compensatory model, the functional specificity of relationships model, and the convoy model.

1. The **task specificity model** says that different groups (family, friends, neighbours) have different abilities and offer different types of support (Litwak 1985). Each group plays a specific role in supporting the older person. For example, a spouse might provide companionship, while adult children provide everyday support, and friends act as confidants.

2. The **hierarchical compensatory model** of support states that people choose all types of support first from their inner family circle. This typically means their spouse and children. They then move outward to get support from less-intimate people if more intimate ties are not available or are unable to meet their needs (Cantor and Little 1985). This model says that a married older person will get help first from a spouse, while a widow or widower will get help first from a child (most often a daughter). The older person will then turn to friends, siblings, or other family members, then to neighbours, and then to formal supports, in that order.

3. The **functional specificity of relationships model** (Simons 1983–84) recognizes that "one tie may provide one type of support or a broad range of support, dependent on how that particular relationship has been negotiated" over the life course (Campbell, Connidis, and Davies 1999, 118). For example, the gender, marital status, parenthood, and proximity of helpers all influence the amount and type of support a person will get.

4. The **convoy model of support** sees people as having a dynamic network of close ties with family and friends (Kahn and Antonucci 1980). This model uses concentric circles to position close relationships around the individual, with the closest ties in the closest circle. Outer circles show ties that are less close (Haines and Henderson 2002). These ties form a "convoy" that travels with individuals throughout life, exchanging social support and assistance. The nature of this convoy can grow and change over time with changing life circumstances.

Penning (1990) compared the ability of the task specificity model and the hierarchical compensatory model to explain older people's use of informal supports. She found only limited support for each model. Older people tended to use a variety of formal and informal supports at the same time and not in a specific hierarchical order. She also found that groups did a variety of tasks that overlapped. For example, relatives and neighbours both helped with household tasks. Penning (1990, 227) said that "it is unlikely that assistance is provided routinely and uniformly on the basis of a set order of preference." She concluded that "the issue of who provides assistance to whom, of what type, and under what conditions is complex."

Denton (1997) used data from Canada's General Social Survey to study the use of formal and informal supports. She found that formal supports compensate for the lack of informal supports, but not in the way put forward by the hierarchical compensatory model. Use of formal supports in this way most often applies to single older people who live alone and have no children. Denton also found that in a smaller proportion of cases caregivers used formal supports to supplement their informal support. This study builds on Penning's earlier work. It shows that formal care both compensates for and supplements informal support.

Campbell, Connidis, and Davies (1999) found support for the functional specificity of relationships model. They found that siblings provide a range of social support for certain groups, including single women, the childless, single men, and widowed women. But siblings provide little support for divorced and married men. In general, siblings give support when they live nearby. Siblings also tend to serve as companions and confidants, and they more often provide practical support to sisters than to brothers. These findings show that particular groups of older adults develop supportive ties with siblings, "not as substitution or compensation for lost ties but based on a lifetime of negotiating unique ties with siblings" (144).

More recently, Haines and Henderson (2002) assessed the convoy model of social support. They found that while the model helps to identify significant supportive relationships, not all strong ties provide support. They also found that weak ties, typically ignored in the convoy model of support, can and do provide instrumental support, emotional support, and companionship. Sims-Gould and her colleagues (2008; also Sims-Gould and Martin-Matthews 2007) report that often a network of individuals provide support. But, they say, current models don't look at how multiple care providers assist *one another* in their work.

Other research findings add another dimension to this complexity of social support. Whether or not an older person lives with someone strongly influences the type of support he or she gets. If an older person lives with someone, that person will likely give him or her support for the activities necessary to daily living (Boaz, Hu, and Ye, 1999; Campbell and Martin-Matthews 2000b). It seems that shared living arrangements (between siblings or friends) may help widowed or childless older people live in the community. Strain and Blandford (2003) report that caregivers who live with an older parent provide daily help with meal preparation and household chores.

Family members sometimes relocate to give or receive care (Cranswick 2003; 1999). For example, in 1996, 470,000 Canadians moved closer to family members either to provide care or because they needed care (Cranswick 1999). Some of these people (130,000 individuals) moved in with their care receiver. In 2001, among caregivers aged 45 to 64, 10 percent of women and 8 percent of men said their care receiver had moved closer to them, with 4 percent of women and 2 percent of men moving in with the older relative needing care (Cranswick 2003).

Studies find that, compared to women, men get less informal support from nonspousal supporters. Women are more likely than men to consult family and friends regarding common ailments. And women say they would consult a relative outside the house for a health emergency. Compared to men, women also report support from more helpers and more help from daughters and relatives for functional disabilities. Older people who have a helping network feel greater subjective well-being.

Many older people turn to formal care services in addition to informal support. Two conditions lead to the use of formal supports along with informal supports. First, some older people have incomplete informal networks and need specific kinds of help (such as someone to shop for them or clean their home). Second, some older people who have intact networks have high health care needs. For example, caregivers who care for older family members with dementia use more personal care

services and in-home services than other caregivers (Hawranik 2002). Ideally, the informal and formal systems work together in these cases to share the overall load.

Ward-Griffin (2002) found that both formal and informal care providers perform physical and emotional care work. Formal care providers, specifically nurses in this study, have professional knowledge and skills that differentiate them from family care providers. However, as Ward-Griffin says, the boundary between professionals and family caregivers blurs when family members develop caregiving skills and knowledge. In other related work, Ward-Griffin (2000) found that in caregiving situations, where nurses and family caregivers worked together, nurses gradually transferred the caregiving labour to the family caregiver. She found that family caregivers did most of the physical and economic care, but got little practical assistance. Ward-Griffin argues for a more equitable sharing of responsibility between family and professional caregivers.

Guberman and her colleagues (2006) support these findings. They say that formal care practitioners tend to see the work of family caregivers as a series of instrumental or clinical tasks, ignoring the intangible emotional or social support family caregivers provide. Many practitioners expect family caregivers to take on the role of "quasi-nurse's aides."

Policy often speaks of partnerships between state programs and informal supports. But a number of researchers ask whether this new focus on the family will provide better care or simply shift the burden of care to families (Keating et al. 1997; Rosenthal 1997). Ward-Griffin and Marshall (2003), for example, see a growing imbalance as the state withdraws formal supports and expects more from informal supporters. Keating and her colleagues (1999) say that the emphasis on family and community care can place a heavy burden on **informal caregivers** who are typically family members.

Harlton and her colleagues (1998) found that older people and policy makers differed in their view of care to older people. Policy makers often believe that family and neighbourhood (informal) supports give older people more control over their lives. But many older people feel that family support makes them more dependent and a burden on their families. They do not feel that family members should provide housing, financial support, or personal care (Kemp and Denton 2003). They preferred state-funded supports, believing that these supports give them the most control over the services they received. Policy makers need to learn more about the views of older clients and their families in order to create programs that meet older people's needs. They must also recognize that family caregivers face significant personal costs—financial and health related—in their caregiving role (Keefe, Légaré and Carrière 2007). Kunemund and Rein (1999) find that generous state-funded social and health care supports strengthen rather than weaken family solidarity.

Rosenthal (1997) notes some further issues related to care of older people. She describes a conflict between the policy to shift care to the family, the increase in the number of older people, and the decrease in available women to provide family care. Middle-aged women (traditional caregivers) have entered the labour force in large numbers. Many now have to juggle work and care for older parents. This added demand leads to stress, absenteeism, and sometimes withdrawal from work (Cranswick 2003). Rosenthal says the government should fund programs and resources to support family care. However, that does not mean caregiver problems (such as juggling multiple responsibilities) should remain personal troubles. The government needs to see them as public issues and provide formal supports to help family caregivers fulfill their roles (Keefe, Légaré and Carrière 2007).

Children as a Source of Informal Support

Adult children stay in touch with older parents. Among adult children 25 to 54 years of age, 7 out of 10 contact their mothers at least once a week by telephone, letters, or through visits (Townsend-Batten 2002). Six out of 10 of this age group stays in frequent contact with their fathers. Daughters, compared to sons, have more contact with their mothers. And both daughters and sons have more frequent contact with mothers than with fathers. This may reflect the kin keeper role that mothers often play in families (Rosenthal 1995). Contact between adult children and parents leads to greater feelings of life satisfaction and well-being for older people (Rowe and Kahn 1998).

The marital status of adult children influences their level of involvement with older parents (Sarkisian and Gerstel 2008). Married sons and daughters are less likely than their single or divorced counterparts to stay in touch with parents. Married children less often provide parents with financial support, emotional support, or practical help. They are also less likely to receive these types of assistance from parents. The marital status of the parent can also influence his or her relationship with adult children, including the support received. For example, adult children provide about the same support to divorced or widowed mothers but provide the least support to divorced fathers (Lin 2008).

Adult children provide much of the support needed by their parents. Research finds that even older adults who reside in long-term care facilities receive informal help from their children (Dupuis and Smale 2004). Keefe and Fancey (2002) report that strong feelings of attachment to a parent and recognition of past help and support lead to caregiving. Other studies report that daughters, compared with sons, provide more care to parents. Even working daughters with children at home spend more than twice as much time as working sons providing care to an older parent (29 hours per month compared to 13 hours per month) (Williams 2005). Daughters also report greater feelings of stress, more sleep disturbances, and more personal health concerns than do sons (Cranswick 2003; Penning 1998). Daughters-in-law often provide care to their husband's parents. They may feel responsible to give care even if they don't feel affection for the parent (Guberman 1999). Single women provided more care than any other type of caregiver (Connidis, Rosenthal, and McMullin 1996). Walker (1996) traces this fact to cultural pressures on women to give care. One woman put it simply: "Who else is going to do it?" (Aronson 1992, 15).

Studies show that adult children and their parents see the amount of support provided by the children differently. Many studies report that older people feel they receive less support than their children say they give. Early work by Bengtson and Kuypers (1971) referred to this as differences in the **developmental stake** or (more recently) **generational stake** (Mandemakers and Dykstra 2008). Older people have a greater stake in the relationship with their children. They have invested more in the relationship and they have more to lose if it fails (Jerrome 1996). So older people tend to emphasize the existence of family harmony and solidarity. Their positive interpretation of the relationship allows them to maintain a feeling of generational continuity within the family. They may de-emphasize the amount of support they receive in order not to see themselves as a burden on their children. This difference in perception can create tensions in the family. Adult children may feel that their parents do not appreciate how much they do for them, even though the children may feel they do as much as they can.

Recent research from the Netherlands (Mandemakers and Dykstra 2008) finds limited and mixed support for the generational stake hypothesis. This study reports discrepancies in parents' and adult children's reports of contact and support but with *both* parents and their adult children underestimating the amount of support they received and overestimating the amount of support they provided. Better-educated parents and children seemed to more accurately estimate relationship contact and support.

Mandemakers and Dykstra also find that parents and adult children in high-quality relationships tend to overestimate the support and contact in their relationship. The authors suggest there may be value in having such a "sunny" outlook on a relationship. They conclude that "people in close relationships harbor 'positive illusions' about each other. They emphasize their partners' virtues, and are motivated to overlook their faults. A certain level of favorable deception seems to be basic to happy relationships" (504).

Research shows that intergenerational interaction has grown in intensity and complexity in recent years. Older people and their children live longer lives and spend more years interacting with one another. Gee (1988) reported that in Canada from the 1830s to the 1950s, the number of years spent parenting declined for women, but the time spent as an adult child increased. Today, people spend more years as an adult child of living parents than as parents of young children. This trend will continue in the future. In some cases, caregivers of older parents will need support themselves as they grow older.

Some Canadian provinces provide family members a **caregiver's wage or allowance**. These programs provide financial payment to caregivers for their work. Currently, three provinces—Nova Scotia, Ontario, and Quebec—offer financial support to caregivers of older family members. These programs have three goals: (1) to reward caregivers for their efforts; (2) to help with the cost of caregiving; and (3) to delay institutionalization of the older person. Controversy exists over these programs. Some writers argue that payment to family members strengthens family values; others claim that payment (at generally low wages) exploits family members who have little choice but to accept the job (Keefe et al. 2008). Finally, policy makers worry that payment will lead to fraud and abuse of the program and exploitation of the older person (Blaser 1998). Payment to family members (who now give care for free) will also increase the government's cost of caring for older people.

Keefe and Fancey (1997) studied the financial support program in Nova Scotia in detail. They compared three groups of family caregivers (mostly daughters). One group received home care support (homemaking and nursing support), a second group received financial support to provide care, and a third group received both types of support. Keefe and Fancey found that paid caregivers tended to be younger women who lived in a nonurban setting with the care receiver. Those who received home care support tended to be sons or spouses who live in an urban setting. The paid caregivers felt more burdened by caregiving. They spent more time and energy on giving care and felt more tired and anxious than the caregivers receiving home support.

The researchers conclude that financial support buys the time and services of family caregivers when they have access to few formal supports. But the findings suggest that financial support helps caregivers cope only with the economic costs. Paid caregivers still experience more personal cost than caregivers who get home help. Some writers feel that financial support programs give public recognition to caregivers' efforts; others fear that these types of programs will lead to a decrease in the natural tendency of families to care for older members (Keefe, Glendinning, and Fancey 2008).

Keefe and Fancey (1997) showed that both types of support (home help and financial support) benefit caregivers. And, in the case of rural caregivers (with few formal services available), financial help makes the most sense. They propose that future programs combine financial support with home help services. This dual program would help caregivers cope with the stress of caregiving and might also lead more families to care for older relatives in the community.

More recently, Keefe and her colleagues (2008) looked at the programs different countries use to compensate family caregivers. They conclude that (1) poor financial compensation may further devalue family caregiving; (2) pay to caregivers may reinforce gender roles (and the expectation that women will provide care); and (3) pay for care may not lead to quality care, especially when the older person needs complex care. Keefe and her colleagues propose multiple measures of compensation and support for caregivers. This would include fair financial payment to caregivers, workplace supports, and backup formal services. As the authors state, "The challenge is to ensure the appropriate balance between these different measures" (203). Keefe and Rajnovich (2007) say policy makers should be less concerned with whether it is the family or the state that assumes responsibility for care. Policy should focus on supporting those who choose to give care.

Researchers say that changes in the family may limit informal caregiving in the future. For example, geographic mobility, immigration, greater numbers of young adult children living at home, smaller modern homes, multigenerational help needs, more pressure on fewer children, women in the workforce, caregiver burnout, and conflicting demands on caregivers may all put pressure on the informal care system. A lower birth rate and smaller numbers of children per family mean that middle-aged children will have fewer siblings to help support their aging parents.

Sources of Informal Support for Childless Older People

Adult children are a primary source of support and well-being for older parents. But who provides this support to older adults who are without children? Studies find that childless older people create a network of supportive family and friends.

Those who have chosen to remain childless report high life satisfaction and happiness (Connidis and McMullin 1999). They have about the same satisfaction with life as married older people who have close relations with their children and higher satisfaction than parents with distant ties to children. Compared to older people who have no children due to circumstances beyond their control, those who remain childless by choice have higher life satisfaction. McMullin and Marshall (1996, 356) report that "compared to parents, childless individuals experience less life stress and similar levels of well-being." Connidis and McMullin (1999) also find that childless older adults report financial benefits, greater freedom, and career flexibility.

Childless older people who report disadvantages point to a lack of companionship, missed experiences, a feeling of incompleteness, and lack of care in old age (Connidis and McMullin 1999). Women who feel disappointed by childlessness also report loneliness and depression (Koropeckyj-Cox 2002). The social networks of older childless people offer less support than the networks of older parents when they become sick (Rubinstein 1996). Childless older people tend to face other disadvantages. They tend to be unmarried, older, female, less financially secure, in poorer health, and living alone. Widows especially face a disadvantage if they have no children. They may lack informal support and may need to rely on formal support. Compared to older people with children, they also face a greater risk of institutionalization (Giranda, Luk, and Atchison 1999).

Research often ignores childless adults or views their lives "through a lens of deficiency" or as the "other" category (in contrast to parents) (Dykstra and Hagestad 2007, 1291). As a result, compared to what we know about seniors with children, we know less about the social networks and relationships of childless older people. We also know less about the varied responses people make to childlessness. Dykstra and Hagestad (2007, 1301) say that for some people, "life without children can have particular advantages, in others it can have disadvantages, and in yet others, no effects at all." They say that research should explore "when childlessness matters and when it does not."

Other Sources of Informal Support: Friends, Siblings, and Pets

Friends can be an important source of support in later life. Studies find that people enjoy friends most in youth and in old age. High-quality friendships in later life lead to high life satisfaction and well-being (O'Connor 1995). Studies show that many older people get more enjoyment out of visits with friends than with family. Researchers say that people in a family may visit one another as a matter of routine or because they feel obliged to see one another. But when older people see their friends, they do so out of choice. Most older people choose friends from their own age group. Older people may have more in common with their friends than with younger family members, and shared interests and experiences lead to greater warmth and good feelings.

While friends can play a vital role in the support network of older people, friendships in later life can also involve tensions and disappointments. Moremen (2008) terms this the "downside of friendship." Some of the women in Moremen's study reported "disruptions" in their friendships when friends did not share their interests, habits, and other friends. A loss of trust in the relationship, dishonesty, or exploitation could also put strain on the friendship. For some women, differences in marital status, socioeconomic status, or geographic location (when a friend moved away) could create stress. Women said they felt anger, betrayal, disappointment, resentment, and sadness when these situations occurred. Many women used an avoidance strategy to deal with strains and problems in the relationship. This often meant not confronting the problem or keeping hurt or angry feelings inside. But sometimes these feelings ended the friendship. Some women resolved these tensions by talking about them; others used humour or agreed to disagree.

In spite of potential problems, friendships help older people overcome distress caused by lost work roles or widowhood (Field 1999). Friends also help each other cope with life difficulties and stressful events. Friends who are the same age often share the same physical limits, the same interests, and the same historical background. Lifelong friends also share cherished experiences and memories. Research shows the importance of close and supportive friendships in the lives of older adults (Davidson, Daly, and Arber 2003; de Jong Gierveld 2003). A variety of relationships, including friendships, create a full and satisfying support network.

Siblings are also an important source of social support for older people (Spitze and Trent 2006). Eighty percent of older adults have at least one living sibling (brother or sister). The sibling bond often lasts throughout a lifetime but its importance often gets overlooked (Campbell, Connidis, and Davies 1999). The supportive role of a sibling will vary by individual need and circumstance. For example, a married older person with many children nearby may make little use of sibling support. Campbell, Connidis, and Davies (1999) found that single people and women make the most use of sibling supports. For example, they tend to get more support from siblings when they get ill. Childless older people, compared to people with children, set up more supportive ties with their siblings (Connidis and Campbell 1995). Childless siblings also tend to give support to their brothers and sisters (Barrett and Lynch 1999). Rubinstein (1996) reports that childless women often build relationships with siblings' children or the children of nonrelatives.

Most adults report having frequent contact with and positive feelings about their siblings (Spitze and Trent 2006). In general, compared to older men, older women tend to have more active sibling ties, with ties between sisters stronger than ties between brothers or a brother and sister (Connidis 2001). In Spitze and Trent's (2006) study of adult sibling ties in two-child families, sisters exchanged advice and kept in touch by phone more often than did other pairs of siblings. Compared to men, women more often report that they help a sibling with child care. They also tend to get help with home repairs (from a brother).

Geographic closeness influences some types of sibling support but not others. For example, companionship requires in-person contact, but confiding and emotional support between siblings can occur over a greater distance (Campbell, Connidis, and Davies 1999). Siblings more often provide emotional support than practical support, even for those who live close by. Strong or weak sibling ties in adulthood tend to continue as such into later life (Miner and Uhlenberg 1997).

Few people think of pets as a source of social support but pets provide their owners with companionship, affection, and friendship. Researchers have studied the potential social support and health benefits pets can provide to older people. This includes older people who live in the community and those in long-term care settings (Banks, Gonser, and Banks 2001; Wood, Giles-Corti, and Balsara 2005). Pet ownership increases social contact, positive interaction with neighbours, and community involvement. Human–pet interaction can help people deal with stress, loneliness, and bereavement (Allen, Blascovich, and Mendes 2002). Pet ownership can also protect a person from cardiovascular disease, improve blood pressure, and increase physical activity (Thorpe et al. 2006).

Compared to other pet owners, dog owners get the most activity benefit from pet ownership (Thorpe et al. 2006). Studies show dog owners do more recreational walking than non-dog owners. Dogs can also act as a "catalyst for social interaction" (McNicholas and Collis 2000; Wood et al. 2005). Compared to people who walk alone, people who walk their dogs more often engage in conversation with neighbours, other dog owners, or even strangers. Dogs can also precipitate the exchange of favours between neighbours (Wood 2000). These casual social exchanges do not generally turn into sources of social support. Still, as Wood and colleagues (2005, 1162) say: "dogs have the greatest capacity to facilitate social interaction and contact as they are the type of pet most likely to venture with their owners into the broader community."

Animal-assisted therapy has been used as an effective therapy for older residents in long-term care homes. This therapy introduces pets, such as dogs, cats, rabbits, or birds, into nursing homes or other residential care settings. Research finds that pets can bring pleasure and comfort to residents in long-term care homes, and reduce their loneliness (Banks and Banks 2002). One study found that having an aquarium in the dining room stimulated residents to eat more at mealtime and to gain weight.

Filan and Llewellyn-Jones (2006) conducted a review of literature on the use of animal-assisted therapy for dementia residents. They found that quiet interaction between residents and dogs lowered blood pressure and increased feelings of relaxation and bonding for residents. Studies suggest that the presence of a dog can reduce agitation and aggression in residents with dementia, and promote positive social behaviours, such as smiling, laughing, and touching (Churchill et al. 1999; Richeson 2003).

Although research supports the value of pets in long-term care settings, pet visits may not suit all residents. Some residents may have allergies. Others may fear dogs, birds, or other animals. An aggressive patient may mishandle or harm an animal. Residents and staff in long-term care homes must see that pets in these settings get good care and treatment.

Caregiver Burden

Many studies report that giving care to a physically disabled or cognitively impaired older person can lead to feelings of **caregiver burden** (problems and stress due to caregiving) (Keating, Dosman, Swindle, and Fast 2008; MacLean 2008). Some research suggests that caregiving spouses suffer a greater burden from caregiving than do adult children (Novak and Guest 1992). They may feel the strain more as they see their partner decline (especially if the person shows mental as well as physical decline). Caregiving places heavy demands on spousal caregivers and they may have limited informal resources to call on for help (Keating, Dosman, Swindle, and Fast 2008). This can increase their feelings of burden. O'Rourke and his colleagues (1996) found that caregivers felt subjective burden (for example, a feeling of hopelessness) apart from specific caregiving demands.

Lai (2007) examined the effects of culture on caregiver burden in a Chinese-Canadian community. Despite a strong Chinese tradition of caring for older family members, these caregivers felt caregiver burden. Caregivers with health problems, those who faced greater care demands, and those who had fewer financial resources all report greater caregiver burden. Recent immigrants, people with a religious belief, and people who felt less committed to **filial piety** all felt a greater burden. Lai cautions, though, that while strong feelings of filial piety may ease caregiver burden, they does not make caregiving easy. In fact, strong filial piety may keep caregivers from using the outside help and resources they need.

Research suggests that the caregiver's interpretation of the situation may lead to greater or lesser feelings of burden. For example, a negative view of dysfunctional behaviour leads to psychological distress and negative feelings about caregiving. Chappell and Reid (2002) found that caregivers who perceived that they had enough social support reported feelings of well-being. O'Rourke and Wenaus (1998, 385) found that spouses who show an "inordinately positive appraisal of their spouse and marriage" suffer the least burden. They propose that spouses who

© 2009 Jupiterimages Corporation

Many middle-aged women find themselves in the role of caregiver to their parents. Caregivers can feel conflicting emotions. They feel love for their parents but they also feel the stress of caregiving. For example, a cognitively impaired parent may act out physically and may not recognize the adult child. The adult child may find roles reversed as the impaired parent becomes the cared-for person in the relationship. A parent with dementia creates unique physical and emotional challenges.

feel less burden may reconstruct their marriage as positive in the past. This helps them cope with stresses they face in the present. "Provision of care thus serves as perceived payment or appreciation for the privilege of sharing their lives in better times" (396). Caregivers who can identify some positive feelings about caregiving have lower depression, less burden, and better self-reported health (Cohen, Colantonio, and Vernich 2002; MacLean 2008).

Spouse caregivers may have health problems themselves, which makes caregiving difficult and adds to their feeling of burden. They may also have fewer resources (financial and social) to call on than would a middle-aged child. People who lived with an impaired older person (many of them spouses), compared with those who did not, felt greater stress and reported poorer psychological well-being. Family caregivers can feel a loss of control and autonomy. One caregiver reports, "I feel like, like now, I'm all on tenterhooks. I feel like I'm on a treadmill, all the time, all the time, and I can't get off this thing" (cited in O'Connor 1999, 226). Caregivers also report stress due to tasks like cleaning, doing laundry, and shopping. Still, O'Connor reports that many spouse caregivers refuse to use outside help. They feel an obligation to their spouse and they feel that they can give the best care (Harris 2005).

MacLean (2008) conducted in-depth interviews with older wives whose husbands with dementia were waiting for placement in a long-term care setting. The study looked at how wives cope with caregiving while awaiting placement. The study found that wives experience multiple "layers of loss." First, wives talked about the loss of communication with their husbands. Women missed having a partner to talk to about household finances or other everyday issues. They even missed simple dinner conversations. They felt that their husband's "true self" had gone.

Second, wives identified the loss of their marriage partnership. In taking on the physical care of their spouse, as well as his household tasks and responsibilities, these women felt their relationship was no longer a "give-and-take" partnership. One woman said: "Well, granted, I'm still his wife, but he's not like my husband … my husband isn't there" (53).

Third, many of the women felt a loss of personal freedom. This involved the loss of contact with friends, or the inability to attend social activities. They missed the everyday freedoms like running down to the mailbox to mail a letter or going shopping. As one woman described it: "I feel I'm sort of tied down … I'm pretty well trapped" (53).

At times these women also lost patience with their spouse. To cope with their situation, they drew on their internal strengths, such as thinking positively. They also remembered their spouse's former self, relied on religious teachings to gain patience, and used external resources like formal care services, or support from friends and family. Most of these women just tried to get through the day—one day at a time. As MacLean explains: "with this simple and primary goal, these women demonstrated their clear understanding that longer term goals are inappropriate when caregiving for a person whose illness experience changes minute to minute, hour to hour, and day after day" (104).

Even after a spouse enters an institution, a caregiver spouse feels caregiver burden. For example, caregiver spouses often felt guilty after institutionalization. Spouses of institutionalized older people, compared with adult children, feel more physical and developmental burden. Physical burden referred to the strain of long visits and travel to the institution. Hallman and Joseph (1999) found that women, compared to men, spend more time travelling to give care. Developmental burden referred to spouses' feelings of being unable to get on with life. One wife told Gladstone (1995, 56): "when you're apart after never being apart it has an effect on you. You seem to be in a turmoil. We'd known each other since we were 14 years old so we were together a long, long time."

Rosenthal and Dawson (1991) identified the concept of **quasi-widowhood**. This term describes married individuals who "feel widowed" because their spouse lives apart in a long-term care setting. These people have lost the physical presence of their spouse and the emotional support and companionship of a partner. Ross, Rosenthal, and Dawson (1994) studied 40 wives who had placed their husbands in nursing homes. These women said that they felt relief after placement but also felt failure, "anger, guilt, sadness, depression and grief" (40). Most women over time adapt to their spouse living in an institution (see also Loos and Bowd 1997). Overall, they express satisfaction with the care their husbands receive (Dawson and Rosenthal 1996). Some women accept the loss of their spouse as a friend and companion, and restructure their lives outside the institution.

Other spouses keep close ties to the institution. Ross, Rosenthal, and Dawson (1997a; 1997b) found that more than 80 percent of the wives in their study visited their husbands at least several times a week; about 20 percent visited every day. This pattern continued over the nine-month period of the study. Most wives said they visited out of love, devotion, and duty. Active visitors over this period, the researchers said, were "holding on to the past." They often had husbands with physical impairments. Active visitors took on a variety of tasks, including planning birthday parties, personalizing their husband's room, and bringing in special foods. Overall, active visitors provided care as a way to maintain their attachment to their husbands and as a way to maintain their role as a wife and supporter. Wives felt most satisfied if they felt useful. But the researchers found that active visitors felt more depressed at the end of nine months and felt dissatisfied with the care their husbands got.

This study by Ross and colleagues suggests that wives who give up the caregiver role do better after their husbands are institutionalized. The researchers found that about two-thirds of spouses gave up some of their caregiving responsibility. They visited less and allowed staff to take on the job of caring. This group began what the researchers call "embracing new realities." They felt less depressed and they felt "sort of like a widow" (Ross, Rosenthal, and Dawson 1994, 29). But healing began to take place as they gained distance from the caregiver role.

Harris (2005) studied spousal caregiving by husbands. The study found that men often continue to care for their wives at home even when their own health declines. Further, compared to husbands who kept their spouse at home, husbands whose wives entered an institution felt more depression (Kramer 2000). Exhibit 13.6 shows the percentage of older Canadians with Alzheimer's disease living in a private household.

Gender and Spousal Caregiving

Compared to older women, older men more often get care from a spouse. Still, husbands play a significant role in caring for their wives in later life (Calasanti and Bowen 2006; Kirsi, Hervonen, and Jylhä 2004). Men make up about 40 percent of spousal caregivers. Studies find that husbands and wives who provide spousal care provide about the same amount and types of care (Ye and Shultz 2000). Research suggests that husbands often see caregiving as an extension of their work role—like a "new career," or a continuation of their authority in the marital relationship (Ribeiro 2007). Husbands often bring problem-solving strategies from their work role to their care role (Harris 2005).

Some men feel uncomfortable providing care that involves "traditionally female" tasks, such as domestic work and personal care. These men report "role incongruence." Many are not prepared for the caregiving role and need to learn new and unfamiliar skills (Harris 2005). Still, they feel satisfaction and a sense of accomplishment in being able to provide care to their spouse (Kirsi et al. 2004).

Calasanti and Bowen (2006) conducted in-depth interviews with spousal caregivers of persons with dementia to examine how gender might affect their caregiving. They found that both men and women "crossed

gendered boundaries" in their caregiving. This happened in two ways.

First, husbands and wives assumed responsibility for domestic and household tasks that were typically done by the other spouse. For example, women took responsibility for the household finances, learned outside home maintenance, or learned how to maintain the car. One woman said: "I never had to put gas in a car, I never had to check the tires, I never had to do anything about an automobile because he did everything. And now I have that and that is hard" (257). Caregiving husbands took on tasks typically done by their wives. Husbands had to do many of these tasks, like cooking and cleaning, every day. "I found out how difficult it is to do all these things [that she used to do]," one husband said (258).

Second, spouses "crossed gender boundaries" when they helped their partner with personal care. Caregivers helped their partner maintain their gendered identity as a man or woman. They did this, for example, by helping their spouse with bathing and grooming. They saw that their spouse wore clean and attractive clothing. Wives experienced this as an extension of familiar tasks. Husbands experienced personal care for their spouse as new and unfamiliar. Still, the authors say, husbands "strove to insure their wives looked like the "ladies" they had been" (259).

Family, friends, and the broader society, often praise men for taking on care work, particularly tasks typically performed by women (Milne and Hatzidimitriadou 2003). Ribeiro and his colleagues (2007) call this "perceived social honour." Milne and Hatzidimitriadou (2003) use the phrase, "isn't he wonderful." Yet, Russell (2006) found that while men were praised for special care tasks, they got little recognition for "unheroic" daily caregiving chores. Many husbands felt their spousal care was invisible, and that others around them did not appreciate how much of their lives was consumed by the demands of caregiving. "For many [men], the locus of care work, the home, represented a location in which they became as invisible as the work they performed" (Russell 2006, 311). This invisibility contributed to an increased sense of social isolation.

Filial Caregiving

Along with spouses, adult children provide most of the informal care to older family members. Most of these adult children (73 percent of men and 63 percent of women aged 45 to 64) juggle jobs along with their caregiving tasks (Cranswick 2003). Caregiving children often feel intense pressure as they try to meet the demands of work, their children, and caregiving (Neal, Wagner, Bonn, and Niles-Yokum 2008). A respondent in one study of middle-aged children said, "I have looked after both parents for twenty-seven years and they have become very dependent on me. We are very tied down and I don't know how much more my nerves and health can stand" (Marshall, Rosenthal, and Synge 1983, 267–68). In another study, a woman said, "[Mother] has been getting more and more forgetful and confused and can't be alone at all. I'm depressed, and I don't sleep well. How can I go to work when she needs constant supervision?" (Brody 1990, ix).

Rosenthal and Matthews (1999) find that many filial caregivers combine managerial care (that is, orchestrating care, managing finances, arranging formal services, and providing financial assistance) with other types of assistance. This amount of care, particularly organizing and coordinating care, contributes to stress for women and to personal and work-related costs for both men and women. Joseph and Hallman (1996) found that adult children can feel stress due to travel time to their care receiver. **Long-distance caregivers** (those who live a long distance from their care receiver) often experience guilt or worry (Baldock 2000; Neal et al. 2008).

Caregiving can bring up the inherent tension between the adult child's personal autonomy and his or her interdependence within a family. Joseph and Hallman (1996) report that caregivers sometimes use vacation time from work to manage their caregiving tasks. Sometimes they need to decrease their work hours, leave work early, or turn down job opportunities (Cranswick 2003). Caregiving can disrupt social and holiday plans, as well as sleep patterns (Campbell 2002). It can cause declines in the caregiver's health. Caregivers report conflicts between family and work responsibilities (Gignac, Kelloway, and Gottlieb 1996; see also Cranswick 1997). For women, this shows up as job dissatisfaction and absenteeism. For men, it shows up as lost job opportunities and absenteeism. Some caregivers, typically adult daughters, may quit their jobs to take care of parents (see Exhibit 13.5). Many caregivers report that they feel disappointment, resentment, and frustration.

Adult children often need to negotiate parent care within their sibling network. Connidis and Kemp (2008) find that in general adult children with fewer family and work responsibilities, and greater proximity to their parents, most often get selected by their siblings to serve as caregiver. Sisters more often than brothers serve in this role. Hequembourg and Brallier (2005) find that caregiving roles among siblings get divided like the domestic tasks in a traditional marriage. Sisters—like wives—also assume the role of "care coordinator."

Even adult children who do not consider themselves primary caregivers feel concern about their parents.

For example, family members often monitor the care their older relative receives in a health care facility. Ross, Carswell, and Dalziel (2002) found that family members provide both direct and indirect care in a facility, including making their relative's environment more home-like (33 percent), providing personal care (26 percent), and acting as advocates for their relatives and watching over their care (40 percent).

Keefe and Fancey (2000) report that more than half of family members saw no change in their perceived responsibility after their care receiver moved to a facility. People who reduced their caregiving tended to cut back on direct supports such as transportation, meals, or laundry service. Some family members felt their responsibility had increased after a relative entered an institution. They said they spent time at the facility visiting or dealing with their relative's affairs.

This increased responsibility often came from changes in the older resident's health. One daughter in Keefe and Fancey's study said about her mother that "as her confusion is getting worse I'm finding myself called upon more to sort out the messes either by phone [to the facility] or leaving our jobs [her husband accompanies her] and going up [to the facility] for the afternoon" (240). This change from direct responsibility to indirect responsibility took time and energy from other responsibilities.

Gladstone and his colleagues (2006) found that family members continued to provide care even after their relative moved into a nursing home. But caregivers rebalanced or refocused their care. As one daughter said: "Once upon a time the balance was physical needs for my mother and now the balance has become the emotional need" (99). Most family members did not identify themselves as "caregivers." Rather, they saw themselves as "family" whose primary role was to provide emotional and social support, and to monitor the quality of care provided in the facility.

Research shows that a good relationship between family members and facility staff enhances the well-being of residents and family members. Gladstone and Wexler (2002b) found a more positive relationship between families and nursing staff in long-term care facilities when the nurses felt their care was recognized and appreciated by family. Family members who created friendly and open relations with staff, who appreciated the difficulties faced by staff, and who recognized the nurses' expertise and experience tended to have better relationships with nursing staff. Family members felt that having a good relationship with staff could mean an extra hug or pat on the shoulder for their family member. It also improved the quality of family visits (Gladstone

● Exhibit 13.5

PATRICIA KEEPS IT GOING

Patricia House's mother and father were no saints. They were strict, prone to anger and proud, but they always were there for her. Now that their faculties are giving way, it's her turn.

Patricia House remembers her mother as a housewife who dressed up for the grocery store; who had four raincoats hanging in the hall closet, each with a matching umbrella, hat and gloves; who taught her the secrets to soothing a cranky baby and baking the perfect pie crust.

That is not the woman now living in her basement.

This Alice House forgets to change her clothes and doesn't notice that she is dirty. She burns pots black on the stove. She asks the same question half-a-dozen times in an hour.

Later tonight, Alice will hang her clothes back up in the closet, and her daughter will quietly slip them off the hangers and throw them in the wash. Alice has been wearing that cardigan, these pants and those beads for five days—a problem if you can't get into the bathtub because of your artificial hip, and if, on occasion, you aren't fast enough to the toilet.

But Alice refuses to let her 44-year-old daughter see her naked, so she gives herself sponge baths, and hand-washes her own underwear, performing neither task well. Patricia steals the dainties off the bathroom doorknob where Alice hangs them, and adds them to the wash. To deal with family complaints that Grandma was smelly, Patricia devised another gentle trick: She takes her mother twice a week to a seniors centre, where she can enjoy a 30-minute soak in a special Jacuzzi.

It is not what Patricia imagined when she lured her parents from Vancouver to Penticton, B.C., two years ago. She asked them to "visit" for Thanksgiving, then declared the move permanent. Her father, then 86 with advanced dementia, lasted 10 days before a run-in with police led her to follow doctors' advice and place him in a nursing home.

Patricia still gets angry thinking about her parents' failure to plan for the future. She had a job she liked in the office of a grocery store, but quit to look after them. With two daughters in their 20s, she and her husband, David, a 51-year-old teacher, were looking forward to freedom. But so often the burden of care falls hardest on one person, and somehow Patricia made more sense than her brothers John, who works in film in New York, and even Douglas, who's near Vancouver.

It was, she suspects, what her parents always assumed. She has never forgotten a conversation overheard when she was 15: Her 89-year-old grandmother leaned forward in bed, and said to her mother, "I hope when you are old, you have someone to look after you."

"Don't worry," Alice House had answered. "Patricia will be there."

Source: Anderssen, Erin. 2004. Focus: Shades of Grey: Part 2, p. F4. *The Globe and Mail*. November 27. Reprinted with permission from The Globe and Mail.

and Wexler 2002a). In good family–staff relationships, family members expressed appreciation to the staff and assisted them with instrumental tasks (Gladstone and Wexler 2000).

Family members use different styles of engagement when interacting with staff (Gladstone et al. 2007). For example, some family members use a positive style of engagement to develop good relationships with staff.

Family members who have a negative style of engagement with staff criticize staff members' work, or question their competence. Some family members assessed the quality of their relationship with staff by judging the amount of information staff provided to them. Ideally, information should flow freely between family and staff. Iwasiw et al. (2003) say that nursing staff in long-term care facilities can benefit from listening to family members about

● **Exhibit 13.6**

PERCENTAGE OF SENIOR WOMEN AND MEN LIVING IN A PRIVATE HOUSEHOLD WITH ALZHEIMER'S DISEASE, 2003

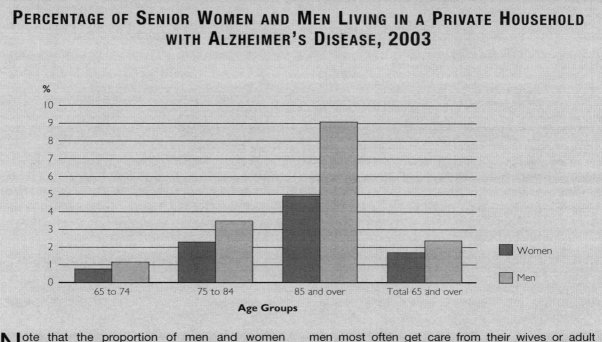

Note that the proportion of men and women with Alzheimer's disease (AD) living in private households increases with each older age group. Men with AD in the oldest age group who live at home outnumber women nearly two to one. These men most often get care from their wives or adult children (mostly daughters or daughters-in-law). The increase in the population aged 85 and over will challenge more families than ever before with the care for Alzheimer's family members at home.

Source: Statistics Canada, Canadian Community Health Survey.

older residents' experiences and needs. This can improve the level of care and the quality of life for residents.

The decision to move a relative into a long-term care home is a difficult one for families. Caron and her colleagues (2006) asked family members to talk about the process they went through to arrive at their decision. Three conditions influenced family members' decision: (1) the amount of care needed by the older relative, (2) the caregiver's ability to provide that amount of care; and (3) the formal supports available.

The placement decision can take a long time. Caron and colleagues (2006) report an average of two years from the family's first thoughts of placement until the actual move occurred. Many caregivers in this study said they did not receive the support they needed from health care professionals during this process.

Women (and Men) in the Sandwich Generation

The **sandwich generation** refers to people—typically women—who have at least one living parent and at least one child living in the household (Rosenthal 2000; Williams 2005). Brody (1981) first proposed that women could get caught in the middle—sandwiched between care for their children and care for their aging parents. "Such women are in middle age, in the middle from a generational standpoint, and in the middle in that the demands of their various roles compete for their time and energy" (471). Gerontologists have generally assumed that these sandwich-generation women feel high levels of stress. But recent studies questioned this view of middle age. They find that relatively few women get caught in the middle like this (Rosenthal, Martin-Matthews, and Matthews 1996).

Based on data from the 1990 General Social Survey, Rosenthal, Martin-Matthews, and Matthews (1996) found that 71 percent of women aged 35 to 39 had the structural potential to be sandwiched between parents and young children (having both an older parent and a child living at home). This number dropped to 51 percent for those aged 45 to 49, and to 24 percent for women aged 50 to 54.

The study found a very low proportion of women in this sandwich generation who actually provided care to an older parent at least monthly and who had a child living at home. The highest percentage in any age group was only 13 percent of women. Most daughters who cared for older parents had grown children who had moved out of the house. Most were also not in the paid labour force. Rosenthal, Martin-Matthews, and Matthews (1996) concluded that relatively few Canadians get "caught in the middle." But they did say that when it does occur, it can create a heavy burden.

Williams (2005) examined data from the 2002 General Social Survey. She focused on adult Canadians aged 45 to 64 who cared for an elderly parent and had single children living at home. That year, approximately 712,000 Canadians fit this description. Eighty percent of these caregivers also worked outside the home. Some of these people reported that they had to change work or home schedules such as shifting or reducing work hours. But only about 1 in 10 of people who cared for an older family member (with or without children at home) reported problems meeting their other commitments.

Williams found that compared to people without children at home, "sandwiched workers" spent more time on care to older relatives. But more than 80 percent of sandwiched workers said they felt satisfied with their work–family balance, and 95 percent said they felt satisfied or very satisfied with life in general (about the same proportion as those with fewer care commitments). The majority of sandwiched workers felt good about giving back to their parent. They also felt that caregiving strengthened their relationship.

Myles (1991; also Rosenthal 2000) said that women who work outside the home and provide care to aging parents feel a "caregiving crunch" because society expects women to serve as caregivers. Research shows that these women experience more stress and greater absenteeism from work (Martin Matthews and Campbell 1995). Researchers say that caregivers need to work out family strategies to cope with stress. They also need workplace supports such as job flexibility, eldercare services, and community supports to help them stay at work. Social policies and services need to provide options to family care (Rosenthal 2000; Williams 2005).

Myles (1991) said that changed workplace norms and more sympathetic personnel practices could help ease this crunch. However, he also called for more radical reform, saying that "nothing short of a revolution in gender relations and in the sexual division of caregiving work is required to solve the problem" (84). Myles's call for change remains, today, mostly unanswered.

Sons as Caregivers

Adult sons make up 15 to 40 percent of adult child caregivers. And adult sons may take a more active role in caregiving in the future. Demographic changes, changes in family size and structure, and women's increased employment outside the home all increase the chances that a man will provide care to an aging parent (Campbell and Carroll 2007; Campbell and Martin-Matthews 2003).

Like middle-aged women, middle-aged men must often balance multiple roles—spouse, father, employee, and adult child. This balancing act can create a strain and feelings of burden. Care given by adult sons, in general, tends to fit with "traditional" roles for men within families. Some sons provide personal care and help with household chores (Campbell and Carroll 2007). But most often men take on financial and managerial work, home maintenance chores, and yard work (Keating et al. 1999). A son will get more involved in caregiving if he lives nearby, has older children (or no children), has few or no siblings, and feels an obligation to help (Campbell and Martin-Matthews 2000a; 2003).

Matthews and Heidorn (1998) studied brothers-only sibling groups. They found that sons kept in contact with their parents and engaged in gender-typical services—yard work or financial advice. They also accepted both informal and formal services as ways to meet their parents' needs. More recent work by Matthews (2002) finds that sons attempt to keep parents as independent as possible. Daughters, by contrast, take a more "hands on" approach to care. This tends to increase their parents' dependence. Hequembourg and Brallier (2005) found that caregiving brothers tended to fall into two categories. Brothers in the first category (helper brothers) assumed a more traditional role in care, providing significantly less care than their sisters, and relying on sisters to assign them specific tasks. Brothers in the second category (co-provider brothers) contributed to the care of their parents in a more equitable way. But even these brothers tended to rely on their sisters to coordinate and assign their caregiving work.

Campbell (2002; also see Campbell and Carroll 2007; Carroll and Campbell 2008) found some common themes in the experiences of adult sons who were providing care to older parents. For example, most men provided care out of a sense of commitment to family. They felt a strong bond to their parent and a desire to repay the parent for past support. Many sons talked about how providing care had brought them emotionally closer to their parent. For most, the caregiving role evolved as a gradual process.

Men experienced a mixture of emotions, including feelings of love, compassion, responsibility, as well as sadness, frustration, and guilt. As one 40-year-old married son said about caring for his mother: "I love my mum [but] sometimes it is frustrating and sometimes it's overwhelming … [There's] a sense of feeling very spread out. I'm using very emotional terms, but, you know, yeah, [it's] so emotionally overwhelming sometimes" (500). Many sons felt that no matter how difficult the tasks might be, they just did what needed to be done. As one son said: "just deal with it … do what you have to do and move on" (Campbell and Carroll 2007, 498).

Campbell (2002) also reports differences between married and never married sons in their involvement in care. In general, married sons more often gave care in limited and traditional ways (visiting, providing help with transportation, home maintenance). In contrast, never married sons (who more often lived with their parent) were more involved in care (including domestic and personal care). Never married sons often had little or no social support, few financial resources, and intense caregiving responsibilities. This made them particularly vulnerable to caregiver stress and burden.

Care for the Caregiver

Many caregivers report feelings of satisfaction and accomplishment (Harris 2005). Greater commitment to and enthusiasm for the caregiving role can lead to greater feelings of well-being (Pierce, Lydon, and Yang 2001). Cohen, Colantonio, and Vernich (2002) found that 73 percent of caregivers could identify at least one positive thing about caregiving. For example, caregivers enjoyed helping their care receiver feel better. They also felt duty and love toward the person receiving the care (Harris 2005). Most spousal caregivers express positive feelings about caregiving. Many adult sons said their relationship with their parent improved after they began caregiving (Campbell 2002).

Sims-Gould and Martin-Matthews (2007) found that caregivers often receive help from others with their caregiving. Spouses, siblings, and siblings-in-law most often serve as direct helpers. And many caregivers—and helpers—provide assistance to each other and to more than one older person at the same time. Many family members pay an emotional and psychological price when they take on informal caregiving. Caregivers of cognitively impaired older people, particularly those caring for relatives with Alzheimer's disease (AD) or other forms of dementia, many of them spouses, feel the most stress (Harris 2005; MacLean 2008).

MacRae (1999; 2002) found that a majority of caregivers at some time felt shame and embarrassment at a care receiver's behaviour. Spouses often tried to cover up the problem of memory loss. Children prepared situations in advance or avoided situations where a parent's memory loss would prove embarrassing. Many family members caring for a person with AD conceal the illness from others to protect the person from negative labelling (MacRae 2002). Caregivers often feel isolated, fatigued, and overwhelmed by the strain of care. Carpentier and Ducharme (2007) found that caregivers who experience distress, frustration, and continuous failure are likely to hold a negative perception of their support network and underestimate the help they receive.

A number of researchers have proposed ways to ease caregiver burden. Some of these proposals are listed below.

1. **Family counselling** can help ease the burden of caregiving. Counselling works best when it takes into account the entire family system—the caregiver's spouse, children, and siblings, as well as the older person. Counselling can help caregivers deal with moral conflicts about how much protection to give a care receiver. Counselling or psychotherapy can also help a caregiver deal with stress and depression (Hébert et al. 2003).

2. **Support groups** give caregivers information about how to cope with caregiving demands as well as emotional support. The Alzheimer's Society, hospitals, and religious institutions offer support groups. Some groups offer support based on a specific disease (e.g., dementia or cancer). Some of these groups have a professional leader; others work as self-help groups. People who attend support groups say they feel relief and an improved ability to manage as caregivers (Hagen, Gallagher, and Simpson 1997). Other forms of support groups that benefit caregivers include telephone support groups (Ploeg et al. 2001; Smith and Toseland 2006) and online supports (including e-mail correspondence support groups). Different types of caregivers appear to benefit from different types of group support (Stewart et al. 2006).

3. **Respite services** in the community give caregivers a break from the demands of caregiving. These services range from friendly visitors who stay with the care receiver for a few hours, to full-day adult day care, to longer institutional respite. Institutional respite programs can last from several days to several weeks, allowing caregivers to take vacations, deal with personal needs like medical treatment, or simply rest.

Chappell (1997) found that regulations, such as a minimum two-night stay for respite admission, as well as lack of funding and slow processing of respite requests, created barriers that sometimes prevented caregivers from getting the help they needed. Gottlieb and Johnson (2000) found that the services, when offered, appear to be "too little, too late." They report little measurable benefit from these respite programs. Yet many family caregivers say they value and want respite. One caregiver, in Chappell's study (1997, 26), who got in-home respite, said, "I kept my sanity. I could breathe again, and I wasn't spinning in circles ... I was more patient, happier, and more caring."

In a study by Dupuis and Smale (2004), caregivers of persons with dementia identified a number of issues related to respite services and programs. These include the need for immediate and readily accessible emergency respite to deal with crises and more hours of in-home respite care. Caregivers also identified the need for meaningful social and recreational respite programs for their family members with dementia.

Researchers suggest that the meaning of respite differs among caregivers and may not just be related to services or organized programs. Almost half of the caregivers in a study by Chappell, Reid, and Dow (2001) defined respite as "stolen moments"— activities or situations that for a short time took them away from the worries of caregiving. None of the caregivers in the study talked about respite in terms of services. Dupuis (2000) finds that caregiving daughters who experienced "leisure moments" in the institution-based caregiving context felt more enjoyment in care. These stolen or leisure moments may provide caregivers with a form of respite that is more a state of mind than a tangible service.

4. **Eldercare programs** at work can help family caregivers cope. These programs include counselling services, information on community services and support, and flexible work schedules. Some research shows that children who provide care, particularly middle-aged caregiving daughters, may quit their jobs to take care of their parent. Other women reduce their work hours. Research finds that employment does not reduce adult daughters' assistance to parents and parents-in-law (Rosenthal et al. 2004). Mothers of working women get the same number of hours of care (formal and informal) as mothers of nonworking women, but the working women often have to pay for personal care and meal services for their parent. These paid services fill in for them while they work.

Gottlieb and his colleagues (1994; see also Martin-Matthews and Campbell 1995) found that women with young children at home who provided care to older parents faced a high risk of personal and job stress. One-quarter of workers who cared for older parents averaged nine hours per week helping with activities of daily living as well as general care. The rest averaged three hours per week of general help such as household chores. More recent Canadian research on working caregivers (Stobert and Cranswick 2004) found that men spend just over 14 hours per month on caregiving. Employed women spend about 26 hours per month giving care. Caregiving for many workers leads to stress and time away from the job. Caregivers also face the constant threat of a breakdown in their support system (e.g., a respite program may be closed for a day). Some caregivers have to cut back on leisure, education, social activities, and volunteering activities.

Although some companies have responded to this problem, more could be done to implement these programs and inform workers about eldercare options. Medjuck, Keefe, and Fancey (1998) studied 37 workplaces in Nova Scotia. They found that only half of the human resources documents they studied contained a family leave policy. Those that had leave policies often had restrictions that limited their usefulness. Less than one-third of the documents referred to an employee assistance program to help employees cope with stress and social issues. This research shows that companies should make eldercare information and programs more available to workers.

Good programs and other interventions cannot completely do away with feelings of burden, nor should they be expected to. Spouses and children feel loss, anger, and frustration as they see a person close to them suffer through an illness. These feelings reflect a legitimate response to a parent's or spouse's suffering. But interventions can help caregivers understand caregiving; they can help caregivers cope with the everyday demands of care; and they can give caregivers social and emotional support. Raina and his colleagues (2004) say that the most effective support programs target caregivers who face the most risk.

Few of the proposals to ease caregiver burden address the large-scale issues of gender inequality or the changing role of women in the labour force. For example, current programs and policies that encourage community care put the burden on female family members. Too often help for caregivers comes into play only when family care breaks down. The rhetoric about family care suggests that the state would like to shift more caregiving to family members. However, Guberman and Maheu (2002) say that practitioners and policy makers must move to a more community-oriented approach to caregiving. In this model families serve as only one of many available resources. Caregiving demands will increase in the future. Researchers propose more studies of how health care policies affect the lives of caregivers.

The Future of Informal Support

Informal supports play a vital role in the well-being of older people. But the availability of informal supports may decrease in the years ahead. At least two changes in Canadian society point to this likelihood.

First, demographic changes may decrease the amount of informal support older people will get in the future. Family size has shrunk, so older people in the future will have fewer children to call on for help. A decrease in the availability of nuclear family supports will increase the risk of institutionalization. Also, the number of children over the age of 65 who care for their parents will increase in the future as more people live longer. Some of these children will be unable to care for their parents, and some may need health care help themselves.

Second, as people live longer, their support networks suffer from the death of a spouse and cohort attrition. Peers die off over time, leaving members of some support networks without help. This makes children a vital source of support for most older people as they age. This could put future pressure on the children of the Baby Boom. In the third and later decades of this century, middle-aged children may find themselves challenged by their parents' care needs.

For those without children, or with geographically distant children, the need for formal support services will also increase.

These trends suggest potential problems with the availability of informal supports in the future. But other trends might lead to stronger informal supports. First, because of longer life expectancy, more spouses will live together longer than ever before. This increased longevity will give married couples more informal support as they age. Greater longevity will also mean the parent–child relationship can endure long into the adult child's middle and later years. This may strengthen the bond within these relationships and increase social support.

Second, current trends in health promotion (better diet, exercise, and a decrease in smoking) may lead to better health in old age. If these trends continue, older people in the future may need less long-term health care support than older people today.

Third, new types of groups based on the mutual needs of older people may develop. Novak and Stone (1985) called these **semiformal structures** because they fall between the informal (voluntary) support structures of the family and the formal (professionalized) structures of the health and social service systems. Semiformal structures include car pools, groups of people in the same building who shop together, friendly visitors, or "daily hello" phone calls. These groups and relationships do not rely on kinship, friendship bonds, or the fee-for-service bond of formal supports. Instead, they are based on a bond of reciprocity and on the fact that they bring mutual benefit to users. More of these groups in the future could make up for losses in older people's social networks.

Both trends—the decrease in informal supports and the increase in alternative forms of support (including home care and semiformal structures)—could strengthen in the future. The well-being of older people in the future will depend on how well alternatives to traditional supports meet their needs.

Researchers caution that current trends in policy may lead to future problems in long-term care. Current policy supports a shift in responsibility for care of older adults from institutions and professionals to "the community." This most often means a shift to the family and, typically, to the middle-aged or older woman. Armstrong (2002) and others worry that this lack of government support for community services to meet the needs of these caregivers could damage personal networks, relationships, and families' ability to care. Women, as well as men, who choose to care for older family members need support at work, good community supports, and institutional care when their care receiver needs it. Fewer institutional beds will leave families without this option.

Rosenthal (1994) said that formal support should play the central part in social support. Families (very often middle-aged women) could then decide how much or how little of this support they need. "We should not overestimate the availability or quality of family care," Rosenthal (421) said. "Some older people do not have family members who are able to provide care." Others may have family members who do not have the time or energy to give more than emotional support. Still others may prefer professional help to family care.

Rosenthal (2000) states her belief in the need for society to take more responsibility in caring for older Canadians:

> "Whether families are or will be capable of providing needed support to older relatives must take second place to the question of who should be responsible for the care of older people. My position, one that is growing stronger over the years as I continue to learn more about older families, is that the care of the elderly is a public, not a private, issue and that responsibility lies with the state. Within that framework, we may then examine the role families might play if they are able and willing" (61).

ABUSE AGAINST OLDER PERSONS

Most older people get support and comfort from their families, but some people face exploitation and abuse. No single definition of abuse against older persons exists. But a broad definition refers to abuse and neglect as "any action or inaction by ANY person, which causes harm to the older or vulnerable person" (Council against Abuse of Older Persons 2008). Abuse against older persons includes physical abuse, psychosocial abuse, financial abuse, neglect (active or passive), institutional abuse, and domestic violence. Research shows that most abuse against older persons comes from family members, and most victims of family violence are women (Turcotte and Schellenberg 2007). In this situation, many abused older people suffer in silence, making the rate of abuse hard to estimate and harder to eliminate. A number of studies of abuse against older persons in Canada discuss research findings, policy issues, and best practice.

Canadian Research Findings

Most Canadian research on abuse against older persons has used convenience samples, sometimes with low response rates. This makes it hard to generalize from the findings. Almost 20 years ago, Podnieks et al. (1990) conducted Canada's first random-sample survey on abuse against older persons. The researchers conducted telephone interviews with a sample of 2,008 people aged 65 and over who lived in private households. These people presented a statistically reliable picture of the 91 percent of seniors who lived on their own in the community. The survey asked about abuse carried out by family members and other intimates.

The sample contained about two-thirds women; 73 percent of respondents owned their own homes

and 52 percent were married. About one-third of the respondents received the Guaranteed Income Supplement (the federal government pension that goes to the poorest seniors); 63 percent reported good or excellent health; and the large majority shopped, cooked, and cleaned for themselves. Relatively few respondents reported feeling lonely, bored, or downhearted. The majority by far (92 percent) said they felt fairly happy or very happy.

Podnieks and her colleagues (1990) defined four categories of abuse in their study: material (financial) abuse, chronic verbal aggression, physical violence, and neglect. The study counted only the most serious and obvious cases. Because of this, the researchers cautioned that their findings probably underestimated the number of abused older people.

The study estimated that about 4 percent of all older people (about 98,000 people) in private dwellings in Canada had experienced abuse since turning age 65. This was similar to the rate (3.2 percent) that Pillemer and Finkelhor (1988) reported at about the same time for a random sample study in the United States. Most of these cases involve passive, verbal, emotional, and financial abuse, rather than physical violence or neglect. This fits with the findings of other research in the 1990s (Wolf 1996).

More recent data from the 1999 General Social Survey (GSS) in Canada finds that 7 percent of older Canadians report some type of emotional or financial abuse, the most common types of abuse (Dauvergne 2003). These findings are significantly higher than earlier work suggested.

At the time of their study, Podnieks and her colleagues (1990) found that about 2.5 percent of older adults in the Canadian study had experienced material abuse; about 1.4 percent of older adults experienced chronic verbal aggression; about 0.5 percent of older adults experienced physical violence; and about 0.4 percent of older adults experienced neglect. The study also found a fifth common form of abuse: denial of access to grandchildren. About 4 percent of older adults reported denial of access at least once since they turned age 65. If the researchers had included this category at the start of their study, the overall rate of abuse would nearly have doubled, to 7 percent of older adults.

Just under 1 percent of older adults in the study suffered from more than one form of abuse. The 1999 GSS finds this to be almost 2 percent of older Canadians (Dauvergne 2003). Rates in the 1999 GSS study run nearly twice as high as the earlier study by Podnieks and her colleagues (1990) reported.

Podnieks and her colleagues (1990; also Turcotte and Schellenberg 2007) found that female victims of abuse outnumber male victims by almost two to one. Also, some types of people faced a higher risk for some types of abuse than for others. For example, people who reported material abuse tended to live more isolated lives and to have poor health. These people faced abuse from varied sources, including spouses, friends, children, and distant relatives.

Neglect can arise from unresolved conflict in a family, bad feelings about a divorce or remarriage, or emotionally distant ties with adult children or step-children. These fractured relationships can lead to withdrawal and, ultimately, neglect by children and other family members. Women who report neglect also have poor health, low morale, and a dependence on others for functional help. They faced abuse from spouses, children, and nonfamily caregivers. Compared to older women, older men run a high risk of abandonment (the most extreme form of neglect) (Stratton and Moore 2007).

Research in Quebec supports these findings. Lithwick and colleagues (1999) looked at 128 mistreatment cases involving older adults (aged 60 or older) in three community service agencies. The researchers found psychological abuse in 70 percent of cases, financial abuse in 41 percent of cases, neglect in 32 percent of cases, and physical abuse in 20 percent of cases. The majority of victims in this study were women (75 percent) while the majority of abusers were men (65 percent). Most abuse came from spouses (48 percent of cases) or adult children (30 percent of cases). More than one-half of these older victims suffered from two to four types of abuse. Fisher and Regan (2006) found a similar pattern of abuse in an American study of older women. Forty-five percent of study participants reported psychological/emotional abuse. Twelve percent reported threats, 4 percent reported physical abuse, and 3 percent reported sexual abuse. Many of these women were victims of multiple or repeat abuse.

Research has often focused on cases in which an adult child caregiver abuses an older person he or she cares for. But more recent studies show that often the abusing child relies on the abused person for housing or financial support (Podnieks 2008). Financial dependence can lead to resentment, anger, and abuse. Pittaway and Gallagher (1995) found that in 56 percent of cases of abused older people (aged 55 and over in their study) the abuser partly or wholly depended financially on the abused person. Bond and his colleagues (1999) studied cases of suspected financial abuse in a sample of mentally incompetent older Canadians. They found that the abused person was more likely to be female, to live in a long-term care facility or to own her own home, and to have a high monthly income. Often the nonpayment of bills in the long-term care facility signalled possible

financial abuse. When community-dwelling seniors suffer financial abuse, it is often at the hands of someone (a family member, friend, or neighbour), they had trusted to do their banking or pay bills (see Exhibit 13.7).

People who report chronic verbal abuse and physical violence have some things in common. They tend to be married, and they report that the abuse came from their spouse. Beaulieu, Gravel, and Lithwick (1999) found that spouses differed from other people in their pattern of abuse. They found that spouses "exercise strong psychological control, and they are the least reluctant to use physical force ... They are neglectful in a quarter of the cases of mistreatment" (8). Abusive husbands can use feelings of jealousy as a pretext for their violent and coercive behaviour (Beaulaurier et al. 2007).

In 2003, Canadian police services recorded approximately 4,000 incidents of violence against older persons (Turcotte and Schellenberg 2007). Family members committed about 30 percent of these incidents. Compared to men, older women showed the highest rates of victimization.

Men more often than women engage in violent abuse in families (Dauvergne 2003). Police data from 2000 show that men made up 80 percent of those accused of violence against older family members. Offenders most often engaged in common assaults (e.g., pushing, slapping, and shoving). Adult children and spouses (most often sons and husbands) account for about 70 percent of family violence against older adults (Dauvergne 2003). Most cases of violence against older people occur in their home—often by a child who lives with the older person.

Researchers have developed several theories to explain the causes of abuse against older persons (Harbison, McKinley, and Pettipas 2006; McDonald and Collins 2000; Podnieks 2008). One theory holds that caregiver stress leads to abuse. A second theory says that abuse exists as part of a larger pattern of violence in some families. Family members who suffered abuse or who witnessed abuse in childhood become abusers themselves. A third theory sees abuse against older persons within marriage as a continuation of earlier spousal abuse into later life. Finally, some theorists say that abuse against older persons fits into a larger societal pattern of ageism and the devaluation of older people (Harbison 1999a; Podnieks 2008).

Aronson, Thornewell, and Williams (1995; see also Harbison 1999b and Neysmith 1995b) take a feminist approach to the study of abuse against older persons. They say that the term "elder abuse" masks the link between abuse against older women and the relative powerlessness of women throughout life. They prefer the term "wife assault in old age" to describe the physical

Exhibit 13.7

OLDER ADULT SUFFERS ABUSE OF TRUST

Dr. Peter Ingram, a psychogeriatric specialist in Winnipeg, describes a case of material abuse. He goes on to explain the options open to him and his patient once he detects the abuse.

Anastasia Kowalchuk (not her real name) is angry. She can't understand why the bank took $12,000 of her money, more than half the 87-year-old woman's savings.

Her niece, who had been visiting from Toronto, took her to the bank where Anastasia hoped to withdraw some money to donate to her community's nursing home, where she plans to move this year. She was shocked to see how little money she had left. With the help of her niece, she asked the bank to find out what had happened.

On a return visit, the bank manager showed her the transaction slip with her signature, authorizing the withdrawal. Although Anastasia's vision is dim from cataracts, she had to agree the signature looked like her own.

Anastasia has had trouble remembering things for some time. She forgets to pay her bills and deposit her pension cheques. When her friend Mary offered to help her with cooking meals and housekeeping two years ago for a small salary, it seemed like a good way to stay out of the nursing home.

When Mary more recently suggested she also help with the banking, Anastasia agreed. Now Mary is acting strangely; she has been shouting at Anastasia and told her not to talk to Sophia or Kateryna, her neighbours. As Anastasia speaks only a little English, she feels isolated without her daily chats in Ukrainian with her two elderly friends. She wishes her husband were alive to explain things. Anastasia's family doctor asked Dr. Ingram and his staff to assess her and look into the situation. A community nurse interviewed Anastasia's niece, neighbours, and someone from the bank. Dr. Ingram concludes that Anastasia may suffer from dementia and material abuse. Dr. Ingram will decide whether Anastasia can manage her finances or whether he should apply for an Order of Supervision. This order allows the Public Trustee to take over Anastasia's finances and ensures the safety of her savings.

Dr. Ingram may find that Anastasia has enough cognitive ability to look after her own affairs. In this case he can only warn her to take more care in managing her finances. If the abuser comes from Anastasia's family, Dr. Ingram says, "often nothing changes."

"This is very frustrating," he says, "and I find it hard to walk away from these people without helping them."

Source: P. Ingram, 1996, "Senior Suffers Abuse of Trust," *Winnipeg Free Press*, January 11, A6. Reprinted with permission.

---

abuse of older women. Beaulieu and her colleagues (1999) support this point. They found that in 40 percent of domestic violence cases the violence had gone on for more than 25 years. Aronson and her colleagues say that studies of abuse against older women must link current abuse to structured social inequalities.

Policy Issues

Policy refers to regulations and guidelines on how to deal with abuse against older persons (MacLean and Williams 1995). Abuse policies attempt to help the older abused person. Policies can include criminal court action, mandatory reporting, guardianship and power of attorney, and mediation to resolve disputes. These methods use public means (by a social worker or police) to improve a family relationship. But this course of action often fails.

The law assumes that two people in a dispute have only a limited relation to each other, but an abused spouse or parent often has a long-term relationship with his or her abuser and he or she may want to maintain this relationship (sometimes at personal risk). For example, a study of the effectiveness of adult protective legislation conducted in the mid-1990s (Bond, Penner, and Yellen 1995) found an unwillingness by both the alleged abuser and the victim to cooperate during investigations, and a general reluctance to report cases of abuse. The researchers found that few cases went to court.

Legal action may do little to improve the abused person's life. A legal outcome, such as removing the abused person from a setting, may cause more stress to the abused person. Likewise, the abused person may reject legal remedies such as jailing an abusing child or spouse on whom he or she depends for help. Pittaway and Gallagher (1995) found that nearly one-fifth (18 percent) of abused older people were afraid to report the abuse because they feared reprisal from the abuser (Beaulaurier et al. 2007).

Researchers support the need for intervention strategies for both the abused older people and their abusers (Lithwick et al. 1999; Nahmiash and Reis 2000; Podnieks 2008). Nahmiash and Reis (2000) examined the effectiveness of intervention strategies in cases of abuse in Canada. The most successful strategies involved concrete help from nurses and other medical professions as well as homemaking services. Other successful interventions helped to empower older people. These included support groups, volunteers who acted as advocates, and information about a person's rights and available resources (see also World Health Organization/International Network for the Prevention of Elder Abuse 2002). The most successful interventions for caregiver abusers involved individual counselling to reduce stress, as well as education and training (Nahmiash and Reis 2000).

Barriers exist to implementing these changes. For example, Wolf (2001) finds that many victims of family violence refuse to join a support group. She suggests that support groups have an older group leader or co-leader, someone familiar with issues these older people face. Other research (Lithwick et al. 1999) finds that many abused older people refuse services that might reduce stress. These included medical services, home care assistance, day-care centres, and respite programs.

A study in British Columbia and Yukon looked at the use of emergency shelter services available to older women who are victims of domestic violence (Hightower et al. 1999). The researchers found that only 2 percent of the women in these shelters were age 60 or older. Only 4 percent of these programs had services especially geared to older women. Hightower and her colleagues (1999; also Beaulaurier et al. 2007) say staff at shelters need to recognize and understand the special needs of elderly abuse victims.

Research in the United States (Beaulaurier et al. 2007) examined the external barriers that older women face when they seek help from domestic abuse. For example, most women in the study felt that their families would not support them if they reported abuse, and the research bore this out. Families typically denied abuse or blamed the victim. One abused woman's mother's said, "you married him knowing he was like that ... so deal with it" (750).

Women also lacked faith in the justice system. They did not feel they would get the help and support they needed. They feared that by reporting abuse they faced greater jeopardy. One woman said, "A restraining order is [a court order] asking him to stay away from you, but it doesn't keep him away from you" (751). Some women did, or said they would, talk to a member of the clergy for guidance. But none of the women who talked to their clergy had been referred later to social services or the police. The authors found that most clergy encouraged these women to maintain "the status quo while offering little practical help" (750).

Many women did not know where to go for community support, or felt no help existed. This applied especially to older victims of domestic violence. Beaulaurier and his colleagues say that "law enforcement responders need to ... involve community providers of domestic violence and elder services in any intervention to create a viable safety net" (754).

Tam and Neysmith (2006) say that the Western definition of elder abuse does not include abuse as defined by other cultures. The researchers interviewed Chinese home care workers who provided services to Chinese seniors and their families in Toronto. Tam and Neysmith find that "disrespect" of older family members is the primary type of elder abuse in the Chinese community. Disrespect involves actions and attitudes that violate traditional Chinese norms or values. The home care workers in their study said that disrespect could include family members being overly bossy or rude, abrupt commands, unnecessary scolding, or dismissive comments.

Older people felt disrespected if family members restricted the older person's space or mobility; for example, some older family members were made to stay in their rooms. In some cases, the family kept the older relative from eating meals with the family, or kept them from taking part in the dinner conversation. Home care workers said these older people showed signs of loneliness and depression because they felt socially isolated. Tam and Neysmith recommend that "researchers be cautious about applying elder abuse categories derived from a Western cultural perspective to understand or account for abuse in other cultures" (149). This recommendation extends to policy makers as well.

Future Issues in Abuse against Older Persons

Abuse and neglect against older persons has existed throughout history. What then accounts for the relatively sudden interest in abuse and neglect? Four social changes account for this interest: (1) the growth of the older population, (2) the increased political power of older people, (3) the women's movement and a critical analysis of the family, and (4) the state's willingness to intervene in family life.

Some authors (Callahan 1986; Crystal 1986) argue that formal service agencies have adopted the cause of abuse against older persons in order to expand their influence and get more funding. This view links the sudden interest in abuse to the expansion of the welfare state. Other authors say that special programs aimed at reducing abuse reinforce negative stereotypes of older people as feeble and helpless (Harbison 1999a). Others (Otto 2000) take a different view. They see health and social service professionals' intervention in child abuse and in abuse against older persons as parallel. In both cases, professionals, on behalf of the state, set out to protect a vulnerable minority. Through this process, abuse against older persons has become a legitimate social problem. The authors see this attention as a first step in creating social policies to protect abused older people.

The research on abuse against older persons supports the idea that older people suffer from varied forms of mistreatment. Some subgroups may have a higher-than-average risk of abuse and may need special attention. This includes older women, those who are physically or cognitively frail, and those who depend upon their abuser for financial security or caregiving (Brandl 2000).

Professionals need more education about abuse and the tools to assess and detect abuse (Podnieks 2008; Reis and Nahmiash 1997; 1998; Trevitt and Gallagher 1996). Still, the research shows that the vast majority of older people do not experience abuse. These findings should make us more aware of abuse and also help keep the issue of abuse in perspective.

Canadian researchers have explored the causes, theories, and responses to abuse against older persons. Research is needed on the role of ethnicity or culture in the abuse and neglect of older Canadians (Kozak, Elmslie, and Verdon 1995). More research is also needed on the health implications of abuse and abuse against older persons in residential settings (Fisher and Regan 2006). Glendenning (1999), for example, reviewed the literature on abuse and neglect in long-term care settings. This review found that the facility environment, the characteristics of the resident, and the characteristics of the staff (including the problem of staff burnout) all influenced the existence of abuse. Future studies need to propose policies and practices to help ensure the safety of a growing and diverse older population within the community and residential settings.

FUTURE RESEARCH ON FAMILY LIFE AND SOCIAL SUPPORT

In the 1980s, research on the family and social supports in later life focused on what Abu-Laban (1980, 196) then called "the 'normal' (or at least the research worthy) aged—[the] gray-haired, Anglo-Celtic, heterosexual, life-long marrieds, who have produced children and grandchildren." Studies reported how this ideal family coped with the normal crises of growing older. These studies then turned to "the support ties of the white-haired, Anglo-Celtic, widowed mother and grandmother" (196).

Researchers now believe that this image takes too narrow a view of family life. First, the literature idealizes marriage and the caregiving spouse, but it says little about the dysfunctions that marriage and the use of informal supports can create. Married couples, for example, make less use of formal services. The caregiver spouse sees care as a normal and expected part of marriage (Davidson, Arber, and Ginn 2000). However, the failure to use available supports can make life harder for both spouses. Also, when spouses rely on each other for support, they can lose contact with friends and relatives. This situation can lead to feelings of burden, isolation, and depression for both spouses. More research on marriage in later life should focus on both the benefits and the problems that marriage can bring. In the late 1990s, Peters and Liefbroer (1997) were among the first to identify the need to look beyond marital status. They proposed studies of partner status, marital history, and individuals' views of marriage.

Second, the structure of the family has changed significantly over the past decades. Sociodemographic changes in family size and structure, patterns of marriage and divorce, changing roles for women, increased life expectancy, and greater diversity in the timing of life course events and transitions means that more families will include older family members. "The dynamic aspect of this is," Rosenthal (2000, 45) says, "a much increased overlap of lives between familial generations." Many older people today have living siblings, adult children, and grandchildren. Families will have more generations alive at one time than ever before. This means that older people today have large reservoirs of potential informal support. We know little about the lives and relationships of older people in these new family structures.

Older people in the future (around 2025), compared with older people today, will have fewer children and fewer siblings. This will give them a smaller pool of close relatives to call on for support and could lead to increased reliance on **fictive kin**. This term refers to close relationships with nonrelatives such as friends, neighbours, and home care workers.

Third, research on older people's family life has almost ignored the lives of certain types of people. Little research has been done on never married older people (Baumbusch 2004; Pudrovska et al. 2006), divorced older people (Lin 2008; Wu and Schimmele 2007), or the childless elderly (Dykstra and Hagestad 2007). We also know little about gender differences in the social support needs of different marital status groups, including those who remarry in later life (Wister and Dykstra 2000). Further research should also look at the social support needs and experiences of older gay and lesbian couples and individuals (Connidis 2003).

Fourth, few studies have compared the family life of older people from different cultural and ethnic backgrounds. More research on ethnicity in old age should look at family relations (Mitchell 2003), informal supports (Keefe, Rosenthal, and Béland 2000), and the use of social services by different ethnic groups. Kobayashi (2000) looked at intergenerational support in Japanese-Canadian families. She found that filial obligation (the obligation to care for a parent) had a significant effect on children's provision of emotional support to parents. But it did not affect the amount of financial or service support children gave. She says that researchers need to study ethnicity and parent–child exchanges and the differences in support given by sons and daughters.

Buchignani and Armstrong-Esther (1999) examined the informal care needs of older Aboriginal people in Alberta. They found that while many had fair or poor health, very few had the financial resources to pay for formal services or to live independently in old age. Adult children, spouses, and sisters provided support. The researchers say that institutional barriers and a lack of available services lead these older Canadians to rely extensively on family care.

Fifth, research in the past several decades focused mostly on older women. Few studies on family and social relations looked at older men. Researchers need to look at male friendships, lone-father families (McQuillan and Belle 2001), widowers, grandfathering, gay men as they age, men's remarriage, as well as men involved in caregiving to family members, particularly adult sons (Campbell and Carroll 2007) and older husbands (Calasanti and Bowen 2006). Studies that have described men show that they face special challenges in old age.

Sixth, some researchers suggest that marriage is becoming increasingly fragile. Current low marriage rates among younger people, increases in common-law and living-apart-together (LAT) relationships, high divorce rates, and fewer remarriages in middle and later life will lead to new and more diverse patterns of family life for older people. These trends may produce more unmarried older people, both men and women. They may also lead to more older people with children from multiple marriages.

An older person in the future may have several sets of children and grandchildren from several marriages. Their children too may have children from several marriages. The study of these family structures in the future will give a more complete picture of family life in old age.

CONCLUSION

Older people live rich social lives. They interact with family members, friends, and neighbours as well as with their spouses. Most older people rely on these networks of family and friends for social, emotional, and health care support. Older people also give to their families and serve as role models for the young. Old age is a time of change—the death of a spouse, for example, creates one of life's greatest stresses. But research shows that most older people cope with the challenges of aging and experience satisfying and rewarding social lives.

Summary

1. The myth persists that middle-aged children abandon their elderly parents, but studies show again and again that children maintain contact with their parents, provide them with help, and get help and support from them when they need it.
2. A good marriage provides support for both partners as they age. Married older people use less formal care, rely less on children and friends for support, and have a lower institutionalization rate than unmarried older people. Older women run a higher risk than older men of losing this support due to widowhood.

3. Never married older adults play vital and supportive roles in the lives of siblings, older parents, and others. They also form friendships and other social relationships to provide themselves with supporters, confidants, and companions.

4. Older divorced men are more likely than older divorced women to remarry. Being divorced in later life often means economic insecurity, particularly for women, and loss of social contact with children for men. There has been a significant increase in the number of divorced older people.

5. Older adults now and in the future will have greater choice in the type of intimate relationships they wish to form. These will include common-law and living-apart-together (LAT) relationships for those older people who want a close and intimate relationship, but not necessarily one within marriage.

6. Widowhood has become an expected life event for women in Canada, although it still creates stress in a woman's life. Researchers disagree about the impact of widowhood on men. Some studies show that widowed men have fewer social supports and that they suffer from isolation, loneliness, and a high risk of suicide. More recent studies suggest that men may need less social support than women and that they adapt in different ways to widowhood.

7. Older people have an interest in sex throughout life. Most people will need to adjust their expectations about sexual performance in later life. But, given good health and a willing partner, older people can enjoy sexual relations into late old age. New attitudes toward sexuality may encourage more sexual activity in later life.

8. Long-term relationships with a committed partner can provide both older gay men and lesbians with companionship, acceptance, and support. Other social network ties with family members and friends also serve an important social support function in their lives.

9. Most older people keep up social contacts with relatives and friends as they age. They also give support as well as receive it. They help their children socially, financially, and emotionally. They help their peers by acting as confidants. Older people, like younger people, get esteem and a sense of purpose from helping others.

10. Grandparenting offers older people one of the most enjoyable roles in old age. It has few responsibilities attached to it, so older people can shape the role to suit their personality, lifestyle, and interests. With increased longevity, many grandparents will live to see their grandchildren grow into adults with children of their own.

11. Older people often depend on informal support networks for emotional and health care support, but informal support can place a burden on family members (particularly women). These burdened caregivers may lose their income from work, their pensions, and even their health due to caregiving demands. Government financial support for caregivers would make caregiving a less burdensome option for many people and would recognize their valuable service to the community.

12. Adult children, most often daughters, provide most of the informal support needed by their older parents. Research shows that strong feelings of attachment to a parent lead to caregiving, and that feelings of closeness between parents and children lead to satisfaction and happiness. Older adults, particularly those without a spouse or children, receive support from sibling and friends as well.

13. Abuse against older people is most often committed by family members. The abuse most often takes the form of material abuse and chronic verbal aggression. A smaller proportion of older people face physical aggression and neglect. Education for police, counsellors, family members, and older adults themselves may help reduce the incidence of abuse. Legal services, mental health services, and shelters could help older people to cope with the aftermath of abuse.

14. Some trends, such as cohort attrition for very old people and smaller families for Baby Boomers, suggest that informal supports will decline in the future. Other trends, such as longer life expectancy for spouses and the development of semiformal structures, suggest that older people will still rely on informal supports in the years ahead. These two trends may counterbalance each other, and older people in the future may develop new types of social supports.

15. Many gaps still exist in the literature on family life in old age. Research on atypical groups of older people—for example, older gay men and lesbians, permanently single and divorced older people—will increase our understanding of family and intimate relations in later life.

Study Questions

1. What are the benefits of marriage in old age? How does divorce affect people in old age? Why do some older people choose to live in common-law or living-apart-together (LAT) relationships?

2. What types of people form the social support networks of older divorced and never married people? Compare and contrast the networks of divorced and never married people.

3. Explain why widows outnumber widowers in the aging population. Why do men seem to suffer more than women socially and psychologically when they lose a spouse?

4. Explain the difference between formal and informal support. What kind of support do most older people get? Describe the benefits of this type of support. How do older people choose their potential support groups?

5. In addition to family, where else do older people look for informal support? How do support networks differ by marital and parental status?

6. What types of help and support do older people provide to family and friends?

7. Discuss the role that grandparents play in the lives of grandchildren. What are the benefits of the grandparent–grandchild tie for grandparents? Explain the different styles of grandparenting.

8. Explain the term "sandwich generation." What are the major difficulties that arise when people take on the role of caregiver to their aged parents?

9. Discuss several things that may ease the burden of caregiving on spouses or adult children.

10. Why do demographers project that the availability of informal supports may decrease in the future? In the absence of informal support, what other types of support are available to the older population?

11. What are the different types of abuse against older persons? How common is this abuse and who is often responsible for abusing an older person? Suggest some ways that abuse against older persons can be prevented, both in the community and in institutions.

12. Why do some gerontologists believe that researchers could expand the scope of studies in aging and the family? What types of issues and trends should this research address?

Key Terms

animal-assisted therapy   therapy that involves introducing pets, such as dogs, cats, rabbits, or birds, into nursing homes or other residential care settings with the objective of improving the health, behaviour, and well-being of the residents. (309)

boomerang children   adult children who return to their parent's home after having moved out at an earlier point in time. (296)

caregiver burden   problems and stress due to caregiving. (309)

caregiver's wage or allowance   financial payment to family caregivers to assist them in their caregiving role. (307)

confidant   someone in whom one confides. (292)

convoy model of support   a model that describes social support as a network of close family and friends who travel together throughout life, exchanging social support and assistance. (304)

developmental stake or **generational stake**   the idea that, compared with their children, older people have a greater investment in the relationship with their children. (306)

eldercare programs   workplace programs that can help family caregivers cope with care for an older family member. (318)

family counselling   counselling with a social worker or psychotherapist that includes parents, children, and siblings. (317)

fictive kin   the close relationships that an older person develops with nonrelatives such as friends, neighbours, and home care workers. (325)

filial piety   a culture value or belief, highly valued in Asian cultures, that younger generations should take care of older family members. (310)

formal support   paid support from professional caregivers such as doctors, nurses, social workers, and home care workers. (302)

functional specificity of relationships model   a model of social support that contends a family or friendship tie may provide one type of support or a broad range of support, depending on the particular relationship between the caregiver and the care receiver. (304)

GRAND (Grandparents Requesting Access and Dignity)   a group that helps grandparents who cannot get access to their grandchildren. (301)

hierarchical compensatory model   a model of social support that contends people choose their supports first from their inner family circle and then move outward to get support from less-intimate people as they need more help. (304)

informal caregivers   unpaid care providers with a tie of kinship or affection toward the care receiver. (305)

informal support   unpaid support from family members, friends, neighbours, and others in the community. (302)

kin keeper   the person in a family who keeps family members in touch with one another. Women generally occupy this role. (298)

LAT (living apart together) couples   couples that have a committed relationship but maintain separate households. (288)

long-distance caregivers   caregivers who live at a significant distance from the care recipient. (313)

primary potential support groups   family and close friends who give help to the older person and who can expect help from the older person. (303)

quasi-widowhood   experiencing feelings of grief, depression, and loss after a spouse is placed in a nursing home. (311)

respite services   services ranging from friendly visitors who stay with the care receiver for a few hours, to full-day adult day care, to longer institutional respite to give caregivers time off. (318)

sandwich generation   people in mid-life who have at least one living parent and at least one child living in the household. (315)

second language of sex   the "language of sex" that develops in a long-term intimate relationship and focuses on responsiveness, caring, and affection. (294)

semiformal structures   forms of organized support, such as car pools, groups of people in the same building who shop together, friendly visitors, or "daily hello" phone callers, that fall between the informal and formal support structures. (319)

skip-generation households   grandparents living with grandchildren without the presence of the middle (parent) generation. (299)

social support   the help and assistance people give to one another. (296)

support groups   groups that give caregivers information about how to cope with caregiving demands and provide emotional support. (317)

task specificity model   a model of social support that contends different groups (of family, friends, neighbours) have different abilities and offer different types of support, each playing a specific role. (304)

Selected Readings

Arber, S., Davidson, K., and Ginn, J. (Eds.), *Gender and Ageing: Changing Roles and Relationships,* Maidenhead, UK: Open University Press, 2003.

> This book contains writings from prominent researchers in the field of gender and aging. It focuses on changing gender roles and relationships. The life course perspective links these readings. This volume will interest university students in sociology, social gerontology, or gender studies, as well as academics and researchers who work in the area of gender, family, and aging.

Connidis, I.A. *Family Ties and Aging.* Thousand Oaks, CA: Sage, 2001.

> This book provides a comprehensive and well-integrated examination of research on family ties and aging. It discusses relationships with spouses, children, and grandchildren, as well as those that are often neglected in the literature, such as the family ties of single, divorced, and childless older adults, as well as older gay men and lesbians. The book highlights the diversity that exists within family relationships based on gender, ethnicity and race, socioeconomic status, and sexual orientation. A good resource for undergraduate and graduate students, academics, practitioners, and policy makers.

Martin-Matthews, A., and Phillips, J. E. (Eds.). 2008. *Aging and Caring at the Intersection of Work and Home Life: Blurring the Boundaries.* New York, NY: Psychology Press, Taylor & Francis Group.

> This edited volume brings together work from various countries on work–life balance in the care of older people. The articles describe the intersections of public and private care, the complexities of family care networks, issues facing long-distance caregivers, financial compensation initiatives for family caregivers, and other work–life balance issues.

Hall, C.M. The Special Mission of Grandparents: Hearing, Seeing, Telling. Westport, CT: Greenwood, 1999.

This book describes the diversity of challenges and satisfactions experienced by grandparents from different cultural and family backgrounds. The book addresses a number of ways grandparents can influence their grandchildren's lives as friends, confidants, and support providers. The author shows that grandparents can have a positive influence on their families.

Van den Hoonaard, D.K. *The Widowed Self: The Older Woman's Journey through Widowhood.* Waterloo, ON: Wilfrid Laurier University Press, 2001.

The author discusses her research on a sample of older Canadian widowed women in a book that combines symbolic interactionist theory and qualitative methods with autobiographical accounts of these women's experiences. The book presents widowhood in the women's own voices.

Websites to Consult

Canadian Network for the Prevention of Elder Abuse (CNPEA)

http://www.cnpea.ca

The CNPEA is a nonprofit organization formed in the late 1990s. Its mandate is to help Canadians recognize and prevent abuse against older people, through communication and collaboration. This website provides information on the signs of abuse, where to go to get help, Canadian laws on abuse, and links to resources to help families and those who are being abused.

CANGRANDS

http://cangrands.com

CANGRANDS is a Canadian not-for-profit organization that provides support for grandparents and others who are raising grandchildren or other kin. This website provides information on health issues and legal concerns. It also connects family caregivers to on-line support and email groups, social events, and other resources that can assist them with their care.

Family Caregiver Alliance (FCA)

http://www.caregiver.org

The FCA is a national service on caregiving in the United States, and a "public voice for caregivers." This website provides education, information, services, research, and advocacy for caregivers and their families. The site provides a wide range of information and resources of use to Canadian caregivers.

© Stuart Forster England / Alamy

Chapter

14

Death and Dying

INTRODUCTION

Draw a line across a piece of paper. Put the word "birth" at the left end of the line. Put the word "death" at the right end of the line. Now put a dot for today's date. Put the date of your birth under the "birth" dot. Now put the date you project for your death under the dot that says "death."

How did you feel about fixing a date for your death? How did you come up with a date? Do people of different ages think the same way about death? Do you look forward to your next birthday? Or do you think about how few years you have left to do the things you want to do? How do older people think and feel about death?

This chapter will look at death in old age. It will focus on (1) attitudes toward death and on where death takes place, (2) ethical questions about death and dying, and (3) mourning and grief.

DEATH AND SOCIETY

Aiken (2001) says that attitudes toward death fall on a continuum. Some societies see death as an enemy, something we fight with all our power. Other societies welcome death and even see it as a transition to a better, even blissful, world. Still others, in the middle, see death as a mystery.

Kastenbaum (1999, xv) says that he misses the old days—"the really old days." In the ancient past, he says, people saw death as a mysterious transition and created myths and stories to explain death to themselves. The Greek Hades, the Christian Heaven or Hell, or the Muslim Paradise all show humans grappling with the meaning of death. For some societies, death meant an eternity of darkness and shadow. For others, as Dante describes in his *Inferno*, it could mean punishment for an evil life. And for Muslims, death means a life of ease and pleasure for believers. As Kastenbaum says, "death was clearly something BIG" (xv) The power of the stories and their central role in religion and culture tell us that people have always wondered about death.

But times have changed and we have a new view of death and dying (one that coexists with some of our traditional views). Science and technology extend life and push death and dying to late old age. Death in Canada today most often takes place in a hospital or nursing home. Motiwala and colleagues (2006) found that 49.2 percent of deaths among older people (aged 66 or older) in Ontario in 2001/02 took place in a hospital, and 30.5 percent of deaths took place in a long-term care facility. Only about one person in five died at home. We rarely

have a direct experience of death. We see graphic scenes of violence and death in the movies or on TV but these images distance us from death (Aiken 2001); they have little impact on our daily lives. We can turn off the TV or leave the theatre if the images scare or depress us.

Today, death challenges our moral and ethical codes. Our legal system grapples with the issue of physician-assisted suicide (PAS), our health care system deals with the long trajectory toward death that we call long-term care, and families cope with institutions such as hospitals and nursing homes where death most often occurs. Death may still fill us with fear. But more often it confronts us with practical choices (to die in an institution or at home? to prolong care or end treatment? to opt for burial, cremation, or freezing of the body until science finds a cure?). We still hear the old stories through our religious traditions and literature, but they lack mystery and sound more like fantasy. Discussions of death and dying today often focus on death and dying in old age.

DEATH IN OLD AGE

In the past, high infant mortality rates, childhood diseases, and high female death rates during childbearing years made death among all age groups a common event. Today, most infants will live to old age. Life expectancy at birth in 2004 stood at 77.6 years for males and 82.4 years for females. Even in old age, life expectancy has increased. A man aged 65 in 2004 could expect to live another 17.7 years (up from 14.6 years in 1979), a woman 21.0 years (up from 19.0 years in 1979) (Statistics Canada 2004b; Statistics Canada Table 2, 2007i; Statistics Canada 2008c).

Longer life expectancy today means that most people die of the diseases of old age—cancer, heart disease, stroke, lung disease, and influenza/pneumonia. These diseases result from a lifetime of accumulated stress on the body (see Exhibit 14.1).

The trajectory of death from these diseases differs from dying in the past. People died earlier in the past and they often died quickly of an acute illness (e.g., smallpox) or accident. Nearly one-third of deaths (29 percent) in 1926 occurred in infants and children under age 5. Today, fewer than 1 percent of deaths occur in young children. Wilkins (2006) reports that in 2002 cancer and circulatory diseases (including stroke) accounted for nearly two-thirds of deaths in Canada.

Motiwala and colleagues (2006) found that the trajectory of death (a slow lingering death, an acute illness, or a sudden accident) affects where a person will die. In their study of deaths among older people they found that

● **Exhibit 14.1**

THE FIVE LEADING CAUSES OF DEATH AT AGE 65 OR OLDER BY SEX, CANADA 2002 (PERCENT)

	Men	Women
Malignant neoplasms (cancer)	30.3	23.7
Heart diseases	26.6	26.3
Cerebrovascular diseases (stroke)	6.8	9.3
Chronic lower respiratory diseases	6.1	4.5
Diabetes	3.7	3.8

Note that cancer and heart disease account for more than half of the deaths among older people in 2002. Compared to women, men tend to have a higher rate of deaths by cancer. In particular, compared to women, men have a higher rate of lung cancer (8.8 percent compared to 5.2 percent). Women have a higher rate of deaths by stroke. This may reflect the fact that more women live into later old age. Very few older people (only 1 percent) die from infectious diseases.

What influences the likelihood of death in later life? The National Population Health Survey (NPHS) found that the following items increase the risk of death: psychological stress, financial stress, low educational level, widowhood, inactivity, smoking, being underweight, and functional limitation. Some of these items seem obvious as influences on death. For example, an underweight person or someone with a functional limitation may have suffered from a life-threatening illness. Further analysis of the NPHS data shows that psychological distress (including financial stress) has an especially strong effect on women (more so than on men). Chronic degenerative diseases (like cancer and heart disease) may overshadow the effects of psychological distress in men.

Source: Adapted from K. Wilkins. (2006). "Predictors of Death in Seniors." *Supplement to Health Reports, 16,* 57–67. Statistics Canada. Cat No. 82-003, p. 59. Citing 2002 Canadian Mortality Database.

a person with cancer has the greatest chance of dying at home because cancer patients and their families can plan for death, and the health care system (including hospice care, palliative care, and home care) has adapted to the demands of this illness. A person with dementia, on the other hand, most often will die in a nursing home or hospital. A person with a major acute illness will likely die in a hospital. Menec and colleagues (2007) studied end-of-life care in Manitoba. They found that where a person died varied by age. People aged 85 and over, compared to people aged 65 to 74, showed the greatest likelihood of dying in a nursing home.

Death in later life today usually comes slowly and predictably. People often experience a decline in function and health over time along with periodic intense crises that lead to death. Dying can include pain, delirium, swallowing problems, loss of mental function, and other forms of discomfort (Ross et al. 2002). Dying in old age makes special demands on health care providers, family members, and older people themselves.

ETHNIC AND CULTURAL DIFFERENCES IN RESPONSE TO DYING

Health care workers, in particular, need sensitivity to an older person's ethnic and cultural background. Duffy and colleagues (2006) studied preferences of older dying patients from different cultural backgrounds. They report that end-of-life values differ for different cultures. Studies in the United States, for example, find that African Americans and people of Hispanic heritage tend not to use hospices; they prefer to continue life-sustaining treatment. Arab Muslims, on the other hand, may not want to prolong life, and prefer to learn about their condition and the likelihood of death. The researchers also found differences between men and women. Hispanic women, for example, preferred to continue life-sustaining measures like dialysis. Hispanic men, on the other hand, preferred little artificial support at the end of life.

This study shows the variety of attitudes and preferences people have at the end of life. Culture plays a role here, as does religion and gender (Cicirelli 2002). Some group preferences come into conflict with the current values of Western medicine. Arab respondents, for example, preferred not to speak about death to a dying relative (though they said they would prefer to be told about their condition if they were dying).

Ellerby and colleagues (2000, 845) found unique issues related to death and dying among Aboriginal people. The researchers report that in one case a son refused to directly translate the word cancer into Ojibway because it would "promote fear and pain." The son further opposed the doctor's attempt to explain the seriousness of the illness. The son said that a direct reference to death might "bring death closer."

These cultural differences can create a dilemma for doctors, nurses, and other caregivers. They want to respect cultural preferences but may feel a professional duty to give the patient information about his or her illness. The doctor in this case felt that he needed to explain about cancer and its life-threatening progress so the patient could make an informed decision. The son preferred a gradual indirect approach. The son proposed to involve other family members in a "sharing circle" that would involved the patient, the family members, and professional caregivers. Aboriginal people use this approach to gain consensus on a decision and to build trust.

This example shows the need for flexibility in response to minority members' needs. Language barriers can make communication difficult, although a trained health interpreter can help. But even with a translator, Ellerby and colleagues (2000) say Aboriginal values (e.g., avoidance of direct reference to disease or death, family consultation in decision making, etc.) often are discounted by Western systems of health care. This observation applies to the treatment of people from other non-Western cultures.

Some writers, for example, express concern about discrimination in end-of-life treatment due to a person's race or ethnicity. A Canadian study of pain relief by Gagliese and colleagues (2005) found that, compared to older whites, older minority-group members receive less pain management at the end of life. These researchers say that Canada's diverse ethnic and racial population calls for sensitivity to patients' cultural

values. They suggest that health care workers receive training that teaches them how to care for people from unfamiliar (usually non-Western) cultures. They also suggest more options for end-of-life care for minority elders (see Exhibit 14.2).

SENIORS' VIEWS OF DEATH AND DYING

Only a small number of studies have looked at how older people feel about death; major theories of aging do not address the subject. According to activity theory, people want to stay active throughout their lives, and substitute new roles and activities for ones that they lose as they age. When people retire, activity theory says that they will have the highest life satisfaction if they find new things to do. This theory says nothing about death.

Disengagement theory says that people want to disengage from social roles as they age. This theory also says that retirement and withdrawal from social responsibilities leads to high life satisfaction. According to this theory, an awareness of impending death starts the process of disengagement. People know that they will die soon, so they ease their way out of social life. Disengagement produces a smooth transition of power from one generation to the next. Death has a less disruptive effect on society if older people disengage from social roles as they age. This theory focuses on the social effects of dying, but it says little about death as a personal experience or about how older people feel about death.

Erikson's (1963) theory of ego development says that the last stage of life leads to a life review. A person looks over his or her life, ties up loose ends, and prepares for death. Erikson describes this as **ego integrity**. "It is the acceptance of one's one and only life cycle as something that had to be and that, by necessity, permitted of [sic] no substitutions" (1963, 268). The integrated person accepts his or her biography and culture, and with this acceptance "death loses its sting" (268). Peck ([1955] 1968) says that in the last part of this last stage a person can achieve **ego transcendence**. People in this stage feel a deep concern for others and for the culture they will leave when they die.

These theories say that older people respond to death in more than one way: Some people deny it, some accept it, and some embrace it. The few studies that have tested these theories have found complex combinations of acceptance and rejection of death.

A study conducted by University of Toronto researchers (cited in Koster and Prather 1999) found

● **Exhibit 14.2**

DEATH AND DYING AMONG THE HUTTERITES

In an article on aging and death, Joseph W. Eaton reprinted the following letter from a Hutterite farmer to his sister. The letter describes the death of their younger brother.

Dear sister, our dear brother came home on September 8, on a Wednesday morning about 5 o'clock. He said that he had a fairly nice trip. He cried a great deal because of pains. He stated that distress teaches one to pray. I went immediately the following day to visit with him. I could hardly look at him, it was so painful to me; he looked so terrible that it made my heart almost break. However, I remained with him until he died, and until the funeral was over.

Two evenings before his death, his home was full of people, approximately 25 were there. He expressed a heavenly pleasure when he saw them all and said he could not express his pleasure in seeing them. It struck me almost as a miracle when I saw this starved and weak body lying there, telling us such a strong story. We listened to him, warned him not to talk so much because it may do him harm. However, he stated, "while I am still alive, I can speak. When I will be dead, then, of course, I won't be able to tell you what I have to say." ...

He stated that dying does not cause him any difficulty; he said that he had a clear conscience and is in peace with God and all people. He asked many people in my presence whether they had something against him. However, everybody replied in the negative. They said to him that they themselves were in peace with him. ...

[Just before his death] his children stood around him with a sad heart, and all realized that his departure will be soon. He called his oldest son, gave him his hand and pressed a kiss on his forehead, and advised him how he should behave in the future. Among other words he told him he should obey his preacher, the boss and the field boss, and if the community entrusted a position to him, he should execute same as well as he could, and not only superficially. ...

[He then calls to his side his daughter, the colony business manager, his wife and his brother.] He said, "I am at peace with God and with all people. I have a clear and good conscience. I am ready to depart, but now everything goes so slow. I have only one desire and that is to go to my Lord." He said quite frequently how good it is to have a clear and peaceful conscience. He advised us also that we should prepare ourselves, because the pleasure was inexpressible.

So I have described to you the events and experiences which I have seen with my own eyes, and it is my request and my wish that we all should prepare ourselves. Blessed by God.

Source: Joseph W. Eaton, 1964, "The Art of Aging and Dying," *The Gerontologist* 4: 94–112. Reproduced with permission of The Gerontological Society of America, 2000.

that people at the end of life had five concerns: avoiding a drawn-out death, getting pain relief, having control of treatment options, staying in touch with loved ones, and becoming a burden. People feared that they would burden family with physical care, that family members would have to witness their death, and that family members would have to make decisions about life-sustaining treatment. Duffy and colleagues (2006) found that older people, regardless of their race or ethnicity, wanted comfort in their last days, they wanted to have their responsibilities taken care of, and they wanted their spiritual beliefs honoured. Most people wanted to say goodbye to relatives and friends, to make plans for their death, and to be "ready to go."

Studies that compare older and younger people find that older people think about death more, but feel less afraid of death than the young. Lavigne and Lévesque (1992) studied older people in long-term care centres in Montreal. They found that about one-third of the people in the study thought of their own death when they heard of the death of a peer. A Canadian study by Gesser and colleagues (1986) studied the fear of death among old and young people. They found that older people showed less fear and more acceptance of death than younger people. They also found that as fear of death decreased, hopelessness decreased and happiness increased. They say that people who get over the fear of death feel satisfied with life. These people find meaning and purpose in the time they have left, and they feel in control of their lives.

Cicirelli (2002) says that older people vary in how they view death in later life. And how a person views death influences how he or she acts in old age. For example, some people see death positively—as a path to a life in heaven or an end to suffering. These people may more easily plan for death because they accept it without fear. On the other hand, people who dread death may avoid making out a will and may refuse to discuss plans for their funeral. Some people will use their increased awareness of death to make the most of the time they have left. Others will use this increased awareness to withdraw from projects and live each day as it comes. What approach to death leads to the best experience of later life? Cicirelli says we don't know the answer to this question. Research on this question has only just begun.

Cicirelli (2002) notes that most studies on the fear of death looked at people in the 65- to 75-year-old range. Few reports exist on the attitudes of very old people (aged 85 and over). Cicirelli (2002) studied a group of 109 people aged 70 to 97 (mean age 80.7). He found that at some point the oldest-old must accept death as inevitable and they must come to terms with it. But his work shows that even among the oldest-old, people vary in their fear of death. Many elders, he found, accept death and view it as a part of life. Others fear death and the dying process. They fear a long illness, life in a nursing home, or dying alone.

Cicirelli (2002) found that age plays a role in a person's attitude toward death. He found that the fear of dying peaks in the early 80s and then tapers off in late old age. People in their 90s have turned a corner in their relationship to death. They "seem to show an increasing acceptance of death, with some actively looking forward to death as a relief from problems of aging" (150).

Tornstam (2005) conducted in-depth interviews with 50 people aged 52 to 97 years old. He found that in general the people in this study did not fear death. "They may fear dying," he writes, "that it will be extended and painful, but not being dead" (57). Some people had little fear of death throughout their lives, but others found that their fear of death decreased as they aged. Other studies reported by Tornstam, field studies in assisted-living settings, found more diverse views of death. Some people showed little fear of death; others accept death because of serious illness or pain. These findings support Cicirelli (2002), who found both acceptance and denial of death among older people. Tornstam considers fear and avoidance of death a barrier to personal development in later life. Acceptance of death, he says, can lead

to "gerotranscendence"—a greater appreciation of life and a more cosmic view of the self.

Religion plays a smaller role in society today than in the past. But people often turn to religious leaders and institutions at the time of death. Church groups, for example, arrange visits to dying church members. Religious leaders spend time with dying people at their bedsides and lead religious services after a person has died. People with different religious beliefs differ in their attitudes to death. Gesser, Wong, and Reker (1986) found that older people more than younger people accepted life after death. "It may be that belief in the afterlife helps the elderly to find meaning and purpose in life, as well as in death. ... Older people overcome their fear of death because they feel that life after death goes on" (20).

Most religions teach that people get the kind of afterlife they deserve. Studies show that people with mild or uncertain religious belief fear death most, while those with strong religious beliefs or no belief at all deal with death best (Wink and Scott 2005). Wink (2006) found that a strong religious belief buffered a person from the fear of death. A general spiritual belief (not associated with conventional religion) did not provide the same buffer. He says that religious people accept social norms and conventional religious explanations of the afterlife. People who held traditional belief in the afterlife but did not practise their religion reported a high fear of death (Wink and Scott 2005). These people may accept enough of religion to believe in an afterlife, but not enough to feel they will have a good one (see Exhibit 14.3).

INSTITUTIONAL DEATH

Religious belief and a sense of purpose can help buffer the fear of death, but how and where a person expects to die also affects how he or she feels about death. In the past, most people died at home, surrounded by family, friends, and neighbours. Some cultures still ensure this kind of death. But, in Canada, a large majority of deaths (for people of all ages) take place in hospitals.

A study at the Baycrest Centre for Geriatric Care in Toronto compared the death rate in the centre's hospital, nursing home, and apartment complex. The study found that the hospital had a death rate more than 20 times greater than that of the nursing home and more than 130 times greater than that of the apartment complex. Shapiro (1983) studied hospital use by a group of more than 3,000 patients aged 68 and over and found that about two-thirds of the sample entered the hospital in the year they died.

● **Exhibit 14.3**

SENIORS TALK ABOUT DEATH AND DYING

Researchers Jacques Grand'Maison and Solange Lefebvre studied older people in the Laurentian region of Quebec from 1988 through the 1990s. They spoke with dozens of older people individually and in groups. They conducted long interviews on social, cultural, moral, and spiritual issues. Their report, *Sharing the Blessings* (1996), contains many excerpts from these interviews. Below you will find reflections on death and dying from their study. These excerpts show the variety of ways that older people think about death and dying. They also show that older people remain committed to a satisfying life even in the face of death.

"For me," a woman, age 59, says, "death is a happy end after a full life. I can't think it's true that you have to suffer when you die. My grandfather died at ninety-four, and he died singing. I've always remembered this. It shows you can be happy, have a beautiful, healthy old age, and don't have to go through all sorts of stages to realize you're happy."

"I try to fight against the anguish of death ...," a woman, age 66, says. "But you can't avoid it; one day you'll die, and I hope there's something on the other side. I'm working at accepting the end."

"I believe in life," a man, age 68, says. "Nothing but Life with a capital L. Life is perhaps God. ... I don't know anymore. ... Death is emptiness, it has no meaning. If you can't enjoy life, you might as well pack and go."

"Death? It's a nagging question," says a man, age 68. "I believe in another life, but I don't know what form it will take. I must say that questions about death become more urgent when someone close to you dies. ... To be honest ... I'm getting older, and it's coming."

"Death has no meaning for me," a woman, age 55, says. "It's a return to nature. Unfortunately this isn't very profound. I saw my parents die, but they continue to live in me. It wasn't so terrible. They're still alive. When I've got troubles, I call on my mother and ask her to do something. But death doesn't affect my existence. I love life, love being alive, I'm content just to be on this earth. It's simply the pleasure of being."

Source: J. Grand'Maison and S. Lefebvre, 1996, *Sharing the Blessings: The Role of Seniors in Today's Society*, trans. from the French by Jane Brierley, Sherbrooke, QC: Mediaspaul. Reprinted with permission of Mediaspaul.

Hospitals will take in more and more dying patients as the population ages, but studies show that many doctors and nurses in hospitals feel uncomfortable with dying patients. Ross and her colleagues (2002) say that acute-care hospitals often marginalize older dying patients. Staff see them as practical problems or "bed blockers." The medical model, based on technology and cure, often fails to meet the needs of the dying older person (Kaufman 2006).

The largest study of dying in hospitals, conducted in the United States, took place in five university hospitals across the country. It included 4,300 patients with a terminal illness (median age of 65) who reported on their experiences. The study found that 38 percent of patients spent 10 or more days in intensive care before their deaths. Forty-six percent of do-not-resuscitate (DNR) orders were written two days before a person died, even though 79 percent of the patients already had a DNR order. Fifty percent of the conscious patients' families reported that the patient experienced severe pain at least half the time in the three days before the person died (Kaufman 2006).

A further study that attempted to improve care for terminally ill hospital patients failed to change treatment patterns. "The startling results," Kaufman (2006, 281) says, "were that interventions aimed at improving physician-patient communication and physician knowledge of patients' end-of-life wishes did not change the practice of medicine ..." She concludes that a "technological imperative shapes activities and choices in the hospital." This condition exists even though health professionals support the idea of death with only appropriate use of high-technology treatment.

Medical staff sometimes feel guilty or angry about dying patients. Because they have spent all of their professional lives learning to keep people alive, they think of death as a failure and avoid dying patients or respond less quickly to their needs. In some cases the medical care system may overrespond to dying patients' physical decline. Latimer and colleagues (1999) studied the medical care given to patients in the last six months of life in the United States and Canada. The study found a sharp increase in doctors' services in the last 60 days of life. This study raises questions about the appropriateness of excessive medical treatment at the end of life. and points to the lack of alternatives to medical treatment within the medical model of health care.

A Quebec (n.d., 20) policy paper says that sometimes "cutting-edge treatments are no longer having much effect and that it would be better for the patient's wellbeing to suggest palliative care. For many physicians, resorting to palliative care is an admission of powerlessness, or even failure." Health care professionals need ongoing training in the care of dying patients. This should include knowledge about pain management and about the unique needs of minority-group older people (Ross et al. 2002).

CHANGES IN THE TREATMENT OF THE DYING

The health care system has begun to change its approach to dying patients of all ages. Two doctors more than any others—Elisabeth Kübler-Ross in the United States and Dame Cicely Saunders in England—started this reform.

Stages of Death and Dying

Kübler-Ross (1969) described five stages that her patients went through before they died. First, she says, people deny that they are dying. They say, "Not me." They may believe that the doctor has the wrong X-rays or someone else's tests. They may go from specialist to specialist looking for a new diagnosis. They may not even hear the doctor tell them they have a fatal illness.

Second, she says, people feel angry. They begin to believe that they will die. "Why me?" they ask. At this point, people blames the doctors or their spouse or God for their illness.

Third, they begin to bargain. They say, "Yes, me, but ..." and try to make deals with the hospital staff. They may promise to be a good patient and to follow doctor's orders, if only they will get better. They may bargain with God, promising to go to worship or to live a more pious life. They may bargain with God for one more summer at the cottage, or for enough time to see a child married, a grandchild born, or their next birthday.

Fourth, they feel depressed. Their illness gets worse, and they know they will die. They say, "Yes, me," and they feel a great sadness. Kübler-Ross says that depression has two stages. In the first stage, people mourn present losses—the loss of family, career, and the things they love, such as a home, car, or cottage. In the second stage, they mourn future losses—the loss of good times to come, the chance to see children or grandchildren grow up, and other future events. People begin to say goodbye in this stage.

Fifth, people accept death. They say, "My time is close now ... it's okay." They say goodbye to family and friends and die in peace.

Kübler-Ross says that at every stage a person holds on to hope. At first, a person may hope the doctor made a mistake; later there may be hope for a remission if the person has cancer, and later still there may be hope for a painless death.

Some writers question the number of Kübler-Ross's stages or their order. Shneidman (1984, 199) rejects Kübler-Ross's stage theory—"the notion that human beings, as they die, are somehow marched in lock step through a series of stages of the dying process"—on clinical grounds. He reports a wide range of emotions, needs, and coping methods that dying people use. "A few of these in some people, dozens in others—experienced in an impressive variety of ways" (199). Kübler-Ross (1969) herself says that patients can skip stages; stages can overlap; and people can go back over the same stage many times. Some responses, such as anger, come up again and again.

Also, different illnesses create different trajectories of death or different patterns of response. Kübler-Ross based her model on cancer patients in a hospital, but cancer patients who have remissions may go through these stages more than once. People with other illnesses show other trajectories. Sometimes, a person can have long plateaus between times of decline; however, someone who dies shortly after an auto accident may not go through any of these stages. Northcott and Wilson (2001) say that the dying process depends on many things—a person's age, illness, and will to live, and the treatments used to fight or manage the disease. Lawton (2001, citing Institute of Medicine 1997), for example, says that "sudden death, steady decline, and episodic decline" all have described unique death trajectories.

All sides of this debate share one thing: They have brought discussion and thinking about death into the open. People who have to cope with death and dying—patients, their families, and medical staff—now have a number of ways to think, and talk, about death. This has helped free many people from the silence that surrounded death and dying only a few years ago.

The Hospice Movement

The idea of a **hospice** dates back to at least the Middle Ages in Europe. Hospices at that time took in travellers who needed food, shelter, and care. Hospices today, however, meet the special needs of dying patients. Dame Cicely Saunders opened the first modern hospice, St. Christopher's, in London, England, in 1967.

St. Christopher's has 52 beds, in-patient and out-patient services, a home visiting program, a day-care centre for the children of staff, and private rooms for older people. The hospice welcomes visitors, including children, and allows families to cook for their dying relatives if they want to. There are also rooms for relatives who want to stay overnight. St. Christopher's does not attempt to extend life; it tries to relieve symptoms and help patients enjoy their last days.

Hospice Program Goals

Saunders says that a "hospice is a program, not a place" (cited in Canadian Medical Association 1987, 34). First, a hospice controls pain. People fear death for many reasons, but often they fear the pain that may accompany death more than death itself. Pain relief ensures that the person will die in comfort, thus relieving much of the fear and anxiety. St. Christopher's pioneered the pain relief techniques now used by hospices around the world.

St. Christopher's created the Brompton mix—a mixture of heroin or morphine, cocaine, Stemetil syrup, and chloroform water—to relieve chronic pain. Medical staff base pain control on two techniques: First, they adjust drug dosage until it relieves a patient's pain. "The aim," Saunders (1984, 268) says, "is to titrate the level of analgesia against the patient's pain, gradually increasing the dose until the patient is pain free." Then, the nurses give the next dose before the previous one has worn off. Hospitals often wait until a person shows signs of pain before they give the next dose of pain reliever. By giving the analgesic "before the patient may think it necessary [usually every four hours] ... it is possible to erase the memory and fear of pain" (268). Patients cared for by this method need lower dosages to maintain a pain-free state because the drug does not have to overcome the pain that has begun. Lower dosages mean that patients stay more alert. Skelton (1982) says that 90 percent of people can get complete pain relief in a hospice setting, and all but 1 to 2 percent can get some help.

Second, a hospice allows a person to die a simple death. The hospice does not use respirators or resuscitators to keep people alive. Staff members make dying a part of life in the hospice. They leave the curtains open around a dying person's bed so that patients can see that their roommates have died. Patients also know they have a say in their treatment; they can ask for medication when they feel they need it, and they can ask to die at home. Saunders (1984) reports that people who die at home often feel more pain than people who die in the hospice, and caregivers often feel burdened by the demands of care. St. Christopher's (and other hospices) agree to re-admit patients whenever the patient or the family needs more support.

Third, a hospice gives people love and care. Staff members focus on the comfort of the patient, taking the time to touch patients and hold them. The hospice will serve special foods that patients like or give them soothing scented baths. The hospice also helps patients do as much for themselves as they can; this increases patients' well-being by giving them a sense of control over their treatment. The family members of dying patients also receive care. The Family Service Project at St. Christopher's offers help to families who find it hard to cope with their grief (see also Levy 1987). Saunders (1984, 269) says that "staff and volunteers visit to assess the need and to offer support, and if more specialized help is indicated, this can be arranged."

Hospices spread to North America during the 1970s and early 1980s; more than 1,000 hospices opened in the United States between 1974 and 1984. Angeli (2001) reports that by 2001 the United States had 2,500 hospices. In Canada, hospice organizations exist in Quebec, Ontario, British Columbia, and Manitoba. Most provinces also have palliative (terminal) care units, palliative care teams, or a palliative care expert on staff in hospitals. The National Hospice Organization in the United States studied family satisfaction with several hundred hospice programs there. The study found high levels of family satisfaction with services (Connor 1998). Taylor (1999) reports rapid growth in hospice care in Canada. She says that an "Angus Reid survey found that 91% of Canadians support hospice care services" and 84 percent "strongly agree that it is important for terminally ill people to be able to spend their final days at home" (4).

Palliative Care

Palliative care is "a program of active compassionate care primarily directed towards improving the quality of life for the dying" (Subcommittee on Institutional Program Guidelines 1989, 1). The Canadian Hospice Palliative Care Association (CHPCA 2007) says that hospice palliative care programs allow patients to gain more control over their lives, manage pain and symptoms more effectively, and provides support to family and informal caregivers. A complete program of palliative care includes symptom control and spiritual support as well as bereavement support and education. Palliative care can take place in a special unit in a hospital, in a nursing home, or in a person's home.

Workers in palliative care programs include nurses, physiotherapists, psychologists, and volunteers. Through the 1990s awareness of palliative care grew throughout the country. Auger (2000) reports that 594 palliative care programs existed in Canada in 1997, with all provinces having some palliative care programs. Ontario had the largest number of programs (303) followed by British Columbia and Yukon (with 75 each), and Nova Scotia (48). In June 2001 Health Canada established the Secretariat on Palliative and End-of-Life Care, which works to develop a national strategy on end-of-life care. It promotes best practices and supports the expansion of palliative care throughout the country.

Most provincial home care programs today offer palliative care services. The Quality End-of-Life Coalition of Canada (2008) reports that all provinces assess home care clients' need for palliative care. Provinces vary in the specific supports they provide, but all provide pharmacists' advice, and nearly all support the costs of medications. Most provinces use a team approach to provide palliative care to clients at home. Still, today only about one-third of dying patients (37 percent) have access to high-quality hospice palliative care at home. The Quality End-of-Life Coalition calls for greater access to palliative care services at home and for the development of more palliative care programs in nursing homes and hospitals.

Recent research finds that the medical model of care dominates end-of-life care. Relatively few physicians have training in palliative care. The Canadian Hospice and Palliative Care Association (2007) estimates that only about 200 physicians in Canada have specialist training in palliative and end-of-life care, and only some provincial health care systems offer palliative care in the community. Compared to people in cities, those in rural settings have less access to palliative care services. Dupere (2006) reports that only about 15 percent of Canadians have access to palliative care services, although 90 percent of people asked said they preferred dying at home (see Exhibit 14.4).

Palliative Care for the Elderly

Palliative care units take in patients of all ages. Patients at Royal Victoria Hospital, for example, ranged from 20 years old to over 90. Studies show that palliative care can help older people as well as younger people, but some older patients have unique needs.

Shedletsky and colleagues (1982) studied the records of 40 older patients (average age 80.6 years) who had died in the extended care wing of a hospital.

Extended care hospital settings take in many older people with long-term illnesses who need constant medical care. These units often have a palliative care treatment philosophy. The researchers found that older extended care patients differed from younger palliative care patients. First, older patients averaged more diagnoses than the younger patients. Second, the younger patients typically had cancer, while the older patients typically suffered from circulatory and respiratory diseases. Third, relatively few younger patients died from respiratory failure, while respiratory failure caused about 50 percent of all deaths in the older group.

Shedletsky and colleagues (1982) found that drug treatment helped about 80 percent of the people with pain and skin problems. The staff reported that just before death, 75 percent of patients felt no pain or distress and 75 percent were conscious or semi-conscious. The staff found, however, that patients with respiratory problems got the least benefit from drug treatment, and this group made up the largest portion of people with discomfort before death. The researchers concluded that some groups of older extended care patients may have special palliative care needs.

Lusk (2007) supports the earlier work of Shedletsky and colleagues. She says that the older population has multiple illnesses and are more likely to die from heart disease, stroke or chronic respiratory diseases. People with dementia have special needs but few of them are referred for palliative care. Lusk says that the medical model places low priority on long-term care facilities so palliative care for older people in these facilities gets little attention. But with an aging society, an increasing number of older people will die in institutions, and the need for palliative care in these settings will increase. Lusk calls for more resources to support palliative care in institutions. In particular, she focuses on the need for staff education, including training in communication and relationship skills as well as team building among staff.

Mori (1991) describes a number of challenges that face palliative care programs. First, health care system funding limits some palliative care services. For example, most hospitals cannot claim reimbursement for services to caregivers. Also, physicians get low pay for home visits, a condition that limits their interest in palliative home care. Northcott and Wilson (2001) say that the system tends to underfund palliative care programs. Only four provinces (British Columbia, Alberta, Saskatchewan, and Manitoba) fund palliative care as a basic service, although an Angus Reid poll found that almost three-quarters of Canadians thought the government should fund palliative care (Sewell 2003) (see Exhibit 14.5).

● **Exhibit 14.4**

THEY'RE BUYING A STAIRWAY TO HEAVEN: MUSIC FOR THE DYING— "ENTERTAINMENT WITH A MISSION!"—IS A BURGEONING NEW INDUSTRY

Do you remember the mix tapes you made for friends and family when you were younger? Bev Foster, a Toronto-based musician, started making mix tapes at the age of 15, but with a particular purpose: to cheer up friends and relatives who were sick. When she grew up, she turned it into a business. The business is Room 217, which makes and markets CDs with a simple goal: to soothe dying people and make their final moments more bearable.

When elderly people are in palliative care and facing the last moments of their lives, Foster's theory goes, they need to hear something "soothing, calming, peaceful." Maybe an arrangement of *Amazing Grace* with a harp, a flute and Foster's singing voice in an echo chamber. Or a piano and cello playing the Beatles' *In My Life.* "I think the biggest effect Room 217 has on people is spiritual," says Foster. She adds that she chose the songs for her CDs by asking 100 seniors the key question: "If you had one month to live, what music would you listen to?" This led to her creating such tracks as the theme from the movie *The Mission,* arranged for the English horn.

Foster is a singer and pianist who was inspired to create Room 217 after the death of her father (the name comes from the number of the hospital room where he died). She has released and self-marketed three CDs so far: the vocal *Celtic Whisperings* (with such non-Celtic songs as *Amazing Grace*); *Spirit Wings,* and the all-instrumental *Deep Waters.* Foster says that the music she and her colleagues make can have a positive impact on dying people not only psychologically, but physically. Their music "helps lessen agitation and makes laboured breathing easier," she says. "We get back comments to this effect from hospital and palliative care staff and family members." ...

What do you think of this new line of products? Would you buy a CD for someone who was dying? Will this business grow as the older population ages and more people die in old age? Do you think that this product will appeal more to younger or older people? How would you propose to market this product (assuming you believed it would help people nearing death)?

Source: Jaime J. Weiman. April 17, 2006. They're buying a stairway to heaven. *Maclean's* Magazine. Reprinted by permission.

Second, health care workers and the public need more knowledge about palliative care. The public needs to know what this option offers. Professionals need to know how to work effectively on a palliative care team. Balfour Mount, one of the founders of palliative care in Canada, says that "most physicians are not trained to deal with death. Even the basics of pain control are not routinely taught at medical school" (Sewell 2003). A 2002 survey found that only two of Canada's 16 medical schools said they felt satisfied with their course work on palliative care (Sewell 2003).

Third, Northcott and Wilson (2001) say that palliative care also challenges some core beliefs that people hold today. People believe in the curative power of modern medicine. They may feel that palliative care gives up on the patient and may feel guilty about choosing palliative care for a dying parent or spouse.

Northcott and Wilson refer to the "California daughter syndrome" (68). A child, who may not have seen a parent for many years, refuses to accept the death of the parent and demands maximum medical treatment. Northcott and Wilson call for the gradual use of palliative care measures as a person approaches death. This, they say, may avoid the appearance that treatment has ended and palliative care has begun.

Fourth, nurses in one study said that the health care system often made it hard for them to deliver palliative care at home (Ross and McDonald, 1994). They blamed bureaucracy, fragmented services, and too much focus on efficiency. These forces interfered with the quality of care they wanted to provide and from giving patients the emotional support they wanted to give. This study points to the tension between the values of palliative care and the curative model that dominates the health care system.

● Exhibit 14.5

THE BENEFITS OF PALLIATIVE CARE

Margaret Murray describes the difference between dying on an acute care hospital ward and on a palliative care ward. She shows the benefits of palliative care to the patient and to the patient's family.

My Aunt Harriet was an attractive, intelligent businesswoman who lost a four-year battle with cancer when she was in her mid-sixties. The initial surgery and radiotherapy gave her a few more years to play tennis and pursue her other interests, but the final year with more surgery and various experiments with chemotherapy was almost straight downhill for her.

About five weeks before she died, Harriet was admitted to a large downtown hospital after her bowel and bladder function failed. Up until her admission, she had been living with my parents, spending her days in the living room with her family, and getting about the house in a wheelchair. After less than two weeks of hospitalization, her change was startling.

One Sunday afternoon, we visited her in hospital and found her slumped in a large chair, her drooping head almost touching the bare overbed table apparently to prevent her from falling. With some difficulty we roused her, and she began to report a conversation with her husband who had been dead for 30 years. We tried to make her as comfortable as possible and to bring her back to the present with quiet conversation. This was only moderately successful. She continued to doze and awaken only enough to plead with us to put her back to bed. Eventually, I approached

her nurse for help, and was told that my aunt should stay up because she "needed the stimulation"! Since she had been alone before our arrival, without company and in no position to look out a window or watch television, this was a remarkable concept.

Although the nurse was never impolite, she left me with the feeling that her care was given with gritted teeth—she did not know how to care for the "difficult" patient, who did not know what was good for her. I wanted to say "She's dying! The complications of immobility are not as important as her need for comfort, dignity and peace." But I felt she wouldn't understand. ...

A few days later, "Auntie Harry" was transferred to the Palliative Care Unit at the [Salvation Army's] Grace Hospital [in Toronto]. On my first visit I found her in a sunny four-bed room, sitting up and brightly awaiting the arrival of her dinner. She had been up once that day, gently lifted into a wheelchair and taken to the lounge where she was introduced to some of the other patients. She enjoyed the brief social interaction, and was returned to bed before she became too tired. Now, she was looking forward to another excursion after supper. Her conversation was relevant and lucid; she was appreciative of her surroundings and had many compliments for the staff. That day I left with the feeling that an enormous burden had been lifted from my shoulders—my aunt was still dying, but somehow it was alright now, for her and for the rest of the family.

Source: M.E. Murray, "Palliative Care," *Canadian Nurse/L'infirmière canadienne* 77(5) (1981), 16–17. Reproduced with permission from *The Canadian Nurse*.

Fifth, many older people will have no one at home to provide palliative care outside the institution. Community-based palliative care programs favour people with a primary caregiver. One study found that most palliative care programs served married women with husbands (Levy 1987, cited in Mori 1991). Older women, many of them widowed, often lack a primary caregiver, which makes them ineligible for palliative care in the community. Also, multiple pathologies in an older patient may make pain control more complex. Frail older people on palliative home care may need the use of respite beds and a day hospital (CMA 1987).

Caregivers of older patients in palliative care programs report feeling stressed and exhausted (Ross et al. 2002). Families need health care and social support to carry out home-based palliative care (Hollander and Chappell 2002). Home care workers can help with cleaning and shopping, and respite care can help family caregivers get the rest they need. Quality community-based end-of-life care depends on a partnership between formal and informal caregivers and the support of institutional care when needed. In Great Britain today, for example, most care at the end of life takes place at home (Eastaugh 1996, cited in Northcott and Wilson 2001). People often go to a hospital for only a short (one- to three-day) stay before they die.

ETHICAL ISSUES

Palliative care and other approaches to the treatment of dying patients raise a variety of ethical questions. Is it ethical to stop actively treating a person's illness? Does the decision not to put someone on a respirator or not to use a heroic life-saving measure contribute to the person's death? Philosophers, physicians, and legal experts have looked at these and other issues related to dying today.

Two ethical questions come up again and again in the writing on death and dying. First, how much information should health care providers give a dying person about his or her condition? Second, when should a doctor allow a person to die?

INFORMED CONSENT

Some years ago, experts debated whether to tell dying patients about their condition or keep this knowledge from them. Today, most experts support an open awareness context; they agree that patients have a right to know about the choice of treatment the physician has made and about alternative treatments, including the choice of no treatment. Some provinces have written the right to know into the law. British Columbia (1996) passed the *Health Care (Consent) and Care Facility (Admission) Act*, which defines the rights of adults with respect to health care treatment. Part 2, Article 4 of the act states that

> Every adult who is capable of giving or refusing consent to health care has
>
> (a) the right to give consent or to refuse consent on any grounds, including moral or religious grounds, even if the refusal will result in death,
>
> (b) the right to select a particular form of available health care on any grounds, including moral or religious grounds,
>
> (c) the right to revoke consent,
>
> (d) the right to expect that a decision to give, refuse or revoke consent will be respected, and
>
> (e) the right to be involved to the greatest degree possible in all case planning and decision making.

The act goes on to define the responsibilities of health care workers. For example, it requires workers to respect the wishes of the patient, to communicate clearly with the patient, and to ensure that the patient consents to treat-ment. Patients need to know their prognosis (the likely outcome of their illness) in order to make good decisions about treatment. For this reason alone, patients have a need as well as a right to know that they are dying.

Euthanasia and Physician-Assisted Suicide

Euthanasia

Doctors sometimes face ethical conflicts when they treat dying patients. Medical ethics says that a doctor should heal and cure patients, but the Hippocratic oath also says that a doctor should first "do no harm." What should a doctor do when machines, surgery, or drugs that extend a person's life also prolong his or her suffering? What should a doctor do when a patient asks to die? And what does the law in Canada say about **euthanasia** (actively helping someone relieve his or her suffering and achieve a painless death)?

First, when is a person dead? When he or she stops breathing? When the heart stops beating? Or when the brain waves stop? Harvard Medical School (1968) gives four criteria for death: the person (1) no longer makes a response, (2) no longer breathes or moves, (3) has no reflexes, and (4) has no sign of brain activity on two EEGs taken 24 hours apart.

All of the states in the United States and the District of Columbia support the *Uniform Determination of Death Act* (UDDA), the result of a 1981 Presidential Commission and a report titled *Defining Death*. The UDDA definition echoes the Harvard definition and recognizes whole-brain death, the irreversible cessation of all functions of the entire brain. This would show up as no breathing or heartbeat unless maintained by artificial means.

But what if a machine keeps someone breathing, or a heart pump keeps someone's heart beating? The UDDA may still define this as death; however, a family may see things differently. The family or some members of a family may not want to end artificial support. When does a family or a doctor have the right to take someone off these machines?

At present, a person in a coma, who lacks the mental competence to refuse treatment, must rely on someone else to act for him or her. Family members, a friend, or a medical doctor often must make this decision. Even if a person has told someone his or her wishes or has written a statement of a wish to end treatment at a certain point, in Canada these instructions have no binding effect on the decision.

Although Northcott and Wilson (2001, 72) say that "health care professionals in Canada are not obliged either to offer or to provide futile care," Canada's *Criminal Code* prohibits euthanasia (the active termination of another person's life). It also lists, as punishable offenses, advising someone to commit suicide or aiding someone who commits suicide. A person can receive life imprisonment for euthanasia and up to 14 years in prison for assisted suicide.

A Special Senate Committee on Euthanasia and Assisted Suicide (Senate of Canada 1995) reviewed the legal prohibitions on assisted suicide and concluded that the laws on euthanasia and physician-assisted suicide (PAS) should remain in place. This continues to make it illegal for a doctor to prescribe a lethal drug or provide a technical method for someone to commit suicide. But the Special Senate Committee did recognize the need to review the penalties in cases of nonvoluntary or voluntary euthanasia (see Exhibit 14.6 for definitions). In this case the person who aids the suicide acts with compassion or mercy. It also called for more research on this topic.

In the early 1980s Canada's Law Reform Commission dealt with the issue of euthanasia and assisted suicide. It reviewed ways to relieve doctors of criminal liability, citing the example of California, which in 1976 passed Bill 3060, called the *Natural Death Act*. This bill allows a person to write a **living will** that authorizes relatives or doctors to withdraw or withhold artificial methods of life support in cases of terminal illness. It also attempts to relieve doctors of responsibility for stopping treatment. By 2009 all of the provinces except New Brunswick and Nunavut had enacted legislation that recognizes advance directives. British Columbia, Saskatchewan, Manitoba, Ontario, Prince Edward Island, Yukon and the Northwest Territories accept out-of-province advance directives as long as they meet local requirements.

Most states in the United States recognize living wills. Kelly et al. (1989) studied physicians in nine countries and found that doctors value having specific directions on the type of care a patient wants. Using the results of the study, the researchers produced a booklet called *Let Me Decide*, which offers a model of a living will and a **health care directive**, sometimes called an **advance directive**. The directive gives specific information to family members and doctors about the amount of treatment the person prefers under different conditions, and state who has the right to make end-of-life decisions (Cramer, Tuokko, and Evans 2001). The person may write out a personal statement about preferences for care as part of the directive.

Directives most often take the form of the **durable power of attorney** and the living will. The power of attorney gives someone (often a lawyer, but also possibly a child, spouse, or other family member) the right to make financial decisions on behalf of the older person if

---

● **Exhibit 14.6**

EUTHANASIA AND ASSISTED SUICIDE: SOME TERMS AND WHAT THEY MEAN

Assisted suicide involves providing the means for someone to commit suicide (e.g., supplying prescription drugs) with or without direct participation in the event.

Euthanasia, sometimes referred to as mercy killing, is a term that comes from the Greek word for "good death." It means helping someone end his or her life. A distinction is often drawn between "passive" and "active" euthanasia.

Active euthanasia means intervening actively to end a person's life—e.g., administering a lethal dose of sedatives to someone with a terminal illness. If performed with the consent of the person concerned, this is called "voluntary euthanasia."

Involuntary euthanasia means the patient has not sought euthanasia and may even oppose the idea.

Nonvoluntary euthanasia means the person lacks the competence to give consent. A person in a coma falls into this category.

Passive euthanasia means withholding or ceasing treatment of someone who is ill or injured and not expected to recover—e.g., turning off life support systems and allowing a person to die "naturally."

Voluntary euthanasia means the person has given consent and has enlisted the aid of a physician or someone else in committing suicide.

Source: National Advisory Council on Aging, "Euthanasia and Assisted Suicide: What They Mean," *Expressions* 10(1) (1994), 2. Courtesy of the National Advisory Council on Aging, Health Canada, 2000.

the person loses his or her mental capacity. The living will refers to health care wishes at the end of life. It directs the person to make decisions on the older person's behalf, if that person can't make the decision. Advance directives allow the older person to maintain autonomy and also help family members make health care decisions and avoid court intervention in decision making.

Studies have looked at the basis for people's end-of-life decisions. Lambert and colleagues (2005) studied a small sample of long-term care residents in Ontario. They asked residents where they got information about end-of-life decisions and how they made these decisions. The researchers found that people made end-of-life decisions based on their personal experiences with death and illness. The people in the study, between ages 72 and 100, rarely used information from experts or from the media. They relied on spiritual, emotional, and social considerations in making their decision.

Some research shows that people put off making an advance directive because they don't want to think about poor health or death (Hamel et al. 2002). Post (2006) says that health professionals should encourage all adults to make out a living will. Education about advance directives can increase a person's knowledge about end-of-life options and increase their use. A study of 116 veterans in Canada assessed the impact of an advance directive program called "Let Me Decide" (Molloy, Russo, et al. 2000). The study included workshops and visits by counsellors to tell veterans about the program. The counsellors encouraged the veterans to fill out advance directive forms. Thirty-six percent of the veterans in this study completed directives, and nearly all veterans in the study felt that they benefited from the program.

Molloy, Guyatt, and their colleagues (2000) conducted a similar education program in Ontario. They paired six nursing homes in a controlled study of the "Let Me Decide" (LMD) program's effects. They found that after the program, 49 percent of the competent residents and 78 percent of families of incompetent residents had filled out advance directives.

In addition, compared to the control homes, the LMD homes reported fewer hospitalizations of residents and less health care resource use. The education program and the advance directives led staff members to know more about residents' preferences, allowing staff in the LMD homes to keep residents in the homes rather than send them to a hospital for treatment. The researchers conclude that programs such as LMD can reduce hospitalization of nursing home residents. LMD also makes a resident's wishes known to staff members. Information about advance directives increases an understanding of their value and increases their use.

Garrett and colleagues (2008) studied the use of end-of-life documents in Canada by people aged 75 and over. They found that two people in five (38.81 percent) had created an advance directive (AD). Women, compared to men, reported a greater likelihood of thinking about or discussing an advance directive. Ppeople in different regions of the country differed in their likelihood of having an AD; people in Ontario showed the greatest likelihood of having thought about, discussed, or put in place a formal end-of-life document. People in the Atlantic Provinces showed the least likelihood of having a document in place.

The researchers say that the decision to create an AD takes place in stages. The researchers found that people who had thought about an advance directive (AD) showed the most likelihood of discussing an AD, and those who had discussed an AD reported the most likelihood of having one in place. This research supports the idea that education and information about end-of-life options could increase the use of advance directives.

Cramer and colleagues (2001) studied health care directive use by 661 older people (median age 82) on Vancouver Island. They found that 28 percent of the people in the study had a power of attorney for health decisions, and 19 percent had a living will for health services. But many of the people in the study had not discussed their end-of-life preferences with their preferred surrogate (e.g., a spouse or a sibling). The researchers see this as a problem and say that people need to make their wishes clear to the person they designate as their surrogate decision maker.

Some provinces have laws that support living wills and require health care workers to follow the instructions in the living will (as long as the instructions do not require illegal activity) (Northcott and Wilson 2001). Lavoie and colleagues (1999) presented nurses with two treatment scenarios. In one, the patient had a living will. In the other, the patient did not. The presence of a living will led nurses to choose a level of care that provided only comfort to the patient. The absence of a living will led nurses to choose an intensive treatment and aggressive therapy. The researchers found that the living will helped nurses choose the more appropriate level of care for patients.

Lawton (2001) reports that family members and physicians sometimes differ in their judgment of a person's will to live and the person's end-of-life preferences. This potential for conflict supports the need for an advance directive. Lawton goes on to say that an advance directive allows a person to think about his or her preferences while in a sound state of mind and allows people to control their own destiny. The courts will honour advance directives but a person's relatives or friends need to make health care professionals aware of the directive and what it says.

Cramer, Tuokko, and Evans (2001) report that most people have heard of advance directives, but relatively few people have them. In their study, they found that only 28 percent of their sample had made out a power of attorney for finances. Only 19 percent said they had a living will for health services. People with more education tended to have these documents in place (see Exhibit 14.7).

Advance directives can ensure that an older person gets the care he or she wants. However, advance directives pose problems that need public discussion.

First, in some cases people may change their minds as they near death, but they will not get a chance to change their advance directive. Lawton (2001) reviewed studies of end-of-life preferences and found support for this concern. The research showed that about 30 percent of people change their preferences over time. Some want more intervention (10 percent) and others less

---

● Exhibit 14.7

A LIVING WILL

The living will format below appears in the California Natural Death Act. The directive below gives an idea of what such a will should contain. Read it over and consider the pros and cons of living wills. Would you fill one out? Would you witness a friend's? Do you think Canada should allow the use of living wills?

Directive to Physician

Directive made this _____ day of _____ (month, year). I _____, being of sound mind, willfully and voluntarily make known my desire that my life shall not be artificially prolonged under the circumstances set forth below, and do hereby declare:

1. If at any time I should have an incurable injury, disease, or illness certified to be a terminal condition by two physicians, and where the application of life-sustaining procedures would serve only to artificially prolong the moment of my death and where my physician determines that my death is imminent whether or not life-sustaining procedures are utilized, I direct that such procedures be withheld or withdrawn and that I be permitted to die naturally.

2. In the absence of my ability to give directions regarding the use of such life-sustaining procedures, it is my intention that this directive shall be honoured by my family and physician(s) as the final expression of my legal right to refuse medical or surgical treatment and accept the consequences from such refusal.

3. If I have been diagnosed as pregnant and that diagnosis is known to my physician, this directive shall have no force or effect during the course of my pregnancy.

4. I have been diagnosed and notified at least 14 days ago as having a terminal condition by _____, M.D., whose address is _____, and whose telephone number is _____. I understand that if I have not filled in the physician's name and address, it shall be presumed that I did not have a terminal condition when I made out this directive.

5. This directive shall have no force or effect five years from the date filled in above.

6. I understand the full import of this directive and I am emotionally and mentally competent to make this directive.

Signed _____
City, County and State of Residence

_____

The declarant has been personally known to me and I believe him or her to be of sound mind.

Witness _____

Source: *California Natural Death Act.* The contents of this document are in the public domain.

(20 percent). He concludes that people need the chance to review and, if necessary, revise their advance directive as they approach death.

Second, subtle forms of coercion may influence an older person's instructions in an advance directive. Older people may propose an end to treatment because they feel that they will burden others with their care. These issues point to the need for better methods of communication between dying people and their caregivers (Fisher, 2006; Lawton 2001).

The Law Reform Commission of Canada (1982) says that doctors should not feel compelled to take heroic measures to keep someone alive and patients should not have to write advance directives to protect themselves from a doctor's fear of prosecution. The commission says that the law and medical ethics distinguish between killing someone and allowing someone to die. A doctor who allows death to happen—for example, by not putting a person on a respirator or by taking someone off a respirator—may or may not cause a person's death. This is **passive euthanasia** because the person may live even without the treatment. Walton and Fleming (1980) say that ethical treatment should offer the most options to the patient. "A passive course of action provides a sensible alternative to aggressive treatment and, at the same time, allows for unexplainable and unforeseen events which may be of great benefit to the patient" (60). Treatment should offer the most options to the patient.

The current law in Canada leaves many questions open. Once treatment has begun, for instance, the law inhibits a doctor from discontinuing treatment. The doctor may know, through an advance directive, that after some time the patient would want treatment discontinued. But, by discontinuing the treatment, the doctor risks legal action. Doctors themselves disagree on how much a physician should assist a person who wishes to die. But at present the law and medical ethics reject **active euthanasia** or physician-assisted suicide—actively helping someone end his or her life either because the person asks for death or to relieve suffering (Steinbock 2005).

St. John and Man-Son-Hing (2002) say that a request for active euthanasia most often comes from someone in pain or with depression. Symptom control can make dying less painful and can reduce the request for active euthanasia. Fisher (2006, 430) says that good palliative care can "decrease the perceived need for euthanasia." Some studies show that women, minorities, and older people sometimes fail to get the pain relief they need (Meier, Myers, and Muskin 1999; Gagleise and colleagues (2005). The medical profession needs to ensure that everyone gets the highest quality palliative care.

Physician-assisted Suicide

In **physician-assisted suicide**, a doctor gives a person the means to commit suicide or gives advice on how to commit suicide. The patients take the action themselves. Controversy exists over this practice.

Supporters and critics of these decisions often argue about the issue of consent. Supporters of assisted suicide say that the patient's right to accept or refuse treatment will protect people from abuse of assisted suicide. Critics of assisted suicide fear that this will lead to "mercy killing" without patients' consent. Krauthammer (1996; also Patel, 2004) reports that this has occurred in the Netherlands. Also, some doctors may consent to patient requests too quickly. Few guidelines exist today for doctors to follow, and medical associations have begun to review their standards in light of recent court actions and social changes (CMA 1995).

Canadian law prohibits a doctor from helping patients end their lives. A case in Canada (*Rodriguez v. British Columbia*) in 1993 supported the *Criminal Code*'s provisions against physician-assisted suicide (Health Canada 1994). At that time, Sue Rodriguez, a 42-year-old mother, had amyotrophic lateral sclerosis (Lou Gehrig's disease). Her health declined and she would soon lose the ability to speak, swallow, or move. She had between two and 14 months to live. She requested a court order from the Supreme Court of British Columbia to allow her to have a physician help her end her life when she chose. She asked the court to declare the *Criminal Code* statute (section 241[b]) invalid. This statue prohibits assisted suicide.

The court held that Rodriguez did not have the right to have a doctor help her end her life. The court split five to four against her request. Some of the dissenting justices proposed procedural guidelines that could allow physician-assisted suicide. A court of appeal supported the majority opinion against Rodriguez's request. The outcome reflects "social divisions about how to reconcile the strongly held values of self-determination and the sanctity of life" (National Advisory Council on Aging 1994, 5). (Sue Rodriguez died peacefully with an anonymous doctor's assistance on February 12, 1994.)

Public debate on this issue will grow. The Catholic Health Association of Canada, for example, opposes assisted suicide and euthanasia (Blouin 1995, cited in Northcott and Wilson 2001), but others support these practices (Humphry 2000). They say that medicine now has the ability to prolong life through technology, which will mean more years of pain and suffering for some patients. Also, the cost of keeping people alive on machines and with expensive medications will also increase. Some people will support active euthanasia on economic grounds, while others see the choice of active euthanasia as a right in modern society.

Only a few countries currently allow voluntary euthanasia or physician-assisted suicide. Humphry (2000) reports that Swiss law has allowed **assisted suicide** since 1937 as long as it relieves suffering and has a humanitarian purpose. But social sanctions keep most doctors in Switzerland from assisting with suicide. On May 20, 1997, the Constitutional Court of Colombia approved legalized euthanasia. The court ruled that "no person can be held criminally responsible for taking the life of a terminally ill patient who has given clear authorization to do so." As of 2007 the country's legislators had not created legislation to govern the process (as is the case in the Netherlands).

Humphry (2000) says that in only two places does assisted suicide have societal support—the Netherlands and the state of Oregon in the United States. Oregon passed the *Death with Dignity Act* in 1994 by popular vote. This act bans voluntary euthanasia (mercy killing), but it supports physician-assisted suicide in cases of advanced terminal illness. The law lays out a detailed process for patients and physicians to follow.

A report in 2006 on the Oregon policy (Oregon 2007) found that 65 people got legal prescriptions for medication and 35 followed through with it. Eleven people, who had filled prescriptions earlier, died in 2006, bringing the total of deaths under this policy to 46 in 2006. Since 1997, 292 people have died under this law.

Studies in Oregon show the need for education about end-of-life options. Silveira and colleagues (2000), for example, studied 728 outpatients in four Oregon clinics. They found that only 23 percent understood assisted suicide and only 32 percent understood active euthanasia. Sixty-two percent of the people in the study did not know the difference between the two. The researchers say that people need education about their options before they can make intelligent decisions about end-of-life care.

The Netherlands began allowing physician-assisted suicide in 1973. In 1984, the Dutch Supreme Court allowed both voluntary euthanasia and physician-assisted suicide. These causes of death account for about 3 percent of all deaths in the Netherlands each year. Regulations exist to guide physicians' practices. In particular, doctors have to report cases where they have assisted with a suicide. However, technically, euthanasia remains illegal in the Netherlands. The courts allow the process, reflecting public opinion, but no law exists that makes it legal (Humphry 2000). Rurup and colleagues

(2005) say that support for euthanasia has increased from 50 percent to almost 90 percent.

The Globe and Mail conducted an online poll in March 2009. The paper asked readers "Would you support making assisted suicide available to terminally ill patients?" Fifty-five percent of almost 20,000 readers favoured this proposition. The Canadian Medical Association (CMA) conducted a study of physicians' views of physician-assisted suicide and found that more than 60 percent of doctors wanted to change the *Criminal Code* to do away with the laws that prohibit physician-assisted suicide (National Advisory Council on Aging 1994c). In 1994, the ethics committee of the CMA supported doctors' right to assist in suicide. The committee also proposed that the CMA set up guidelines for physicians who choose to assist a patient in suicide. But CMA members rejected the committee's recommendation, voting to ban doctors from engaging in physician-assisted suicide. Disagreement exists, even within the medical profession, over the practice. Humphry (2000, 59) says that "the medical profession almost everywhere is split down the middle on the issue of euthanasia."

This debate over physician-assisted suicide will continue as Canadians sort out the implications of changing the law. Humphry (2000, 59) says that "in every nation where there have been scientific surveys of public opinion, it has become obvious that the general *public want action*, while the *politicians* (who actually make the laws) are either *against law reform or afraid of a religious backlash* if they follow the public's wishes." It seems unlikely that Canada will change its law to allow assisted suicide. But other approaches to end-of-life illness, such as hospice and palliative care, will get more attention. Likewise, people need to learn more about advance directives so that they can get the end-of-life care that they want (see Exhibit 4.8).

MOURNING AND GRIEF

When an older person dies, he or she often leaves behind children, sometimes a spouse, and other family members (such as grandchildren or siblings). These survivors need to adjust to the loss, and society can help with this adjustment. Funeral practices and rituals structure the grieving process. They prescribe what mourners should say, what they should wear, and in some cultures even how they should sit.

Mourners in Christian cultures wear black; mourners in some Asian cultures wear white. North American society values silent, unemotional grieving;

● Exhibit 14.8

A FAMILY'S RESPONSE TO DEATH AND DYING

The academic discussions of the right to decide on prolonging life often focus on medical and legal issues. But every day in Canada, people, along with their physicians and nursing staff, make decisions about their older family members. These decisions, at their best, take place within a context of openness and trust between families and health care professionals. The following case shows how one family decided against aggressive treatment.

Mrs. Walker, 78, moved into an apartment in the Beth Sharon Senior Complex in early December. The complex offered her a supportive environment. It had a security system, access for a wheelchair, and a chance to socialize with other residents.

Mrs. Walker had played an active part in her community for many years as a hospital volunteer and businessperson. So, when she moved into her apartment complex, she joined the Beth Sharon Seniors Group and regularly attended their afternoon teas in a nearby centre. On January 10, as she left for the tea, she lost her balance, fell down a flight of stairs, and severely injured her head. When an ambulance arrived, she was found to be unconscious and was taken to a nearby hospital for emergency treatment.

Mrs. Walker's daughter, Phyllis, a nurse, rushed to the hospital when she was called. The neurosurgeon on

staff had already completed a CAT scan and showed it to Phyllis. "I don't like the look of this," he said. "There appears to be severe bleeding at the base of the brain stem. She's not likely to be well again, or indeed function on her own."

Phyllis left the ward to talk with her sister and other family members. They agreed that they would not press for an operation to remove the blood clot. Surgery would almost certainly lead to the necessity of a respirator and other artificial means of life support. Over the next few days, as the family waited for some change in their mother's condition, Phyllis would suggest various actions or ask for another test. Each time the surgeon in charge would ask a simple question, "Would your mother like us to do that?" And each time Phyllis agreed that her mother would not want aggressive treatment to prolong her life. The decision to wait became harder to sustain as Mrs. Walker's breathing faltered. But the family stayed with its decision, based on Mrs. Walker's many discussions with them. Family members and close friends supported the family's decision to follow their mother's wishes.

Sixteen days after entering the hospital, and without regaining consciousness, Mrs. Walker died. She was cremated, in accordance with her request, and her family held a memorial service to celebrate her life.

Chinese families hire professional mourners to make loud wailing noises at the funeral. Jewish tradition requires that the family "sit shiva" for seven days after a funeral. According to this custom, mourners tear their clothes, sit on low chairs to deny themselves physical comfort, cover the mirrors in their home, and light a candle that burns for one week. The mourning family accepts visitors throughout the week, and 10 men gather at the house each day for prayer. Mourning continues in less intense stages for a year until the unveiling of a commemorative stone on the grave of the deceased.

Each culture has its own funeral rituals and mourning practices, but all have a common purpose: to help the bereaved family cope with grief and re-establish community bonds after the loss of a community member.

Regardless of the culture a person belongs to or the type of funeral he or she attends, each bereaved person has to work through personal feelings of grief.

Some research in North America shows that mourners go through stages of grief. Early work by Lindemann (1944) describes three such stages: an initial response phase, an intermediate phase, and a recovery phase.

First, the bereaved person feels shock and disbelief. He or she may report feeling cold and numb, and some people say they feel dazed, empty, and confused. These feelings protect a person from feelings of sorrow. People in this phase often fear that they will break down in public. This phase can last for several weeks.

Second, the person will begin to review what has happened. This takes three forms: (1) The bereaved person obsessively reviews one or two scenes related to the death, or may be very self-critical about something that he or she should have said or done. (2) The bereaved person searches for a meaning for the death. Religious people may find solace in knowing that God willed this death. (3) The bereaved person searches for the deceased. This may mean that a widow goes to places where she expects to see her spouse. She may also feel his presence while watching TV, eating dinner, or lying in bed. Some people even call out to their spouses and expect an answer. This phase lasts about a year.

Third, the bereaved person begins to recover. Survivors look for social contacts. They may join a club or go on a cruise. They feel that they have come through an ordeal and say they feel stronger and more competent than before. This stage begins around the second year after the death.

Kastenbaum (2001) says that grief affects a person's physical as well as psychological well-being. Some research shows that grief throws the body's neuroendocrine system out of balance. Acute grief can lead to illness and may even lead to death. Grief affects a person's entire life, including his or her social relations.

Sometimes a person can show a delayed emotional response to a parent's or a spouse's death. The person seems to cope well, displaying lots of zest and energy, but may have internalized the grief. This delay can lead to emotional upset and physical illness later.

The case of Joanna will show the cost of morbid grieving. While her husband was in the hospital dying of brain cancer, she visited him every day. At the same time, she carried on a career in real estate and worked on a master's degree. For two years, she ran herself into the ground. She went to the hospital twice a day, at noon and at supper time, to feed her husband his meals, then would jump in her car and show another house or run home to work on a paper.

When her husband died, she was determined that nothing was going to stop her. "I didn't allow myself time to grieve," she says. "After his death, I travelled. At Christmas I went to Spain, Hawaii, or wherever. At Easter I went somewhere. I went to Europe. There was never a day—I didn't allow myself any time at all. Do you get the picture? No time to breathe."

To keep going she used pills and alcohol. Then she started collecting pills and drinking more. "That was my way of coping, my way of standing the pain. I needed some kind of anesthetic," she says. At the end of this downward spiral, Joanna drove the front of her car through a restaurant window. She got out of her car, walked through the window frame, sat down at a booth in the restaurant, and waited for the police to take her away (Novak 1985).

Like Joanna, some people will feel disbelief, shock, numbness, sadness, or guilt. A person can also feel abandoned, isolated, angry, and depressed. Research shows that people who have problems with grieving may turn to alcohol and drugs (Connor 1998). Still, only a small percentage of people go through morbid grieving (and few people show Joanna's extreme denial). Northcott and Wilson (2001) say that the pattern of grieving depends on how a person dies, whether the death takes place suddenly or over time, and the age of the person. Forewarning about a spouse's death, for example, may allow a person to work out some grief. Surviving spouses can plan for the future, and this eases adjustment to widowhood. Burton and colleagues (2006) found that a sudden death led to a greater risk of depression. They also found that strong emotions may come and go for many months after a spouse's death, especially among highly stressed caregivers who experienced extreme stress before their care receiver's death.

Loss of a Spouse in Old Age

Widows and widowers face some common problems. These include not enough time to grieve, a lack of emotional support after the official mourning period, and lack of support from adult children during grieving. Kahana (2006) says that widowhood signals the end of a woman's former identity (as a wife) and begins the need to build a new identity. MacDougall (1998, 1–2), a widow, says that "part of the pain has to do with our sense of self; without our life-long partner, it becomes necessary to redefine our place in the world. When one has been part of a couple for a very long time, the adjustment can seem impossible."

Older spouses may show a delayed and more extreme grief reaction than younger spouses. Research shows that bereavement can go on months after the formal mourning period. Northcott and Wilson (2001, 156) say that "grief is never truly over." Many women hold onto the wife role for years after their husbands' deaths. Onrust and Cuijpers (2006) reviewed 11 studies for evidence of depression and anxiety in widowhood. The studies contained data on 3,481 widows and 4,685 non-widows. They found a high rate of major depressive disorder among the widows in the first year of widowhood; almost 22 percent of the widowed group showed high rates of depression and 12 percent showed post-traumatic stress disorder.

The Changing Lives of Older Couples (CLOC) study in the United States included over 1,500 people before widowhood (Mancini et al., 2006). The researchers then conducted a three-wave longitudinal study at 6, 18, and 48 months after the death of a study participant's spouse.

This study, for the first time, detailed the frequency and variety of reactions to a spouse's death. Because it looked at pre-loss mental health, the study could assess the effect of loss on psychological well-being.

The study found five responses to the loss of a spouse:

1. chronic grief (low pre-loss depression, high post-loss depression after 6 to 18 months);

2. common grief or recovery (low pre-loss depression and high post-loss depression at 6 months with improvement at 18 months);

3. resilience (low pre- and low post-loss depression at 6 and 18 months);

4. depressed-improved (high pre-loss depression and low post-loss depression at 6 and 18 months); and

5. chronic depression (high pre-loss depression and high post-loss depression at 6 and 18 months).

Only a small group (about 15.6 percent) showed chronic grief—low pre-loss depression, but high post-loss depression. This study distinguished these people from those who showed chronic depression—high pre- and high post-loss depression. This group made up 7.8 percent of the study population. The largest group in this study (45.7 percent) reported low pre- and low post-loss depression after 6 to 18 months. This result may surprise some people. It shows that those in good mental health before a spouse's death cope reasonably well with their grief.

Some people, the depressed-improved group, felt less depressed after their spouse's death. These people may have suffered through an unpleasant marriage and the spouse's death may have come as a relief. The study found that a majority of spouses either recovered from their grief (10.7 percent) after 6 to 18 months or coped well with their grief and showed low depression at 6 to 18 months (45.7 percent).

Wolff and Wortman (2006) studied the effects of widowhood on nutrition and health. They report that compared to women, men show a greater decline in health. Women in married couples often oversee the nutritional and health needs of the couple (for example, women tend to make appointments for medical checkups) Therefore, the loss of a wife often leaves a man without the motivation to stay fit and healthy.

Wolff and Wortman say that widowers may increase smoking and drinking. The researchers write (citing Umberson, 1987; 1992) "that men are hurt more by widowhood because with the loss of their wives, widowed men have lost a social agent who is concerned with the

preservation of their health" (Wolff and Wortman, 2006, 99–100). Shear (2006, 107) says that health problems related to bereavement "can be chronic, serious, and debilitating."

Compared with men, a smaller proportion of women remarry after their spouse dies. This, in part, reflects the smaller number of eligible men compared with eligible women in later life. Also, men tend to remarry younger women. Women who do remarry say they want a companion and the feeling that they add to another person's happiness. Talbott (1998) found that many older widows reported an interest in men but they also reported negative attitudes toward remarriage and an increased enjoyment of their independence.

Sexual relations after the death of a spouse also differ by gender. Wolff and Wortman (2006 citing Hustins, 2001) say that only 7 percent of widows had some sexual relationship by the end of their first year of bereavement. By contrast 54 percent of men reported a sexual relationship in this time. Even among older widowed men (65 and over) 31 percent said they had a sexual relationship within two years of bereavement. Only 4 percent of older widowed women reported a sexual relationship in this time (Davidson, 2001).

Shear (2006) says that recovery from grief alternates between coping with stress due to loss and rebuilding a satisfying life. Rebuilding can include doing new things, going new places, and taking on new roles. Some women, for example, experience widowhood as a release, allowing them to rediscover parts of their identities they had lost in marriage. One woman said she would not marry again (for the fourth time). "I'm tired of taking care of sick old men," she said. "I want to enjoy myself for a while" (personal communication with author).

Hallam and colleagues report that spouses who have died continue to influence the living in many ways. People sometimes talk to dead spouses, ask them for advice, or try to imagine what they would do in a situation the surviving spouse is facing. One woman said she felt her husband lie down next to her in bed some months after his funeral. Widows or widowers will sometimes decide against remarriage because of the close tie that still exists with their dead spouse. More research on bereavement in old age will show how this experience differs from bereavement in younger people.

CONCLUSION

This chapter has touched on some of the complex issues related to death and dying. Each religion has its own views on issues such as euthanasia, funeral practices, and mourning. Each culture shapes its members' beliefs about the meaning of death, about life after death, and about care for the sick and dying. People will respond in unique ways to their own death and to the deaths of people they know and love. Today, changes in technology, the management of terminal illness, and the meaning of death raise new questions about death and dying.

The study of death and dying can help people understand these issues and make better choices for themselves. An incident in the life of the lead author of this book, Mark Novak, made this clear to him.

After my father's funeral, my mother, my sister, my father's brothers, and I got into a rented limousine and drove to the cemetery. The funeral director stopped the cars in the funeral procession at the cemetery gate. We saw the hearse pull ahead and stop a hundred yards away. I turned around to talk to one of my uncles in our car. A few minutes later, the director waved all the cars on. We stopped behind the hearse and got out. It was empty. The director led us to the graveside. We stood close to the grave, but we could not see the coffin or any earth. A blanket of fake grass covered the earth that had come from the grave. Another blanket covered the coffin. Relatives and friends gathered to the side and behind us. The director said some prayers and a few kind words. My mother, my sister, and I stood and stared at the fake grass. I think we were supposed to leave. But I motioned to the director to pull the grass back. He looked surprised. I told him to pull the grass back. He did. We saw the corner of the coffin and the corner of the grave, and we started to cry.

I tell this story because my knowledge of death and dying gave me the confidence to act. I felt I should do something, and I knew what I had to do.

Those of us in the field of aging use our knowledge of aging each day. We use it to better understand our families and friends, and we use it to understand the changes we go through as we age. Knowledge about aging allows us to plan for our future with less fear and denial. The study of aging can make old age a better time of life for each of us and for the people we love.

Summary

1. Attitudes to death vary by age, religion, and culture. Older people generally accept death more than younger people. Like younger people, older people say they want to continue living if they feel their life has meaning.

2. People with either no religious belief or a very strong one seem to cope with death best.

3. Death occurs more often in old age today than in the past, and it also occurs more often in an institution. These trends will increase as the population ages.

4. Elisabeth Kübler-Ross reports five stages of dying. Not everyone goes through all of these stages in the order Kübler-Ross describes, but her writings encouraged a more open discussion of death and dying when they first appeared.

5. Dame Cicely Saunders opened the first modern hospice in England in 1967. St. Christopher's Hospice offers an alternative to hospital care for the dying. Hospices offer pain control and a home-like setting for death.

6. Palliative care units in hospitals offer the same comfort and care as a hospice. Some of these units will help patients die in their own homes. They also assure patients that they can return to the hospital at any time.

7. Most experts and patients prefer an open awareness context for dying. They agree that patients have a right to know about the choice of treatment the physician has made and about alternative treatments, including the choice of no treatment. Doctors today need to understand their own feelings about death and dying, so they can give their patients the kind of care that their patients prefer.

8. Doctors say that proper pain control would end the fear that leads people to ask for euthanasia. The law in Canada today does not require doctors to take heroic measures to keep a terminally ill patient alive. Canada needs clearer guidelines to help doctors decide about stopping treatment for people in certain situations, although Canadian law does prohibit active euthanasia. Judicial review of cases would lead to more rational decisions about termination of life.

9. Health care directives relieve doctors of criminal liability. They give family members and doctors specific information about the amount of treatment a person prefers and state who has the right to make decisions on behalf of the patient.

10. Death leads to grief and mourning for survivors. Culture and religion help people cope with feelings of grief. Funerals, for example, bring the community together and give mourners support. Still, each person has to work through feelings of grief in his or her own way. Researchers say that mourners go through stages of grief and that if all goes well they will emerge from grieving to carry on their life.

Study Questions

1. Researchers have proposed three theories that describe how older people respond to death. List and explain each of these theories.

2. Describe the means that older people use to buffer their fear of death.

3. How has population aging changed the context of dying?

4. Describe how Elisabeth Kübler-Ross and Dame Cicely Saunders each influenced thinking about death and dying.

5. Explain the main function of a hospice. What methods do hospices use to help people enjoy their last days?

6. Compare and contrast palliative care units and hospices. Why do researchers think that, compared with a normal hospital, palliative care units cost less money to care for dying patients?

7. What moral issues did the Sue Rodriguez case raise? What conflict did this case raise between the medical profession and the Canadian legal system? How can Canadian society resolve this conflict for the future?

8. Describe the three stages of grief. Describe successful grief work. How do older and younger people differ in their grieving patterns?

Key Terms

active euthanasia   intervening actively to end a person's life. (347)

advance directive   a precise statement of the desired treatment and care, including what medical actions are to be taken under what conditions and a declaration of who has the right to decide. (344)

assisted suicide   suicide made possible with the help of someone, who may or may not participate directly in the event; in the case of physician-assisted suicide, a doctor provides the person with the means or advice on how to commit suicide. (348)

durable power of attorney   the power that gives someone, usually a lawyer, child, friend, or other family member, the right to make decisions on behalf of the ill person. (344)

ego integrity   the acceptance of the notion that one's life cycle is something complete and unique. (334)

ego transcendence   a late stage of psychosocial development, in which people feel a deep concern for others and for the culture they will leave when they die. (334)

euthanasia   ending the life of a person suffering a terminal illness or incurable condition. (343)

health care directive   instructions with specific information for family members and doctors about the amount of treatment the person prefers under different conditions. (344)

hospice health   care services that meet the special needs of dying patients. (339)

living will   a legal document that specifies the limits of health care treatment desired in case of a terminal illness. (344)

palliative care   care directed toward improving the quality of life for the dying, including symptom control and spiritual support as well as bereavement support and education. (339)

passive euthanasia   withholding or ceasing treatment of someone who is ill or injured and not expected to recover. (347)

physician-assisted suicide (PAS)   when a physician provides a patient with advice about how to commit suicide or with the technical means (e.g., lethal medications) to commit suicide. (347)

Selected Readings

Cicirelli, Victor G. *Older Adults' Views on Death.* New York: Springer, 2006.

> The author describes how older adults understand death and dying. He shows that people hold many different beliefs about death and looks at how culture, religion, and family influence peoples' views of death. The author also describes older peoples' fear of death and death's meaning in later life.

Kastenbaum, R.J. *Death, Society, and Human Experience,* 10th ed. Boston: Allyn and Bacon, 2009.

> This classic text in the field, offers up-to-date information on hospice care, end-of-life decisions, euthanasia, and bereavement. The book also covers unusual topics like survival after death. The book is well written with good summaries of the research on death and dying.

Northcott, H.C., and D.M. Wilson. *Dying and Death in Canada.* Aurora, ON: Garamond Press, 2001.

> This book reviews the history of death and dying in Canada. The authors present current information on causes of death, gender differences in causes of death, and ages at death. The book looks at the relationship between modern medicalized approaches to death and dying in Canada and other cultural traditions (Muslim, Jewish, and Asian). The authors present case studies of how Canadians cope with and respond to death. This is a readable and insightful book.

Websites to Consult

Canadian Hospice Palliative Care Association

http://www.chpca.net

> This site provides information on palliative care services in Canada. It also provides links to educational resources and interest groups.

Quality End-of-Life Care Coalition

http://www.chpca.net/qelccc.htm

> Thirty groups concerned about quality of life issues sponsor this website. Members include the Alzheimer Society of Canada, CARP: Canada's Association for the Fifty-Plus, and the Canadian Medical Association. The site includes annual reports on quality end-of-life issues, a media kit, and information resources.

Senator Sharon Carstairs on Palliative Care

http://www.sen.parl.gc.ca/scarstairs/PalliativeCare/PalliativeCare_e.asp

This site contains information on government actions related to palliative care in Canada. It includes an archive of speeches and motions in the Canadian Senate on palliative care. The site also links to many other health-related websites.

Right to Die Society of Canada

http://www.righttodie.ca

This organization supports individuals' right to die and legislation that would legalize euthanasia and assisted suicide. The site makes a strong case for this view but also presents other information on this topic, including a listing of laws in Canada related to euthanasia and assisted suicide. The sites links to a newsletter and to other information.

References

Aadlandsvik, R. 2007. "Education, Poetry, and the Process of Growing Old." *Educational Gerontology* 33(8), 665–78.

AARP. 2007. *AARP Profit from Experience: Perspectives of Employers, Workers and Policymakers in the G7 Countries on the New Demographic Realities,* http://assets.aarp.org/rgcenter/econ/intl_older_worker.pdf, accessed March 2008.

Abu-Laban, Sharon McIrvin. 1980. "Social Supports in Older Age: The Need for New Research Directions." *Essence* 4: 95–209.

Adams, R. 2003. "Strength Training: A Natural Prescription for Staying Healthy and Fit." *Gerontology Research Centre News* 22(1): 1–4.

Adler, G., and S. Rottunda. 2006. "Older Adults' Perspectives on Driving Cessation." *Journal of Aging Studies* 20(3): 227–35.

Aiken, L.R. 2001. *Dying, Death, and Bereavement*, 4th ed. Mahwah, NJ: Lawrence Erlbaum.

Albert, M.S., and R.J. Killiany. 2001. "Age-Related Cognitive Change and Brain-Behavior Relationships." In J.E. Birren and K.W. Schaie, eds., *Handbook of the Psychology of Aging*, 5th ed. San Diego: Academic Press.

Aldwin, C.M., A. Spiro, and C.L. Park. 2006. "Health, Behavior, and Optimal Aging: A Life Span Developmental Perspective." In J. E. Birren and K.W. Schaie eds., *Handbook of the Psychology of Aging*, 6th edition (85–104). Burlington, MA: Elsevier Academic Press.

Allen, K.R., and K.L. Wilcox. 2000. "Gay/Lesbian Families over the Life Course." In S.J. Price, P.C. McKenry, and M.J. Murphy, eds., *Families Across Time: A Life Course Perspective*, (51–63). Los Angeles, CA: Roxbury Publishing.

Allen, K., J. Blascovich, and W. Mendes. 2002. "Cardiovascular Reactivity and the Presence of Pets, Friends and Spouses: The Truth about Cats and Dogs." Psychosomatic Medicine, 64(5): 727–39.

Allen, P.A., B. Bucur, and M.D. Murphy. 2006. "Information-Processing Theory. In R. Schulz, L.S. Noelker, K. Rockwood, and R.L. Sprott, eds., *The Encyclopedia of Aging,* 4th ed. 588–591. New York: Springer.

Alwin, Duane F., Scott M. Hofer, and Ryan J. McCammon. 2006. "Modeling the Effects of Time Integrating Demographic and Developmental Perspectives." In Robert H. Binstock and Linda K. George, eds., *Handbook of Aging and the Social Sciences*, 6th ed., 20–38. Burlington, MA: Academic Press.

Alzheimer Society of Canada. 2004. Introduction to "Alzheimer Care: Safely Home—Alzheimer Wandering Registry." http://www.alzheimer.ca/english/care/wandering-intro.htm, accessed July 30, 2004.

American Association of Retired Persons. 1998. *Aging Everywhere.* Washington, DC: American Association of Retired Persons.

Aminzadeh, F., and N. Edwards. 2000. "Factors Associated with Cane Use among Community Dwelling Older Adults." *Public Health Nursing* 176: 474–83.

Aminzadeh, F., W.B. Dalziel, F.J. Molnar, and J. Alie. 2004. "An Examination of the Health Profile, Service Use and Care Needs of Older Adults in Residential Care Facilities." *Canadian Journal on Aging* 23(3): 281–94.

Amoako, E.P., L. Richardson-Campbell, and L. Kennedy-Malone. 2003. "Self-Medication with Over-the-Counter Drugs among Elderly Adults." *Journal of Gerontological Nursing* 29(8): 10–15.

Anderson, G.F., and P.S. Hussey. 2000. "Population Aging: A Comparison among Industrialized Countries." *Health Affairs* 19(3): 191–203.

Andrew, M.K., and K. Rockwood, K. (2007). "Psychiatric Illness in Relation to Frailty in Community-dwelling Elderly People without Dementia: A Report from the Canadian Study of Health and Aging." *Canadian Journal on Aging* 26(1): 33–38.

Andrews, G.J., N. Gavin, S. Begley, and D. Brodie. 2003. "Assisting Friendships, Combating Loneliness: Users' Views on a 'Befriending' Scheme." *Ageing and Society* 23(3): 349–62.

Andrews, M. 2000. "Ageful and Proud." *Ageing and Society* 20 (Part 6): 791–95.

Angeli, E.A.G. 2001. "Spiritual Care in Hospice Settings." In D.O. Moberg, ed., *Aging and Spirituality,* 113–24. Binghamton, NY: Haworth Pastoral Press.

Angus Reid. 2000. "Health Care in Canada." Opinion poll. Angus Reid Group.

Antonucci, T.C. 2001. "Social Relations: An Examination of Social Networks, Social Support, and Sense of Control." In J.E. Birren and K.W. Schaie, eds., *Handbook of the Psychology of Aging,* 5th ed. San Diego: Academic Press.

Apt, N.A. 2002. "Ageing and the Changing Role of the Family and the Community: An African Perspective." *International Social Security Review* 55(1): 39–47.

Armstrong, H., W. Clement, Z. Lin, and S. Prus. 2006. *Contrasting Inequalities: Comparing Correlates of Health in Canada and the United States. Social and Economic Dimensions of an Aging Population.* SEDAP Research Paper No. 167. Hamilton, ON: McMaster University.

Armstrong, P. 2002. "Guidelines for Examining Women, Work, and Caring in the New Millennium." *Centres of Excellence for Women's Health Research Bulletin* 3(1): 15–18.

Armstrong, P., and H. Armstrong. 2001. *The Double Ghetto: Canadian Women and Their Segregated Work, 3rd Edition.* Don Mills, ON: Oxford University Press.

Armstrong-Esther, C.A. 1994. "Health and Social Needs of Native Seniors." In National Advisory Council on Aging, *Aboriginal Seniors' Issues,* 39–48. Cat. No. H71-2/1-15-1994E. Ottawa: Minister of Supply and Services.

Arnsten, Amy. 2008. "Arnsten Lab: Yale University Department of Neurobiology." http://info.med.yale.edu/neurobio/arnsten/Research.html, accessed May 18, 2008.

Aronson, J. 1992. "Women's Sense of Responsibility for the Care of Old People: 'But Who Else Is Going to Do It?'" *Gender and Society* 6(1): 8–29.

Aronson, J. 2002. "Frail and Disabled Users of Home Care: Confident Consumers or Disentitled Citizens?" *Canadian Journal on Aging* 21(1): 11–25.

Aronson, J., and C. Sinding. 2000. "Home Care Users' Experiences of Fiscal Constraints: Challenges and Opportunities for Case Management." *Care Management Journals* 2(4): 220–25.

Aronson, J., C. Thornewell, and K. Williams. 1995. "Wife Assault in Old Age: Coming Out of Obscurity." *Canadian Journal on Aging* 14(Suppl. 2): 72–88.

Arsenault, N. 1997. "Typologies and the Leisure Learner." *Aging International* 4(2/3): 64–74.

Artibise, A. 1977. *Winnipeg: An Illustrated History.* Toronto: Lorimer.

Atchley, R.C. 1982. "The Process of Retirement: Comparing Women and Men." In M. Szinovacz, ed., *Women's Retirement,* 153–68. Beverly Hills: Sage.

Atchley, R.C. 1985. *Social Forces and Aging.* 4th ed. Belmont, CA: Wadsworth.

Au, D.W.H., T.F. Crossley, and M. Schellhorn. 2004. *The Effect of Health Changes and Long-term Health on the Work Activity of Older Canadians. Social and Economic Dimensions of an Aging Population.* Research Paper No. 119. Hamilton, ON: McMaster University.

Auger, J.A. 2000. *Social Perspectives on Death and Dying.* Halifax, NS: Fernwood Publishing.

Bäckman, L., B.J. Small, and A. Wahlin. 2001. "Aging and Memory: Cognitive and Biological Perspectives." In J.E. Birren and K.W. Schaie, eds., *Handbook of the Psychology of Aging,* 5th ed. San Diego: Academic Press.

Bäckman, L, B.J. Small, A.Wahlin, and M. Larsson. 2000. "Cognitive Functioning in Very Old Age." In F.I.M. Craik and T.A. Salthouse, eds., *The Handbook of Aging and Cognition,* 2nd ed., 499–558. Mahwah, NJ: Lawrence Erlbaum Associates.

Baker, M., J. Gruber, and K. Milligan.2003. "Early Retirement Provisions and the Labor Force Behavior of Older Men: Some Evidence from Canada." *Journal of Labor Economics, 17*: 724–56.

Baldock, C.V. 2000. "Migrants and Their Parents: Caregiving from a Distance." *Journal of Family Issues* 21: 205–24.

Baldwin, B. 2006. "A Shaky Third Pillar: The Vulnerability of Retirement Incomes." In L. O. Stone, ed., *New Frontiers of Research on Retirement,* 383–406. Ottawa: Minister of Industry. Statistics Canada. Catalogue No. 75-511-XIE.

Ballantyne, P.J., and V.W. Marshall. 1995. "Wealth and the Life Course." In V.W. Marshall, J.A. McMullin, P.J. Ballantyne, J. Daciuk, and B.T. Wigdor, eds.,

Contributions to Independence over the Adult Life Course, 49–83. Toronto: Centre for Studies of Aging, University of Toronto.

Baltes, P.B. 1992. "Wise, and Otherwise." *Natural History* (February): 50–51.

Baltes, P.B. 1993. "Aging Mind: Potential and Limits." *Gerontologist* 33(5): 580–94.

Baltes, P.B. 1997. "On the Incomplete Architecture of Human Ontogeny: Selection, Optimization, and Compensation as Foundations of Developmental Theory." *American Psychologist* 52: 366–80.

Baltes, P.B., and K.W. Schaie. 1982. "Aging and IQ—The Myth of the Twilight Years." In Steven H. Zarit, ed., *Readings in Aging and Death: Contemporary Perspectives*, 2nd ed., 97–101. New York: Harper and Row.

Baltes, P.B., J. Smith, U.M. Staudinger, and D. Sowarka. 1990. "Wisdom: One Facet of Successful Aging?" In M. Perlmutter, ed., *Late Life Potential*, 63–81. Washington, DC: Gerontological Society of America.

Banks, M.R., and W.A. Banks. 2002. "Effects of Animal-Assisted Therapy on Loneliness in an Elderly Population in Long-Term Care Facilities." *Journals of Gerontology Series A* 57(7): 428–32.

Banks, W.A., and M.R. Banks. 2003. "Putting More Heart in the Nursing Home: What We Learned from the Dogs." *Geriatrics and Aging* 6(2): 66.

Banks, M., P. Gonser, and W. Banks. 2001. "Animal Assisted Therapy in the Treatment of Loneliness in Long-Term Care Facility Residents." *The Gerontologist* 57A(7): M428–M432.

Barer, M.L., R.G. Evans, and C. Hertzman. 1995. "Avalance or Glacier?: Health Care and the Demographic Rhetoric." *Canadian Journal on Aging* 14(2): 193–224.

Barer, M.L., R.B. Evans, C. Hertzman, and J. Lomas. 1986. "Toward Efficient Aging: Rhetoric and Evidence." Paper prepared for presentation at the 3rd Canadian Conference on Health Economics, Winnipeg.

Barer, M.L., C. Hertzman, R. Miller, and M.V.B. Pascall. 1992. "On Being Old and Sick: The Burden of Health Care for the Elderly in Canada and the United States." *Journal of Health Politics, Policy, and Law* 17(4): 163–82.

Barrett, A.E., and S.M. Lynch. 1999. "Caregiving Networks of Elderly Persons: Variations by Marital Status." *Gerontologist* 39(6): 695–704.

Bass, S.A., and F.G. Caro. 1996. "The Economic Value of Grandparent Assistance." *Generations* 20(1): 29–38.

Bassett, R., V. Bourbonnais, and I. McDowell. (2007). "Living Long and Keeping Well: Elderly Canadians Account for Success in Aging. *Canadian Journal on Aging* 26(2): 113–26.

Basting, A. 2003. "Reading the Story behind the Story: Context and Content in Stories by People with Dementia." *Generations* 23(3): 25–29.

Battle, K. 1997. "Pension Reform in Canada." *Canadian Journal on Aging* 16(3): 519–52.

Baumbusch, J.L. 2004. "Unclaimed Treasures: Older Women's Reflections on Lifelong Singlehood." *Journal of Women and Aging*, 16(1–2): 105–21.

Baumgarten, M., P. Lebel, H. Laprise, C. Leclerc, and C. Quinn. 2002. "Adult Day Care for the Frail Elderly: Outcomes, Satisfaction, and Cost." *Journal of Aging and Health* 14(2): 237–59.

Bayer K. 2005. "Cosmetic Surgery and Cosmetics: Redefining the Appearance of Age." *Generations* 29(3): 13–18.

BC Housing. 2008. "Shelter Aid for Elderly Renters." http://www.bchousing.org/programs/SAFER, accessed December 16, 2008.

Beaujot, R., and K. McQuillan. 1982. *Growth and Dualism: The Demographic Development of Canadian Society.* Toronto: Gage.

Beaulaurier, R.L., L.R. Seff, F.L. Newman, and B. Dunlop. 2007. "External Barriers to Help Seeking for Older Women Who Experience Intimate Partner Violence," *Journal of Family Violence* 22: 747–55.

Beaulieu, M., S. Gravel, and M. Lithwick. 1999. "Older Adult Mistreatment: Dynamics in Personal Relationships." *Gerontology Research Centre News* (Simon Fraser University), February.

Beaupré, P., P. Turcotte, and A. Milan. 2006ba. "Junior Comes Back Home: Trends and Predictors of Returning to the Parental Home." *Canadian Social Trends* (Winter): 28–34. Statistics Canada. Cat. #11-008.

Beaupré, P., P. Turcotte, and A. Milan. 2006ab. "When Is Junior Moving Out? Transitions from the Parental Home to Independence." *Canadian Social Trends* (Winter): 9–15. Statistics Canada, Cat. #11-008.

Beausoleil, N., and G. Martin. 2002. "Activité physique, santé et vieillissement chez des femmes francophones de l'Ontario." *Canadian Journal on Aging* 21(3): 443–54.

Beck, M., D. Glick, J. Gordon, and L. Picker. 1991. *Newsweek,* November 11, 60–63.

Becker, B. 2001. "Challenging 'Ordinary Pain': Narratives of Older People Who Live with Pain." In G. Kenyon, P. Clark, and B. de Vries, eds., *Narrative Gerontology: Theory, Research, and Practice,* 91–112. New York: Springer.

Béland, D. 2004. *Pension Reform and Financial Investment in the United States and Canada.* SEDAP Research Paper No.120. Hamilton, ON: McMaster University.

Béland, D., and J. Myles. 2003. *Stasis Amidst Change: Canadian Pension Reform in an Age of Retrenchment.* SEDAP Research Paper No. 111. Hamilton, ON: McMaster University.

Béland, F. 1987. "Living Arrangement Preferences among Elderly People." *Gerontologist* 27: 797–803.

Béland, F., and E. Shapiro. 1994. "Ten Provinces in Search of a Long Term Care Policy." In V. Marshall and B. McPherson, eds., *Aging: Canadian Perspectives,* 245–67. Peterborough, ON: Broadview Press.

Belanger, A., L. Martel, J-M. Bertholet, R. Wilkins. 2002. "Gender Differences in Disability-Free Life Expectancy for Selected Risk Factors and Chronic Conditions in Canada." *Journal of Women & Aging* 14(1/2): 61–83.

Bengtson, V.L., E.O. Burgess, and T.M. Parrott. 1997. "Theory, Explanation, and a Third Generation of Theoretical Development in Social Gerontology." *Journals of Gerontology Series B* 52(2): S72–88.

Bengtson, V.L., and J.A. Kuypers. 1971. "Generational Differences and the Developmental Stake." *International Journal of Aging and Human Development* 2: 249–60.

Bengtson, V.L., C.J. Rice, and M.L. Johnson. 1999. "Are Theories of Aging Important? Models and Explanations in Gerontology at the Turn of the Century." In V.L. Bengtson and K.W. Shaie, eds., *Handbook of Theories of Aging,* 3–20. New York: Springer Publishing.

Bengtson, V.L., and K.W. Schaie, eds. 1999. *Handbook of Theories of Aging.* New York: Springer.

Benoit, C.M. 2000. *Women, Work and Social Rights.* Scarborough, ON: Prentice Hall Allyn and Bacon Canada.

Bennett, K.M. 2007. "No Sissy Stuff": Towards a Theory of Masculinity and Emotional Expression in Older Widowed Men. *Journal of Aging Studies* 21: 347–356.

Berger, E.D., and Denton, M.A. 2004. "The Interplay between Women's Life Course Work Patterns and Financial Planning for Later Life." *Canadian Journal on Aging* 23(Supplement1): S99-S113.

Berger, P.L., and T. Luckmann. 1966. *The Social Construction of Reality.* New York: Doubleday.

Bergob, M. 2004. "Drug Use among Senior Canadians." Statistics Canada, http://www.statcan.ca/english/ads/11-008-XIE/drugs.html, accessed August 4, 2004.

Berkner, Lutz. 1972. "The Stem Family and the Development Cycle of the Peasant Household: An Eighteenth-Century Austrian Example." *American Historical Review* 77: 398–418.

Berman, L., and I. Sobkowska-Ashcroft. 1986. "The Old in Language and Literature." *Language and Communication* 6: 139–45.

Berman, L., and I. Sobkowska-Ashcroft. 1987. *Images and Impressions of Old Age in the Great Works of Western Literature (700 b.c.–1900 a.d.).* Lewiston, NY: Edwin Mellen Press.

Bernard, A., and C. Li. 2006. *Death of a Spouse: The Impact on Income for Senior Men and Women.* Statistics Canada. Ottawa: Minister of Industry.

Bess, I. 1999a. "Seniors behind the Wheel." *Canadian Social Trends* (Autumn): 2–7.

Bess, I. 1999b. "Widows Living Alone." *Canadian Social Trends* (Summer): 2–5.

Bhat, A.K., and R. Dhruvarajan. 2001. "Ageing in India: Drifting Intergenerational Relations, Challenges and Options." *Ageing and Society* 21(Part 5): 621–40.

Bieman, C.S., and R.E. Bouchard. 1998. "Age-Biased Interpretation of Memory Successes and Failures in Adulthood." *Journals of Gerontology Series B* 53(2): P105–P111.

Biggs, Simon, J. Hendricks, and A. Lowenstein. 2003. "The Need for Theory in Gerontology: Introduction." In J. Simon Biggs, Ariela Lowenstein, and Jon Hendricks, eds., *The Need for Theory: Critical Approaches to Social Gerontology,* 1–12. Amityville, New York: Baywood Publishing Company.

Binstock, R.H. 2005. "Old-Age Policies, Politics, and Ageism." *Generations 29(3):* 73–78.

Birren, J.E. and K.W. Schaie, eds. 2006. *Handbook of the Psychology of Aging,* 6th edition. Burlington, MA: Elsevier Academic Press.

Black, C., N.P. Roos, B. Havens, and L. MacWilliam. 1995. "Rising Use of Physician Services by the Elderly: The Contribution of Morbidity." *Canadian Journal on Aging* 14(2): 225–44.

Blackwell, T. 2002. "Ottawa to Test Safety Devices for Elderly Drivers." *National Post,* September 17, A8.

Blakeney, M. 1992. "Canadians in Subsidized Housing." *Canadian Social Trends* (Winter): 20–24.

Blanchard-Fields, F., and R.P. Abeles. 1996. "Social Cognition and Aging." In J.E. Birren, and K.W. Schaie, eds., *Handbook of the Psychology of Aging,* 4th ed., 159–61. San Diego: Academic Press.

Blandford, A.A., and N.L. Chappell. 1990. "Subjective Well-Being among Native and Non-Native Elderly Persons: Do Differences Exist?" *Canadian Journal on Aging* 9: 386–99.

Blaser, C.J. 1998. "The Case against Paid Family Caregivers: Ethical and Practical Issues." *Generations* 22(3): 65–69.

Blau, Z.S. 1973. *Old Age in a Changing Society.* New York: New Viewpoints.

Blouin, M. 1995. "Care-in-Dying: A Call to Action." *Catholic Health Association of Canada Review* 23(1): 23.

Boaz, R.F., J. Hu, and Y. Ye. 1999. "The Transfer of Resources from Middle-Aged Children to Functionally Limited Elderly Parents: Providing Time, Giving Money, Sharing Space." *Gerontologist* 39(6): 648–57.

Bocksnick, J.G., and B.L. Hall. 1994. "Recreation Activity Programming for the Institutionalized Older Adult." *Activities, Adaptation and Aging* 19(1): 1–25.

Bolger, Joe. 1980. "Bill C-12 and the Debate over Public Service Pension Indexing." Unpublished master's essay. Ottawa: Carleton University.

Boon, S.D., and Shaw, M.J. 2007. "Grandchildren's perceptions of grandparents' health: Worries and impact on their own lives." *Journal of Intergenerational Relationships,* 5(1): 57–78.

Bond, J.B. Jr., R. Cuddy, G.L. Dixon, K.A. Duncan, and D.L. Smith. 1999. "Financial Abuse of Mentally Incompetent Older Adults: A Canadian Study." *Journal of Elder Abuse and Neglect* 11(4): 23–38.

Bond, J.B., Jr., R.L. Penner, and P. Yellen. 1995. "Perceived Effectiveness of Legislation Concerning Abuse of the Elderly: A Survey of Professionals in Canada and the United States." *Canadian Journal on Aging* 14 (Suppl. 2): 118–35.

Boon, S.D., and M.J. Brussoni. 1998. "Popular Images of Grandparents: Examining Young Adults' Views of Their Closest Grandparents." *Personal Relationships* 5: 105–19.

Borell, K., and Ghazanfareeon Karlsson, S. 2003. Reconceptualizing Intimacy and Ageing: Living Apart Together. In S. Arber, K. Davidson, and J. Ginn, eds., *Gender and Ageing: Changing Roles and Relationships,* 47–62. Maidenhead, UK: Open University Press.

Borovoy, A. 1982. "Guardianship and Civil Liberties." *Health Law in Canada* 3(3): 51–52.

Botwinick, J. 1984. *Aging and Behavior,* 3rd ed. New York: Springer.

Bourque, Paul, Joëlle Dionne, and Sarah Pakzad. 2006. "La douleur arthritique, les limites et les inca-pacitiés fonctionnelles chez les personnes âgées." *Canadian Journal on Aging* 25(4): 401–12.

Bourque, P., D. Pushkar, L. Bonneville, and F. Beland. 2005. "Contextual Effects on Life Satisfaction of Older Men and Women." *Canadian Journal on Aging* 24(1): 31–44.

Bowd, A.D. 2003. "Stereotypes of Elderly Persons in Narrative Jokes." *Research on Aging* 25(1): 22–23.

Bowles, N.L., and L.W. Poon. 1982. "An Analysis of the Effect of Aging on Memory." *Journal of Gerontology* 37(2): 212–19.

Boyd, M., and D. Norris. 1999. "The Crowded Nest: Young Adults at Home." *Canadian Social Trends* (Spring): 2–5.

Brandl, B. 2000. "Power and Control: Understanding Domestic Abuse in Later Life." *Generations* 24: 39–45.

Braun, P., and R. Sweet. 1983–84. "Passages: Fact or Fiction?" *International Journal of Aging and Human Development* 18(3): 161–76.

Bravo, G., M-F. Dubois, M. Charpentier, P. De Wals, and A. Emond. 1999. "Quality of Care in Unlicensed Homes for the Aged in the Eastern Townships of Quebec." *Canadian Medical Association Journal* 160(10): 1441–48.

Bravo, Gina, Michael Gagnon, Sheila Wildeman, David T. Marshall, Mariane Pâquet, and Marie-France Dubois. 2005. "Comparison of Provincial and Territorial Legislation Governing Substitute

Consent for Research." *Canadian Journal on Aging* 24(3): 237–249.

Bravo, G., P. Gauthier, P.M. Roy, H. Payette, and P. Gaulin. 1996. "Comparison of Group- versus a Home-Based Exercise Program in Osteopenic Women." *Journal of Aging and Physical Activity* 4(2): 51–64.

Breytspraak, L.M. 1995. "The Development of Self in Later Life." In M. Novak, ed., *Aging and Society: A Canadian Reader*, 92–103. Toronto: Nelson Canada.

Brillon, Y. 1992. "Editorial: The 'Right' to Age in an Institution." *Canadian Journal on Aging* 12(1): 7–11.

Brimacombe, C.A.E., Q. Nyla, N. Nance, and L. Garrioch. 1997. "Is Age Irrelevant? Perceptions of Young and Old Adult Eyewitnesses." *Law and Human Behavior* 21(6): 619–34.

Bringle, R.G., & Kremer, J.F. 1993. "Evaluation of an intergenerational service learning project for undergraduates." *Educational Gerontology, 19*(5): 407–416.

Brink, S. 2001. "Digital Divide or Digital Dividend? Ensuring Benefits to Seniors from Information Technology." In J. Jessome, C. Parks, and M. MacLellan, eds., *Seniors and Technology*, 19–32. Cat. No. 0-662-30932-4. Ottawa: Minister of Public Works and Government Services Canada.

British Columbia. 1996. *Health Care (Consent) and Care Facility (Admission) Act.* Revised Statutes and Consolidated Regulations of British Columbia. Victoria: Queen's Printer. http://www.qp.gov.bc.ca/statreg/stat/H/96181_01.htm, accessed May 6, 2009.

Brockmann, H., and T. Klein. 2004. " Love and Death In Germany: The Marital Biography and Its Effect on Mortality." *Journal of Marriage and Family* 66(3): 567–581.

Brody, E.M. 1981. "'Women in the Middle' and Family Help to Older People." *Gerontologist* 18: 471–80.

Brody, E.M. 1990. *Women in the Middle: Their Parent-Care Years.* New York: Springer.

Bronnum-Hansen, H., and K. Juel. 2001. "Abstention from Smoking Extends Life and Compresses Morbidity: A Population-Based Study of Health Expectancy among Smokers and Never Smokers in Denmark." *Tobacco Control* 10(3): 273–78.

Bronowski, J. 1976. *The Ascent of Man.* London: BBC Publishing.

Brotman, S. 1998. "The Incidence of Poverty among Seniors in Canada: Exploring the Impact of Gender, Ethnicity, and Race." *Canadian Journal on Aging* 17(2): 166–85.

Brotman, S., B. Ryan, S. Collins, L. Chamberland, R. Cormier, D. Julien, E. Meyer, A. Peterkin, and B. Richard. 2007. "Coming out to Care: Caregivers of Gay and Lesbian Seniors in Canada." *The Gerontologist* 47(4): 490–503.

Brotman, S., B. Ryan, and R. Cormier. 2002. "Mental Health Issues of Particular Groups: Gay and Lesbian Seniors." In *Writings in Gerontology: Mental Health and Aging*, 56–67. Cat. No. H71-2/1-18-2002E. Ottawa: Minister of Public Works and Government Services Canada.

Brown, R.L. 1995. "Security for Social Security—Raise the Age of Entitlement?" In E.M. Gee and G.M. Gutman, eds., *Rethinking Retirement*, 69–73. Vancouver: Gerontology Research Centre, Simon Fraser University.

Browne, A., M. Blake, M. Donnelly, and D. Herbert. 2002. "On Liberty for the Old." *Canadian Journal on Aging* 21(2): 283–93.

Brugman, G. M. 2006. "Wisdom and Aging." In In J.E. Birren and K.W. Schaie, eds., *Handbook of the Psychology of Aging*, 6th ed., 445–76. Burlington, MA: Elsevier Academic Press.

Bryant, T., P. McGowan, I. Brown, D. Raphael, T. Cogan, L. Richard, C. Dallaire, L. Thompson, S. Laforest, and J. Young. 2004. "What do Canadian Seniors Say Supports their Quality of Life? Findings from a National Participatory Research Study." *Canadian Journal of Public Health* 95(4): 299–303.

Bryden, K. 1974. *Old Age Pensions and Policy-Making in Canada.* Montreal: McGill-Queen's University Press.

Buchignani, N., and C. Armstrong-Esther. 1999. "Informal Care and Older Native Canadians." *Ageing and Society* 19(1): 3–32.

Buckley, N.J., F.T. Denton, A.L. Robb, and B.G. Spencer, B.G. 2005. *Socioeconomic Influences on the Health of Older Canadians: Estimates Based on Two Longitudinal Surveys.* Social and Economic Dimensions of an Aging Population. SEDAP Research Paper No. 139. Hamilton, ON: McMaster University.

Bugos, J.A., W.M. Perlstein, C.S. McCrae, T.S. Brophy, and P.H.Bedenbaugh. 2007. "Individualized Piano Instruction Enhances Executive Functioning and

Working Memory in Older Adults." *Aging and Mental Health 11(4)*, 464–71.

Burke, M.A. 1991. "Implications of an Aging Society." *Canadian Social Trends* (Spring): 6–8.

Burke, M.A., J. Lindsay, I. McDowell, and G. Hill. 1997. "Dementia among Seniors." *Canadian Social Trends* (Summer): 24–27.

Burton, A.M., W.E. Haley, and B.J. Small. 2006. "Bereavement After Caregiving or Unexpected Death: Effects on Elderly Spouses." *Aging and Mental Health 10*(3): 319–26.

Burtless, Gary and Joseph Quinn. 2001. "Retirement Trends and Policies to Encourage Work among Older Americans." In Peter Budetti, Richard Burkhauser, Janice Gregory and H. Allan Hunt, eds., *Ensuring Health and Income Security for an Aging Workforce*, 375–416. Kalamazoo, MI: Upjohn Institute.

Butler, R.N. 1969. "Age-ism: Another Form of Bigotry." *Gerontologist* 9: 243–46.

Butler, R.N. 1975. *Why Survive? Being Old in America.* New York: Harper and Row.

Butler, R.N. 1993. "Dispelling Ageism: The Cross-Cutting Intervention." *Generations* 17(2): 75–78.

Butler, R.N., and M.I. Lewis. 1976. *Sex after 60: A Guide for Men and Women for Their Later Years.* New York: Harper and Row.

Byszewski, A. 2002. "Driving and Dementia: A Toolkit to Assist Physicians in Dealing with the Issue." *Geriatrics and Aging* 5(4): 68–73.

Cairney, J. 2000. "Socio-Economic Status and Self-Rated Health among Older Canadians." *Canadian Journal on Aging* 19(4): 456–78.

Calasanti, T.M. 1988. "Participation in a Dual Economy and Adjustment to Retirement." *International Journal of Aging and Human Development* 26: 13–27.

Calasanti, T. 2004a. "Feminist Gerontology and Old Men." *Journal of Gerontology: Social Sciences* 59B(6): S305–S314.

Calasanti, T. 2004b. "New Directions in Feminist Gerontology: An Introduction." *Journal of Aging Studies* 18(1): 1–8.

Calasanti T. 2005. "Ageism, Gravity, and Gender: Experiences of Aging Bodies." *Generations* 29(3): 8–12.

Calasanti, T., and M.E. Bowen, 2006. "Spousal Caregiving and Crossing Gender Boundaries: Maintaining Gendered Identities." *Journal of Aging Studies* 20: 253–63.

Calasanti, T., and K.J. Kiecolt. 2007. "Diversity among Late-Life Couples." *Generations 31*(3): 10–17.

Calasanti, T.M., and K.F. Slevin. 2001. *Gender, Social Inequalities, and Aging.* Walnut Creek, CA: AltaMira Press.

Callahan, J.J. 1986. "Guest Editor's Perspective." *Pride Institute Journal of Long-Term Home Health Care* 5: 2–3.

Campbell, L.D. 2002. "Men Who Care: Exploring the Male Experience of Filial Caregiving." Paper presented at the International Symposium Reconceptualising Gender and Ageing, University of Surrey, Guildford, U.K., June 25–27.

Campbell, L.D., and M.P. Carroll. 2007. "The Incomplete Revolution: Theorizing Gender When Studying Men Who Provide Care to Aging parents." *Men and Masculinities* 9(4): 491–508.

Campbell, L.D., I.A. Connidis, and L. Davies. 1999. "Sibling Ties in Later Life: A Social Network Analysis." *Journal of Family Issues* 20(1): 114–48.

Campbell, L.D., and A. Martin-Matthews. 2000a. "Caring Sons: Exploring Men's Involvement in Filial Care." *Canadian Journal on Aging* 19(1): 57–79.

Campbell, L.D., and A. Martin-Matthews. 2000b. "Primary and Proximate: The Importance of Coresidence and Being Primary Provider of Care for Men's Filial Care Involvement." *Journal of Family Issues* 21(8): 1006–30.

Campbell, L.D., and A. Martin-Matthews. 2003. "The Gendered Nature of Men's Filial Care." *Journals of Gerontology Series B* 58(6): S350–58.

Campbell, S. 2004. "Defining Information Literacy in the 21st Century." Paper presented at the World Library and Information Congress: 70th IFLA General Conference and Council, Buenos Aires, Argentina, August 22–27, 2004.

Campolieti, M. 2001. "Disability Insurance and the Labour Force Participation of Older Men and Women in Canada." *Canadian Public Policy* 27(2): 179–94.

Canada. 1984. *Canada Health Act,* R.S.C. 1985, c. C-6. Ottawa: Queen's Printer. http:// www.laws.justice. gc.ca/en/C-6/index.html, accessed August 4, 2004.

Canada Coordinating Committee. 1999. *Canada, a Society for All Ages.* Ottawa: Canada Coordinating Committee.

Canada Mortgage and Housing Corporation. 2002a. "Housing Conditions of Women and Girls, and Female-Led Households." *Research Highlights.* Special Studies on 1996 Census Data, Socio-Economic Series, Issue 55-9. http://www.cmhc-schl.gc.ca/publications/ en/rh-pr/socio/socio055-9-e.pdf, accessed on December 7, 2003.

Canada Mortgage and Housing Corporation. 2002b. "Housing the Boom, Bust and Echo Generations." *Research Highlights.* Special Studies on 1996 Census Data, Socio-Economic Series, Issue 77. http://www.cmhc-schl.gc.ca/ publications/en/rh-pr/socio/socio77-e.pdf, accessed December 7, 2003.

Canada Mortgage and Housing Corporation. 2002c. "Seniors' Housing Conditions." *Research Highlights.* Special Studies on 1996 Census Data, Socio-Economic Series, Issue 55-8. http://www.cmhc-schl.gc.ca/publications/en/rh-pr/socio/socio055-8e.pdf, accessed December 7, 2003.

Canada Mortgage and Housing Corporation. 2003a. "Housing Needs of Low-Income People Living in Rural Areas: Literature Review." *Research Highlights.* Socio-Economic Series 03-023. http://www.cmhc-schl.gc.ca/odpub/pdf/63352.pdf, accessed May 7, 2009.

Canada Mortgage and Housing Corporation. 2003b. "Housing Needs of Low-Income People Living in Rural Areas." *Research Highlights.* Socio-Economic Series 116. http://www.cmhc-schl.gc.ca/odpub/pdf/63119.pdf, accessed May 7, 2009.

Canada Mortgage and Housing Corporation. 2003c. "Housing Options for Elderly or Chronically Ill Shelter Users." *Research Highlights.* Socio-Economic Series 03-019. http://www.cmhc-schl.gc.ca/publications/en/ rh-pr/socio/socio03-019-e.pdf, accessed December 6, 2003.

Canada Mortgage and Housing Corporation. 2003d. "Improving Quality and Affordabiity: Flexhousing." http://www.cmhc-schl.gc.ca/en/imquaf/flho/index.cfm, accessed December 6, 2003.

Canada Mortgage and Housing Corporation. 2005a. "2001 Census Housing Series: Issue 9 Revised: The Housing Conditions of Canada's Seniors." *Research Highlights.* Socio-Economic Series 05-020. http://www.cmhc-schl.gc.ca/odpub/pdf/63820.pdf, accessed May 7, 2009.

Canada Mortgage and Housing Corporation. 2005b. "A Legal Framework for Supportive Housing for Seniors: Options for Canadian Policy Makers." *Research Highlight*s. Socio-Economic Series 05-020.

http://www.cmhc-schl.gc.ca/odpub/pdf/63975.pdf, accessed May 7, 2009.

Canada Mortgage and Housing Corporation. 2006a. "2001 Census Housing Series. Issue 10. Aging, Residential Mobility and Housing Choices." *Research Highlights.* Socio-Economic Series 06-001. http://www.cmhc-schl.gc.ca/odpub/pdf/64992.pdf, accessed May 7, 2009.

Canada Mortgage and Housing Corporation. 2006b. "Senior Housing for Seniors: A Feasibility Study." *Research Highlights.* Socio-Economic Series 06-023. http://www.cmhc-schl.gc.ca/odpub/pdf/65308.pdf, accessed May 7, 2009.

Canada Mortgage and Housing Corporation. 2007. "Supportive Housing for Homeless and Hard-to-House Seniors: An In-Depth Case Study." *Research Highlights.* Socio-Economic Series 07-017. http://www.cmhc-schl.gc.ca/odpub/pdf/65672.pdf, accessed May 7, 2009.

Canada Mortgage and Housing Corporation. 2008a. "Impacts of the Aging of the Canadian Population on Housing and Communities." *Research Highlights.* Socio-Economic Series 08-003. http://www.cmhc-schl.gc.ca/odpub/pdf/65913.pdf, accessed May 7, 2009.

Canada Mortgage and Housing Corporation. 2008b. "Adapting Homes to Extend Independence." *Research Highlights.* Socio-Economic Series 08-009. http://www.cmhc-schl.gc.ca/odpub/pdf/66004.pdf, accessed May 7, 2009.

Canada Mortgage and Housing Corporation. 2008c. "About Your House—General Series: Garden Suites." http://www.cmhc.ca/en/co/renoho/refash/refash_026.cfm, accessed May 7, 2009.

Canada Mortgage and Housing Corporation. 2008d. "Residential Rehabilitation Assistance Program (RRAP)—Conversion." http://www.cmhc-schl.gc.ca/en/co/prfinas/prfinas_009.cfm, accessed May 7, 2009.

Canada Mortgage and Housing Corporation. 2008e. "CHS—Public Funds and *National Housing Act* (Social Housing) 2007." http://www.cmhc-schl.gc.ca/odpub/esub/64689/64689_2008_ A0l.pdf, accessed May 7, 2009.

Canada Mortgage and Housing Corporation. 2008f. "Life Leases." http://www.cmhc-schl.gc.ca/en/inpr/afhoce/tore/afhoid/fite/lile/index.cfm, accessed May 7, 2009.

Canada Mortgage and Housing Corporation. 2008g. "Designing Flexible Housing." http://www.cmhc-schl.gc.ca/en/inpr/afhoce/tore/afhoid/cohode/deflho/index.cfm, accessed May 7, 2009.

Canada Mortgage and Housing Corporation. 2008h. "Reverse Mortgages." http://www.cmhc-schl.gc.ca/en/inpr/afhoce/tore/afhoid/fite/remo/index.cfm, accessed May 7, 2009.

Canada Revenue Agency. 2008. *How Much Can I Contribute*? http://www.cra-arc.gc.ca/tax/individuals/topics/rrsp/contributing/limits-e.html, accessed March 1, 2008.

Canadian Association of University Teachers. 1991. "Mandatory Retirement." *CAUT Bulletin* 38: 1–5.

Canadian Council on Social Development. 1999. "Social Spending across the Life Course: Summary Report." http://www.ccsd.ca/pubs/hc/spend.htm, accessed July 26, 2004.

Canadian Council on Social Development. 2008. "Stats and Facts: A Profile of Economic Security in Canada."http://www.ccsd.ca/factsheets/economic_security/poverty/index.htm accessed May 7, 2009.

Canadian Healthcare Association (CHA). 2004. *Stitching the Patchwork Quilt Together: Facility-Based Long-Term Care within Continuing Care—Realities and Recommendations.* Ottawa: CHA.

Canadian Institute for Health Information. 2003. *National Health Expenditure Trends, 1975–2003.* Ottawa: Canadian Institute for Health Information.

Canadian Institute for Health Information. 2008. *Number of Physicians by Province/Territory, Canada, 2006 (Figure).* http://www. secure.cihi.ca/cihiweb/dispPage.jsp?cw_page=statistics_a_z_e#P, accessed May 7, 2009.

Canadian Medical Association. 1995. "Policy Summary: Joint Statement on Resuscitative Intervention (Update 1995)." *Canadian Medical Association Journal* 153(11): 1652a–52c.

Canadian Study of Health and Aging Working Group. 1994. "Canadian Study of Health and Aging: Study Methods and Prevalence of Dementia." *Canadian Medical Association Journal* 150(6): 899–913.

Cantor, M.H., and V. Little. 1985. "Aging and Social Care." In R.H. Binstock and E. Shanas, eds., *Handbook of Aging and the Social Sciences*, 745–81. New York: Van Nostrand Reinhold.

Carey, B., and A. Yamada. 2002. *Getting Older, Getting Poorer? A Study of the Earnings, Pensions, Assets, and Living Arrangements of Older People in Nine Countries.* Labour Market and Social Policy Occasional Paper No. 60. Paris: Organization for Economic Co-operation and Development.

Caron, C.D., F. Ducharme, and J. Griffith. 2006. "Deciding on Institutionalization for a Relative with Dementia: The Most Difficult Decision for Caregivers." *Canadian Journal on Aging* 25(2): 193–205.

Carpentier, N., and F. Ducharme. 2007. "Social Network Data Validity: The Example of the Social Network of Caregivers of Older Persons with Alzheimer-type Dementia." *Canadian Journal on Aging,* 26(supplement 1): 103–116.

Carr, D. 2004a. "Gender, Preloss Marital Dependence, and Older Adults' Adjustment to Widowhood." *Journal of Marriage and Family* 66(1): 220–35.

Carr, D. 2004b. "The Desire to Date and Remarry among Older Widows and Widowers." *Journal of Marriage and Family* 66(4): 1051–68.

Carrière, Y. 2000. "The Impact of Population Aging and Hospital Days: Will There Be a Problem?" In E.M. Gee and G.M. Gutman, eds., *The Overselling of Population Aging: Apocalyptic Demography, Intergenerational Challenges, and Social Policy,* 26–44. Don Mills, ON: Oxford University Press.

Carroll, M., and L.D. Campbell. 2008. "Who Now Reads Parsons and Bales?: Casting a Critical Eye on the "Gendered Styles of Caregiving" Literature." *Journal of Aging Studies* 22: 24–31.

Carstensen, L.L., J.A. Mikels, and M. Mather. 2006. "Aging and the Intersection of Cognition, Motivation, and Emotion." In J.E. Birren and K.W. Schaie, eds., *Handbook of the Psychology of Aging*, 6th ed., 343–62. Burlington, MA: Elsevier Academic Press.

Cattan, M., M. White, J. Bond, and A. Learmouth. 2005. "Preventing Social Isolation and Loneliness Among Older People: A Systematic Review of Health Promotion Interventions." *Aging and Society* 25(1): 41–67.

Cavanaugh, J.C. 1983. "Comprehension and Retention of Television Programs by 20- and 60-Year Olds." *Journal of Gerontology* 38: 190–96.

Cerella, J. 1990. "Aging and Information-Processing Rate." In J.E. Birren and K.W. Schaie, eds., *Handbook of the Psychology of Aging*, 3rd ed., 201–22. San Diego: Academic Press.

CFLRI (Canadian Fitness and Lifestyle Research Institute). 2004. *Physical Activity Monitor.* Ottawa: CFLRI. http://www.cflri.ca/pdf/e/2004pam.pdf, accessed May 7, 2009.

Chalmers, L. and A. Milan. 2005. "Marital Satisfaction During the Retirement Years." *Canadian Social Trends,* (Spring): 14–17.

Chan, C.G., and G.H. Elder, Jr. 2000. "Matrilineal Advantage in Grandchild–Grandparent Relations." *Gerontologist* 40(2): 179–90.

Chan, L. 2003. "Is Spirituality Healthful?" *Wellness Options* 4(12): 26–27.

Chan, P., and S.R. Kenny. 2001. "National Consistency and Provincial Diversity in Delivery of Long-Term Care in Canada." *Journal of Aging and Social Policy* 13(2–3): 83–99.

Chapman, S.A. 2005. "Theorizing About Aging Well: Constructing a Narrative." *Canadian Journal on Aging* 24(1): 9–18.

Chappell, N.L. 1997. *National Respite Project: Evaluation Report.* Victoria: Centre on Aging, University of Victoria.

Chappell, N.L. 1999a. "Director's Perspective." *Centre on Aging Bulletin* 7(2): 1–3.3. Centre on Aging, University of Victoria.

Chappell, N.L. 1999b. "Editorial: Canadian Association on Gerontology Policy Statement on Home Care in Canada." *Canadian Journal on Aging* 18(3): i–iii.

Chappell, N.L. 2005. "Perceived Change in Quality of Life Among Chinese Canadian Seniors: The Role of Involvement in Chinese Culture." *Journal of Happiness Studies* 6: 69–91.

Chappell, N.L., and M.J. Penning. 1979. "The Trend Away from Institutionalization: Humanism or Economic Efficiency?" *Research on Aging* 1: 361–87.

Chappell, N.L., and R.C. Reid. 2002. "Burden and Well-Being among Caregivers: Examining the Distinction." *Gerontologist* 42(6): 772–80.

Chappell, N.L., R.C. Reid, and E. Dow. 2001. "Respite Reconsidered: A Typology of Meanings Based on the Caregiver's Point of View." *Journal of Aging Studies* 15(2): 201–16.

Chappell, N.L., L.A. Strain, and A.A. Blandford. 1986. *Aging and Health Care: A Social Perspective.* Toronto: Holt, Rinehart, and Winston of Canada.

Chard, J. 1995. "Women in a Visible Minority." In Statistics Canada, *Women in Canada: A Statistical Report*, 3rd ed., 133–46. Cat. No. 89-503E. Ottawa: Minister of Supply and Services.

Chard, J. 2000. "Women in a Visible Minority." In C. Lindsay, ed., *Women in Canada 2000: A Gender-Based Statistical Report*, 219–46. Cat. No. 89-503-XPE. Ottawa: Statistics Canada.

Chard, J., J. Badets., and L.H. Leo. 2000. "Immigrant Women." In C. Lindsay, ed., *Women in Canada 2000: A Gender-Based Statistical Report*, 189–217. Cat. No. 89-503-XPE. Ottawa: Minister Responsible for Statistics Canada.

Charness, N. 1981. "Aging and Skilled Problem Solving." *Journal of Experimental Psychology: General* 110(1): 21–38.

Charness, N. 1985. "Aging and Problem-Solving Performance." In N. Charness, ed., *Aging and Human Performance*, 225–59. Chichester, U.K.: John Wiley and Sons.

Charness, N.H. 1993. "Whither Technology and Aging?" *Gerontology News* (April): 2ff.

Charness, N., and J.I.D. Campbell. 1988. "Acquiring Skill at Mental Calculation in Adulthood: A Task Decomposition." *Journal of Experimental Psychology: General* 117: 115–29.

Chawla, R.K. and T. Wannell. 2004. "Housing Costs of Elderly Families." *Perspectives.* Statistics Canada Catalogue No. 75-001-XIE.

Che-Alford, J., and K. Stevenson. 1998. "Older Canadians on the Move." *Canadian Social Trends* 48: 15–18.

Che-Alford, J., and B. Hamm. 1999. "Under One Roof: Three Generations Living Together." *Canadian Social Trends* (Summer): 6–9.

Cheal, D. 2002. "Introduction: Contextualizing Demographic Concerns." In D. Cheal, ed., *Aging and Demographic Change in Canadian Context*, 3–21. Toronto: University of Toronto Press.

Checkland, D., and M. Silberfeld. 1993. "Competence and the Three A's: Autonomy, Authenticity, and Aging." *Canadian Journal on Aging* 12(4): 453–68.

Chee, Y.K. 2000. "Elder Care in Korea: The Future Is Now." *Ageing International* 26(1/2): 25–37.

Chen, J., and F. Hou. 2002. "Unmet Needs for Health Care." *Health Reports* 13(2): 23–34.

Chen, J., F. Hou, C. Sanmartin, C. Hould, S. Tremblay, and J.M. Berthelot. 2002. "Unmet Health Care Needs." *Canadian Social Trends* (Winter): 18–22.

Chené, A. 1994. "Community-Based Older Learners: Being with Others." *Educational Gerontology* 20: 765–81.

Cherlin, A., and F.F. Furstenberg. 1985. "Styles and Strategies of Grand-Parenting." In V.L. Bengtson and J.F. Robertson, eds., *Grandparenthood*, 97–116. Beverly Hills: Sage.

Chernoff, R. 2002. "Health Promotion for Older Women: Benefits of Nutrition and Exercise Programs." *Topics in Geriatric Rehabilitation* 18(1): 59–67.

Chevan, A. 1996. "As Cheaply as One: Cohabitation in the Older Population." *Journal of Marriage and the Family* 58(3): 656–67.

Chi, I. 2001. "Commentary: Asian Perspectives on Sociological Issues for the Millennium." *Canadian Journal on Aging* 20 (Suppl. 1): 118–24.

Chipperfield, J.G., and B. Havens. 2001. "Gender Differences in the Relationship between Marital Status Transitions and Life Satisfaction in Later Life." *Journals of Gerontology Series B* 56(3): P176–86.

Chipperfield, J.G., B. Havens, and W.D. Doig. 1997. "Method and Description of the Aging in Manitoba Project: A 20-Year Longitudinal Study." *Canadian Journal on Aging* 16(4): 606–25.

Chipperfield, J. G., D. W. Campbell, and R. P. Perry. 2004. "Stability in Perceived Control: Implications for Health among Very Old Community-Dwelling Adults." *Journal of Aging and Health* 16(1): 116–147.

Choi, H. and N.F. Marks. 2008. "Marital conflict, Depressive Symptoms, and Functional Impairment." *Journal of Marriage and Family* 70(2): 377–90.

Chou, P.H.B., and A.V. Wister. 2005. "From Cues to Action: Information Seeking and Exercise Self-Care among Older Adults Managing Chronic Illness." *The Canadian Journal on Aging* 24(4): 395–408.

Chui, T., K. Tran, and H. Maheux. 2007. *Immigration in Canada: A Portrait of the Foreign-born Census Year 2006.* Statistics Canada. Ottawa: Minister of Industry.

Churchill, M., J. Safaoui, B.W. McCabe, and M.M. Baun. 1999. "Using a Therapy Dog to Alleviate the Agitation and Desocialization of People with Alzheimer's Disease." *Journal of Psychosocial Nursing* 37: 16–22.

Cicirelli, V.G. 2002. *Older Adults' Views on Death.* New York: Springer.

CIHR Institute of Aging. 2008. http://www.cihr-irsc. gc.ca/e/8643.html, accessed May 7, 2009.

Clarfield, M. 2002. "Is Old Age a Disease or Just Another of Life's Stages?" *Geriatrics and Aging* 5(1): 58–59.

Clark, D.O., Stump, T.E., & Damush, T.M. (2003). "Outcomes of an exercise program for older women recruited through primary care." *Journal of Aging and Health,* 15(3), 567–85.

Clark, F., A.F. Heller, C. Rafman, and J. Walker. 1997. "Peer Learning: A Popular Model for Seniors' Education." *Educational Gerontology* 23(8): 751–62.

Clark, G.T. 1993. *Personal Meanings of Grief and Bereavement.* Doctoral dissertation. Edmonton: University of Alberta.

Clark, P.G. 1993. "Moral Discourse and Public Policy in Aging: Framing Problems, Seeking Solutions, and 'Public Ethics.'" *Canadian Journal on Aging* 12(4): 485–508.

Clark, W. 2000. "Patterns of Religious Attendance." *Canadian Social Trends* (Winter): 23–26.

Clark, W. 2002. "Time Alone." *Canadian Social Trends* (Autumn): 2–6.

Clark, W. 2003. "Pockets of Belief: Religious Attendance Patterns in Canada." *Canadian Social Trends* (Spring): 2–5.

Clark, W. 2005. "What do Seniors Spend on Housing?" *Canadian Social Trends* (Fall): 2–7.

Clark, W., and S. Crompton, S. 2006. "Till Death Do Us Part? The Risk of First and Second Marriage Dissolution." *Canadian Social Trends* (Summer): 24–34.

Clark, W., and G. Schellenberg. 2006. "Who's Religious?" *Canadian Social Trends* (Summer): 2–9.

Clarke, P., and A. Colantonio. 2005. "Wheelchair Use Among Community-Dwelling Older Adults: Prevalence and Risk Factors in a National Sample." *Canadian Journal on Aging* 24(2): 191–98.

Clarke, P.J., V.W. Marshall, C.D. Ryff, and C.J. Rosenthal. 2000. "Well-Being in Canadian Seniors: Findings from the Canadian Study of Health and Aging." *Canadian Journal on Aging* 19(2): 139–59.

Cohen, C.A., A. Colantonio, and L. Vernich. 2002. "Positive Aspects of Caregiving: Rounding out the Caregiver Experience." *International Journal of Geriatric Psychiatry* 17(2): 184–88.

Cohen, G.D. 1999. "Marriage and Divorce in Later Life: Editorial." *American Journal of Geriatric Psychiatry* 7(3): 185–87.

Cohen, Gene D. 2005. *The Mature Mind: The Positive Power of the Aging Brain.* New York: Basic Books.

Cohen, G.D., S. Perlstein, J. Chapline, J. Kelly, K. M. Firth, and S. Simmens. 2006. "Impact of Professionally Conducted Cultural Programs on the Physical Health, Mental Health, and Social Functioning of Older Adults." *Gerontologist* 46(6): 726–34.

Cohen, Gene D., S. Perlstein, J. Chapline, J.Kelly, K.M. Firth, and S. Simmens. 2007. "Impact of Professionally Conducted Cultural Programs on the Physical Health, Mental Health, and Social Functioning of Older Adults—2-Year Results." *Journal of Aging, Humanities and the Arts*1(1–2), 5–22.

Cohn, R. 1982. "Economic Development and Status Change of the Aged." *American Journal of Sociology* 87: 1150–61.

Colcombe, S.J. and A.F. Kramer. (2003). "Fitness Effects on the Cognitive Function of Older Adults." *Psychological Science* 14:125–30.

Coleman, D., and S.E. Iso-Ahola. 1993. "Leisure and Health: The Role of Social Support and Self-Determination." *Journal of Leisure Research* 25: 111–28.

Collings, P. 2000. "Aging and Life Course Development in an Inuit Community." *Arctic Anthropology* 37(2): 111–25.

Collings, P. 2001. "'If You Got Everything, It's Good Enough': Perspectives on Successful Aging in a Canadian Inuit Community." *Journal of Cross-Cultural Gerontology* 16(2): 127–55.

Colson, E., and T. Scudder. 1981. "Old Age in Gwembe District, Zambia." In P.T. Amoss and S. Harrell, eds., *Other Ways of Growing Old: Anthropological Perspectives*, 125–53. Stanford, CA: Stanford University Press.

Columbia News. 2008. "New MRI Approach Can Identify Sources of Memory Loss in Humans and Mice." http://www.columbia.edu/cu/news/00/12/MRI.html, accessed May 7, 2009.

Comeau, T.D., and C.L. Kemp. 2007. "Intersections of Age and Masculinities in the Information Technology Industry." *Ageing and Society* 27(2): 215–232.

Commission on the Future of Health Care in Canada. 2002. *Building on Values: The Future of Health Care in Canada: Final Report* (Romanow Report). Ottawa: Government of Canada. http://www.hc-sc.gc.ca/english/pdf/care/romanow_e.pdf, accessed July 10, 2003.

Conde, H., and J.T. McDonald. 2007. *The Health Services Use Among Older Canadians in Rural and Urban Areas.* Social and Economic Dimensions of an Aging Population. SEDAP Research Paper No. 178. Hamilton, ON: McMaster University.

Conference of Deputy Ministers of Health. 1999. *Toward a Healthy Future: Second Report on the Health of Canadians.* Ottawa: Government of Canada. http://www.hc-sc.gc.ca/hppb/phdd/report/toward/ index.html, accessed May 7, 2009.

Conn, D.K. 2002. "An Overview of Common Mental Disorders among Seniors." In *Writings in Gerontology: Mental Health and Aging,* 19–31. Ottawa: National Advisory Council on Aging.

Connelly, M.P., and M. MacDonald. 1990. *Women and the Labour Force.* Cat. No. 98-125. Ottawa: Minister of Supply and Services.

Connidis, I.A. 1983. "The Pros, Cons and Worries of Aging." Paper presented at the Canadian Association on Gerontology 12th Annual Scientific and Educational Meeting, Moncton.

Connidis, I.A. 2001. *Family Ties and Aging.* Thousand Oaks, CA: Sage.

Connidis, I.A. 2003. "Bringing Outsiders in: Gay and Lesbian Family Ties over the Life Course." In Arber, S., K. Davidson, and J. Ginn, eds., *Gender and Ageing: Changing Roles and Relationships*, 79–94. Maidenhead, UK: Open University Press.

Connidis, I.A. 2006. "Intimate Relationships: Learning from Later Life Experience." In T. Calasanti and K. Slevin, eds., *Age Matters.* New York: Routledge.

Connidis, I.A., and L.D. Campbell. 1995. "Closeness, Confiding, and Contact among Siblings in Middle and Late Adulthood." *Journal of Family Issues* 16(6): 722–45.

Connidis, I.A., and C.L. Kemp. 2008. "Negotiating Actual and Anticipated Parental Support: Multiple Sibling Voices in Three-Generation Families." *Journal of Aging Studies* 22: 229–38.

Connidis, I.A., and J.A. McMullin. 1999. "Permanent Childlessness: Perceived Advantages and Disadvantages among Older Persons." *Canadian Journal on Aging* 18(4): 447–65.

Connidis, I.A., C.J. Rosenthal, and J.A. McMullin. 1996. "Impact of Family Composition on Providing Help to Older Parents." *Research on Aging* 18(4): 402–29.

Connor, S.R. 1998. *Hospice: Practice, Pitfalls, and Promise.* Washington, DC: Taylor and Fancis.

Conroy, N., M. Lamontagne, L.O. Stone, and P. Moloney. 2006. "Additional topics for future research." In L.O. Stone, ed., *New Frontiers of Research on Retirement*, 429–444. Statistics Canada. Catalogue No. 75-511-XIE. Ottawa: Minister of Industry.

Cooke, M. 2006. "Policy Changes and the Labour Force Participation of Older Workers: Evidence from Six Countries." *Canadian Journal on Aging* 25(4): 387–400.

Cooley, M.E. 2002. "Sex over Sixty." *Expression* 15(2). Ottawa: National Advisory Council on Aging.

Cooney, T., and K. Dunne. 2001. "Intimate Relationships in Later Life, Current Realities, Future Prospects." *Journal of Family Issues* 22(7): 838–58.

Corbeil, J-P. 1995. "Sport Participation in Canada." *Canadian Social Trends* (Spring): 18–23.

Corbett, David (with Richard Higgins). (2007). *Portfolio Life.* San Francisco: John Wiley and Sons.

Cotman, C.W., and N.C. Berchtold. 2002. "Exercise: A Behavioral Intervention to Enhance Brain Health and Plasticity." *Trends in Neuroscience* 25, 295–301.

Cott, C.A., and M.T. Fox. 2001. "Health and Happiness for Elderly Institutionalized Canadians." *Canadian Journal on Aging* 20(4): 527–35.

Cott, C.A., and M.A.M. Gignac. 1999. "Independence and Dependence for Older Adults with Osteoarthritis or Osteoporosis." *Canadian Journal on Aging* 18(1): 1–25.

Council Against Abuse of Older Persons. 2008. http://www.caaop.com/en/what_is_abuse.php, accessed May 7, 2009.

Cousins, S.O. 1993. "Turn of the Century Tomboys: Does Older Women's Efficacy for Late Life Exercise Originate in Childhood?" In E. Beregi, I.A. Gergely, and K. Rajczi, eds., *Recent Advances in Aging Science, 1911–1916.* Bologna: Monduzzi Editore.

Cousins, S.O. 1995. "Social Support for Exercise among Elderly Women in Canada." *Health Promotion International* 10(4): 273–82.

Cousins, S.O. 1996. "Exercise Cognition among Elderly Women." *Journal of Applied Sport Psychology* 8: 131–45.

Cousins, S.O. 1997. "Elderly Tomboys? Sources of Self-Efficacy for Physical Activity in Later Life." *Journal of Aging and Physical Activity* 5(3): 229–43.

Cousins, S.O. 2000. "'My Health Couldn't Take It': Older Women's Beliefs about Exercise Benefits and Risks." *Journals of Gerontology Series B* 55(5): P283–94.

Cousins, S.O. 2001. "Thinking Out Loud: What Older Adults Say about Triggers for Physical Activity." *Journal of Aging and Physical Activity* 9(4): 347–63.

Cousins, S.O., and A. Burgess. 1992. "Perspectives on Older Adults in Physical Activity and Sports." *Educational Gerontology* 18: 461–81.

Cousins, S.O., and N. Keating. 1995. "Life Cycle Patterns of Physical Activity among Sedentary and Active Older Women." *Journal of Aging and Physical Activity* 3: 340–59.

Cowgill, D.O. 1972. "A Theory of Aging in Cross-Cultural Perspective." In D. Cowgill and L. Holmes, eds., *Aging and Modernization*, 1–13. New York: Appleton-Century-Crofts.

Cowgill, D.O. 1974. "Aging and Modernization: A Revision of the Theory." In J.F. Gubrium, ed., *Late Life.* Springfield, IL: Charles C. Thomas.

Cowgill, D.O., and L.D. Holmes, eds. 1972. *Aging and Modernization.* New York: Appleton-Century-Crofts.

Coyte, P.C. 2000. "Home Care in Canada: Passing the Buck." Paper commissioned by the Dialogue on Health Reform. http://www.utoronto.ca/hpme/dhr, accessed May 7, 2009.

CPP Investment Board. 2009. *The 2008 Annual Report.* http://www.cppib.ca/files/PDF/Annual_reports/ar_2008_Online.pdf, accessed May 16, 2009.

Craik, F.I.M. 2000. "Age-Related Changes in Human Memory." In D.C. Park and N. Schwarz, eds., *Cognitive Aging: A Primer*, 75–92. Philadelphia: Taylor and Francis.

Cramer, K., H. Tuokko, and D. Evans. 2001. "Extending Autonomy for Health Care Preferences in Late Life." *Aging Neuropsychology and Cognition* 8(3): 213–24.

Cranswick, K. 1997. "Canada's Caregivers." *Canadian Social Trends* (Winter). Cat. No. 11-008XPE. http//www.statcan.ca/English/ads/11-008-XIE/pdf, accessed August 29, 2004.

Cranswick, K. 1999. "Help Close at Hand: Relocating to Give or Receive Care." *Canadian Social Trends* (Winter): 11–12.

Cranswick, K. 2003. "Caring for an Aging Society." Statistics Canada, 89-582-XIE. http://www.statcan.ca/english/freepub/89-582-XIE/index.htm, accessed May 7, 2009.

Cranswick, K., and D. Thomas. 2005. "Elder Care and the Complexities of Social Networks." *Canadian Social Trends* (Summer): 10–15.

Crilly, R.G., S. Lytwynec, M. Kloseck, J.M. Smith, T. Olsen, B. Gold, S. Masse. 2005. "Patient Outcomes After Discharge from a Geriatric Day Hospital." *Canadian Journal on Aging* 24(3): 305–10.

Crowley, C., and Henry S. Lodge. 2004. *Younger Next Year.* New York: Workman Publishing.

Crowther, M.R., M.W. Parker, W.A. Achenbaum, W.L. Larimore, and H.G. Koenig. 2002. "Rowe and Kahn's Model of Successful Aging Revisited: Positive Spirituality—The Forgotten Factor." *Gerontologist* 42(5): 613–20.

Crystal, S. 1986. "Social Policy and Elder Abuse." In K.A. Pillemer and R.S. Wolf, eds., *Elder Abuse: Conflict in the Family.* Dover, MA: Auburn House.

Cujec, B., H. Quan, Y. Jin, and D. Johnson. 2004. "The Effect of Age upon Care and Outcomes in Patients Hospitalized for Congestive Heart Failure in Alberta, Canada." *Canadian Journal on Aging* 23(3): 255–67.

Cullinane, P. 2006. "Late-Life Civic Engagement Enhances Health for Individuals and Communities." *Journal of Active Aging* 5(6): 66–73.

Cumming, E., and W.E. Henry. 1961. *Growing Old: The Process of Disengagement.* New York: Basic Books.

Curtis, J., W. McTeer, and P. White. 1999. "Exploring Effects of School Sport Experiences on Sport Participation in Later Life." *Sociology of Sport Journal* 16(4): 348–65.

Cusack, S.A., W.J.A. Thompson, and M.E. Rogers. 2003. "Mental Fitness for Life: Assessing the Impact of an 8-Week Mental Fitness Program on Healthy Aging." *Educational Gerontology* 29(5): 393–403.

Cutler, Stephen J. 2006. "Technological change and aging." In Robert H. Binstock and Linda K. George, eds., *Handbook of Aging and the Social Sciences,* 6th ed., 257–76. Burlington, MA: Academic Press.

Cvitkovich, Y., and A. Wister. 2001. "Importance of Transportation and Prioritization of Environmental Needs to Sustain Well-Being among Older Adults." *Environment and Behavior* 33(6): 809–29.

Czaja, S.J. and C.C. Lee. 2006. "Human Factors Engineering." In R. Schulz, L.S. Noelker, K. Rockwood, and R.L. Sprott, eds., *The Encyclopedia of Aging,* 4th ed., 549–52. New York: Springer.

Daigneault, G., P. Joly, and J-Y. Frigon. 2002. "Previous Convictions or Accidents and the Risk of Subsequent Accidents of Older Drivers." *Accident Analysis and Prevention* 34(2): 257–61.

d'Anglure, B.S. 1994. "Recycling the 'Elders' in the Inuit Social Life." In National Advisory Council on Aging, *Aboriginal Seniors' Issues,* 59–64. Cat. No. H71-2/1-15-1994E. Ottawa: Minister of Supply and Services.

Dauvergne, M. 2003. "Family Violence against Seniors." *Canadian Social Trends* (Spring): 10–14.

Davidson, K., S. Arber, and J. Ginn. 2000. "Gendered Meanings of Care Work within Late Life Marital Relationships." *Canadian Journal on Aging* 19(4): 536–53.

Davidson, K., T. Daly, and S. Arber. 2003. "Exploring the Social Worlds of Older Men." In S. Arber, K. Davidson, and J. Ginn, eds., *Gender and Ageing: Changing roles and relationships,* 168–85. Maidenhead, UK: Open University Press.

Davies, S., and M. Denton. 2002. "Economic Well-Being of Older Women Who Became Divorced or Separated in Mid- or Later Life." *Canadian Journal on Aging* 21(4): 477–93.

Davis, C., D. Flett, L. Johnson, L. Gosselin, L. Holmes, and E. Gerrits. 2000. *Supportive Housing for Seniors.* Ottawa: Canada Mortgage and Housing Corporation.

Davis, I. 1996. "Grandparenting Denied." *Maturity* (March/April): 25–26.

Dawson, P., and C.J. Rosenthal. 1996. "Wives of Institutionalized Elderly Men: What Influences Satisfaction with Care?" *Canadian Journal on Aging* 15(2): 245–63.

De Coster, C., Bruce, S., and Kozyrskyi, A. 2005. "Use of Acute Care Hospitals by Long-Stay Patients: Who, How Much, and Why?" *Canadian Journal on Aging,* 24(Suppl.1): 97–106.

De Jong Gierveld, J. 2003. "Social Networks and Social Well-Being of Older Men and Women Living Alone." In S. Arber, K. Davidson, and J. Ginn, eds., *Gender and Ageing: Changing Roles and Relationships,* 95–110. Maidenhead, UK: Open University Press.

De Jong Gierveld, J., and B. Havens. 2004. "Cross-National Comparisons of Social Isolation and Loneliness: Introduction and Overview." *Canadian Journal on Aging* 23(2): 109–13.

Del Balso, Michael, and Alan D. Lewis. 2008. *First Steps: A Guide to Social Research,* 4th edition. Toronto: Nelson Publishing.

Delisle, M.A. 1988. "What Does Solitude Mean to the Aged?" *Canadian Journal on Aging* 7: 358–71.

Dennis, W. 1968. "Creative Productivity between the Ages of 20 and 80 Years." In B.L. Neugarten, ed., *Middle Age and Aging*, 106–14. Chicago: University of Chicago Press.

Denton, F.T., C.H. Feaver, and B.G. Spencer. 1986. "Prospective Aging of the Population and Its Implications for the Labour Force and Government Expenditures." *Canadian Journal on Aging* 5: 75–98.

Denton, F.T., C.H. Feaver, and B.G. Spencer. 1998. "The Future Population of Canada, Its Age Distribution, and Dependency Relations." *Canadian Journal on Aging* 17(1): 83–109.

Denton, F.T., A. Gafni, and B.G. Spencer. 2001. *Exploring the Effects of Population Change on the Costs of Physician Services.* SEDAP Research Paper No. 43. Hamilton, ON: McMaster University.Denton, F.T., and B.G. Spencer. 1995. "Demographic Change and the Cost of Publicly Funded Health Care." *Canadian Journal on Aging* 14(2): 174–92.

Denton, F.T., and B.G. Spencer. 1997. "Population Aging and the Maintenance of Social Support Systems." *Canadian Journal on Aging* 16(3): 485–98.

Denton, F.T., and B.G. Spencer. 1999. *Population Aging and Its Economic Costs: A Survey of the Issues and Evidence.* SEDAP Research Paper No. 1. Hamilton, ON: McMaster University.

Denton, F.T., and B.G. Spencer. 2000. "Population Aging and Its Economic Costs: A Survey of the Issues and Evidence." *Canadian Journal on Aging* 19(Suppl. 1): 1–31.

Denton, F.T., and B.G. Spencer. 2002. "Some Demographic Consequences of Revising the Definition of 'Old Age' to Reflect Future Changes in Life Table Probabilities." *Canadian Journal on Aging* 21(3): 349–56.

Denton, F.T., and B.G. Spencer. 2003. *Population Change and Economic Growth: The Long-Term Outlook.*

SEDAP Research Paper No. 12. Hamilton, ON: McMaster University.

Denton, M. 1997. "The Linkages between Informal and Formal Care of the Elderly." *Canadian Journal on Aging* 16(1): 30–50.

Denton, M., and L. Boos. 2007. "The Gender Wealth Gap: Structural and Material Constraints and Implications for Later Life." *Journal of Women and Aging* 19(3/4): 105–120.

Denton, M., and K. Kusch. 2006. *Well-Being Throughout the Senior Years: An Issues Paper on Key Events and Transitions in Later Life.* SEDAP Research Paper No. 165. Hamilton, ON: McMaster University.

Denton, M.A., C.L. Kemp, S. French, A. Gafni, A. Joshi, C.J. Rosenthal, and S. Davies. 2004. Reflexive Planning for Later Life. *Canadian Journal on Aging* 23(Supplement1): S71–S82.

Desrosiers, J., Hebert, R., Payette, H., Roy, P-M., Tousignant, M., Cote, S., and Trottier, L. 2004. "Geriatric Day Hospital: Who Improves the Most?" *Canadian Journal on Aging, 23*(3): 217–229.

Devine, B.A. 1980. "Old Age Stereotyping: A Comparison of Nursing Staff Attitudes toward the Elderly." *Journal of Gerontological Nursing* 6: 25–32.

Diachun, L.L., A.C. Dumbrell, K. Byrne, and J. Esbaugh. 2006. "... But Does It Stick? Evaluating the Durability of Improved Knowledge Following an Undergraduate Experiential Geriatrics Learning Session." *Journal of the American Geriatrics Society* 54(4): 696–70. http://www.sc.gc.ca/seniors-aines/nfa-cnv/pdf/aging_e.pdf, accessed December 31, 2007.

Dixon, R.A. 2000. "Concepts and Mechanisms of Gains in Cognitive Aging." In D.C. Park and N. Schwarz, eds., *Cognitive Aging: A Primer,* 23–41. Philadelphia: Taylor and Francis.

Dixon, R.A., and L. Bäckman. 1993. "The Concept of Compensation in Cognitive Aging: The Case of Prose Processing in Adulthood." *International Journal of Aging and Human Development* 36(3): 199–217.

Dixon, R.A., and A-L. Cohen. 2001. "The Psychology of Aging: Canadian Research in an International Context." *Canadian Journal on Aging* 20(Suppl. 1): 125–48.

Dominion Bureau of Statistics. 1964. *Census of Canada (1961 Census). Bulletin* 7: 1–4. Ottawa: Queen's Printer.

Donahue, P.J.D. 2001. *Fraud in Ethnocultural Seniors' Communities.* SEDAP Research Paper No. 37. Hamilton, ON: SEDAP Research Program, McMaster University.

Dowd, J.J. 1980. *Stratification among the Aged.* Monterey, CA: Brooks/Cole.

Downs, K.J.M., M. Coleman, and L. Ganong. 2000. "Divorced Families over the Life Course." In S.J. Price, P.C. McKenry, and M.J. Murphy, eds., *Families across Time: A Life Course Perspective,* 24–36. Los Angeles: Roxbury Publishing Company.

Doyle, V. 1994. "Choice, Control and the Right to Age in Place." In G. Gutman and A.V. Wister, eds., *Progressive Accommodation for Seniors: Interfacing Shelter and Services,* 33–44. Vancouver: Gerontology Research Centre.

Doyle-Baker, P.K. (2007). "Mall Walking: A New Strategy for Physical Activity Among Older Adults." *WellSpring, 18*(1).

Dubois, M-F., G. Bravo, and M. Charpentier. 2001. "Which Residential Care Facilities Are Delivering Inadequate Care? A Simple Case-Finding Questionnaire." *Canadian Journal on Aging* 20(3): 339–55.

Dubé, V. and C. Dionne. 2005. "Looking, and Looking, for Work." *Perspectives on Labour and Income,*6(5): 10–14.

Duclos, E., and R. Langlois, R. 2003. *Disability Supports in Canada, 2001.* Statistics Canada. Catalogue No. 89-580-XIE. Ottawa: Minister of Industry. http://www.dsp-psd.pwgsc.gc.ca/Collection/Statcan/89-580-X/89-580-XIE2003001.pdf, accessed May 7, 2009.

Duffy, S.A., F.C. Jackson, S.M. Schim, D.L. Ronis, K.E. Fowller. 2006. "Racial/ethnic Preferences, Sex Preferences, and Perceived Discrimination Related to End-of-Life Care." *Journal of the American Geriatrics Society* 54(1):150–57.

Dumas, J. 1990. *Current Demographic Analysis: Report on the Demographic Situation in Canada 1988.* Statistics Canada. Cat. No. 91-209E. Ottawa: Minister of Supply and Services.

Dunn, P.A. 1997. "A Comparative Analysis of Barrier-Free Housing: Policies for Elderly People in the United States and Canada." In L.A. Patalan, ed., *Shelter and Service Issues for Aging Populations: International Perspectives,* 37–53. New York: Haworth Press.

Dupere, D. 2006. "Palliative Care." In R. Schulz, L.S. Noelker, K. Rockwood, and R.L. Sprott, eds., *The Encyclopedia of Aging,* 4th ed., 899–901. New York: Springer.

Dupuis, J. 2003. "Federal Housing Policy: An Historical Perspective." *The Parliamentary Research Branch of the Library of Parliament, Ottawa.* http://www.//dsp-psd.pwgsc.gc.ca/Collection-R/LoPBdP/PRB-e/PRB0255-e.pdf, accessed December 11, 2008.

Dupuis, J., D.R. Weiss, and C. Wolfson. 2007. "Gender and Transportation Access among Community-Dwelling Seniors." *Canadian Journal on Aging* 26(2): 149–58.

Dupuis, S.L. 2000. "Institution-Based Caregiving as a Container for Leisure." *Leisure Sciences* 22(4): 259–80.

Dupuis, S.L., and B.J.A. Smale. 1995. "An Examination of Relationship between Psychological Well-Being and Depression and Leisure Activity Participation among Older Adults." *Society and Leisure* 18(1): 67–92.

Dupuis, S.L., and B.J.A. Smale. 2004. *In Their Own Voices: Dementia Caregivers Identify the Issues.* Final report prepared for the Minstry of Health and Long-Term Care and the Ontario Senior's Secretariat as part of Initiative No. 6 of Ontario's Alzheimer Strategy. Waterloo, ON: Murray Alzheimer Research and Education Program.

Durkheim, E. 1951. *Suicide: A Study in Sociology.* New York: Free Press.Dykstra, P.A., and J. De Jong Gierveld. 2004. "Gender and Marital-History Differences in Emotional and Social Loneliness among Dutch Older Adults." *Canadian Journal on Aging* 23(2): 141–55.

Dykstra, Pearl A., and G.O. Hagestad. 2007. "Roads Less Taken: Developing a Nuanced View of Older Adults Without Children." *Journal of Family Issues 28* (10): 1275–1310.

Eastaugh, A.M. 1996. "Approaches to Palliative Care by Primary Health Care Teams: A Survey." *Journal of Palliative Care* 12(4): 47–50.

Eaton, B., M.J. Stones, and K. Rockwood. 1986. "Poor Mental Status in Older Hospital Patients: Prevalence and Correlates." *Canadian Journal on Aging* 5: 231–39.

Eden Alternative. 2008. "It Can Be Different." http://www.edenalt.org, accessed May 7, 2009.

Edwards, N., E. Gallagher and D. Lockett. 2003. "Steady As You Go (SAYGO): A Falls-Prevention Program for Seniors Living in the Community." *Canadian Journal on Aging* 22(2): 207–16.

Edwards, N., D. Lockett, F. Aminzadeh, and R.C. Nair. 2003. "Predictors of Bath Grab-Bar Use among Community-Living Older Adults." *Canadian Journal on Aging* 22(2): 217–27.

Edwards, P, and Mawani, A. 2006. *Healthy Aging in Canada: A New Vision, A Vital Investment From Evidence to Action.* A Background Paper Prepared for the Federal, Provincial and Territorial Committee of Officials (Seniors). http://www.hc-sc.gc.ca/seniors-aines/pubs/haging_newvision/pdf/vision-rpt_e.pdf, accessed December 31, 2007.

Ehrenreich, Barbara. 2001. *Nickel and Dimed: On (Not) Getting By in America.* New York: Henry Holt and Company.

Eke, B. 2004. "Intergenerational impact of the AIDS pandemic in Nigeria." *Journal of Intergenerational Relationships 2(3–4),* 39–52.

Ekerdt, D.J. 1986. "The Busy Ethic: Moral Continuity between Work and Retirement." *The Gerontologist* 26(3); 239–44.

Ekerdt, D.J., and J.F. Sergeant. 2006. "Retirement." In R. Schulz, L.S. Noelker, K. Rockwood, and R.L. Sprott, eds., *The Encyclopedia of Aging,* 4th ed., 1032–1037. New York: Springer.

Ekos Research Associates. 1998. Ottawa. *Rethinking Generations: Preliminary Findings.*

Elder, G.H., Jr., and M.K. Johnson. 2003. "The Life Course and Aging: Challenges, Lessons, and New Directions." In R. A. Settersten, Jr., ed., *Invitation to the Life Course: Toward New Understandings of Later Life,* 49–81. Amityville, New York: Baywood Publishing Company.

Elderhostel. 1981. *Annual Report.* Boston: Elderhostel.

Elderhostel. 2003. "What Is Elderhostel?" http://www.elderhostel.org/about/what_is.asp, accessed May 7, 2009.

Elderhostel. 2007a. *About Us.* http://www.elderhostel.org/about/default.asp, accessed May 7, 2009.

Elderhostel. 2007b. *The Learning in Retirement Movement.* http://www.elderhostel.org/ein/learning_na.asp, accessed May 7, 2009.

Elgar, F.J., G. Worrall, and J.C. Knight. 2002. "Functional Assessment of Elderly Clients of a Rural Community–Based Long-Term Care Program: A 10-Year Cohort Study." *Canadian Journal on Aging* 21(3): 455–63.

Ellerby, J.H., J. McKenzie, S. McKay, G.J. Gariepy, J.M. Kaufert. 2000. "Bioethics for Clinicians: 18. Aboriginal Cultures." *CMAJ: Canadian Medical Association Journal, 163*(7): 845–50.

Elliott, S., and D. Umberson. 2008. "The Performance of Desire: Gender and Sexual Negotiation in Long-Term Marriages." *Journal of Marriage and Family* 70: 391–406.

Elo, A.E. 1965. "Age Changes in Master Chess Performance." *Journal of Gerontology* 20: 289–99.

Engelman, M. 2000. "Here's to the Belleville Ladies: Creativity in Aging." *Activities, Adaptation and Aging* 24(4): 19–26.

Enman, A., and M.H. Rogers. 2002. "Aging Well in Rural Places." *The Guardian* (Charlottetown), June 4, D19.

Erikson, E.H. 1963. *Childhood and Society,* 2nd ed. New York: W.W. Norton.

Erikson, E.H. 1982. *The Life Cycle Completed.* New York: W.W. Norton.

Estabrooks, P.A., and A.V. Carron. 2000. "Predicting Scheduling Self-Efficacy in Older Adult Exercisers: The Role of Task Cohesion." *Journal of Aging and Physical Activity* 8(1): 41–50.

Estes, C.L. 2001. "Political Economy of Aging: A Theoretical Framework." In C.L. Estes, ed., *Social Policy and Aging: A Critical Perspective,* 1–22. Thousand Oaks, CA: Sage Publications.

Estes, Carroll L. 2003. "Theoretical Perspectives on Old Age Policy: A Critique and a Proposal." In Simon Biggs, Ariela Lowenstein, and Jon Hendricks, eds., *The Need for Theory: Critical Approaches to Social Gerontology,* 219–43. Amityville, New York: Baywood Publishing Company.

Evans, J.G. 1996. "Health Care for Older People: A Look across a Frontier." *Journal of the American Medical Association* 275(18): 1449–50.

Evans, R.G., K.M. McGrail, S.G. Moran, M.L. Barer, and C. Hertzman. 2001. "Apocalypse No: Population Aging and the Future of Health Care Systems." *Canadian Journal on Aging* 20(Suppl. 1): 160–91.

Fast, J., N. Keating, P. Otfinowski, and L. Derksen. 2004. "Characteristics of Family/Friend Care Networks of Frail Seniors." *Canadian Journal on Aging 23*(1): 5–20.

Feeley, D. 2006. *Quality and Cost International Programs.* http://www.academyhealth.org/2006/feeleyd, accessed June 19, 2008.

Ferraro, K.F. 2006. "Health and Aging." In Robert H. Binstock and Linda K. George, eds., *Handbook of*

Aging and the Social Sciences, 6th ed. Burlington, MA: Academic Press.

Ferrucci, L., G. Izmirlian, S.G. Léveillé, C.L. Phillips, M.C. Corti, D.B. Brock, and J.M. Guralnik. 1999. "Smoking, Physical Activity, and Active Life Expectancy." *American Journal of Epidemiology* 149(7): 645–53.

Field, D. 1999. "Continuity and Change in Friendships in Advanced Old Age: Findings from the Berkeley Older Generation Study." *International Journal of Aging and Human Development* 48(4): 325–46.

Filan, S.L., and R.H. Llewellyn-Jones. 2006. "Animal-Assisted Therapy for Dementia: A Review of the Literature." *International Psychogeriatrics* 18(4): 597–611.

Fillit, H.M., R.N. Butler, A.W. O'Connell, M.S. Albert, J.E. Birren, C.W. Cotman, W.T. Greenough, P.E. Gold, A.F. Kramer, L.H. Kuller, T.T. Perls, B.G. Sahagan, and T. Tully. 2002. "Achieving and Maintaining Cognitive Vitality With Aging." *Mayo Clinic Proceedings;* 77:681–96. http://www.mayoclinicproceedings.com/pdf%2F7707%2F7707r%2Epdf, accessed November 4, 2008.

Fingerman, K.L. 2004. "The Role of Offspring and In-Laws in Grandparents' Ties to Their Grandchildren." *Journal of Family Issues* 25(8): 1026–49.

Finlayson, M., and B. Havens. 2001. "Changes over Time in Long-Term Care Use, ADL, and IADL among the Oldest-Old Participants of the Aging in Manitoba Longitudinal Study." *Canadian Journal on Aging* 20(2): 271–90.

Finlayson, M., and J. Kaufert. 2002. "Older Women's Community Mobility: A Qualitative Exploration." *Canadian Journal on Aging* 21(1): 75–84.

Finlayson, M., L. Lix, G.S. Finlayson, and T. Fong. 2005. "Trends in the Utilization of Specific Health Care Services among Older Manitobans: 1985 to 2000." *Canadian Journal on Aging* 24(Suppl.1): 15–27.

Fischer, D.H. 1978. *Growing Old in America*, expanded ed. New York: Oxford University Press.

Fisher, R. 2006. "Euthanasia and Physician-Assisted Suicide: Are They Next?" *Caregiving* 9(6): 427–31.

Fisher, B. S., and S.L. Regan. 2006. "The Extent and Frequency of Abuse in the Lives of Older Women and Their Relationship with Health Outcomes." *The Gerontologist* 46(2): 200–9.

Fitzpatrick, J.A., and K.S. Wampler. 2000. "Marital Relationships: A Life Course Perspective." In S.J. Price, P.C. McKenry, and M.J. Murphy, eds., *Families across Time: A Life Course Perspective*, 92–104. Los Angeles: Roxbury Publishing Company.

Foisy, P. 1995. "Variations in Age-Related Deficits among Episodic Memory Tasks: An Archival Study." *Canadian Journal on Aging* 14(4): 686–96.

Foote, D.K., and D. Stoffman. 1998. *Boom, Bust, and Echo 2000: Profiting from the Demographic Shift in the New Millennium.* Toronto: Macfarlane Walter and Ross.

Forbes, W.F., J.A. Jackson, and A.S. Kraus. 1987. *Institutionalization of the Elderly in Canada.* Toronto: Butterworths.

Foundations Project. 1980. "Foundations for Gerontological Education." *Gerontologist* 20: Part II.

Fox, P.L. 1995. "Environmental Modifications in the Homes of Elderly Canadians with Disabilities." *Disability and Rehabilitation: An International Multidisciplinary Journal* 17(1): 3–49.

Freeman, A. 1994. "CPP Dips into Surplus Fund." *The Globe and Mail,* April 21, B1–2.

Freedman, Marc. 2007. *Encore: Finding Work that Matters in yhe Second Half of Life.* New York: PublicAffairs.

French, Howard W. 2006. "As China Ages, A Shortage of Cheap Labor Looms." The *New York Times.* June 30, 2006. http://www.nytimes.com, accessed April 26, 2007.

French, S.E., M. Denton, A. Gafni, A. Joshi, J. Lian, P. Raina, C.J. Rosenthal, and D.J. Willison. 2000. "Independence of Older Persons: Meaning and Determinants." In F.T. Denton, D. Fretz, and B.G. Spencer, eds., *Independence and Economic Security in Old Age,* 59–84. Vancouver: UBC Press.

Frideres, J. 1994. "The Future of Our Past: Nartie Elderly in Canadian Society." In National Advisory Council on Aging, *Aboriginal Seniors' Issues,* 17–37. Cat. No. H17-2/1-15-1994E. Ottawa. Minister of Supply and Services.

Friend, R.A. 1996. "Older Lesbian and Gay People: A Theory of Successful Aging." In R. Berger, ed., *Gay and Grey: The Older Homosexual Man*, 2nd ed., 277–98. New York: Harrington Park.

Fries, James F. 1980. "Aging, Natural Death, and the Compression of Morbidity." *New England Journal of Medicine* 303: 130–36.

Fries, J. 2006. "Compression of Morbidity." In R. Schulz, L.S. Noelker, K. Rockwood, and R.L. Sprott, eds., *The Encyclopedia of Aging*, 4th ed., 257–259. New York: Springer.

Fries, J.F., and L.M. Crapo. 1981. *Vitality and Aging.* San Francisco: W.H. Freeman.

Frohlich, N., C. De Coster, and N. Dik. 2002. *Estimating Personal Care Home Bed Requirements.* Manitoba Centre for Health Policy. Department of Community Health Sciences. Faculty of Medicine, University of Manitoba. Manitoba Health. http://www.mchp-appserv.cpe.umanitoba.ca/reference/pch2020.pdf, accessed May 7, 2009.

Fry, Christine L. 2005. "Globalization and the Experiences of Aging." *Gerontology and Geriatrics Education* 26(1): 9–22.

Fry, P.S. 2000. "Religious Involvement, Spirituality and Personal Meaning for Life: Existential Predictors of Psychological Well-Being in Community-Residing and Institutional Care Elders." *Aging and Mental Health* 4(4): 375–87.

Fuller-Thomson, E. 2005. "Canadian First Nations Grandparents Raising Grandchildren." *International Journal of Aging and Human Development* 60(4): 331–42.

Funderburk, B., J.A. Damron-Rodriguez, L.L. Storms, and D. Solomon. 2006. "Endurance of Undergraduate Attitudes toward Older Adults." *Educational Gerontology* 32(6): 447–462.

Gagan, D. 1983a. "Geographical and Social Mobility in Nineteenth-Century Ontario: A Microstudy." In P.W. Ward, ed., *The Social Development of Canada: Readings.* Richmond, BC: Open Learning Institute.

Gagan, D. 1983b. "Land, Population, and Social Change: The 'Critical Years' in Rural Canada West." In P.W. Ward, ed., *The Social Development of Canada: Readings.* Richmond, BC: Open Learning Institute.

Gagliese, L., R. Nissim, M. Jovellanos, N. Weizblit, W. Ellis, M.M. Martin, and G. Rodin. 2005. "Aging and Cultural Disparities in Pain at the End of Life." *Geriatrics and Aging 18(6):* 34–36.

Galenson, D.W. 2006. *Old Masters and Young Geniuses: The Two Life Cycles of Artistic Creativity.* Princeton: Princeton University Press.

Gall, T.L., and D.R. Evans. 2000. "Preretirement Expectations and the Quality of Life of Male Retirees in Later Retirement." *Canadian Journal of Behavioural Science* 32(3): 187–97.

Gallo, W.T., E.H. Bradley, J.A. Dubin, R.N. Jones, T.A. Falba, H-M. Teng, and S.V. Kasl. 2006. "The Persistence of Depressive Symptoms in Old Workers Who Experience Involuntary Job Loss: Results from the Health and Retirement Survey." *Journal of Gerontology: SOCIAL SCIENCES 61b*(4): S221–8.

Garfinkel, H. 1967. *Studies in Ethnomethodology.* Englewood Cliffs, NJ: Prentice-Hall.

Garrett, D.D., H. Tuokko, K.I. Stjduhar, J. Lindsay, and S. Buehler 2008. "Planning for End-of-Life Care: Findings from the Canadian Study of Health and Aging." *Canadian Journal on Aging* 27(1): 11–21.

Gatz, M., and M.A. Smyer. 2001. "Mental Health and Aging at the Outset of the Twenty-First Century." In J.E. Birren and K.W. Schaie, eds., *Handbook of the Psychology of Aging,* 5th ed. San Diego: Academic Press.

Gauthier, S., I. McDowell, and G. Hill. 1990. "Canadian Study of Health and Aging (CaSHA)." *Psychiatry Journal of the University of Ottawa* 15(4): 227–29.

Gazzaley, A., J.W. Cooney, J. Rissman, and M. D'Esposito. 2005. "Top-down Suppression Deficit Underlies Working Memory Impairment in Normal Aging." *Nature Neuroscience 8*(10): 1298–300.

Gearon, C.J. 2003. "Visiting the 'Kids' Gets Harder." *AARP Bulletin* 44(2): 6.

Gee, E.M. 1988. "The Changing Demography of Intergenerational Relations in Canada." Paper presented at the 17th Annual Scientific and Educational Meeting of the Canadian Association on Gerontology, Halifax, October.

Gee, E.M. 1995. "Population Aging: A Contested Terrain of Social Policy." In E.M. Gee and G.M. Gutman, eds., *Rethinking Retirement,* 13–29. Vancouver: Gerontology Research Centre, Simon Fraser University.

Gee, E.M., and G.M. Gutman, eds. 2000. *The Overselling of Population Aging: Apocalyptic Demography, Intergenerational Challenges, and Social Policy.* Don Mills, ON: Oxford University Press.

Gee, E.M., and M.M. Kimball. 1987. *Women and Aging.* Toronto: Butterworths.

Gee, E.M., and S.A. McDaniel. 1993. "Social Policy for an Aging Society." *Journal of Canadian Studies* 28(1): 139–53.

Gee, E.M., K.M. Kobayashi, and S.G. Prus. 2004. "Examining the Healthy Immigrant Effect in Mid- to Later Life: Findings from the Canadian

Community Health Survey." *Canadian Journal on Aging* 23 (Supplement 1): S61–S69.

Genoe, M.R., and J.F. Singleton. 2006. "Older Men's Leisure Experiences across Their Lifespan." *Topics in Geriatric Rehabilitation* 22(4): 348–56.

George, M.V., M.J. Norris, F. Nault, S. Loh, and S.Y. Dai. 1994. *Population Projections for Canada, Provinces and Territories 1993–2016.* Cat. No. 91-520. Ottawa: Ministry of Industry, Science and Technology.

Gesser, G., P.T.P. Wong, and G.T. Reker. 1986. "Death Attitudes across the Life-Span: The Development and Validation of the Death Attitude Profile (DAP)." Personal communication.

Gibson, H.B. 2000. "It Keeps Us Young." *Ageing and Society* 20(Part 6): 773–79.

Gibson, K.J., W.J. Zerbe, and R.E. Franken. 1993. "The Influence of Rater and Ratee Age on Judgments of Work-Related Attributes." *Journal of Psychology* 127(3): 271–80.

Gigliotti, C.M., and S.E. Jarrott. 2005. "Effects of Horticulture Therapy on Engagement and Affect." *The Canadian Journal on Aging* 24(4): 367–77.

Gignac, M.A.M., C. Cott, and E.M. Badley. 2000. "Adaptation to Chronic Illness and Disability and Its Relationship to Perceptions of Independence and Dependence." *Journals of Gerontology Series B* 55(6): P362–72.

Gignac, M.A.M., E.K. Kelloway, and B.H. Gottlieb. 1996. "The Impact of Caregiving on Employment: A Mediational Model of Work–Family Conflict." *Canadian Journal on Aging* 15(4): 525–42.

Gilbart, E.E., and J.P. Hirdes. 2000. "Stress, Social Engagement, and Psychological Well-Being in Institutional Settings: Evidence Based on the Minimum Data Set 2.0." *Canadian Journal on Aging* 19(Suppl. 2): 50–66.

Gillis, K.J., and J.P. Hirdes. 1996. "The Quality of Life Implications of Health Practices among Older Adults: Evidence from the 1991 Canadian General Social Survey." *Canadian Journal on Aging* 15(2): 299–314.

Gilmour, H., and Park, J. 2006. "Dependency, Chronic Conditions and Pain in Seniors." *Supplement to Health Reports, 16*: 21–31. Statistics Canada. Cat. No. 82-003.

Giranda, M., J.E. Luk, and K.A. Atchison. 1999. "Social Networks of Elders without Children." *Journal of Gerontological Social Work* 31(1/2): 63–83.

Gladstone, J.W. 1989. "Grandmother–Grandchild Contact: The Mediating Influence of the Middle Generation Following Marriage Breakdown and Remarriage." *Canadian Journal on Aging* 8: 355–65.

Gladstone, J.W. 1995. "The Marital Perceptions of Elderly Persons Living or Having a Spouse Living in a Long-Term Care Institution in Canada." *Gerontologist* 35(1): 52–60.

Gladstone, J., and E. Wexler. 2000. "Family Perspective of Family/Staff Interaction in Long-Term Care Facilities." *Geriatric Nursing* 21(1): 16–19.

Gladstone, J., and E. Wexler. 2002a. "Exploring the Relationships between Families and Staff Caring for Residents in Long-Term Care Facilities: Family Members' Perspectives." *Canadian Journal on Aging* 21(1): 39–45.

Gladstone, J., and E. Wexler. 2002b. "The Development of Relationships between Families and Staff in Long-Term Care Facilities: Nurses' Perspectives." *Canadian Journal on Aging* 21(2): 217–28.

Gladstone, J.W., S.L. Dupuis, and E. Wexler. 2007. "Ways that Families Engage with Staff in Long-Term Care Facilities." *Canadian Journal on Aging* 26(4): 391–402.

Glass, P-Y. 1995. "He Didn't Know She'd Live Forever." *Winnipeg Free Press,* December 29, 1.

Glendenning, F. 1999. "Elder Abuse and Neglect in Residential Settings: The Need for Inclusiveness in Elder Abuse Research." *Journal of Elder Abuse and Neglect* 10(1–2): 1–11.

The Globe and Mail. 1993. "Will We Still Feed Them, When They're 64?" Editorial, November 15, A12.

Glor, E.D. 1991. "An Effective Evaluation of a Small-Scale Seniors Health Promotion Centre: A Case Study." *Canadian Journal on Aging* 10: 64–73.

Godbey, G., and Burnett-Wolle, S. 2007. "Looking Below the Surface: Keys to Promoting Physical Activity." *Journal of Active Aging* 6(1): 40–43.

Gold, D.P., D. Andres, J. Etezadi, T. Arbuckle, and A. Schwartzman. 1995. "Structural Equation Model of Intellectual Change and Continuity and Predictors of Intelligence in Older Men." *Psychology and Aging* 10(2): 294–303.

Goldberg, D.L. 2003. "Grandparent–Grandchild Access: A Legal Analysis." Paper presented to Family, Children, and Youth Section, Department of Justice Canada. Minister of Justice and Attorney General of Canada.

Goodman, C. 1999. "Retirement Patterns in Canada." *Horizons* 2(2): 16–17.

Gordon, S.A., T.J. Overend, and A.A. Vandervoort. 2001. "Country Line Dancing: An Aerobic Activity for Older Women?" *Journal of Aging and Physical Activity* 9(4): 364–71.

Gott, M., and S. Hinchliff. 2003a. "How Important Is Sex in Later Life? The Views of Older People." *Social Science and Medicine* 56(8): 1617–28.

Gott, M., and S. Hinchliff. 2003b. "Sex and Ageing: A Gendered Issue." In S. Arber, K. Davidson., and J. Ginn, eds., *Gender and Ageing: Changing Roles and Relationships*, 63–78. Open University Press: Maidenhead, England.

Gottlieb, B.H. 2002. "Older Volunteers: A Precious Resource under Pressure." *Canadian Journal on Aging* 21(1): 5–9.

Gottlieb, B.H., and J. Johnson. 2000. "Respite Programs for Caregivers of Persons with Dementia: A Review with Practice Implications." *Aging and Mental Health* 4(2): 119–29.

Gottlieb, B.H., E.K. Kelloway, and M. Fraboni. 1994. "Aspects of Eldercare That Place Employees at Risk." *Gerontologist* 34(6): 815–21.

Government of Canada. 1982. *Better Pensions for Canadians (Green Paper)*. Ottawa: Minister of Supply and Services.

Government of Canada. 1999. "Help Given to Children in Parents' Senior Years." *Info-Age* 20 (January).

Grand'Maison, J., and S. Lefebvre. 1996. *Sharing the Blessings: The Role of Seniors in Today's Society*. Trans. Jane Brierly. Sherbrooke: Mediaspaul.

Grant, B.C. 2002. "Physical Activity: Not a Popular Leisure Choice in Later Life." *Loisir et société/Society and Leisure* 25(2): 285–302.

Grant, M.J., A.S. Ross, C.M. Button, T.E. Hannah, and R. Hoskins. 2001. "Attitudes and Stereotypes about Attitudes across the Lifespan." *Social Behavior and Personality* 29(8): 749–62.

Gruber, J., and D. Wise. 1999a. "Social Security Programs and Retirement around the World." *Research in Labor Economics* 18: 1–40

Gruber, J., and D. Wise. 1999b. "Social Security, Retirement Incentives, and Retirement Behavior: An International Perspective." *EBRI Issue Brief No. 209* (May): 1–22.

Guberman, N. 1999. "Daughters-in-Law as Caregivers: How and Why Do They Come to Care?" *Journal of Women and Aging* 11(1): 85–102.

Guberman, N. and P. Maheu. 2002. "Conceptions of Family Caregivers: Implications for Professional Practice." *Canadian Journal on Aging* 21(1): 27–37.

Guberman, N., J. Lavoie, J. Pepin, S. Lauzon, and M. Montejo. 2006. "Formal Service Practitioners' Views of Family Caregivers' Responsibilities and Difficulties." *Canadian Journal on Aging* 25(1): 43–54.

Guillemard, A.M. 1997. "Re-Writing Social Policy and Changes within the Life Course Organisation. A European Perspective." *Canadian Journal on Aging* 16(3): 441–64.

Guillemard, A-M. 2006. "What Age for Employment? The Need for a New Social Organization of the Working Age." In L. O. Stone, ed., *New Frontiers of Research on Retirement*, 49–64. Statistics Canada. Catalogue No. 75-511-XIE. Ottawa: Minister of Industry.

Guppy, N. 1989. "The Magic of 65: Issues and Evidence in the Mandatory Retirement Debate." *Canadian Journal on Aging* 8: 174–86.

Gureje, O., Ogunniyi, A., Kola, L., and Afolabi, E. 2006. "Functional Disability in Elderly Nigerians: Results from the Ibadan Study of Aging." *Journal of the American Geriatrics Society* 54(11): 1784–89.

Ha, J. 2008. "Changes in Support from Confidants, Children, and Friends Following Widowhood." *Journal of Marriage and Family* 70(2): 306–18.

Haber, Carole. 2006. "Old Age Through the Lens of Family History." In Robert H. Binstock and Linda K. George, eds., *Handbook of Aging and the Social Sciences*, 6th ed., 59–75.Burlington, MA: Academic Press.

Haber, C., and B. Gratton. 1994. *Old Age and the Search for Security: An American Social History*. Bloomington: Indiana University Press.

Hagen, B., E.M. Gallagher, and S. Simpson. 1997. "Family Caregiver Education and Support Programs: Using Humanistic Approaches to Evaluate Program Effects." *Educational Gerontology* 23(2): 129–42.

Hagestad, G.O. 1985. "Continuity and Connectedness." In V.L. Bengtson and J.F. Robertson, eds., *Grandparenthood*, 31–48. Beverly Hills: Sage.

Hagestad, G.O., and Uhlenberg, P. 2005. "Social Separation of Old and Young: A Root of Ageism." *Journal of Social Issues* 61(2): 343–60.

Haines, V.A., and L.J. Henderson. 2002. "Targeting Social Support: A Network Assessment of the Convoy Model of Social Support." *Canadian Journal on Aging* 21(2): 243–56.

Hall, B.L. 1993. "Elderly Vietnamese Immigrants: Family and Community Connections." *Community Alternatives* 5(2): 81–96.

Hall, S.S. 2007. "Small and Thin: The Controversy Over the Fetal Origins of Adult Health." *The New Yorker*, November 19: 52–57.

Hall, M., and B. Havens. 2002. "Social Isolation and Social Loneliness." In *Writing in Gerontology: Mental Health and Aging*, No. 18, 33–44. Ottawa: National Advisory Council on Aging.

Hall, M., D. Lasby, G. Gumulka, and C. Tryon. 2006. *Caring Canadians, Involved Canadians: Highlights from the 2004 Canada Survey of Giving, Volunteering and Participating*. Statistics Canada. Ottawa: Minister of Industry.

Hall, R., and P.C. Coyte. 2001. "Determinants of Home Care Utilization: Who Uses Home Care in Ontario?" *Canadian Journal on Aging* 20(2): 175–92.

Hallam, E., J. Hockey, and G. Howarth. 1999. *Beyond the Body: Death and Social Identity.* London: Routledge.

Hallman, B.C., and A.E. Joseph. 1999. "Getting There: Mapping the Gendered Geography of Caregiving to Elderly Relatives." *Canadian Journal on Aging* 18(4): 397–414.

Hamel, C.F., L.W. Guse, P.G. Hawranik, and J.B. Bond. 2002. "Advance Directives and Community-Dwelling Older Adults." *Western Journal of Nursing Research* 24(2): 143–58.

Hamilton, K., and T. Brehaut. 1992. *Older Women: A Study of the Housing and Support Service Needs of Older "Single" Women.* A Report for the Canada Mortgage and Housing Corporation. Charlottetown: Renaissance Communications.

Harbison, J. 1999a. "Models of Intervention for 'Elder Abuse and Neglect': A Canadian Perspective on Ageism, Participation, and Empowerment." *Journal of Elder Abuse and Neglect* 10(3–4): 1–17.

Harbison, J. 1999b. "Changing Career of 'Elder Abuse and Neglect' as a Social Problem in Canada: Learning from Feminist Frameworks?" *Journal of Elder Abuse and Neglect* 11(4): 59–80.

Harbison, J., P. McKinley, and D. Pettipas. 2006. "Older People as Objects not Subjects: Theory and Practice in Situations of Elder Abuse." In R. Alaggia

and C. Vine (eds.), Cruel but not Unusual: Violence in Canadian Families, A Sourcebook of History, Theory and Practice, 689–743. Waterloo, ON: Wilfrid Laurier Press.

Harbison, J., and M. Morrow. 1998. "Re-examining the Social Construction of 'Elder Abuse and Neglect': A Canadian Perspective." *Ageing and Society* 18: 691–711.

Hardy, M. 2006. "Older Workers." In J.E. Birren and K. W. Schaie, eds., *Handbook of the Psychology of Aging*, 6th ed., 201–18. Burlington, MA: Elsevier Academic Press.

Harlton, S.V., N. Keating, and J. Fast. 1998. "Defining Eldercare for Policy and Practice: Perspectives Matter." *Family Relations* 47(3): 281–88.

Harris, P.B. 2005. "The Voices of Husbands and Sons Caring for a Family Member with Dementia." In B. J. Kramer and E. H. Thompson, Jr., eds., *Men as Caregivers*, 213–33. Amherst, New York: Prometheus Books.

Hartley, A. 2006. "Changing Role of the Speed of Processing Construct in the Cognitive Psychology of Human Aging." In J.E. Birren and K.W. Schaie (Eds.), *Handbook of the Psychology of Aging,* 6th ed., 183–207. Burlington, MA: Elsevier Academic Press.

Harvard Medical School. 1968. "A Definition of Irreversible Coma: Report of the Ad Hoc Committee of the Harvard Medical Schoolto Examine the Definition of Brain Death." *Journal of the American Medical Association* 205(5): 677–79.

Havens, B. 1995. "Canadian Long-Term Care Use: What Is the Future?" In S.R. Ingman, X. Pei, C.D. Ekstrom, H.J. Friedsam, and K.R. Bartlett, eds., *An Aging Population, an Aging Planet, and a Sustainable Future.* Denton, TX: Texas Institute for Research and Education on Aging, University of North Texas.

Havens, B., and M. Hall. 2001. "Social Isolation, Loneliness, and the Health of Older Adults in Manitoba, Canada. *Indian Journal of Gerontology* 15(1-2): 126–44.

Havens, B., M. Hall, G. Sylvestre, and T. Jivan. 2004. "Social Isolation and Loneliness: Differences between Older Rural and Urban Manitobans." *Canadian Journal on Aging* 23(2): 129–40.

Hawranik, P. 2002. "Inhome Service Use by Caregivers and Their Elders: Does Cognitive Status Make a

Difference?" *Canadian Journal on Aging* 21(2): 257–72.

Hayward, L.M. 2001. *Mid-Life Patterns and the Residential Mobility of Older Men.* SEDAP Research Paper No. 64. Hamilton, ON: McMaster University.

Hayward, L., S. Davies, R. Robb, M. Denton, and G. Auton. 2004. "Publicly Funded and Family-Friend Care in the Case of Long-Term Illness: The Role of the Spouse." *Canadian Journal on Aging* 23 (supplement 1): S39–S48.

He, Y.H., A. Colantonio, and V.W. Marshall. 2003. "Later-Life Career Disruption and Self-Rated Health: An Analysis of General Social Survey Data." *Canadian Journal on Aging* 22(1): 45–57.

Health and Welfare Canada. 1984. *Alzheimer's Disease: A Family Information Handbook.* Ottawa: Minister of Supply and Services.

Health and Welfare Canada. 1988. *Active Health Report: The Active Health Report on Seniors.* Cat No. H-39-124/1988E. Ottawa: Minister of Supply and Services.

Health and Welfare Canada. 1991. *Mental Health Problems among Canada's Seniors: Demographic and Epidemiologic Considera-tions.* Ottawa: Supply and Services.

Health Canada. 1994. *Suicide in Canada: Update of the Report of the Task Force on Suicide in Canada.* Cat. No. 39-107/1995E. Ottawa: Minister of National Health and Welfare.

Health Canada. 1998. *Principles of the National Framework on Aging: A Policy Guide.* Ottawa: Division of Aging and Seniors. Minister of Public Works and Government Services Canada.

Health Canada. 1999a. *Canada's Physical Activity Guide to Healthy Active Living for Older Adults: Handbook.* Ottawa: Canada's Communications Group.

Health Canada. 1999b. "Canada's Seniors. No. 13: Living in Institutions—In All Provinces." http://www.hc-sc.gc.ca/seniors-aines/pubs/factoids/1999/pdf/entire_e.pdf, accessed July 26, 2004.

Health Canada. 1999c. "Many Seniors in All Provinces." *Canada's Seniors, Snapshot No. 3.* http://www.hc-sc.gc.ca/seniors-aines/pubs/factoids/1999/pdf/entire_e.pdf, accessed July 26, 2004.

Health Canada. 2001a. "Canada's Seniors. No.1: A Growing Population." http://www.hc-sc.gc.ca/seniors-aines/pubs/factoids/2001/ no01_e.htm, accessed December 27, 2003.

Health Canada. 2001b. "Canada's Seniors. No. 2: Canada's Oldest Seniors." http://www.hc-sc.gc.ca/seniors-aines/pubs/factoids/2001/ no02_e.htm, accessed December 27, 2003.

Health Canada. 2001c. "Canada's Seniors. No. 24: Travel in Canada and around the World." http://www.hc-sc.gc.ca/seniors-aines-pubs/factoids/2001/no24_e.htm, accessed August 17, 2004.

Health Canada. 2002a. *Dare to Age Well!: Healthy Aging, Physical Activity and Older Adults.* Cat. No. H39-612/2002-4E. Ottawa: Minister of Public Works and Government Services Canada.

Health Canada. 2002b. Division of Aging and Seniors. *Dare to Age Well: Workshop on Health Differences across Twenty-one Ethnocultural Groups in Canada.* Social and Economic Dimensions of an Aging Population. SEDAP Research Paper No. 143. Hamilton, ON: McMaster University

Health Canada. 2002c. *Healthy Aging: Tobacco Use and Smoking Cessation among Seniors.* Cat. No. H39-612/2002-E. Minister of Public Works and Government Services Canada.

Health Canada. 2002d. *A Report on Mental Illnesses in Canada.* Ottawa: Health Canada Editorial Board.

Health Canada. 2003. *Custom Tabulations.* Economic Research Analysis Section, Policy Research Division, Strategic Policy Directorate, Population and Public Health Branch, Health Canada.

Health Canada. 2006. "Obesity." It's Your Health. Minister of Health. Cat. No. H13-7/20-2006E-PDF. http://www.healthcanada.gc.ca/iyh, accessed January 18, 2008.

Heaphy, B., A.K.T. Yip, and D. Thompson. 2004. "Ageing in a Non-Heterosexual Context." *Ageing and Society* 24: 881–902.

Heath, Y., and R. Gifford. 2001. "Post-Occupancy Evaluation of Therapeutic Gardens in a Multi-Level Care Facility for the Aged." *Activities, Adaptation and Aging* 25(2): 21–43.

Hébert, R., N. Dubuc, M. Buteau, J. Desrosiers, G. Bravo, L. Trottier, C. St-Hilaire, and C. Roy. 2001. "Resources and Costs Associated with Disabilities of Elderly People Living at Home and in Institutions." *Canadian Journal on Aging* 20(1): 1–21.

Hébert, R., L. Lévesque, J. Vézina, J.P. Lavoie, F. Ducharme, C. Gendron, M. Préville, L. Voyer, and M.F. Dubois. 2003. "Efficacy of a Psychoeducative Group Program for Caregivers of Demented

Persons Living at Home: A Randomized Controlled Trial." *Journals of Gerontology Series B* 58(1): S58–67.

Hendricks, J. 1982. "The Elderly in Society: Beyond Modernization." *Social Science History* 6: 321–45.

Hendricks, J. 1997. "Bridging Contested Terrain: Chaos or Prelude to a Theory." *Canadian Journal on Aging* 16(2): 197–217.

Hendricks, J. 2005. "Ageism: Looking across the Margin in the New Millennium." *Generations* 29(3): 5–7.

Hendrix, C.C., and K.M. Sakauye. 2001. "Teaching Elderly Individuals on Computer Use." *Journal of Gerontological Nursing* 27(6): 47–53.

Henkens, Kene. 2003. "Stereotyping Older Workers and Retirement: The Manager's Point of View." WANE Working Paper #5. London, ON: University of Western Ontario.

Henripin, J. 1972. *Trends and Factors of Fertility in Canada*. Ottawa: Statistics Canada (Dominion Bureau of Statistics).

Henripin, J., and Y. Peron. 1972. "The Demographic Transition of the Province of Quebec." In D. Glass and R. Revelle, eds., *Population and Social Change*, 213–31. London: Edward Arnold.

Henry, R.G., R.B. Miller, and R. Giarrusso. 2005. "Difficulties, Disagreements, and Disappointments in Late-Life Marriages." *International Journal of Aging and Human Development* 61(3): 243–64.

Hequembourg, A., and S. Brallier. 2005. "Gendered Stories of Parental Caregiving among Siblings." *Journal of Aging Studies* 19: 53–71.

Hering, M., and M. Kpessa. 2007. *Private Pensions and Income Security in Old Age: An Uncertain Future – Conference Report*. SEDAP Research Paper No. 180. Hamilton, ON: McMaster University.

Hess, T.M. 2006. "Attitudes toward aging and their effects on behavior." In J. E. Birren and K.W. Schaie, eds., *Handbook of the Psychology of Aging*, 6th ed., 379–406. Burlington, MA: Elsevier Academic Press.

Hicks, Peter. 2002. *Preparing for Tomorrow's Social Policy Agenda*. Social Research and Demonstration Corporation Working Paper Series 02-04.

Hightower, J., M.J. Smith, C.A. Ward-Hall, and H.C. Hightower. 1999. "Meeting the Needs of Abused Older Women? A British Columbia and Yukon Transition House Survey." *Journal of Elder Abuse and Neglect* 11(4): 39–57.

Hilton, J.M., and D.P. Macari. 1997. "Grandparent Involvement Following Divorce: A Comparison in Single-Mother and Single-Father Families." *Journal of Divorce and Remarriage* 28(1/2): 203–24.

Hirdes, J.P., and K.S. Brown. 1996. "A Survival Analysis of Institutional Relocation in a Chronic Care Hospital." *Canadian Journal on Aging* 15(4): 514–24.

Hodge, G., and L. McKay. 1992. *Small Town Seniors and Their Freedom to Move*. Final report on Seniors' Independence Project No. 4687-9-88/029. Vancouver: Gerontology Research Centre, Simon Fraser University.

Hofer, S.M., and M.J. Sliwinski. 2006. "Design and Analysis of Longitudinal Studies on Aging." In In J. E. Birren and K. W. Schaie, eds., *Handbook of the Psychology of Aging*, 6th ed., 15–37. Burlington, MA: Elsevier Academic Press.

Hodgson, L.G. 1995. "Adult Grandchildren and Their Grandparents: The Enduring Bond." In J. Hendricks, ed., *The Ties of Later Life*, 155–70. Amityville, NY: Baywood.

Hoenig, H., D.H. Taylor, Jr., and F.A. Sloan. 2003. "Does Assistive Technology Substitute for Personal Assistance among the Disabled Elderly?" *American Journal of Public Health* 93(2): 330–37.

Holladay, S., D. Denton, D. Harding, M. Lee, R. Lackovich, and M. Coleman. 1997. "Granddaughters' Accounts of the Influence of Parental Mediation on Relational Closeness with Maternal Grandmothers." *International Journal of Aging and Human Development* 45(1): 23–38.

Holladay, S., R. Lackovich, M. Lee, M. Coleman, D. Harding, and D. Denton. 1998. "(Re)constructing Relationships with Grandparents: A Turning Point Analysis of Granddaughters' Relational Development and Maternal Grandmothers." *International Journal of Aging and Human Development* 46(4): 287–303.

Hollander, M.J. 2001. *Comparative Cost Analysis of Home Care and Residential Care Services*. http://www.homecarestudy.com/reports/summaries/ss01-es.html, accessed July 12, 2003.

Hollander, M.J. 2003. *Unfinished Business: The Case for Chronic Home Care Services. A Policy Paper*. Victoria, BC.

Hollander, M.J., and N. Chappell. 2002. *Overview of the National Evaluation of the Cost-Effectiveness of Home Care*. Victoria: Hollander Analytical Services and the Centre on Aging at the University of Victoria. http://www.homecarestudy.com/overview/index.html#cost, accessed May 7, 2009.

Holmén, K., E. Kjerstin, L. Andersson, B. Winblad. 1992. "Loneliness among Elderly People Living in Stockholm: A Population Study." *Journal of Advanced Nursing* 17(1): 43–51.

Holmes, E.R., and L.D. Holmes. 1995. *Other Cultures, Elder Years.* 2nd ed. Thousand Oaks, CA: Sage.

Homans, George C. 1961. *Social Behaviour: Its Elementary Forms.* New York: Harcourt Brace Jovanovich.

Hooyman, N.R., C.V. Browne, R. Ray, and V. Richardson. 2002. "Feminist Gerontology and the Life Course: Policy, Research, and Teaching Issues." *Gerontology and Geriatrics Education* 22(4): 3–26.

Horgas, A.L., H-U. Wilms, and M.M. Baltes. 1998. "Daily Life in Very Old Age: Everyday Activities as Expression of Successful Living." *Gerontologist* 38(5): 556–68.

Horn, J.L., and R.B. Cattell. 1966. "Age Differences in Primary Mental Ability Factors." *Journal of Gerontology* 21(2): 210–20.

Horn, J.L., and R.B. Cattell. 1967. "Age Differences in Fluid and Crystallized Intelligence." *Acta Psychologica* 26(2): 107–29.

Hosler, I. 2007. "Stepping Out: Mall Walking and Older Adults." *WellSpring, 18*(1).

House of Commons Canada. 1983. *Report of the Parliamentary Task Force on Pension Reform* (Frith Commission). Ottawa: Supply and Services Canada.

Hoyer, W.J., and P. Verhaeghen. 2006. "Memory Aging." In J. E. Birren and K. W. Schaie, eds., *Handbook of the Psychology of Aging,* 6th ed., 209–232. Burlington, MA: Elsevier Academic Press.

HSBC (HSBC Insurance Holdings, Ltd.). 2006. *The Future of Retirement in a World of Rising Life Expectancies.* http://www.hsbc.com/1/PA_1_1_S5/content/assets/retirement/hsbc_future_of_retirement.pdf, accessed May 7, 2009.

Hughes, K. 2001. "Restructuring Work, Restructuring Gender: The Movement of Women into Non-traditional Occupations in Canada." In V. Marshall, W.R. Heinz, H. Kruger, and A. Verma, eds., *Restructuring Work and the Life Course,* 84–106. Toronto: The University of Toronto Press.

Hughes, E.C., and H.M. Hughes. 1952. *Where Peoples Meet.* Glencoe, IL: Free Press.

Hultsch, D.F., and F. Deutsch. 1981. *Adult Development and Aging: A Life-Span Perspective.* New York: McGraw-Hill.

Hultsch, D.F., and R.A. Dixon. 1983. "The Role of Pre-Experimental Knowledge in Text Processing in Adulthood." *Experimental Aging Research* 9(1): 7–22.

Human Behavior Magazine. 1977. "Retirement to the Porch." In S.H. Zarit, ed., *Readings in Aging and Death: Contemporary Perspectives,* 2nd ed., 158. New York: Harper and Row.

Human Resources Development Canada. 2003a. "Income Security Programs: Table of Rates in Effect July–September 2003." http://www.hrdc-drhc.gc.ca/isp/oas/ tabrates2003.pdf, accessed August 24, 2003.

Human Resources Development Canada. 2003b. "The ISP Stats Book: Statistics Related to Income Security Programs." http://www.sdc.gc.ca/en/isp/statistics/pdf/ispstatbook2003.pdf, accessed August 10, 2004.

Hummert, M. L., T.A. Garstka, and L. O'Brien. 2002. "Using the Implicit Association Test to Measure Age Differences in Implicit Social Cognitions." *Psychology and Aging* 17: 482–495.

Humphry, D. 2000. *Supplement to Final Exit.* Junction City, OR: Norris Lane Press.

Hurd Clarke, L. 2005. "Remarriage in Later Life: Older Women's Negotiation of Power, Resources, and Domestic Labour." *Journal of Women and Aging* 17(4): 21–41.

Hurd Clarke, L. 2006. "Older Women and Sexuality: Experiences in Marital Relationships across the Life Course." *Canadian Journal on Aging* 25(2): 129–140.

Hurd Clarke, Laura, and M. Griffin. 2007. "The Body Natural and the Body Unnatural: Beauty Work and Aging." *Journal of Aging Studies* 21(3): 187–201.

Hutlock, T. 2003. "'Smart Technology' Future Is Now." *Nursing Homes Long Term Care Management, 52*(1), 84+.

Ibbott, P., D. Kerr, and R. Beaujot. 2006. "Probing the Future Of Mandatory Retirement in Canada." *Canadian Journal on Aging 25(2),* 161–78.

Idler, Ellen. 2006. "Religion and Aging." In Robert H. Binstock and Linda K. George, eds., *Handbook of*

Aging and the Social Sciences, 6th ed., 277–300. Burlington, MA: Academic Press.

"Impact of Smoking on Life Expectancy and Disability." 2001. *The Daily,* June 22. http://www.statcan.ca/english/edu/feature/smk.htm, accessed May 7, 2009.

Institute of Medicine. 1997. *Approaching Death.* Washington, DC: National Academy Press.

Iwasiw, C., D. Goldenberg, N. Bol, and E. MacMaster. 2003. "Resident and Family Perspectives: The First Year in a Long-Term Care Facility." *Journal of Gerontological Nursing* 29(1): 45–54.

Jacoby, S. 1999. "Great Sex: What's Age Got to Do with It?" *Modern Maturity* (October): 41ff.

Janicki, M.P., A.J. Dalton, P. McCallion, D.D. Baxley, and A. Zendell. 2005. "Group Home Care for Adults with Intellectual Disabilities and Alzheimer's Disease." *Dementia* 4(3), 361–85.

Jametti, M. 2007. *Underfunding of Defined Benefit Pension Plans and Benefit Guarantee Insurance—An Overview of Theory and Empirics.* SEDAP Research Paper No. 200. Hamilton, ON: McMaster University.

Jerrome, D. 1996. "Continuity and Change in the Study of Family Relationships." *Ageing and Society* 16(1): 93–104.

Joffres, C. 2002. "Barriers to Residential Planning: Perspectives from Selected Older Parents Caring for Adult Offrspring with Lifelong Disabilities." *Canadian Journal on Aging* 21(2): 303–11.

Johnson, T. 2006. "China Fears Aging Population Will Strain Benefits System." *San Jose Mercury News,* 20A, December 13.

Johnston, D.W. 1999. *Cyberseniors: Exploring the Use of Communication and Information Technologies by Older Adults.* M.A. thesis, University of Calgary, Graduate Program in Communication Studies.

Jones, H.E., and H.S. Conrad. 1933. "The Growth and Decline of Intelligence." *Genetic Psychology Monographs* 12: 223–98.

Joseph, A.E., and B.C. Hallman. 1996. "Caught in the Triangle: The Influence of Home, Work, and Elder Location on Work–Family Balance." *Canadian Journal on Aging* 15(3): 393–412.

Joseph, A.E., and A. Martin-Matthews. 1993. "Growing Old in Aging Communities." *Journal of Canadian Studies* 28(1): 14–29.

Kahana, E. 2006. "Loss." In R. Schulz, L.S. Noelker, K. Rockwood, and R.L. Sprott, eds., *The Encyclopedia of Aging,* 4th ed., 707–9. New York: Springer.

Kahn, R.L., and T.C. Antonucci. 1980. "Convoys over the Life Course: Attachments, Roles, and Social Support." *Life-Span Development and Behavior* 3: 253–86.

Kalbach, W.E., and W.W. McVey. 1979. *The Demographic Bases of Canadian Society,* 2nd ed. Toronto: McGraw-Hill Ryerson.

Kalish, R.A. 1979. "The New Ageism and the Failure Models: A Polemic." *Gerontologist* 19: 398–402.

Kam, P. K. 2003. "Powerlessness of Older People in Hong Kong: A Political Economy Analysis." *Journal of Aging and Social Policy* 15(4): 81–111.

Kapsalis, C., and P. Tourigny. 2004. "Duration of Non-Standard Employment." *Perspectives on Labour and Income,* 15(12): 5–13. http://www.statcan.ca/english/freepub/75-001-XIE/11204/art-1.htm, accessed May 7, 2009.

Karlawish, J. 2004. "Ethics of Research in Dementia." In S. Gauthier, P. Scheltens, and J.L. Cummings, eds., *Alzheimer's Disease and Related Disorders Annual 2004,* 123–36. London: Martin Dunitz.

Kastenbaum, R.J. 1999. "Foreword." In B. de Vries, ed., *End of Life Issues,* xv–xvii. New York: Springer.

Kastenbaum, R.J. 2001. *Death, Society, and Human Experience.* Boston: Allyn and Bacon.

Kastenbaum, R.J., and B. Ross. 1975. "Historical Perspectives on Care." In J.G. Howells, ed., *Modern Perspectives in the Psychiatry of Old Age,* 421–459. New York: Brunner/Mazel.

Katz, I.R. 1999. "Expanding the Place of Geriatric Mental Health within Health Systems: Integrated Care, Prevention, and Rehabilitation." *Gerontologist* 39: 626–30.

Katz, M.B. 1975. *The People of Hamilton, Canada West: Family and Class in a Mid-Nineteenth-Century City.* Cambridge, MA: Harvard University Press.

Katz, S. 1996. *Disciplining Old Age: The Formation of Gerontological Knowledge.* Charlottesville, VA: University Press of Virginia.

Katz, Stephen. 2003. "Critical Gerontological Theory: Intellectual Fieldwork and the Nomadic Life Of Ideas." In Simon Biggs, Ariela Lowenstein, and Jon Hendricks, eds., *The Need for Theory: Critical Approaches to Social Gerontology,* 15–31.

Amityville, New York: Baywood Publishing Company.

Katz, S., and B. Marshall. 2003. "New Sex for Old: Lifestyle Consumerism and the Ethics of Aging Well." *Journal of Aging Studies* 17(1): 3–16.

Katzmarzyk, P., Gledhill, N., and Shephard, R. 2000. "The Economic Burden of Physical Inactivity in Canada." *Canadian Medical Association Journal* 163(11): 1435–40.

Kaufman, S.R. 2006. "Death and Dying." In R. Schulz, L.S. Noelker, K. Rockwood, and R.L. Sprott, eds., *The Encyclopedia of Aging*, 4th ed., 280–83. New York: Springer.

Kaye, L.W., and A. Monk. 1984. "Sex Role Traditions and Retirement from Academe." *Gerontologist* 24: 420–26.

Keating, N.C. 1991. *Aging in Rural Canada.* Toronto: Butterworths.

Keating, N.C. 1996. "Legacy, Aging, and Succession in Farm Families." *Generations* 20(3): 61–64.

Keating, N., D. Dosman, J. Swindle, and J. Fast. 2008. "Sharing the Work: Care Networks of Frail Seniors in Canada." In A. Martin-Matthews and J. E. Phillips, eds., *Aging and Caring at the Intersection of Work and Home Life*, 165–184. New York, NY: Psychology Press.

Keating, N.C., J.E. Fast, I.A. Connidis, M.J. Penning, and J. Keefe. 1997. "Bridging Policy and Research in Eldercare." *Canadian Journal on Aging/Canadian Public Policy* 16(Suppl.): 22–41.

Keating, N.C., J.E. Fast, J. Frederick, K. Cranswick, and C. Perrier. 1999. *Eldercare in Canada: Context, Content, and Consequences.* Cat. No. 89-570-XPE. Ottawa: Minister of Industry.

Keefe, J.M., and P. Fancey. 1997. "Financial Compensation or Home Help Services: Examining Differences among Program Recipients." *Canadian Journal on Aging* 16(2): 254–78.

Keefe, J.M., and P. Fancey. 2000. "Care Continues: Responsibility for Elderly Relatives Before and After Admission to a Long-Term Care Facility." *Family Relations* 49(3): 235–44.

Keefe, J.M., and P.J. Fancey. 2002. "Work and Eldercare: Reciprocity between Older Mothers and Their Employed Daughters." *Canadian Journal on Aging* 21(2): 229–41.

Keefe, J., and Rajnovich, B. 2007. "To Pay or Not to Pay: Examining Underlying Principles in the Debate on Financial Support for Family Caregivers." *Canadian Journal on Aging* 26(supplement 1): 77–90.

Keefe, J., C. Glendinning, and P. Fancey. 2008. "Financial Payments for Family Carers: Policy Approaches and Debates." In A. Martin-Matthews and J. E. Phillips, eds., *Aging and Caring at the Intersection of Work and Home Life*, 184–206. New York: Psychology Press.

Keefe, J., J. Légaré, and Y. Carrière. 2007. "Developing New Strategies to Support Future Caregivers of the Aged in Canada: Projections of Need and their Policy Implications." *Canadian Public Policy* 33(suppl.): S66–S80.

Keefe, J.M., C. Rosenthal, and F. Béland. 2000. "Impact of Ethnicity on Helping Older Relatives." *Canadian Journal on Aging* 19: 317–42.

Keith, P. 2003. "Resources, Family Ties, and Well-Being of Never-Married Men and Women." *Journal of Gerontological Social Work* 42(2): 51–75.

Kelley, M.L., and M.J. MacLean. 1997. "I Want to Live Here for the Rest of My Life: The Challenge of Case Management for Rural Seniors." *Journal of Case Management* 6(4): 174–82.

Kelly, J.L., G. Elphick, V. Mepham, and D.W. Molloy. 1989. *Let Me Decide.* Hamilton: McMaster University Press.

Kelly, L.E., V.J. Knox, and W.L. Gekoski. 1998. "Women's Views of Institutional versus Community-Based Long-Term Care." *Research on Aging* 20(2): 218–45.

Kemp, C. 2003. "The Social and Demographic Contours of Contemporary Grandparenthood: Mapping Patterns in Canada and the United States." *Journal of Comparative Family Studies* 34(2): 187–212.

Kemp, C.L. 2004. "'Grand' Expectations: The Experiences of Grandparents and Adult Grandchildren." *Canadian Journal of Sociology* 29(4): 499–525.

Kemp, C.L. 2005. "Dimensions of Grandparent-Adult Grandchild Relationships: From Family Ties To Intergenerational Friendships." *Canadian Journal on Aging* 24(2): 161–78.

Kemp, C.L., and M. Denton. 2003. "The Allocation of Responsibility for Later Life: Canadian Reflections on the Roles of Individuals, Government, Employers, and Families." *Ageing and Society* 23(6): 737–60.

Kenyon, G.M. 1992. "Editorial: Why Is Ageism a Serious Social Problem and What Can Be Done about It?" *Canadian Journal on Aging* 11(1): 2–5.

Kenyon, Gary M., Jan-Eric Ruth, and Wilhelm Mader. 1999. "Elements of a Narrative Gerontology." In V.L. Bengtson and K. W. Schaie, eds. *Handbook of Theories of Aging*, 40–58. New York: Springer Publishing Company.

Kertzer, D.I. 1995. "Toward a Historical Demography of Aging." In D.I. Kertzer and P. Laslett, eds., *Aging in the Past: Demography, Society, and Old Age*, 363–83. Berkeley: University of California Press.

Kieran, P. 2001. "Early Retirement Trends." *Perspectives on Labour and Income* 13(4): 7–13.

Kind, V., M. Silverstein, G.H. Elder, V.L. Bengtson, and R.D. Conger. 2004. "Relations with Grandparents: Rural Midwest versus Urban Southern California." *Journal of Family Issues* 24(8), 1044–1069.

King, V., and G.H. Elder, Jr. 1997. "The Legacy of Grandparenting: Childhood Experiences with Grandparents and Current Involvement with Grandchildren." *Journal of Marriage and the Family* 59(4): 848–59.

King, V., and M.E. Scott. 2005. "A Comparison of Cohabiting Relationships among Older and Younger Adults." *Journal of Marriage and Family* 67(2): 271–85.

Kinsella, K., and V.A. Velkoff. 2001. *An Aging World: 2001*. U.S. Census Bureau, Series P95/01-1. Washington, DC: U.S. Government Printing Office. http://www.census.gov/prod/2001pubs/p95-01-1.pdf, accessed May 7, 2009.

Kirsi, T., Hervonen, A., and Jylha, M. 2004. "Always One Step Behind: Husbands' Narratives About Taking Care of Their Demented Wives." *Health: An Interdisciplinary Journal for the Social Study of Health, Illness and Medicine* 8(2): 159–81.

Klassen, T.R., and C.T. Gillin. 1999. "The Heavy Hand of the Law: The Canadian Supreme Court and Mandatory Retirement." *Canadian Journal on Aging* 18(2): 259–76.

Knapp, J.L., and P. Stubblefield. 2000. "Changing Students' Perceptions of Aging: The Impact of an Intergenerational Service Learning Course." *Educational Gerontology*, 26(7): 611–21.

Knight, B.G., B. Kaskie, G.R. Shurgot, and J. Dave. 2006. "Improving the Mental Health Of Older Adults." In J. E. Birren and K. W. Schaie, eds., *Handbook of the*

Psychology of Aging, 6th ed., 407–24. Burlington, MA: Elsevier Academic Press.

Kobayashi, K.M. 2000. *The Nature of Support from Adult Sansei (Third Generation) Children to Older Nisei (Second Generation) Parents in Japanese Canadian Families*. SEDAP Research Paper No. 18. Hamilton, ON: McMaster University.

Kobayashi, K.M., A. Martin-Matthews, C. Rosenthal, and S. Matthews. 2001. *The Timing and Duration of Women's Life Course Events: A Study of Mothers with at Least Two Children*. SEDAP Research Paper No. 55. Hamilton, ON: McMaster University.

Kobayashi, Karen M., Steven Prus, and Zhiqiu Lin. 2008. *Ethnic Differences in Health: Does Immigration Matter?* SEDAP Research Paper No. 230. Hamilton, ON: McMaster University.

Koncelik, J.A. 2003. "The Human Factors of Aging and the Micro-Environment: Personal Surroundings, Technology and Product Development." *Journal of Housing for the Elderly, 17*(2), 117–34.

Kornhaber, A. 2002. *The Grandparent Guide.* Chicago: Contemporary Books.

Koropeckyj-Cox, T. 2002. "Beyond Parental Status: Psychological Well-Being in Middle and Old Age." *Journal of Marriage and the Family 64*(4): 957–71.

Koster, J., and J. Prather. 1999. "Around the World: Canada." *AARP Global Aging e-Report*, April. E-mail communication.

Kozak, J.F., T. Elmslie, and J. Verdon. 1995. "Epidemiological Perspectives on the Abuse and Neglect of Seniors: A Review of the National and International Research Literature." In M.J. MacLean, ed., *Abuse and Neglect of Older Canadians: Strategies for Change*, 129–41. Toronto: Thompson Educational Publishing.

Kozyrskyi, A.L. 2003. "Romanow on Pharmaceuticals: A Strong Case for Access to Quality Medication Therapy." *Canadian Journal on Aging* 22(1): 25–28.

Kramer, B.J. 2000. "Husbands Caring for Wives with Dementia: A Longitudinal Study of Continuity and Change." *Health and Social Work* 25: 97–107.

Kramer, A.F., M. Fabiani, and S.J. Colcombe. 2006. "Contributions of Cognitive Neuroscience to the Understanding of Behavior and Aging." In J. E. Birren and K. W. Schaie, eds., *Handbook of the Psychology of Aging*, 6th ed., 57–83. Burlington, MA: Elsevier Academic Press.

Kraus, H., and W. Raab. 1961. *Hypokinetic Disease.* Springfield, IL: Charles C. Thomas.

Krause, N. 2006. "Social Relationships in Late Life." In Robert H. Binstock and Linda K. George, eds., *Handbook of Aging and the Social Sciences* 6th ed., 181–200. Burlington, MA: Academic.

Krauthammer, C. 1996. "First and Last, Do No Harm." *Time,* April 15, 61.

Krueger, P., K. Brazil, L. Lohfeld, J. daPonte, and M. Slobodnik. 2000. *Canadian Journal of Public Health* 91(6): 445–48.

Kruk, E. 1995. "Grandparent–Grandchild Contact Loss: Findings from a Study of 'Grandparent Rights' Members." *Canadian Journal on Aging* 14(4): 737–54.

Kübler-Ross, Elisabeth. 1969. *On Death and Dying.* New York: Macmillan.

Kuhl, D., and M. Westwood. 2001. "A Narrative Approach to Integration and Healing Among the Terminally Ill." In G. Kenyon, P. Clark, and B. de Vries, eds., *Narrative Gerontology: Theory, Research, and Practice,* 311–30. New York: Springer.

Kunemund, H., and M. Rein. 1999. "There Is More to Receiving Than Needing: Theoretical Arguments and Empirical Explorations of Crowding In and Crowding Out." *Ageing and Society* 19(1): 93–121.

Kunzmann, U. 2006. "Wisdom." In R. Schulz, L.S. Noelker, K. Rockwood, and R.L. Sprott, eds., *The Encyclopedia of Aging,* 4th ed., 1230–34. New York: Springer.

Labillois, M. 1994. "Aboriginal Housing: A Personal Perspective." In National Advisory Council on Aging, *Aboriginal Seniors' Issues,* 11–15. Cat. No. H71-2/1-15-1994E. Ottawa: Minister of Supply and Services.

Labouvie-Vief, G. 1985. "Intelligence and Cognition." In J.E. Birren and K.W. Schaie, eds., *Handbook of the Psychology of Aging,* 2nd ed., 500–530. New York: Van Nostrand Reinhold.

Lacy, W.B., and J. Hendricks. 1980. "Developmental Models of Adult Life: Myth or Reality." *International Journal of Aging and Human Development* 11: 89–110.

Lachman, M.E. 2000. Promoting a Sense of Control over Memory Aging. In L. Bäckman, R. D. Hill, and A. Stigsdotter-Neely, eds., *Cognitive Rehabilitation in Old Age,* 106–20. New York: Oxford University Press.

Lai, D.W.L. 2000. "Depression among the Elderly Chinese in Canada." *Canadian Journal on Aging* 19(3): 409–29.

Lai, D. W. L. 2007. "Cultural Predictors of Caregiving Burden of Chinese-Canadian Family Caregivers." *Canadian Journal on Aging* 26(supplement 1): 133–48.

Lai, D. W. L., K.T. Tsang, N. Chappell, D.C.Y. Lai, and S.B.Y. Chau. 2007. "Relationships between Culture and Health Status : A Multi-Site Study of the Older Chinese in Canada." *Canadian Journal on Aging* 26(3): 171–84.

Lalive d'Epinay, C.J., and J.F. Bickel. 2003. "Do 'Young-Old' Exercisers Feel Better Than Sedentary Persons? A Cohort Study in Switzerland." *Canadian Journal on Aging* 22(2): 155–65.

Lalonde, Marc. 1974. *A New Perspective on the Health of Canadians.* Ottawa: Minister of Supply and Services.

Lam, N., M.J. Prince, and J. Cutt. 1996. "Restoring the Canada Pension Plan: Simulating the Future and Stimulating the Social Policy Debate." In J.B. Burbridge et al., eds., *When We're 65: Reforming Canada's Retirement Income System,* 129–70. Toronto: C.D. Howe Institute.

Lamb, R., and E.M. Brady. 2005. "Participation in Lifelong Learning Institutes: What Turns Members On?" Educational Gerontology *31:* 207–24.

Lambert, H.C., M. McColl, J. Gilbert, J. Wong, G. Murray, and S.E.D. Shortt. 2005. "Factors Affecting Long-Term-Care Residents' Decision-Making Processes as They Formulate Advance Directives." *Gerontologist* 45(5): 626–33.

Lancaster, L.C., and D. Stillman. 2002. *When Generations Collide.* New York: HarperCollins.

Larkin-Lieffers, P.A. 2000. "Older Adult and Public Library Computer Technology: A Pilot Study in a Canadian Setting." *Livri* 50(4): 225–34.

Latimer, E.A., D. Verrilli,and W.P. Welch. 1999. "Utilization of Physician Services at the End of Life: Differences between the United States and Canada." *Inquiry 36*(1): 90–100.

Lavigne, P.C., and L. Lévesque. 1992. "Reactions of the Institutionalized Elderly upon Learning of the Death of a Peer." *Death Studies* 16(5): 451–61.

Lavoie, M., D. Blondeau, and G. Godin. 1999. "Intentions to Select a Given Level of Care When Confronted with an Ethical Issue: The Impact of a Living Will." *Journal of Applied Social Psychology* 29(4): 772–85.

Lavoie, M., and J. Oderkirk. 1993. "Social Consequences of Demographic Change." *Canadian Social Trends* (Winter): 2–5.

Law Reform Commission of Canada. 1982. *Euthanasia, Aiding Suicide and Cessation of Treatment.* Working Paper 28. Ottawa: Minister of Supply and Service.

Lawton, M.P. 1976. "The Relative Impact of Enriched and Traditional Housing on Elderly Tenants." *Gerontologist* 16: 237–42.

Lawton, M.P. 1980. *Environment and Aging.* Monterey, CA: Brooks/Cole.

Lawton, M.P. 1982. "Environmental Research: Issues and Methods." In R. Bayne and B. Wigdor, eds., *Research Issues in Aging: Report of a Conference, 1980.* Hamilton, ON: Gerontology Research Council of Ontario.

Lawton, M.P. 2001. "Quality of Life and the End of Life." In J.E. Birren and K.W. Schaie, eds., *Handbook of the Psychology of Aging,* 5th ed. San Diego: Academic Press.

Lawton, M.P., and L. Nahemow. 1973. "Ecology and the Aging Process." In C. Eisdorfer and M.P. Lawton, eds. *The Psychology of Adult Development and Aging,* 619–74. Washington, DC: American Psychological Association.

Lazowski, D-A., N.A. Ecclestone, A.M. Myers, D.H. Paterson, C. Tudor-Locke, C. Fitzgerald, G. Jones, N. Shima, and D.A. Cunningham. 1999. "Randomized Outcome Evaluation of Group Exercise Programs in Long-Term Care Institutions." *Journals of Gerontology Series A* 54(12): M621–28.

Leacy, F., ed. 1983. *Historical Statistics of Canada.* 2nd ed. Ottawa: Minister of Supply and Services.

LeBlanc, L.S., and J.A. McMullin. 1997. "Falling through the Cracks: Addressing the Needs of Individuals between Employment and Retirement." *Canadian Public Policy* 23(3): 289–304.

Lee, G.R., and A. DeMaris. 2007. "Widowhood, Gender, and Depression." *Research on Aging* 29(1): 56–72.

Lee, G.R., M.C. Willetts, and K. Seccombe. 1998. "Widowhood and Depression: Gender Differences." *Research on Aging* 20: 611–30.

Lee, J.A. 1987. "The Invisible Lives of Canada's Gray Gays." In V.W. Marshall, ed., *Aging in Canada,* 2nd ed., 138–55. Toronto: Fitzhenry and Whiteside.

Lefrancois, R., G. Leclerc, M. Dube, S. Hamel, and P. Gaulin. 2001. "Valued Activities of Everyday Life Among the Very Old: A One-Year Trend." *Activities, Adaptation and Aging,* 25(3-4): 19-34.

Lehman, H.C. 1953. *Age and Achievement.* Princeton, NJ: Princeton University Press.

Lehman, H.C. 1968. "The Creative Production Rates of Present versus Past Generations of Scientists." In B.L. Neugarten, ed., *Middle Age and Aging,* 99–105. Chicago: University of Chicago Press.

Lehto, X.Y., J.T. O'Leary, and G. Lee. 2001. "Mature International Travelers: An Examination of Gender and Benefits." *Journal of Hospitality and Leisure Marketing* 9(1–2): 53–72.

Leigh, G.K. 2000. "Cohabiting and Never-Married Families across the Life Course." In S.J. Price, P.C. McKenry, and M.J. Murphy, eds., *Families across Time: A Life Course Perspective,* 77–89. Los Angeles: Roxbury Publishing Company.

Leithman, G. 2005. *Retirement Planning: Do Financial Means Influence Life Satisfaction? Comparative Study of Male and Female Retirees.* UMI Dissertation Services, ProQuest Information and Learning, Ann Arbor, Michigan.

Lemon, B.W., V.L. Bengtson, and J.A. Peterson. 1972. "An Exploration of the Activity Theory of Aging: Activity Types and Life Satisfaction among In-Movers to a Retirement Community." In C.S. Kart and B.B. Manard, eds., *Aging in America: Readings in Social Gerontology,* 15–38. Sherman Oaks, CA: Alfred.

Leon, D., and Y. Ben-Shlomo. 1997. "Pre-adult Influences on Cardiovascular Disease and Cancer." In N D. Kuh and Y. Ben-Shlomo, eds., *A Life Course Approach to Chronic Disease Epidemiology,* 45–77. New York: Oxford University Press.

Lesemann, F. 2001. "Twenty Years of Canadian Social Research on Aging: An Attempted Understanding." *Canadian Journal on Aging* 20(Suppl. 1): 58–66.

Lévesque, L., S. Cossette., L. Potvin, and M. Benigeri. 2000. "Community Services and Caregivers of a Demented Relative: Users and Those Perceiving a Barrier to Their Use." *Canadian Journal on Aging* 19(2): 186–209.

Levinson, D.J. 1978. *The Seasons of a Man's Life.* New York: Knopf.

Levitt, S.D., and S.J. Dubner. 2005. *Freakonomics.* New York: William Morrow.

Levy, J.A. 1987. "A Life Course Perspective on Hospice and the Family." *Marriage and Family Review* 11: 39–64.

Lewis, David L., David Jewell, Irene Turpie, Christopher Patterson, Barbara McCoy, and Julia Baxter. 2005. "Translating Evidence Into Practice: The Case of Dementia Guidelines in Specialized Geriatric Services." *Canadian Journal of Aging* 24(3): 251–60.

Li, S-C., U. Lindenberger, B. Hommel, G. Aschersleben, W. Prinz, and P.B. Baltes. 2004. "Transformations in the Couplings among Intellectual Abilities and Constituent Cognitive Processes across the Life Span." *Psychological Science* 15(3): 155–63.

Li, J, 2006. "Separation, Linkage and Blurring in the Public and Private Pillars of Canada's Retirement Income System." In L.O. Stone, ed., *New Frontiers of Research on Retirement*, 95–111. Ottawa: Minister of Industry. Statistics Canada. Catalogue no. 75-511-XIE.

Liang, J., N. M. Krause, and J. M. Bennett. 2001. "Social Exchange and Well-Being: Is Giving Better Than Receiving?" *Psychology and Aging* 16: 511–23.

Light, L.L., and J.L. Capps. 1986. "Comprehension of Pronouns in Young and Older Adults." *Developmental Psychology* 2: 580–85.

Light, L.L., E.M. Zelinski, and M. Moore. 1982. "Adult Age Differences in Reasoning from New Information." *Journal of Experimental Psychology: Learning, Memory and Cognition* 8: 435–47.

Lin, J. 2005. "The Housing Transitions of Seniors." *Canadian Social Trends* (Winter): 22–26. Statistics Canada, Cat. No. 11-008.

Lin, I-Fen. 2008. "Consequences of Parental Divorce for Adult Children's Support of Their Frail Parents." *Journal of Marriage and Family 70*(1): 113–28.

Lincoln, Y., and E. Guba. 2000. "Paradigmatic Controversies, Contradictions, and Emerging Confluences." In N. Denzin and Y. Lincoln, eds., *Handbook of Qualitative Research*, 2nd ed., 163–87. Thousand Oaks, CA: Sage.

Lindberg, D.A. 2005. "Integrative Review of Research Related to Meditation, Spirituality, and the Elderly." *Geriatric Nursing* 26(6): 372–77.

Lindemann, E. 1944. "Symptomatology and Management of Acute Grief." *American Journal of Psychiatry* 101: 141–48.

Lindsay, C. 1999. *A Portrait of Seniors in Canada*, 3rd ed. Cat. No. 89-519-XPE. Ottawa: Statistics Canada.

Lindenberger, U., and P.B. Baltes. 1994. "Sensory Functioning and Intelligence in Old Age: A Strong Connection." *Psychology and Ageing 9*: 339–55.

Lindsay, C., and M. Almey, 2006. "Senior Women." In *Women in Canada,* 5th edition. A Gender-based Statistical Report, 265–90. Statistics Canada, Social and Aboriginal Statistics Division. Catalogue No. 89-503-XIE. Ottawa: Minister of Industry.

Lithwick, M., M. Beaulieu, S. Gravel, and S.M. Straka. 1999. "Mistreatment of Older Adults: Perpetrator-Victim Relationships and Interventions." *Journal of Elder Abuse and Neglect* 11(4): 95–112.

Little, D. 2002. "Review of Smoking in the Elderly." *Geriatrics and Aging* 5(9): 9–13.

Litwak, E. 1985. *Helping the Elderly: The Complementary Roles of Informal Networks and Formal Systems.* New York: Guilford Press.

Litwak, E., and C.F. Longino, Jr. 1987. "Migration Patterns among the Elderly: A Developmental Perspective." *Gerontologist* 27: 266–72.

Litwin, H. 2000. "Activity, Social Network and Well-Being: An Empirical Examination." *Canadian Journal on Aging* 19(3): 343–62.

Liu, L.L., and D.C. Park. 2003. "Technology and the Promise of Independent Living for Adults: A Cognitive Perspective." In N. Charness and K. W. Schaie, eds., Impact of Technology on Successful Aging, 262–89. New York: Springer.

Lo, O. 1996. "Condominium Living." *Canadian Social Trends* (Summer): 27–30.

Longino, C.F., Jr. 2005. *"The Future of Ageism: Baby Boomers at the Doorstep." Generations 29*(3): 79–83.

Longino, C. F. Jr., and D. E. Bradley, 2006. "Internal and International Migration." In Robert H. Binstock and Linda K. George, eds., *Handbook of Aging and the Social Sciences,* 6th edition, 76–93. Burlington, MA: Academic Press.

Loos, C., and A. Bowd. 1997. "Caregivers of Persons with Alzheimer's Disease: Some Neglected Implications of the Experience of Personal Loss and Grief." *Death Studies* 21(5): 501–14.

Lord, S., and N. Luxembourg. 2006. "Mobility of Elderly Residents Living in Suburban Territories: Mobility Experiences in Canada and France." *Journal of Housing for the Elderly* 20 (4): 103–21.

Lovering, M.J., C.A. Cott, D.L. Wells, J. Schleifer Taylor, and L.M. Wells. 2002. "A Study of a Secure Garden in the Care of People with Alzheimer's Disease." *Canadian Journal on Aging* 21(3): 417–27.

Luchak, A.A., and I.R. Gellatly. 2001. "What Kind of Commitment Does a Final-Earning Pension Plan Elicit?" *Relations Industrielles/ Industrial Relations* 56(2): 394–417.

Lucas, J.A. 2006. "Adult Day Care." In R. Schulz, L.S. Noelker, K. Rockwood, and R.L. Sprott, eds., *The Encyclopedia of Aging,* 4th ed., 17–20. New York: Springer.

Luffman, J. 2005. "Out-of-Pocket Spending on Prescription Drugs." *Perspectives,* September: 5-13. Statistics Canada–Catalogue No. 75-001-SIE.

Lusk, C. 2007. "The Need for Palliative/End-of-Life Care Programs in LTC." *Canadian Nursing Home* 18(4): 9–15.

MacAuley, J. 2005. "CARP Takes Action to End Mandatory Retirement." *50Plus Magazine,* February.

Ma, A., and I. Chi. 2005. "Utilization and Accessibility of Social Services for Chinese Canadians." *International Social Work 48:* 148–60.

MacCourt, P., H. Tuokko, and M. Tierney. 2002. "Editorial: Canadian Association on Gerontology Policy Statement on Issues in the Delivery of Mental Health Services to Older Adults." *Canadian Journal on Aging* 21(2): 165–74.

MacDougall, B. 1998. "A Time to Grieve." *Expression* 12(1): 1–2. Ottawa: National Advisory Council on Aging.

Mace, N.L., and P.V. Rabins. 1981. *The Thirty-Six-Hour Day.* Baltimore: Johns Hopkins University Press.

MacGregor, D. 2005. "The Ass and the Grasshopper: Canadian Universities and Mandatory Retirement." *Time's Up! Mandatory Retirement in Canada.* Toronto: James Lorimer and Company.

MacKnight, C., B.L. Beattie, H. Bergman, W.B. Dalziel, J. Feightner, B. Goldlist, D.B. Hogan, F. Molnar, and K. Rockwood. 2003. "Response to the Romanow Report: The Canadian Geriatrics Society." *Geriatrics Today* 6(1): 11–15.

MacLean, E. 2008. *Getting through The Day: A Coping Process of Drawing Upon Resources While Caring for a Spouse with Dementia Awaiting Long Term Care Placement.* Master's Thesis, School of Nursing, McMaster University, Hamilton, ON, Canada.

MacLean, M.J., and R. Bonar. 1983. "The Normalization Principle and the Institutionalization of the Elderly." *Canada's Mental Health* 31: 16–18.

MacLean, M.J., and R.M. Williams. 1995. "Introduction." In M.J. MacLean, ed., *Abuse and Neglect of Older Canadians: Strategies for Change,* xi–xxii. Toronto: Thompson Educational Publishing.

MacRae, H. 1999. "Managing Courtesy Stigma: The Case of Alzheimer's Disease." *Sociology of Health and Illness* 21(1): 54–70.

MacRae, H. 2002. "The Identity Maintenance Work of Family Members of Persons with Alzheimer's Disease." *Canadian Journal on Aging* 21(3): 405–15.

Madden, D.J. 2001. "Speed and Timing of Behavioral Processes." In J.E. Birren and K.W. Schaie, eds., *Handbook of the Psychology of Aging,* 5th ed. San Diego: Academic Press.

Maddox, G.L. 1988. "Overview." In *Aging around the World: A Report on the President's Symposium on Aging in Tomorrow's World: An International Perspective.* Washington, DC: Gerontological Society of America.

Mahoney, D., B. Tarlow, and R. Jones. 2003. "Effects of an Automated Telephone Support System on Caregiver Burden and Anxiety: Findings from the REACH TLC Intervention Study." *The Gerontologist* 43, 556–67.

Malcolm, M., W.C. Mann, M.R. Tomita, L.F. Fraas, K.M. Stanton, and L. Gitlin. 2001. "Computer and Internet Use in Physically Frail Elders." *Physical and Occupational Therapy in Geriatrics* 19(3): 15–32.

Mamdani, M., S.V. Parikh, P.C. Austin, and R.E. Upshur. 2000. "Use of Antidepressants among Elderly Subjects: Trends and Contributing Factors." *American Journal of Psychiatry* 157(3): 360–67.

Mancer, K. 2003. *Life Lease Housing in Canada: A Preliminary Exploration of Some Consumer Protection Issues.* Ottawa: Canada Mortgage and Housing Corporation.

Mancini, A.D., and G.A. Bonanno. 2006. "Marital Closeness, Functional Disability, and Adjustment in Late Life." *Psychology and Aging* 21 (3): 600–10.

Mandemakers, J.J., and P.A. Dykstra. 2008. "Discrepancies in Parent's and Adult Child's Reports of Support and Contact." *Journal of Marriage and Family* 70: 495–506.

Manga, P. 1993. "Health Economics and the Current Health Care Cost Crisis: Contributions and Controversies." *Health and Canadian Society* 1(1): 177–203.

Manitoba Regional Health Authority. 2008. "Senior Centres." Support Services to Seniors. http://www.wrha.mb.ca/community/seniors/centres.php, accessed May 7, 2009.

Mann, R. 2007. "Out of the Shadows?: Grandfatherhood, Age and Masculinities." *Journal of Aging Studies* 21: 281–91.

Manton, K.G., X. Gu, V.L. Lamb. 2006. "Change in Chronic Disability from 1982 to 2004/2005 as Measured by Long-Term Changes in Function and Health in the U.S. Elderly Population." *Proceedings of the National Academy of Sciences of the United States of America* 103(48): 18374–79.

Marmen, L., and S. Delisle. 2003. "Health Care in French Outside Quebec." *Canadian Social Trends* (Winter): 24–27.

Marshall, V.W. 1995. "Rethinking Retirement: Issues for the Twenty-First Century." In E.M. Gee and G.M. Gutman, eds., *Rethinking Retirement*, 31–50. Vancouver: Gerontology Research Centre, Simon Fraser University.

Marshall, V.W. 2001. "Canadian Research on Older Workers." Paper presented for a symposium, "Problems of Older Workers," at the International Association of Gerontology 17th World Congress, Vancouver, July.

Marshall, V.W., P.J. Clarke, and P.J. Ballantyne. 2001. "Instability in the Retirement Transition: Effects on Health and Well-Being in a Canadian Study." *Research on Aging* 23(4): 379–409.

Marshall, Victor, Walter R. Heinz, Helga Krueger, and Anil Verma., eds. 2001. *Restructuring Work and the Life Course.* Toronto: University of Toronto Press.

Marshall, V.W., C.J. Rosenthal, and J. Synge. 1983. "Concerns about Parental Health." In E.W. Markson, ed., *Older Women: Issues and Prospects*, 253–73. Lexington, MA: D.C. Heath.

Marsiske, M., and J.A. Margrett. 2006. "Everyday Problem Solving and Decision Making." In J.E. Birren and K. W. Schaie eds., *Handbook of the Psychology of Aging*, 6th edition, 315–42. Burlington, MA: Elsevier Academic Press.

Martel, L., and A. Bélanger. 2000. "Dependence-Free Life Expectancy in Canada." *Canadian Social Trends* (Autumn): 26–29.

Martel, L., A. Bélanger, and J-M. Berthelot. 2002. "Loss and Recovery of Independence among Seniors." *Health Reports* 13(4): 35–48.

Martel, L., and É. Caron-Malenfant. 2008. *Portrait of the Canadian Population in 2006: Findings.* Statistics Canada, 2006 Census Analysis Series. http://www12.statcan.ca/english/census06/ analysis/popdwell/index.cfm, accessed July 9, 2008.

Martel, L., J. He, and E. C. Malenfant. 2006. *Report on the Demographic Situation in Canada 2003 and 2004.* Statistics Canada Demography Division. Ottawa: Minister of Industry.

Martin-Matthews, A. 2006. "Canadian Research on Aging." In R. Schulz, L.S. Noelker, K. Rockwood, and R.L. Sprott, eds., *The Encyclopedia of Aging*, 4th ed., 148–52. New York: Springer.

Maser, Karen. 2003. "An Introduction to Canada's Retirement Income Programs." *Canada's Retirement Income Programs: A Statistical Overview (1990–2000).* Statistics Canada Catalogue No. 74-507-XIE.

Maser, K., and J. Begin. 2003. *Canada's Retirement Income Programs: A Statistical Overview (1990–2000).* Ottawa: Minister of Industry.

Matthews, A.M. 1987. "Widowhood as an Expectable Life Event." In V.W. Marshall, ed., *Aging in Canada: Social Perspectives*, 2nd ed., 343–66. Toronto: Fitzhenry and Whiteside.

Matthews, A.M., K.H. Brown, C.K. Davis, and M.A. Denton. 1982. "A Crisis Assessment Technique for the Evaluation of Life Events: Transition to Retirement as an Example." *Canadian Journal on Aging* 1: 28–39.

Matthews, A.M., and L.D. Campbell. 1995. "Gender Roles, Employment and Informal Care." In S. Arber and J. Ginn, eds., *Connecting Gender and Aging: A Sociological Approach*, 129–43. Buckingham, U.K.: Open University Press.

Matthews, A.M., and Joseph A. Tindale. 1987. "Retirement in Canada." In K.S. Markides and C.L. Cooper, eds., *Retirement in Industrialized Societies: Social, Psychological and Health Factors*, 43–75. Toronto: John Wiley and Sons.

Matthews, A.M., J.A. Tindale, and J.E. Norris. 1985. "The Facts on Aging Quiz: A Canadian Validation and Cross-Cultural Comparison." *Canadian Journal on Aging* 3: 165–74.

Matthews, S.H. 2002. *Sisters and Brothers/Daughters and Sons: Meeting the Needs of Older Parents.* Bloomington, IN: Unlimited Publishing.

Matthews, S.H., and J. Heidorn. 1998. "Meeting Filial Responsibilities in Brothers-Only Sibling Groups." *Journals of Gerontology Series B* 53(5): S278–86.

Maurier, W.L., and H.C. Northcott. 2000. *Aging in Ontario: Diversity in the New Millennium.* Calgary: Detselig Enterprises.

Maxwell, R., and J.P. Silverman. 1977. "Information and Esteem: Cultural Considerations in the Treatment of the Aged." In W.H. Watson and R.J. Maxwell, eds., *Human Aging and Dying: A Study in Socio-cultural Gerontology*, 15–45. New York: St. Martin's Press.

Mays, H.J. 1983. "A Place to Stand: Families, Land and Permanence in Toronto Gore Township, 1820–1890." In W.P. Ward, ed., *The Social Development of Canada: Readings.* Richmond, BC: Open Learning Institute.

McAuley, E., S. Elavsky, G.J. Jerome, J.F. Konopack, and D.X. Marquez. 2005. "Physical Activity-Related Well-Being in Older Adults: Social Cognitive Influences." *Psychology and Aging* 20(2): 295–302.

McCrae, R., and P. Costa, Jr. 1990. *Personality in Adulthood.* New York: Guilford.

McDaniel, S. 1986. *Canada's Aging Population.* Toronto: Butterworths.

McDaniel, S. 2003. "Intergenerational Interlinkages: Public, Family, and Work." In D. Cheal, ed., *Aging and Demographic Change in Canadian Context*, 22–71. Toronto: University of Toronto Press.

McDaniel, S., and R. Lewis, 1997. "Did They or Didn't They? Intergenerational Supports in Canada's Past and a Case Study of Brigus, Newfoundland, 1920–1949." In L. Chambers and E-A. Montigny, eds., *Family Matters: Papers in Post-Confederation Canadian Family History*, 475–97. Toronto: Canadian Scholars Press.

McDill, T., S.K. Hall, and S.C. Turell. 2006. "Aging and Creating Families: Never Married Heterosexual Women over Forty." *The Journal of Women and Aging* 18(3): 37–50.

McDonald, L. 1997. "The Invisible Poor: Canada's Retired Widows." *Canadian Journal on Aging* 16(3): 553–83.

McDonald, L. 2002. *The Invisible Retirement of Women.* SEDAP Research Paper No. 69. Hamilton, ON: McMaster University.

McDonald, L. 2006a. "Gender and Family—Major Dimensions of Retirement Research." In L.O. Stone, ed., *New Frontiers of Research on Retirement*, Chapter 9, 129–36. Ottawa: Minister of Industry. Statistics Canada. Catalogue no. 75-511-XIE.

McDonald, L. 2006b. "Gendered Retirement: The Welfare of Women and the 'New' Retirement." In L.O. Stone, ed., *New Frontiers of Research on Retirement*, Chapter 10, 137–64. Ottawa: Minister of Industry. Statistics Canada. Catalogue no. 75-511-XIE.

McDonald, L., and M.Y.T. Chen. 1995. "The Youth Freeze and the Retirement Bulge: Older Workers and the Impending Labour Shortage." *Journal of Canadian Studies* 28(1): 75–101.

McDonald, L., and A. Collins. 2000. *Abuse and Neglect of Older Adults: A Discussion Paper.* Ottawa: Health Canada, National Clearing-house on Family Violence.

McDonald, L., J. Dergal, and L. Cleghorn. 2007. "Living on the Margins: Older Homeless Adults in Toronto." *Journal of Gerontological Social Work* 49 (1/2): 19-46.

McDonald, L., and P. Donahue. 2000. "Poor Health and Retirement Income: The Canadian Case." *Aging and Society* 20 (Pt. 5): 493–522.

McDonald, L., P. Donahue, and V. Marshall. 2000. "The Economic Consequences of Unexpected Early Retirement." In F.T. Denton, D. Fretz, and B.G. Spencer, eds., *Independence and Economic Security in Old Age*, 267–92. Vancouver: UBC Press.

McDonald, L, P. Donahue, and B. Moore. 1998. *The Economic Casualties of Retiring to Caregive.* Program for Research on the Independence and Economic Security of the Older Population. Research Paper No. 28. McMaster University.

McDonald, L., P. Donahue, and B. Moore. 2000a. "The Poverty of Retired Widows." In F.T. Denton, D. Fretz, and B.G. Spencer, eds., *Independence and Economic Security in Old Age*, 328–45. Vancouver: UBC Press.

McDonald, L., P. Donahue, and B. Moore. 2000b. "Retirement through Unemployment: What Social Work Needs to Know." *Canadian Social Work Review* 17(1): 69–85.

McDonald, L., and A.L. Robb. 2004. "The Economic Legacy of Divorce and Separation for Women in Old Age." *Canadian Journal on Aging* 23 (Suppl. 1): S83–S97.

McDonald, Lynn P., T. Sussman, and P. Donahue. 2007. *When Bad Things Happen to Good People: The Economic Consequences of Retiring to Caregive.*

SEDAP Research Paper No. 202, Hamilton, ON: McMaster University.

McDonald, P.L., and R.A. Wanner. 1984. "Socioeconomic Determinants of Early Retirement in Canada." *Canadian Journal on Aging* 3: 105–16.

McDonald, P.L., and R.A. Wanner. 1990. *Retirement in Canada.* Toronto: Butterworths.

McDougall, G.J. 2000. "Memory Improvement in Assisted Living Elders." *Issues in Mental Health Nursing* 21(2), 217–33.

McFadden, S.H. 1996. "Religion, Spirituality, and Aging." In J.E. Birren and K.W. Schaie, eds., *Handbook of the Psychology of Aging*, 4th ed., 162–77. San Diego: Academic Press.

McFadgen, L., and L. Zimmerman. 1995. "Women's Retirement: Shifting Ground." In E.M. Gee and G.M. Gutman, eds., *Rethinking Retirement*, 93–118. Vancouver: Gerontology Research Centre, Simon Fraser University.

McFarland, P.L., and S. Sanders. 2003. "A Pilot Study About the Needs of Older Gays and Lesbians: What Social Workers Need to Know." *Journal of Gerontological Social Work* 40(3): 67–80.

McGoldrick, A.E., and C.L. Cooper. 1988. *Early Retirement.* Gower: Brookfield, VT.

McGuire, F.A., F.D. Dottavio, and J.T. O'Leary. 1987. "The Relationship of Early Life Experiences to Later Life Leisure Involvement." *Leisure Sciences* 9: 251–57.

McHugh, K. 2003. "The 'Ageless Self'? Emplacement of Identities in Sun Belt Retirement Communities." *Journal of Aging Studies* 14: 103–15.

McInnis, R.M. 1977. "Childbearing and Land Availability: Some Evidence from Individual Household Data." In R. Lee, ed., *Population Patterns in the Past*, 201–27. New York: Academic Press.

McKeen, N. A., J.G. Chipperfield, and D.W. Campbell. 2004. "Longitudinal Analysis of Discrete Negative Emotions and Health-Service Use in Elderly Individuals." *Journal of Aging and Health* 16(2): 204–27.

McKie, C. 1993. "Population Aging: Baby Boomers into the 21st Century." *Canadian Social Trends* (Summer): 2–6.

McMellon, C.A., and L.G. Schiffman. 2002. "Cybersenior Empowerment: How Some Older Individuals Are Taking Control of Their Lives." *Journal of Applied Gerontology* 21(2): 157–75.

McMullin, J. A. 2005. "Patterns of Paid and Unpaid Work: The Influence of Power, Social Context, and Family Background." *Canadian Journal on Aging* 24 (3): 225–36.

McMullin, J.A., and V.W. Marshall. 1996. "Family, Friends, Stress, and Well-Being: Does Childlessness Make a Difference?" *Canadian Journal on Aging* 15(3): 355–73.

McMullin, J.A., and V.W. Marshall. 1999. "Structure and Agency in the Retirement Process: A Case Study of Montreal Garment Workers." In C.D. Ryff and V.W. Marshall, eds., *The Self and Society in Aging Processes*, 305–38. New York: Springer.

McMullin, J.A., and V.W. Marshall. 2001. "Ageism, Age Relations, and Garment Industry Work in Montreal." *Gerontologist* 41(1): 111–22.

McMullin, J.A., and T.L. Tomchick. 2004. *To be Employed or Not to be Employed?: An Examination of Employment Incentives and Disincentives for Older Workers in Canada.* WANE Working Paper #7. London, ON: University of Western Ontario.

McPherson, B.D. 2001. "Commentary: Are There Two Solitudes in Canadian Gerontology?" *Canadian Journal on Aging* 20 (Suppl. 1): 76–81.

McPherson, B.D., and C. Kozlik. 1987. "Age Patterns in Leisure Partricipation: The Canadian Case." In V.W. Marshall, e., *Aging in Canada,* 2nd ed. Toronto: Fitzhenry and Whiteside.

McQuillan, K., and M. Belle. 2001. "Lone-Father Families in Canada, 1971–1996." *Canadian Studies in Population* 28(1): 67–88.

McWilliam, C.L., W.L. Diehl-Jones, J. Jutai, and S. Tadrissi. 2000. "Care Delivery Approaches and Seniors' Independence." *Canadian Journal on Aging* 19(Suppl. 1): 101–24.

Mead, G.H. 1934. *Mind, Self, and Society: From the Standpoint of a Social Behaviorist.* Chicago: University of Chicago Press.

Medjuck, S., J.M. Keefe, and P.J. Fancey. 1998. "Available But Not Accessible: An Examination of the Use of Workplace Policies for Caregivers of Elderly Kin." *Journal of Family Issues* 19(3): 274–99.

Mehrotra, C.M. 2003. "In Defense of Offering Educational Programs for Older Adults." *Educational Gerontology* 29: 645–55.

Meier, D.E. 1999. "Should It Be Legal for Physicians to Expedite Death? No: A Change of Heart on Assisted Suicide." *Generations* 23(1): 58–60.

Meier, E.E., H. Myers, and P.R. Muskin. 1999. "When a Patient Requests Help Committing Suicide." *Generations* 23(1): 61–68.

Melenhorst, A., A. Fisk, E. Mynatt, and W. Rogers. 2004. "Potential Intrusiveness of Aware Home Technology: Perceptions of Older Adults." *Proceedings of the Human Factors and Ergonomics Society* 48: 266–70.

Melzer, D., B. McWilliams, C. Brayne, T. Johnson, and J. Bond. 2000. "Socioeconomic State and the Expectation of Disability in Old Age: Estimates for England." *Journal of Epidemiology and Community Health* 54(2): 28–92.

Menec, V.H. 2003. "Relation between Everyday Activities and Successful Aging: A 6-Year Longitudinal Study." *Journals of Gerontology Series B* 58(2): S74–82.

Menec, V.H., L. Lix, and J. MacWilliam. 2003. "Living Longer, Living Healthier? Trends in the Health Status of Older Manitobans." Paper presented at the 32nd Annual Scientific and Educational Meeting of the Canadian Association on Gerontology, Toronto, October 30–November 1.

Menec, V.H., L. Lix, and L. MacWilliam. 2005. "Trends in the Health Status of Older Manitobans, 1985 to 1999." *Canadian Journal on Aging* 24(Suppl. 1): 5–14.

Menec, V.H., L. Lix, S. Nowicki, and O. Ekuma. 2007. "Health Care Use at the End of Life Among Older Adults: Does It Vary by Age?" *Journals of Gerontology: Series A: Biological Sciences and Medical Sciences* 62A(4): 400–7.

Mercado, R., A. Páez, and K.B. Newbold. 2007. *Policy Areas Impinging on Elderly Transportation Mobility: An Explanation with Ontario, Canada as Example.* SEDAP Research Paper No. 187. Hamilton, ON: McMaster University.

Metge, C., R. Grymonpre, M. Dahl, and M. Yogendran. 2005. "Pharmaceutical Use among Older Adults: Using Administrative Data to Examine Medication-Related Issues." *Canadian Journal on Aging* 24(Suppl. 1): 81–95.

Meyer, V.B.J.F., and C.K. Pollard. 2006. "Applied Learning and Aging: A Closer Look at Reading." In J.E. Birren and K.W. Schaie eds., *Handbook of the Psychology of Aging*, 6th edition, 233–60. Burlington, MA: Elsevier Academic Press.

Michalos, A.C., A.M. Hubley, B.D. Zumbo, and D. Hemingway. 2001. "Health and Other Aspects of the Quality of Life of Older People." *Social Indicators Research* 54(3): 239–74.

Miedema, B., and S. Tatemichi. 2003. "Gender, Marital Status, Social Networks, and Health: Their Impact on Loneliness in the Very Old." *Geriatrics Today* 6(2): 95–99.

Milan, A.M., and B. Hamm. 2003. "Across the Generations: Grandparents and Grandchildren." *Canadian Social Trends* (Winter): 2–7.

Miles, C.C., and W.R. Miles. 1932. "The Correlation of Intelligence Scores and Chronological Age from Early to Late Maturity." *American Journal of Psychology* 44: 44–78.

Millar, W.J. 1999. "Older Drivers: A Complex Public Health Issue." *Health Reports* 11(2): 59–71.

Milligan, Kevin. 2007. *The Evolution of Elderly Poverty in Canada.* SEDAP Research Paper No. 170. Hamilton, ON: McMaster University.

Milligan, K., and T. Schrile. 2006. *Public Pensions and Retirement: International Evidence in the Canadian Context.* HRDC-IC-SSHRC. http://www.strategis.ic.gc.ca/epic/site/eas-aes.nsf/en/ra02019e.html, accessed May 7, 2009.

Mills, T.L. 1999. "When Grandchildren Grow Up: Role Transition and Family Solidarity among Baby Boomer Grandchildren and Their Grandparents." *Journal of Aging Studies* 13(2): 219–39.

Milne, A., and E. Hatzidimitriadou, 2003. "'Isn't He Wonderful?': Exploring the Contributions and Conceptualization of Elder Husbands as Carers." *Ageing International* 28: 389–407.

Milner, C. 2006. "Marketing Successfully to Age 40-Plus Women." *Journal on Active Aging* 5(4): 22–26.

Miner, S., and P. Uhlenberg. 1997. "Intergenerational Proximity and the Social Role of Sibling Neighbors after Midlife." *Family Relations* 46(2): 145–53.

Minerva Senior Studies Institute. 2003. "Fall 2003 Programs and Courses." http://www.minerva.macewan.ca/minerva.pdf, accessed November 26, 2003.

Minkler, M., and C.L. Estes. 1999. *Critical Gerontology: Perspectives from Political and Moral Economy.* Amityville, NY: Baywood.

Minkler, M., and M. Holstein. 2005. "Successful Aging." In E.B. Palmore, L. Branch, and D.K. Harris, eds., *Encyclopedia of Ageism,* 306–9. New York: The Haworth Pastoral Press.

Mireles, D.E., and N. Charness. 2002. "Computational Explorations of the Influence of Structured Knowledge on Age-Related Cognitive Decline." *Psychology and Aging* 17(2): 245–59.

Mitchell, B.A. 2003. "Would I Share a Home with an Elderly Parent? Exploring Ethno-cultural Diversity and Intergenerational Support Relations during Young Adulthood." *Canadian Journal on Aging* 22(1): 69–82.

Mitchell, E. 1996. "Yo, Van Gogh! What's Up?" *Time,* February 26, 60.

Mitchell, L., N.P. Roos, and E. Shapiro. 2005. "Patterns in Home Care Use in Manitoba." *Canadian Journal on Aging* 24(Suppl.1): 59–68.

Mitchell, L.A., L.A. Strain, and A.A. Blandford. 2007. "Indicators of Home Care Use in Urban and Rural Settings." *Canadian Journal on Aging* 26(3): 275–280.

Mittelman, K., S. Crawford, S. Holliday, G. Gutman, and G. Bhakthan. 1989. "The Older Cyclist: Anthropometric, Physiological, and Psychosocial Changes Observed during a Trans-Canada Cycle Tour." *Canadian Journal on Aging* 8: 144–56.

Mo, L., J. Legare, and L. Stone. 2006. *The Diversification and the Privatization of the Sources of Retirement Income in Canada.* SEDAP Research Paper No. 159. Hamilton, ON: McMaster University.

Moberg, D.O. 1997. "Religion and Aging." In K.F. Ferraro, ed., *Gerontology: Perspectives and Issues,* 2nd ed., 193–220. New York: Springer.

Moberg, D.O. 2001. "The Reality and Centrality of Spirituality." In D.O. Moberg, ed., *Aging and Spirituality,* 3–20. New York: Haworth Press.

Moen, P. and D. Spencer. 2006. "Converging Divergences in Age, Gender, Health, and Well-Being: Strategic Selection in the Third Age." In Robert H. Binstock and Linda K. George, eds., *Handbook of Aging and the Social Sciences,* 6th ed., 127–44. Burlington, MA: Academic Press.

Moen, P., and P. Roehling. 2005. *The Career Mystique: Cracks in the American Dream.* Boulder, CO: Rowman and Littlefield.

Moen, P., V. Fields, H.E. Quick, and H. Hofmeister. 2000. "A Life-Course Approach to Retirement and Social Integration." In K. Pillemer, P. Moen, E. Wethington, and N. Glasgow, eds., *Social Integration in the Second Half of Life,* 75–107. Baltimore: Johns Hopkins University Press.

Moen, P., K. Pillemer, E. Wethington, N. Glasgow, and G. Vesey. 2000. "Closing Thoughts and Future Directions." In K. Pillemer, P. Moen, E. Wethington, and N. Glasgow, eds., *Social Integration in the Second Half of Life,* 287–304. Baltimore: Johns Hopkins University Press.

Molloy, D.W., G.H. Guyatt, R. Russo, R. Goeree, B.J. O'Brien, M. Bédard, A.Willan, J. Watson, C. Patterson, C. Harrison, T. Standish, D. Strang, P.J. Darzins, S. Smith, and S. Dubois. 2000. "Systematic Implementation of an Advance Directive Program in Nursing Homes: A Randomized Controlled Trial." *Journal of the American Medical Association* 283(11): 1437–44.

Molloy, D.W., R. Russo., D. Pedlar, and M. Bédard. 2000. "Implementation of Advance Directives among Community-Dwelling Veterans." *Gerontologist* 40(2): 213–17.

Monserud, M. A. 2008. "Intergenerational Relationships and Affectual Solidarity between Grandparents And Young Adults." *Journal of Marriage and Family* 70: 182–95.

Montague, A. 1989. *Growing Young: Second Edition.* Westport, CT: Bergin & Garvey.

Montgomery, P.R., A.J. Kirshen, and N.P. Roos. 1988. "Long-Term Care and Impending Mortality: Influence upon Place of Death and Hospital Utilization." *Gerontologist* 28: 351–54.

Montigny, E-A. 1997. *Foisted upon the Government? State Responsibilities, Family Obligations, and the Care of the Dependent Aged in Late Nineteenth-Century Ontario.* Montreal and Kingston: McGill-Queen's University Press.

Moodie, S. 1853. *Life in the Clearings Versus the Bush.* New York: DeWitt and Davenport.

Moore, A.J., and D.C. Stratton. 2002. *Resilient Widowers: Older Men Speak for Themselves.* New York: Springer.

Moore, E.G. 1995. "Aboriginal Women in Canada." In Statistics Canada, *Women in Canada: A Statistical Report,* 3rd ed., 147–62. Cat. No. 89-503E. Ottawa: Minister of Supply and Services.

Moore, E.G., and M.A. Pacey. 2003. *Geographic Dimensions of Aging in Canada 1991–2001.* SEDAP Research Paper No. 97. Hamilton, ON: McMaster University.

Moore, E.G., and M.A. Pacey. 2004. "Geographic Dimensions of Aging in Canada, 1991–2001." *Canadian Journal on Aging* 23(Suppl. 1): S5–S21.

Moore, E.G., M.W. Rosenberg, and S.H. Fitzgibbon. 1999. "Activity Limitations and Chronic Conditions in Canada's Elderly, 1986–2011." *Disability and Rehabilitation* 21(5/6): 196–210.

Moorman, S.M., A. Booth, and K.L. Fingerman. 2006. "Women's Romantic Relationships After Widowhood." *Journal of Family Issues* 27(9): 1281–304.

Moremen, R.D. 2008. "The Downside of Friendship: Sources of Strain in Older Women's Friendships." *Journal of Women and Aging* 20(1/2): 169–87.

Morgan, Jay. (2007). *Accredited Senior Centers: A Snapshot.* http://www.ncoa.org/ content.cfm?sectionID=369&detail=1307, accessed May 7, 2009.

Morris, J.N., I. Carpenter, K. Berg, and R.N. Jones. 2000. "Outcome Measures for Use with Home Care Clients." *Canadian Journal on Aging* 19(Suppl. 2): 87–105.

Morissette, R. and Y. Ostrovsky. 2007. "Pensions and Retirement Savings of Families." *Perspectives on Labour and Income* 19(4): 5–18.

Morissette, R., and Z. Zhang. 2004. "Retirement Plan Awareness." *Perspectives on Labour and Income* 5(1): 11–18.

Motiwala, S.S., R. Croxford, D.N. Guerriere, and P.C. Coyte. 2006. "Predictors of Place of Death for Seniors in Ontario: A Population-Based Cohort Analysis." *Canadian Journal on Aging* 25(4): 363–71.

Mundorf, N., J. Mundorf, and W. Brownell. 2006. "Communication Technologies and Older Adults." In R. Schulz, L.S. Noelker, K. Rockwood, and R.L. Sprott, eds., *The Encyclopedia of Aging,* 4th ed., 242–47. New York: Springer.

Musick and Wilson. 2003. "Volunteering and Depression: The Role of Psychological and Social Resources in Different Age Groups." *Social Science and Medicine* 56: 259–69.

Myers, A.M., and G. Gonda. 1986. "Research on Physical Activity in the Elderly: Practical Implications for Program Planning." *Canadian Journal on Aging* 5: 175–87.

Myles, J. 1982. "Social Implications of a Changing Age Structure." In G. Gutman, ed., *Canada's Changing Age Structure: Implications for the Future.* Vancouver: Simon Fraser University Publications.

Myles, J. 2000. "The Maturation of Canada's Retirement Income System: Income Levels, Income Inequality, and Low Income among Older Persons." *Canadian Journal on Aging* 19(3): 287–316.

Myles, J. 2002. "Editorial: Back to Bismarck? The Public Policy Implications of Living Longer." *Canadian Journal on Aging* 21(3): 325–29.

Myles, J. 2006. "From Pension Policy to Retirement Policy: Towards a New Social Agenda? In L.O. Stone, ed., *New Frontiers of Research on Retirement,* 65–82. Statistics Canada. Catalogue No. 75-511-XIE. Ottawa: Minister of Industry.

Myles, J., and M. Boyd. 1982. "Population Aging and the Elderly." In D. Forcese and S. Richer, eds., *Social Issues: Sociological Views of Canada,* 258–85. Scarborough, ON: Prentice-Hall.

Myles, J., and D. Street. 1995. "Should the Economic Life Course Be Redesigned? Old Age Security in a Time of Transition." *Canadian Journal on Aging* 14(2): 335–59.

Myles, J., and L. Teichroew. 1991. "The Politics of Dualism: Pension Policy in Canada." In J. Myles and J. Quadagno, eds., *States, Labor Markets, and the Future of Old-Age Policy,* 84–104. Philadelphia: Temple University Press.

Naglie, G., M. Silberfeld, K. O'Rourke, B. Fried, N. Durham, C. Bombardier, and A. Detsky. 1995. "Convening Expert Panels to Identify Mental Capacity Assessment Items." *Canadian Journal on Aging* 14(4): 697–705.

Nagnur, D., and M. Nagrodski. 1988. "Cardiovascular Disease, Cancer and Life Expectancy." *Canadian Social Trends* (Winter): 25–27.

Nahmiash, D., and M. Reis. 2000. "Most Successful Intervention Strategies for Abused Older Adults." *Journal of Elder Abuse and Neglect* 12(3–4): 53–70.

Namazi, K.H., and M. McClintic. 2003. "Computer Use Among Elderly Persons in Long-Term Care Facilities." *Educational Gerontology* 29(6): 535–50.

Narushima, Miya. 2005. "'Payback Time': Community Volunteering Among Older Adults as a Transformative Mechanism." *Ageing and Society* 25(4): 567–84.

Nason, J.D. 1981. "Respected Elder or Old Person: Aging in a Micronesian Community." In P.T. Amoss and S. Harrell, eds., *Other Ways of Growing Old: Anthropological Perspectives,* 155–73. Stanford, CA: Stanford University Press.

National Advisory Council on Aging. 1993a. "Competency and Risk." *Expression* 9(2): 3–4. Ottawa: National Advisory Council on Aging.

National Advisory Council on Aging. 1993b. "Freedom and Responsibility: Home Alone." *Expression* 9(2): 2. Ottawa: National Advisory Council on Aging.

National Advisory Council on Aging. 1993c. "Rights and Limits to Risk." *Expression* 9(2): 1–8. Ottawa: National Advisory Council on Aging.

National Advisory Council on Aging. 1993d. "The Freedom to Drive a Car." *Expression* 9(2): 7. Ottawa: National Advisory Council on Aging.

National Advisory Council on Aging. 1994. "Euthanasia and Assisted Suicide: What They Mean." *Expression* 10(1): 2. Ottawa: National Advisory Council on Aging.

National Advisory Council on Aging. 1995. *The NACA Position on Community Services in Health Care for Seniors: Progress and Challenges.* Ottawa: National Advisory Council on Aging.

National Advisory Council on Aging. 1996. "Are Seniors Heavier Users of Hospital Care?" Aging Vignette No. 29. http://www.hc-sc.gc.ca/ seniors-aines/pubs/ vignette/pdf/vig21-33_e.pdf, accessed August 5, 2004.

National Advisory Council on Aging. 2000a. "Choice." *Expression* 14(1): 5. Ottawa: National Advisory Council on Aging.

National Advisory Council on Aging. 2000b. "The 'New' Retirement." *Expression* 13(2): 5.

National Advisory Council on Aging. 2001a. "Seniors a Target." *Expression* 14(2). Ottawa:

National Advisory Council on Aging. 2001b. *Seniors in Canada: A Report Card.* Cat. No. H88-3/29-2001E. Minister of Public Works and Government Services Canada.

National Advisory Council on Aging. 2002. "AIDS and Age." *Expression* 15(4): 7. Ottawa: National Advisory Council on Aging.

National Advisory Council on Aging. 2002–03. "Let's Get Moving!" *Expression* 16(1): 1–8. Ottawa: National Advisory Council on Aging.

National Advisory Council on Aging. 2004. "The Seniors of Canada's Far North." *Expression,* 17(2).

National Advisory Council on Aging (NACA). 2006. *Seniors in Canada: 2006 Report Card.* Cat. No. HP30-1/2006E. Ottawa: Minister of Public Works and Government Services Canada.

National Center for Education Statistics. 2007. *The Condition of Education 2007.* U.S. Department of Education, Washington, DC: U.S. Government Printing Office. http://nces.ed.gov/ pubs2007/2007064.pdf.

National Council on Disability. 1993. *Study on the Financing of Assistive Technology Devices and Services for Individuals with Disabilities.* Washington, DC.

National Council of Welfare. 1979. *Women and Poverty.* Ottawa: Minister of Supply and Services.

National Council of Welfare. 1989. *A Pension Primer.* Cat. No. H68-23/1989E. Ottawa: Minister of Supply and Services.

National Council of Welfare. 1990. *Women and Poverty Revisited.* Ottawa: Minister of Supply and Services. Cat. No. H68-25/1990E.

National Council of Welfare. 1996. *A Pension Primer.* Cat. No. H68-23/1996E. Ottawa: Minister of Supply and Services.

National Council of Welfare. 2006. *Poverty Profile, 2002 and 2003.* Volume 124. The National Institute on Aging. 2009. "Alzheimer's Disease Medications Fact Sheet." http://www.nia.nih.gov/Alzheimers/ Publications/medicationsfs.htm, accessed May 15, 2009.

National Union of Public and General Employees. 2006. http://www.nupge.ca/news_2006/n14jy06a.htm, accessed May 7, 2009.

Neal, M. B., D.L. Wagner, K.J.B. Bonn, and K. Niles-Yokum. 2008. "Caring from a Distance: Contemporary Care Issues." In A. Martin-Matthews and J. E. Phillips, eds. *Aging and Caring at the Intersection of Work and Home Life,* 107–128. New York, NY: Psychology Press.

Nemeth, M. 1994. "Amazing Greys." *Maclean's,* January 10, 32–33.

Neugarten, B. L. 1985. "Interpretive Social Science and Research on Aging." In A. S. Rossi, ed., *Gender and the Life Course.* New York: Aldine de Gruyter.

Neugarten, B.L., R.J. Havighurst, and S. Tobin. 1968. "Personality and Patterns of Aging." In B.L. Neugarten, ed., *Middle Age and Aging,* 173–77. Chicago: University of Chicago Press.

Neugarten, B.L., J.W. Moore, and J.C. Lowe. 1968. "Age Norms, Age Constraints, and Adult Socialization." In B.L. Neugarten, ed., *Middle Age and Aging,* 22–28. Chicago: University of Chicago Press.

Neuman, W.L. 2003. *Social Research Methods: Qualitative and Quantitative Approaches.* 5th ed. Boston: Allyn and Bacon.

Neuman, W.L., and K. Robson. 2009. *Basics of Social Research: Qualitative and Quantitative Approaches, Canadian Edition.* Toronto, ON: Pearson Education Canada.

New York Times News Service. 2007. "China Faces Economic Dilemma as Boomers near Early Retirement." Wire-International, A3. March 23. LexisNexis Academic.

New Brunswick. 2008. "New Brunswick Human Rights Commission. Supreme Court Issues Decision on Mandatory Retirement Case (08/07/22)." Communications New Brunswick. News Release. http://www.gnb.ca/cnb/news/hrc/2008e1074hr.htm, May 16, 2009.

Newall, N.E. 2005. *Regret in Later Life: Exploring Relationships between Regret, Perceived Control and Health in Older individuals.* Ann Arbor, MI: UMI Dissertation Services, ProQuest Information and Learning.

Newbold, K.B. 2007. *Return and Onwards Migration among Older Canadians: Findings from the 2001 Census.* SEDAP Research Paper No. 171. Hamilton, ON: McMaster University.

Neysmith, S.M. 1984. "Poverty in Old Age: Can Pension Reform Meet the Needs of Women?" *Canadian Woman Studies* 5: 17–21.

Neysmith, S.M. 1995. "Power in Relationships of Trust: A Feminist Analysis of Elder Abuse." In M.J. MacLean, ed., *Abuse and Neglect of Older Canadians: Strategies for Change*, 43–54. Toronto: Thompson Educational Publishing.

Ng, C. F., H.C. Northcott, and S.M. Abu-Laban. 2007. "Housing and Living Arrangements of South Asian Immigrant Seniors in Edmonton, Alberta." *Canadian Journal on Aging* 26(3): 185–194.

Norland, J.A. 1976. *The Age–Sex Structure of Canada's Population.* Cat. No. 99-703. Ottawa: Statistics Canada.

Norland, J.A. 1994. *Profile of Canada's Seniors.* Cat. No. 96-312E. Ottawa: Statistics Canada and Prentice-Hall Canada.

Normand, J. 2000. "The Health of Women." In Statistics Canada, *Women in Canada 2000: A Gender-Based Statistical Report.* Cat. No.89-503-XPE. Ottawa: Minister Responsible for Statistics Canada.

Norris, J.E. 1993. "'Why Not Think Carnegie Hall?' Working and Retiring among Older Professionals." *Canadian Journal on Aging* 12(2): 182–99.

Norris, J.E. 1998. "Editorial: A Psychology of Aging: Who Needs It?" *Canadian Journal on Aging* 17(4): i–xi.

Northcott, H.C., and D.M. Wilson. 2001. *Dying and Death in Canada.* Aurora, ON: Garamond Press.

Nosek, B.A., M.R. Banaji, and A.G. Greenwald. 2002. "Harvesting Implicit Group Attitudes and Beliefs from a Demonstration Web Site." *Group Dynamics: Theory, Research, and Practice* 6: 101–15.

Novak, M. 1985. *Successful Aging: The Myths, Realities, and Future of Aging in Canada.* Markham, ON: Penguin.

Novak, M. 1985–86. "Biography after the End of Metaphysics." *International Journal of Aging and Human Development* 22(3): 189–204.

Novak, M., N. Chappell, and C. Miles-Tapping. 1990. "Nursing Assistant Stress and the Cognitively Impaired Elderly." Paper presented at the 43rd Scientific Meeting of the Gerontological Society of America, Boston, November.

Novak, M., and C. Guest. 1985. "Social Correlates of Caregiver Burden." Paper presented at the Canadian Association on Gerontology 14th Annual Scientific and Education Meeting, Hamilton, Ontario, October.

Novak, M. and C. Guest. 1992. "A Comparison of the Impact of Institutionalization on Spouse and Nonspouse Caregivers." *Journal of Applied Gerontology* 11: 379–94.

Novak, M., and L.O. Stone. 1985. "Changing Patterns of Aging." Paper presented at the Annual Meeting of the Canadian Sociology and Anthropology Association, Montreal. June.

Novelli, Bill and Boe Workman. 2006. *50+: Igniting a Revolution to Reinvent America.* New York: St. Martin's Press.

O'Brien, C., and A. Goldberg. 2000. "Lesbians and Gay Men Inside and Outside Families." In N. Mandell and A. Duffy, eds., *Canadian Families: Diversity, Conflict, and Change*, 115–45. Toronto: Harcourt Brace.

O'Brien, C., and A. Goldberg. 2005. "Lesbians and Gay Men Inside and Outside Families." In V. Zawilski and C. Levine-Rasky, eds., *Inequality in Canada: A Reader on the Intersections of Gender, Race, and Class,* 126–46. Don Mills, ON: Oxford University Press.

O'Brien, S.J., and P.R. Conger. 1991. "No Time to Look Back: Approaching the Finish Line of Life's

Course." *International Journal of Aging and Human Development* 33(1): 75–87.

O'Brien, S.J., and P.A. Vertinsky. 1991. "Unfit Survivors: Exercise as a Resource for Aging Women." *Gerontologist* 31: 347–57.

O'Connor, B.P. 1995. "Family and Friend Relationships among Older and Younger Adults: Interaction Motivation, Mood, and Quality." *International Journal of Aging and Human Development* 40(1): 9–29.

O'Connor, B.P., and R.J. Vallerand. 1994. "Motivation, Self-Determination, and Person–Environment Fit as Predictors of Psychological Adjustment among Nursing Home Residents." *Psychology and Aging* 9(2): 189–94.

O'Connor, D. 1999. "Living with a Memory-Impaired Spouse: (Re)cognizing the Experience." *Canadian Journal on Aging* 18(2): 211–35.

O'Rand, A. 1990. "Stratification and the Life Course." In R.H. Binstock and L. K. George, eds., *Handbook of Aging and the Social Sciences* 3rd ed. San Diego: Academic Press.

O'Rand, Angela M. 2006. "Stratification and the Life Course: Life Course Capital, Life Course Risks, and Social Inequality." In Robert H. Binstock and Linda K. George, eds., *Handbook of Aging and the Social Sciences* 6th ed., 145–62. Burlington, MA: Academic Press.

O'Rourke, N., B.E. Haverkamp, H. Tuokko, S. Hayden, and B.L. Beattie. 1996. "The Relative Contribution of Subjective Factors to Expressed Burden among Spousal Caregivers of Suspected Dementia Patients." *Canadian Journal on Aging* 15(4): 583–96.

O'Rourke, N., and C.A. Wenaus. 1998. "Marital Aggrandizement as a Mediator of Burden among Spouses of Suspected Dementia Patients." *Canadian Journal on Aging* 17(4): 384–400.

OECD. 2001. *Ageing and Income: Financial Resources and Retirement in 9 OECD Countries.* Paris.

OECD. 2007. *OECD Regions at a Glance: Health Resources—Hospitals.* http://www.fiordiliji.sour-ceoecd.org/pdf/regions_glance/33.pdf, accessed May 7, 2009.

Ogrodnik, L. 2007. *Seniors as Victims of Crime 2004 and 2005.* Canadian Centre for Justice Statistics. Statistics Canada. Ottawa: Ministry of Industry. Cat No. 85F0033MIE.

Oh, K.M., and A.M. Warnes. 2001. "Care Services for Frail Older People in South Korea." *Ageing and Society* 21(Part 6): 701–20.

Onrust, S.A., and P. Cuijpers. 2006. "Mood and Anxiety Disorders in Widowhood: a Systematic Review." *Aging and Mental Health* 10(4): 327–34.

Ontario Ministry of Health and Long-Term Care. 2004. "Seniors' Care: Supportive Housing." http://www.health.gov.on.ca/english/ public/program/ltc/13_housing.html, accessed August 28, 2004.

Ontario Ministry of Labour. 2006. *Facts and Figures: Mandatory Retirement.* http://www.labour.gov.on.ca/english/news/2006/06-126b_2.html, accessed May 7, 2009.

Ontario Provincial Police. 1997. Phonebusters—A National Task Force Combating Telemarketing Fraud. http://consumerinformation.ca/app/oca/ccig/abstract.do?abstractNo=RP000021&language=eng, accessed May 23, 2009.

Oppong, Christine. 2006. "Familial Roles and Social Transformations: Older Men and Women in Sub-Saharan Africa." *Research on Aging* 28(6): 654–68.

Oregon. 2007. *Summary of Oregon's Death with Dignity Act—2006.* http://egov.oregon.gov/DHS/ph/pas/docs/year9.pdf, accessed May 7, 2009.

Osnos, Evan. 2007. "China's Getting Old Before It Becomes Rich." *San Jose Mercury News,* January 30, 7A.

Otto, J. 2000. "The Role of Adult Protective Services in Addressing Abuse." *Generations* 24: 33–38.

Ouellet, P. 1986. "The Leisure Participation and Enjoyment Patterns of French and English-Speaking Members of Senior Citizens' Clubs in New Brunswick, Canada." *Canadian Journal on Aging* 5: 257–68.

Owram, D. 1996. *Born at the Right Time: A History of the Baby-Boom Generation.* Toronto: University of Toronto Press.

Pacey, M.A. 2002. *Living Alone and Living with Children: The Living Arrangements of Canadian and Chinese-Canadian Seniors.* SEDAP Research Paper No. 74. Hamilton, ON: McMaster University.

Palameta, B. 2001. "Who Contributes to RRSPs? A Re-Examination." *Perspectives on Labour and Income* 13(3): 7–13.

Palmore, E.B. 1971. "Attitudes toward Aging as Shown in Humor." *Gerontologist* 11: 181–86.

Palmore, E.B. 1977. "Facts on Aging: A Short Quiz." *Gerontologist* 17: 315–20.

Palmore, E.B. 1988. *The Facts on Aging Quiz: A Handbook of Uses and Results.* New York: Springer.

Paré, I. 2000. "Des projets-pilotes prometteurs en santé." *Le Devoir*, October 27.

Paris, H. 1989. *The Corporate Response to Workers with Family Responsibilities.* Report 43-89. Ottawa: Conference Board of Canada.

Park, D.C. 2000. "The Basic Mechanisms Accounting for Age-Related Decline in Cognitive Function." In D.C. Park and N. Schwarz, eds., *Cognitive Aging: A Primer,* 3–21. Philadelphia: Taylor and Francis.

Park, D.C., and A.H. Gutchess. 2000. "Cognitive Aging and Everyday Life." In D.C. Park and N. Schwarz, eds., *Cognitive Aging: A Primer,* 217–32. Philadelphia: Taylor and Francis.

Park, D.C., and M.L. Meade. 2006. "Memory: Everyday." In R. Schulz, L.S. Noelker, K. Rockwood, and R.L. Sprott, eds., *The Encyclopedia of Aging,* 4th ed., 744–47. New York: Springer.

Park, D.C., G. Lautenschlager, T. Hedden, N.S. Davidson, A.D. Smith, and P.K. Smith. 2002. "Models of Visuospatial and Verbal Memory across the Adult Life Span." *Psychology and Aging* 17: 299–320.

Parliament, J-A. 1987. "Increased Life Expectancy, 1921–1986." *Canadian Social Trends* (Summer): 15–19.

Parmelee, P.A., and M.P. Lawton. 1990. "The Design of Special Environments for the Aged." In J.E. Birren and K.W. Schaie, eds., *Handbook of the Psychology of Aging,* 3rd ed. 464–88. San Diego: Academic Press.

Parsons, J., and J.A. Tindale. 2001. "Parents Who Sue Their Adult Children for Support: An Examination of Decisions by Canadian Court Judges." *Canadian Journal on Aging* 20(4): 451–70.

Parsons, T. 1937. *The Structure of Social Action.* New York: McGraw-Hill.

Parsons, T. 1951. *The Social System.* New York: Free Press.

Patel, K. 2004. "Euthanasia and Physician-Assisted Suicide Policy in the Netherlands and Oregon: A Comparative Analysis." *Journal of Health and Social Policy* 19(1): 37–55.

Patterson, C.J. 2000. "Family Relationships of Lesbians and Gay Men." *Journal of Marriage and the Family* 62 (4): 1052–69.

Peck, R.C. [1955] 1968. "Psychological Aspects of Aging." In J.E. Anderson, ed. *Proceedings of a Conference on Planning Research, Bethesda, MD, April 24–27, 1955.* Washington, DC: American Psychological Association. Excerpted in "Psychological Developments in the Second Half of Life," in B.L. Neugarten, ed., *Middle Age and Aging.* Chicago: University of Chicago Press, 1968.

Penning, M.J. 1990. "Receipt of Assistance by Elderly People: Hierarchical Selection and Task Specificity." *Gerontologist* 30: 220–27.

Penning, M.J. 1998. "In the Middle: Parental Caregiving in the Context of Other Roles." *Journals of Gerontology Series B* 53(4): S188–97.

Penning, M.J. 2002. "Hydra Revisited: Substituting Formal for Self- and Informal In-Home Care among Older Adults with Disabilities." *Gerontologist* 42(1): 4–16.

Perfect, T.J., and Z.R.R. Dasgupta. 1997. "What Underlies the Deficit in Reported Recollective Experience in Old Age?" *Memory and Cognition* 25(6): 849–58.

Perlman, D. 2004. "European and Canadian Studies of Loneliness among Seniors." *Canadian Journal on Aging* 23(2): 181–88.

Perodeau, G.M., and G.G. du Fort. 2000. "Psychotropic Drug Use and the Relation between Social Support, Life Events, and Mental Health in the Elderly." *Journal of Applied Gerontology* 19(1): 23–41.

Peters, A., and A.C. Liefbroer. 1997. "Beyond Marital Status: Partner History and Well-Being in Old Age." *Journal of Marriage and the Family* 59(3): 687–99.

Peterson, S., E. Shapiro, and N.P. Roos. 2005. "Regional Variation in Home Care Use in Manitoba." *Canadian Journal on Aging* 24(Suppl.1): 69–80.

Pfeiffer, E., A. Verwoerdt, and H.S. Wang. 1968. "Sexual Behavior in Aged Men and Women, I: Observations on 254 Community Volunteers." *Archives of General Psychiatry* 19: 753–58.

Phillips, L. H., M. Kliegel., and M. Martin. 2006. "Age and Planning Tasks: The Influence of Ecological Validity." *International Journal of Aging and Human Development* 62(2): 175–84.

Philpot, H.J. 1871. *Guide Book to the Canadian Dominion Containing Full Information for the Emigrant, the Tourist, the Sportsman and the Small Capitalist.* London: E. Stanford.

Pierce, T., J.E. Lydon, and S. Yang. 2001. "Enthusiasm and Moral Commitment: What Sustains Family Caregivers of Those with Dementia." *Basic and Applied Social Psychology* 23(1): 29–41.

Pillemer, K., and D. Finkelhor. 1988. "The Prevalence of Elder Abuse: A Random Sample Survey." *Gerontologist* 28: 51–57.

Pittaway, E. and E. Gallagher. 1995. *A Guide to Enhancing Service for Abused Older Canadians*. Victoria: Centre on Aging, University of Victoria.

Ploeg, J., L. Biehler, K. Willison, B. Hutchinson, and J. Blythe. 2001. "Perceived Support Needs of Family Caregivers and Implications for a Telephone Support Service." *Canadian Journal of Nursing Research* 33(2): 43–61.

Ploeg, J., L. Campbell, M. Denton, A. Joshi, and S. Davies. 2004. "Helping to Build and Rebuild Secure Lives and Futures: Financial Transfers from Parents to Adult Children and Grandchildren." *Canadian Journal on Aging* 23(Supplement1), S131–S144.

Ploeg, J., L. Campbell, C. Kemp, C. Rosenthal, and L. de Witt. 2007. "The Unwritten Rules Guiding Inheritance Decisions." Paper presented at the 36th Annual Scientific and Education Meeting of the Canadian Association on Aging, Calgary, Alberta, November 1–3, 2007.

Podnieks, E. 2008. "Elder Abuse: The Canadian Experience." *Journal of Elder Abuse & Neglect* 20 (2): 126–50.

Podnieks, E., K. Pillemer, J.P. Nicholson, T. Shillington, and A. Frizzel. 1990. *National Survey on Abuse of the Elderly in Canada*. Toronto: Ryerson Polytechnic Institute.

Poirier, D. 1992. "Power of Social Workers in the Creation and Application of Elder Protection Statutory Norms in New Brunswick and Nova Scotia." *Journal of Elder Abuse and Neglect* 4: 13–33.

Poirier, S., and G. Barbeau. 1999. "In-Home Medication Inventory among Elderly Receiving Home Care Services." *Journal of Geriatric Drug Therapy* 12(3): 43–54.

Policy Research Initiative. 2004. *Views on Life-Course Flexibility and Canada's Aging Population*. Ottawa: PRI Project: Population Aging and Life-Course Flexibility.

Policy Research Initiative. 2005. *Encouraging Choice in Work and Retirement: Project Report, 24. http:// policyresearch.gc.ca/doclib/Encour_Choice_E.pdf*. Ottawa: PRI Project: Population Aging and Life-Course Flexibility.

Poon, P. 2005. "Who's Missing Out on the GIS?" *Perspectives on Labour and Income*, 6(10): 5–14.

Post, L.F. 2006. "Living Wills and Durable Powers of Attorney." In R. Schulz, L.S. Noelker, K. Rockwood, and R.L. Sprott, eds., *The Encyclopedia of Aging*, 4th ed., 668–71. New York: Springer.

Prager, J. 2003. "Aging and Productivity: What Do We Know?." In D. Cheal, ed., *Aging and Demographic Change in Canadian Context*, 133–89. Toronto: University of Toronto Press.

Prentice, A., P. Bourne, G.C. Brandt, B. Light, W. Mitchinson, and N. Black. 1996. *Canadian Women: A History*, 2nd ed. Toronto: Harcourt Brace.

Press, I., and M. McKool. 1972. "Social Structure and Status of the Aged: Toward Some Valid Cross-Cultural Generalizations." *Aging and Human Development* 3: 297–306.

Préville, M., R. Hébert, R. Boyer, and G. Bravo. 2001. "Correlates of Psychotropic Drug Use in the Elderly Compared to Adults Aged 18–64: Results from the Quebec Health Survey." *Aging and Mental Health* 5(3): 216–24.

Préville, M., R. Hébert, G. Bravo, and R. Boyer. 2002. "Predisposing and Facilitating Factors of Severe Psychological Distress among Frail Elderly Adults." *Canadian Journal on Aging* 21(2): 195–204.

Price, S.J., P.C. McKenry, and M.J. Murphy. 2000. "Families across Time: A Life Course Perspective." In S.J. Price, P.C. McKenry, and M.J. Murphy, eds., *Families across Time: A Life Course Perspective*, 2–22. Los Angeles: Roxbury Publishing Company.

Pringle, D. 1998. "Aging and the Health Care System: Am I in the Right Queue?" *Forum Collection Series*. Ottawa: National Advisory Council on Aging.

Proulx, C., H. Helms, and C. Buehler. 2007. "Marital Quality and Personal Well-Being: A Meta-Analysis." *Journal of Marriage and Family* 69(3): 576–93.

Province of Manitoba 2008. *Grand Relations*. http:// www.gov.mb.ca/index.html, accessed May 7, 2009.

Prull, M.W., J.D.E. Gabrieli, and S.A. Bunge. 2000. "Age-Related Changes in Memory: A Cognitive Neuroscience Perspective." In F.I.M. Craik and T.A. Salthouse, eds., *The Handbook of Aging and Cognition*, 2nd ed., 91–153. Mahwah, NJ: Lawrence Erlbaum Associates.

Prus, S.G. 2000. "Income Inequality as a Canadian Cohort Ages: An Analysis of the Later Life Course." *Research on Aging* 22(3): 211–37.

Prus, S.G. 2004. "A Life Course Perspective on the Relationship between Socio-economic Status and Health: Testing the Divergence Hypothesis." *Canadian Journal on Aging* 23(Supplement 1): S145–S153.

Prus, S.G., and R.L. Brown. 2008. *Age-Specific Income Inequality and Life Expectancy: New Evidence.* SEDAP Research Paper 229. Hamilton, ON: McMaster University.

Prus, S., and Z. Lin. 2005. *Ethnicity and Health: An Analysis of Physical Health Differences across Twenty-one Ethnocultural Groups in Canada.* SEDAP Research Paper No. 143. Hamilton, ON: McMaster University.

Public Health Agency of Canada. 2009. *Canada's Physical Activity Guide to Healthy Active Living for Older Adults.* http://www.phac-aspc.gc.ca/pau-uap/paguide/older/index.htmlaccessed May 21, 2009.

Pudrovska, T., S. Schieman, and D. Carr. 2006. "Strains of Singlehood in Later Life: Do Race and Gender Matter?" *Journal of Gerontology: SS 61B* (6): S315–S322.

Pyper, W. 2006. "Aging, Health and Work." *Perspectives on Labour and Income* 7(2): 5–15.

Pyper, W. 2008. "RRSP Investments." *Perspectives on Labour and Income* 20(1): 5–11.

Quadagno, J., and J. Reid. 1999. "The Political Economy Perspective in Aging." In V.L. Bengtson and K.W. Schaie, eds., *Handbook of Theories of Aging*, 344–58. New York: Springer Publishing.

Quality End-of-Life Care Coalition of Canada. 2008. *Hospice Palliative Home Care in Canada: A Progress Report.*

Quebec. n.d. *Quebec End-of-Life Palliative Care Policy.* (English Translation).

Quirouette, C.C., and D. Pushkar. 1999. "Views of Future Aging among Middle-Aged, University Educated Women." *Canadian Journal on Aging* 18(2): 236–58.

Raina, P., C. McIntyre, B. Zhu, I. McDowell, L. Santaguida, B. Kristjansson, A. Hendricks, H. Massfeller, and L. Chambers, 2004. "Understanding the Influence of the Complex Relationships Among Informal and Formal Supports on the Well-Being of Caregivers of Persons with Dementia." *Canadian Journal on Aging, 23*(supplement 1): S49–S60.

Randall, W.L., and G.M. Kenyon. 2004. "Time, Story, and Wisdom: Emerging Themes inNarrative Gerontology." *Canadian Journal on Aging* 23(4): 333–46.

Ray, Ruth E. 2003. "The Perils and Possibilities of Theory." In Simon Biggs, Ariela Lowenstein, and Jon Hendricks, eds., *The Need for Theory: Critical Approaches to Social Gerontology,* 33–44. Amityville, New York: Baywood Publishing Company.

Ray, Ruth E. 2008. "Coming of Age in Critical Gerontology: Introduction." *Journal of Aging Studies,* Special Issue 22 (2): 97–100.

Raz, N. 2000. "Aging of the Brain and Its Impact on Cognitive Performance: Integration of Structural and Functional Findings." In F.I.M. Craik and T.A. Salthouse, eds., *The Handbook of Aging and Cognition*, 2nd ed., 1–90. Mahwah, NJ: Lawrence Erlbaum Associates.

RCMP (Royal Canadian Mounted Police). 2007. *Phonebusters.* http://www.phonebusters.com, accessed May 7, 2009.

Rea, W., D. Mackay, and S. LeVasseur. 2008. *Changing Patterns in Canadian Home Ownership and Shelter Costs, 2006 Census.* Statistics Canada. Catalogue No. 97-554-X. Ottawa: Ministry of Industry.

Reis, M., and D. Nahmiash. 1997. "Abuse of Seniors: Personality, Stress, and Other Indicators." *Journal of Mental Health and Aging* 3(3): 337–56.

Reis, M., and D. Nahmiash. 1998. "Validation of the Indicators of Abuse (IOA) Screen." *Gerontologist* 38(4): 471–80.

Reker, G.T. 2001–02. "Prospective Predictors of Successful Aging in Community-Residing and Institutionalized Canadian Elderly." *Ageing International* 27(1): 42–64.

Rhodes, R.E., A.D. Martin, and J.E. Taunton. 2001. "Temporal Relationships of Self-Efficacy and Social Support as Predictors of Adherence in a 6-Month Strength-Training Program for Older Women." *Perceptual and Motor Skills* 93(3): 693–703.

Ribeiro, O., C. Paúl, and C. Nogueira, C. 2007. "Real Men, Real Husbands: Caregiving and Masculinities in Later Life." *Journal of Aging Studies* 21: 302–313.

Richard, C.A., and A.H. Brown. 2006. "Configurations of Informal Social Support among Older Lesbians." *Journal of Women and Aging* 18 (4): 49–65.

Richard, L., S. Laforest, F. Dufresne, and J.P. Sapinski. 2005. "The Quality of Life of Older Adults Living in an Urban Environment : Professional and Lay Perspectives." *Canadian Journal on Aging* 24(1): 19–30.

Richardson, R., S. Lowenstein, and M. Weissberg. 1989. "Coping with the Suicidal Elderly: A Physician's Guide." *Geriatrics* 44(9): 43–47, 51.

Richeson, N. E. 2003. "Effects of Animal-Assisted Therapy on Agitated Behaviors and Social Interactions of Older Adults with Dementia." *American Journal of Alzheimer's Disease and Other Dementias* 18: 353–58.

Riediger, M., S-C Li, and U. Lindenbergert. 2006. "Selection, Optimization, and Compensation as Developmental Mechanisms of Adaptive Resource Allocation: Review and Preview." In In J. E. Birren and K. W. Schaie eds., *Handbook of the Psychology of Aging*, 6th edition, 289-313. Burlington, MA: Elsevier Academic Press.

Riegel, K.F. 1975. "Adult Life Crises: A Dialectic Interpretation of Development." In N. Datan and L.H. Ginsberg, eds., *Life-Span Developmental Psychology: Normative Life Crisis*. New York: Academic Press.

Riegel, K.F. 1976. "The Dialectics of Human Development." *American Psychologist* 31: 689–700.

Riley, M.W. 1971. "Social Gerontology and the Age Stratification of Society." *Gerontologist* 11: 79–87.

Riley, M.W. 1987. "On the Significance of Age in Sociology." *American Sociological Review* 52: 1–14.

Riley, M.W. 1994. "Aging and Society: Past, Present and Future." *Gerontologist* 34: 436–46.

Riley, M.W., A. Foner, and J.W. Riley, Jr. 1999. "The Aging and Society Paradigm." In V.L. Bengtson and K.W. Schaie, eds., *Handbook of Theories of Aging*, 327–43. New York: Springer Publishing.

Riley, M.W., A. Foner, and J. Waring. 1988. "Sociology of Age." In N. Smelser, ed., *Handbook of Sociology*. Beverly Hills: Sage.

Riley, M.W., M.E. Johnson, and A. Foner, eds. 1972. *Aging and Society*. Vol. 3: A Sociology of Age Stratification. New York: Russell Sage Foundation.

Rix, S. E. 2004. *Aging and Work: A View from the United States*. Washington, DC: AARP Public Policy Institute. http://www.research.aarp.org/econ/2004_02_work.pdf, accessed May 7, 2009.

Rix, Sara E. 2006. *Update on the Aged 55+ Worker: 2005*. Washington, DC: AARP Public Policy Institute. http://www.assets.aarp.org/rgcenter/econ/dd136_worker.pdf, accessed May 7, 2009.

Robb, R., M. Denton, A. Gafni, A. Joshi, J. Lian, C. Rosenthal, and D. Willison. 1999. "Valuation of Unpaid Help by Seniors in Canada: An Empirical Analysis." *Canadian Journal on Aging* 18(4): 430–46.

Roberge, D., F. Ducharme, P. Lebel, R. Pineault, and J. Losielle. 2002. "Qualité des soins dispensés en unités de courte durée gériatriques: la perspective des aidants familiaux." *Canadian Journal on Aging* 21(3): 393–403.

Roberto, K.A., K.R. Allen, and R. Blieszner. 2001. "Grandfathers' Perceptions and Expectations of Relationships with Their Adult Grandchildren." *Journal of Family Issues* 22 (4): 407–26.

Robertson, A. 2000. "'I Saw the Handwriting on the Wall': Shades of Meaning in Reasons for Early Retirement." *Journal of Aging Studies* 14(1): 63–79.

Robinson, T.E. 1998. *Portraying Older People in Advertising*. New York: Garland.

Robinson, S.P, L. Mullane, and M.B. Lakin. 2007. *Framing New Terrain: Older Adults and Higher Education*. Washington, DC: American Council on Education. http://www.acenet.edu/Content/NavigationMenu/ProgramsServices/CLLL/Reinvesting/Reinvestingfinal.pdf, accessed May 7, 2009.

Robson, W.B.P. 1996. "Ponzi's Pawns: Young Canadians and the Canada Pension Plan." In J.B. Burbridge et al., eds., *When We're 65: Reforming Canada's Retirement Income System*, 27–56. Toronto: C.D. Howe Institute.

Robson, W.B.P. 2001. *Will the Baby Boomers Bust the Health Budget? Demographic Change and Health Care Financing Reform*. Commentary No. 148. Toronto: C.D. Howe Institute.

Rose, M.R. 1993. "Evolutionary Gerontology and Critical Gerontology: Let's Just Be Friends." In T.R. Cole, W.A. Achenbaum, P.L. Jakobi, and R. Kastenbaum, eds., *Voices and Visions of Aging: Toward a Critical Gerontology*, 64–75. New York: Springer.

Rosenberg, M.W., and A.M. James. 2000. "Medical Services Utilization Patterns by Seniors." *Canadian Journal on Aging* 19 (Suppl.1): 125–42.

Rosenmayr, L., and E. Kockeis. 1963. "Propositions for a Sociological Theory of Aging and the Family." *International Social Science Journal* 15: 410–26.

Rosenthal, C.J. 1983. "The Anglo-Canadian Family: A Perspective on Ethnicity and Support to the Elderly." Paper presented at the 12th Annual Scientific and Educational Meeting of the Canadian Association on Gerontology, Moncton.

Rosenthal, C.J. 1986. "Family Supports in Later Life: Does Ethnicity Make a Difference?" *Gerontologist* 26: 19–24.

Rosenthal, C.J. 1994. "Editorial: Long-Term Care Reform and 'Family' Care: A Worrisome Combination." *Canadian Journal on Aging* 13(3): 419–27.

Rosenthal, C.J. 1995. "The Comforter." In M. Novak, ed., *Aging and Society: A Canadian Reader*, 326–31. Scarborough, ON: Nelson Canada.

Rosenthal, C.J. 1997. "Changing Contexts of Family Care in Canada." *Ageing International* 24(1): 13–31.

Rosenthal, C.J. 2000. "Aging Families: Have Current Changes and Challenges Been 'Oversold'?" In E.M. Gee and G.M. Gutman, eds., *The Overselling of Population Aging: Apocalyptic Demography, Intergenerational Challenges, and Social Policy*, 45–63. Don Mills, ON: Oxford University Press.

Rosenthal, C., and P. Dawson. 1991. "Wives of Institutionalized Husbands." *Journal of Aging and Health* 3(3): 315–34.

Rosenthal, C.J., L. Hayward, A. Martin-Matthews, and M. Denton. 2004. "Help to Older Parents and Parents-In-Law: Does Paid Employment Constrain Women's Helping Behaviour?" *Canadian Journal on Aging* 23(supplement 1): S115–S130.

Rosenthal, C.J., V.W. Marshall, and J. Synge. 1980. "The Succession of Lineage Roles as Families Age." *Essence* 4: 179–93.

Rosenthal, C.J., A. Martin-Matthews, and S.H. Matthews. 1996. "Caught in the Middle? Occupancy in Multiple Roles and Help to Parents in a National Probability Sample of Canadian Adults." *Journals of Gerontology Series B* 51(6): S274–83.

Ross, M.M., A. Carswell, and W.B. Dalziel. 2002. "Family Caregiving in Long-Term Care Facilities: Visiting and Task Performance." *Geriatrics Today* 5(4): 179–82.

Ross, M.M., and B. McDonald. 1994. "Providing Palliative Care to Older Adults: Context and Challenges." *Journal of Palliative Care* 10(4): 5–10.

Ross, M.M., C.J. Rosenthal, and P. Dawson. 1994. "The Continuation of Caregiving Following the Institutionalization of Elderly Husbands." In National Advisory Council on Aging, *Marital Disruption in Later Life,* 23–32. Cat. No. H71-3/17-1994E. Ottawa: Minister of Supply and Services.

Ross, M.M., C.J. Rosenthal, and P.G. Dawson. 1997a. "Spousal Caregiving in the Institutional Setting: Task Performance." *Canadian Journal on Aging* 16(1): 51–69.

Ross, M.M., C.J. Rosenthal, and P. Dawson. 1997b. "Spousal Caregiving in the Institutional Setting: Visiting." *Journal of Clinical Nursing* 6(6): 473–83.

Roterman, M. 2006. "Seniors' Health Care Use." *Supplement to Health Reports, 16*: 33–45. Statistics Canada. Cat No. 82-003.

Roth, D. 2005. "Culture Change in Long-Term Care: Educating the Next Generation." *Journal of Gerontological Social Work* 45(1–2): 233–48.

Rowe, G., and H. Nguyen. 2003. "Older Workers and the Labour Market." *Perspectives on Labour and Income* 15(1): 55–58.

Rowe, J.W., and R.L. Kahn. 1991. "Human Aging: Usual and Successful." In H. Cox, ed., *Aging*, 7th ed. Guilford, CT: Dushkin. Originally published in *Science* 237 (1987): 143–49.

Rowe, J.W., and R.L. Kahn, 1998. *Successful Aging.* New York: Dell Publishing.

Rozanova, J., H.C. Northcott, and S.A. McDaniel. 2006. "Seniors and Portrayals of Intra-Generational and Inter-Generational Inequality in *The Globe and Mail*." *Canadian Journal on Aging 25(4):* 373–86.

Rubinstein, R.L. 1996. "Childless, Legacy, and Generativity." *Generations* 20(3): 58–60.

Rubio, M., and E. Waterson, eds. 1986. *Selected Journals of L.M. Montgomery.* Vol. 1: 1889–1910. Toronto: Oxford University Press.

Rudman, D. L., J. Friedland, M. Chipman, and P. Sciortino. 2006. "Holding On and Letting Go: The Perspectives of Pre-Seniors and Seniors on Driving Self-Regulation in Later Life." *Canadian Journal on Aging* 25(1): 65–76.

Rurup, M.L., B.D. Onwuteaka-Phiupsen, G. Van Der Wal, A.Van Der Heide, and P.J. Van Der Maas. 2005. "A 'Suicide Pill' for Older People: Attitudes of Physicians, the General Population, and Relatives of Patients Who Died after Euthanasia or Physician Assisted Suicide in the Netherlands." *Death Studies* 29: 519–34.

Ryan, E.B., A.P. Anas, M.L. Hummert, and I.A. Laver. 1998. "Young and Older Adults' Views of Telephone Talk: Conversation Problems and Social Uses." *Journal of Applied Communication Research* 26(1): 83–98.

Ryan, E.B., A.P. Anas, M. Beamer, S. Bajorek. "Coping with Age-Related Vision Loss in Everyday Reading Activities. *Educational Gerontology* 29(1): 37–54.

Ryan, M.C. 1998. "The Relationship between Loneliness, Social Support, and Decline in Cognitive Function in the Hospitalized Elderly." *Journal of Gerontological Nursing* 24(3): 19–27.

Sacco, V.F., and R.M. Nakhaie. 2001. "Coping with Crime: An Examination of Elderly and Nonelderly Adaptations." *International Journal of Law and Psychiatry* 24(2/3): 305–23.

Sainsbury, R.S., and M. Coristine. 1986. "Affective Discrimination in Moderately to Severely Demented Patients." *Canadian Journal on Aging* 5: 99–104.

Saint-Arnaud, J. 1993. "Autonomy, Self-Determination, and the Decision-Making Process Concerning End-of-Life Treatment." In National Advisory Council on Aging, *Ethics and Aging*, 33-49. Cat. No. H71-3/16-1993E. Ottawa: Minister of Supply and Services.

Salthouse, Timothy, A. 2006. "Theoretical Issues in the Psychology of Aging." In James E. Birren and K. Warner Schaie, eds. *Handbook of the Psychology of Aging*. 6th ed., 3–13. Burlington, MA: Elsevier Academic Press.

Salthouse, T.A., and F.I.M. Craik. 2000. "Closing Comments." In F.I.M. Craik and T.A. Salthouse, eds., *The Handbook of Aging and Cognition*, 2nd ed., 689–703. Mahwah, NJ: Lawrence Erlbaum Associates.

Salvatori, P., M. Tremblay, J. Sandys, and D. Maraccio. 1998. "Aging with an Intellectual Disability: A Review of Canadian Literature." *Canadian Journal on Aging* 17(3): 249–71.

Sarkisian, N., and N. Gerstel. 2008. "Till Marriage Do Us Part: Adult Children's Relationships with Their Parents." *Journal of Marriage and Family* 70 (2): 360–76.

Saskatchewan Health Services Utilization Research Commission. 1998, *Hospital and Home Care Study*. Summary Report No. 10. Saskatoon: Saskatchewan Health.

Saunders, C. 1984. "St. Christopher's Hospice." In E.S. Shneidman, ed., *Death: Current Perspectives*, 3rd ed., 266–71 Palo Alto, CA: Mayfield.

Saunders, L.D., A. Alibhai, D.B. Hogan, C.J. Maxwell, H. Quan, and D. Johnson. 2001. "Trends in the Utilization of Health Services by Seniors in Alberta." *Canadian Journal on Aging* 20(4): 493–516.

Scarth, W. 2003. *Population Aging, Productivity, and Growth in Living Standards*. SEDAP Research Paper No. 90. Hamilton, ON: McMaster University.

Schaie, K.W. 1990. "The Optimization of Cognitive Functioning in Old Age: Predictions Based on Cohort-Sequential and Longitudinal Data." In P.B. Baltes and M.M. Baltes, eds., *Successful Aging: Perspectives from the Behavioral Sciences*, 94–117. Cambridge, UK: Cambridge University Press.

Schaie, K.W. 2006. "Intelligence." In R. Schulz, L.S. Noelker, K. Rockwood, and R.L. Sprott, eds., *The Encyclopedia of Aging*, 4th ed., 600–2. New York: Springer.

Schellenberg, G. 1994. *Older Workers and Canada's Aging Labour Force*. Ottawa: One Voice—the Seniors Network (Canada) Ltd.

Schellenberg, G. 1995. "Summary of Address to Statistics Canada Symposium on Greying of the Workforce." *Perspectives on Labour and Income* 7(1): 33–38.

Schellenberg, G. 2004. *The Retirement Plans and Expectations of Non-Retired Canadians Aged 45 to 59*. Ottawa: Minister of Industry. Statistics Canada No. 11F0019 No. 223.

Schellenberg, G., and Ostrovsky, Y. 2008. "Retiring Together, or Not." *Perspectives on Labour and Income*, 9(4): 5–11.

Schellenberg, G., M. Turcotte and B. Ram. 2005. "What Makes Retirement Enjoyable?" *Canadian Social Trends* (Fall):12–14.

Schellenberg, G., M. Turcotte, and B. Ram, 2006. "The Changing Characteristics of Older Couples and Joint Retirement in Canada. In L.O. Stone, ed., *New Frontiers of Research on Retirement*, 199–218. Ottawa: Minister of Industry. Statistics Canada. Catalogue no. 75-511-XIE.

Schembari, P. 2003. "Terms and Conditions of Registered Pension Plans." In Statistics Canada. *Canada's Retirement Income Programs: A Statistical Overview (1990–2000)*. Minister of Industry. http://www.statcan.ca/english/freepub/74-507-XIE/0010074-507-XIE.pdf, accessed May 7, 2009.

Schiff, M., and N. Gnaedinger. 1997. *Adapting Municipal Housing to Meet the Needs of Older Tenants with Dementia*. Ottawa: Canada Mortgage and Housing Corporation.

Schroots, J.F. 1995. "Psychological Models of Aging." *Canadian Journal on Aging* 14(1): 44–66.

Schultz, S. E., and J. A. Kopec, 2003. "Impacts of Chronic Conditions." *Health Reports* 14: 41–53.

Schulz, J.H. 1991. "Epilogue: The 'Buffer Years': Market Incentives and Evolving Retirement Policies." In J. Myles and J. Quadagno, eds., *States, Labor Markets, and the Future of Old-Age Policy*, 295–308. Philadelphia: Temple University Press.

Schulz, J.H. 2001. *Economics of Aging.* 7th ed. Auburn House, Westport, CT.

Schulz, J.H., and A. Borowski, A. 2006. "Economic Security in Retirement: Reshaping the Public-Private Pension Mix." In Robert H. Binstock and Linda K. George, eds., *Handbook of Aging and the Social Sciences,* 6th ed., 360–79. Burlington, MA: Academic Press.

Schulz-Hipp, P.L. 2001. "Do Spirituality and Religiosity Increase with Age?" In D.O. Moberg, ed., *Aging and Spirituality*, 85–98. New York: Haworth Press.

Scialfa, Charles T., and Geoff R. Fernie. 2006. "Adaptive Technology." In James E. Birren and K. Warner Schaie, eds., *Handbook of the Psychology of Aging*, 6th ed., 425–441. Burlington, MA: Elsevier Academic Press. ScienceDaily. 2009. http://www.sciencedaily.com/aboutus.htm, accessed May 18, 2009.

Seeman, T.E., L.F., Dubin, and M. Seeman. 2003. "Religiosity/Spirituality and Health: A Critical Review of the Evidence for Biological Pathways." *American Psychologist* 58: 53–63.

Selody, J. 2007. "How Vulnerable Are Private Pensions? Is There a Funding Crisis?" In M. Hering and M. Kpessa, *Private Pensions and Income Security in Old Age: An Uncertain Future—Conference Report.* SEDAP Research Paper No. 180. Hamilton, ON: McMaster University.

Senate of Canada. 1995. *Of Life and Death.* Report of the Special Senate Commmittee on Euthanasia and Assisted Suicide. Ottawa: Queen's Printer of Canada.

Seniors Today. 1995. "National Alzheimer Registry Created." *Seniors Today,* July 1, 3.

Sermat, V. 1978. "Sources of Loneliness." *Essence* 2: 271–76.

Service Canada. 2007. *Income Security Programs Information Card –October–December 2007.* Catalogue No.: ISPB-258-10-07E. http://www.hrsdc.gc.ca/en/isp/statistics/rates/octdec07.shtml, accessed May 7, 2009.

Service Canada. 2008. *Canada Pension Plan (CPP) Payment Rates.* http://www.142.236.54.114/en/isp/pub/factsheets/rates.shtml, accessed May 7, 2009.

Service Canada. 2009. "Income Security Programs Information Card. 2009." Catalogue No.: ISPB-258-04-09E, http://www.hrsdc.gc.ca/eng/isp/statistics/rates/aprjun09.shtml, May 16, 2009.

Settersten, Richard A. Jr. 2003. "Propositions and Controversies in Life-Course Scholarship." In R.A. Settersten, Jr., ed., *Invitation to the Life Course: Toward New Understandings of Later Life, 15–45.* Amityville, New York: Baywood Publishing Company.

Settersten, Richard A. 2006. "Aging and the Life Course." In Robert H. Binstock and Linda K. George, eds., *Handbook of Aging and the Social Sciences,* 6th Edition, 3–19. Burlington, MA: Academic Press.

Sevick, Mary Ann, Terrance McConnell, and Melissa Muender. 2003. "Conducting Research Related to Treatment of Alzheimer's Disease." *Journal of Gerontological Nursing* 29(2): 6–12.

Sewell, D. 2003. "Giving the Gift of Peace." *Reader's Digest Canada.* http://www.readersdigest.ca/mag/2003/08/palliative.html, accessed May 7, 2009.

Shanas, Ethel. 1967. "Family Help Patterns and Social Class in Three Societies." *Journal of Marriage and the Family* 29: 257–66.

Shanas, E. 1979. "The Family as a Social Support System in Old Age." *Gerontologist* 19: 169–74.

Shapiro, E. 1992. "Editorial: We've Come a Long Way but Are We There?" *Canadian Journal on Aging* 11(3): 206–9.

Shapiro, E., and B. Havens. 2000. "Bridging the Knowledge Gap: From Evidence to Policy and Practice That Fosters Seniors' Independence." *Canadian Journal on Aging* 19(Suppl. 1): 176–90.

Shapiro, E., and N.P. Roos. 1986. "High Users of Hospital Days." *Canadian Journal on Aging* 5: 165–74.

Shapiro, E., and R.B. Tate. 1988a. "Survival Patterns of Nursing Home Admissions and Their Policy Implications." *Canadian Journal of Public Health* 79: 268–74.

Shapiro, E., and R. Tate. 1988b. "Who Is Really at Risk of Institutionalization?" *Gerontologist* 28: 237–45.

Shapiro, E., and R.B. Tate. 1997. "The Use and Cost of Community Care Services by Elders with Unimpaired Cognitive Function with Cognitive

Impairment/No Dementia and with Dementia." *Canadian Journal on Aging* 16(4): 665–81.

Sharkey, J.R., and N.E. Schoenberg. 2002. "Variations in Nutritional Risk among Black and White Women who Receive Home-Delivered Meals." *Journal of Women & Aging* 14(3/4): 99–119.

Sharp, H.S. 1981. "Old Age among the Chipewyan." In P.T. Amoss and S. Harrell, eds., *Other Ways of Growing Old: Anthropological Perspectives*, 99–109. Stanford, CA: Stanford University Press.

Shear, K. 2006. "Bereavement." In R. Schulz, L.S. Noelker, K. Rockwood, and R.L. Sprott, eds., *The Encyclopedia of Aging*, 4th ed., 107–110. New York: Springer.

Shedletsky, R., R. Fisher, and G. Nadon. 1982. "Assessment of Palliative Care for Dying Hospitalized Elderly." *Canadian Journal on Aging* 1: 11–15.

Shenk, D., K. Kuwahara, and D. Zablotsky. 2004. "Older Women's Attachments to Their Home and Possessions." *Journal of Aging Studies* 18: 157–69.

Sheppard, H.L. 1991. "Early Retirement: Questions and Speculations." In J. Myles and J. Quadagno, eds., *States, Labor Markets, and the Future of Old-Age Policy*, 290–94. Philadelphia: Temple University Press.

Shidler, S. 1998. "Participation of Chronically Ill Older Adults in Their Life-Prolonging Treatment Decisions: Rights and Opportunity." *Canadian Journal on Aging* 17(1): 1–23.

Shields, M., and L. Martel. 2006. "Healthy Living Among seniors." *Supplement to Health Reports* 16: 7–20. Statistics Canada. Cat. No. 82-003.

Shields, M., and S. Shooshtari. 2001. "Determinants of Self-Perceived Health." *Health Reports* 13(1): 35–52.

Shiota, M. N., and R.W. Levenson. 2007. "Birds of a Feather Don't Always Fly Farthest: Similarity in Big Five Personality Predicts More Negative Marital Satisfaction Trajectories in Long-Term Marriages." *Psychology and Aging* 22(4): 666–75.

Shneidman, E.S. 1984. "Malignancy: Dialogues with Life-Threatening Illnesses." In E.S. Shneidman, ed., *Death: Current Perspectives*, 3rd ed., 195–219. Palo Alto, CA: Mayfield.

Shrestra, L.B. 2000. "Population Aging in Developing Countries." *Health Affairs* 19(3): 204–12.

Silberfeld, M. 1992. "The Use of 'Risk' in Decision-Making." *Canadian Journal on Aging* 11(2): 124–36.

Silberfeld, M. 1994. "Evaluating Decisions in Mental Capacity Assessments." *International Journal of Geriatric Psychiatry* 9: 365–71.

Silberfeld, M., R. Grundstein Amando, D. Stephens, and R. Deber. 1996. "Family and Physicians' Views of Surrogate Decision-Making: The Roles and How to Choose." *International Psychogeriatrics* 8(4): 589–96.

Silveira, M.J., A. DiPiero, M.S. Gerrity, and C. Feudtner. 2000. "Patients' Knowledge of Options at the End of Life: Ignorance in the Face of Death." *Journal of the American Medical Association* 284(19): 2483–88.

Silverstein, M., and J.D. Long. 1998. "Trajectories of Grandparents' Perceived Solidarity with Adult Grandchildren: A Growth Curve Analysis over 23 Years." *Journal of Marriage and the Family* 60(4): 912–23.

Simmons, L.W. 1960. "Aging in Preindustrial Societies." In C. Tibbitts, ed., *Handbook of Social Gerontology: Societal Aspects of Aging*. Chicago: University of Chicago Press.

Simmons, L.W. 1970. *The Role of the Aged in Primitive Society*. New Haven, CT: Yale University.

Simons, R.L. 1983–84. "Specificity and Substitution in the Social Networks of the Elderly." *International Journal of Aging and Human Development* 18: 121–39.

Simonton, D.K. 1977. "Creative Productivity, Age, and Stress: A Biographical Time-Series Analysis of 10 Classical Composers." *Journal of Personality and Social Psychology* 35(11): 791–804.

Simonton, D.K. 1988. "Age and Outstanding Achievement: What Do We Know after Over a Century of Research?" *Psychological Bulletin* 104: 251–67.

Simonton, D.K. 1990. "Creativity and Wisdom in Aging." In J.E. Birren and K.W. Schaie, eds., *Handbook of the Psychology of Aging*, 3rd ed., 320–29. San Diego: Academic Press.

Simonton, D.K. 2006. "Creativity." In R. Schulz, L.S. Noelker, K. Rockwood, and R.L. Sprott, eds., *The Encyclopedia of Aging*, 4th ed., 269–70. New York: Springer.

Sims-Gould, J., and A. Martin-Matthews. 2007. "Family Caregiving or Caregiving Alone: Who Helps the Helper?" *Canadian Journal on Aging* 26 (supplement 1): 27–46.

Sims-Gould, J., A. Martin-Matthews, and C.J. Rosenthal. 2008. "Family Caregiving and Helping at the Intersection of Gender and Kinship: Social Dynamics in the Provision of Care to Older Adults in Canada." In A. Martin-Matthews and J. E. Phillips, eds., *Aging and Caring at the Intersection of Work and Home Life*, 65–84. New York, NY: Psychology Press.

Skelton, D. 1982. "The Hospice Movement: A Human Approach to Palliative Care." *Canadian Medical Association Journal* 126: 556–58.

Skinner, M.W., and M.W. Rosenberg. 2002. *Health Care in Rural Communities: Exploring the Development of Informal and Voluntary Care*. SEDAP Research Paper No. 79. Hamilton, ON: McMaster University.

Slaughter, S., and J. Bankes. 2007. "The Functional Transitions Model: Maximizing Ability in the Context of Progressive Disability Associated with Alzheimer's Disease." *Canadian Journal on Aging* 26(1): 39–48.

Smale, B.J.A., and S.L. Dupuis. 1993. "The Relationship between Leisure Activity Participation and Psychological Well-Being across the Lifespan." *Journal of Applied Recreation Research* 18(4): 281–300.

Smale, B., and S.L. Dupuis. 2003a. *In Their Own Voices: A Profile of Dementia Caregivers in Ontario. Stage 1: Survey Results*. Waterloo, ON: University of Waterloo.

Smale, B., and S.L. Dupuis. 2003b. *In Their Own Voices: A Profile of Dementia Caregivers in Ontario. Stage 2: The Focus Group*. Waterloo, ON: University of Waterloo.

Smith, A.D. 2006. "Cognitive Processes." In R. Schulz, L.S. Noelker, K. Rockwood, and R.L. Sprott, eds., *The Encyclopedia of Aging*, 4th ed., 229–32. New York: Springer.

Smith, R., L. Magee, A.L. Robb, and J.B. Burbidge. 2000. "The Independence and Economic Security of Older Women Living Alone." In F.T. Denton, D. Fretz, and B.G. Spencer, eds. *Independence and Economic Security in Old Age*, 293–327. Vancouver: UBC Press.

Smith, T.L., and R.W. Toseland. 2006. "The Effectiveness of a Telephone Support Program for Caregivers of Frail Older Adults." *The Gerontologist* 46(5): 620–29.

Snell, J.G. 1990. "Filial Responsibility Laws in Canada: An Historical Study." *Canadian Journal on Aging* 9: 268–77.

Snell, J.G. 1993. "The Gendered Construction of Elderly Marriage, 1900–1950." *Canadian Journal on Aging* 12(4): 509–23.

Snowdon, D. 2001. *Aging with Grace: What the Nun Study Teaches Us About Leading Longer, Healthier, and More Meaningful Lives*. Bantam Books, New York, NY.

Sobczak, J. 2002. "Staying Stronger Longer." *Quality in Aging* 3(2): 6–10.

Sorcinelli, A., L. Shaw, A. Freeman, and K. Cooper. 2007. "Evaluating The Safe Living Guide: A Home Hazard Checklist for Seniors." *Canadian Journal on Aging* 26(2): 127–38.

Sorrell, J.M. 2006. "Developing Programs for Older Adults in a Faith Community." *Journal of Psychosocial Nursing and Mental Health Services* 44(11): 15–18.

Sparks, B., V. Temple, M. Springer, and K.P. Stoddart. 2000. "Service Provision to Older Adults with Developmental Disabilities: A Survey of Service Providers." *Canadian Journal on Aging* 19(2): 210–22.

Special Senate Committee on Euthanasia and Assisted Suicide. 1995. *Of Life and Death—Final Report*. http://www.parl.gc.ca/35/1/parlbus/commbus/senate/com-e/euth-e/rep-e/lad-tc-e.htm, accessed May 7, 2009.

Speechley, M., S. Belfry, M.J. Borrie, K.B. Jenkyn, R. Crilly, D. Gill, S. McLean, P. Stolee, A. A. Vandervoort, and G. R. Jones. 2005. "Risk Factors for Falling among Community-Dwelling Veterans and Their Caregivers." *Canadian Journal on Aging* 24(3): 261–74.

Spitze, G., and K. Trent. 2006. "Gender Differences in Adult Sibling Relations in Two-Child Families." *Journal of Marriage and Family* 68(4): 977–92.

St-Arnaud, J., M.P. Beaudet, and P. Tully. 2005. "Life Expectancy." *Health Reports* 17(1): 43–47. Statistics Canada. Catalogue No. 82-003.

St. John, P., and M. Man-Son-Hing. 2002. "Requests for Physician-Assisted Suicide in Older Persons: An Approach." *Geriatrics Today* 5(2): 81–83.

Standish, T.I.M., D.W. Molloy, A. Cunje, and D.L. Lewis. 2007. "Do the ABCS 135 Short Cognitive Screen and Its Subtests Discriminate between Normal Cognition, Mild Cognitive Impairment, and Dementia?" *International Journal of Geriatric Psychiatry* 22(3): 189–94.

Statistics Canada. 1968. *1966 Census of Canada*. Vol. 1 (1–11). Ottawa: Queen's Printer.

Statistics Canada. 1973. *Census of Canada (1971 Census). Bulletin* 1: 2–3. Ottawa: Information Canada.

Statistics Canada. 1978. *Vital Statistics.* Vol. III: Births–Deaths, 1975 and 1976. Cat. No. 84-204. Ottawa: Health Division, Vital Statistics and Diseases Registry Section, Statistics Canada, Ministry of Supply and Services.

Statistics Canada. 1981. *Canada Year Book, 1980–81.* Ottawa: Minister of Supply and Services.

Statistics Canada. 1986. *The Labour Force, August 1986.* Cat. No. 71-001. Ottawa: Minister of Supply and Services.

Statistics Canada. 1989. *Canada Year Book 1990.* Cat. No. 11-402E/1990. Ottawa: Minister of Supply and Services.

Statistics Canada. 1991. *Population Projections 1990–2011.* Ottawa: Statistics Canada, Demography Division.

Statistics Canada. 1992. "Age, Sex, and Marital Status." *1991 Census of Canada.* Cat. No. 93-310. Ottawa: Statistics Canada.

Statistics Canada. 1996. *Canada's Retirement Income Programs: A Statistical Overview.* Cat. No. 74-507-XPB. Ottawa: Minister of Industry.

Statistics Canada. 1998. *Labour Force Update: Older Workers* 2(2). Ottawa: Statistics Canada, Household Surveys Division.

Statistics Canada. 1999. *Canada Year Book.* Cat. No. 11-402E/1999. Ottawa: Ministry of Industry, Science, and Technology.

Statistics Canada. 2000a. "Stress and Well-Being." *Health Reports* 12(3). Cat. No. 82-003-XIE. http://www.statcan.ca/english/freepub/ 82-003-XIE/art2.pdf, accessed November 23, 2003.

Statistics Canada. 2000b. "Taking Risks/Taking Care." *Health Reports* 12(3). Cat. No. 82-003-XIE. http://www.statcan.ca/english/freepub/ 82-003-XIE/art1.pdf, accessed November 23, 2003.

Statistics Canada 2001a. "Bring Your Families to Canada." http://142.206.72.67/02/02a/ 02a_005_e.htm#t01, accessed July 26, 2004.

Statistics Canada. 2001b. *Changing Conjugal Life in Canada.* Cat. No. 89-576-XIE. Ottawa: Statistics Canada.

Statistics Canada. 2001c. "How Healthy Are Canadians?" *Health Reports* 12(3). Cat. No. 82-003. http://www.statcan.ca/english/freepub/ 82-003-XIE/free.htm, accessed July 28, 2004.

Statistics Canada. 2001d. "Internet Use among Older Canadians." http://www.statcan.ca:8096/ bsolc/english/bsolc?catno=56F0004M2001004, accessed September 15, 2004.

Statistics Canada. 2001e. "Trends in Early Retirement." *The Daily*, September 19, 2001. http://www.statcan.ca/Daily/English/010919/d010919c.htm, accessed August 10, 2004.

Statistics Canada. 2002a. "Median Age, Canada, 1901–2011." http://www12.statcan.ca/ english/ census01/Products/Analytic/companion/age/cdamedaget.cfm, accessed September 27, 2003.

Statistics Canada. 2002b. "Median Age Reaches All-Time High." http://www12.statcan.ca/english/census01/Products/Analytic/companion/age/canada.cfm#median_age, accessed July 26, 2004.

Statistics Canada. 2003a. "Aboriginal Peoples of Canada: A Demographic Profile." *2001 Census: Analysis Series.* Cat. No. 96F0030XIE2001007. http://www12.statcan.ca/english/census01/products/analytic/companion/abor/pdf/96F0030XIE2001007.pdf, accessed May 7, 2009.

Statistics Canada. 2003b. "Average Earnings by Sex and Work Pattern." *Canadian Statistics.* http://www.statcan.ca/english/Pgdb/labor01a.htm, accessed May 7, 2009.

Statistics Canada. 2003c. *Canada's Retirement Income Programs: A Statistical Overview (1990-2000).* Minister of Industry. http://www.statcan.ca/english/freepub/74-507-XIE/0010074-507-XIE.pdf, accessed May 7, 2009.

Statistics Canada. 2003d. *Canadian Community Health Survey: Mental Health and Well-Being.* Cat. No. 82-617-XIE. Ottawa: Ministry of Industry. http//www.statcan.ca:8096/bsolc/English/bsolc?catno=82-617-X, accessed August 2, 2004.

Statistics Canada. 2003e. "Gender Differences in Low Income." http://www.hc-sc.gc.ca/seniors-aines/pubs/factoids/2001/no15_e.htm, accessed August 10, 2004.

Statistics Canada. 2003f. "General Social Survey: Social Support and Aging." *The Daily*, September 2. http://www.statcan.ca/Daily/ English/030902/d030902a.htm, accessed September 2, 2004.

Statistics Canada. 2003g. "Grandparents and Grandchildren." *The Daily*, December 9, 2003.

http://www.statcan.can/Daily/English/031209/d031209b.htm, accessed August 18, 2004.

Statistics Canada. 2003h. "Pain or Discomfort That Affects Activities, by Age Group and Sex, Household Population Aged 12 and Over, Canada." *Health Indicators* 2003(1). Cat. No. 82-221-XIE.

Statistics Canada. 2003i. *PALS (Participation and Activity Limitation Survey).* http://www.statcan.gc.ca/pub/89-577-x/index-eng.htm, accessed May 22, 2009.

Statistics Canada. 2003j. "The People: Break-up." *Canada e-Book.* Cat. No. 11-404-XIE. Ottawa: Statistics Canada.

Statistics Canada. 2003k. "The People: Common-Law." *Canada e-Book.* Cat. No. 11-404-XIE. Ottawa: Statistics Canada.

Statistics Canada. 2003l. "The People: Hospitals." *Canada e-Book.* http://142.206.72.67/02/02b/02b_008c_e.htm, accessed December 19, 2003.

Statistics Canada. 2003m. "The People: Widowhood." *Canada e-Book.* http://ww43.statcan.ca/02/02d/02d_00le_e.htm, accessed August 22, 2008.

Statistics Canada. 2003n. *Perspectives on Labour and Income.* Ottawa: Mininster of Industry.

Statistics Canada. 2003o. "Population and Growth Components, 1851–2001 Censuses." http://www.statcan.ca/english/Pgdb/demo03.htm, accessed May 7, 2009.

Statistics Canada. 2003p. "Population by Sex and Age Group." CANSIMII, Table 051-0001. http://www.statcan.ca/english/Pgdb/demo10a.htm, accessed May 7, 2009.

Statistics Canada. 2003q. "Reasons for Part-Time Work by Sex and Age Group." *Canadian Statistics.* http://www.statcan.ca/english/Pgdb/ labor63a.htm, accessed October 10, 2003.

Statistics Canada. 2003r. "Religion and Age Groups for Population, for Canada, Provinces, Territories, Census Metropolitan Areas 1 and Census Agglomerations, 2001 Census." http://www12.statcan.ca/english/census01/products/highlight/Religion/Page.cfm?Lang=E&Geo=PR&View=1a&Code=01&Table=1&StartRec=1&Sort=2&B1=Canada&B2=1, accessed May 7, 2009.

Statistics Canada. 2003s. "Retirement Savings through RRSPs and RPPs." *Canadian Statistics.* http://www.statcan.ca/english/Pgdb/labor55.htm, accessed May 7, 2009.

Statistics Canada. 2003t. "The Retirement Wave." *The Daily,* February 21, 2003. http://www.statcan.ca/Daily/English/030221/d030221f.htm, accessed May 7, 2009.

Statistics Canada. 2003u. "Satisfaction with Life, by Age Group and Sex, Household Population Aged 15 and Over, Canada Excluding Territories, 2002." *Canadian Community Health Survey: Mental Health and Well-Being 2002,* Table 21. Cat. No. 82-617-XIE. Ottawa: Ministry of Industry. http://www.statcan.ca/english/freepub/82-617-XIE/htm/51100115.htm, accessed May 7, 200-.

Statistics Canada. 2003v. "Social Support and Mortality among Seniors." *The Daily*, May 23. Health Statistics Division.

Statistics Canada. 2004a. "Deaths, 2002." *The Daily, September 27,* http://www.statcan.ca/Daily/English/040927/d040927a.htm, accessed May 7, 2009.

Statistics Canada. 2004b. "Divorces." *The Daily*, May 4. http://www.statcan.ca/Daily/ English/040504/d040504a.htm.

Statistics Canada. 2004c. "The People: Hospitals." *The Canada e-Book (11-404-XIE)* (based on the *2001 Canada Year Book (11-402-XPE).*http://www43.statcan.ca/02/02b/02b_008a_e.htm, accessed May 7, 2009.

Statistics Canada. 2004d. "Profile of Disability in 2001." *Canadian Social Trends,* Spring, 14–18. Cat. No.11.-008.

Statistics Canada. 2004e. "Study: Economic Consequences of Widowhood." *The Daily,* July 22, 2004. http://www.statcan.ca/Daily/English/040722/do40722b.htm, accessed August 22, 2008.

Statistics Canada. 2005a. *Income in Canada——2005.* http://www.statcan.ca/english/freepub/75-202-XIE/2005000/tablesectionlist.htm, accessed March 8, 2008.

Statistics Canada, 2005b, *Population Projections for Canada, Provinces and Territories, 2005–2031,* Statistics Canada. Catalogue No. 91-520-XIE, http://www.statcan.ca/english/freepub/91-003-XIE/2007001/tables/table2-en.htm, accessed May 7, 2009.

Statistics Canada. 2005c. *Projections of the Aboriginal Populations, Canada, Provinces and Territories: 2001 to 2017.* Ottawa: Minister of Industry. Cat. No. 91-547-XIE.

Statistics Canada. 2006a. "Canada's Retirement Income Programs." *The Daily*, February 7, http://www.statcan.gc.ca/daily-quotidien/060207/dq060207b-eng.htm, accessed May 22, 2009.

Statistics Canada. 2006b. *Caring Canadians, Involved Canadians: Highlights from the 2004 Canada Survey of Giving, Volunteering and Participating.* Ottawa: Minister of Industry.

Statistics Canada. 2007a. *2001 Census.* http://www12.statcan.ca/english/census01/release/release5.cfm, accessed May 7, 2009.

Statistics Canada. 2007b. "2006 Census: Families, Marital Status, Households and Dwelling Characteristics." *The Daily*, September 12. http://www.Statcan.ca/Daily/English/070912/d070912a.htm, accessed September 12, 2008.

Statistics Canada. 2007c. "Canada's Population by Age and Sex." *The Daily*, October 26, 2006. http://www.statcan.ca/Daily/English/061026/d061026b.htm, accessed May 7, 2009.

Statistics Canada. 2007d. "Centenarians: Women Outnumber Men Four to One." http://www12.statcan.ca/english/census01/Products/Analytic/companion/age/canada.cfm#centenarians, accessed May 7, 2009.

Statistics Canada. 2007e. *Infant Mortality Rates, by Province And Territory (Both Sexes).* http://www40.statcan.ca/l01/cst01/health21a.htm, accessed December 26, 2007.

Statistics Canada. 2007f. *Participation and Activity Limitation Survey 2006: Tables 2006.* Ottawa: Minister of Industry, http://www.statcan.ca/english/freepub/89-628-XIE/2007003/series1-en.htm, accessed May 7, 2009.

Statistics Canada. 2007g. *Portrait of the Canadian Population in 2006, by Age and Sex, 2006 Census Age and Sex, 2006 Census. Ottawa: Minister of Industry.*Statistics Canada. 2007X.

Statistics Canada. 2007h. *Portrait of the Canadian Population in 2006, Population and Dwelling Counts, 2006 Census.* Ottawa: Minister of Industry.

Statistics Canada. 2007i. "Table 2. Life Expectancy at Birth by Sex in Canada and Provinces, 1971, 2004 and 2031." *Demographics at a Glance.* Catalogue No. 91-003-XWE. Based on Statistics Canada, 2005, *Population Projections for Canada, Provinces and Territories, 2005–2031*, Statistics Canada. Catalogue No. 91-520-XIE, Demography Division, and Health

Statistics Division. http://www.statcan.ca/english/freepub/91-003-XIE/2007001/tables/table2-en.htm, accessed May 7, 2009.

Statistics Canada. 2007j. *Participation and Activity Limitation Survey.* http://www.statcan.ca/english/freepub/89-628-XIE/2007003/series1-en.htm, accessed May 7, 2009.

Statistics Canada. 2008a. 2006 Census website. *Participation and Activity Limitation Survey.* http://www.statcan.ca/english/freepub/89-628-XIE/2007003/series1-en.htm, accessed May 7, 2009.

Statistics Canada. 2008b. *Canada's Changing Labour Force, 2006 Census—Census year 2006.* Ottawa: Minister of Industry.

Statistics Canada. 2008c. *Canadian Vital Statistics, Birth and Death Databases and Demography Division (population estimates)* (CANSIM Table 102-0511). Table 36a2-HLT Life Expectancy, Abridged Life Table, at Age 65, by Sex, Canada, Provinces and Territories, 2002 and 2003. http://www.statcan.ca/english/freepub/82-401-XIE/2006000/tables/dt005.htm, accessed May 7, 2009.

Statistics Canada. 2008d. *Low Income Cut-offs for 2007 and Low Income, 2006/2007,* Catalogue No. 75F0002M. http://www.statcan.gc.ca/pub/75f0002m/75f0002m2008004-eng.pdf, accessed May 16, 2009.

Statistics Canada. 2008e. Report on the Demographic Situation in Canada, 2005 and 2006. Catalogue No. 91-209-X. Minister of Industry, 2008.

Statistics Canada. 2008f. "Suicides and Suicide Rate, by Sex and by Age Group." http://www40.statcan.ca/l01/cst01/perhlth66b.htm, accessed May 7, 2009.

Stein, P. 1981. "Understanding Single Adulthood." In P.J. Stein, ed., *Single Life: Unmarried Adults in Social Context*, 9–21. New York: St. Martin's.

Steinbock, B. 2005. "The Case for Physician Assisted Suicide: Not (Yet) Proven." *Journal of Medical Ethics* 31(4): 235–41.

Stelmach, L., C. Konnert, and K. Dobson. 2001. "Obtaining Informed Consent from Continuing Care Residents: Issues and Recommendations." *Canadian Journal on Aging* 20(3): 385–406.

Stevens-Ratchford, R., and T. Diaz. 2003. "Promoting Successful Aging through Occupation. An Examination of Engagement in Life: A Look at

Aging in Place, Occupation and Successful Aging." *Activities, Adaptation and Aging* 27(3/4): 19–37.

Stewart, M., A. Bamfather, A. Neufeld, S. Warrne, N. Letourneau, and L. Liu. 2006. "Accessible Support for Family Caregivers of Seniors with Chronic Conditions: From Isolation to Inclusion." *Canadian Journal on Aging* 25(2): 179–92.

Stine-Morrow, E.A.L., J.M. Parisi, D.G. Morrow, J. Greene, and D.C. Park. 2007. "Engagement Model of Cognitive Optimization through Adulthood." *Journals of Gerontology: Series B: Psychological Sciences and Social Sciences* 62B(Special Issue 1): 62–69.

Stobert, S., and K. Cranswick. 2004. "Looking after Seniors: Who Does What for Whom?" *Canadian Social Trends* (Autumn) 74: 2–6.

Stobert, S., D. Dosman, and N. Keating. 2006. *Aging Well: Time Use Patterns of Older Canadians.* Statistics Canada. Catalogue No. 89-622-XIE, No. 2 Ottawa: Minister of Industry.

Stone, D.S. 2003. "Disability, Dependence, and Old Age: Problematic Constructions." *Canadian Journal on Aging* 22(1): 59–67.

Stone, L.O., ed. 2006. *New Frontiers of Research on Retirement.* Statistics Canada. Catalogue No. 75-511-XIE. Ottawa: Minister of Industry.

Stone, L.O., and A.S. Harvey, 2001. "Gender Differences in Transtions to Total-work Retirement." In V. Marshall, W.R. Heinz, H. Kruger, and A. Verma, eds., *Restructuring Work and the Life Course,* 258–69. Toronto: The University of Toronto Press.

Stones, L., and M. Stones. 1996. *Sex May Be Wasted on the Young.* North York, ON: Captus.

Stones, M.J., L.D. Clyburn, M.C. Gibson, and M.G. Woodbury. 2006. "Predicting Diagnosed Depression and Anti-Depressant Treatment in Institutionalized Older Adults by Symptom Profiles: A Closer Look at Anhedonia and Dysphoria." *Canadian Journal on Aging* 25(2), 153–59.

Strain, L.A. 2001. "Senior Centres: Who Participates?" *Canadian Journal on Aging* 20(4): 471–91.

Strain, L.A., and A.A. Blandford. 2003. "Caregiving Networks in Later Life: Does Cognitive Status Make a Difference?" *Canadian Journal on Aging* 22(3): 261–73.

Strain, L.A., C.C. Grabusic, M.S. Searle, and N.J. Dunn. 2002. "Continuing and Ceasing Leisure Activities

in Later Life: A Longitudinal Study." *Gerontologist* 42(2): 217–23.

Stratton, D.C., and A.J. Moore. 2007. "Fractured Relationships and the Potential for Abuse of Older Men." *Journal of Elder Abuse and Neglect* 19 (1/2): 75–97.

Street, D., and I. Connidis. 2001. "Creeping Selectivity in Canadian Women's Pensions." In J. Ginn, D. Street, and S. Arber, eds., *Women, Work, and Pensions: International Issues and Prospects,* 158–78. Buckingham, U.K.: Open University Press.

Sullivan, T., and P.M. Baranek. 2002. *First Do No Harm: Making Sense of Canadian Health Reform.* Vancouver: UBC Press.

Sullivan, T., and C. Mustard. 2001. "Canada: More State, More Market?" In J.B. Davis, ed., *The Social Economics of Health Care.* London: Routledge.

Sutton, D., M.A.M. Gignac, and C. Cott. 2002. "Medical and Everyday Assistive Device Use among Older Adults with Arthritis." *Canadian Journal on Aging* 21(4): 535–48.

Synge, J. 1980. "Work and Family Support Patterns of the Aged in the Early Twentieth Century." In V.W. Marshall, ed., *Aging in Canada: Social Perspectives,* 135–44. Toronto: Fitzhenry and Whiteside.

Szinovacz, M.E. 1982. "Introduction: Research on Women's Retirement." In M. Szinovacz, ed., *Women's Retirement.* Beverly Hills, CA: Sage.

Szinovacz, M. 2006. "Families and Retirement." In L.O. Stone, ed., *New Frontiers of Research on Retirement,* 165–98. Statistics Canada. Catalogue No. 75-511-XIE. Ottawa: Minister of Industry.

Talbott, M.M. 1998. "Older Widows' Attitudes towards Men and Remarriage." *Journal of Aging Studies* 12(4): 429–49.

Tam, S., and S. Neysmith. 2006. "Disrespect and Isolation: Elder Abuse in Chinese Communities." *Canadian Journal on Aging* 25(2): 141–51.

Tamblym, R., and R. Perreault. 2000. "Prescription Drug Use and Seniors." *Canadian Journal on Aging* 19(Suppl. 1): 143–75.

Tan, J.W., and R.D. Brown. 2005. "Effect of Viewing a Landscape on Physiological Health of Elderly Women." *Journal of Housing for the Elderly* 19 (3–4): 187–202.

Tasse, L. 1993. "Promised Lands: The Social Role and Filiation of Elderly Algonquins of Kitigan Zibi."

International Review of Community Development 29(69): 25–36.

Taylor, K. 1999. "Hospice Palliative Care: A Growing Movement in B.C." *Gerontology Research Centre News* (February): 4–5.

Taylor, P.S. 1995. "Grandma! Grandpa! Back to Work!" *Saturday Night,* June, 18.

Taylor, M.A., and D. Doverspike. 2003. "Retirement Planning and Preparation." In G.A. Adams and T.A. Beehr, eds., *Retirement: Reasons, Processes, and Results*, 53–82. New York: Springer.

TD Bank Financial Group 2004. 2005. "Retirement, What Retirement? According to TD Waterhouse RSP Poll 1/3 Canadians Plan to Keep on Working." Toronto: TD Bank. http://www.tdassetmangement.com/Content/InvResources/PressRoom/p_LibraryItem.asp?LIID=351&CAT=30, accessed January 5, 2005.

The Latest for Seniors. 2008. "Changes to Seniors Benefits –2008." http://www.seniors.gc.ca/content.jsp?lang=enandauxPageId=142#3, accessed May 7, 2009.

Thomas, D. 2001. "Evolving Family Living Arrangements of Canada's Immigrants. Evolving Family Living Arrangements Of Canada's immigrants." *Canadian Social Trends* (Summer): 16–22.

Thomas, L.E. 1982. "Sexuality and Aging: Essential Vitamin or Popcorn?" *Gerontologist* 22, 240–43.

Thompson, E. P. 1971. "The Moral Economy of the English Crowd in the Eighteenth Century." *Past and Present* 50: 76–136.

Thornton, R., and L.L. Light. 2006. "Language Comprehension and Production in Normal Aging." In J. E. Birren and K.W. Schaie, eds., *Handbook of the Psychology of Aging,* 6th ed., 261–67. Burlington, MA: Elsevier Academic Press.

Thorpe, R.J., Jr., R.A. Kreisle, L.T. Glickman, E.M. Simonsick, A.B. Newman, and S. Kritchevsky. 2006. "Physical Activity and Pet Ownership in Year 3 of the Health ABC Study." *Journal of Aging and Physical Activity* 14(2): 154–68.

Tibbetts, J. 2007. "Fewer Grad Students Leading to Professor Shortage."CanWest News Service. December 9, 2007. http://www2.canada.com/ottawacitizen/news/story.html?id=ffd41b3e-4a47-47c4-bbdc-2b910bd97a4b&k=36637, accessed May 16, 2009.

Tierney, M.C. 1997. "Editorial: How Safe Are Cognitively Impaired Seniors Who Live Alone?" *Canadian Journal on Aging* 16(2): 177–89.

Tierney, M.C., and J. Charles. 2002. "The Care and Treatment of People with Dementia and Cognitive Impairment: An Update." In *Writings in Gerontology: Mental Health and Aging,* 97–112. Ottawa: National Advisory Council on Aging.

Tindale, J. 1991. *Older Workers in an Aging Work Force.* Cat. No. H71-2/1-10-1991E. Ottawa: Minister of Supply and Services.

Tompa, E. 1999. *Transitions to Retirement: Determinants of Age of Social Security Take Up.* SEDAP Research Paper No. 6. Hamilton, ON: McMaster University.

Tornstam, L. 2005. *Gerotranscendence: A Developmental Theory of Positive Aging.* New York: Springer.

Tourigny, A., P.J. Durand, L. Bonin, R. Hebert, and L. Rochette. 2004. "Quasi-Experimental Study of the Effectiveness of an Integrated Service Delivery Network for the Frail Elderly." *Canadian Journal on Aging* 23(3): 231–46.

Tournier, Paul. 1972. *Learning to Grow Old.* London: SCM Press.

Townsend-Batten, B. 2002. "Staying in Touch: Contact between Adults and their Parents." *Canadian Social Trends* (Spring): 9–12.

Townson, Monica. 2006a. *Growing Older, Working Longer: The New Face of Retirement.* Ottawa: Canadian Centre for Policy Alternatives.

Townson, M. 2006b. "The Impact Of Precarious Employment On Financial Security In Retirement." In L. O. Stone, ed., *New Frontiers of Research on Retirement*, 355–382. Statistics Canada. Catalogue No. 75-511-XIE. Ottawa: Minister of Industry.

Townson, M. 2006c. "New Vulnerable Groups and Living Standards In The Retirement Years." In L. O. Stone, ed., *New Frontiers of Research on Retirement*, 345–54. Statistics Canada. Catalogue No. 75-511-XIE. Ottawa: Minister of Industry.

Trevitt, C., and E. Gallagher. 1996. "Elder Abuse in Canada and Australia: Implications for Nurses." *International Journal of Nursing Studies* 33(6): 651–59.

Trottier, H., L. Martel, C. Houle, J-M. Berthelot, and J. Legare. 2000. "Living at Home or in an Institution: What Makes the Difference for Seniors?" *Health Indicators* 11(4): 49–62.

Tsiantar, D. 2007. "Wrinkles in Living Color." *Time,* April 16, Global 1–2.

Tudor-Locke, C., A.M. Myers, C.S. Jacob, G. Jones, D. Lazowski, and N.A. Ecclestone. 2000. "Development and Formative Evaluation of the Centre for Activity and Ageing's Home Support Exercise Program for Frail Older Adults." *Journal of Aging and Physical Activity* 8(1): 59–75.

Turcotte, M. 2006. "Passing on the Ancestral Language." *Canadian Social Trends* (Spring): 20–26.

Turcotte, M. and G. Schellenberg. 2005. "Job Strain and Retirement." *Perspectives on Labour and Income* 6(7): 13–17.

Turcotte, M., and G. Schellenberg. 2007. *A Portrait of Seniors 2006. Statistics Canada. Catalogue No. 89-519-XIE.* Ottawa: Ministry of Industry.

Turnbull, C. 1961. *The Forest People.* New York: Simon and Schuster.

Twigg, Julia. 2004. "The Body, Gender, and Age: Feminist Insights in Social Gerontology." *Journal of Aging Studies* 18(1): 59–73.

"Two-Wheel Adventurers Brook No Complaints." 1999. *Fifty Plus, Victoria Times Colonist* advertising feature, October 5.

Underhill, C. 2006. "Training through the Ages." *Perspectives on Labour and Income* 7(10): 17–27.

Underhill, S.C., V.W. Marshall, and S. Deliencourt. 1997. *Options 45+ HRCC Survey Final Report.* Toronto: Institute for Human Development, Life Course and Aging, University of Toronto; and Ottawa: One Voice: Canadian Seniors Network.

United Nations. 2002. *World Population Aging: 1950–2050.* Department of Economic and Social Affairs. Population Division.http://www.un.org/esa/population/publications/worldageing19502050/index.htm, accessed May 7, 2009.

Vaillant, George E. 2002. *Aging Well.* Boston: Little, Brown and Company.

Valentijn, S. A., M.P.J. van Boxtel, S.A.H. van Hooren, H. Bosma, H.J.M. Beckers, R.W.H.M. Ponds, and J. Jolles. 2005. "Change in Sensory Functioning Predicts Change in Cognitive Functioning: Results From a 6-Year Follow-Up in the Maastricht Aging Study." *Journal of the American Geriatrics Society* 53(3): 374–80.

van den Hoonaard, D.K. 1999. "No Regrets: Widows' Stories about the Last Days of Their Husbands' Lives." *Journal of Aging Studies* 13(1): 59–72.

van den Hoonaard, D. 2002. "Attitudes of Older Widows and Widowers in New Brunswick, towards New Partnerships." *Ageing International* 27 (4): 79–92.

Vanderburgh, R.M. 1988. "The Impact of Government Support for Indian Culture on Canada's Aged Indians." In E. Rathbone-McEwan and B. Havens, eds., *North American Elders: United States and Canadian Perspectives,* 221–33. New York: Greenwood.

Van der Veen, R. 1990. "Third Age or Inter-Age Universities?" *Journal of Educational Gerontology* 5: 96–105.

Vares, T., A. Potts, N. Gavey, and V.M. Grace. 2007. "Reconceptualizing Cultural Narratives of Mature Women's Sexuality in the Viagra Era." *Journal of Aging Studies* 21: 153–64.

Veall, M.R. 2007. *Which Canadian Seniors Are Below the Low-Income Measure?* SEDAP Research Paper No. 186. Hamilton, ON: McMaster University.

Venne, R.A. 2001. "Population Aging in Canada and Japan: Implications for Labour Force and Career Patterns." *Canadian Journal of Administrative Sciences* 18(1): 40–49.

Verwoerdt, A., E. Pfeiffer, and H.S. Wang. 1969. "Sexual Behavior in Senescence—Changes in Sexual Activity and Interest of Aging Men and Women." *Journal of Geriatric Psychiatry* 2: 163–80.

Victorino, C.C., and A.H. Gauthier. 2005. "Are Canadian Seniors Becoming More Active? Empirical Evidence Based on Time-Use Data." *Canadian Journal on Aging* 24(1): 45–56.

Vintners, H.V. 2001. "Aging and the Human Nervous System." In J.E. Birren and K.W. Schaie, eds., *Handbook of the Psychology of Aging,* 5th ed. San Diego: Academic Press.

Vogler, George P. 2006. "Behavior Genetics and Aging." In James E. Birren and K. Warner Schaie, eds., *Handbook of the Psychology of Aging,* 6th ed., 41–55. Burlington, MA: Elsevier Academic Press.

von Kondratowitz, H-J. 2003. "The Legacy of Social Constructionism for Social Gerontology." In Simon Biggs, Ariela Lowenstein, and Jon Hendricks, eds., *The Need for Theory: Critical Approaches to Social Gerontology,* 45–62. Amityville, New York: Baywood.

Vosko, L.F., N. Zukewich, and C. Cranford. 2003. "Precarious Jobs: A New Typology Of Employment." *Perspectives on Labour and Income* 4(10): 16–26.

Wagner, D.L. 1995. "Senior Center Research in America: An Overview of What We Know." In

D. Shollenberger, ed., *Senior Centers in America: A Blueprint for the Future*. Washington, DC: National Council on the Aging and National Eldercare Institute on Multipurpose Senior Centers and Community Focal Points.

Wahl, J., and S. Purdy. 2001. *Elder Abuse: The Hidden Crime*. 7th ed. Toronto: Advocacy Centre for the Elderly.

Waldrop, D.P., and J.A. Weber. 2001. "From Grandparent to Caregiver: The Stress and Satisfaction of Raising Grandchildren." *Families in Society* 82(5): 361–472.

Walker, Alan. 2005. "Towards an International Political Economy of Ageing." *Ageing and Society* 25 (6): 815–39.

Walters, W.H. 2002. "Place Characteristics and Later-Life Migration." *Research on Aging* 24(2): 243–77.

Wannell, T. 2007a. "Public Pensions and Work." *Perspectives on Labour and Income* 8(8): 12–19.

Wannell, T. 2007b. "Young Pensioners." *Perspectives on Labour and Income* 8(2): 5–14.

Whitehead, M. J., and C. A. Quinlan. 2002. *Canada: An Information Literacy Case Study*. White Paper prepared for UNESCO, the U.S. National Commission on Libraries and Information Science, and the National Forum on Information Literacy, for use at the Information Literacy Meeting of Experts, Prague, The Czech Republic. http://www. nclis.gov/ libinter/infolitconf&meet/papers/quinlan-fullpaper. pdf, accessed April 27, 2008.

Wiener, J.M., and L.H. Illston. 1996. "The Financing and Organization of Health Care for Older Americans." In R.H. Binstock and L.K. George, eds., *Handbook of Aging and the Social Sciences*, 427–45. San Diego: Academic Press.

Wilcox, S., Evenson, K.R., Aragaki, A., Wassertheil-Smoller, S., Mouton, C. P., and Loevinger, B.L. 2003. "Effects of Widowhood On Physical And Mental Health, Health Behaviours, And Health Outcomes: The Women's Health Initiative." *Health Psychology*, 22(5): 513-522.

Wilkins, K. 2006. "Predictors of Death in Seniors." *Supplement to Health Reports*, 16: 57-67. Statistics Canada. Cat No. 82-003.

Wilkins, K., and M.P. Beaudet. 2000. "Changes in Social Support in Relation to Seniors' Use of Home Care." *Health Reports* 11(4): 39–48.

Wilkins, S. 2001. "Aging, Chronic Illness and Self-Concept: A Study of Women with Osteoporosis." *Journal of Women and Aging* 13(1): 73–92.

Willert, A., and M. Semans. 2000. "Knowledge and Attitudes About Later Life Sexuality: What Clinicians Need to Know About Helping the Elderly." *Contemporary Family Therapy* 22: 415–435.

Williams, C. 2005. "The Sandwich Generation." *Canadian Social Trends* (Summer): 16–21.

Williams, A.P., J. Barnslety, S. Leggat, R. Deber, and P. Baranek. 1999. "Long-Term Care Goes to Market: Managed Competition and Ontario's Reform of Community-Based Services." *Canadian Journal on Aging* 18(2): 125–53.

Wink, P. 2006. "Who Is Afraid of Death? Religiousness, Spirituality, and Death Anxiety in Late Adulthood." *Journal of Religion, Spirituality and Aging* 18(2–3): 93–110.

Wink, P., and Scott, J. 2005. "Does Religiousness Buffer Against the Fear of Death and Dying in Late Adulthood? Findings from a Longitudinal Study." *Journals of Gerontology: Series B: Psychological Sciences and Social Sciences* 60B(4): P207–14.

Wister, A.V. 2005. *Baby Boomer Health Dynamics. How Are We Aging?* Toronto: University of Toronto Press.

Wister, A.V., and P.A. Dykstra. 2000. "Formal Assistance among Dutch Older Adults: An Examination of the Gendered Nature of Marital History." *Canadian Journal on Aging* 19(4): 508–35.

Wister, A.V., and G. Gutman. 1997. "Housing Older Canadians: Current Patterns, Preferences and Policies." *Journal of Housing for the Elderly* 12(1/2): 19–35.

Wister, A.V., and C. Moore. 1998. "First Nations Elders in Canada: Issues, Problems and Successes in Health Care Policy." In A.V. Wister and G. Gutman, eds., *Health Systems and Aging in Selected Pacific Rim Countries: Cultural Diversity and Change*, 103–24. Vancouver: Gerontology Research Centre, Simon Fraser University.

Wister, A.V., and Z. Romeder. 2002. "The Chronic Illness Context and Change in Exercise Self-Care among Older Adults: A Longitudinal Analysis." *Canadian Journal on Aging* 21(4): 521–34.

Wister, A.W., and D. Wanless. 2007. "A Health Profile of Community-Living Nonagenarians in Canada." *Canadian Journal on Aging* 26(1): 1–18.

Witcher, C. 2006. "Designing Health-Promotion Messages for Older Adults in Rural Areas." *WellSpring* 17(2), 1–4.

Wolf, R.S. 1996. "Understanding Elder Abuse and Neglect." *Aging* 367: 4.

Wolf, R.S. 2001. "Support Groups for Older Victims of Domestic Violence." *Journal of Women & Aging* 13(4): 71–83.

Wood, S., B. Giles-Corti, and M. Bulsara. 2005. "The Pet Connection: Pets as a Conduit for Social Capital?" *Social Science and Medicine* 61: 1159–73.

World Health Organization. 1984. "Health Promotion: A World Health Organization Document on the Concept and Principles." *Canadian Public Health Association Digest* 8: 101–2.

World Health Organization/International Network for the Prevention of Elder Abuse. 2002. *Missing Voices: Views of Older Persons on Elder Abuse.* Geneva: World Health Organization.

Worswick, C. 2005. *Mandatory Retirement Rules and the Retirement.* Statistics Canada. Family and Labour Studies Division. Ottawa: Minister of Industry.

Wu, Z., and C.M. Schimmele. 2007. "Uncoupling in Later Life." *Generations* 31(3): 41–46.

Wylde, M.A. 1998. "How to Effectively Research and Market Technology to Older People." In G.M. Gutman, ed., *Technology Innovation for an Aging Society: Blending Research, Public and Private Sectors,* 41–50. Vancouver: Gerontology Research Centre, Simon Fraser University.

Yee, J.L., and R. Schulz. 2000. "Gender Differences in Psychiatric Morbidity among Family

Caregivers: A Review and Analysis." *The Gerontologist* 40: 147–64.

Young, B.W., P.L. Weir, J.L. Starkes, and N. Medic. 2008. "Does Lifelong Training Temper Age-Related Decline in Sport Performance? Interpreting Differences between Cross-Sectional and Longitudinal Data." *Experimental Aging Research* 34(1): 27–48.

Young, H.M., S.K. Sikma, L.S. Johnson Trippett, J. Shannon, and B. Blachly. 2006. "Linking Theory and Gerontological Nursing Practice in Senior Housing." *Geriatric Nursing* 27(6): 346–54.

Zacks, R.T., L. Hasher, and K.Z.H. Li. 2000. "Human Memory." In F.I.M. Craik and T.A. Salthouse, eds., *The Handbook of Aging and Cognition,* 2nd ed., 293–357. Mahwah, NJ: Lawrence Erlbaum Associates.

Zhang, A. 2001. "China Faces the Challenge of an Aging Society." *Beijing Review* July 19, 12–15.

Zimmer, Z., and N. Chappell, 1997. "Rural-Urban Differences in Seniors' Neighbourhood Preferences." In L.A. Patalan, ed., *Shelter and Service Issues for Aging Populations: International Perspectives,* 105–24. New York: Haworth Press.

Zimmer, Z., and N.L. Chappell. 1999. "Receptivity to New Technology among Older Adults." *Disability and Rehabilitation* 21(5/6): 222–30.

Zimmer, Z., T. Hickey, and M.S. Searle. 1997. "Pattern of Change in Leisure Activity Behavior among Older Adults with Arthritis." *Gerontologist* 37(3): 384–92.

Zimmer, Z., and A. Myers. 1997. "Receptivity to Protective Garments among the Elderly." *Journal of Aging and Health* 9(3): 355–72.

Zimmerman, L., B. Mitchell, A. Wister, and G. Gutman. 2000. "Unanticipated Consequences: A Comparison of Expected and Actual Retirement Timing among Older Women." *Journal of Women and Aging* 12(1–2): 109–28.

Zuckerman, H. 1977. *Scientific Elite: Studies of Nobel Laureates in the United States.* New York: Free Press.

Zuzanek, J., and S.J. Box. 1988. "Life Course and the Daily Lives of Older Adults in Canada." In K. Altergott, ed., *Daily Life in Later Life: Comparative Perspectives,* 147–85. Newbury Park, CA: Sage.

Index